Second Edition

Programming in RPG/400

by Judy Yaeger

A Division of
DUKE COMMUNICATIONS
INTERNATIONAL

Loveland, Colorado

Library of Congress Cataloging-in-Publication Data

Yaeger, Judy, 1943-
Programming in RPG/400 / by Judy Yaeger. — 2nd ed.
p. cm.
Includes index.
ISBN 1-882419-23-5
1. RPG/400 (Computer program language)   I. Title.
QA76.73.26Y34 1995
005. 2'45—dc20

95-11169
CIP

Copyright © 1993, 1995 by DUKE PRESS
DUKE COMMUNICATIONS INTERNATIONAL
Loveland, Colorado

All RPG specifications forms are reproductions of those forms produced by IBM. Sample screen formats are reproductions of those found on the AS/400.

ISBN 1-882419-23-5

3 4 5 6 CP 9 8 7 6

To my husband John, for his enduring love, friendship, humor and support, and to my students, who have made teaching fun.

Acknowledgments

A second edition of a book builds on the first; without the help of all the individuals involved in the original edition of this text, this present edition would not be possible. However, some people deserve special thanks for this second edition. First, I would like to thank all those readers who took the time and effort to suggest improvements and to point out errors that managed to slip into the first edition, despite my best efforts. Catharine Minor, of Memphis, Tennessee; Bernadette Cinkoske, of Indianapolis, Indiana; and Patty Hunter of Billings, Montana, especially come to mind. Roger Pence, of *NEWS 3X/400*, was most helpful in providing suggestions for the RPG IV sections added to the book and in serving as technical editor for the project as a whole. I am especially grateful to Janet Robbins; the accuracy of this current edition owes much to her sharp editorial eye. And finally, to Dave Bernard, for his editorial leadership; to Sharon Hamm, for her help in the editing process; to Steve Adams, for the cover design; to Jan Caufman, for her work in production; and to the other fine people at Duke Communications, thanks.

Table of Contents

Preface XIII

Chapter 1: Introduction to Programming and RPG 1
    Chapter Overview 1
    Programming 1
    History of RPG 1
    Program Variables 4
    Data Files and the Data Hierarchy 5
    Programming Specifications 6
    The Program Development Cycle 9
    Program Entry and Testing 10
    Chapter Summary 12
    Terms 14
    Discussion/Review Questions 14
    Exercises 15

Chapter 2: Getting Started 17
    Chapter Overview 17
    Specifications Forms in RPG 17
    Program Specifications for Example Program 18
    File Description Specifications 18
    Input Specifications 20
    Record Identification Entries 21
    Field Description Entries 22
    Output Specifications 23
    Record Identification Entries 24
    Field Description Entries 26
    Calculation Specifications 28
    Indicators and Calculations 30
    RPG Operations 31
    Internal Documentation 32
    The Completed Program 33
    Output Editing 35
    Edit Codes 35
    Edit Words 37
    Chapter Summary 38

Terms 40
Discussion/Review Questions 40
Exercises 41
Programming Assignments 41

Chapter 3: Arithmetic and Assignment Operations 43
Chapter Overview 43
Numeric Literals and Fields 43
Arithmetic Operations 44
Numeric Truncation and Field Sizes 49
Result Field Size for Addition 50
Result Field Size for Subtraction 51
Result Field Size for Multiplication 51
Result Field Size for Division 51
Rounding 52
Effective Commenting on Calculations 54
Putting It All Together 54
Assignment Operations 57
Character Literals 59
Figurative Constants 63
Chapter Summary 65
Terms 66
Discussion/Review Questions 66
Exercises 67
Programming Assignments 67

Chapter 4: Top-Down, Structured Program Design 71
Chapter Overview 71
Structured Design 71
Sequential Flow of Control 72
Relational Comparisons 73
Selection Operations 74
IF and Page Overflow 78
Operations for Iteration 80
Loops and Early Exits 86
Unstructured Operations 87
Top-Down Design 90
Defining Subroutines 91
Scope Terminators 92
Control-Break Logic 94
Chapter Summary 100
Terms 102
Discussion/Review Questions 102
Exercises 103
Programming Assignments 104

Chapter 5: Externally Described Files 107
    Chapter Overview 107
    The AS/400 Approach to Database Files 107
    Physical and Logical Files 108
    Introduction to DDS 109
    Defining Physical Files 110
    Data Types and Data Storage 111
    Defining Logical Files 114
    Simple Logical Files 114
    Record Selection/Omission 116
    Logical Files with Multiple-Record Formats 119
    Join-Logical Files 120
    Creating Database Files 122
    RPG Programming with Externally Defined Files 123
    Additional Database File Concepts 124
    Externally Described Printer Files 127
    Putting It All Together 131
    Chapter Summary 134
    Terms 135
    Discussion/Review Questions 135
    Exercises 136
    Programming Assignments 136

Chapter 6: File Access and Record Manipulation 141
    Chapter Overview 141
    Operations for Input Files 141
    Sequential Access 141
    Random Access 147
    Referencing Composite Keys 148
    Operations for Output Files 151
    Update Files and I/O Operations 154
    File and Record Locking 157
    I/O Errors 160
    Chapter Summary 161
    Terms 163
    Discussion/Review Questions 163
    Exercises 163
    Programming Assignments 164

Chapter 7: Interactive Applications 169
    Chapter Overview 169
    Batch and Interactive Programs 169
    Display Files 169
    Additional DDS Keywords 178
    File-Level Keywords 179
    Record-Level Keywords 179

Field-Level Keywords 180
Conditioning Indicators 184
Interactive File Maintenance 187
Screen Design and CUA 195
Chapter Summary 196
Terms 198
Discussion/Review Questions 198
Exercises 198
Programming Assignments 199

Chapter 8: Tables and Arrays 201
Chapter Overview 201
Tables 201
Table Definition 202
Compile-Time Tables 203
Pre-Runtime Tables 205
Table Look-Ups 206
Two Related Tables 206
Multiple Related Tables 209
Range Tables 212
Changing Table Values 213
Arrays 214
Runtime Arrays and Input Data 216
Calculations with Arrays 218
Using Arrays 222
Array Look-Ups 225
Indicators as Array Elements 226
Output with Arrays 227
Chapter Summary 228
Terms 229
Discussion/Review Questions 229
Exercises 230
Programming Assignments 231

Chapter 9: Advanced Data Definition 235
Chapter Overview 235
Named Constants 235
*LIKE DEFN (Field Definition) 237
Data Structures 238
Simple Data Structures 239
Multiple-Occurrence Data Structures 242
Initialization and Reinitialization of Variables 247
File-Information Data Structures 251
Program-Status Data Structures 253
Error Handling and *PSSR 254
Chapter Summary 257

Terms 259
Discussion/Review Questions 259
Exercises 259
Programming Assignments 260

Chapter 10: Interactive Programs: Advanced Techniques 265
Chapter Overview 265
Subfiles 265
Subfile Record Formats 268
Subfile Control-Record Formats 269
Loading the Entire Subfile 271
Loading the Subfile a Page at a Time 275
Subfiles and Change 283
Uses of Subfiles 286
On-Line Help 286
Chapter Summary 289
Terms 291
Discussion/Review Questions 291
Exercises 291
Programming Assignments 292

Chapter 11: Byte- and Bit-Level Operations 293
Chapter Overview 293
Field Character Inspection 293
Field Character Manipulation 299
Using Arrays for String Manipulation 303
Working with Bits 306
Chapter Summary 309
Terms 310
Discussion/Review Questions 310
Exercises 310
Programming Assignments 311

Chapter 12: Interprogram Communications 313
Chapter Overview 313
Modular Programming 313
Calling Programs 313
Passing Data Between Programs 317
Calling QCMDEXC 320
Data Areas 321
Data-Area Data Structures 322
Using *NAMVAR DEFN 322
Chapter Summary 325
Terms 327
Discussion/Review Questions 327
Exercises 327
Programming Assignments 328

Chapter 13: Looking Backward: RPG II 331
    Chapter Overview 331
    RPG II: An Initial Look 331
    RPG's Fixed-Logic Cycle 336
    The Fixed-Logic Cycle and Control Breaks 337
    Decisions in RPG II 342
    Resulting Indicators and Arithmetic 346
    Iteration and RPG II 347
    Chapter Summary 350
    Terms 351
    Discussion/Review Questions 351
    Exercises 351
    Programming Assignments 354

Chapter 14: Looking Forward: RPG IV 357
    Chapter Overview 357
    Introduction to RPG IV 357
    Modifications to File Specifications 360
    Modifications to Extension Specifications 362
    Introducing Definition Specifications 362
    Modifications to Input Specifications 368
    Modifications to Calculation Specifications 369
    Modifications to Output Specifications 376
    Putting It All Together 377
    Pseudocode for Invoice Program 378
    Chapter Summary 383
    Terms 385
    Discussion/Review Questions 385
    Exercises 385
    Programming Assignments 386

Appendix A: Developing Programs on the AS/400 389
    The Programmer Menu 390
    Programming Development Manager (PDM) 391

Appendix B: Source Entry Utility (SEU) 399
    SEU Overview 399
    Using Prompts 400
    Working Within the Edit Display 402
    Function Keys in SEU 403
    SEU's Command Line 403
    Working with a Split Screen 404
    Exiting SEU 405

Appendix C: Program Testing and Debugging 407
    Syntax Errors 407
    Logic Errors 408

Runtime Errors 408
Diagnosing Abends 408
Diagnosing Infinite Loops 409
Output Errors 410
Detecting Output Errors 410
Correcting Output Errors 411
Debug 413
Breakpoints 414
Trace Commands 414

Appendix D: Data Files 417
Case 1: CompuSell 417
Case 2: Wexler University 421
Case 3: GTC, Inc. 426
Miscellaneous Files 427

Appendix E: RPG IV and RPG/400 431
Chapter 1 Modifications 431
Chapter 2 Modifications 431
Chapter 3 Modifications 434
Chapter 4 Modifications 435
Chapter 5 Modifications 435
Chapter 6 Modifications 436
Chapter 7 Modifications 436
Chapter 8 Modifications 436
Chapter 9 Modifications 439
Chapter 10 Modifications 442
Chapter 11 Modifications 442
Chapter 12 Modifications 444
Chapter 13 Modifications 444

Glossary 447

Index 465

Preface

This second edition is designed to provide a transition from RPG/400 to RPG IV, the version of RPG that participates in IBM's Integrated Language Environment (ILE). Look for the new final chapter (Chapter 14: Looking Ahead: RPG IV), which summarizes the key features of RPG IV. In addition, although the content of the original chapters still focuses on RPG/400, a new appendix (Appendix E: RPG IV and RPG/400) points out how the material in each chapter is affected by the new version of the language. These effects consist of "Mandatory Changes" — features of RPG/400 that will not work with the RPG IV compiler — and "Optional Changes" — enhancements to RPG/400 that can be used, but are not required by the compiler.

Other changes to the text include revised figures (reworked for increased clarity) and a section on externally described printer files (added to Chapter 5: Externally Described Files). Finally, numerous small (but annoying) code inaccuracies have been corrected.

The purpose of this book is to instruct students in the syntax of RPG/400 and the programming methods used by today's RPG programmers — and to prepare them for the time when RPG IV has been more universally adopted. Its primary purpose is to serve as a classroom text for a first course that introduces students to RPG programming, but it is also suitable for those experienced programmers who wish to learn another language.

The book attempts to bridge the gap between academia and the business world by presenting all the facets of RPG/400 needed by a professional programmer. The material is introduced gradually, and it is organized such that students will be able to write simple procedural programs by the end of Chapter 2. Each successive chapter includes additional facts about RPG and programming techniques to make students increasingly knowledgeable about RPG and, as the term progresses, increasingly proficient at programming.

Each chapter includes a brief overview to orient students to the material contained in the chapter and a chapter summary reiterating the major points covered. In addition, the chapters contain discussion/review questions, exercises, and programming assignments. A major challenge for a programming instructor is to help students develop their analytical and problem solving skills, so that they can apply concepts to new situations. The end-of-chapter material is designed to make students think, rather than simply repeat memorized terms or recode algorithms presented within the chapters.

The assignments at the ends of the chapters are arranged in order of increasing difficulty, so that instructors can assign programs appropriate to their time schedules and their students' abilities. Some of the programs are difficult and will require time and effort on the part of the students to develop correct solutions. Unfortunately, there is no easy way to learn to become a good programmer, nor can you learn to deal with program complexity by merely reading or talking about it. Those students interested in becoming

MIS professionals must recognize that they have chosen a rewarding but demanding and challenging profession, and they need to realize that they must be willing to devote the effort required to succeed in that profession.

To provide students with a sense of application system development, and not just stand-alone programs, most of the programming assignments are part of three application systems described in Appendix D. By working on these assignments, students should gain a sense of how data files are repeatedly used by numerous applications for different, related purposes.

Although a complete introduction to using the AS/400 is beyond the scope of this text, Appendices A and B introduce students to working on the system using the Programmer Menu, PDM, and SEU. Appendix C tries to provide some insights into program testing and debugging, often a bewildering process for beginning programmers.

Depending on the length of your term and the pace you wish to set, instructors may choose to present this material over two terms or to omit some of the more technical chapters less central to RPG/400. If you have already installed V3R1 of OS/400 on your system, you should direct students to read the appropriate section from Appendix E as you present each chapter; they should also read Chapter 14. If you still work with an RPG/400 compiler, you simply may want students to read Chapter 14 at the end of the term to acquaint them with the features of RPG IV. Chapters 1-9 and 13 definitely should be presented to provide students with the minimal information needed by entry-level RPG programmers.

An instructor's manual is available to those instructors adopting this text for classroom use; the manual includes answers to the review questions, solutions to the exercises, and solutions to the programming assignments. The manual also comes with a diskette containing all the data files needed by the programming assignments and the source code of solutions to the programming assignments, as well.

Chapter 1

Introduction to Programming and RPG

Chapter Overview

This chapter introduces you to RPG as a programming language. It also explains general programming and computer-related concepts that you need to know as you begin learning to program in RPG/400.

Programming

Computer programming involves writing instructions for a computer that tell it how to process, or manipulate, data. In many programming languages, these instructions depict a step-by-step procedure needed to produce a specific result or product, such as a sales report. These kinds of languages are called **procedural languages**. Procedural languages require that you explicitly state each processing step or instruction for the computer. Moreover, you must accurately describe the order or sequence in which the computer is to execute these steps for the program to produce correct results.

The computer is a binary device. Designed with electronic components that can depict only two states — on or off, or flow of current or no flow — computers internally store and manipulate instructions (and data) as patterns of **bits**, or **binary digits**. Programmers originally were forced to write computer instructions as strings of 1s and 0s, using machine language. Humans, however, do not function as well at this low representation level. Fortunately, advances in computer science soon led to the development of **high-level languages (HLLs)**.

Programs written in HLLs require translation into the bit patterns of machine language before a computer can actually execute their instructions. The computer itself can accomplish this translation using a special program called a **compile**r. A compiler translates a program written in an HLL into machine language that the computer can understand.

History of RPG

IBM introduced the **Report Program Generator (RPG)** programming language in the early 1960s. RPG filled a niche for providing quick solutions to a common business task: generating reports needed within the business. By designing RPG to be relatively easy to learn and to use, IBM set the stage for today's **Fourth Generation Languages (4GLs)**.

Unlike the procedural languages in use at the time, RPG did not require the programmer to detail each processing step required. Instead, the language included a fixed-logic cycle that automatically executed the normal cycle of read-calculate-write found in most report programs. In RPG, the programmer's job was to describe accurately to the computer the files, record layouts, calculations, and output desired for a specific program; the RPG compiler supplied the needed missing steps to provide a standard machine-language program for the computer to execute. RPG required that these descriptive specifications appear in a specific sequence within a program and that entries within a program line appear in fixed locations, or columns, within each line.

Another unique characteristic of RPG was its use of a special class of built-in variables called **indicators**. These variables, many of which simply had numbers for names, were predefined to the computer and could have only one of two values — '1' or '0' (corresponding to "on" or "off"). These indicators could be set on or off in one part of the program; their status would then be referenced in another part of the program to determine what processing was to occur.

By the late 1960s, RPG had gained popularity, especially in small- and medium-sized data processing departments. Programmers were stretching the language beyond its original intended use, using the language for complex computations and complicated file updating, as well as for report generation. Accordingly, IBM introduced an enhanced version of the language, RPG II, when it released its System/3 computer. Although other computer vendors saw the popularity of RPG and developed RPG II compilers for their minicomputers, RPG remained, for the most part, a language associated with IBM installations.

During the 1970s, several trends in data processing became apparent. First, as computers became cheaper and more powerful, and as operating systems became more sophisticated, interest in interactive programs began to mushroom. In **interactive applications**, a user interacts with the computer directly through a terminal or workstation to control the actions of a computer program as it is running. Previously, programs had involved **batch processing**, in which the computer processed a "batch" of data (typically representing business transactions) without user intervention.

A second emerging trend was a growing interest in a database approach to data management. With a database approach, programmers define data independently of programs, in a central data dictionary. The files storing the data are rigorously designed and organized to minimize redundancy and to facilitate accessing data stored in separate files. Any program can use these database files without having to define the data within the program itself.

Finally, a third trend during that decade was an increasing concern with program design. This trend resulted in a methodology called **structured design**. As companies' libraries of developed programs continued to grow, the need to revise those programs to fit evolving business needs grew as well. It became apparent that computer professionals had paid too little attention to the initial design of programs. Poorly designed programs were causing inefficiencies in program maintenance. Experts attributed much of this inefficiency to "spaghetti code," that is, programs that included undisciplined, haphazard transfer of control from one portion of the program to another.

Advocates of structured design recommended restricting indiscriminate flow of control within a program and using only those operations that kept tight controls on that flow. With this emphasis on structured design, concepts of modular programming and code reusability also began to emerge.

IBM addressed all these trends when it introduced the System/38 minicomputer in 1979. This computer's architecture was unique in that the design of the computer and its operating system had a built-in database approach; the S/38 required data files to be predefined at a system level before a program could reference or use those files. This requirement alone forced IBM to release a new version of RPG to allow external file definition. IBM called this version RPG III.

IBM made several other major changes to RPG at this time as well. First, they added features that made it easier for programmers to develop interactive applications. Second, they included structured operations for looping and decision logic to address the issues of structured design. Finally, to support modular code and reusability, IBM revamped the language to include the capability to perform calls to other programs and to pass data between programs.

In 1988, IBM announced its successor computer to the S/38 — the Application System/400. With the new computer came a new version of RPG, RPG/400. Despite its changed name, RPG/400 was really just a minor upgrade of RPG III, with a few new operations and enhancements. Following RPG/400's initial release, IBM periodically added additional features to the language, but these changes were also relatively minor. Meanwhile, a growing number of critics accused RPG of being difficult to understand because of its short data names, abbreviated operation codes, and rigidly fixed format. These critics contended that the language was showing its age in its limited choice of data types (e.g., no direct support for date data types), its inability to handle multidimensional arrays, and its patchwork approach to data definition.

To address some of these criticisms, in 1994, concurrent with the release of V3R1 of the AS/400's operating system, IBM introduced a version of RPG sufficiently unlike earlier versions that it warranted a change in name: RPG IV. In addition to trying to address the criticisms mentioned above, IBM included RPG as part of its newly introduced Integrated Language Environment (ILE), which allows program modules to be first compiled and then bound together into executable programs. This change supported the growing interest in developing reusable units of code and improving system performance. Moreover, it allowed the programmer to develop an application using modules written in different languages and then bind these modules into a single application.

These changes have quieted, but not suppressed RPG's critics. However, given the large base of existing RPG applications and IBM's present willingness to support RPG, it is likely that the language will continue to evolve and will remain the primary language for application development on the AS/400 throughout this decade.

If you compared RPG programs written 20 years ago with those written by RPG professionals today, you would be struck by their great design differences. These differences are not due solely to the use of operations unavailable in the past, although the new operations enabled the changes. The biggest change is that RPG, originally a language that emphasized specification instead of procedure, has been transformed by programming practices into a procedural language. Today's programmers virtually ignore RPG's fixed-logic cycle — the feature that made the language unique in the 1960s. And most modern programmers use RPG's indicators only in those instances where the language absolutely requires their use.

Most RPG texts start by instructing students in RPG II, and introduce RPG III or RPG/400 only after thoroughly indoctrinating the students in the fixed-logic cycle and the use of indicators. This book begins by teaching RPG as today's programmers use it. Only after you have mastered modern RPG will you become familiar with features of the language common in the past.

You may wonder why, if RPG programming has changed so much, you as a student need to bother at all with features of RPG II. The reason is simple. For better or worse, most companies are still using some programs that were written 10 or more years ago. Because your first job in the computer profession probably will involve maintenance programming, you no doubt will be working with some programs based on RPG II. Accordingly, you will need to understand the features of this language version so you can modify such programs when you encounter them. Chapter 13 of this text points out the important differences between RPG II and RPG/400 that you will need to know to round out your understanding of this language. Chapter 14 tries to give you a taste of what RPG programs will look like in the future as programmers adopt RPG IV.

Now that you have an understanding of RPG's evolution, we can turn to some basic programming concepts that you need to know before you begin to learn RPG programming.

Program Variables

Computer programs would be of little value if you needed a different program each time you wanted to change the values of the data to be processed. For example, assume you were developing a payroll program, and one processing step was to multiply hours worked by pay rate. If you had to rewrite this step to state explicitly the number of hours worked and the hourly pay rate for each employee, you would be better off calculating wages by hand or with a calculator. The power and value of computer programming rests in the concept of variables.

A **program variable** represents a location in the memory of the computer that can store data. When a programming instruction involves the manipulation of a variable, the computer checks the value stored at that memory location and uses that value in the calculation. Thus, you can tell the computer to take the value stored in variable HRS and multiply that by the value stored in variable RATE and store the answer in variable GRSPAY. If HRS contained 35 and RATE 6, GRSPAY would become 210. If HRS contained 40 and RATE 5, GRSPAY would become 200.

RPG generally uses the term **field** rather than **variable**. The language requires that you define all fields by naming them, assigning them a fixed length that determines the amount of memory allocated for storing each field's values, and declaring whether the values are to consist of **alphanumeric** (character) or **numeric data**. You will learn the methods RPG uses to define fields in subsequent chapters of this book.

Data Files and the Data Hierarchy

In the business world, data processing typically centers on processing sets of data from files stored on disk or tape. Files of data of temporary importance, generated during the course of the day's business, are **transaction files**. Once you have processed a transaction file, you typically have no further use for it. In contrast, most companies have sets of data that are of long-term importance to the company. These files, called **master files**, contain vital information about customers, products, accounts, and so on. Although you may update or change master files, companies regard master files as permanent files of data.

All files, transaction or master, are organized into a data hierarchy of file-record-field. A **file** is a collection of data about a given kind of entity or object. For example, a business might have a customer master file that contains information about its customers. A file, in turn, is broken down into **records** that contain data about one specific instance of the entity. Data about customer #20 would be stored in a record within the customer file; data about customer #321 would be stored in a separate record within that file.

Finally, each record contains several discrete pieces of data about each entity instance. For example, a customer record might contain the customer's account number, last name, first name, street address, city, state, zip code, phone number, date of last order, credit limit, and so on. Each of these items is a **field**. A field generally represents the smallest unit of data that we want to manipulate within a program. Figure 1.1 illustrates this data hierarchy.

All records within a file usually contain the same fields of data. Because you define these fields to be fixed in length, if an alphanumeric value (for example, a person's last name) is shorter than the space allocated for it, blanks, or spaces, occupy the unused positions to the right of the value. If a numeric value is smaller than the space allocated for it, the system stores zeros in the unused positions. If quantity-on-hand, for example, was 6 positions long and had a value of 24, the value would be stored in the file as 000024. Note that numeric values are stored as "pure" numbers, without dollar signs, commas, or decimal points.

Figure 1.1
Example of
the Data Hierarchy

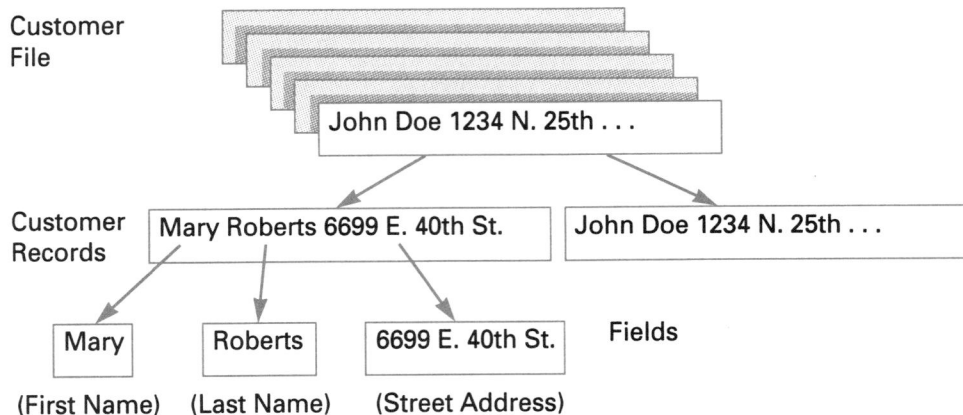

A file occasionally may contain different record types, each with its distinct format. In this case, each record usually contains a code field whose value signals which format that record represents. Figure 1.2 illustrates a data file with multiple record formats.

Figure 1.2
Order File with
Multiple Record Formats

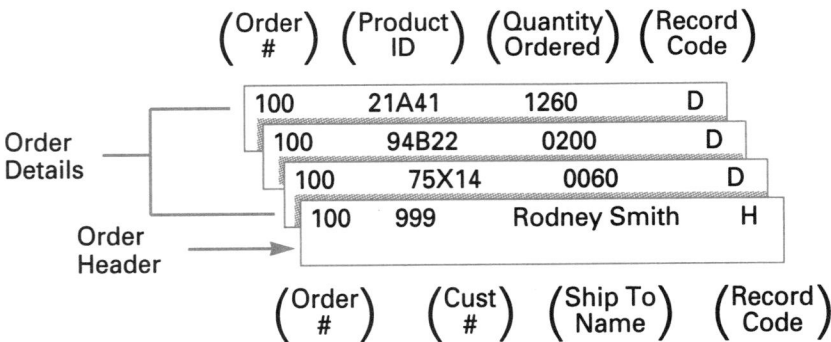

Programming Specifications

In many installations, programmers work from specifications given to them by systems analysts. These specifications detail the desired output of a program, the required input, and a general statement of the processing required. The programmer must then develop the instructions needed to generate the appropriate output from the given input, ensuring that the correct data manipulations take place.

Analysts often provide **record layouts** to describe the record formats of input files to be used by a program. One method of presenting a record layout shows the beginning and ending position of data fields within records; other methods list fields in the order in which they appear in records and give the length of each field or the positions of the fields within records. These methods, illustrated in Figure 1.3, include information about the number of decimal positions of numeric data.

Figure 1.3
Alternate Methods of
Describing Record Layouts

Item Number	Description	Quantity on Hand 0 decimals	Unit Cost 2 decimals	Vendor Code	Reorder Point 0 decimals
1 5	6 25	27 35	36 40	41 43	44 52

Field	Length	Decimal Positions
Item Number	5	
Description	20	
Quantity on Hand	9	0
Unit Cost	5	2
Vendor Code	3	
Reorder Point	9	0

Field	Positions	Decimal Positions
Item Number	1- 5	
Description	6- 25	
Quantity on Hand	27- 35	0
Unit Cost	36- 40	2
Vendor Code	41- 43	
Reorder Point	44- 52	0

When the desired output includes a report, a **printer spacing chart (PSC)** provides the details of the desired report layout. The position of lines within the chart indicates the desired line spacing for the report. The printer spacing chart shows all constants (report headings or titles, column headings, and so on) that the report should include and where on the report they should appear. Printer spacing charts generally represent variable information with Xs, where each X represents one character of data.

We often want numeric data presented with special formats to facilitate comprehension. The printer spacing chart can depict the desired formatting, or **output editing**. Although there is no single accepted convention for indicating desired output editing, programmers generally recognize the notation presented in this chapter section (and used throughout this book).

Commas, decimal points, and other insertion characters included within the Xs signal that these characters are to appear in the printed output. A zero within the Xs signals that **zero suppression** is desired.

Zero suppression simply means that leading, nonsignificant zeros are not printed. Thus, 000123 would print as ҏҏҏ123 if zero suppression were in effect (ҏ = blank). The location of the 0 within the Xs indicates the extent to which blanks, rather than leading zeros, are to print. X0XX signals "suppress up to and including the hundred's place but no farther." With that format, 0001 should print as ҏҏ01. A zero at the end of the format — e.g., XXX0 — signals that zero suppression should continue to the right-most digit; with that format, a value of 0000 should print as all blanks.

Dollar signs can appear two ways in output: as fixed or as floating dollar signs. A **fixed dollar sign** is positioned in a set column of the output, regardless of the number of significant digits in the number following the sign. A

floating dollar sign prints next to the left-most significant digit of the number; its position varies, or "floats," depending on the value of the number it is associated with. In a printer spacing chart, you can denote a fixed dollar sign by adding a single dollar sign to the immediate left of the Xs representing a numeric field. To signal a floating dollar sign, use two dollar signs, one at the far left of the Xs and the other in place of the zero suppression character.

PSC Notation	Meaning
$XXXX.XX	Fixed dollar sign, no zero suppression, no comma.
$X,XX0.XX	Fixed dollar sign, zero-suppress to unit's place, insert commas.
X,XX.XX	Floating dollar sign, zero-suppress to unit's place, insert commas.
XX0	No dollar sign or decimal; complete zero suppression.

Printer spacing charts also indicate how the analyst wants negative values to print. A single hyphen at the left signals a fixed negative sign. Two hyphens, one to the left and one in place of a zero, indicate a floating negative sign. A single hyphen or CR to the right of the Xs signals a fixed, trailing negative sign or Credit notation.

PSC Notation	Meaning
XXX	No sign to be displayed.
–XX0	Fixed sign, complete zero suppression.
–XX–.XX	Floating sign, zero-suppress to unit's place.
XX0.XX–	Zero-suppress, trailing negative sign.
XX0.XXCR	Zero-suppress, indicate negative value with CR.

Figure 1.4 illustrates a printer spacing chart that includes headings, lines of detailed information, departmental subtotals, and a grand total. Note that the chart indicates that slashes should be inserted within the date and that asterisks are to appear to the right of totals.

Figure 1.4
Sample Printer Spacing Chart

```
            1         2         3         4         5         6         7         8
   12345678901234567890123456789012345678901234567890123456789012345678901234567890
   XX/XX/XX                                                        PAGE XXØX
                                 MONTHLY SALES REPORT
                     SLSPSN.                                          SALES
          DEPT.        NO.         SLSPSN. NAME                      AMOUNT
          XX          XXXX        XXXXXXXXXXXXXXXXXXXXXXXXXX        XX,XXØ.XX
                      XXXX        XXXXXXXXXXXXXXXXXXXXXXXXXX        XX,XXØ.XX

                                             DEPARTMENT TOTAL    X,XXX,XXØ.XX*

          XX          XXXX        XXXXXXXXXXXXXXXXXXXXXXXXXX        XX,XXØ.XX
                      XXXX        XXXXXXXXXXXXXXXXXXXXXXXXXX        XX,XXØ.XX

                                             DEPARTMENT TOTAL    X,XXX,XXØ.XX*

                                             GRAND TOTAL      $XXX,XXX,XX$.XX**
```

The Program Development Cycle

The programmer's job is to develop a solution to a data processing problem represented by the program specifications. The generally accepted method for achieving this solution is called the **Program Development Cycle**. This cycle, which summarizes the sequence of activities required in programming, can be summarized as follows:

- Define the problem.
- Design the solution.
- Write the program.
- Enter the program.
- Test and debug the program.
- Document the program.
- Maintain the program.

The cycle starts with *problem definition*. It should be obvious that unless you understand the problem, as described in the programming specifications, you have little chance of coming up with a correct solution.

Once you understand the problem, you need to design a solution to the problem. *Program design* requires working out the solution, or **algorithm**, to the problem before expressing the solution in a given programming language. Formal design tools such as program flow charts, Warnier-Orr diagrams, or pseudocode can help clarify and illustrate program logic. Some programmers develop their own methods of sketching out a program solution. Regardless of the method used, the importance of designing a solution *before* writing the program cannot be overemphasized. Developing a correct, well-structured design for a program represents the challenge of programming; this is the stage where most of your thinking should take place. Time spent at the design stage results in time saved fixing problems later in the cycle.

Writing the program is translating the design into a program using a particular programming language. This stage is often called "coding." Beginning programmers may find this task difficult because they are unfamiliar with the rules of the language. Once you have mastered the syntax of a language, however, coding becomes almost a mechanical process that requires relatively little thought. The challenge of programming lies in design.

Entering the program consists of inputting the program statements into the computer. Years ago, program statements were punched onto cards; today, most program entry is done interactively on a terminal, using a system utility called an **editor**.

Testing the program is required to determine the existence of syntax errors or logic errors in your solution. **Syntax errors** are errors in your use of the rules of the language. These errors are flagged by the computer, either as you enter the statements, or later, when the computer tries to translate your statements into machine language. **Logic errors** are errors of design; it is up to the programmer to detect such errors through rigorous program testing by running the program with sets of test data and carefully checking the accuracy of the program's output. **Debugging** means correcting any errors discovered. Testing should continue until you are convinced that the program is working correctly.

Documenting the program refers to providing material useful for understanding, using, or modifying the program. Some documentation, such as system and program flowcharts, user manuals, or operator instructions may be **external** to the program. **Internal documentation** refers to comments included within the code itself. Such comments make the program more understandable to other programmers. Although documentation appears as one of the final stages in the cycle, documentation is best developed as you progress through the stages of the cycle. For example, it is easiest to provide comments within a program as you are actually entering the program, rather than waiting until the program is completely tested and running.

Program maintenance is making modifications once the program is actually being used, or "in production." Estimates are that up to 70 percent of a programmer's time is spent modifying existing programs. The need for maintenance may arise from a "bug" discovered in the program or from changing user needs. Because maintenance is a way of life, any program you develop should be designed with future maintenance ease in mind. This means, among other things, that your code's logic should be clear, the variable names well-chosen, and the internal comments appropriate and sufficient.

Program Entry and Testing

To complete the program entry and testing stages, you need to eliminate all program errors. These errors fall into two general classes: syntax errors and logic errors. Syntax errors represent violation of the rules of the language itself; they are relatively easily detected and corrected. Logic errors are errors in your program that cause the program to produce incorrect results; these problems are detected by extensively testing the program with sets of test data and correcting any program statements that are causing incorrect processing.

As mentioned earlier, you typically enter a program by interacting with the system's editor. Your program statements are called **source code**; the set of statements for one program constitute a **source member** on the AS/400.

The AS/400 editor will detect some syntax errors as you enter your program and will allow you to correct them immediately. Other syntax errors become apparent when you attempt to **compile** your program. Compiling means translating the source code into machine language, or **object code**. The AS/400 has a program, called a compiler, that accomplishes this translation, provided that you have not violated any rules of RPG in writing your program. If syntax errors prevent the translation from completing, the compiler provides you with a list of the syntax errors it encountered. All such errors need to be fixed before you can progress to the next stage of testing.

Once your program has successfully compiled, you need to run it with test data to determine whether or not it is working correctly. Note that the computer executes the object code, or the translated version of your program. Errors discovered at this stage require that you back up, make changes to the program using the editor, and then recompile your program prior to additional testing.

Figure 1.5 illustrates this iterative process. If you forget to recompile your program after making changes to the source code, the program runs your *old* version of the program, because you have not created a new object incorporating those changes.

Figure 1.5

Flowchart Illustrating Steps
Required to Enter, Test, and
Debug a Program

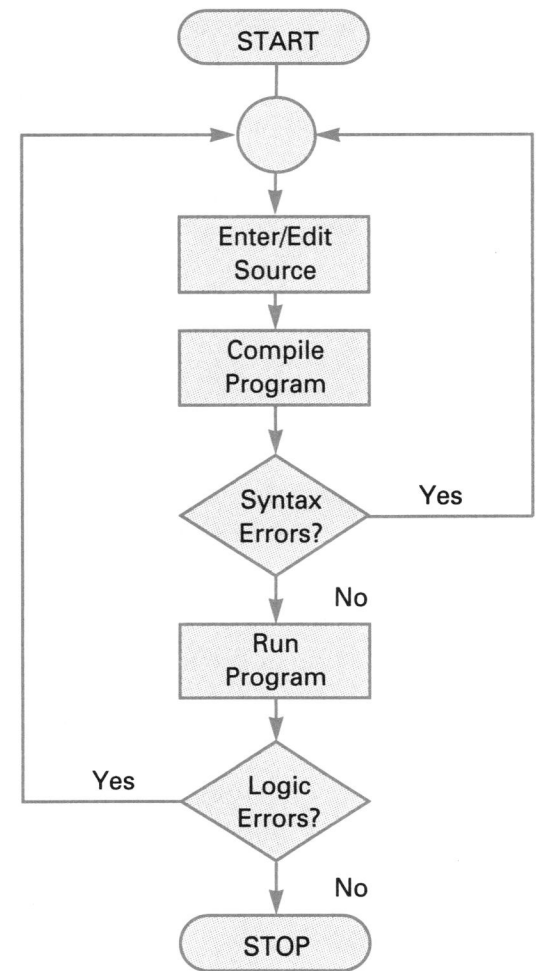

Chapter Summary

RPG (Report Program Generator) is a high-level programming language introduced by IBM in the early 1960s to provide an easy way to produce commonly needed business reports. IBM has added enhancements to the language since its introduction to expand the functionality of RPG. Programmers originally used RPG's fixed-logic cycle and built-in indicators to minimize the need for explicit procedural instructions within their programs. As processing requirements have grown more complex and concerns for program understandability have increased, programmers have moved away from the fixed-logic cycle and now tend to explicitly include all processing instructions within their programs.

Variables enable programs to process different sets of data. RPG provides this flexibility through fixed-length fields that may represent character or numeric data. Data is typically organized in a hierarchy of files, records, and fields. Relatively temporary data files that often need to be processed only a single time are called transaction files, while files of data of lasting importance to the company are called master files.

The process of developing a program is often described as the Program Development Cycle. The cycle begins with problem definition. The problem often is presented through programming specifications, which include record layouts of files to be used by the program, printer spacing charts that describe the layout of desired reports, and an overview of needed processing.

In addition to defining the problem, the Program Development Cycle includes designing the solution, writing the program, entering the program, testing and debugging, documenting, and — eventually — maintaining the program once it is in production. Too often, programmers short-cut the design stage and try to develop their logic as they write the program. This approach often leads to programs that are poorly designed or full of errors that must be corrected.

You enter an RPG program as source code using the AS/400's editor. The program is stored as a source member within a source file on the system. Because computers actually execute machine language instructions, your source program needs to be translated to an object program of machine language before the computer can run it. A special program called a compiler performs this translation. As part of its translation, the compiler flags any entries in your source program that it cannot understand. These kinds of errors are called syntax errors, because they are caused by your misuse of the rules of the language. Syntax errors prevent the creation of an object program.

Once your program has successfully compiled, you need to correct any logic errors in the program that are preventing the program from working correctly to produce the desired results. Each time you use the editor to correct a problem in your program, you must recompile the program before running it to incorporate the changes into the object program.

Terms

algorithm	high-level languages (HLLs)	program variable
alphanumeric data	indicator	record
batch processing	interactive applications	record layouts
bits (binary digits)	internal documentation	Report Program Generator
compile	logic errors	(RPG)
compiler	master files	source code
debugging	numeric data	source member
editor	object code	structured design
external documentation	output editing	syntax errors
field	printer spacing chart (PSC)	transaction files
file	problem definition	zero suppression
fixed dollar sign	procedural languages	
floating dollar sign	program design	
Fourth Generation	Program Development Cycle	
Languages (4GLs)	program maintenance	

Discussion/Review Questions

1. What was the original purpose of RPG?

2. What's an indicator?

3. What trends emerged in the 1970s to influence the enhancements included in RPG III?

4. Do you think that a programming language that requires revisions over time is poorly designed in the first place? Why or why not?

5. Give an example of a syntax error and a logic error in your native language (e.g., English).

6. Would it make sense to describe a person's complete address (street address, city, state, zip code) as one field? Why or why not?

7. Would you define each letter in a person's last name as a separate field? Why or why not?

8. Keeping in mind the fact that all records within a file generally have the same, fixed number of fields, how do you think your school handles the problem of storing information about what courses you've taken?

9. Differentiate between source code and object code.

10. How many times do you need to compile a program?

11. Would you build a house without a blueprint? Is this a good analogy to writing a program without first designing it? Why or why not?

Exercises

1. Develop a list of data fields you think your school might store in its student master file. Design a record layout for this file that includes the length needed for each field, an indication of the data type (character or numeric), and the number of decimal positions of numeric fields.

2. For each printer spacing chart (PSC) notation that follows, show how the data value associated with each should appear when printed.

	PSC Notation	Data Value
a.	XXXXX	98100
b.	XXXXX	01254
c.	XX,XX0	31331
d.	XX,XX0	00010
e.	XX,XX0	01000
f.	XX,XX0	00000
g.	$XX,X0X	00872
h.	XX,XX	00298
i.	XX,XX	00000
j.	–XX,X–X	–07254
k.	–XX,X–X	00451
l.	XX,X0XDB	–00923
m.	XX,XX0–	–91486
n.	XX,XX0–	00000

Chapter 2

Getting Started

Chapter Overview

This chapter introduces you to RPG specifications forms. You will learn how to write simple read/write programs using a procedural approach. You will also learn how to include comment lines to document your program. Finally, this chapter teaches you RPG's techniques of output editing to control the appearance of values on reports.

Specifications Forms in RPG

RPG programs consist of different kinds of lines, called specifications; each type of specification has a particular purpose. You use **File Description Specifications**, for example, to identify the files your program uses, and **Calculation Specifications** to detail the arithmetic operations to be performed by your program. Each kind of specification has a different identifier, or form type, which must appear in position 6 of each program line. A File Specification line of code, for example, must include an F in position 6.

Not every program requires the use of every kind of specification. However, all those that you use must appear in a specific order, or sequence, within your program, with all program lines representing the same kind of specification grouped together. You will learn this order as you are introduced to the details of each kind of specification.

RPG programs are characterized by fixed-position entries within these specification forms. **Fixed-position**, or **fixed-form**, means that the location of an entry within a program line is critical to its interpretation by the RPG compiler. If you use coding sheets to develop your program, the sheets have headings to help you make the correct entries in the correct locations. **Source Entry Utility (SEU)**, the AS/400 editor you use to enter your program, also can provide you with prompts to facilitate making your entries in the proper location. (Appendix B provides more information about SEU.)

As you begin to work with specifications, don't be overwhelmed by what appear to be hundreds of entries with multiple options. Fortunately, many entries are optional, and you will use them only for complex processing or for achieving specific effects. This book will introduce these entries gradually, initially providing you with just those entries needed to write simple programs. As your mastery of the language grows, you will learn how to use additional specification entries required to develop more complex programs.

When you begin writing your first program, you will notice that an entry does not always take up all the positions allocated for it within a specification. When that happens, a good rule of thumb is that alphabetic entries start at the left-most position of the allocated space, with unused positions to the right; numeric entries are usually right-adjusted, with unused positions to the left.

Program Specifications for Example Program

In this chapter, you will learn the minimal entries needed to procedurally code a simple read/write program. To help you understand how to write such a program, we will walk through writing an RPG program to solve the following problem.

You have a file, SALES; records in the file are laid out as follows:

Field	Positions	Decimal Positions
Salesperson number	1- 4	0
Salesperson name	5 -34	
Item sold	35 -50	
Date of sale	51 -56	0
Sale price	57 -63	2

You want to produce a report laid out as follows:

```
          1         2         3         4         5         6         7         8
 12345678901234567890123456789012345678901234567890123456789012345678901234567890

     PAGE XX0X                   WEEKLY SALES REPORT              DATE XX/XX/XX

 SLSM.                                         DATE OF                        SALE
 NO.                NAME                        SALE      ITEM SOLD           PRICE

 XXXX    XXXXXXXXXXXXXXXXXXXXXXXXXXXXXX    XX/XX/XX    XXXXXXXXXXXXXXXX    XX,XX0.XX
 XXXX    XXXXXXXXXXXXXXXXXXXXXXXXXXXXXX    XX/XX/XX    XXXXXXXXXXXXXXXX    XX,XX0.XX
```

When you compare the desired output to the input record layout, you should note that all of the output fields are present on the input records. No data transformation or generation needs to take place within the program. The processing required, then, consists of reading each record from the input file, writing that data to the report with appropriate headings, and formatting the variable data.

File Description Specifications

Generally, RPG programs begin with File Description Specifications. All file specifications include an F in position 6. These specifications describe the files your program uses and define how the files will be used within the program. Each file used by a program requires its own file specification line. In our illustrative problem, file SALES contains the data we want to process.

The output of the program is a report. Although you generally think of a report as hard-copy, rather than a file *per se*, on the AS/400 you produce a report through a printer file. We normally use a system-supplied printer file, QPRINT, as the destination file for our report lines. This file then resides as a spooled file in an output queue, where it will wait for you to release it to the printer. Your instructor will tell you which printer file to use in your programs and explain how to work with spooled files in the output queue. Appendix A of this text also contains helpful information about working with output on the AS/400.

You need to code one file specification for each file the program uses. Although you can describe the files in any order, it is customary to describe the input file first.

FILENAME (positions 7-14)
First, in positions 7-14, labeled FILENAME on the sheet, enter the name of the file. In RPG, file names can be a maximum of eight characters long. They must begin with an uppercase alphabetic character or $, #, or @; the remaining characters may be uppercase alphabetic characters, numbers, or any of the three special characters #, $, and @. A file name cannot contain blanks embedded within the permissible characters. Our practice problem input file is called SALES. The report file is QPRINT.

Note that you code file names, like other alphabetic entries, beginning in the left-most position allowed for that entry — in this case, position 7. Simply leave blank any unneeded positions to the right of the name.

FILE TYPE (position 15)
Position 15 specifies the type of file, or how the file will be used by the program. The two types we will initially work with are input (type I) and output (type O). An **input file** contains data to be read by the program; an **output file** is the destination for writing operations of the program. In our example, SALES is an input file, while QPRINT is an output file.

FILE DESIGNATION (position 16; input files only)
Every input file requires an entry for file designation (position 16). File designation refers to the way the program will access, or retrieve, the data in the file. In our example, we are going to retrieve data by *explicitly* reading records within our program, rather than by using the built-in retrieval of RPG's fixed-logic cycle. In RPG terminology, that makes the file **full procedural**, so F is the appropriate entry for position 16.

FILE FORMAT (position 19)
The next required entry is file format. An F in position 19 stands for fixed format, which means that file records will be described within this program and that each record has the same, fixed length. Although it is preferable to describe files externally, for simplicity's sake we will start with

program-described files and progress to externally described files later (Chapter 5). Because our files will be program described, an F is appropriate for the files of our sample program. All files, regardless of type, require an entry for File Format.

RECORD LENGTH (positions 24-27)
You need to define the record length for each program-described file. Records of data files can be of almost any length; it is important that you code the correct value for this specification. Because SALES has a record length of 63, we enter 63 in positions 24-27. Note that record length is coded right-adjusted within the positions allocated for this entry. This is typical of most RPG entries requiring a numeric value.

Most printers support a line of 132 characters. As a result, records of printer files (which correspond to lines of report output) are 132 positions long. Accordingly, output file QPRINT is assigned a record length of 132 on the File Specification.

DEVICE (positions 40-46)
A final required entry is Device. Database files are stored on disk. Accordingly, DISK is the appropriate entry for the SALES file. The device associated with printer files is PRINTER. These device names are entered left-adjusted in positions 40-46.

There are no other file specification entries required to describe the files used by our sample program. The completed file specifications for the program are shown below.

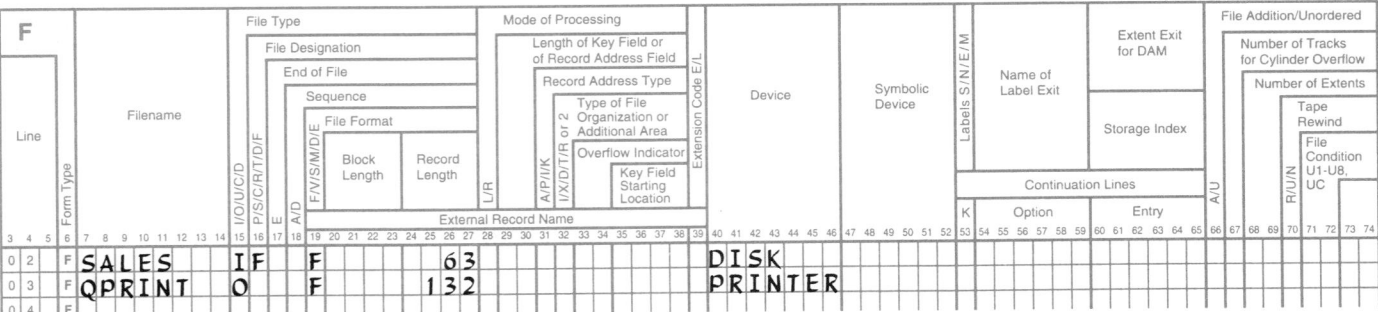

Input Specifications

Input Specifications, identified by an I in position 6, come after File Specifications. Input Specifications describe the records within program-described input files and define the fields within the records. Every program-described input file defined on the File Specifications must be represented by a set of Input Specification lines.

Input Specifications use two types of lines: lines representing record identification entries, which describe the input records at a general level, and lines representing field description entries, which describe the specific fields within the records. The record identification line must precede the field entries for that record.

Record Identification Entries

FILE NAME (positions 7-14)

A record identification line must contain the name of the input file in positions 7-14. This name must match the entry on the File Description Specification, in our case, SALES. The file name is a left-adjusted entry.

SEQUENCE (positions 15-16)

The next required record identification entry is Sequence, in positions 15-16. This entry signals whether or not the system should check the order of records in the file as the records are read during program execution. Sequence checking is relevant only when a file contains multiple record formats (that is, records with different field layouts). When sequence checking is not appropriate, code any two alphabetic characters in positions 15-16 to signal that sequence checking is not required. Many programmers use NS to signal "no sequence." Because the SALES file contains a single record format, we enter NS in positions 15-16.

The complete record identification specification is illustrated below. Note that with the specification coded this way, the compiler will issue a warning that a record identification indicator is missing from the line. Although record identification indicators are relevant in fixed-logic processing (discussed in Chapter 13), they are not used in modern RPG programming. Simply ignore the compiler warning; it will not prevent your program from successfully compiling.

I	Line	Form Type	Filename	Sequence	Number (1/N)	Option (O)	Record Identifying Indicator or **	Record Identification Codes 1 Position	Not (N)	C/Z/D	Character	2 Position	Not (N)	C/Z/D	Character	3 Position	Not (N)	C/Z/D	Character	Stacker Select P/B/L/R	Field Location From	To	Decimal Positions	Field Name	Control Level (L1-L9)	Matching Fields or Chaining Fields	Field Record Relation	Field Indicators Plus	Minus	Zero or Blank
	O R A N D																													
0 1	I	SALES		NS																										
0 2	I																													

Field Description Entries

Field description entries immediately follow the record description entry. You define each field within a record by giving it a valid name, specifying its length, and declaring its data type. Although you can define the fields of a record in any order, convention dictates that fields be described in order from the start of the record to the record's end.

FIELD LOCATION (positions 44-51)
You define a field's length by specifying the beginning position and ending position of a field within the input record. The beginning position is coded as the "from" location (positions 44-47 of the Input Specifications). The ending position is the "to" location (positions 48-51). If the field is one byte long, the "from" and "to" entries will be identical, since the field begins and ends in the same location of the record.

Enter the beginning and ending positions right-adjusted within the positions allocated for these entries. You do not have to enter leading, nonsignificant zeros.

DECIMAL POSITIONS (position 52)
The decimal position entry determines the data type of the field it is associated with. To define a field as a **character field**, leave the decimal position entry blank. To define a field as a **numeric field**, include a decimal position entry in position 52. In RPG, a field must be numeric to be used in arithmetic calculations, or to be edited for output, so it is important not to overlook the decimal position entry. If a numeric field represents **integer data** (i.e., whole numbers), the appropriate entry for its decimal positions is 0 (zero).

FIELD NAME (positions 53-58)
The last required entry for a field description specification is a name for the field being described. This name, entered left-adjusted in positions 53-58, must adhere to the rules for valid field names in RPG. A valid field name

- is maximally six characters long;
- is composed of uppercase alphabetic letters, digits, or special characters #, @, and $;
- does not begin with a digit; and
- does not include embedded blanks.

Although not a requirement of RPG, it is good programming practice to choose field names that reflect the data that they represent, to the extent that this can be done with a six-character name limit. ITEMNO is far superior to X for a field that will store item numbers. Choosing good variable names can prevent your use of incorrect variables as you write your program and can help clarify your program's processing to others who may have to modify that program.

The complete Input Specifications for our sample sales report program are shown below.

I	Filename		Sequence	Number (1/N)	Record Identifying Indicator or *	Record Identification Codes			Field Location		Decimal Positions	Field Name	Control Level (L1-L9)	Matching Fields or Chaining Fields	Field Record Relation	Field Indicators		
Line		Form Type	O R / A N D	Option (O)		Position 1	Position 2	Position 3 / Stacker Select / P/B/L/R	From	To						Plus	Minus	Zero or Blank
0 1	I	SALES	NS															
0 2	I								1	4	0	SLSMNO						
0 3	I								5	34		NAME						
0 4	I								35	50		ITEM						
0 5	I								51	56	0	SDATE						
0 6	I								57	63	2	PRICE						
0 7	I																	

In the above Input Specifications for our sample program, we defined SLSMNO (salesman number), SDATE (date of sale) and PRICE (sale price) as numeric by including decimal position entries in position 52.

Output Specifications

Although Calculation Specifications follow immediately after Input Specifications in RPG programs, we will first discuss **Output Specifications**, since their required entries in many ways parallel those required on Input Specifications. Every program-described output file on the File Specifications needs a set of Output Specifications that provide details about the output required. All Output Specification lines require an O in position 6.

Output Specifications, like Input Specifications, include two kinds of lines: record identification lines, which deal with the output at the record level, and field description lines, which describe the content of a given output record. When output is a report, rather than a data file, "record" translates to "report line." Most reports include several different report-line formats; each needs definition on the Output Specifications.

To refresh your memory, our output file, QPRINT, is to contain a weekly sales report, formatted as shown in the printer spacing chart repeated below.

```
          1         2         3         4         5         6         7         8
12345678901234567890123456789012345678901234567890123456789012345678901234567890
    PAGE XX0X                    WEEKLY SALES REPORT              DATE XX/XX/XX

    SLSM.                                 DATE OF                          SALE
    NO.            NAME                    SALE      ITEM SOLD            PRICE

    XXXX     XXXXXXXXXXXXXXXXXXXXXXXXX    XX/XX/XX   XXXXXXXXXXXXXXX    XX,XX0.XX
    XXXX     XXXXXXXXXXXXXXXXXXXXXXXXX    XX/XX/XX   XXXXXXXXXXXXXXX    XX,XX0.XX
```

The desired report includes four different kinds of lines, or record formats. Three of the lines are headings, which should appear at the top of the page of the report, while the fourth is a detail line of variable information. The term **detail line** means that one line is to print for each record in an input file. The line prints detailed information about the data records being processed.

The complete Output Specifications to produce the above report are shown in the following figure. You should refer to this figure again as you read about the required Output Specification entries.

Line	Filename or Record Name	Type	Space/Skip	Output Indicators	Field Name or EXCPT Name or Constant Name	Edit Codes	End Position in Output Record	Constant or Edit Word
01	QPRINT	E	202		HEADS			
02							8	'PAGE'
03					PAGE		13	
04							50	'WEEKLY SALES REPORT'
05							64	'DATE'
06					UDATE	Y	73	
07		E	1		HEADS			
08							5	'SLSM.'
09							48	'DATE OF'
10							77	'SALE'
11		E	2		HEADS			
12							3	'NO.'
13							21	'NAME'
14							46	'SALE'
15							61	'ITEM SOLD'
16							77	'PRICE'
17		E	1		DETAIL			
18					SLSMNO		4	
19					NAME		37	
20					SDATE	Y	48	
					ITEM		67	
					PRICE	1	79	

Record Identification Entries

Output Specifications require a record identification entry for each different line of the report. Each of these lines, representing a record format, must be followed with detailed information about what that record format (or report line) contains. Because our report has four different kinds of lines to describe, we have four record-format descriptions in our Output Specifications.

FILE NAME (positions 7-14)
The first record identification entry requires a file name entry in positions 7-14. This file name serves to associate the record being described with the output file described on the File Specifications. Thus QPRINT, our output file, appears as the file name entered on the first record-format line of the Output Specifications. Although the Output Specifications include four record-format descriptions, because each describes a format to be written to the same file, QPRINT, you do not have to repeat the file name entry on subsequent record-format entry lines.

TYPE (position 15)
Each record-format description requires an entry in position 15 to indicate the type of line being described. In this context, "type" refers to how RPG is to handle printing the line. Because we will be using procedural techniques to generate the report instead of relying on RPG's fixed-logic cycle, all the record-format lines are Exception lines. As a consequence, we enter an E in position 15 of each line.

EXCPT NAME (position 32-37)
In RPG/400, it is common practice to provide a name in positions 32-37 for each exception line. Although not required, such names allow you to control printing without the use of indicators. By using EXCPT names, you can easily reference lines to print from within your Calculation Specifications.

Moreover, you can assign the same name to lines that need to be printed as a group at the same time. Because our report has three lines that should print together at the top of a page, we have given each the name HEADS. The fourth line, which will print the variable information from our data file, is identified as DETAIL. Note that HEADS and DETAIL are arbitrarily assigned names, not RPG-reserved terms. Exception-line names follow the same rules of naming as do field names, and are coded left-adjusted within the allocated area of the specification form.

SPACE AND SKIP ENTRIES (positions 17-22)
One more set of entries is needed to complete the record-format line definitions. These entries describe vertical alignment of a given line within a report page or relative to other report lines. Two kinds of entries control this vertical alignment: SPACE entries and SKIP entries. Each variant offers a "before" and an "after" option.

For accurate placement of report lines, it is important to understand the differences between SPACE and SKIP entries. SPACE is analogous to the carriage return on a typewriter, or the Enter key on a computer. Each SPACE is the equivalent of hitting the Return (or Enter) key. SPACE BEFORE (position 17) is like hitting the Return key prior to typing a line, while SPACE AFTER (position 18) equates to hitting Return *after* you type a line. Valid values for SPACE are 0, 1, 2, or 3. The same record-format line can include both a SPACE BEFORE and a SPACE AFTER entry.

On the AS/400, if both the SPACE BEFORE and SPACE AFTER entries are left blank, the system defaults to SPACE 1 AFTER printing, the equivalent of single-spacing. If you have either a SPACE BEFORE or a SPACE AFTER entry explicitly coded and the other blank, the blank entry defaults to 0.

In contrast to SPACE, SKIP entries instruct the printer to "SKIP TO" the designated line on a page. SKIP 3 BEFORE printing causes the printer to advance to the third line on a page prior to printing; SKIP 20 AFTER printing causes the printer to advance to the 20th line on the page *after* printing a line. If the printer is already past that position on a given page, a SKIP entry causes the paper to advance to the designated position on the *next* page. Most often you will have a SKIP BEFORE entry only for the first heading line of a report. Programmers most often use SKIP entries to advance to the top of each new report page.

Because we want the first heading of our report to print on the second line of a page, we code a SKIP 02 BEFORE entry in positions 19-20 of the record-format line describing that line. The SPACE 2 AFTER entry (position 18) for that same heading line will advance the printer head to be in the correct position for the second HEADS line. The second HEADS line, with its SPACE 1 AFTER entry, positions the printer head for the third HEADS line, which in turn, with its SPACE 2 AFTER entry, positions the printer head for the first DETAIL line of data to print. Because the report detail lines are to print single-spaced, line DETAIL contains a SPACE 1 AFTER entry.

Field Description Entries

Each record-format line of the Output Specifications is followed by field description entries that describe the contents of the line. Each field-level specification identifies an item to appear as part of the record format it is associated with, indicates where the item is to appear within the record format, and specifies any special output formatting for that item.

Field-level items to be included within a record format may be entered in any order, although conventionally programmers enter them in the order in which they actually are to appear in the output.

FIELD NAME (positions 32-37)
The name of each field whose value is to appear as part of the output record is coded in positions 32-37. Any field appearing as part of the Output Specifications must have been defined earlier in the program.

In our sample program, most of the fields to print are part of the DETAIL record format. These are the same fields — SLSMNO, NAME, SDATE, ITEM, and PRICE — that we defined as part of our input record. By including these field names in the output, each time our program processes a successive record from the input file, each DETAIL line printed will contain the data values present in those fields of the input record.

In addition to the input fields, two RPG/400 reserved words, which function as built-in, predefined fields, appear as part of the report headings. In the first HEADS line, notice the field name PAGE. RPG supplies this field to automatically provide the correct page numbers for a report. PAGE, a 4-byte numeric field, has an initial value of 1; that value is automatically incremented by 1 each time the report begins a new page.

The UDATE field, also appearing as part of the first HEADS line, is another RPG reserved word. UDATE, a 6-byte numeric field, stores the current date in MMDDYY format. Anytime your program needs to access the date on which the program is running, you can simply use UDATE as a field. Reserved words UDAY, UMONTH, and UYEAR allow you to access the day, month, and year portions of the current date individually.

CONSTANTS (positions 45-70)

In addition to fields, whose values change through the course of a program's execution, report output typically contains **constants**, or **literals**: characters that do not change, and instead represent the actual values that are to appear on the report. Enter each constant, enclosed with apostrophes, in positions 45-70 of the Output Specifications. The left-apostrophe should appear in position 45; that is, enter constants left-adjusted within positions 45-70. A constant can be up to 24 characters long. A constant cannot appear on the same Output Specification line as a field; each needs its own line.

In our sample program, the first heading is to contain the word PAGE, as well as the page number. Accordingly, 'PAGE' is coded as a constant within the first HEADS line. Also part of this first heading is the title, WEEKLY SALES REPORT. Although several words make up this constant, the group of words is small enough to fit within the space allocated on the specification form, so it can be entered as a single constant, enclosed in apostrophes.

The second and third report lines, or record formats, consist of column headings for the report. These, too, are handled as constants, with the appropriate values entered in positions 45-70. Notice that the column heading lines are broken up into conveniently sized logical units, and that each unit is then coded as a separate constant.

Note also that blank, or unused, positions in output lines can be ignored unless they appear within a string of characters you wish to handle as a single constant (e.g., 'DATE OF', or 'ITEM SOLD').

END POSITION IN OUTPUT RECORD (positions 40-43).

You denote where a field or constant appears within a line by coding its end position (position of its right-most character) within the line. Specify an end position by entering a numeric value that represents the actual position desired for the right-most character of the field or constant. Such an entry should be right-adjusted within positions 40-43.

For example, because we want the 'E' in constant 'PAGE' to appear in column 8 of the first heading line, we coded 8 in position 43 of the specification entry for the constant 'PAGE'. The printer spacing chart indicates that the right-most digit of the page number should appear in column 13 of the report line. Accordingly, 13 is the specified end position for field PAGE within its Output Specification line.

Our Output Specifications include an end position for each field or constant that is part of our report. If you omit an end position for a field or constant, that item is output immediately adjacent to the previous item with no blanks separating the items.

EDIT CODES (position 38)

Three of the fields appearing in the output — UDATE, SDATE, and PRICE — have an entry in position 38, Edit Codes. An **edit code** formats numeric values to make them more readable. The Y edit code associated with UDATE and SDATE causes slashes to be inserted within the date printed. Thus, if SDATE has a value of 122093, it will print as 12/20/93.

Edit code 1 causes commas and a decimal point to be inserted within the printed value of PRICE and signals that if PRICE is 0, the zero balance should appear on the report, rather than being completely suppressed. RPG includes a large selection of editing alternatives to allow you to print or display values with a format most appropriate to your needs. A detailed discussion of these editing features appears at the end of this chapter.

Calculation Specifications

We have now defined the files to be used by our application, the format of the input records to be processed, and the desired output of the application. All we need to complete our program is to describe the processing steps required to obtain the input and write the report. We use Calculation Specifications to describe these processing steps.

Before coding the Calculation Specifications, you need to develop the logic required to produce the desired output. Generally this stage of the Program Development Cycle, designing the solution, would be completed prior to any program coding, but we delayed program design to introduce you to some of the RPG Specifications, to give you a taste of the language.

We can sketch out the required processing of our program using pseudocode. **Pseudocode** is simply stylized English that details the underlying logic needed for a program. Although there is no single standard for the format used with pseudocode, key control words generally are capitalized, and indentation is used to show the scope of control of the logic structures. It is always a good idea to work out the design of your program prior to actually coding it in RPG. Pseudocode is language-independent and allows you to focus on what needs to be done, rather than on the specific syntax requirements of a programming language.

Our program exemplifies a simple read/write program, in which we want to read a record, write a line on the report, and repeat the process until there are no more records in the file, a condition called **end-of-file**. This kind of application is called "batch" processing, because once the program begins, a batch of data, accumulated in a file, directs its execution. Batch programs can run unattended because they do not require control or instructions from a user.

The logic required by our read/write program is quite simple.

> *Correct Algorithm:*
> Write report headings
> Read a record
> WHILE there are more records
>   Write a detail line
>   Read the next record
> ENDWHILE
> End program

Note that WHILE indicates a repeated process, or loop. Within the loop the processing requirements for a single record are detailed (in this case, simply writing a report line) and then the next record is input. Because we want to print report headings just once at the beginning of the report, rather than once for each record, that step is listed at the beginning of the pseudocode, outside the loop.

You may wonder why there are two read statements in the pseudocode. Why can't there just be a single read, as the first step within the WHILE, as shown below?

> *Incorrect Algorithm:*
> Write report headings
> WHILE there are more records
>   Read the next record
>   Write a detail line
> ENDWHILE
> End program

The above algorithm would work fine as long as each READ operation retrieved a data record from the file. The problem is that eventually the system will try to read an input record and fail because there are no more records in the file to read. Once a program has reached end-of-file, it should not attempt to process any more input data. The incorrect algorithm above would inappropriately write a detail line after reaching end-of-file.

The correct algorithm places the read statement as the last step within the WHILE, so that as soon as end-of-file is detected, no further writing will occur. As a result, the algorithm requires an initial read (often called a **priming read**) *prior* to the WHILE to "prime" the processing cycle.

After you have designed the program, it is a simple matter to express that logic in a programming language — once you have learned its syntax. The Calculation Specifications in the following figure show the correct algorithm expressed in RPG.

C	Form Type	Control Level (L0-L9, LR,SR, AN/OR)	Indicators And Not	And Not	Not	Factor 1	Operation	Factor 2	Result Field Name	Length	Decimal Positions	Operation Extender (H,N,P)	Resulting Indicators Arithmetic Plus	Minus	Zero	Comments
0 1	C						EXCPTHEADS									
0 2	C						READ SALES								9 0	
0 3	C					*IN90	DOWEQ*OFF									
0 4	C						EXCPTDETAIL									
0 5	C						READ SALES								9 0	
0 6	C						ENDDO									
0 7	C						MOVE *ON		*INLR							
0 8	C						RETRN									
0 9	C															

Calculation Specifications specify what processing needs to be done. Calculation Specifications include a C in position 6 of the specification line. Each Calculation Specification contains an operation, entered in positions 28-32 of the coding form. Depending on the operation, specifications may also include a value in factor 1 (positions 18-27), factor 2 (positions 33-42), and/or the result field (positions 43-48). Indicators also may be associated with operations in positions 54-59, as discussed below.

The Calculation Specifications execute sequentially from beginning to end, unless the computer encounters an operation that redirects flow of control. Our program uses six operations: EXCPT, READ, DOWxx, ENDDO, MOVE, and RETRN. Because some of these operations involve RPG indicators, you should learn more about indicators before considering each specific operation.

Indicators and Calculations

An **indicator** in RPG is a built-in character variable with only two possible values: '0' (*OFF) and '1' (*ON). Indicators signal whether certain events have occurred during processing and can be used, in turn, to control subsequent processing. RPG provides 99 numbered indicators (01, 02, 03, ..., 98, 99) for you to use in your program.

Many RPG operations can turn on an indicator or indicators, depending on what happens during the operation's execution. You code these indicators within the area of the Calculation Specifications labeled "Resulting Indicators." This area is divided into three two-position areas (positions 54-55, 56-57, and 58-59) for indicator specifications. Many RPG operations require coding an indicator in one of these three areas to signal the results or effect of the operation when the program is running; other operations optionally allow you to associate indicators with their execution.

In turn, you can use these indicators as fields with operations that control subsequent processing. To reference an indicator as a field, you simply add *IN as a prefix to the indicator name. Thus, *IN90 is indicator 90 treated as a field. If the indicator has been turned on, its value will be '1' (also expressed as *ON); otherwise, its value is '0' (or *OFF).

With that overview of indicators, we can look at the specific operations used within the calculations of our program. The intent here is to provide you with sufficient information to understand our basic program and to write similar programs. Several of the operations described below are discussed in more detail in subsequent chapters of this book.

RPG Operations

EXCPT (Calculation Time Output)

An EXCPT operation directs the program to output an E line or lines from the output specifications. This operation never includes a value in factor 1 (positions 18-27) or the result field (positions 43-48). The use of factor 2 (positions 33-42) is optional. If factor 2 is blank, the operation causes the system to output all *unnamed E lines.* Generally, however, RPG/400 programmers name their E lines and use the EXCPT operation with an E-line name in factor 2 to state explicitly which line or lines are to be involved in the output operation. In the sample program, the first EXCPT operation has HEADS as a factor 2 entry. As a result, the heading lines of our report will print. A second EXCPT specifies DETAIL in factor 2. When the program executes this line of code, our exception line named DETAIL prints.

READ (Read Sequentially)

READ is an input operation that instructs the computer to retrieve the next sequential record from the input file named in factor 2 (positions 33-42), in this case, our SALES file. The file must appear as an input-capable file on the File Specifications.

Notice that each READ statement has a two-digit number entered in positions 58-59, the "Equal" indicator position, at the far right of the specification. This number — in our case, 90 — designates which RPG indicator we want to turn on when a READ operation encounters end-of-file (runs out of records). You can use any one of RPG's indicators for this purpose, but most programmers use indicators in the 90s for end-of-file signals.

DOWxx (Do While)

The DOWxx operation establishes a loop in RPG. The end of the loop is signaled by an ENDDO. Note that this DOWxx and ENDDO correspond to the WHILE and ENDWHILE statements in our pseudocode. In our program, the *xx* of the DOWxx is replaced with EQ, a relational code standing for "equal." The DOWEQ of our program reads, "Do while indicator 90 is off," and is the direct equivalent of the pseudocode statement, "While there are more records...," since indicator 90 will come on only when our READ operation runs out of records.

ENDDO (End Do Group)

This operation serves to mark the end of the scope of a DO operation. All the program statements between the DO operation and its associated ENDDO are repeated as long as the DO operation is in effect.

MOVE (Move)

MOVE is an operation used to assign a value to a variable. In the sample program, by moving *ON to *INLR we are turning on a special indicator called Last Record. *INLR plays a special function within RPG. If it is on when our program ends, it signals the computer to close the files and free up the memory associated with this program. If LR is not on, our program continues to tie up some of the system's resources even though the program is no longer running.

RETRN (Return to Caller)

RETRN returns control to the program that called it — either the computer's operating system or perhaps another program. Program execution stops when a RETRN is encountered. Although your program will end correctly without this instruction (provided you have turned on LR), including it is a good practice: RETRN clearly signals the end-point of your program and allows the program to become part of an application system of called programs. (Chapter 12 deals with called programs in detail.)

Internal Documentation

You might think that once you have a program written and running, you are done with it forever and can move forward, developing new programs. Actually, about 70 percent of all programming is maintenance programming rather than new applications development. Maintenance programming involves modifying existing programs to fix problems, to address changing business needs, or to satisfy user requests for modifications.

Because of the high probability that any program you write will be revised sometime in the future either by yourself or by some other programmer in your company, it is your responsibility to make your program as understandable as possible to facilitate these future revisions.

One good way to help others understand what your program does is to include explanatory documentation internal to your program through the use of **comment lines**. In RPG, an asterisk (*) in position 7 of any line, regardless of the specification type, designates that line to be a comment. When the RPG compiler encounters a commented line, it skips that line and does not try to translate it into machine code. Comments exist within the program at a source-code level only, for the benefit of programmers who may have to work with the program later.

Most companies require overview documentation at the beginning of each program. This documentation states the function or purpose of the program, any special instructions or peculiarities of the program that those working with it should know, the program's author, and the date when the program was written. If the program is revised, entries detailing the revisions, including the author and the date of the revisions, usually are added to that initial documentation. If a program uses several indicators, many programmers will provide an indicator "dictionary" as part of their initial set of comments to state the function or role of each indicator used within the program.

In addition to this overview documentation, you should include comments throughout your program as needed to help explain specific processing steps that are not obvious. In adding such comments, assume that anyone looking at your program has at least a basic proficiency with RPG; your documentation should help clarify your program to such a person. Documenting trivial, obvious aspects of your program is a waste of time. On the other hand, failing to document difficult-to-grasp processing can cost others valuable time. Inaccurate documentation is worse than no documentation because it supplies false clues that may mislead the person responsible for program modification.

Appropriately documenting a program is an important learned skill. If you are uncertain about what to document, ask yourself, "What would I want to know about this program if I were looking at it for the first time?"

The Completed Program

The completed sample program is shown in the figure below. Note that the order of the program statements are File-Input-Calculations-Output. RPG requires this order. Also note that blank comment lines or lines of asterisks can be used to visually break the program into logical units, and that using lowercase lettering within internal documentation makes it stand out from program code.

```
            1         2         3         4         5         6         7
   1234567890123456789012345678901234567890123456789012345678901234567890
      F*****************************************************************
      F*  This program produces a weekly sales report.  The      *
      F*  report data come directly from input file SALES.        *
      F*     Author:  J. Yaeger    Date Written: 10/10/92.        *
      F*                                                          *
      F*     Indicator 90:  End-of-file SALES                     *
      F*****************************************************************
      FSALES    IF  F     63           DISK
      FQPRINT   O   F    132           PRINTER
      I*****************Input Specs*************************
      ISALES    NS
      I                                      1    4ØSLSMNO
      I                                      5   34 NAME
      I                                     35   5Ø ITEM
      I                                     51   56ØSDATE
      I                                     57   632PRICE
      C*****************Calculations***********************
      C                 EXCPTHEADS
      C                 READ SALES                        90
      C*
      C        *IN9Ø    DOWEQ*OFF
      C                 EXCPTDETAIL
      C                 READ SALES                        90
      C                 ENDDO
      C*
      C                 MOVE *ON      *INLR
      C                 RETRN
      O***************Output Specifications******************
      OQPRINT  E  202           HEADS
      O                                   8 'PAGE'
      O                        PAGE     13
      O                                  50 'WEEKLY SALES REPORT'
      O                                  64 'DATE'
      O                        UDATE Y   73
      O        E  1            HEADS
      O                                   5 'SLSM.'
      O                                  48 'DATE OF'
      O                                  77 'SALE'
      O        E  2            HEADS
      O                                   3 'NO.'
      O                                  21 'NAME'
      O                                  46 'SALE'
      O                                  61 'ITEM SOLD'
      O                                  77 'PRICE'
      O        E. 1            DETAIL
      O                        SLSMNO    4
      O                        NAME     37
      O                        SDATE Y  48
      O                        ITEM     67
      O                        PRICE 1  79
```

Now that you have seen how to write a complete RPG program, we can return to the concept of output editing to learn RPG's editing features in greater detail.

Output Editing

Output editing refers to formatting output values by suppressing leading zeros and adding special characters, such as decimal points, commas, and dollar signs, to make the values easier for people looking at the output to comprehend. RPG allows numeric fields (but not character fields) to be edited as part of the Output Specifications. You often will use editing to obtain the output format requested in a printer spacing chart.

Editing is used in part because of the way numbers are stored in RPG. For example, if AMT, a field six bytes long with two decimal positions, is assigned the value 31.24, that value is stored as 003124. Although the computer keeps track of the decimal position, a decimal point is not actually stored as part of the numeric value. If you were to specify that AMT print without editing, the number would print as 003124; the non-significant zeros would appear, and there would be no indication of where the decimal point should be.

Edit Codes

To make it easier to specify the most commonly wanted kinds of editing, RPG includes several built-in edit codes you can use to indicate how you want a field's value to print. You associate an edit code with a field by entering the code in position 38 of the Output Specification containing that field. All commonly used edit codes automatically result in zero-suppression — that is, printing blanks in place of nonsignificant leading zeros — since that is a standard desired format.

Some editing decisions vary with the application. Do you want numbers to print with commas inserted? How do you want to handle negative values? Ignore them and omit any sign? Print a floating minus sign to the left of a negative value? Print CR immediately after the value? Or print – after the value? And if a field has a value of zero, do you want to print zeros or leave that spot on the report blank? A set of 16 edit codes, 1 through 4, A through D, and J through Q, cover all combinations of these three options (commas, sign handling, and zero balances).

The table below details the effects of the 16 codes. Note that this table also appears in the upper right-hand corner of Output Specification Sheets to jog your memory.

Commas	Zero Balances to Print	No Sign	CR	Right –	Floating –
Yes	Yes	1	A	J	N
Yes	No	2	B	K	O
No	Yes	3	C	L	P
No	No	4	D	M	Q

Thus, if you want commas, zero balances to print, and a floating negative sign, you would use edit code N.

Value	1	2	3	4	A	B	C	D
1234∧56	1,234.56	1,234.56	1234.56	1234.56	1,234.56	1,234.56	1234.56	1234.56
1234∧56-	1,234.56	1,234.56	1234.56	1234.56	1,234.56CR	1,234.56CR	1234.56CR	1234.56CR
0234∧56-	234.56	234.56	234.56	234.56	234.56CR	234.56CR	234.56CR	234.56CR
0000∧00	.00		.00		.00		.00	
000000∧	0		0		0		0	

To give you a clear understanding of the effects of each of these edit codes, the two parts of this table demonstrate how various values would appear if printed with each of the edit codes. Notice that if you use edit codes 1-4 with a field containing a negative value, that field will print like a positive number.

Value	J	K	L	M	N	O	P	Q
1234∧56	1,234.56	1,234.56	1234.56	1234.56	1,234.56	1,234.56	1234.56	1234.56
1234∧56-	1,234.56-	1,234.56-	1234.56-	1234.56-	-1,234.56	-1,234.56	-1234.56	-1234.56
0234∧56-	234.56-	234.56-	234.56-	234.56-	-234.56	-234.56	-234.56	-234.56
0000∧00	.00		.00		.00		.00	
000000∧	0		0		0		0	

There are two additional useful edit codes: Y and Z. Edit code Y results in slashes printing as part of a date. Thus, if you run the program on December 11, 1993, UDATE will contain 121193. If edited with Y code, this date will print as 12/11/93. Although normally used to edit dates, edit code Y can be used with any field for which slash-insertion is appropriate.

Edit code Z simply zero suppresses leading non-significant zeros. Z does *not* enable the printing of a decimal point or a negative sign, so that if a field contained 0234∧56–, the Z edit code would cause it to print as 23456. Z, if used at all, should be limited to integer (whole number) fields.

One additional edit code, X, originally was designed to convert positively signed values to unsigned values; because the AS/400 now does this automatically, this edit code has become obsolete. X is the only edit code that does not suppress leading zeros.

You occasionally will want dollar signs to print as part of your report. As mentioned in Chapter 1, dollar signs may be positioned in a fixed column of the report, or they may be placed just to the left of the first significant digit of the values they are associated with. This latter type of dollar sign is called a floating dollar sign.

Fixed Dollar Sign	Floating Dollar Sign
$ 12.34	$12.34
$6,342.11	$6,342.11
$ .00	$.00

Generally, you want to use a dollar sign in addition to one of the editing codes. To specify a floating dollar sign, code '$' in the constant/edit word positions (columns 45-70) of the output specifications *on the same line* as the field and its edit code. To specify a fixed dollar sign, code '$' as a constant *on its own line* with its own end position.

One additional feature can be used along with edit codes; an asterisk, coded in the constant/edit position (45-70) on the same line as the field and edit code specifies that insignificant leading zeros be replaced by asterisks, rather than simply suppressed. This feature is sometimes called **check-protection**, because its most common use is in printing checks to prevent tampering with the check's face value. For example, a check worth $12.15 might include the amount written as $****12.15.

Edit Words

You would think that given the variety of edit codes built into RPG, you would be able to find a code to fit your every need. Unfortunately, that is not the case. Social Security and telephone numbers represent good examples of values that we are used to seeing in a format that an edit code cannot supply. RPG includes an alternative to edit codes, called **edit words**, that can help in this kind of situation.

An edit word is coded in the constant/edit word portion of the Output Specifications on the same line as the field it is to be used with. Edit words and edit codes are never used together for the same field, since they perform the same function. An edit word supplies a template into which a number is inserted. The template is enclosed with apostrophes. Within the template, a blank position indicates where a digit should appear, while a 0 indicates how far zero-suppression should take place. With no zero in the edit word, the default is to zero-suppress to the first significant digit.

Commas *or any other character* can be used as insertion characters within the template. They will print in the specified place, provided they are to the right of a significant digit. To print an insertion character to the left of the first significant digit, you can add a 0 to the left of the insertion character (see example 3 below). A dollar sign at the left of the edit word signals a fixed dollar sign; a dollar sign adjacent to a zero denotes a floating dollar sign. To indicate a blank as an insertion character, use an ampersand (&).

Examine the figure below to see how edit words work.

This value	with this edit word	prints as
999999999	'ƀƀƀ-ƀƀ-ƀƀƀƀ'	999-99-9999
999999999	'ƀƀƀ&ƀƀ&ƀƀƀƀ'	999 99 9999
1234123412	'0(ƀƀƀ)ƀƀƀ-ƀƀƀƀ'	(123)412-3412
00012ₐ14	'ƀƀƀƀ$0.ƀƀ'	$12.14
00012ₐ14	'$ƀƀƀƀ0.ƀƀ'	$ 12.14
05612ₐ14	'$ƀƀ,ƀƀ0.ƀƀ'	$ 5,612.14

You can duplicate the effects of any edit code with an edit word. In general, RPG programmers use edit words only when there is not an edit code that provides the format they want for their output.

Chapter Summary

RPG programs are written as fixed-form specifications. Different specification forms convey different kinds of information to the RPG compiler, which translates the program into machine language.

File Specifications contain descriptions of all files used within a program. Input Specifications provide detailed information about each program-described input file used by a program. There are two kinds of Input Specification lines: one that contains record identification entries, to generally describe a record format within a file, and one that contains field identification entries to define the fields comprising the record. Each field is described on a separate line.

Calculation Specifications center on operations, or processing steps, to be accomplished by the computer. Each Calculation Specification must include an RPG operation and may include additional entries, depending on the specific operation. The computer executes operations in the order they are given on the Calculation Specifications, unless the computer encounters an operation that specifically alters this flow of control.

Output Specifications provide details about each program-described output file. You use two kinds of Output Specification lines: a record identification line, to describe an output record format at a general level, and field description lines, to describe each field or constant that appears as part of a record format. When the output is a report, you need a record identification line and corresponding field identification entries for each kind of line to appear on the report.

It generally is customary to edit numeric values that are printed. RPG supplies ready-made edit codes for common editing requirements and allows you to create special editing formats by using edit words.

An important part of programming is documenting the program. Comment lines, signaled by an * in position 7 of a specification line, can appear anywhere within a program. Such lines are ignored by the RPG compiler.

Terms

Calculation Specifications	File Description	output editing
character field	Specifications	output file
check-protection	fixed-position/fixed-form	Output Specifications
comment lines	full procedural	priming read
constants/literals	indicator	pseudocode
detail line	input file	Source Entry Utility (SEU)
edit code	Input Specifications	
edit words	integer data	
end-of-file	numeric field	

Discussion/Review Questions

1. What's a fixed-form language? Can you give an example of a free-form language?

2. Why do reports generated by RPG programs need to appear on File Specifications?

3. Why don't you need to enter a File Designation for output files?

4. Which of the following are invalid RPG variable names? Why?

```
X         1STQTR  #3      ABC      QTY-OH
CUSTNO    .@END   SALES   $AMT     CUSTNUM
CUST#     DAY1    YR END  YR_END   YEAREND
```

5. What is an indicator? What specific methods of turning on indicators were introduced in this chapter? How can you use indicators to control processing?

6. Describe the difference between a skip and a space entry on the Output Specifications.

7. How could you obtain five blank lines between detail lines of a report?

8. What is the advantage of giving the same name to several Exception lines of output?

9. What are some fields that are automatically provided by RPG for your use?

10. Why do you often need two read statements within a program?

11. What is the correct order of specifications within an RPG program?

12. What is the purpose of each kind of RPG specification introduced in this chapter?

13. What is LR? Why is it used?

14. What is maintenance programming? What programming techniques can you adopt to facilitate maintenance programming?

15. Why does RPG include both edit codes and edit words? What exceptions are there to the rule that an edit code and an edit word or constant should never appear together on the same Output Specification line?

Exercises

1. A program uses data from file CUST to generate a report that reflects all the data in the file. CUST record layout is as follows:

    Customer number: 1- 5

    Customer name: 6-25

    Last order date: 26-31 (MMDDYY format)

    Balance owed: 32-41 (2 decimal positions)

    Write the File Specifications for this program.

2. Given the above problem definition, write the Input Specifications.

3. Design a report for the application in Exercise 1, using the printer spacing chart (PSC) notation of Chapter 1.

4. Develop Output Specifications based on your printer spacing chart from Exercise 3 and the File Specifications of Exercise 1.

Programming Assignments

All four of the programming assignments below center on a single company: CompuSell. CompuSell is a mail-order company specializing in computers and computer supplies. A description of the company and the record layouts of its data files appear in Appendix D.

1. The company would like you to write a program to produce a listing of all its customers. Use data file CSCSTP, the customer master file for CompuSell, as your input file. The listing should exactly match the format described in the printer spacing chart below:

```
         1         2         3         4         5         6         7         8         9        10
123456789012345678901234567890123456789012345678901234567890123456789012345678901234567890

    XX/XX/XX              COMPUSELL CUSTOMER LISTING          PAGE XX0X

CUST.                                          LAST ORDER      BALANCE
NUMBER      FIRST NAME      LAST NAME             DATE          DUE

XXXXXX      XXXXXXXXXX      XXXXXXXXXXXXXXX      XX/XX/XX      X,XX0.XX
XXXXXX      XXXXXXXXXX      XXXXXXXXXXXXXXX      XX/XX/XX      X,XX0.XX
```

2. CompuSell wants an inventory listing, formatted as shown in the following printer spacing chart. Write the program to produce this report, exactly matching the printer spacing chart specifications. The input file is CSINVP; its record layout is given in Appendix D.

```
         1         2         3         4         5         6         7         8         9        10
123456789012345678901234567890123456789012345678901234567890123456789012345678901234567890

    XX/XX/XX                    COMPUSELL INVENTORY LISTING              PAGE XX0X
                                YOUR NAME
PROD.                            WEIGHT    QTY. ON     AVERAGE     CURRENT      SELLING
NUM.       DESCRIPTION          LBS.  OZS.  HAND        COST        COST         PRICE

XXXXXX     XXXXXXXXXXXXXXXXXXXXXX  X0    XX    XX0X     X,XX0.XX    X,XX0.XX    $X,XX$.XX
XXXXXX     XXXXXXXXXXXXXXXXXXXXXX  X0    XX    XX0X     X,XX0.XX    X,XX0.XX    $X,XX$.XX
```

Programming Assignments Continued

Programming Assignments continued

3. CompuSell wants to send out two separate mailings to each of its customers contained in file CSCSTP (see Appendix D for record layout). Accordingly, the company asks you to write a label-printing program that will print 2-across labels. Each of the labels reading across should represent the same customer. The printer will be loaded with continuous label stock when this program is run. Each label is 5 print lines long. The desired format for the labels is shown below. Note that the information in the parentheses is included to let you know what should appear on the label. It should not appear within your output.

```
            1         2         3         4         5         6         7         8         9        10
   12345678901234567890123456789012345678901234567890123456789012345678901234567890123456789012345678901234567890
 1
 2     XXXXXXXXXX XXXXXXXXXXXXXX          XXXXXXXXXX XXXXXXXXXXXXXX      (first, last name)
 3     XXXXXXXXXXXXXXXXXXXX               XXXXXXXXXXXXXXXXXXXX           (street address)
 4     XXXXXXXXXXXXXX  XX XXXXX-XXXX       XXXXXXXXXXXXXX  XX XXXXX-XXXX  (city, state, zip)
 5
 6
 7     XXXXXXXXXX XXXXXXXXXXXXXX          XXXXXXXXXX XXXXXXXXXXXXXX
 8     XXXXXXXXXXXXXXXXXXXX               XXXXXXXXXXXXXXXXXXXX
 9     XXXXXXXXXXXXXX  XX XXXXX-XXXX       XXXXXXXXXXXXXX  XX XXXXX-XXXX
10
```

4. CompuSell wants a phone and address listing of all its suppliers. Write a program to produce this listing. Your input file, CSSUPP, is described in Appendix D.

```
            1         2         3         4         5         6         7         8
   12345678901234567890123456789012345678901234567890123456789012345678901234567890

        COMPUSELL SUPPLIER LIST AS OF XX/XX/XX              PAGE XX0X

        NAME/ADDRESS                 PHONE             CONTACT PERSON

   XXXXXXXXXXXXXXXXXXXXXXXXXX     (XXX) XXX-XXXX    XXXXXXXXXXXXXXXXXXXXXXXXXXXXXX
   XXXXXXXXXXXXXXXXXXXX
   XXXXXXXXXXXXXX XX XXXXX-XXXX


   XXXXXXXXXXXXXXXXXXXXXXXXXX     (XXX) XXX-XXXX    XXXXXXXXXXXXXXXXXXXXXXXXXXXXXX
   XXXXXXXXXXXXXXXXXXXX
   XXXXXXXXXXXXXX XX XXXXX-XXXX


   XXXXXXXXXXXXXXXXXXXXXXXXXX     (XXX) XXX-XXXX    XXXXXXXXXXXXXXXXXXXXXXXXXXXXXX
   XXXXXXXXXXXXXXXXXXXX
   XXXXXXXXXXXXXX XX XXXXX-XXXX
```

Chapter 3

Arithmetic and Assignment Operations

Chapter Overview

Now that you can write simple read/write programs in RPG, you're ready to learn how to perform arithmetic calculations in your programs. RPG was designed as a business language, and as such, its mathematical capabilities don't extend much beyond the four basic arithmetic operations — addition, subtraction, multiplication, and division.

You will also learn how to determine the appropriate size for fields that store the results of arithmetic operations and how to round calculations to avoid truncation. This chapter also teaches you how to assign values to character and numeric fields. You will also learn how to use numeric and character literals and figurative constants.

Numeric Literals and Fields

You can perform mathematical operations on **numeric fields** or **numeric literals**; numeric fields are used to store the results of calculations. Before looking at specific arithmetic operations, you should understand more about these two RPG data constructs.

A numeric literal is a number *per se*; its value remains fixed throughout the program. A numeric literal can be up to 10 positions long (the maximum length of a factor 1 or factor 2 entry). The literal may include a decimal point and/or a sign. If the numeric literal includes a sign, the sign must be the leftmost character of the literal. If the numeric literal does not include a sign, the computer assumes the literal represents a positive number.

Other than a decimal point and a sign, the literal may include only the digits 0 through 9. You should never use commas, dollar signs, or percent signs in a numeric literal. Numeric literals are not enclosed in apostrophes. Some examples of valid numeric literals follow:

−401230.12	0.0715
102	1
+3	−1
3.1416	.123456789

When entered as factor 1 or factor 2 on a Calculation Specification, numeric literals should be *left-adjusted*; this is the one exception to the rule that numeric values are right-adjusted on specification forms.

All fields used in your program need to be defined by giving them a valid name, specifying their length, and — for numeric variables — designating the number of decimal positions they are to have. As you know, input fields are defined on the Input Specifications, so that any numeric input field can be used in calculations without further definition. Often, however, you need additional fields to serve as work fields or to store results of calculations for printing. One way of defining such fields is within a calculation in which the field appears as a result. Fields defined in this manner must follow the same rules of naming as input fields (page 22).

Positions 49-51 (length) of the Calculation Specifications can be used to assign a length to an undefined field appearing as the result field of that calculation. If the field is numeric — as it must be, if it is the result of an arithmetic operation — also code the appropriate number of decimal positions in position 52 of the calculation. RPG/400 allows numeric fields a maximum length of 30 positions, up to nine of which may be decimal positions. All numeric fields are signed and can store negative values without special specification. Recall, however, that negative values will print without a sign unless you use an appropriate edit code with the field on output.

Good programming practice suggests that you define a given field only once within your program. If you define a field twice and give inconsistent definitions, you will receive an error message from the compiler.

Arithmetic Operations

RPG does not include a wealth of mathematical operations. The four basic arithmetic operations — add, subtract, multiply, and divide — with a few additional extras, represent the range of RPG's mathematical offerings. Moreover, complex mathematical procedures need to be represented a single operation at a time to be executed within an RPG program. Although the language has proven itself adequate to handle most of the mathematical processing required in the business environment, you probably wouldn't want to use RPG to calculate rocket trajectories.

Arithmetic operations, like all other operations of RPG, are coded in positions 28-32 of the Calculation Specifications. All require a result-field entry in positions 43-48, and most also include an entry in factor 2 or entries in both factor 1 and factor 2. The exact format of each RPG arithmetic operation is described below.

ADD (Add)

To add the values of two numbers and store the result in a numeric field, use the ADD operation. Factor 1 (positions 18-27) and factor 2 (positions 33-42) contain the values to be added; these values may be represented as either numeric fields or numeric literals. Remember to define the result field if you have not already done so within the program.

C				Factor 1	Operation	Factor 2	Result Field Name	Length		Comments
01	C	*	Sample	calculations	showing	the ADD	operation.			
02	C			REGPAY	ADD	OTPAY	TOTPAY	62		
03	C			25	ADD	QTY	NEWQTY	30		
04	C			RATE1	ADD	.045	RATE2	43		
05	C									

Addition often is used to accumulate or count. For example, to count the number of customers in a file, you would increment a counter field (i.e., add 1 to it) each time you processed a customer record. Or, to accumulate employees' salaries, you would add each salary to a field representing the grand total of salaries.

There are two ways to represent such counting or accumulating. With the older method, the result field also appears in factor 1 or factor 2. More recent versions of RPG allow you to omit repeating the result field as a factor. The following examples show both formats for counting and accumulating.

C				Factor 1	Operation	Factor 2	Result Field Name	Length		Comments
01	C	*	The	calculations	below	show two	equivalent	ways	of	incrementing
02	C	*	a	counter.						
03	C			CNT	ADD	1	CNT	30		
04	C				ADD	1	CNT	30		
05	C	*	The	calculations	below	show two	equivalent	ways	of	accumulating
06	C	*	net	pay.						
07	C			NETPAY	ADD	TOTNET	TOTNET	82		
08	C				ADD	NETPAY	TOTNET	82		
09	C									

The two examples above would produce identical results (i.e., the value of CNT would be greater by 1 following either calculation, and TOTNET would have the current value of NETPAY added to it, with either calculation). The shorter format, however, in which factor 1 is omitted, is more commonly used today.

To demonstrate how a complex calculation needs to be broken down into single steps, let's assume you need to add FICA, state tax, federal tax, and insurance payments to calculate payroll withholding for an employee. This calculation will take three separate additions, as shown below.

C		Indicators			Factor 1	Operation	Factor 2	Result Field				Resulting Indicators			Comments
Line	Form Type	Control Level (L0-L9, LR,SR, AN/OR)	And (Not)	And (Not) (Not)	Factor 1	Operation	Factor 2	Name	Length	Decimal Positions	Operation Extender (H,N,P)	Arithmetic — Plus/Minus/Zero; Compare 1>2/1<2/1=2; Lookup(Factor 2)is High/Low/Equal			Comments
0 1	C				FICA	ADD	STTAX	WITHLD	62						
0 2	C					ADD	FEDTAX	WITHLD							
0 3	C					ADD	INSUR	WITHLD							
0 4	C														

SUB (Subtract)

The SUB operation is used to subtract factor 2 from factor 1. The result of the subtraction is stored in the result field. As with addition, in subtraction factor 1 and factor 2 can be fields or numeric literals, while the result must be a numeric field. *Unlike* addition, in subtraction the order of the factors is important. In algebra, this operation would be expressed as:

$$\text{Result} = \text{Factor 1} - \text{Factor 2}$$

If you mentally substitute a minus sign for the SUB operation, you are unlikely to accidentally instruct the computer to calculate the opposite of what you want.

C		Indicators			Factor 1	Operation	Factor 2	Result Field				Resulting Indicators			Comments
Line	Form Type	Control Level (L0-L9, LR,SR, AN/OR)	And (Not)	And (Not) (Not)	Factor 1	Operation	Factor 2	Name	Length	Decimal Positions	Operation Extender (H,N,P)	Arithmetic — Plus/Minus/Zero; Compare 1>2/1<2/1=2; Lookup(Factor 2)is High/Low/Equal			Comments
0 1	C				GROSS	SUB	WITHLD	NETPAY	62						
0 2	C				65	SUB	AGE	WRKYRS	20						
0 3	C														

You can also decrement a counter or decrease the value of an accumulator by omitting factor 1. This format says, in effect, "Subtract factor 2 from the result field and store the answer in the result field."

Line	Form Type	Factor 1	Operation	Factor 2	Result Field Name	Length	Decimal Positions
01	C		SUB	1	CTR	2	0
02	C		SUB	AMT	RMDER	6	2
03	C						

MULT (Multiply)

The MULT operation allows you to multiply the contents of factor 1 and factor 2 and store the answer in the result field. Numeric fields and/or literals can serve as the multipliers, while the result must be stored in a numeric field.

Line	Form Type	Factor 1	Operation	Factor 2	Result Field Name	Length	Decimal Positions
01	C	SALES	MULT	TAXRAT	SLSTAX	5	2
02	C	60	MULT	HRS	MIN	5	0
03	C	GROSS	MULT	.0751	FICA	9	2
04	C						

A second format for the MULT operation exists, in which you omit factor 1. With this format, the value of the result field is multiplied by factor 2 and the product is stored in the result field. This format, used within a loop, can be useful for **exponentiation** (raising a value to a power), an operation not directly supported within RPG.

Line	Form Type	Factor 1	Operation	Factor 2	Result Field Name	Length	Decimal Positions
01	C		MULT	NUM	PWR	15	0
02	C						

DIV (Divide)

RPG uses the DIV operation to divide factor 1 by factor 2, storing the quotient in the result field. As with the SUB operation, if you aren't sure what gets divided by what, mentally substitute a "divided by" sign (/) for the DIV operation to avoid reversing the factors. In algebra, this operation would be expressed as:

Result = Factor 1 / Factor 2

The DIV operation supports a second format — as do ADD, SUB, and MULT — in which you leave factor 1 blank. In this case, the result field is divided by factor 2 and the quotient is stored in the result field, replacing the original value.

C		Indicators			Factor 1	Operation	Factor 2	Result Field				Resulting Indicators			Comments
			And	And				Name	Length			Arithmetic			
												Plus	Minus	Zero	
Line												Compare			
												1>2	1<2	1=2	
			Not	Not	Not							Lookup(Factor 2)is			
												High	Low	Equal	
0 1	C				TOTAMT	DIV	CNT	AVGAMT	62						
0 2	C				HRPTS	DIV	CRDTS	GPA	32						
0 3	C					DIV	2	BINCAL	80						
0 4	C														

Remember that division by zero is mathematically impossible. If factor 2 is 0 or a field whose value is zero at the time of the division, a runtime error condition results.

MVR (Move Remainder)

Occasionally, when dividing, you would like to be able to access the remainder of a division operation to use in a subsequent calculation or to print. RPG offers the MVR operation for this purpose.

Factors 1 and 2 are not used with this operation; the remainder is simply stored in the result field, which must be an integer field. If you use MVR, it must *immediately* follow a DIV operation. The following example demonstrates a use of this operation.

```
C  *Convert total minutes to hours and minutes by dividing total
C  *minutes by 60 to get hours and moving the remainder into a
C  *minutes field.
C        TOTMIN    DIV  60            HRS     30
C                  MVR                MIN     20
C
```

SQRT (Square Root)

The final RPG arithmetic operation is SQRT, used for calculating the square root of a numeric value. This operation does not use factor 1. Factor 2 contains a numeric constant or numeric field whose square root you want to calculate, while the result must be a numeric field to store the answer. If the value of factor 2 is 0, the result will be 0; if factor 2 is a negative number, an error condition results, since the square root of a negative value is an imaginary number.

```
C                  SQRT SQFT          FEET    50
C
```

Numeric Truncation and Field Sizes

With all arithmetic operations, one of your jobs as a programmer is to determine appropriate length and decimal position entries for result fields. It is important to allow sufficient room because otherwise, should a calculation produce an answer too big to store in the result field, **truncation** will occur.

Truncation is the loss of digits from the right or the left ends of a result field. The AS/400 stores the result of any arithmetic operation in the result field based on decimal position alignment. If the value to be stored is too large for the result field, truncation occurs. This digit loss may occur from left-most or right-most digits of the answer (or both), depending on the number of defined digit positions to the left and right of the decimal position in the result field. Digit loss from the left is called **high-order truncation**, while loss from the right is **low-order truncation**. The table below illustrates how truncation works.

Calculated Value to Be Stored	Result Field Definition		Stored Result
	Length	Decimal Position	
413.29	4	1	413.2
413.29	4	2	13.29
413.29	4	0	0413
413.29	4	3	3.290

From the examples above, you can see that truncation can occur for significant (left-most) or insignificant (right-most) digits, depending on the calculated value and the number of digit positions to the right and the left of the decimal position in the result field. You should also notice that if the answer has fewer digits (left or right of decimal position) than the result field, the system simply zero-fills the unneeded positions.

Truncation is important to understand, because if it occurs during a program's execution, the program simply continues to run without issuing a warning that digits have been lost. Losing 1/1000 of a dollar may not be the end of the world (although on a large run it could add up), but losing $10,000 would probably cause your company some distress. How do you determine the size of a result field to ensure that truncation does not inadvertently occur?

Fortunately, some straightforward rules of result field definition, if followed, guarantee that your result fields will always be large enough to store the calculated answers. These rules vary with the operation.

Result Field Size for Addition

To avoid truncation when adding, you should define the result field with *one more* position *left of the decimal* than the larger of factor 1 and factor 2's integer digit positions. Positions to the right of the decimal in the result field should equal the larger of the decimal positions of factor 1 and factor 2. For example, if you're adding two fields, one defined as 3 with 2 decimal positions (i.e., 1 to the left, 2 to the right of the decimal) and one defined as 6 with 3 decimal positions (i.e., 3 to the left, 3 to the right of the decimal), your result field should be defined as 7 with 3 decimal positions (4 to left, 3 to the right).

To see why this rule eliminates the possibility of truncation, simply do the addition with the largest possible values the addends can contain — 9.99 and 999.999 — and you will understand its basis.

When you are using addition to count or accumulate, the value of the result keeps getting larger and larger each time the calculation is performed (for example, when accumulating individuals' calculated gross pay figures to generate a grand total gross pay). In this case, to determine the needed size of the result field you need to have an approximate idea of how many times the calculation will be performed (i.e., how many employees you will process). Once you have this estimate, follow the rule for multiplication, given below.

Result Field Size for Subtraction

To eliminate the chance of truncation with subtraction, follow the rule given for addition. This advice may seem strange at first, until you realize that you must provide for the possibility of subtracting a negative number, which essentially turns the problem into one of addition. Thus, to avoid high-order truncation when subtracting, define the result field to have 1 more digit position to the left of the decimal position than the larger of the high-order positions of factor 1 and factor 2. And define the result field to have the same number of decimal positions as the larger of the number of decimal positions of factor 1 and factor 2.

Result Field Size for Multiplication

When multiplying, to determine the needed number of digit positions in a result field, add the number of positions to the left of the decimal positions of the two multipliers and use that to determine the number of high-order digits in the result. The sum of the number of positions to the right of the decimal in the multipliers represents the number of positions your result field must have to the right of the decimal. For example, if you were multiplying 999.99 by 99.99, your result field would require 5 places to the left of the decimal and 4 to the right to store the answer without truncation. In RPG, this would mean a field 9 positions long, with 4 decimal positions.

Result Field Size for Division

When dividing by a value of 1 or greater, the maximum required positions to the left of the decimal in the result is the number of left-of-decimal positions in the dividend (the value *being* divided). To understand this, recognize that dividing any value by 1 yields the original value; dividing by any value greater than one will give you a value smaller than the original value. When dividing by values less than 1, computing the number of digit positions in the result becomes a more complicated process; the smaller the divisor, the more significant positions needed in the result field. If you are working with divisors less than 1, your safest approach is to hand-calculate with some representative values to get a sense of the size needed to store your answer.

Because few divisions work out evenly, there is no way to guarantee that you will provide enough decimal positions to avoid low-order truncation. Generally, you choose the number of decimal positions for the result field based on the degree of significance, or accuracy, the calculation warrants. Because most business data processing deals with calculations involving dollars and cents, it usually makes sense to carry out intermediate calculations with the maximum needed or the maximum allowable number of decimal positions (whichever is smaller) and then to reduce that to two decimal positions in the final calculation.

When you are using the MVR operation, the definition you give the result field should depend on the definitions of the factors and result field of the division operation whose remainder you want to capture. The system will carry out the division until the answer has the same number of decimal positions as the result field; what is left at that point will be moved into the remainder field. To make sure you have your remainder field appropriately defined, manually perform some representative calculations that mirror what you want the computer to do, since there is no simple rule of thumb to guide you in this matter.

Rounding

When you store a value in a result field that has fewer decimal positions than the calculated answer, common business practice dictates that you should always round your answer, rather than allow the system to truncate it. Rounding is sometimes called **half-adjusting** because of the technique computers use to accomplish this feat. The computer adds half the value of your right-most desired decimal position to the digit immediately to the right of that decimal position before storing the answer in the result field. Because the value added is half the value of the least-significant digit position of your result, the term half-adjust came into being.

For example, assume the computer has calculated an answer of 3.14156 that you want to store, in rounded form, in a result field defined as 4 with 3 decimal positions. The computer will add 0.0005 to the answer (i.e., 1/2 of 0.001, the lowest decimal position you are retaining in your result), giving 3.14206. It then stores this value in the result field, truncated to three decimal positions, as 3.142. If you had defined the result as 3 with two decimal positions, the computer would add 0.005 (1/2 of 0.01) to 3.14156, giving 3.14656, and store that answer in the result as 3.14.

Fortunately, even if you don't completely understand how the computer rounds, the method RPG uses to specify that rounding should take place is simple; just enter an H, for half-adjust, in position 53 of the calculation whose result you want rounded. Note that the computer associates a rounding instruction with the specific calculation for which the rounding is specified, rather than associating it with the result field. Consequently, you need to include the H in every calculation line where you want rounding to occur, even if those calculations use the same result field. The compiler will *not* warn you if you inadvertently omit an H entry.

Line	Form Type	Control Level (L0-L9, LR,SR, AN/OR)	Indicators And Not	Indicators And Not	Not	Factor 1	Operation	Factor 2	Result Field Name	Length	Decimal Positions	Operation Extender (H,N,P)	Resulting Indicators Arithmetic Plus	Minus	Zero	Comments
0 1	C					* In the below calcs, field INTRST is defined just once, but										
0 2	C					* still requires an H on the second specification if the										
0 3	C					* result of that calculation is to be rounded.										
0 4	C					RATE	MULT	LOAN	INTRST	62		H				
0 5	C					TOTAMT	DIV	NUM	AVGAMT	52		H				
0 6	C															
0 7	C					RATEB	MULT	LOAN	INTRST			H				
0 8	C															

Although you need to round most often when multiplying or dividing, you can specify rounding for ADD and SUB operations, as well as for MULT and DIV. It is important to note that if you want to capture the remainder of a DIV operation with a subsequent MVR operation, you cannot round that division.

Recognize that you do not always need to round when multiplying. Consider the following calculation, for example:

Line	Form Type	Control Level (L0-L9, LR,SR, AN/OR)	Indicators And Not	Indicators And Not	Not	Factor 1	Operation	Factor 2	Result Field Name	Length	Decimal Positions	Operation Extender (H,N,P)	Resulting Indicators Arithmetic Plus	Minus	Zero	Comments
0 1	C					QTYOH	MULT	UNTPR	VALUE	62						
0 2	C															

If QTYOH (quantity on hand) is an integer (whole number), and UNTPR (unit price) is stored as dollars and cents (e.g., 4 with 2 decimal positions), the resulting answer will never have more than 2 decimal positions, so you do *not* need to round the answer to store it in VALUE.

Sometimes students, out of uncertainty or laziness, decide to play it safe by rounding all arithmetic operations, regardless of whether the rounding is needed. Avoid this practice. The RPG compiler will issue a warning message about unnecessary half-adjusting, and rounding when uncalled for reflects poorly on your programming skills and/or style.

Effective Commenting on Calculations

One characteristic of good programmers is that they write code realizing that other programmers will have to work with and probably revise the code in the future. In addition to following the guideline to avoid "tricky" code, and to code instead for clarity and straightforwardness, good programmers make liberal use of comments to internally document programs, as discussed in Chapter 2.

In addition to using comment lines to document logic that would otherwise be difficult to follow, most professional RPG programmers take advantage of positions 60-74 on Calculation Specifications to add short comments that provide additional explanation about what a given line or block of code accomplishes. This comment area can provide a running commentary of the code, which makes it easier to follow the program's logic. Using lowercase type for these comments makes them stand out clearly from the code itself.

Putting It All Together

You have learned how each RPG arithmetic operation works, and you understand the importance of correctly defining the size of result fields and appropriately rounding calculations. Now it's time to demonstrate the use of these concepts to give you a better flavor of RPG's approach to solving arithmetically oriented programming problems.

As you know, RPG is limited to performing a single arithmetic operation at a time. Complex calculations must be broken down into individual steps, with each step involving a single operation. Sometimes this method requires that you define work fields — fields that do not appear in the program output — to store results of intermediate calculations.

The following sample problem demonstrates how to use the arithmetic operations of RPG to express more complex calculations. A retail store wants you to write a routine to calculate selling prices for items it has received. The store uses a 60 percent markup for its goods. In addition to the required selling price, the store would like you to generate a projection of gross profit for each item and a grand total projected gross profit for all items received. The gross-profit projections should assume that the store will sell all the items at the price calculated by your program.

An input file, NEWITEMS, contains records with the following format:

Field	Position	Decimal Positions
Item Description	1-30	
Item Cost	31-36	2
Quantity Received	37-40	0

The printer spacing chart below depicts the desired report.

```
         1         2         3         4         5         6         7         8         9        10
1234567890123456789012345678901234567890123456789012345678901234567890123456789012345678901234567890

XX/XX/XX                       GROSS PROFIT PROJECTION                        PAGE XX0X

                                         SELLING            PER UNIT             TOTAL
        ITEM                     COST      PRICE     QTY.     PROFIT         GROSS PROFIT

    XXXXXXXXXXXXXXXXXXXXXXXXXXX  X,XX0.XX  XX,XX0.XX  X,X0X  X,XX0.XX       XX,XXX,XX0.XX
    XXXXXXXXXXXXXXXXXXXXXXXXXXX  X,XX0.XX  XX,XX0.XX  X,X0X  X,XX0.XX       XX,XXX,XX0.XX

                        GRAND TOTAL GROSS PROFIT PROJECTED:    $XXX,XXX,XXX,XX$.XX
```

Pseudocode of a solution for this problem is as follows:

```
Print headings
Read a record
WHILE more records exist
      Calculate per unit profit (cost * .6)
      Calculate selling price (cost + per unit profit)
      Calculate total item gross profit (quantity * per unit profit)
      Accumulate grand total gross profit
      Write detail line
      Read a record
ENDWHILE
Print grand total line
End program
```

Notice in the pseudocode that all calculations need to fall within the loop, because each needs to be performed for each data record. Printing headings is done just once before the loop, while printing the grand total line is done just once, following the loop. The pseudocode also shows that the details of the required calculations have been worked out.

The File Specifications for this problem present no new challenges. Note that on the Input Specifications QTY must include a 0 decimal positions entry, since that field will be used in arithmetic operations.

Input Specifications (I)

Line	Form Type	Filename	Sequence	Number (1/N)	Option (O)	Record Identifying Indicator or **	From	To	Decimal Positions	Field Name
0 1	I	NEWITEMS	NS							
0 2	I						1	30		DESC
0 3	I						31	36	2	COST
0 4	I						37	40	0	QTY
0 5	I									

In the Calculation Specifications that follow, note that the multiplication to obtain unit profit (UNTPFT) is rounded, while the multiplication to calculate gross profit (GRPFT) is not. This difference is based on the relative number of decimal positions the two multiplication operations generate, given the number of decimal positions in factors 1 and 2.

Also note that to calculate grand total gross profit (TOTPFT), in each pass through the loop it is necessary to add the gross profit of the current item (GRPFT) to the accumulator TOTPFT.

The calculations also demonstrate (a bit excessively) how comments can be used in positions 60-74 to try to clarify the calculations.

Calculation Specifications (C)

Line	Form Type	Indicators	Factor 1	Operation	Factor 2	Result Field Name	Length	Decimal Positions	Operation Extender (H,N,P)	Resulting Indicators	Comments
0 1	C			EXCPTHEADS							Write headings
0 2	C			READ	NEWITEMS					90	Priming read
0 3	C	*									
0 4	C		*IN90	DOWEQ	*OFF						Start loop
0 5	C		COST	MULT	.6	UNTPFT	62		H		Unit profit
0 6	C		COST	ADD	UNTPFT	SELLPR	72				Selling price
0 7	C		UNTPFT	MULT	QTY	GRPFT	102				Gross profit
0 8	C			ADD	GRPFT	TOTPFT	142				Grand total
0 9	C			EXCPTDETAIL							Write detail
1 0	C			READ	NEWITEMS					90	
1 1	C			ENDDO							End of loop
1 2	C	*									
1 3	C			EXCPTTOTAL							Write total
1 4	C			MOVE	*ON	*INLR					
1 5	C			RETRN							
1 6	C										

Details of the coding for the heading lines are omitted, because there is nothing new there to consider. Do note that the total line (TOTAL) appears in the output with a SPACE 1 BEFORE entry. That spacing is required to obtain one blank line between the last detail line to print and the total line. Also note that a floating dollar sign is associated with field TOTPFT, as requested in the printer spacing chart.

Line	Filename or Record Name	Type (H/D/T/E)	Space Before/After	Skip Before/After	Output Indicators And / And	Field Name or EXCPT Name or Constant Name	End Position in Output Record	Edit Codes	Constant or Edit Word
0 1	O QPRINT	E	0 2			HEADS			
0 2	O					. . .			
0 3	O	E	1			DETAIL			
0 4	O					DESC	30		
0 5	O					COST 1	41		
0 6	O					SELLPR 1	53		
0 7	O					QTY 1	62		
0 8	O					UNTPFT 1	74		
0 9	O					GRPFT 1	92		
1 0	O	E	1			TOTAL			
1 1	O						52		'GRAND TOTAL GROSS'
1 2	O						70		'PROFIT PROJECTED:'
1 3	O					TOTPFT 1	92		'$'
1 4	O								

Assignment Operations

This chapter began by introducing you to the arithmetic operations available in RPG. You also need to become familiar with a second class of operations called **assignment operations**. Assignment operations are those that allow you to simply assign a value to a variable. RPG has four assignment operations, two used for numeric fields and two that most often are used with character fields.

Z-ADD (Zero and Add)
The most commonly used assignment operation for numeric fields is Z-ADD. The Z-ADD operation always involves a factor 2 value and a result field. You can interpret this operation as "zero out the result field and add factor 2 to it."

The effect of this operation is to assign the value of factor 2 to the result field. The most common use of this operation is to initialize or reinitialize a counter or accumulator to zero. Although RPG automatically initializes all numeric variables to 0 at the start of program execution, good programming practice recommends that you explicitly initialize all counters and accumulators for clarity's sake. For example, in the sample program computing gross profit (page 56), initializing field TOTPFT by appropriately coding the statement Z-ADD 0 TOTPFT just before the DOW loop would clarify the use of that field. You can also use Z-ADD to assign the value of *any* numeric literal or numeric field to the result field.

C		Indicators						Result Field			Resulting Indicators		
Line	Form Type	Control Level (L0-L9, LR,SR, AN/OR)	And / Not	And / Not	/ Not	Factor 1	Operation	Factor 2	Name	Length	Decimal Positions	Operation Extender (H,N,P)	Arithmetic / Compare / Lookup / Comments	
0 1	C	* Set CTR to zero.												
0 2	C						Z-ADD0		CTR	30				
0 3	C	* Assign CTR the same value as that of field N.												
0 4	C						Z-ADDN		CTR	30				
0 5	C	* Set MAX to 20.												
0 6	C						Z-ADD20		MAX	20				
0 7	C	* Zero out SLSTOT.												
0 8	C						Z-ADD0		SLSTOT	62				
0 9	C													

Z-SUB (Zero and Subtract)

Like Z-ADD, Z-SUB requires a factor 2 and a result field entry. The Z-SUB operator works similarly to Z-ADD, except that after zeroing out the result field, it *subtracts* the value of factor 2 from the result field. Because this operation assigns the negative value of factor 2 to the result field, its effect is to reverse the sign of a field.

C		Indicators						Result Field			Resulting Indicators		
Line	Form Type	Control Level (L0-L9, LR,SR, AN/OR)	And / Not	And / Not	/ Not	Factor 1	Operation	Factor 2	Name	Length	Decimal Positions	Operation Extender (H,N,P)	Arithmetic / Compare / Lookup / Comments	
0 1	C						Z-SUB20		MIN	20				
0 2	C	* Following the above operation, MIN has a value of -20.												
0 3	C						Z-SUB-15		X	20				
0 4	C	* Following the above operation, X had a value of 15, because												
0 5	C	* to subtract a negative value, you change the sign and add.												
0 6	C						Z-SUBPOSVAL		NEGVAL					
0 7	C						Z-SUBNEGVAL		POSVAL					

Character Literals

Before we look at operations used to assign values to character result fields, one feature of RPG not yet mentioned needs to be introduced: **character literals**. Earlier in this chapter you learned how numeric literals could be used in factor 1 or factor 2 in conjunction with arithmetic operations. You also saw how a numeric literal could be used with Z-ADD and Z-SUB to assign numeric values to numeric result fields.

RPG allows you to use character literals in factor 1 and/or factor 2 of the Calculation Specifications when working with character-oriented operations. To indicate that a value is a character literal (and not a field name), simply enclose it with apostrophes. There is no restriction on what characters can comprise the literal; any character that you can represent via the keyboard — including a blank — is acceptable.

The limit to the length of a character literal is the room allowed for it in factor 1 or factor 2. Since each of those factors is maximally 10 characters long, eight is the maximum length for a character literal used on the Calculation Specifications. (The required apostrophes will take up two positions.)

C			Indicators				Factor 1	Operation	Factor 2		Result Field			Resulting Indicators		Comments
			And	And							Name	Length		Arithmetic		
														Plus / Minus / Zero		
Line														Compare		
														1>2 / 1<2 / 1=2		
														Lookup(Factor 2)is		
														High / Low / Equal		
0 1	C						* Examples of character literals.									
0 2	C							. . .	'aBcd 12'							
0 3	C							. . .	' '							
0 4	C							. . .	'14521'							
0 5	C							. . .	'45%'							
0 6	C															

Recognize that you cannot use a character literal — one enclosed within apostrophes — with an arithmetic operation even if all the characters of the literal are digits. Numeric literals do not use apostrophes.

MOVE (Move)

The primary use of the MOVE operation is to assign a value specified in factor 2 to a character result field. Factor 1 is not used with MOVE. Unlike the arithmetic operators and Z-ADD and Z-SUB, which always store results based on decimal-point alignment, the MOVE operation transfers characters from the sending field in factor 2 to the receiving field in the result, character by character, moving through the fields from right to left.

If factor 2 is larger than the result field, the excess characters will be truncated from the left. If factor 2 is smaller than the result field, whatever was in the result field prior to the MOVE will remain in the positions not used in the MOVE operation. Study the figure below to gain an understanding of MOVE.

```
C* If factor 2 and result field are the same length, all characters
C* are copied to the result.
C                     MOVE  'ABCD'     EXMPLE    4
C* EXMPLE now contains 'ABCD'.
C* If the result field is smaller than factor 2, as below,
C* left truncation occurs.
C                     MOVE  'ABCDEFG'  EXMPLE
C* EXMPLE now contains 'DEFG'.
C* If the result field is larger than factor 2, as below,
C* carry-over characters appear to the left.
C                     MOVE  '12'       EXMPLE
C* EXMPLE now contains 'DE12'.
C* If factor 2 is a field, its contents are moved from the right.
C* Assume NAME is a 10-position character field containing
C* 'CHAUNCEY  '.
C                     MOVE  NAME       EXMPLE
C* EXMPLE now contains 'EY  ', the four right-most characters
C* of NAME.
C
```

The possibility of carry-over characters in the result field following the move of a smaller data item to the result has meant that programmers often have had to blank out result fields to prevent such leftovers from corrupting their data. In a recent release of RPG/400 (V2R2), IBM has added an extension to the MOVE operation that allows you to automatically pad unused portions of the result field with blanks: Simply enter a P in position 53 of the Calculation Specification that contains the MOVE.

```
C* Assume EXMPLE contains 'ABCD'.
C                     MOVE  '12'       EXMPLE           P
C* After the MOVE, EXMPLE contains '  12' because the Pad entry
C* blanks out unused positions of the result field.
C
```

Programmers sometimes use the MOVE operation to convert a value's data type from character to numeric. This use arises because occasionally fields that actually contain numeric data are defined without a decimal position to allow them to be used with operators valid only for character fields. (Some of these operations are discussed in Chapter 11.) To allow that value to be subsequently used in arithmetic calculations, the programmer would then move that character field's value to a numeric field.

```
C* Store a numeric value in character field ALPHA.
C                  MOVE '1234'      ALPHA     4
C* Execute desired character operations on ALPHA.
C                  ...
C* Then move the value to a numeric field so that it can be used
C* with arithmetic operations or edited for output.
C                  MOVE ALPHA       NUMER     40
C
```

In general, avoid using MOVE for assigning values to numeric fields when Z-ADD is the appropriate operation. The MOVE operator disregards decimal positions of numeric fields during the value transfer, since it transfers on a strict right-to-left basis, and as a result you may inadvertently change the values of numeric fields in ways that you may not want. The sample code in the following figure demonstrates how this change in value may occur.

```
C* Assume X, three positions long with 2 decimal positions, contains
C* 1.23, and that Y, 5 long with 1 decimal position, contains zeros.
C                  MOVE X           Y
C* Y now contains 0012.3, because decimal positions are disregarded
C* in a move.
C
```

MOVEL (Move Left)

The MOVEL operation, which requires a factor 2 and a result entry, works like a MOVE except that data transfer starts with the left-most characters of the sending and receiving fields and moves data, character by character, from left to right.

Except for this directional difference, MOVEL works the same way as MOVE. If factor 2 is larger than the result field, truncation of characters (excess *right-most*, in this case) occurs; if the result field is larger than factor 2, carry-over values will remain in the unused (*right-most*) positions of the result. V2R2 of RPG/400 added the Pad option to the MOVEL operation so that you now can easily eliminate such carry-over values, if you wish.

Line	Form Type	Control Level (L0-L9, LR,SR, AN/OR)	Indicators			Factor 1	Operation	Factor 2	Result Field		Decimal Positions	Operation Extender (H,N,P)	Resulting Indicators			Comments
			And	And					Name	Length			Arithmetic / Compare / Lookup			

```
C* If factor 2 and result field are the same length, all characters
C* are copied to the result.
C            MOVEL'ABCD'      EXMPLE   4
C* EXMPLE now contains 'ABCD'.
C* If the result field is smaller than factor 2, as below,
C* right truncation occurs.
C            MOVEL'ABCDEFG' EXMPLE
C* EXMPLE now contains 'ABCD'.
C* If the result field is larger than factor 2, as below,
C* carry-over characters appear to the right.
C            MOVEL'12'        EXMPLE
C* EXMPLE now contains '12CD'.
C* If factor 2 is a field, its contents are moved from the left.
C* Assume NAME is a 10-position character field containing
C* 'CHAUNCEY   '.
C            MOVELNAME        EXMPLE
C* EXMPLE now contains 'CHAU', the four left-most characters of name.
C* Assume EXMPLE contains 'ABCD'.
C            MOVEL'12'        EXMPLE        P
C* After the MOVEL, EXMPLE contains '12  ' because of the Pad entry.
```

Unless you have a specific reason, avoid using MOVEL to assign values to numeric fields. Like MOVE, MOVEL disregards decimal position alignment and you may inadvertently change your field values if you move values between numeric fields of different lengths and decimal positions.

Although at one time RPG programmers extensively used MOVE and MOVEL to split fields into smaller units or to rearrange subfields within fields, this usage has become unnecessary with the introduction of data structures (Chapter 9) and string operators (Chapter 11). Nevertheless, you may still encounter code like the following example, in which a date stored in YYMMDD format is switched to MMDDYY format.

C		Indicators			Factor 1	Operation	Factor 2	Result Field				Resulting Indicators			Comments

Line	Form Type	Control Level (L0-L9, LR,SR, AN/OR)	And	And	Factor 1	Operation	Factor 2	Name	Length	Decimal Positions	Operation Extender (H,N,P)	Arithmetic Plus/Compare 1>2	Minus/1<2	Zero/1=2 Lookup High/Low/Equal	Comments
0 1	C				* Assume DTYMD contains a date, 921025, in YYMMDD format.										
0 2	C					MOVE	DTYMD	MMDD	4						
0 3	C				* The above MOVE puts '1025' in MMDD.										
0 4	C					MOVEL	DTYMD	YY	2						
0 5	C				* The above MOVEL puts '92' in YY.										
0 6	C					MOVEL	MMDD	DTMDY	6	P					
0 7	C				* The above MOVEL puts '1025 ' in DTMDY.										
0 8	C					MOVE	YY	DTMDY							
0 9	C				* DTMDY now contains '102592'.										
1 0	C														
1 1	C														

Figurative Constants

RPG includes a special set of reserved words called **figurative constants.** Figurative constants are implied literals that can be used without a specified length. Figurative constants assume the length and decimal positions of the fields they are associated with. RPG's figurative constants are *BLANK (or *BLANKS), *ZERO (or *ZEROS), *HIVAL, *LOVAL, *OFF, *ON, and *ALL.

Moving *BLANK or *BLANKS causes a character field to be filled with blanks. Moving *HIVAL fills a character field with X'FFFF...'(all bits on) and a numeric field with all 9s and a plus sign. Moving *LOVAL fills a character field with X'0000...' (all bits off) and a numeric field with all 9s and a negative sign. Programmers often assign *HIVAL or *LOVAL to a field to ensure that the field's value will be greater than (or less than, for *LOVAL) any other value they may compare to that field.

C		Indicators			Factor 1	Operation	Factor 2	Result Field				Resulting Indicators			Comments

Line	Form Type	Control Level (L0-L9, LR,SR, AN/OR)	And	And	Factor 1	Operation	Factor 2	Name	Length	Decimal Positions	Operation Extender (H,N,P)	Arithmetic Plus/Compare 1>2	Minus/1<2	Zero/1=2 Lookup High/Low/Equal	Comments
0 1	C				* Examples of using figurative constants.										
0 2	C					MOVE	*BLANKS	LNAME	25						
0 3	C					MOVE	*HIVAL	RECKEY	6						
0 4	C					MOVE	*LOVAL	RECKEY	6						
0 5	C														

RPG allows you to assign *ZERO (or *ZEROS) both to numeric and to character fields to fill the fields with 0s. Moving *ZERO to a numeric field has the same effect as Z-ADD *ZERO (or Z-ADD 0); using the Z-ADD operation is preferable, because Z-ADD is an operation more appropriate to numeric data types than is MOVE.

Moving figurative constant *ALL, immediately followed by one or more characters within quotes, causes the string within the quotes to be cyclically repeated through the entire length of the result field. Note that when used with *ALL, both MOVE and MOVEL begin data placement from the left.

Line	Form Type	Control Level (L0-L9, LR,SR, AN/OR)	Indicators And Not	Indicators And Not	Indicators Not	Factor 1	Operation	Factor 2	Result Field Name	Result Field Length	Decimal Positions	Operation Extender (H,N,P)	Resulting Indicators	Comments
0 1	C						MOVE	*ALL'-'	UNDRLN	80				
0 2	C	* The above operation fills UNDRLN with hyphens.												
0 3	C						MOVE	*ALL'ab'	CHRFLD	9				
0 4	C	* CHRFLD now contains 'ababababa'.												
0 5	C						MOVEL	*ALL'ab'	CHRFLD					
0 6	C	* CHRFLD now contains 'ababababa'.												
0 7	C						Z-ADD	*ALL'1'	NBRFLD	8	2			
0 8	C	* NBRFLD value now is 111111.11.												
0 9	C													

Finally, figurative constants *OFF and *ON represent character '0' and character '1', respectively. Although *OFF and *ON can be used with any character field of any length, most often programmers use *OFF and *ON to change the value of an RPG indicator or to compare with an indicator's value. *ON is the equivalent of '1', while *OFF equates to '0'.

Line	Form Type	Control Level (L0-L9, LR,SR, AN/OR)	Indicators And Not	Indicators And Not	Indicators Not	Factor 1	Operation	Factor 2	Result Field Name	Result Field Length	Decimal Positions	Operation Extender (H,N,P)	Resulting Indicators	Comments
0 1	C	* Turn on indicator 90.												
0 2	C						MOVE	*ON	*IN90					
0 3	C	* Turn off indicator 40.												
0 4	C						MOVE	*OFF	*IN40					
0 5	C	* Loop while indicator 90 is on.												
0 6	C						*IN90	DOWEQ	*ON					
0 7	C							...						
0 8	C													

Chapter Summary

RPG has a limited number of arithmetic operators to use for computations. The format of RPG specifications requires that only a single operator be used at a time. Only numeric fields or literals can be used as factors in arithmetic. Do not enclose numeric literals with apostrophes; apostrophes signal the presence of a character literal, which cannot participate in arithmetic operations.

If the size of the result of an arithmetic operation exceeds the length of the field to receive the result, the computer aligns the answer in the result field based on the locations of the decimal positions and then truncates those digits for which there is not enough room. This truncation may be high-order or low-order, depending on the size of the result field. You can avoid low-order truncation by rounding your answer; you should routinely round when the size of the result field warrants it.

You should use assignment operations Z-ADD and Z-SUB to assign values to numeric fields. Operations MOVE and MOVEL should primarily be used to manipulate character data. MOVE and MOVEL function almost identically, except that MOVE moves data starting at the right-most position of the data items while MOVEL starts at the left.

Figurative constants are built-in literals with specified values. The length of a figurative constant automatically adjusts to match that of the field it is used with. Figurative constants include *BLANK, *BLANKS, *ZERO, *ZEROS, *HIVAL, *LOVAL, *OFF, *ON, and *ALL.

The summary table below shows the RPG operations from this chapter to help you recall the appropriate format for Calculation Specifications based on those operations.

Required Format of Arithmetic and Assignment Operations				
Data Types	**Factor 1**	**Operation**	**Factor 2**	**Result**
numeric	field/ literal	**ADD**	FIELD/LITERAL	FIELD
numeric	field/ literal	**SUB**	FIELD/LITERAL	FIELD
numeric	field/ literal	**MULT**	FIELD/LITERAL	FIELD
numeric	field/ literal	**DIV**	FIELD/LITERAL	FIELD
numeric	—	**MVR**	—	FIELD
numeric	—	**SQRT**	FIELD/LITERAL	FIELD
numeric	—	**Z-ADD**	FIELD/LITERAL	FIELD
numeric	—	**Z-SUB**	FIELD/LITERAL	FIELD
character/numeric	—	**MOVE**	FIELD/LITERAL	FIELD
character/numeric	—	**MOVEL**	FIELD/LITERAL	FIELD

Uppercase = required entry; lowercase = optional entry.

Terms

assignment operations
character literals
exponentiation
figurative constants

half-adjusting
high-order truncation
low-order truncation
numeric fields

numeric literals
truncation

Discussion/Review Questions

1. What is a literal? Why would you use a literal within an arithmetic operation? (Give some examples.) Can you think of any disadvantages to using literals in calculations?

2. Which of the values below would not constitute valid numeric literals in RPG?

+124.22	44%	−10.2
$23.44	1,210.34	.9931
'75.22'	4512	−.012345678

3. Why do you think RPG has relatively limited mathematical capabilities ?

4. Why does it make sense that the result of a Calculation Specification cannot be a literal?

5. What two mathematical impossibilities will result in a program error if your program tries to execute them?

6. Summarize the rules of thumb for determining how large to define result fields for arithmetic operations.

7. When should you round an arithmetic operation?

8. Why should you use Z-ADD rather than MOVE to assign values to numeric fields?

9. What is a figurative constant? What are possible uses for figurative constants? How does *ALL work?

10. Discuss the difference between MOVE and MOVEL.

Exercises

1. Write the calculations to discount field OPRICE (6 positions, 2 decimal positions) by 10 percent to give NPRICE.

2. Write the calculations to convert a temperature in Fahrenheit to Centigrade, using the following formula:

   $$C = 5(F - 32)/9$$

   Assume F is 3 positions with 0 decimal positions.

3. Write the calculations to convert a measurement taken in inches (INCH, 5 positions with 0 decimal positions) into the same measurement expressed as yards, feet, and inches.

4. Code the calculations needed to determine the cost of wall-to-wall carpeting for a room. Field LENGTH (3 positions, 1 decimal) contains the room length in feet; field WIDTH (3 positions, 1 decimal) contains the room's width in feet; and field COST (4 positions, 2 decimals) contains the cost per square yard of the selected carpet.

5. Write the calculations to determine the Economic Order Quantity, EOQ, using the formula

   $$EOQ = \text{square root of } (2DO/C),$$

   where D represents annual demand for product;

   O represents costs to place one order;

   and C represents carrying costs.

   Assume D is 5 positions, 0 decimal positions; O is 5 positions, 2 decimal positions; and C is 6 positions, 2 decimal positions.

Programming Assignments

1. Wexler University wants a program that will produce a student grade report. Input file, WUEXAMP (described in Appendix D), contains information about students in a class and five exam grades for each student.

   The program will need to calculate an average exam grade for each student. The school also wants to know the average exam grade for the class as a whole (i.e., the average of the averages). The desired report layout is shown below. Notice that just the initial of the student's first name is to print with the last name.

```
          1         2         3         4         5         6         7         8
 12345678901234567890123456789012345678901234567890123456789012345678901234567890

    XX/XX/XX           WEXLER U. STUDENT GRADE REPORT          PAGE XXØX

                                 EXAM  EXAM  EXAM  EXAM  EXAM   AVG.
    STUDENT NO.        NAME        1     2     3     4     5    GRADE
    XXX-XX-XXXX    X. XXXXXXXXXXXXXX  XØX   XØX   XØX   XØX   XØX    XØX
    XXX-XX-XXXX    X. XXXXXXXXXXXXXX  XØX   XØX   XØX   XØX   XØX    XØX
    XXX-XX-XXXX    X. XXXXXXXXXXXXXX  XØX   XØX   XØX   XØX   XØX    XØX

                                 CLASS AVERAGE  XØX
```

Programming Assignments Continued

Programming Assignments continued

2. CompuSell, the computer mail-order company, extends financing to some of its preferred customers. All financing is done for 12 months at a fixed rate of 14 percent. The company charges interest on the total amount financed, rather than on the unpaid balance remaining after each successive payment. Accordingly, the monthly payment is determined by calculating the interest due on the unpaid balance, adding the interest to the unpaid balance, and dividing that sum by 12.

   Write a program for CompuSell that will calculate monthly charges for each customer in the input file CSCSFINP, described in Appendix D.

   The format of the desired report is shown below. Note that purchase date is to print as DD-MM, and that the report requires a count of customers in the file.

```
         1         2         3         4         5         6         7         8
1234567890123456789012345678901234567890123456789012345678901234567890123456789012345678901234567890

    XX/XX/XX                COMPUSELL FINANCE REPORT              PAGE XXØX

    CUST.          PURCHASE        PURCHASE          DOWN           BALANCE          MONTHLY
    NUM.           AMOUNT          DATE              PAYMENT        OWED             PAYMENT

    XXXXXX         X,XXØ.XX        ØX-XX             X,XXØ.XX       X,XXØ.XX         X,XXØ.XX
    XXXXXX         X,XXØ.XX        ØX-XX             X,XXØ.XX       X,XXØ.XX         X,XXØ.XX

                      TOTALS            $XXX,XX$.XX    $XXX,XX$.XX      $XXX,XX$.XX

    NUMBER OF CUSTOMERS PROCESSED XXØ
```

3. Wexler University wants a program to generate a payroll register for its hourly employees. Appendix D describes the input file for this program: WUHRLYP. The file contains information about regular and overtime hours worked and pay rate for hourly employees.

   The school pays time and a half for overtime hours. Gross pay is the sum of regular and over time pay. Net pay is gross pay less deductions for taxes and FICA. Eighteen percent federal tax is withheld; 5 percent state tax; and 7.51 percent for FICA.

   The format of the desired payroll register is shown below. Note that just the initial of the first name is to print as part of the employee's name.

```
         1         2         3         4         5         6         7         8         9        1Ø
1234567890123456789012345678901234567890123456789012345678901234567890123456789012345678901234567890

    PAGE XXØX                                                            XX/XX/XX

                            WEXLER U. PAYROLL REGISTER

                                     GROSS        FEDERAL       STATE                       NET
        SOC. SEC.       NAME         PAY          TAX           TAX          FICA           PAY

        XXX-XX-XXXX  X. XXXXXXXXXXXXXXX    X,XXØ.XX     X,XXØ.XX      XXØ.XX       XXØ.XX       X,XXØ.XX
        XXX-XX-XXXX  X. XXXXXXXXXXXXXXX    X,XXØ.XX     X,XXØ.XX      XXØ.XX       XXØ.XX       X,XXØ.XX


                  GRAND TOTALS       $XXX,XX$.XX  $XXX,XX$.XX   $XX,XX$.XX  $XX,XX$.XX    $XXX,XX$.XX
```

Programming Assignments Continued

Programming Assignments continued

4. Ida Lapeer, Interior Decorator, wants a program that will estimate material costs for interior painting jobs based on data in file BIDS, described at the end of Appendix D.

Coverage per gallon represents the number of square feet of surface area that can be painted by one gallon. All room measurements were taken in terms of feet and inches (e.g., 14'10"). The percent figure given for windows and doors represents Ida's estimate of wall surface that will *not* need paint because of doors or windows. In calculating costs, include the cost of painting the ceiling, as well as all four walls of the room.

Calculate final needed coverage to the nearest square foot and gallons needed to the nearest 100th of a gallon. Paint cost should be based on that figure. Ida has found that 5 percent of her paint costs represents a good estimate of other miscellaneous job costs, such as masking tape, brushes and rollers, and so on.

Your program should produce the report depicted in the printer spacing chart below.

```
          1         2         3         4         5         6         7         8         9         10
 1234567890123456789012345678901234567890123456789012345678901234567890123456789012345678901234567890

        XX/XX/XX                     IDA LAPEER MATERIAL COST ESTIMATES

    JOB      PAINT     COST      COVERAGE    SQ. FEET    GALLONS     ----- ESTIMATED COSTS -----
    NO.      CODE    PER GAL.    PER GAL.    TO COVER    NEEDED     PAINT       MISC.       TOTAL

    XXXX    XX-XXX    XØ.XX        XØX        X,XØX      XØ.XX     X,XXØ.XX     XXØ.XX    XX,XXØ.XX
    XXXX    XX-XXX    XØ.XX        XØX        X,XØX      XØ.XX     X,XXØ.XX     XXØ.XX    XX,XXØ.XX
```

Chapter 4

Top-Down, Structured Program Design

Chapter Overview

This chapter focuses on program design and introduces you to RPG operations that allow you to write well-designed programs using a top-down, structured approach. Loops, decision logic, and subroutines receive special attention.

Structured Design

Programming problems typically can be solved in many different ways, each of which might produce correct output. Correct output, however, although an important goal, should not be the only goal of the programmer. Producing code that is readable and easily changed is also important to programmers who are concerned with quality.

Changes in user requirements and processing errors discovered as programs are used dictate that programmers spend a lot of their time maintaining existing programs rather than developing new code. A well-designed, well-documented program facilitates such maintenance, while a poorly designed program can be a maintenance nightmare.

Structured design is one development methodology that has become widely accepted over the past 20 years to facilitate quality program design. One important aspect of structured design is limiting control structures within your program to three basic logic structures: sequence, selection (also called decision), and iteration (also called repetition or looping).

Sequence lets you instruct the computer to execute operations serially. **Selection** lets you establish alternate paths of instructions within a program; which alternate the program executes depends on the results of a test or condition within the program. And **iteration** permits instructions within the program to be repeated until a condition is met or is no longer met. Figure 4.1 illustrates these control structures in flowchart symbols so that you can understand easily how flow of control works with each structure.

Each of these control structures has a single entry point and a single exit point. Together, the structures can serve as basic building blocks to express the complex logic required to solve complicated programming problems, while maintaining the tight control over program flow that facilitates program maintenance. Structured programming sometimes is called

Figure 4.1
Flowcharts Illustrating
Basic Control Structures

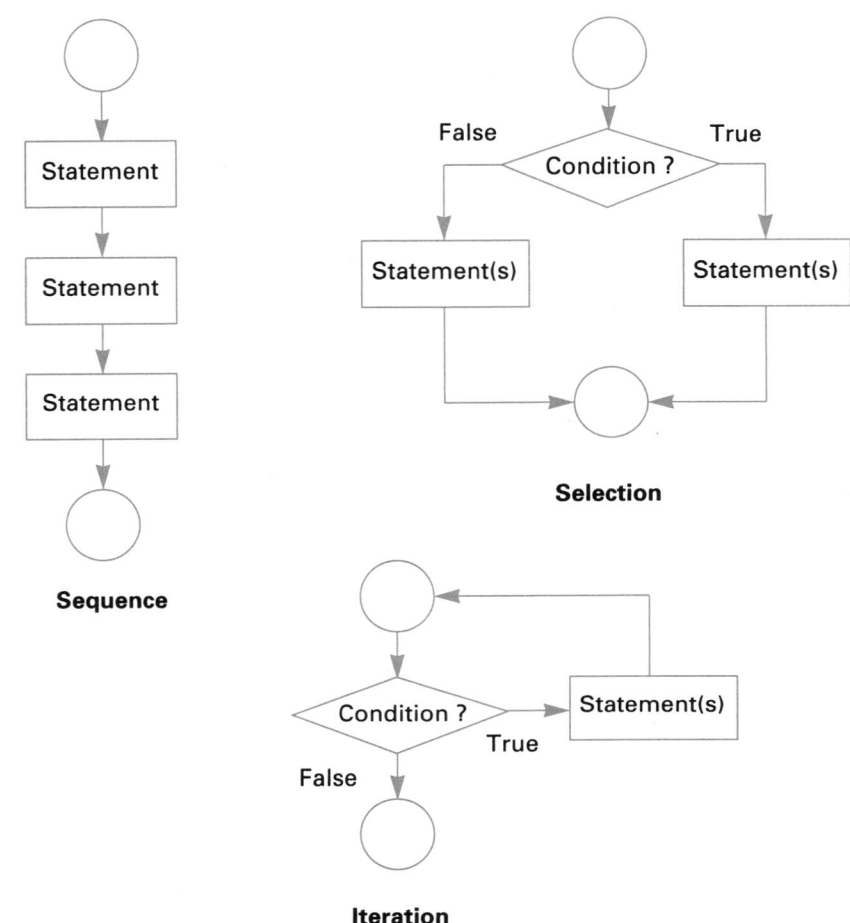

"GOTO-less programming," because this methodology discourages the indiscriminate use of GOTOs. GOTOs are the single operation most responsible for "spaghetti code."

Sequential Flow of Control

Sequential flow of control is inherent in RPG — and other programming languages — by default. The order in which you describe your operations on the Calculation Specifications determines the order in which the computer executes them. The computer continues to execute the program statements in their order of occurrence unless it encounters an operation that explicitly transfers control to a different location within the program.

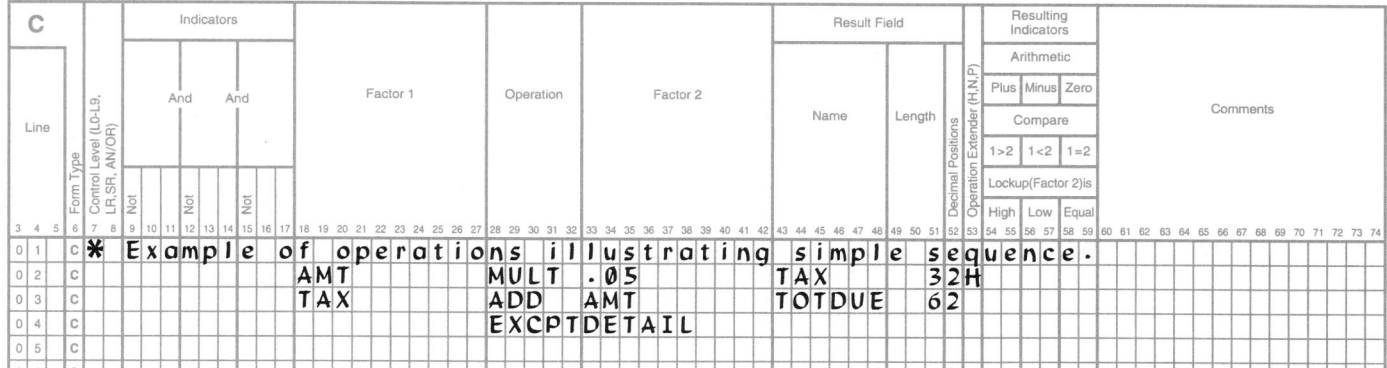

Relational Comparisons

To diverge from a sequential flow of control requires the use of explicit operations. RPG/400 includes a variety of operations to allow you to express both decision and iteration logic. Both kinds of operations involve testing a condition to determine the appropriate course of action. This testing involves a **relational comparison** between two values. To allow you to express the comparison, RPG/400 includes six two-letter **relational codes** that are used with several of the operations to be discussed. The codes are:

GT	Greater than
LT	Less than
EQ	Equal to
NE	Not equal to
LE	Less than or equal to
GE	Greater than or equal to

The way the computer evaluates whether or not a comparison is true depends on the data type of the items being compared. If you are comparing two numeric items (whether fields or literals), the system compares them based on algebraic values. The length and number of decimal positions in the items being compared do not affect the outcome of the comparison. For example, 2.25 is equal to 00002.250000, while 00000002.12345 is smaller than 9. A positive value is always larger than a negative value. Only the algebraic values of the data items themselves determine the result of a relational comparison between numeric fields.

You can also perform relational tests between character values. This kind of comparison takes place somewhat differently from numeric comparisons. When you compare two character literals or fields, the system performs a character-by-character comparison, moving from left to right, until it finds an unmatched pair or has finished checking. When it encounters a character difference, the difference is interpreted in terms of the collating sequence of **EBCDIC**, the data-representation format used by IBM. In EBCDIC, A is less than B, B less than C, and so on; lowercase letters are "smaller" than uppercase letters; letters are smaller than digits; and blank is smaller than any other displayable character.

If you are comparing two character items of unequal sizes, the system blank-pads the smaller item to the right before making the character-by-character comparison. To understand character comparisons, consider the examples below. (In the examples, ƀ represents a blank within the data item.)

ART is less than BART
ARTHUR equals ARTHURƀƀƀƀ
ARTƀƀƀƀ is less than ARTHUR
Al is less than AL
123 is greater than ABC

You can use indicators in relational comparisons, provided you preface the indicator with *IN. You can compare one indicator with another (in which case you're trying to determine whether their values are the same), or you can compare an indicator with character literals '1' and '0' or figurative constants *ON and *OFF, all of which represent the possible values an indicator may assume.

RPG does not allow you to compare a numeric data item with a character data item.

Selection Operations

Now that you understand how RPG makes relational comparisons, you can learn how the relational operators are used with those RPG operations that determine flow of program control. First we will look at the options for sending control to alternate statements within a program — **decision** (or selection) **operations**.

IFxx (If)

The primary decision operator is IFxx, where *xx* represents one of the six relational codes discussed earlier. The general format of the IF operation is:

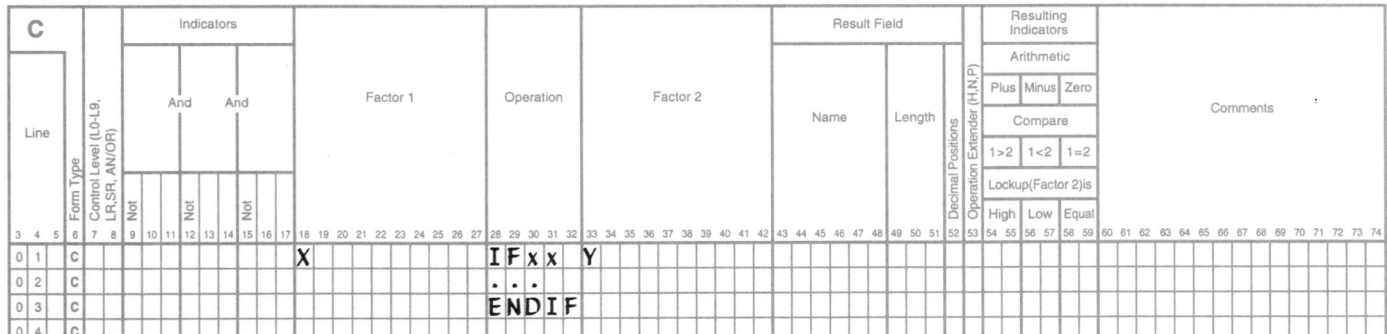

The value in factor 1 is compared to that in factor 2; if the relationship between the two values matches that specified by the relational operator coded in place of *xx*, all the calculations between the IF statement and its ENDIF (or a generic END) statement are executed. If the relationship is not true, those statements are bypassed.

For example, if you wanted to count all senior citizens, you could write the following lines. The IF below can be read, "If AGE is greater than or equal to 65 ..."

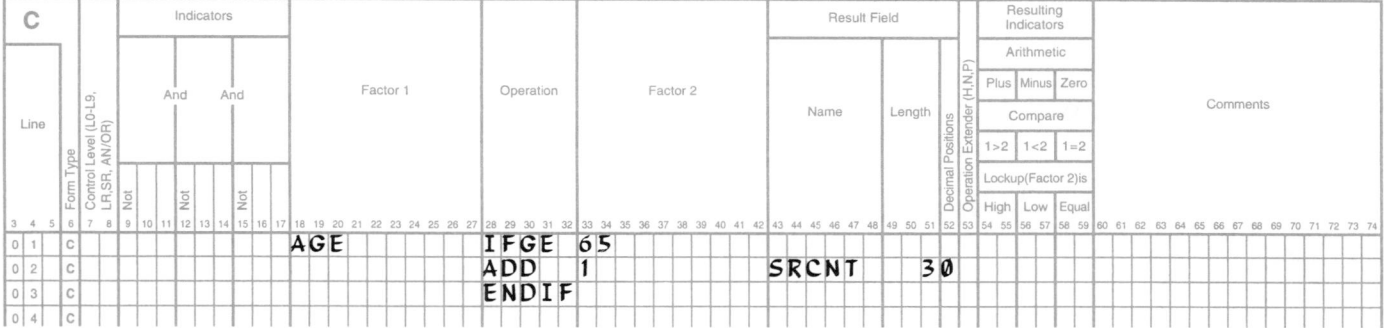

You can also use the IF operation with an ELSE to set up an alternate path of instructions, should the IF fail. For example, if you were asked to calculate pay, and wanted to pay time-and-a-half for any hours over 40, you could code the following:

```
C * If no overtime hours, total pay is hours * rate.
C          HRS       IFLE 40
C          HRS       MULT RATE        TOTPAY    62H
C                    ELSE
C * Figure regular pay and overtime pay, then add for total pay.
C          40        MULT RATE        REGPAY    62
C          HRS       SUB  40          OTHRS     20
C          RATE      MULT 1.5         OTRATE    42H
C          OTHRS     MULT OTRATE      OTPAY     62H
C          OTPAY     ADD  REGPAY      TOTPAY
C                    ENDIF
```

Sometimes you want to execute a series of instructions based on multiple tests or conditions. RPG includes the ANDxx and ORxx variants of the

IF to allow such multiple conditions. When an AND is used to set up a compound condition, both relationships must be true for the IF to evaluate as true. When you use an OR to connect two relational tests, the IF evaluates to true if one or the other (or both) of the conditions is true.

Line	Form Type	Control Level	And Not	And Not	Not	Factor 1	Operation	Factor 2	Result Field Name	Length	Dec Pos	Op Ext	Resulting Indicators	Comments
0 1	C					AGE	IFGE	65						
0 2	C					STATUS	ANDEQ	'R'						
0 3	C	* This block of code executes only if AGE >= 65 and STATUS = R.
0 4	C						...							
0 5	C						ELSE							
0 6	C	* If one or both conditions are not met, this code executes
0 7	C	* instead.
0 8	C						...							
0 9	C						ENDIF							
1 0	C	*
1 1	C	*
1 2	C					AGE	IFGE	65						
1 3	C					STATUS	OREQ	'R'						
1 4	C	* This block executes if one or both conditions are true.
1 5	C						...							
1 6	C						ELSE							
1 7	C	* This block executes only if both conditions are false.
1 8	C						...							
1 9	C						ENDIF							
2 0	C													

IFs also can be nested. That is, you can build IFs within IFs, with or without ELSEs. Each IF requires an ENDIF (or END) in the appropriate spot to indicate the end-point of that IF's influence. The pseudocode below illustrates a nested IF; the code that follows expresses that same logic in RPG.

```
IF age is greater than or equal to 65
    IF sex is female
        life expectancy is 84
    ELSE
        life expectancy is 79
    ENDIF
ELSE
    IF sex is female
        life expectancy is 81
    ELSE
        life expectancy is 78
    ENDIF
ENDIF
```

Line	Form Type	Control Level (L0-L9, LR,SR, AN/OR)	Indicators And Not	Indicators And Not	Indicators Not	Factor 1	Operation	Factor 2	Result Field Name	Length	Decimal Positions	Operation Extender (H,N,P)	Resulting Indicators	Comments
0 1	C					* This code assigns values to LIFE based on age and sex.								
0 2	C					AGE	IFGE	65						
0 3	C					SEX	IFEQ	'F'						
0 4	C						Z-ADD84		LIFE	30				
0 5	C						ELSE							
0 6	C						Z-ADD79		LIFE					
0 7	C						ENDIF							
0 8	C						ELSE							
0 9	C					SEX	IFEQ	'F'						
1 0	C						Z-ADD81		LIFE					
1 1	C						ELSE							
1 2	C						Z-ADD78		LIFE					
1 3	C						ENDIF							
1 4	C						ENDIF							
1 5	C													

Sometimes a program's logic requires that nesting takes place only on the ELSE branches of the decision structure. The following example of assigning commission rates typifies this kind of construct, sometimes called **CASE logic**.

Line	Form Type	Control Level (L0-L9, LR,SR, AN/OR)	Indicators And Not	Indicators And Not	Indicators Not	Factor 1	Operation	Factor 2	Result Field Name	Length	Decimal Positions	Operation Extender (H,N,P)	Resulting Indicators	Comments
0 1	C					* Using nested IFs to assign a value to rate based on								
0 2	C					* level of sales.								
0 3	C					SALES	IFLE	5000						
0 4	C						Z-ADD.005		RATE	44				
0 5	C						ELSE							
0 6	C					SALES	IFLE	10000						
0 7	C						Z-ADD.0075		RATE					
0 8	C						ELSE							
0 9	C					SALES	IFLE	20000						
1 0	C						Z-ADD.01		RATE					
1 1	C						ELSE							
1 2	C						Z-ADD.015		RATE					
1 3	C						ENDIF							
1 4	C						ENDIF							
1 5	C						ENDIF							
1 6	C													

IF and Page Overflow

Before we look at other RPG decision operations, one topic remains to be discussed in conjunction with IF logic: that of page overflow. In the reports we have written up to now, we have included page headings only on the first page. Since most business reports span multiple pages, we need a way to determine when it's time to advance to a new page and reprint heading lines.

RPG has built-in indicators called **overflow indicators**. The special indicators that may be used to signal overflow are OA, OB, OC, OD, OE, OF, OG, and OV. If you associate one of them with the report file on the File Specifications in positions 33-34, that indicator will automatically come on when the printer reaches the overflow line at the bottom of the page.

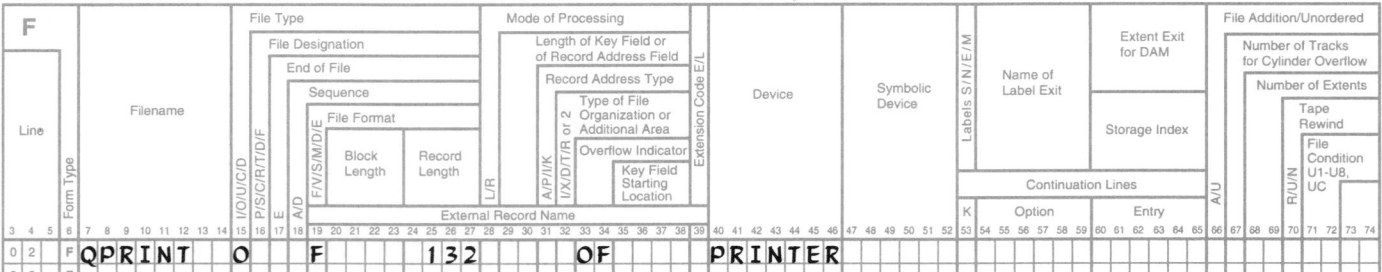

By referencing the status of that indicator in an IF statement just prior to printing a detail line, you can advance the page and print headings each time they are needed, as signaled by the overflow indicator. You will also need to turn that indicator off, since it does not go off automatically.

```
C* Demonstration of how to handle headings within a process loop.
C          *INOF     IFEQ *ON
C                    EXCPTHEADS
C                    MOVE *OFF      *INOF
C                    ENDIF
C                    EXCPTDETAIL
C                    ...
```

Although you can express even the most complex programming decision with just the IF operation, nested IFs can be difficult to set up and hard for others to interpret. To overcome this problem, RPG/400 has two selection operations to allow you to simplify coding of CASE logic: SELEC and CAS.

SELEC (Select)

The SELEC operation appears on a line alone to identify the start of a CASE construct. The SELEC is followed by one or more WHxx lines, each of which specifies a condition to be tested; each WHxx is followed by one or more calculations to be performed when that condition is met. When the program executes, it checks the WHxx conditions sequentially, starting with the first. As soon as it encounters a true condition, the computer executes the operation(s) following that WHxx statement and then sends control to the end of the SELEC construct, signaled by an ENDSL (or END) operation.

The following code uses SELEC to express the same logic shown above with nested IFs.

```
C* Using SELEC to assign a value to RATE based on level of sales.
C                              SELEC
C                    SALES     WHLE  5000
C                              Z-ADD .005        RATE      44
C                    SALES     WHLE  10000
C                              Z-ADD .0075       RATE
C                    SALES     WHLE  20000
C                              Z-ADD .01         RATE
C                              OTHER
C                              Z-ADD .015        RATE
C                              ENDSL
C
```

Notice in the above example that the reserved word OTHER means "in all other cases." OTHER, if used, should be the final "catch-all" condition listed. When a SELEC includes an OTHER, the computer will always perform one of the sets of calculations. When the SELEC is composed only of WHxx conditions, if none of the conditions are met, none of the operations within the SELEC will be performed.

Although not illustrated in the example above, just as in IFxx operations, multiple operations can follow each WHxx line — as many operations as are needed to accomplish the desired processing on that branch of the CASE structure. You also can couple the WHxx conditions with ANDxx and/or ORxx operations to create compound selection criteria.

CASxx

The CASxx structure is nearly identical to SELEC, with one important difference: Instead of coding alternate sets of operations in-line following each condition, the CASxx operation sends control to **subroutines** elsewhere in the program. The name of the subroutine to invoke is entered as the result field on the line that specifies the condition to be met to execute the subroutine.

Subroutines will be discussed in detail a little later in this chapter. For now, recognize that a subroutine is a set of operations coded elsewhere within the calculations and invoked as a unit by referencing the subroutine's name. After performing the subroutine, the program returns control to the statement immediately following the one that invoked the routine. In the case of the CAS operation, control returns to the Calculation Specification immediately following the ENDCS.

C		Indicators			Factor 1	Operation	Factor 2	Result Field			Resulting Indicators	Comments

```
01 C* Using CASxx to send control to different subroutines
02 C* based on the level of sales.
03 C       SALES     CASLE5000        SRLOW
04 C       SALES     CASLE10000       SRMED
05 C       SALES     CASLE20000       SRHI
06 C                 CAS              SRVHI
07 C                 ENDCS
08 C
```

Note that as with SELEC, the first condition that evaluates to true causes the operation(s) associated with that condition (in this case, executing a subroutine) to be performed, and then control jumps to the end of the logic structure to bypass the remaining comparisons. ENDCS (or END) signals the end of the CAS operation. CASxx also allows you to specify a subroutine to be performed if none of the tested conditions prove to be true. To include this option, simply use CAS without a relational operator.

Operations for Iteration

The third logical construct of structured programming is iteration. Iteration allows your program to repeat a series of instructions, a common necessity in programming. In batch processing, for example, you want to execute a series of instructions repeatedly, once for every record in a transaction file. You already have used one RPG operation that enables iteration, or looping: the DOWxx.

DOWxx (Do While)

The DOWxx operation establishes a loop, based on a comparison. The value of the field or literal coded in factor 1 of the operation is compared with that of factor 2; the *xx* of the DOW determines the nature of the comparison. The *xx* can be any one of the six relational codes: EQ, NE, GT, LT, GE, LE. All the operations coded between this operator and its end statement (ENDDO or END) are repeated as long as the condition specified in the relational comparison remains true.

You have already used DOWxx to repeat processing until an end-of-file indicator is turned on. You can use the DOWxx for other kinds of repetition as well. Assume you want to add all the numbers between 1 and 100. With a counter field, NUM, and an accumulator, SUM, you can use DOWxx to easily accomplish this summation, as shown in the following code.

```
C *  This routine adds all the numbers from 1 to 100.
C *  Begin by initializing NUM and SUM to 0.
C                       Z-ADD0          NUM            30
C                       Z-ADD0          SUM            40
C *  Loop while NUM is less than 100.
C            NUM        DOWLT100
C *  Increment NUM by 1.
C                       ADD   1         NUM
C *  Add NUM to accumulator SUM.
C                       ADD   NUM       SUM
C                       ENDDO
C
```

Like RPG's decision operations, the DOWxx operation allows you to use ANDxx and ORxx to form compound conditions to control the looping.

C			Indicators			Factor 1	Operation	Factor 2	Result Field			Resulting Indicators	Comments

The coding-form contents:

```
01 C                    *IN90        DOWEQ*OFF
02 C                    *IN99        ANDEQ*OFF
03 C                                 . . .
04 C  * This code would be repeated as long as both 90 and 99 are off.
05 C                                 . . .
06 C                                 ENDDO
07 C
```

DOUxx (Do Until)

The DOUxx is a structured iteration operation very similar to DOWxx. Like the DOWxx, it includes a field or literal in factors 1 and 2, and repetition is based on a comparison of these factors' values; the *xx* (any of the six relational codes) provides the basis for the comparison.

There are two major differences between a DOWxx and a DOUxx. First, the DOWxx repeats *while* the specified condition *remains* true, whereas the DOUxx operation repeats *until* the condition *becomes* true. Second, a DOWxx is a **leading-decision loop**, which means the comparison is made before the instructions within the loop are executed for the first time. If the comparison evaluates to false, the computer completely bypasses the instructions within the loop. A DOUxx, in contrast, is a **trailing-decision loop**. Because the comparison is made after the instructions within the loop have been executed, the instructions will always execute at least once. In contrast, instructions within a loop controlled by a DOWxx may not be executed at all.

Figure 4.2 presents flowcharts of a DOWxx and a DOUxx operation to illustrate their differences.

Figure 4.2
Flowcharts Illustrating the
Difference Between
DOWxx (Do While) and
DOUxx (Do Until)

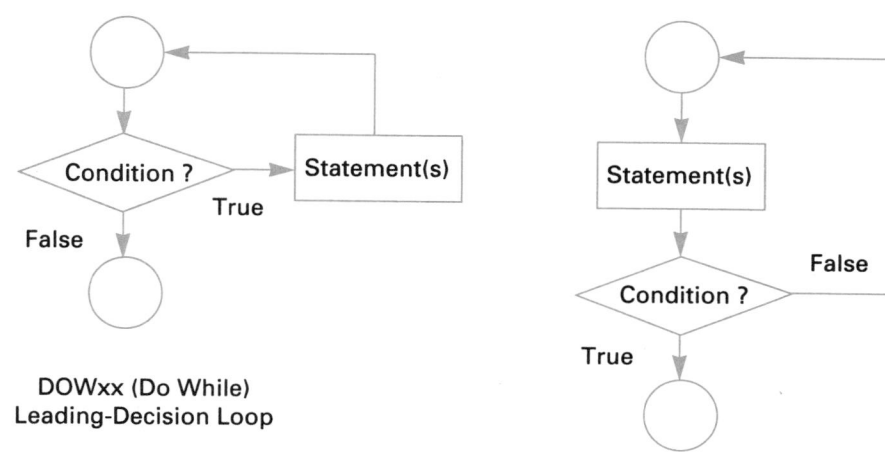

DOWxx (Do While)
Leading-Decision Loop

DOUxx (Do Until)
Trailing-Decision Loop

DOWxx and DOUxx are often equally suited to setting up a looping structure. For instance, you could use DOUxx to solve the add-the-numbers problem; all you would need to change is the DO operation and the relational operator.

Line		Form Type	Control Level (L0-L9, LR,SR, AN/OR)	Not	And	Not	And	Not		Factor 1		Operation		Factor 2			Name		Length	Decimal Positions	Operation Extender (H,N,P)	Plus	Minus	Zero		Comments
0 1	C	*	This code adds all the numbers from 1 to 100.																							
0 2	C	*	Initialize NUM and SUM to 0.																							
0 3	C											Z-ADD 0					NUM		30							
0 4	C											Z-ADD 0					SUM		40							
0 5	C	*	Loop until NUM equals 100.																							
0 6	C									NUM		DOUEQ 100														
0 7	C	*	Increment NUM by 1.																							
0 8	C											ADD	1				NUM									
0 9	C	*	Add NUM to the accumulator SUM.																							
1 0	C											ADD	NUM				SUM									
1 1	C											ENDDO														
1 2	C																									

DO (Do)
Often, as in our example above, you want a loop to execute a specific number of times. To implement this kind of logic with DOUxx or DOWxx, you need to define a field to serve as a counter. Each time through the loop, you increment the counter as part of your loop instructions and check the value

of this counter after each repetition to determine whether or not another iteration is needed.

RPG offers an operation designed specifically for count-controlled loops: DO. Like DOUxx and DOWxx, the end point of a DO structure is signaled by ENDDO or END. Unlike those operations, the DO automatically increments a counter to ensure the repetition is done the desired number of times.

The format of the DO is a little more complicated than that of DOWxx or DOUxx because it provides more options and defaults. In general, a count-controlled operator in any language allows you to specify four things: a field to serve as a counter; the starting value of the counter; the maximum value of the counter for looping to continue; and the amount to be added to the counter at the end of each repetition of the loop.

Although RPG gives you the option to specify these four values, you can also omit any of them. You can omit the initial value for the counter and/or the increment value for the counter. RPG assumes a default value of 1 for both. That is, it will start the counter at 1 and add 1 to it at the start of each additional pass through the loop, unless you specify differently.

You also can omit designating a field to serve as the counter. In this case, the system still keeps track of the number of repetitions with an internal counter, but you are unable to reference directly the counter's value for calculations or printing.

You can also omit specifying an upper limit for the counter; again, the default value is one. To specify a different limit, enter a numeric integer field or literal in factor 2. If your factor 2 entry is a field, the value of the field determines the number of repetitions.

Line	Form Type				Factor 1	Operation	Factor 2	Result Field Name	Length		Resulting Indicators	Comments
0 1	C					DO	50					
0 2	C	* Whatever is here would be done 50 times.										
0 3	C					...						
0 4	C					ENDDO						
0 5	C	*										
0 6	C	*										
0 7	C					DO	ITR					
0 8	C	* The number of repetitions is dependent upon the value of ITR.										
0 9	C					...						
1 0	C					ENDDO						
1 1	C											

If you need to know what iteration the computer is currently executing — for example, to print the value or use it in a calculation — you need to designate a field to be used as the counter. You must define this field as an integer numeric field (e.g., a numeric field with 0 decimal positions). To designate that the field is the counter used by the DO, enter it in the result field position of the DO line.

The code below shows the add-the-numbers problem implemented with DO. NUM is the counter field the system automatically increments by one on each pass through the loop.

C		Indicators			Factor 1	Operation	Factor 2	Result Field			Resulting Indicators		Comments

```
01  C* This routine will add all the numbers from 1 to 100
02  C* using a DO.
03  C              Z-ADD0        SUM      40
04  C* Loop until NUM exceeds 100.
05  C              DO    100     NUM      30
06  C* Add NUM to SUM.
07  C              ADD   NUM     SUM
08  C              ENDDO
09  C
10  C
```

If you want the counter to start at a value other than 1, you can enter an alternate starting value (as either a literal or a field) in factor 1 of the DO statement. And if you want to use an increment amount other than 1, code this value (again, as a literal or field) in factor 2 of the ENDDO statement.

For example, we can easily change our sample solution to add all the even numbers from 1 to 100 if we set NUM's starting value to 2 and the increment value to 2, as shown on the following page.

```
C          Indicators    And  And  Factor 1      Operation  Factor 2    Result Field              Resulting
                                                                        Name      Length          Indicators

01 C* This routine will add all the even numbers from 2 to 100
02 C* using DO.
03 C                                   Z-ADD0          SUM     40
04 C* Loop until NUM exceeds 100. The 2 in factor 1 states
05 C* the starting value of NUM.
06 C              2         DO    100       NUM     30
07 C* Add NUM to the accumulated SUM.
08 C                        ADD   NUM       SUM
09 C                        ENDDO2
10 C* The 2 following ENDDO specifies the increment value
11 C* for NUM.
12 C
```

Loops and Early Exits

You sometimes may want to skip the remaining instructions within a loop to begin the next iteration or cycle. In other cases, you may want to exit the loop completely before the repetition is terminated by the relational comparison. Two RPG/400 operations — ITER and LEAVE — provide you with these capabilities.

When the computer encounters an ITER within a loop, control skips past the remaining instructions in the loop and causes the next repetition to begin. LEAVE terminates the looping process completely and sends control to the statement immediately following the loop's ENDDO statement. Both these statements can be used with all variants of the DO operation: DOWxx, DOUxx, and DO.

Assume, for example, you are processing a file of customer records and printing a report line for those customers whose balance due exceeds zero. If amount due equals zero, you simply want to cycle around and read the next record from the file. The following code illustrates a solution that uses LEAVE and ITER.

C			Indicators									Result Field			Resulting Indicators		

```
0 1  C *This routine processes all records in CUSTFILE and
0 2  C *prints a detail line for those customers whose AMTDUE
0 3  C *is not equal to zero.
0 4  C              *IN90     DOWEQ*OFF
0 5  C                        READ CUSTFILE                              90
0 6  C                        SELEC
0 7  C              *IN90     WHEQ *ON
0 8  C                        LEAVE
0 9  C              AMTDUE    WHEQ 0
1 0  C                        ITER
1 1  C                        OTHER
1 2  C                        EXCPTDETAIL
1 3  C                        ENDSL
1 4  C                        ENDDO
1 5  C
```

Unstructured Operations

Two operations in RPG can be used for both selection and iteration. Both operations should be used with great care, however, because neither has built-in constraints to limit how it directs the flow of control. The operations are GOTO and CABxx.

GOTO/TAG

You often will encounter GOTOs when maintaining older programs written in RPG II, when structured operations were not yet available. The GOTO operation is used to divert control to a different location within your program. Factor 2 of the GOTO contains a label that identifies the location to which control should transfer. That same label must appear as the factor 1 entry of a TAG operation somewhere within the program. TAG, a non-executable operation, simply marks a program line as a label statement that identifies the location. The same rules for forming RPG field names apply to RPG labels.

You can use GOTO to branch around a sequence of instructions if the TAG is below the GOTO, or to set up a loop if the TAG is above the GOTO.

```
C* This GOTO branches around instructions by sending
C* control to SKIP.
C                    GOTO SKIP
C                    ...
C         SKIP       TAG
C                    ...
C         LOOP       TAG
C                    ...
C* This GOTO creates a loop by sending control back up
C* to LOOP.
C                    GOTO LOOP
C
```

The above instructions show the GOTO used to set up unconditional transfer of control. More often, GOTOs are used with IF logic to transfer control based on some conditional test, as shown below.

```
C* This GOTO branches around instructions by sending
C* control to SKIP if A is greater than B.
C         A          IFGT B
C                    GOTO SKIP
C                    ENDIF
C                    ...
C         SKIP       TAG
C*
C         LOOP       TAG
C                    ...
C* This GOTO creates a loop by sending control back up
C* to LOOP if indicator 40 is on.
C         *IN40      IFEQ *ON
C                    GOTO LOOP
C                    ENDIF
C
```

CABxx

The CABxx (Compare and Branch) operation is simply a GOTO in disguise. CABxx combines a conditional test and the transfer of control in a single operation. CABxx compares the value of factor 1 with the value of factor 2 based on the relational code included in the CABxx operation; if the comparison is true, control is transferred to the label designated in the result field. The label specified must appear as the factor 1 of a TAG operation somewhere within the program.

Line	Form Type	Control Level (L0-L9, LR,SR, AN/OR)	Indicators And Not	Indicators And Not	Not	Factor 1	Operation	Factor 2	Result Field Name	Length	Decimal Positions	Operation Extender (H,N,P)	Resulting Indicators	Comments
0 1	C					* This CAB branches around instructions by sending								
0 2	C					* control to SKIP if A is greater than B.								
0 3	C					A	CABGTB		SKIP					
0 4	C						. . .							
0 5	C					SKIP	TAG							
0 6	C					*								
0 7	C					LOOP	TAG							
0 8	C						. . .							
0 9	C					* This CAB creates a loop by sending control back up								
1 0	C					* to LOOP is indicator 10 is on.								
1 1	C					*IN40	CABEQ*ON		LOOP					
1 2	C													

With both CABxx and GOTO, transfer of control is unidirectional; flow simply continues on from the tag. Use of GOTO and CAB often makes programs harder to follow, because these operators do not keep as tight a rein on flow of control as do the structured operators, with their single-entry, single-exit points.

Generally, the appropriate use of SELEC and IF should make CAB and GOTO unnecessary. If you do use CABs or GOTOs to bypass instructions, try to send control from multiple CABs to a single-tag exit point. The first example that follows illustrates poor use of CABs, while the second example demonstrates how CABs can be used to send control to a single exit point, making the flow of control easier to follow.

```
C* Demonstration of poor program design caused by
C* misuse of CAB operations.
C
C           *IN20     CABEQ*ON        LABL1
C
C           *IN15     CABEQ*ON        LABL2
C
C           LABL1     TAG
C
C           X         CABGTY          LABL3
C
C           LABL2     TAG
C
C           LABL3     TAG
C
```

```
C* Better use of CABs because flow of control is
C* easier to follow.
C
C           *IN20     CABEQ*ON        EXIT
C
C           *IN15     CABEQ*ON        EXIT
C
C           X         CABGTY          EXIT
C
C           EXIT      TAG
C
```

Top-Down Design

Up to this point, this chapter has concentrated on structured design. A second design concept, top-down methodology, usually goes hand in hand with a structured approach. **Top-down design** means developing your program solution starting with a broad "outline" and then successively breaking the big pieces into smaller and smaller units. This technique is sometimes called **hierarchical decomposition**.

Hierarchical decomposition is the method your English teacher recommended for writing research papers: Work out an outline, starting with your main topics; then subdivide these into subtopics, and so on, until you have decomposed to a level of sufficient detail to allow you to write the paper (or in programming terms, the individual instructions of your program).

Top-down design allows you to handle problems of great complexity by allowing you to initially ignore the detailed requirements of processing. Top-down design goes hand in hand with the concept of modular program development, which advocates that your program be structured into logical units, or modules. In top-down design the first, or upper-level, design modules you develop are chiefly concerned with controlling flow to and from lower-level modules you develop later.

Each module should be as independent of the others as possible, and the statements within a module should be working together to perform a single function. Structural decomposition gives you a way of dealing with complexity; when used with a modular approach, structural decomposition results in programs of functionally cohesive subroutines that are easier to maintain later.

Defining Subroutines

One vehicle for top-down modular program design in RPG is the subroutine. A subroutine, as mentioned earlier, is a block of code with an identifiable beginning and end. Subroutines are identified by the (optional) letters SR in positions 7-8 of a line, along with the name of the subroutine in factor 1 and the operation BEGSR. The lines of code comprising the executable portion of the subroutine follow. The last line of a subroutine is a line containing ENDSR as the operation to signal the endpoint of that block of code. The code below shows the skeleton of a subroutine.

C	Form Type	Control Level (L0-L9, LR,SR, AN/OR)	Indicators				Factor 1	Operation	Factor 2	Result Field			Resulting Indicators			Comments
			And	And						Name	Length	Decimal Positions / Operation Extender (H,N,P)	Arithmetic / Plus Minus Zero / Compare / 1>2 1<2 1=2 / Lookup(Factor 2)is / High Low Equal			
0 1	C	SR					CALCTX	BEGSR								
0 2	C							. . .								
0 3	C							ENDSR								
0 4	C															

Subroutines are coded as the last entries on the Calculation Specifications, following all other calculations. The order in which you list the subroutines does not matter. A program can have up to 254 subroutines; each must have a unique name, formed with the same rules that apply to RPG fields.

EXSR (Execute Subroutine)

You have already learned one way to send control to a subroutine for execution: the CASxx operation. A second, more common, method is to use EXSR (Execute Subroutine). Enter the name of the subroutine to be performed in factor 2, as shown below.

Line	Form Type	Control Level (L0-L9, LR,SR, AN/OR)	And Not	And Not	Not	Factor 1	Operation	Factor 2	Result Field Name	Length	Decimal Positions	Operation Extender (H,N,P)	Resulting Indicators Arithmetic Plus	Minus	Zero / Compare 1>2	1<2	1=2 / Lookup(Factor 2)is High	Low	Equal	Comments
0 1	C					* The EXSR causes control to drop to SR CALCTX.															
0 2	C						EXSR	CALCTX													
0 3	C					* Control returns here when the subroutine finishes executing.															
0 4	C						. . .														
0 5	C						. . .														
0 6	C					* Subroutines appear at the end of calculation specifications.															
0 7	C	SR				CALCTX	BEGSR														
0 8	C					GROSS	MULT	.0751	FICA	62H											
0 9	C					GROSS	MULT	.045	STTAX	62H											
1 0	C					GROSS	IFGT	50000													
1 1	C					GROSS	MULT	.31	FEDTAX	72H											
1 2	C						ELSE														
1 3	C					GROSS	MULT	.25	FEDTAX	H											
1 4	C						ENDIF														
1 5	C						ENDSR														
1 6	C																				

When the computer encounters an EXSR operation (or a CASxx), control drops to the named subroutine. Upon completion of the subroutine, control *returns* to the operation immediately following the calculation that invoked the subroutine. The fact that control returns makes it possible to maintain tighter flow of control with CAS and EXSR than with CABxx and GOTO operations, which transfer control unidirectionally to other locations within the program.

Subroutines cannot contain other subroutines. Subroutines may execute other subroutines, but a subroutine should never execute itself. This latter coding technique, called **recursion**, is permitted in some programming languages but is treated as an error by the RPG compiler. Additionally, control of flow should always return from the end point of a subroutine; never branch out of the middle of a subroutine with a GOTO or CABxx operation to a location in a different subroutine or in the main portion of your program.

Scope Terminators

Before we begin to apply the concepts covered in this chapter, some clarification on END statements is in order. You probably noticed that in the material presenting decision and looping operations, a generic END statement was mentioned as an alternative to the operation-specific END statements (e.g., ENDIF, ENDCS) as a way to signal the end of the structured operation's scope.

When IBM first introduced structured operations into RPG, the language provided only a single END operation to use with all structured operations. With later releases of the language, as IBM introduced additional structured operations, the company also introduced operation-specific ENDs to make structured code easier to read. For the sake of compatibility among programs written prior to these releases, IBM still allows you to use plain END as the scope terminator of any structured operation, and you will encounter its use when you maintain older programs.

However, in any code that *you* write, use the operation-specific ENDs. Their use makes your code easier to understand and also allows the RPG compiler to check your logic for correct span of control within nested structured operations, as the code below illustrates.

Page 1 of 2

```
C* Code written with generic ENDS; compiler assumes first END
C* belongs with IF, regardless of your intent.
C           *IN90      DOWEQ*ON
C                      ...
C           *IN50      IFEQ *OFF
C                      ...
C                      END
C                      ...
C                      END
C* Code using operation-specific ENDs; compiler will signal that
C* the structured operations are incorrectly nested.
C           *IN90      DOWEQ*ON
C                      ...
C           *IN50      IFEQ *OFF
C                      ...
C                      ENDDO
C                      ...
C                      ENDIF
```

C		Indicators			Factor 1	Operation	Factor 2	Result Field			Resulting Indicators			Comments
		And	And					Name	Length		Arithmetic			
Line	Form Type	Control Level (LO-L9, LR,SR, AN/OR)	Not	Not	Not						Decimal Positions	Operation Extender (H,N,P)	Plus Minus Zero	Compare 1>2 1<2 1=2	Lookup(Factor 2)is High Low Equal
0 1	C	*	Code using operation-specific ENDs with correct nesting;											
0 2	C	*	this code will pass the compiler's scrutiny.											
0 3	C				*IN90	DOWEQ	*ON							
0 4	C					. . .								
0 5	C				*IN50	IFEQ	*OFF							
0 6	C					. . .								
0 7	C					ENDIF								
0 8	C					. . .								
0 9	C					ENDDO								
1 0	C													

Note that use of the generic END is not an alternative to ENDSR. RPG has allowed subroutine use from early on and has required an ENDSR statement to match each BEGSR operation from the start.

Control-Break Logic

To demonstrate how top-down structured design can be used to help develop an easily maintained program, the techniques discussed will be applied to solve a common business programming problem: generating a report that includes subtotals.

Assume you have a file of sales records. Each record contains a salesperson's identification number, department, the amount of a given sale, and the date of the sale. A given salesperson may have many records in the file — depending on how successful a salesperson (s)he is — and the data file is ordered by salesperson, so that all the records for a given salesperson are adjacent to one another in the file. You are asked to write a program that will include the details of each sales transaction and a subtotal of each salesperson's sales. The desired report format is shown in the following illustration.

```
             1         2         3         4         5
    12345678901234567890123456789012345678901234567890

        XX/XX/XX       SALES REPORT     PAGE XXØX

            SLSM.                  AMT.

            XXXX                 X,XXØ.XX
            XXXX                 X,XXØ.XX

                      TOTAL      XX,XXØ.XX*

            XXXX                 X,XXØ.XX
            XXXX                 X,XXØ.XX
            XXXX                 X,XXØ.XX

                      TOTAL      XX,XXØ.XX*

                GRAND TOTAL     XXX,XXØ.XX**
```

This kind of problem is often referred to as a **control-break problem**, because the solution involves checking the input records for a change, or a "break," in the values of a control field. That occurrence signals the need for a subtotal and triggers special processing associated with printing the subtotal and preparing for the next control group.

Because the computer has only a single record in memory at a time, to be able to determine when a change in the control field's value has occurred, you need to define a work field to hold the current value of the control field. Each time a record is read, its control field value can then be compared with that work field; a comparison revealing that the two values are no longer equal signals that the first record of a new group has just been read. Before continuing with the detail processing of that record, it is necessary to "break" away from detail processing and complete any processing required by such a change. Typically that processing entails printing a subtotal line, rolling over an accumulator, zeroing out that accumulator, and storing the new control field value in the work field.

With that overview of control-break logic, let's develop the pseudocode for the calculations required by the program, using a top-down design strategy. Our design now also will include a provision for printing headings at the top of each page.

```
Do Initialization Routine
WHILE not end-of-file
        IF change in slsm
                Do Slsmbreak Routine
        ENDIF
                Do Detail Process Routine
        Read next record
ENDWHILE
Do Termination Routine
END program
```

The above pseudocode works out the "main-line" logic of the program. Notice that at several spots in the pseudocode, "Do" statements indicate that a number of processing steps need to be performed, but the details are not yet spelled out. That is the essence of top-down design.

Once you determine that the main-line logic is correct, you can develop the logic of the additional modules, or routines. They are shown below.

Initialization Routine
Read first record
Set up hold area
Print headings
END Initialization Routine

Slsmbreak Routine
Print slsm line
Add slsmtot to grand total
Zero out slsmtot
Move new value to hold area
END Slsmbreak Routine

Detail Process Routine
IF page overflow
        Print headings
ENDIF
Print detail line
Accumulate sales in slsmtot
END Detail Process Routine

Termination Routine
Do Slsmbreak Routine
Print grand total
END Termination Routine

Notice the processing in Slsmbreak is representative of control-break logic in general. Also notice that Slsmbreak is invoked from within Termination. The break routine needs to execute one last time to print the very last salesperson's subtotal line before printing the grand total.

The complete RPG program, including the calculations reflecting the logic expressed in the pseudocode, is shown below.

```
          1         2         3         4         5         6         7
1234567890123456789012345678901234567890123456789012345678901234567890234
       F***************************************************************
       F* This program produces a Sales Report listing subtotals for *
       F* each salesperson.                                           *
       F*  Author: Yaeger        Date Written:  Dec. 1992             *
       F***************************************************************
       FSALESFILIF  F    19              DISK
       FQPRINT   O  F   132        OF    PRINTER
```

```
                 1         2         3         4         5         6         7
        12345678901234567890123456789012345678901234567890123456789012345678901234

        ISALESFILNS  Ø1
        I                                        1    4 SLSMAN
        I                                        5    7 DEPT
        I                                        8  132SALES
        I                                       14  19ØSALDAT
        C*************************************************************
        C*  Calculations required to produce the Sales Report.
        C*  Main-line logic.
        C*************************************************************
        C                    EXSR INIT
        C*
        C          *IN9Ø     DOWEQ*OFF
        C          SLSHLD    IFNE SLSMAN                        Check for
        C                    EXSR SLSBRK                        control break
        C                    ENDIF
        C                    EXSR DETL
        C                    READ SALESFIL                90
        C                    ENDDO
        C*
        C                    EXSR TERM
        C                    MOVE *ON        *INLR
        C                    RETRN
        C*************************************************************
        C* Subroutine to read first record, set up hold, and print
        C* first page headings.
        C*************************************************************
        CSR        INIT      BEGSR
        C                    READ SALESFIL                90
        C                    MOVE SLSMAN     SLSHLD 4
        C                    EXCPTHEADS
        C                    ENDSR
        C*************************************************************
        C* Subroutine done when salesman changes; print subtotal,
        C* rollover accumulator, zero out accumulator, and reset hold.
        C*************************************************************
        CSR        SLSBRK    BEGSR
        C                    EXCPTBRKLIN
        C                    ADD  SALTOT     GNDTOT 82
        C                    Z-ADDØ          SALTOT
        C                    MOVE SLSMAN     SLSHLD
        C                    ENDSR
        C*************************************************************
        C* Subroutine executed for each input record.
        C*************************************************************
        C          DETL      BEGSR
        C          *INOF     IFEQ *ON                           Page overflow
        C                    EXCPTHEADS
        C                    MOVE *OFF       *INOF
        C                    ENDIF
        C                    EXCPTDETAIL
        C                    ADD  SALES      SALTOT 62          Saleman Tot.
        C                    ENDSR
        C*************************************************************
        C* Subroutine done at end of file; execute SLSBRK one last
        C* time and print grand total line.
        C*************************************************************
        CSR        TERM      BEGSR
        C                    EXSR SLSBRK
        C                    EXCPTTOTAL
        C                    ENDSR
        O*************************************************************
```

```
         1         2         3         4         5         6         7
1234567890123456789012345678901234567890123456789012345678901234567890123 4
OQPRINT  E  2Ø2              HEADS
0                           UDATE  Y    17
0                                       33  'SALES REPORT'
0                                       40  'PAGE'
0                           PAGE        45
0        E  2               HEADS
0
0                                       19  'SLSM.'
0                                       37  'AMT.'
0        E  1               DETAIL
0                           SLSMAN      18
0                           SALES 1     39
0        E 12               BRKLIN
0                                       24  'TOTAL'
0                           SALTOT1     39
0                                       40  '*'
0        E                  TOTAL
0                                       26  'GRAND TOTAL'
0                           GNDTOT1     39
0                                       41  '**'
```

Programmers often are faced with coding solutions to multiple-level control-break problems, in which two or more different control fields of the input file are to be associated with subtotal lines. For example, our sample problem could have specified a need for department subtotals in addition to the salesperson subtotals. If the input file were ordered by department, and within department by salesperson, producing the desired report would take little additional programming effort, because the logic of multiple-level control-break problems follows directly from that of a single-level problem.

To code a multiple-level control-break problem, set up a work field for each control field to hold the value of the group being processed. Code a separate break subroutine for each level; typically, the same processing steps take place in each kind of break (e.g., printing a subtotal line, rolling over an accumulator, zeroing out the accumulator, and moving the new control field value into the work field), but using variables appropriate to that level.

Then, prior to the detail processing of each record, check each control field to see if its value has changed, checking from major (biggest grouping) to minor (smallest grouping); if a break has occurred, execute the appropriate break subroutines, starting with the minor (smallest grouping) and finishing with the break routine that corresponds to the control field that triggered the break processing.

The pseudocode that follows illustrates the logic of a two-level control-break problem.

Mainline Logic for Two-level Control Break
Do Initialization Routine
WHILE not end-of-file
    IF change in dept
        Do Slsmbreak Routine
        Do Deptbreak Routine

```
            ELSE
                  IF change in slsm
                        Do Slsmbreak Routine
                  ENDIF
            ENDIF
            Do Detail Process Routine
            Read next record
      ENDWHILE
      Do Termination Routine
      END program
```

Initialization Routine
Read first record
Set up hold areas for dept and slsm
Do headings
END Initialization Routine

Slsmbreak Routine
Print slsm line
Add slsmtot to depttot
Zero out slsmtot
Move new slsm value to slsm hold area
END Slsmbreak Routine

Deptbreak Routine
Print dept line
Add depttot to grandtot
Zero out depttot
Move new dept value to dept hold area
END Deptbreak Routine

Detail Process Routine
IF page overflow
      Print headings
ENDIF
Print detail line
Add sales to slsmtot
END Detail Process Routine

Termination Routine
Do Slsmbreak Routine
Do Deptbreak Routine
Print grand total
END Termination Routine

Especially notice the order in which the pseudocode checks for changes in the control fields, the order in which it executes the break subroutines, and the parallels between the Slsmbreak and Deptbreak routines. Once you understand the logic of a two-level break problem, you could write a program with any number of level breaks, because the required processing steps can be exactly modeled on those required for a two-level control break.

Chapter Summary

The goal for this chapter has been to give you a basic understanding of structured design and how it is often used with a top-down, modular approach to program development. Structured program design means developing your program logic with flow of control tightly managed, generally by using only structured operations. Top-down methodology requires that you approach designing your program hierarchically, working out its broad logic first — concentrating primarily on flow of control — and later attending to the detailed processing requirements. Both design concepts encourage a modular approach to programming, in which you design your program around subroutines of statements that form functionally cohesive units of code.

RPG provides structured operations IFxx, CASxx, and SELEC to implement decision logic, and structured operations DOWxx, DOUxx, and DO to implement looping logic. All these structured operations have a single entry and a single exit point that help maintain tight flow of control within a program. Although operations CABxx and GOTO also can be used to branch or loop, carelessness in their use to alter flow of control can lead to programs that are very difficult to understand.

Most of the structured operations of RPG require the use of one of six relational operators that are used to control the operations' execution. The operators are GT, LT, EQ, NE, LE, and GE.

The table on the following page can help you remember the specific format required of the operations covered in this chapter.

Required Format for Decision and Iteration Operations

Factor 1	Operation	Factor 2	Result
FIELD/LITERAL	**IFxx**	FIELD/LITERAL	—
FIELD/LITERAL	**ANDxx**	FIELD/LITERAL	—
FIELD/LITERAL	**ORxx**	FIELD/LITERAL	—
—	**ELSE**	—	—
—	**ENDIF**	—	—
—	**SELEC**	—	—
FIELD/LITERAL	**WHxx**	FIELD/LITERAL	—
—	**OTHER**	—	—
—	**ENDSL**	—	—
FIELD/LITERAL	**CASxx**	FIELD/LITERAL	SRNAME
—	**ENDCS**	—	—
FIELD/LITERAL	**DOWxx**	FIELD/LITERAL	—
FIELD/LITERAL	**DOUxx**	FIELD/LITERAL	—
—	**ITER**	—	—
—	**LEAVE**	—	—
field/literal	**DO**	field/literal	field
—	**ENDDO**	field/literal	—
FIELD/LITERAL	**CABxx**	FIELD/LITERAL	LABEL
—	**GOTO**	LABEL	—
LABEL	**TAG**	—	—
—	**EXSR**	SRNAME	—
SRNAME	**BEGSR**	—	—
—	**ENDSR**	—	—

Uppercase = required entry; lowercase = optional entry.

xx = one of the six relational operators.

Terms

CASE logic	leading-decision loop	sequence
control-break problem	overflow indicators	structured design
decision operations	recursion	subroutines
EBCDIC	relational codes	top-down design
hiearchical decomposition	relational comparison	trailing-decision loop
iteration	selection	

Discussion/Review Questions

1. Characterize structured design.

2. If RPG did not include a NE relational operation, what alternate way could you express the following logic in RPG? "If balance due ≠ 0, execute the calculation routine."

3. What does "tight" flow of control mean?

4. How is GOTO different from EXSR?

5. Describe how RPG compares numeric values.

6. Describe how RPG compares character values.

7. Now that RPG has a SELEC operation, can you always avoid writing nested IF statements? Explain your answer.

8. Describe the differences between IFxx and CABxx.

9. What's the difference between ANDxx and ORxx?

10. How would you decide whether to use SELEC or CASxx?

11. Why does RPG need looping operations other than DO? Are both DOWxx and DOUxx essential from a logical standpoint?

12. Describe how ITER and LEAVE work. Would they be considered structured options? Explain.

13. Characterize a control-break problem.

14. In control-break processing, why is a "hold" or work field needed to store the value of the control field?

15. Can you think of an alternative way to handle page advance other than referencing an overflow indicator?

Exercises

1. Use IFs to code the calculations needed to determine property tax based on a property's value, stored in VALUE (6 positions, 0 decimal positions). Use the information below as the basis for your calculations:

Property Value	Property Tax
$0- $50,000	1% of value
$50,001- $75,000	$50 plus 2% of value
$75,001-$100,000	$70 plus 2.5% of value
over $100,000	$100 plus 3% of value

2. Solve the problem described in Exercise 1 using operation SELEC.

3. Write a routine to determine traffic fines based on the values of two input fields: OVER (miles over speed limit) and OFFENS (number of offenses). Fines are to be determined as follows:

MPH Over Limit	Fine
1-10	$25
11-20	$40
21-30	$70
over 30	$100

If the speeder is a first-time offender, there is no additional fine. However, second-time offenders are fined an additional $25 if they are no more than 20 miles over the limit and an additional $50 if they are more than 20 miles over the limit. Third-time offenders are fined an additional $50 if they are no more than 20 miles over the limit and an additional $100 if they are going more than 20 miles over the limit.

4. Use DO to write the calculations needed to obtain the squares, cubes, and square roots of all numbers from 1 to 50.

5. A program to update a master file needs a routine that checks the update code stored in CODE and sends control to one of three different subroutines (ADDSR, CHGSR, and DLTSR), depending on whether the code is A, C, or D (Add, Change, or Delete records). Invalid codes should cause subroutine ERRSR to execute. Write this routine twice, each time using a different structured operator.

Programming Assignments

1. Wexler University wants a summary report of its student population that shows how many in-district, out-of-district, and international students there are at the freshman, sophomore, junior, senior, and graduate levels. The input file for this program is the school's student master file WUSTDP. The record layout for this file is given in Appendix D. The records in the file are ordered by Social Security number.

   Note that district code is a code field where I = in-district; O = out-of-district; and F = international student status. The classification field differentiates G (graduate) from U (undergraduate) students. The school subdivides undergraduates based on earned credits: Students with fewer than 30 credits are freshmen; those with 30-59 credits are sophomores; those with 60-89 credits are juniors; and those with 90 or more credits are seniors.

   The school wants the summary report to be formatted as shown in the printer spacing chart below:

```
          1         2         3         4         5         6         7         8
1234567890123456789012345678901234567890123456789012345678901234567890123456789012345678

   XX/XX/XX                        WEXLER U.                    PAGE XXØX
                         STUDENT POPULATION SUMMARY REPORT

                      -----------------RESIDENCY------------
      CLASSIFICATION  IN-DISTRICT   OUT-OF-DISTRICT  INTERNATIONAL   TOTAL
      --------------  -----------   ---------------  -------------   -----
         FRESHMEN       X,XØX           X,XØX            X,XØX       XX,XØX
         SOPHOMORES     X,XØX           X,XØX            X,XØX       XX,XØX
         JUNIORS        X,XØX           X,XØX            X,XØX       XX,XØX
         SENIORS        X,XØX           X,XØX            X,XØX       XX,XØX

         TOTAL         XX,XØX          XX,XØX           XX,XØX       XX,XØX
```

2. Wexler University needs a report to determine how equitable its faculty salaries are across sexes. Because salaries vary with academic rank and length of employment, they want average salaries broken down by rank, as well as by sex, and they also would like average-length-of-employment figures. The input file, WUINSTP, is described in Appendix D. The desired report is shown below.

```
          1         2         3         4         5         6         7         8
1234567890123456789012345678901234567890123456789012345678901234567890123456789012345678

   WEXLER UNIVERSITY FACULTY SALARY REPORT  XX/XX/XX


                      AVERAGE SALARIES AND LENGTH OF EMPLOYMENT
                              MALE                      FEMALE
      RANK            SALARY      YEARS    N       SALARY      YEARS    N
      ------------    -----------------------      -----------------------
      INSTRUCTOR      XXX,XXØ.XX    ØX    (ØX)     XXX,XXØ.XX    ØX    (ØX)
      ASSISTANT       XXX,XXØ.XX    ØX    (ØX)     XXX,XXØ.XX    ØX    (ØX)
      ASSOCIATE       XXX,XXØ.XX    ØX    (ØX)     XXX,XXØ.XX    ØX    (ØX)
      PROFESSOR       XXX,XXØ.XX    ØX    (ØX)     XXX,XXØ.XX    ØX    (ØX)

      ALL             XXX,XXØ.XX    ØX    (XØX)    XXX,XXØ.XX    ØX    (XØX)


          NOTE: N=NUMBER IN EACH CATEGORY
```

Programming Assignments Continued

Programming Assignments continued

3. The municipal water company needs a program that will calculate monthly water charges. The rates for city residents are:

> $.035 per unit for the first 500 units
> $.030 per unit for the next 500 units
> $.027 per unit for all units beyond 1,000

In addition, there is a service fee of $10.00 per month for all customers, regardless of usage. Water users who are not residents of the city pay 1.5 times the total bill.

An input file, MWC001P, described in Appendix D, contains customer information and old and new meter readings. Determine usage from the old and new meter readings. Note that the meters are like car odometers; when they reach their maximum value (9,999), the next unit's usage causes them to read 0000. You must take this feature into account in your calculations. You may assume that no one will ever use more than 9,999 units of water per month.

Output should appear as shown on the printer spacing chart below.

```
          1         2         3         4         5         6         7
 1234567890123456789012345678901234567890123456789012345678901234567890

   XX/XX/XX                                          PAGE XXØX
                   GOTHAM CITY WATER BILLING REPORT

   CUST.                      RES.   OLD    NEW            AMOUNT
   NUM.      NAME             CODE   METER  METER  USAGE   OWED

   XXXXX   XXXXXXXXXXXXXXXXXXX  X    XXXX   XXXX   X,XØX   X,XXØ.XX
   XXXXX   XXXXXXXXXXXXXXXXXXX  X    XXXX   XXXX   X,XØX   X,XXØ.XX
```

4. ACME manufacturing company wants you to write a payroll program. Each record in the input file, ACP001, described in Appendix D, represents *one day's* work for an employee. Records are accumulated for a week, so there will be several records per employee. Records in the file are ordered by Social Security number.

The company uses both an hourly rate and a piece rate to pay its employees. Everyone gets $5.50 per hour worked. Additionally, if a person produces 0-500 units during the week, (s)he receives 25 cents per unit; if (s)he produces 501-1,000 units, (s)he receives 30 cents per unit; if over 1,000 units, 40 cents per unit. After using these figures to calculate gross pay, a 4.6 percent state tax and a 15 percent federal tax must be subtracted from gross pay to obtain net pay.

Your program is to generate the report illustrated in the accompanying printer spacing chart.

Programming Assignments Continued

Programming Assignments continued

```
         1         2         3         4         5         6         7         8         9
1234567890123456789012345678901234567890123456789012345678901234567890123456789012345678901234567890

XX/XX/XX                          ACME PAYROLL REPORT                        PAGE XXØX


                     HOURS            GROSS      STATE     FED.      NET
SOC. SEC.    NAME     WORKED   UNITS    PAY        TAX      TAX      PAY

XXX-XX-XXXX  XXXXXXXXXXXXXXXX   ØX    X,XØX   X,XXØ.XX   XØ.XX   XXØ.XX  X,XXØ.XX
XXX-XX-XXXX  XXXXXXXXXXXXXXXX   ØX    X,XØX   X,XXØ.XX   XØ.XX   XXØ.XX  X,XXØ.XX
XXX-XX-XXXX  XXXXXXXXXXXXXXXX   ØX    X,XØX   X,XXØ.XX   XØ.XX   XXØ.XX  X,XXØ.XX

             AVERAGE GROSS PAY:  $X,XXØ.XX
             AVERAGE UNITS PER EMPLOYEE:  X,XØX
             AVERAGE UNITS PER HOUR:  X,XØX
```

5. Wexler University's faculty members run a credit union. They want you to write a program to calculate monthly payments for loan applicants. The monthly payment is to be calculated using the formula shown below. Note that I represents **monthly interest rate** and N represents number of **months** for the loan. Also note that the N in the formula is an exponent, not a multiplier. The formula to be used in calculating payment amount is:

$$\text{PAYMENT} = \text{LOAN AMT} * (I * (1 + I)^N) / ((1 + I)^N - 1)$$

Records in input file WULOANP, described in Appendix D, contain information about the loan amounts, interest rates, and length of loan. Generate a report formatted as shown below:

```
         1         2         3         4         5         6         7         8
12345678901234567890123456789012345678901234567890123456789012345678901234567890

DATE XX/XX/XX         WEXLER U. FACULTY CREDIT UNION          PAGE XXØX
                      NEW LOAN APPLICANTS REPORT

LOAN      CUSTOMER          LOAN      ANNUAL     NO. OF    MONTHLY
NUM.        NAME           AMOUNT    INT. RATE   MONTHS    PAYMENT

XXXXX   XXXXXXXXXXXXXX    XX,XXØ.XX    XØ.XX%      XØX     XX,XXØ.XX
XXXXX   XXXXXXXXXXXXXX    XX,XXØ.XX    XØ.XX%      XØX     XX,XXØ.XX

        GRAND TOTALS    X,XXX,XXØ.XX                    X,XXX,XXØ.XX
```

Chapter 5

Externally Described Files

Chapter Overview

In this chapter you will learn how the AS/400 handles database files. The chapter explains the differences between physical and logical files and discusses field-reference files. You will learn how to define database files at a system level and how to access these definitions from within RPG programs. You will also learn about externally described printer files.

The AS/400 Approach to Database Files

The AS/400, like its predecessor the S/38, is unique in the way it handles data. Unlike other systems, which require additional, costly software to provide them with database capabilities, the AS/400 was designed with database applications in mind. Its operating system automatically treats all data files as part of a large relational database system. One consequence of this approach is that all data files need to be defined to the system independently of application programs. Even those applications that on the surface seem to be "creating" files are actually creating records and storing them in a file that must have been defined to the AS/400 prior to program execution.

These files may be defined on the system at a record level (i.e., not broken down into individual fields) or at a field level. If you define a file only to the record level, any RPG program that uses that file must subdivide that record into the appropriate logical fields on the Input or Output Specifications. On the other hand, if you have externally defined the file at a field level, you do not need to code those field definitions within your application programs that use the file; the definitions will be brought into the program at compile time. This latter technique, called **external file description**, is almost universally practiced by RPG/400 programmers today.

There are several advantages to defining data files external to application programs. First, if you design the files using database design principles, externally defined files can reduce the need for duplication of data across files. (This kind of duplication is called **redundancy.**) Because all programs using a given file use the same field definitions and names, externally defined files impose a standardization among programmers and across applications.

External file description increases programmer efficiency, because programmers don't need to duplicate the file definition effort each time they need to reference a file within a program. And finally, if it is necessary to add a field to a file's records or to change a field's definition (e.g., expand zip code to 9 digits), these changes need to be made only in a single place (in the external file definition), rather than in every program using that file. This feature simplifies system maintenance.

Physical and Logical Files

The AS/400 allows you to define two kinds of database files: **physical files** and **logical files**. Physical files actually store data records. If you define the physical file at a field level and one of those fields is designated the key, you subsequently can access records stored in that file in either **key sequence** or **arrival sequence** (first-in, first-out). If you do not define a **key field**, access is limited to arrival sequence.

Logical files describe how data *appears* to be stored in the database. Logical files do not actually contain data records; instead, they store access paths, or pointers, to records in physical files. Because you generally want these access paths to be based on values of key fields, logical files typically have one or more fields designated as a key. A logical file is always based on one or more physical files. Depending on which fields are specified and which are named as keys, the apparent record images and processing order of a logical file may vary greatly from that of the physical file(s) underlying it. Logical files correspond to users' views of data, or **subschemas**, in database terminology.

To understand the relationship between physical and logical files, consider the illustration below, which shows records of an employee master physical file and two logical files based on the physical file. Employee number is the key field to the physical file. One of the logical files is keyed on a **composite**, or **concatenation**, of department and employee number, while the other has zip code as the key field.

The illustration shows the order in which the records would appear to an application program for each file if you stipulated sequential retrieval by key.

```
Physical File EMPMST (keyed on employee number)
Emp. no.   Last Name   First Name   Dept.   Salary   Street          City        St   Zip
111111111  Jones       Mary         MKT     54000    123 W. 45th     Decatur     MI   49065
222222222  Smith       Sam          ACT     61500    4422 N. Oak     Paw Paw     MI   49045
333333333  Adams       Arnold       MKT     34950    1120 W. Main    Kalamazoo   MI   49008
444444444  Houston     Wanda        MIS     29500    290 S. State    Kalamazoo   MI   49007
555555555  Jacobs      David        ACT     43275    9911 S. 88th    Mattawan    MI   49069
666666666  Salinger    Carol        MIS     38500    1300 Maple Lk.  Paw Paw     MI   49065
777777777  Riley       Thomas       MKT     24600    8824 E. Drake   Kalamazoo   MI   49008


Logical File EMPMSTL1(keyed on department and employee number)
222222222  Smith       Sam          ACT     61500
555555555  Jacobs      David        ACT     43275
444444444  Houston     Wanda        MIS     29500
666666666  Salinger    Carol        MIS     38500
111111111  Jones       Mary         MKT     54000
333333333  Adams       Arnold       MKT     34950
777777777  Riley       Thomas       MKT     24600
```

```
Logical File EMPMSTL2 (keyed on zip code)
Houston    Wanda      290 S. State   Kalamazoo  MI  49007
Adams      Arnold     1120 W. Main   Kalamazoo  MI  49008
Riley      Thomas     8824 E. Drake  Kalamazoo  MI  49008
Smith      Sam        4422 N. Oak    Paw Paw    MI  49045
Jones      Mary       123 W. 45th    Decatur    MI  49065
Salinger   Carol      1300 Maple Lk. Paw Paw    MI  49065
Jacobs     David      9911 S. 88th   Mattawan   MI  49069
```

Although the actual data records are stored *only in the physical file* (remember that the logical files store only access paths to records), programs can use logical files just as though the logical files themselves contained the data.

You might use the first logical file to produce a salary report of employees, broken down by department, while the second logical file could be used to print mailing labels for employees, ordered by zip code. Note that logical file records do not need to include all the fields present in the physical records upon which they are based; what fields appear within a logical file depend on the logical file's definition.

Introduction to DDS

The procedure for creating database file definitions is similar to that of creating an RPG program. The first step is to enter SEU to create a source member of definition statements. Most installations use a special file, QDDSSRC, to store members representing externally described files. The source type of a physical file member is PF, whereas that of a logical file member is LF. SEU automatically provides prompts appropriate to the member type you specify.

Because the source statements require entries in specific fixed positions, using a special specification form called **Data Description Specifications (DDS)** to first develop your definitions can help prevent syntax errors.

DDS sheets resemble RPG coding sheets, for good reason: AS/400 file definitions were closely modeled after RPG. All DDS Specifications include an A in position 6. As in RPG, an asterisk in position 7 of a DDS source line signals a comment line. You can use comment lines throughout the file definition. Minimally, you should include a few comment lines at the beginning of each file definition to identify the nature of the file.

In addition to comment lines, DDS specifications include *record format descriptions*, which define a record type within the file; *field definition lines*, which describe fields within records; and perhaps *key specifications*, which designate which fields are to serve as keys to the file. The particular nature of these specifications depends on whether you are defining a physical file or a logical file.

DDS also extensively uses a variety of **keywords**, each with a special meaning. Some keywords, which apply to the file as a whole, are called **file-level keywords**; some apply to a specific record format within the file and are called **record-level keywords**; and some, which are associated only with a specific field, are called **field-level keywords**.

Although all externally defined files share those general features mentioned above, the details of a DDS definition depend on the type of file you are defining. Accordingly, let's first look at using DDS to define physical files.

Defining Physical Files

A physical file's source statements define the data contents that file will have. Physical files can contain only a single record format, or type. That means that every record within a physical file must have an identical record layout. Because of this requirement, a physical file's DDS may contain only one record type, or format. The record format is signaled by an R in position 17 (Name Type), and a name for the record format is entered in positions 19-28 (Name).

Following the record-format specification, you must enter lines to define each field the record contains. Following the field definitions, you optionally can designate a key for the file. A K in position 17 denotes a key field. If you list a key field, its contents determine the sequence in which you can retrieve records from the file. The example below illustrates the DDS code for the employee master file EMPMST.

	Form Type	And/Or/Comment (A/O/*)	Not (N)	Indicator	Not (N)	Indicator	Not (N)	Indicator	Name Type (Ø/R/K/S/O)	Reserved	Name	Reference (R)	Length	Data Type (Ø/A/P/S/B A/S/X/Y/N/J/W)	Decimal Positions	Usage (Ø/O/I/B/H/M)	Location Line	Pos	Functions
A											**** Employee master physical file EMPMST ****								
A																UNIQUE			
A									R		EMPREC								
A											EMPNO		9	S	0				TEXT('Employee number')
A											LNAME		15	A					TEXT('Last name')
A											FNAME		10	A					TEXT('First name')
A											DEPT		3	A					TEXT('Department')
A											SALARY		6	P	0				TEXT('Annual salary')
A											STREET		15	A					TEXT('Street')
A											CITY		15	A					TEXT('City')
A											STATE		2	A					TEXT('State')
A											ZIP		5	S	0				TEXT('Zip code')
A									K		EMPNO								

Let's look at the details of that definition. First, UNIQUE is a file-level keyword. (All file-level keywords appear at the beginning of the DDS specifications, prior to the record-format specification line.) UNIQUE stipulates that the file cannot contain records with duplicate key values. When you include this keyword, attempts to write a record to the file with a key value identical to a record already in the file will cause the system to generate an error message. Use of UNIQUE is optional; without its use, the system permits records with duplicate key values.

The record-format line is next. Note the R in position 17, and the format name, EMPREC, left-justified in positions 19-28. Although the AS/400 actually allows record-format names (and field names, for that matter) to be up to 10 characters long and to include underscores (as well as those characters permissible in RPG), for compatibility with RPG, it is best to follow RPG's rules for file names. That is, limit record-format names to eight characters and field names to six characters, and use only alphabetic characters, digits, and #, $, and @.

You define the fields of a record on successive lines below the record-format line. The field name begins in position 19. Next, you specify the length of the field, right-adjusted in positions 30-34 (Length). As in RPG, any numeric field definition must include a decimal position entry (positions 36-37). You can use position 35 (Data Type) to specify data type. Possible types are A (character data), P (packed decimal), S (signed, or zoned decimal), and B (binary). If this position is left blank, the system defaults assume character data (A) for those fields with no decimal position entry and packed decimal (P) for those with an entry for decimal positions. (An explanation of what all these types mean follows shortly.)

Following the definition of all the fields to appear within the record, you may designate one or more fields as the record key by coding a K in position 17 and specifying the name of the key field in positions 19-28. In our example, EMPNO is named as the key field of the file. Notice that you must define the key field as part of the record prior to the K specification.

If you list more than one key line, you are specifying a composite or concatenated key. For composite keys, list the key fields in order from major to minor. Note that fields need not be adjacent to one another within the record to be key components.

The TEXT keyword entries are optional ways to provide documentation. In our example, TEXT is used with each field to explain what the field represents. You must enclose text comments with apostrophes and surround them with parentheses. Although text comments are not required, it makes good sense to include them, especially if your field names are somewhat cryptic. TEXT also can appear as a record-level keyword to document the record format.

Data Types and Data Storage

As mentioned a few paragraphs ago, you can assign a data type to each field of a physical file. The permissible types are **character** (A) for alphanumeric data; and **zoned decimal** (S), **packed decimal** (P) and **binary** (B) for numeric data. You have learned earlier in this book that RPG differentiates between just two data types —character and numeric — in determining what operations are allowable and whether output editing may occur. What, then, is the significance of the subtypes of numeric data — zoned decimal, packed decimal, and binary? These distinctions refer to how numeric data is represented and stored within the database.

An explanation of data representation must begin with EBCDIC. You know that computers manipulate data in binary form. You also probably know that any numeric value can be converted from its familiar decimal, or base 10, value to a corresponding value in binary, or base 2, notation. At first glance, then, data representation should be a simple matter of converting values from one base to another. The problem is that many characters and values that we want to represent to the computer are not numbers — letters of the alphabet, for example, or $ and {.

IBM developed a coding scheme to allow any data character — numeric or non-numeric — to be represented to the computer. This coding scheme is called EBCDIC (Extended Binary Coded Decimal Interchange Code). EBCDIC assigns a unique 8-bit binary pattern to each representable character. Capital A, for example, is 11000001 in EBCDIC, while the digit 1 is represented as 11110001. The left-most four bits are often called **zone** or **high-order bits**, while the right-most four bits are **digit** or **low-order bits**. Because eight bits comprise a byte, it takes one byte of storage to store each character in EBCDIC. All non-numeric, or character, data values are stored this way.

Numbers can be handled slightly differently. The EBCDIC codes for the digits 0-9 are shown below.

Digit	EBCDIC
0	11110000
1	11110001
2	11110010
3	11110011
4	11110100
5	11110101
6	11110110
7	11110111
8	11111000
9	11111001

The first thing you should notice is that the zone bits of all digits are identical — 1111. This means that the zone portion is redundant for numeric data; that is, if the system knows the data is numeric, it knows that the zones of the data are all 1s. Two forms of numeric data storage take advantage of this redundancy.

The first form, zoned (or signed) decimal, takes a full byte to store each digit of a numeric value, except that the zone of the right-most digit is used to store the sign of the data: 1111 represents a plus sign (+), while 1101 represents a negative sign (–). Zoned-decimal representation, then, is almost identical to character representation, except that the sign is represented as part of the right-most digit's byte. It takes one byte of storage to store each digit of a number in zoned-decimal format.

The second form of numeric representation, packed decimal, takes greater advantage of the redundancy built into digit representation by simply not bothering to store the zones of numbers. Data in packed format can take as little as half the amount of storage it would take to store the same number in zoned-decimal format. In packed format, only the digit, or low-order, bits of a number are stored, with the sign of the number represented by an additional four bits. These sign bits always occupy the right-most four-bit positions of a packed decimal value.

Study the figure below to understand the differences in data representation between these two formats. Notice the location of the signs in both representations, and the elimination of the zone bits in the packed format.

Value to Represent	Zoned Decimal
+ 136	11110001 11110011 11110110
– 136	11110001 11110011 11010110
	(sign)

	Packed Decimal
+ 136	00010011 01101111
– 136	00010011 01101101
	(sign)

The third form for representing numbers, binary format, dispenses completely with EBCDIC and stores the number as its direct binary equivalent. This format can result in the greatest savings in storage: It takes just two bytes of storage to store any number 1-4 digits long, and four bytes of storage to store any number 5-9 digits long.

Programmers seldom use binary format, however. It adds overhead during processing, because the computer must convert the binary values to packed decimal before the values can be used in calculations. The system also converts zoned-decimal values to packed decimal before using them in calculations. Although some programmers prefer to define numeric fields as zoned decimal (type S) because it's easier to print or view the raw data in the file when the data is stored in this format, the AS/400 works most efficiently with numbers stored in packed-decimal format.

The length of the entry you give a field in DDS represents the number of digit positions in the value to be represented, but the number of bytes of storage it will take to actually store the value may vary, given the data type. Packed fields take $(n+1)/2$ bytes of storage (rounded to the nearest whole byte), where n = number of digit positions in the data value. The formula derives from the fact that in packed format, the sign and each digit require a half-byte of storage; you need to round up to the nearest whole byte because data storage is allocated in byte-sized units. A number eight positions long would have a length of 5 if stored in packed format. (So would a number nine positions long. Because it takes the same amount of storage, many programming experts recommend that you always define packed numeric fields with an odd number of digit positions.) An 8-digit number would have a length of 4 if binary was the type specified for it. For zoned-decimal format, length corresponds exactly to digit positions in the value to be stored.

Now that you understand the basics of defining physical files, you are ready to learn about logical files on the AS/400. Although you could, in theory, "get by" using only physical files to define your data, you are just scratching the surface of the AS/400's database capabilities until you begin to use logical files.

Defining Logical Files

As discussed above, logical files define access paths to data actually stored in physical files. You can use a logical file to restrict user views to a subset of fields contained in a physical file, to change the retrieval order of records from a file (by changing the designated key field), or to combine data stored in two or more separate physical files into a single logical file. Although the data actually is stored in physical files, once you have defined logical files to the system you can reference these logical files in RPG programs as though the logical files themselves actually contained records. The advantage of using logical files is that they can provide alternate ways to look at data, including different orders of record access, without redundantly storing the actual data on the system.

Simple Logical Files

A logical file based on a single physical file is called a simple logical file. The method of defining simple logical files is similar to that of defining physical files: You first specify a record format, follow that with a list of fields (optional), and follow that with one or more (optional) key fields. Because logical files provide views of physical files, you must include the key word PFILE beginning in position 45 (Functions) on the record-format line, followed, in parentheses, by the name of the physical file upon which the logical record format is based.

The easiest way to code a simple logical file is to use the same record-format name within the logical file as the record-format name in the physical file the logical file is based on. With this method, the system assumes the record layouts of the files are identical. As a result, you do not need to include fields within your logical record description. However, you can still designate one or more fields as a key, and this key does not have to match the key of the physical file. The following example shows a logical file based on employee master file EMPMST.

A				Conditioning											Location					

```
A * Logical file EMPMSTL3, keyed on last name.
A   R EMPREC                                    PFILE(EMPMST)
A   K LNAME
A
```

With this definition, all the fields defined within the physical file are included within the logical file. Because the logical file is keyed on last name, keyed sequential access of this logical file will retrieve the employee records in alphabetic order by last name. This kind of logical file definition is widely used to change the retrieval order of records in a file. Its effects are identical to that of physically sorting file records into a different order, but without the system overhead that a physical sort requires.

If you want to restrict the logical file so that it includes only some of the fields from the physical file, provide the logical file with a record-format name different from that of the record name in the physical file and then list just those fields to be included in the logical file. Again, you may designate one or more of these fields to serve as the key to the file. The logical file defined below would produce the logical view of employee data organized by department and employee number illustrated earlier in the chapter.

A				Conditioning											Location					

```
A *Logical file EMPMSTL1, keyed on department and within department,
A *employee number. Restricts fields accessible within the
A *logical file.
A   R EMPRECL1                                  PFILE(EMPMST)
A     EMPNO
A     LNAME
A     FNAME
A     DEPT
A     SALARY
A   K DEPT
A   K EMPNO
A
```

Notice that you do not need to specify length, type, and decimal positions for the fields in a logical file; these field attributes are already given in the physical file on which the logical file is based.

If you wanted to limit access to only name and address information in the employee master file and retrieve the records in zip-code order, you could define a logical file like the one that follows. Again, the data view resulting from this logical file was illustrated earlier.

```
A *Logical file EMPMSTL2, keyed on zip code.
A          R EMPRECL2                           PFILE(EMPMST)
A            LNAME
A            FNAME
A            STREET
A            CITY
A            STATE
A            ZIP
A          K ZIP
A
```

Record Selection/Omission

You can define logical files to exclude certain records contained in the physical file, or to include only a subset of the records contained in the physical file, by using Omit or Select specifications. You can use this feature only if the logical file contains a key specification. Your specifications base record exclusion or inclusion on actual data values present in selected fields of the physical file records. For example, assume you want to omit the MIS department from the salary report. You simply designate department as an omit field (O in position 17) and then in position 45 provide the basis for the omission. In this case, since you want to omit a specific department, simply use the field-level keyword VALUES, followed by the value or values you want to omit. If the field type is character, you must enclose each value with apostrophes.

If you wanted to *include only* the MIS and ACT departments, you could change the O in position 17 of the select/omit field to an S, and specify MIS and ACT as values. In that case, the logical file would *contain* only employees of the MIS and ACT departments. Other departments would be excluded.

Sequence Number	Form Type	And/Or/Comment (A/O/*)	Not (N)	Indicator	Not (N)	Indicator	Not (N)	Indicator	Name Type (b/R/K/S/O)	Reserved	Name	Reference (R)	Length	Data Type (b/A/P/S/B A/S/X/Y/N/I/W)	Decimal Positions	Usage (b/O/I/B/H/M)	Location Line	Pos	Functions
	A										*Logical file EMPMSTL4, keyed on department and within department,								
	A										*employee number. MIS department employees are excluded from								
	A										*the file.								
	A								R		EMPMSTL4								PFILE(EMPMST)
	A										EMPNO								
	A										LNAME								
	A										FNAME								
	A										DEPT								
	A										SALARY								
	A								K		DEPT								
	A								K		EMPNO								
	A								O		DEPT								VALUES('MIS')
	A																		

Sequence Number	Form Type	And/Or/Comment (A/O/*)	Not (N)	Indicator	Not (N)	Indicator	Not (N)	Indicator	Name Type (b/R/K/S/O)	Reserved	Name	Reference (R)	Length	Data Type (b/A/P/S/B A/S/X/Y/N/I/W)	Decimal Positions	Usage (b/O/I/B/H/M)	Location Line	Pos	Functions
	A										*Logical file EMPMSTL5, keyed on department, and within								
	A										*department, employee number. Only MIS and ACT departments								
	A										*are included within the file.								
	A								R		EMPMSTL5								PFILE(EMPMST)
	A										EMPNO								
	A										LNAME								
	A										FNAME								
	A										DEPT								
	A										SALARY								
	A								K		DEPT								
	A								K		EMPNO								
	A								S		DEPT								VALUES('MIS' 'ACT')
	A																		

Besides VALUES, two additional keywords allow you to specify the basis of record inclusion or exclusion: RANGE and COMP. Keyword RANGE, followed by parentheses containing two values, allows you to specify the beginning value and the ending value of a *range* of values upon which the selection or omission is to be based. In the example that follows, only employees with zip codes 49400 through 50000 will be included in the logical file.

```
A*Logical file EMPMSTL6, selecting specified records based on a
A*range of zip codes.
A          R EMPRECL6                     PFILE(EMPMST)
A            LNAME
A            FNAME
A            STREET
A            CITY
A            STATE
A            ZIP
A          K ZIP
A          S ZIP                          RANGE(49400 50000)
A
```

With keyword COMP, you can specify that a comparison between a field's value and a given value serve as the basis of selection or omission. You specify the nature of the comparison by using one of eight relational operators: EQ (equal to), NE (not equal to), LT (less than), NL (not less than), GT (greater than), NG (not greater than), LE (less than or equal to), and GE (greater than or equal to). To use this feature, enter field-level keyword COMP; follow the keyword with parentheses containing first the relational operator and then a literal indicating the comparison value. In the following example, employees with zip codes below 49500 would be omitted from the logical file.

```
A*Logical file EMPMSTL7, omitting those employees whose zip codes
A*are less than 49500.
A          R EMPRECL7                     PFILE(EMPMST)
A            LNAME
A            FNAME
A            STREET
A            CITY
A            STATE
A            ZIP
A          K ZIP
A          O ZIP                          COMP(LT 49500)
A
```

You can designate multiple select and/or omit fields, set up alternate criteria using ORs (O in position 7), or list multiple criteria using ANDs (A in position 7) so that several specifications must hold true for record inclusion/exclusion to occur. (See IBM's reference manual, *Programming: Data Description Specifications Reference* (SC41-9620), for additional details.)

Logical Files with Multiple-Record Formats

You also can define logical files based on two or more physical files. One way to do this is to define logical files with multiple-record formats, where each format is based on a different physical file.

Consider the following scenario. You have a student master physical file that contains student number, name, major, date admitted (and so on). As students take courses, each course is recorded in a second physical file containing student number, course identification, semester taken, grade received, and so on. Partial definitions of these physical files are shown below.

```
A* Physical file definition for student master file STUDMST.
A          R STUDREC
A            STUDNO        9S 0      TEXT('Student Number')
A            LNAME        20A        TEXT('Last Name')
A            FNAME        10A        TEXT('First Name')
A            MAJOR         6A        TEXT('Major')
A            ADMDTE        6S 0      TEXT('Date Admitted')
A          K STUDNO
```

```
A* Physical file of student courses taken, STUDCRS.
A          R CRSREC
A            STUDNO        9S 0      TEXT('Student Number')
A            CRSID         6A        TEXT('Course Identifier')
A            SMSTER        3A        TEXT('Semester Taken')
A            GRADE         2A        TEXT('Grade Received')
A          K STUDNO
A          K CRSID
```

Now assume you want to produce a report that shows the name, number, and major for each student, followed immediately with a list of all the courses (s)he has taken and the grade received in each course. One way to handle this would be to define a logical file based on the two physical files. The logical file definition is shown below.

Sequence Number	Form Type	And/Or/Comment (A/O/*)	Not (N)	Indicator	Not (N)	Indicator	Not (N)	Indicator	Name Type (b/R/K/S/O)	Reserved	Name	Reference (R)	Length	Data Type (b A/P/S/B A/S/X/Y/N/I/W)	Decimal Positions	Usage (b/O/I/B/H/M)	Line	Pos	Functions
	A	*									Logical file over STUDMST and STUDCRS physical files.								
	A								R		STUDREC								PFILE(STUDMST)
	A								K		STUDNO								
	A								R		CRSREC								PFILE(STUDCRS)
	A								K		STUDNO								
	A								K		SMSTER								
	A																		

Notice that the logical file contains two record formats, one based on physical file STUDMST and the other on physical file STUDCRS. Both record formats use the student number as the major key; the second format, CRSREC, also has semester as the minor portion of a concatenated key.

With this definition, sequentially reading the logical file will retrieve first a student record (that student with the lowest student number); then, one by one, each record from the course file for that student, arranged in semester order; then the next student's record, followed by the courses, in semester order, for that student; and so on. The logical file gives the appearance that the two physical files have been merged together, with records grouped by student, and within that grouping arranged by semester. In reality, the data remains in the two separate physical files. The logical file interconnects them by building access paths to the records in both files.

Join-Logical Files

You can define a second kind of logical file based on two or more physical files: a **join-logical file**. In contrast to a logical file with multiple-record formats, in which data from different physical files remain on separate records in the logical file, a join-logical file combines fields from different physical files into a single record. To use this format, there must be a matching field across the physical files upon which the joining can be based.

Take, for example, the case where you want to generate invoice lines based on an inventory physical file whose records contain part number, description, unit cost, and selling price and an order physical file that contains order number, part number and quantity ordered. You could set up a logical file to combine the description and price information from the inventory file with the order number and quantity ordered information from the order file by joining the two files on part number.

Sequence Number	Form Type	And/Or/Comment (A/O/*)	Not (N)	Indicator	Not (N)	Indicator	Not (N)	Indicator	Name Type (b/R/K/S/O)	Reserved	Name	Reference (R)	Length	Data Type (b A/P/S/B A/S/X/Y/N/I/W)	Decimal Positions	Usage (b/O/I/B/H/M)	Location Line	Pos	Functions
	A	*									Physical file of inventory, INVENT								
	A								R		INVREC								
	A										PARTNO		6A						TEXT('Part Number')
	A										DESCRP		30A						TEXT('Description')
	A										UNTCST		5P	2					TEXT('Unit Cost')
	A										SELPRC		5P	2					TEXT('Selling Price')
	A										OHQTY		5P	0					TEXT('On-hand Quantity')
	A								K		PARTNO								
	A																		

Sequence Number	Form Type	And/Or/Comment (A/O/*)	Not (N)	Indicator	Not (N)	Indicator	Not (N)	Indicator	Name Type (b/R/K/S/O)	Reserved	Name	Reference (R)	Length	Data Type (b A/P/S/B A/S/X/Y/N/I/W)	Decimal Positions	Usage (b/O/I/B/H/M)	Location Line	Pos	Functions
	A	*									Physical file of orders, ORDERS								
	A								R		ORDREC								
	A										ORDRNO		6A						TEXT('Order Number')
	A										CUSTNO		5A						TEXT('Customer Number')
	A										PRTNO		6A						TEXT('Part Number')
	A										QTYORD		3P	0					TEXT('Quantity Ordered')
	A								K		ORDRNO								
	A								K		PRTNO								
	A																		

```
A* Join logical file connecting INVENT and ORDERS
A          R ORDLINE                    JFILE(ORDERS INVENT)
A          J                            JOIN(ORDERS INVENT)
A                                       JFLD(PRTNO PARTNO)
A            ORDRNO
A            CUSTNO
A            PARTNO
A            DESCRP
A            SELPRC
A            QTYORD
```

In the logical file above, keyword JFILE signals which physical files are used by the logical file. The next two lines specify the nature of the join. Notice that the join specification requires a J in position 17 of the specification line. Keyword JOIN designates which files are used in this join. Because we expect every record from ORDERS to appear in the logical file, we list that file first.

The JFLD keyword indicates which fields' values are to be matched across the physical files named in the JOIN parameter. Following the join-level entries are the fields comprising the logical record. Notice that some fields within the logical record come from INVENT, while others come from ORDERS. Records from these two files are "joined" together to create a single, logical-record image.

Creating Database Files

The first step in actually creating a physical or logical file is to enter the DDS statements using SEU. As mentioned earlier, it is standard practice to use source file QDDSSRC for storing database source members. Also recall that the source type is PF for physical file and LF for logical file.

Once you have entered your DDS code, you must compile it to create the file as an object on the system. If you are working from PDM or the Programmer's Menu, follow the same procedure to compile a database object that you use to create a program object.

If you compile by directly entering a command at a command line, rather than by working through menus, the appropriate commands are CRTPF (Create Physical File) and CRTLF (Create Logical File).

If the system encounters syntax errors while trying to create your file, you will receive a message indicating that the creation was not successful. Otherwise, the system will tell you the job completed normally and that the database object now exists. Once the file object exists, you may use it to store data. You can enter data into physical files by using a system utility called **Data File Utility (DFU)**, by writing values to the file through a program, or by copying records to the file from another file.

Note that you must create a physical file before you can create logical files based on that physical file; failure to do so will result in error messages. If you want to change the definition of a physical file after you have created a logical file based on that definition, you must first delete the logical file object (though not the source) before the system will allow you to delete the physical file object and create a new one.

You should be aware of one additional caveat: If you want to change a physical file's definition after you have stored data in the file, deleting the file deletes the data in the file as well. You can avoid such data loss by copying it temporarily to a different file; your instructor can provide you with this information, should you need it.

RPG Programming with Externally Defined Files

Now that you understand how to define and create files on the AS/400, you will find that it is simple to reference these external definitions for input files used by your programs. Basically, all you need to do is make a few minor modifications to your File Specifications and eliminate your Input Specifications.

On the File Specifications in position 19, instead of an F for Fixed Format, code an E for Externally Defined. Next, omit a record-length entry, because the system will supply that information automatically, based on the external definition. And finally, if the file is keyed and you want to access records based on keys, code a K in position 31. Omitting the K results in record retrieval based on arrival sequence (i.e., the order in which the records were originally written to the file). The following figure illustrates a File Specification for an externally described file.

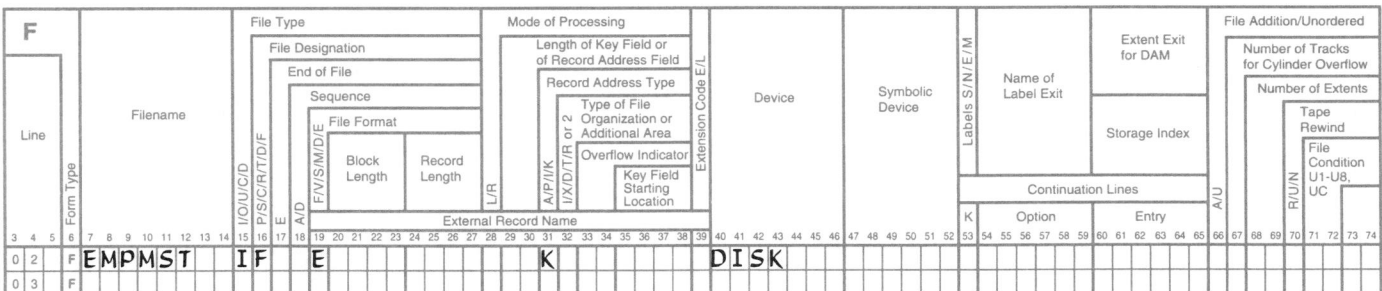

EMPMST is a physical file. If you wanted to use a logical file, you would enter the logical file name; the remaining entries would be identical to those shown for the physical file. At a program level, there is no distinction made between physical and logical files.

If your input file is externally described, you do not need to code Input Specifications for that file. When you compile your program, the system will copy the file's definition into your source listing where the input specifications would normally appear. Obviously then, when you use external definition, the file must exist before your program will successfully compile.

Less obviously, if you make changes in a physical or logical file definition after you have compiled a program using that file, you must recompile the program before the system will allow the program to run. This feature, called **level checking**, prevents you from running a program based on an obsolete or inaccurate definition of a database file.

Calculation and Output Specifications may use any fields defined as part of the externally described input file just as though the fields were defined internally as part of the Input Specifications. You also can externally describe database files used as output; in that case, Output Specifications are unnecessary and writing to the file can take place directly from your calculations. Chapter 6 explores this concept in detail.

Additional Database File Concepts

The purpose of this chapter has been to provide the beginning RPG programmer with a basic understanding of externally defined files on the AS/400. The AS/400 provides features for defining data far beyond what has been covered here. Variants on join-logical files, for instance, can be much more complex than the simple examples illustrated. In addition to the keywords used in this chapter, the AS/400 offers 30 or so other keywords used with data file definition. Some of these keywords allow you to establish data validity checks for interactive data entry, while others allow you to specify how the field will be edited upon output to the screen.

Finally, the AS/400 allows you to create a centralized **data dictionary** of fields in a physical file (sometimes called a **field-reference file**). You never actually use this file for data storage; its sole purpose is to provide field definitions for use in subsequent file creation. You reference this file to define fields within database files.

Consider the examples of physical files that were part of the student records application system illustrated earlier in this chapter. Instead of defining each field within the physical database files, we could have first created a physical file containing the definitions of *all* the fields that the student record system will need to store. This file — a field-reference file — is illustrated in the following figure.

```
A.....Field reference file STUDREF for the student records system
A          R FLDREC
A            STUDNO            9S 0        TEXT('Student Number')
A            LNAME            20A          TEXT('Last Name')
A            FNAME            10A          TEXT('First Name')
A            MAJOR             6A          TEXT('Major')
A            ADMDTE            6S 0        TEXT('Date Admitted')
A            CRSID             6A          TEXT('Course Identifier')
A            SMSTER            3A          TEXT('Semester Taken')
A            GRADE             2A          TEXT('Grade Received')
A          . . .
A
```

Once you have created the reference file, you can create physical database files whose field definitions are obtained from the reference file. To use this feature, simply include in your physical file the file-level keyword REF, with the name of the field-reference file in parentheses. You can then define any field in this physical file whose definition already exists in the reference file by simply coding an R in position 29 (Reference) and omitting the length, type, decimal entry, and relevant keyword information for that field.

The two physical files that follow illustrate the use of a field-reference file.

```
A.....Physical file definition for student master file STUDMST
A                                              REF(STUDREF)
A          R STUDREC
A            STUDNO          R
A            LNAME           R
A            FNAME           R
A            MAJOR           R
A            ADMDTE          R
A          K STUDNO
A
```

```
A* Physical file of student courses taken, STUDCRS
A                                          REF(STUDREF)
A          R CRSREC
A            STUDNO    R
A            CRSID     R
A            SMSTER    R
A            GRADE     R
A          K STUDNO
A          K CRSID
```

Field-reference files can enforce a uniformity and consistency throughout an application system that facilitates program development and maintenance. Using such files, however, requires a thoughtful, structured approach to application system development, since your data needs should be determined prior to any file creation or application development. The casual approach that many companies take toward developing new systems does not allow them to take advantage of field-reference files.

Another related topic of concern to programmers is database design. A crucial step in application system development is determining the file structure for the system. What data fields will you need to store? What physical and logical files will you need? How do you determine what fields belong in what files? Whole books have been written on the subject of relational database design. Although this topic is beyond the scope of this book, realize that every professional programmer should have a solid understanding of relational database design.

As systems become complex and the number of files used in a system grows, it becomes increasingly important for an IS department to have file-naming conventions that provide some information about the function and type of each file. Although working with a maximum of eight-character file names poses some restrictions on your ability to assign good file names, many installations use an agreed-upon mnemonic prefix to denote the system within which the file was designed to be used and a short alphabetic mnemonic code — often related to the key of the file — to uniquely identify each file within the system. Some companies also use a suffix of P, L, or F to denote whether the file is a physical, logical, or field-reference file and a number to differentiate between similar files.

Externally Described Printer Files

In addition to allowing the external definition of database files, RPG lets you define reports externally. Although programmers use this feature less often than they use externally described database files, a significant number of programmers prefer to handle all their report programs by externally describing the reports.

There are two primary advantages to externally describing printer files. First, this method lets you modify a report format without changing the source code of the program that produces the report, a wise approach to application maintenance. Second, if you externally define printer files, you can use a system utility, Report Layout Utility (RLU), to help you design the layout of the report visually on the terminal; you don't need to use paper and printer spacing chart forms. RLU then generates the DDS required to describe the report so you don't have to do the grunt work of figuring out line position and spacing entries. (The details of using RLU fall outside the scope of this text; those persons interested in developing printer files with this method should consult the IBM manual *RLU User's Guide and Reference*, SC09-1416.)

You use DDS to define printer files at the source level, the same as you do for database files. The source members of printer files, like database files, are generally stored in QDDSSRC; a printer file's type, however, is PRTF. Once you have entered the source code through SEU (or via RLU), you compile the source to create a printer file object. Once the object exists, it can receive output from a program for printing. The DDS code for a printer file is analogous to that of a database file, except that its focus is the definition of record formats of information to be sent to the printer. Printer files, like logical files, may contain multiple record formats, each defining a different set of output lines. The DDS may also include keyword entries at the file level, the record level, and/or the field level to define the position and/or appearance of the output.

To illustrate how you would externally define a printer file, let's reconsider the sales report from Chapter 4. Recall that the desired report includes headings, individual sales figures, a sales total for each salesperson, and a grand total for all salespersons. The printer spacing chart for the report is reproduced on the following page.

```
          1         2         3         4         5
12345678901234567890123456789012345678901234567890

XX/XX/XX     SALES REPORT    PAGE XXØX

        SLSM.               AMT.

        XXXX                X,XXØ.XX
        XXXX                X,XXØ.XX

                    TOTAL   XX,XXØ.XX*

        XXXX                X,XXØ.XX
        XXXX                X,XXØ.XX
        XXXX                X,XXØ.XX

                    TOTAL   XX,XXØ.XX*

              GRAND TOTAL   XXX,XXØ.XX**
```

The RPG program in Chapter 4 defined five exception lines, grouped as HEADS, DETAIL, BRKLIN, and TOTAL, to generate this output. You would follow much the same procedure to externally describe this report in DDS.

The following figure illustrates the DDS for the sales report. First, you need to define one record format for each line or group of lines to be printed in a single output operation. Then, for each of those record formats, you

Page 1 of 2

Sequence Number	Form Type	And/Or/Comment (A/O/*)	Not (N)	Indicator	Not (N)	Indicator	Not (N)	Indicator	Name Type (W/R/K/S/O)	Reserved	Name	Reference (R)	Length	Data Type (W A/P/S/B A/S/X/Y/N/I/W)	Decimal Positions	Usage (W/O/I/B/H/M)	Line	Pos	Functions
	A	*									Printer file SALESRPT, externally describing the sales report.								
	A								R		HEADS								SKIPB(2)
	A																	10	DATE EDTCDE(Y)
	A																	22	'SALES REPORT'
	A																	37	'PAGE'
	A																	42	PAGNBR EDTCDE(3)
	A																		SPACEA(2)
	A																	15	'SLSM.'
	A																	34	'AMT'
	A																		SPACEA(2)
	A								R		DETAIL								SPACEA(1)
	A										SLSMAN		4				15		
	A										SALES		6		2		32		EDTCDE(1)
	A								R		BRKLIN								SPACEB(1) SPACEA(2)
	A																	20	'TOTAL'
	A										SALTOT		6		2		31		EDTCDE(1)
	A																	40	'*'
	A																		
	A																		
	A																		

Page 2 of 2

Sequence Number	Form Type	And/Or/Comment (A/O/*)	Not (N)	Indicator	Not (N)	Indicator	Not (N)	Indicator	Name Type (#/R/K/S/O)	Reserved	Name	Reference (R)	Length	Data Type (#/A/P/S/B A/S/X/Y/N/J/I/W)	Decimal Positions	Usage (#/O/I/B/H/M)	Line	Pos	Functions
	A								R		TOTAL								
	A																	16	'GRAND TOTAL'
	A										GNDTOT		8		2			30	EDTCDE(1)
	A																	40	'**'
	A																		
	A																		

need to specify what fields and/or literals are to print as part of that format, what line spacing each format should follow, where within a line the variable or constant data should appear, and what editing (if any) should be associated with the numeric fields.

You must begin each record-format definition with an R in position 17, followed by the name of the format in positions 19-28. Next, for each record format, you need to define all the information that is to print as part of that format. Specify fields in positions 19-28, just as for database files. Constants are coded in positions 45-80 and must be enclosed in apostrophes.

To define each field within the DDS, provide its length in positions 30-34 and, for numeric fields, its number of decimal positions in positions 36-37; blanks in the decimal position columns signal a character field. Thus, in our example, SLSMAN is defined as a 4-byte character field, while SALES is a 6-byte numeric field with two decimal positions. Literals 'SALES REPORT' and 'PAGE' are simply entered within apostrophes starting in position 45.

You also need to specify where within the report line each piece of information is to appear. Use positions 42-44 for this purpose. Note that in DDS, unlike in RPG, you must specify the field or constant's *beginning position* (where it starts within the line), rather than its *ending position*. Thus, in our example, because SALES REPORT begins in column 22 of the first heading, you code 22 in positions 43-44 of the DDS line for that constant.

DDS handles the system date and the report page numbers a little bit differently than RPG does. RPG includes two built-in variables, UDATE and PAGE, which supply the system date and page number, respectively. In DDS the same information is accessible through the keywords DATE and PAGNBR. As shown in the example, you enter these keywords on their own lines in DDS.

The same edit codes and edit words available in RPG to modify the appearance of numeric output are available within DDS. However, you indicate desired editing through the use of keywords EDTCDE or EDTWRD, followed by the appropriate edit code or word enclosed within parentheses. In our example, DATE will print with slashes as a result of the EDTCDE(Y) entry, while fields SALES, SALTOT, and GNDTOT will print with commas and zero balances because of keyword EDTCDE(1). EDTCDE(3) specifies that PAGNBR, a 4-digit numeric value, should be zero-suppressed and printed without commas.

The easiest way to specify line positioning on a page in DDS is to use four keywords: SPACEA, SPACEB, SKIPA, and SKIPB. The meaning of these keywords — space after or before and skip after or before — corresponds exactly to the meaning of those terms in RPG. The number of lines to space (for SPACEA or SPACEB) or the line to skip to (for SKIPA and SKIPB) is designated within parentheses following the keyword. You can use these keywords at the record level or at the field level. If you want line positioning to change *within* a record format, you would use the appropriate keyword at a field level; whereas if line positioning is to change for the record format as a whole, use the keyword at the record level.

In our previous example, because we want the headings to begin on the second line of each new page, we use the keyword entry SKIPB(2) at the record-format level (that is, on the line containing the R entry or the lines immediately following that entry and before any field or constant entry). But recall that record format HEADS contains information about two heading lines for our report, and we want to position the second line two lines below the first heading. The SPACEA(2) keyword entry immediately following the PAGNBR keyword entry produces the desired line spacing; immediately following the printing of the page number, the paper would advance two lines. Printing would then continue with the constant 'SLSM.'. Note that multiple keywords can appear on the same code line, as shown by the record-level entry SPACEB(1) SPACEA(2) for record format BRKLIN.

Other optional features of externally described printer files (e.g., changing fonts, printing bar codes, using indicators, defining fields by reference) are beyond the scope of this text. But with this introduction, you should be able to use DDS to externally describe most common types of printed output.

How does external definition of printed output affect an RPG program? First, in the File Specification entry for the report file, include the actual name of the printer file, rather than the generic output file QPRINT. In addition, change the file format entry (position 19) to E — for Externally Described. And finally, omit any entry for record length. You may, however, still associate an overflow indicator with this file by specifying an indicator in positions 33-34 of the File Specification, but the indicator cannot be OA-OF or OV. The following figure illustrates a File Specification for an externally described printer file.

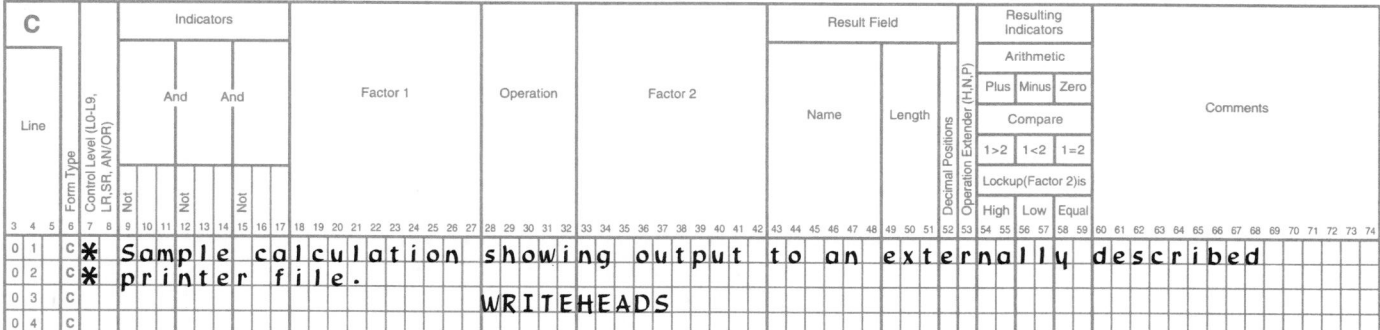

The externally described printer file eliminates the need for Output Specifications in your program. How then do you direct the computer to print at the appropriate times as it executes your program? Instead of using the EXCPT operation, which references lines defined on Output Specifications, use the WRITE operation, with the name of the appropriate record format of your printer file specified in factor 2. The figure below illustrates the WRITE operation.

Putting It All Together

Now that you have seen how database files and printer files can be externally described and you have a sense of how this approach to file definition affects RPG programs, we can rewrite our control-break program from Chapter 4 to take advantage of external definition. First, let's externally define the input file SALESFIL. The DDS for this file is shown in the following example. Because the file is keyed on SLSMAN, data records later stored in the file will be kept ordered by salesperson number, a necessary condition for our control break report.

```
A *  Definition of physical file SALESFIL.
A       R SALESREC
A         SLSMAN        4A        TEXT('Salesperson number')
A         DEPT          3A        TEXT('Department')
A         SALES         6S 2      TEXT('Sales amount')
A         SALDAT        6S 0      TEXT('Date of sale')
A       K SLSMAN
```

We have already developed the DDS for the printer file SALESRPT. Remember that you must compile or create an object of each externally described file before it can be used. (Additionally, remember that the physical file initially is empty; you would need to put actual data records into the file before it could meaningfully be used as input.) With those files externally described, our RPG program becomes considerably shorter, as shown below. In addition, we can now make changes to our report layout or to our data file definition without having to modify the RPG program.

```
         1         2         3         4         5         6         7         8
12345678901234567890123456789012345678901234567890123456789012345678901234567890
     F*****************************************************************
     F* This program produces a Sales Report listing subtotals for *
     F* each salesperson.                                          *
     F*   Author:  Yaeger        Date Written:  Dec. 1992          *
     F*                                                            *
     F* Modified, Nov., 1994, by Yaeger                            *
     F*   Changed program-described files to externally described. *
     F*****************************************************************
     FSALESFILIF E           K        DISK
     FSALESRPTO  E             10      PRINTER
     C*****************************************************************
     C* Calculations required to produce the Sales Report.
     C* Main-line logic.
     C*****************************************************************
     C                   EXSR INIT
     C*
     C          *IN90    DOWEQ*OFF
     C          SLSHLD   IFNE SLSMAN                    Check for
     C                   EXSR SLSBRK                    control break
     C                   ENDIF
     C                   EXSR DETL
     C                   READ SALESFIL              90
     C                   ENDDO
     C*
     C                   EXSR TERM
     C                   MOVE *ON     *INLR
     C                   RETRN
```

```
              1         2         3         4         5         6         7         8
     1234567890123456789012345678901234567890123456789012345678901234567890123456789Ø

     C************************************************************
     C* Subroutine to read first record, set up hold, and print
     C* first page headings.
     C************************************************************
     CSR           INIT      BEGSR
     C                       READ SALESFIL                         90
     C                       MOVE SLSMAN    SLSHLD  4
     C                       WRITEHEADS
     C                       ENDSR
     C************************************************************
     C* Subroutine done when salesman changes; print subtotal,
     C* rollover accumulator, zero out accumulator, and reset hold.
     C************************************************************
     CSR           SLSBRK    BEGSR
     C                       WRITEBRKLIN
     C                       ADD  SALTOT    GNDTOT 82
     C                       Z-ADDØ         SALTOT
     C                       MOVE SLSMAN    SLSHLD
     C                       ENDSR
     C************************************************************
     C* Subroutine executed for each input record.
     C************************************************************
     C             DETL      BEGSR
     C             *IN1Ø     IFEQ *ON                  Page overflow
     C                       WRITEHEADS
     C                       MOVE *OFF      *IN1Ø
     C                       ENDIF
     C                       WRITEDETAIL
     C                       ADD  SALES     SALTOT 62  Salesman Tot.
     C                       ENDSR
     C************************************************************
     C* Subroutine done at end of file; execute SLSBRK one last
     C* time and print grand total line.
     C************************************************************
     CSR           TERM      BEGSR
     C                       EXSR SLSBRK
     C                       WRITETOTAL
     C                       ENDSR
```

Chapter Summary

The AS/400 defines data files independently of your programs. Such files, defined through DDS statements, exist as objects on the system and may be used by any program as externally described files. Physical files contain data records, while logical files provide access paths, or pointers, to the physical file records. A logical file is always associated with one or more physical files. Both physical and logical files may contain a key that allows records to be retrieved based on the value of the key. The key can consist of one or several data fields; in the latter case, the key is called a composite, or concatenation.

A physical file may contain only a single-record format or type. Logical files may contain multiple-record formats, based on records from two or more physical files. A logical file also may contain a single-record format that actually combines data fields stored in different physical files; this kind of file is called a join-logical file. Logical files also can be used to specify which records should be selected for inclusion or omitted from inclusion based on data values of the records in the physical file upon which the logical file is based.

A special kind of physical file, a field-reference file, can be used to record field definitions. Physical database files then can reference this file rather than having the field definitions included directly within the physical files themselves.

Numeric data can be stored in a physical file in one of three formats: zoned decimal, packed decimal, or binary. Zoned decimal is easiest to view but takes up the most room on disk. Packed decimal, the data format native to the AS/400, eliminates redundant high-order bits in storing digit values. Both zoned-decimal and packed-decimal formats use EBCDIC representation. Binary format stores the binary equivalent of a numeric value without first representing the number in EBCDIC.

Database design is an important part of application system design and development. A well-planned database can facilitate application development and maintenance; a poorly designed database can plague programmers for years. Once database files exist, using them within RPG programs is simple: Reference the file as Externally Described on the File Specifications. The system then will import the file's record definition to your program when you compile the program.

Some programmers use externally described printer files to define report formats. This practice offers several advantages: Report formats can be changed without modifying programs, RLU can be used to design the reports and generate the DDS, and Output Specifications can be eliminated from your programs.

Terms

arrival sequence	field-level keywords	low-order bits
binary data type	field-reference file	packed-decimal data type
character data type	file-level keywords	physical files
composite key	high-order bits	record-level keywords
concatenation	join-logical file	redundancy
Data Description	key field	subschemas
Specifications (DDS)	key sequence	zoned-decimal data type
data dictionary	keywords	
Data File Utility (DFU)	level checking	
external file description	logical files	

Discussion/Review Questions

1. Explain the advantages of externally describing database files. Do externally described printer files share the same advantages?

2. Explain the difference between a logical file and a physical file.

3. What does concatenation mean? What's a concatenated key?

4. What are the advantages of logical files? Why not just create lots of physical files to store records in different orders or to present different combinations of data fields?

5. How does the system know whether you intend a keyword to be a file-level, record-level, or field-level keyword?

6. Why might you use UNIQUE as a keyword in a physical file?

7. Express the following values in zoned-decimal and packed-decimal format: +362 and –51024

8. How many bytes will it take to store 389,241,111 in zoned decimal? In packed decimal? In binary?

9. Provide several practical examples for using logical files.

10. Explain the differences between keywords COMP, RANGE, and VALUES.

11. If Select and Omit specifications were not available in logical file definitions, how could you produce a report that included only the employees of the ACT and MIS departments and excluded other employees?

12. What is a join-logical file?

13. Explain the difference between arrival sequence and key sequence of sequential record retrieval.

14. Assume you wanted to write a program that used an externally described logical file that was based on a join of two physical files. What order would you use to create the four objects required to execute the program? Why?

15. Some programmers argue that standards in file and field naming and the use of features like field-reference files reduces their opportunities to be creative and should not be enforced. How would you respond to them?

Exercises

1. A library wants a database file to store book title; author's last name, first name, and middle initial; catalog number; publisher; date published; number of pages; and number of copies owned. Code a physical-file definition to store this data after determining what you believe to be the appropriate fields, and the length and type for each field. Consider what the key field (if any) should be, and whether UNIQUE is appropriate.

2. The library wants to be able to access the catalog information described in Exercise 1 based on author's name. Among other things, they want to be able to print out listings by author such that all books by the same author will appear together. Define a logical file that will enable this kind of access.

3. The library also wants to store a description of each book. Because the books' descriptions vary greatly in length, from a few words to a long paragraph, the person designing the library's database suggested storing the descriptions in a separate physical file, where each record contained the catalog number, a description line number, and 40 characters of description. Define this physical file.

4. Define a multiple-record-format logical file that will combine the information in the physical files from Exercises 1 and 3 such that the initial book information will be followed sequentially by the lines of description, in order, for that book.

5. Define a field-reference file for the library based on the data requirements of Exercises 1 and 3 and then rewrite the physical-file definitions to take advantage of the field-reference file.

Programming Assignments

Note: All of the following assignments involve producing reports that either can be defined as part of your RPG program or described externally; your instructor will tell you which technique to use.

1. This assignment includes several parts.
    a) Create a physical file for Wexler University's student master file (file WUSTDP, in Appendix D). Key this file on student number and specify that keys be unique.
    b) Enter records in the file, following your instructor's directions.
    c) Design a report for Wexler University that provides a listing of student information. Include student number, first and last name, credits earned, major, date admitted, and grade-point average in your report layout.
    d) Write a program to produce the report you designed in part c, with your input file the externally described file you defined in part a. The report should show students listed in order by Social Security number.
    e) Create a logical file over WUSTDP with last name and first name as a concatenated key.

Programming Assignments Continued

Programming Assignments continued

    f) Modify your program from part d to use this logical file as the input file. The resulting report should list the students in alphabetical order by last name, and within last name, by first name.

2. This assignment includes several parts.

    a) Create a physical file for CompuSell's customer master file (CSCSTP in Appendix D). Key the file on customer number and specify that keys be unique.

    b) Enter records in the file, following your instructor's directions.

    c) Write a program using the file you created as input to produce the report shown below. All the customers should be listed, in order of customer number.

    d) Create a logical file over the customer file keyed on last name, and within last name, by first name.

    e) Modify your program to use the file you created in part d as the input file. The report should now list customers in name order.

    f) Create another logical file over the customer file, this time keyed on balance due and selecting only those customers with a balance greater than zero.

    g) Modify your program to use the file you created in part f as the input file. The report should now list customers in balance-owed order and include only those customers who owe the company money.

```
          1         2         3         4         5         6         7         8
 1234567890123456789012345678901234567890123456789012345678901234567890123456789Ø

     XX/XX/XX    COMPUSELL REPORT OF CUSTOMER BALANCES        PAGE XXØX

     CUST. NO.      FIRST NAME      LAST NAME        BALANCE OWED

      XXXXX        XXXXXXXXXX     XXXXXXXXXXXXXX      -X,XX-.XX
      XXXXX        XXXXXXXXXX     XXXXXXXXXXXXXX      -X,XX-.XX
      XXXXX        XXXXXXXXXX     XXXXXXXXXXXXXX      -X,XX-.XX

                                    TOTAL          $XXX,XX$.XX
```

3. This assignment includes several parts.

    a) Create a physical file for Wexler University's student master file (file WUSTDP, in Appendix D). Key this file on student number and specify that keys be unique.

    b) Create a physical file for Wexler University's department file (WUDPTP, in Appendix D), keyed on department code.

    c) Enter records in both files, following the directions of your instructor.

    d) Create a multiple-record-format logical file based on the department file and the student master file, with formats keyed on department code, and department of major and earned credits, respectively.

    e) Use the logical file from part d as an input file to produce the report shown below. *Hint*: you will have to use control-break logic. You may assume that the student major has been validated so there will never be a student who does not belong within an existing department. However, there may be departments that

Programming Assignments Continued

Programming Assignments continued

do not currently have students enrolled in their programs. In that case, print the message shown in the printer spacing chart. Note that the date admitted should print in MM/DD/YY format.

```
          1         2         3         4         5         6         7         8         9
 123456789012345678901234567890123456789012345678901234567890123456789012345678901234567890

   XX/XX/XX              WEXLER U.  DEPARTMENTAL LISTING OF STUDENTS            PAGE XX0X


 DEPARTMENT                      STUDENTS
           SOC. SEC.     NAME: LAST       FIRST       CREDITS   GPA    DATE ADMIT.

 XXXXXXXXXXXXXXXXXXXX
           XXX-XX-XXXX   XXXXXXXXXXXXXX XXXXXXXXXX      X0X     0.XX     XX/XX/XX
           XXX-XX-XXXX   XXXXXXXXXXXXXX XXXXXXXXXX      X0X     0.XX     XX/XX/XX
           XXX-XX-XXXX   XXXXXXXXXXXXXX XXXXXXXXXX      X0X     0.XX     XX/XX/XX

 XXXXXXXXXXXXXXXXXXXX
           (NO MAJORS AT THIS TIME)

 XXXXXXXXXXXXXXXXXXXX
           XXX-XX-XXXX   XXXXXXXXXXXXXX XXXXXXXXXX      X0X     0.XX     XX/XX/XX
           XXX-XX-XXXX   XXXXXXXXXXXXXX XXXXXXXXXX      X0X     0.XX     XX/XX/XX
           XXX-XX-XXXX   XXXXXXXXXXXXXX XXXXXXXXXX      X0X     0.XX     XX/XX/XX
```

4. Wexler University wants you to put together a University Catalog that lists all the courses of all departments. The format of the catalog is shown below. You will need to do the following to generate the catalog:

   a) Create three physical files: one for the department file (WUDPTP), one for the course file (WUCRSP) and one for the course description file (WUCRSDSP). Appendix D describes the layouts of these files.

   b) Put records in the files, following your instructor's directions.

   c) Create a multiple-record-format logical file over the three physical files.

   d) Use the file to generate the catalog. You can assume that every course belongs to a department, and that every department offers at least one course. However, some courses may not have a description.

Start each department on a new page. Use the system year in the catalog heading. Each course is identified by a course identification consisting of the department code and the course number; the course title follows the identification.

Programming Assignments Continued

Programming Assignments continued

```
          1         2         3         4         5         6         7
1234567890123456789012345678901234567890123456789012345678901234567890
   XXØX
                   WEXLER UNIVERSITY CATALOG
                        19XX

DEPARTMENT
XXXXXXXXXXXXXXXXXXXX  CHAIR: XXXXXXXXXXXXXXXXXXXXXXXXXXX
      FOR INFORMATION CALL (XXX)XXX-XXXX OR VISIT ROOM XXXXXXXXXX


COURSES:
      XXXXXX  XXXXXXXXXXXXXXXXXXXXXXXXXX      X CREDITS
      XXXXXXXXXXXXXXXXXXXXXXXXXXXXXXXXXXXXXXXXXXXXXXX
      XXXXXXXXXXXXXXXXXXXXXXXXXXXXXXXXXXXXXXXXXXXXXXX
      XXXXXXXXXXXXXXXXXXXXXXXXXXXXXXXXXXXXXXXXXXXXXXX

      XXXXXX  XXXXXXXXXXXXXXXXXXXXXXXXXX      X CREDITS
      XXXXXXXXXXXXXXXXXXXXXXXXXXXXXXXXXXXXXXXXXXXXXXX
      XXXXXXXXXXXXXXXXXXXXXXXXXXXXXXXXXXXXXXXXXXXXXXX
      XXXXXXXXXXXXXXXXXXXXXXXXXXXXXXXXXXXXXXXXXXXXXXX
      XXXXXXXXXXXXXXXXXXXXXXXXXXXXXXXXXXXXXXXXXXXXXXX
      XXXXXXXXXXXXXXXXXXXXXXXXXXXXXXXXXXXXXXXXXXXXXXX

      XXXXXX  XXXXXXXXXXXXXXXXXXXXXXXXXX      X CREDITS
      XXXXXXXXXXXXXXXXXXXXXXXXXXXXXXXXXXXXXXXXXXXXXXX
      XXXXXXXXXXXXXXXXXXXXXXXXXXXXXXXXXXXXXXXXXXXXXXX
```

Chapter 6

File Access and Record Manipulation

Chapter Overview

This chapter introduces you to RPG's operations for reading, writing, and updating records. You will learn both sequential and random file access techniques. The chapter also discusses file maintenance — adding, deleting, and changing records in a file — and record locking considerations in update procedures.

Operations for Input Files

File access refers to how records can be retrieved, or read, from an input file. RPG offers several alternative operations for accessing data from full procedural database files. Several of these operations are appropriate for sequential processing; you can use others for random access processing.

Sequential Access

In **sequential access**, records are retrieved in either key order, if the file is keyed and so noted in position 31 on the File Specifications, or in arrival or FIFO order (First-In-First-Out) for non-keyed files. Reading generally starts with the first record in the file, with each subsequent read operation retrieving the next record in the file until eventually you reach end-of-file. This kind of sequential access is especially suited for batch processing.

READ (Read a Record)
As you know, the READ operation retrieves records sequentially. A file name in factor 2 designates which file the READ accesses. An indicator in positions 58-59 comes on to signal end-of-file when the READ finds no additional records in the file.

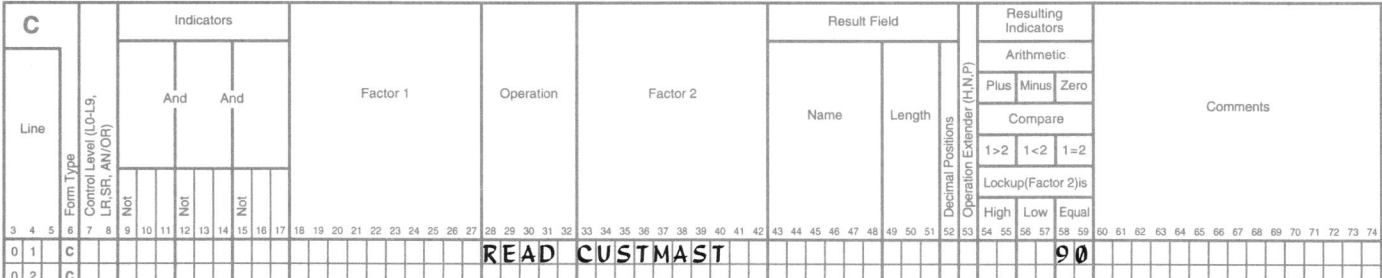

For externally described files, factor 2 can actually be a record-format name, rather than a file name. However, if the read encounters a record format different from that named in factor 2 — as could be the case when the input file is a logical file with multiple formats — the operation ends in error. You optionally can code an indicator in positions 56-57 to detect such errors and appropriately handle them, as shown below, or you can use other error-handling techniques (discussed in Chapter 9).

C		Indicators					Factor 1	Operation	Factor 2	Result Field				Resulting Indicators			Comments
			And	And						Name	Length			Arithmetic			
														Plus	Minus	Zero	
Line	Form Type	Control Level (L0-L9, LR,SR, AN/OR)	Not	Not	Not							Decimal Positions	Operation Extender (H,N,P)	Compare			
														1>2	1<2	1=2	
														Lookup(Factor 2)is			
														High	Low	Equal	
0 1	C							READ	CUSTREC1						80	90	
0 2	C		*IN80					IFEQ	*ON								
0 3	C							EXCPT	ERROR								
0 4	C							ENDIF									
0 5	C																

If your program does not include some way to handle this kind of error, however, the program will terminate before reaching its normal ending point after issuing an error message. (This kind of abnormal ending is often called an **abend**). Accordingly, unless you have a specific reason for reading a record format, rather than the file, and unless you explicitly want to include an error handler, you are better off using a file name as factor 2.

RPG/400 includes additional operations that provide variations on sequential record access. Some of these operations control where in the file sequential reading will next occur, while others determine the nature of the reading itself.

SETLL (Set Lower Limit)

The SETLL (Set Lower Limit) operation provides flexibility related to where sequential reading occurs within a file. SETLL allows you to begin sequential processing at a record other than the first one in the file. It also can be used to reposition the file once end-of-file has been reached. The general format of a SETLL is:

C		Indicators								Result Field				Resulting Indicators			
			And	And	Factor 1	Operation	Factor 2			Name	Length			Arithmetic			Comments
Line														Plus	Minus	Zero	
														Compare			
														1>2	1<2	1=2	
	Form Type	Control Level (L0-L9, LR,SR, AN/OR)	Not	Not	Not				Decimal Positions	Operation Extender (H,N,P)				Lookup(Factor 2)is			
														High	Low	Equal	
0 1	C					Factor1	SETLL	Factor2									
0 2	C																

SETLL positions a file at the first record whose *key* is greater than or equal to the value specified in factor 1. Factor 1 can be a literal, field name, figurative constant, or KLIST (discussed shortly). Factor 2 can be a file name or record format name (if the file is externally described). Notice that no indicator is required in conjunction with this operation. You can, however, use any or all three resulting indicator positions, if you wish. Each indicator position signals a different outcome of the SETLL operation.

An indicator in the High (HI) position (54-55) comes on if the value of factor 1 is greater than the highest key in the file. An indicator in the Low (LO) position (56-57) comes on if some system error occurs upon execution of the operation. An indicator in the Equal (EQ) position (58-59) comes on if a record is found in the file whose key exactly matches the value of factor 1.

The SETLL does *not* actually retrieve a record; it simply positions the file to determine what record the next sequential read will access. An unsuccessful SETLL causes the file to be positioned at end-of-file.

SETLL has two common uses in RPG programming. The first is to reposition the file to the beginning during processing by using figurative constant *LOVAL as factor 1. The next sequential read operation then retrieves the first record in the file.

C		Indicators								Result Field				Resulting Indicators			
			And	And	Factor 1	Operation	Factor 2			Name	Length			Arithmetic			Comments
Line														Plus	Minus	Zero	
														Compare			
														1>2	1<2	1=2	
	Form Type	Control Level (L0-L9, LR,SR, AN/OR)	Not	Not	Not				Decimal Positions	Operation Extender (H,N,P)				Lookup(Factor 2)is			
														High	Low	Equal	
0 1	C					*LOVAL	SETLL	CUSTMAST									
0 2	C						READ	CUSTMAST								90	
0 3	C																

The second common use of SETLL is to position the file to the first record of a group of records with identical key values preparatory to processing that group of records. (Details of this use are described in conjunction with the READE operation.)

You also can use SETLL to determine whether or not a record exists in a file without actually reading it. If you simply need to check for the presence of a record with a given key, without accessing the data contained in the record, using a SETLL is more efficient than doing a READ operation.

C		Indicators						Factor 1	Operation	Factor 2		Result Field				Resulting Indicators				Comments
			And		And							Name	Length			Arithmetic				
																Plus	Minus	Zero		
Line																Compare				
																1>2	1<2	1=2		
																Lookup(Factor 2)is				
			Not		Not		Not									High	Low	Equal		
0 1	C							CUSTNO	SETLL	CUSTMAST								10		
0 2	C							*IN10	IFEQ	*ON										
0 3	C								EXSR	CUSFND										
0 4	C								ELSE											
0 5	C								EXSR	NOCUS										
0 6	C								ENDIF											
0 7	C																			

SETGT (Set Greater Than)

The SETGT operation works similarly to SETLL. The primary difference is that this operation positions the file to a record whose key value is *greater* than the value of factor 1, rather than greater than or equal to the value of factor 1.

C		Indicators						Factor 1	Operation	Factor 2		Result Field				Resulting Indicators				Comments
			And		And							Name	Length			Arithmetic				
																Plus	Minus	Zero		
Line																Compare				
																1>2	1<2	1=2		
																Lookup(Factor 2)is				
			Not		Not		Not									High	Low	Equal		
0 1	C							Factor1	SETGT	Factor2										
0 2	C																			

Like the SETLL operation, factor 1 can be a field, literal, figurative constant or KLIST; factor 2 can be a file name or record format name. Like SETLL, SETGT does not require the use of resulting indicators. You can, however, include indicators in the HI and/or LO positions. An indicator in the HI position (54-55) comes on with SETGT if the positioning is *not* successful (in which case the file would be positioned at end-of-file); an indicator in the LO position (56-57) comes on if an error occurs during the operation. You cannot use an indicator in the EQ position (58-59) with the SETGT operation.

To understand the value of this operation, assume you have a logical file over your orders file, keyed on order date in YYMMDD format, and you want to generate a report of orders from the last six months of 1992. By using the SETGT operation with June 30 as the factor 1 value, the system will position the file to the first record of July, regardless of what date that happens to be. The code below illustrates this example.

Line	Form Type	Control Level (L0-L9, LR,SR, AN/OR)	And Not	And Not	Not	Factor 1	Operation	Factor 2	Result Field Name	Length	Decimal Positions	Operation Extender (H,N,P)	Plus	Minus	Zero	1>2	1<2	1=2	High	Low	Equal	Comments
0 1	C					920630	SETGT	ORDERS														
0 2	C						READ	ORDERS													90	
0 3	C					*IN90	DOWEQ	*OFF														
0 4	C						...															
0 5	C						READ	ORDERS													90	
0 6	C						ENDDO															
0 7	C						...															
0 8	C																					

SETGT also is used with *HIVAL to position the file to end-of-file preparatory to a READP operation (discussed in the next section). Remember that a SETGT, like a SETLL, merely positions the file; it does not actually retrieve a record from the database.

READE (Read Equal Key)

The READE sequentially reads the next record in a full procedural file if the key of that record matches the value in factor 1. If the record's key does not match, or if the file is at end-of-file, the indictor you specify in the EQ position (58-59) comes on. The operation requires an indicator in this position. You may also use an indicator in the LO position (56-57) to signal the occurrence of an error during the operation.

Factor 1 can be a field, literal, figurative constant, or KLIST name (KLISTs are described later in this chapter). Factor 1 also may be omitted, provided that the file previously has been positioned using SETLL, SETGT, READ, READE (with factor 1 specified), or other input-related operations that position the file. Factor 2 may be a file name or record-format name.

Programmers use this operation within a loop to identically process sets of records with duplicate keys in a file. Programmers often precede the first READE with a SETLL operation to position the file initially, preparatory to processing those records with keys identical to that specified by the SETLL.

Assume, for example, that you want to list all orders received on a specific date, and that the order file is keyed on date. Further assume that the date whose orders are to print is stored in field INDATE. The following processing would be appropriate:

C		Indicators			Factor 1	Operation	Factor 2	Result Field			Resulting Indicators	Comments

```
Line  Form Type
0 1 C              INDATE      SETLLORDERS                          50
0 2 C        *IN50             IFEQ *ON
0 3 C              INDATE      READEORDERS                          90
0 4 C        *IN90             DOWEQ*OFF
0 5 C                          EXCPTORDLN
0 6 C              INDATE      READEORDERS                          90
0 7 C                          ENDDO
0 8 C                          ELSE
0 9 C                          EXCPTNOORDS
1 0 C                          ENDIF
1 1 C
```

The code above uses the value of INDATE to position the ORDERS file to a key value that matches that of INDATE. If the match exists, indicator 50 comes on. If indicator 50 is on, the program does an initial READE of the file and then sets up a loop with DOW; within the loop the program uses EXCPT to write an order line and then reads the next equal record. The loop continues as long as the READE is successful. If the initial SETLL failed (signaled by indicator 50 remaining off), flow bypasses the loop, drops down to the ELSE, and writes a "no orders" line using EXCPT.

READP (Read Prior Record) and REDPE (Read Prior Equal)
The READP and REDPE operations are sequential reading operations that have their parallels in READ and READE, respectively. The only difference between READP and READ, and between REDPE and READE, is directionality; the PRIOR operations move "backwards" through the file. You do not use a factor 1 entry with READP; a factor 1 entry is optional for REDPE, subject to the same constraints as READE. Both PRIOR operations require a factor 2 entry, which may be a file or record-format name.

Like READ and READE, both READP and REDPE *require* the use of an indicator in the EQ position (58-59). This indicator comes on at beginning-of-file for the READP, or when the key of the prior sequential record does not match the factor 1 value for REDPE. With both operations, you have the option to use an indicator in the LO position (56-57) to signal an error.

You must first position the file with some input operation before using READP or REDPE with a blank factor 1. Programmers often use a SETGT for this initial positioning before beginning the reverse transversal through the file.

The concept of "backwards" sequential access is relatively easy to grasp; it is harder to visualize why such processing might be desired. Let's consider an example to get a sense of when these operations might be appropriate.

Imagine the following scenario. As part of an order-processing program, the program is to assign order numbers sequentially. Each day the program is run, the number assigned to the first order number is to be one larger than the number of the last order processed the previous day. Assume also that the order file is keyed on order number. The following code will determine the appropriate starting value for the day's orders.

C		Indicators			Factor 1	Operation	Factor 2		Result Field				Resulting Indicators			Comments

```
01 C           *HIVAL      SETGTORDERS
02 C                       READPORDERS                              90
03 C           *IN90       IFEQ *OFF
04 C                       ADD  1            ORD#
05 C                       ELSE
06 C                       EXSR ERROR
07 C                       ENDIF
08 C
```

In the above code, SETGT positions the file at end-of-file. The **READP** operation retrieves the last record in the file (e.g., the record with the highest order number). Adding 1 to ORD#, then, gives you the value for the first new order of the day.

In general, the PRIOR read operations might be used any time you want to process files in descending key order, since ordinarily the AS/400 organizes keyed files in sequence by ascending key value.

Random Access

All the operations discussed so far in this chapter have dealt with retrieving database records sequentially. Often, however, you want to be able to read a specific record, determined by its key value, without having to read through the file sequentially to reach that record. This kind of access is called **random access**. Random access lets you "reach into" a file and extract just that record you want.

CHAIN (Random Retrieval from a File)
RPG supports random access of full procedural database files through the CHAIN operation. CHAIN requires a factor 1 entry. The literal or data item name of factor 1 contains the key value of the record to be randomly read.

Factor 2, also required, contains the name of the file (or record format) from which the record is to be randomly retrieved. A required indicator in the HI position (54-55) comes on if the random read is *unsuccessful*, that is, if no record in the file matches the specified key value of factor 1. You have the option of including an error indicator in the LO position (56-57).

C	Form Type	Control Level (L0-L9, LR,SR, AN/OR)	Indicators			Factor 1	Operation	Factor 2	Result Field		Decimal Positions	Operation Extender (H,N,P)	Resulting Indicators			Comments
			And	And					Name	Length			Arithmetic / Compare / Lookup			
Line			Not	Not	Not								Plus Minus Zero / 1>2 1<2 1=2 / High Low Equal			
3 4 5	6	7 8	9 10 11	12 13 14	15 16 17	18 19 20 21 22 23 24 25 26 27	28 29 30 31 32	33 34 35 36 37 38 39 40 41 42	43 44 45 46 47 48 49 50 51		52	53	54 55 56 57 58 59		60 61 62 ... 74	
0 1	C					CUSTNO	CHAIN	CUSTMAST					90			
0 2	C					*IN90	IFEQ	*ON								
0 3	C						EXSR	NOREC								
0 4	C						ELSE									
0 5	C						EXSR	RECFND								
0 6	C						ENDIF									
0 7	C															

In the example shown above, CUSTNO contains the key value of the CUSTMAST record you want to read. If the CHAIN does not find a record with that key value, indicator 90 comes on and the program executes subroutine NOREC; if the record is found, indicator 90 stays off and the program executes subroutine RECFND.

When the file contains records with duplicate keys, such that more than one record would qualify as a match, the system retrieves the first record that matches.

If the CHAIN is successful (signaled by the resulting indicator remaining *OFF), the system positions the file to the record immediately following the retrieved record. Accordingly, issuing a READ or READE to the file following a successful CHAIN results in sequentially accessing the file starting with the record *immediately following* the CHAINed record. Because of this, the CHAIN operation can be used to position the file in a manner similar to SETLL. The primary difference between these two approaches is that a successful CHAIN actually reads a record, whereas a successful SETLL merely repositions the file without retrieving a record.

If a CHAIN operation is unsuccessful, it cannot be followed with a sequential read operation without first successfully repositioning the file with another CHAIN, SETLL, or SETGT operation.

Referencing Composite Keys

As discussed in Chapter 5, both physical and logical files can have keys based on more than one field. This kind of key is called a **composite** or **concatenated key**. The existence of composite keys raises a puzzling question: What can you use as a factor 1 search argument for CHAIN, SETLL, READE, etc., when the records in the file you are trying to access are keyed on more than a single field value? That is, how can you indicate a corresponding composite value in a single data-item entry? RPG solves this problem with the KLIST operation.

KLIST (Define a Composite Key) and KFLD (Define Parts of a Key)
The KLIST operation allows you to define a field for accessing records based on a composite key. Factor 1 specifies the name you wish to give the KLIST. No entries other than factor 1 are used with KLIST.

At least one KFLD operation must immediately follow a KLIST operation. Each KFLD entry declares a field that is to participate in the concatenation; the field is entered as the result field of the operation. The order in which the KFLDs are listed determines the order in which they are concatenated to form the KLIST.

To understand how to form and use KLISTs, consider the following example. Assume you have a database file of student grades, STUDGRDS, which contains one record per student per course taken. The records contain four fields — STUDNO, CRSENO, GRADE, and SEMSTR — and the file has a composite key based on STUDNO, SEMSTR, and CRSENO. You are writing a program that requires you to randomly access the STUDGRDS file to retrieve a grade that a given student received in a given class. The student, semester, and course you want to find are stored in fields STUD, SEM, and CRSE, respectively.

Line	Form Type	Control Level (L0-L9, LR,SR, AN/OR)	And Not	And Not	And Not	Factor 1	Operation	Factor 2	Name	Length	Decimal Positions	Operation Extender (H,N,P)	Resulting Indicators			Comments
0 1	C					STUCRS	KLIST									
0 2	C						KFLD		STUD							
0 3	C						KFLD		SEM							
0 4	C						KFLD		CRSE							
0 5	C						...									
0 6	C					STUCRS	CHAIN STUDGRDS						90			
0 7	C						...									
0 8	C															

In the above example, STUCRS is the KLIST name that stores the combined values of student number (STUD), semester (SEM), and course (CRSE). That KLIST is then used to chain to the STUGRDS file.

The KFLDs may have, but do not need to have, the same names as those of the file records' composite key. However, each KFLD field must agree in length, type, and decimal positions with the field it corresponds to in the file's composite key. Each KFLD is associated with a composite key field based on the ordinal positions of the corresponding fields. That is, the first KFLD field is matched to the first (or high-order) field of the composite key, and so on.

KLIST and KFLD are declarative operations, providing definitions rather than executable operations. You can declare a KLIST anywhere within a program, but it is good programming practice to include it at the beginning of the calculations or as part of an initialization subroutine. You can use the same KLIST name to access different database files — provided it is appropriate to do so. You can also use one KLIST multiple times to access the same file within a program. A KLIST name can serve as the factor 1 value in CHAIN, READE, REDPE, SETLL, SETGT, and DELET operations.

Partial Key Lists

KLIST offers an additional feature that makes processing groups of logically associated records relatively simple. Use the example above, but this time instead of wanting information about a grade for one course for one student, assume you want to be able to access *all* the records in STUDGRDS for a particular student for a given semester, perhaps to print out his/her grades earned that semester.

Line	Form Type		Indicators And Not	And Not	And Not	Factor 1	Operation	Factor 2	Result Field Name	Length			Resulting Indicators	Comments
0 1	C					* Define partial KLIST.								
0 2	C					STUK	KLIST							
0 3	C						KFLD		STUD					
0 4	C						KFLD		SEM					
0 5	C					* Use KLIST to access correct student and semester.								
0 6	C					STUK	CHAINSTUDGRDS						90	
0 7	C					*IN90	IFEQ *OFF							
0 8	C					* Loop through records for that student/semester.								
0 9	C					*IN90	DOWEQ*OFF							
1 0	C						EXSR PRTGRD							
1 1	C					* READE fails when no more records for that student/semester.								
1 2	C					STUK	READESTUDGRDS						90	
1 3	C						ENDDO							
1 4	C						ELSE							
1 5	C						EXSR NOTFND							
1 6	C						ENDIF							
1 7	C													
1 8	C													

The above code accomplishes the desired processing. First, it defines KLIST STUK with only the student number and semester as the KFLDs of the list. STUK, then, is a partial KLIST, since the file it will be used with is keyed on a composite of student number, semester, and course number.

Using STUK, the program chains to the STUDGRDS file to read the first course for the given student in the given semester. If the CHAIN is successful (signaled by indicator 90 remaining off), the program sets up a loop that continues until indicator 90 comes on. Within the loop, the program executes subroutine PRTGRD to print grades and then executes a READE to bring in the next course for the student being processed. If the original CHAIN fails, control drops to the ELSE and the program executes subroutine NOTFND to indicate that the student/semester was not in the file.

Note that the same effects could have been achieved by issuing a SETLL to position the file and then, provided the operation was successful, using a READE to read the first record of the set. A successful CHAIN reads a record and positions the file to the desired location in one operation.

RPG/400 allows you to access a database file based on a partial key list, provided the portion you want to use is the major, or high-order, key field(s). That is, given STUDGRDS keyed on STUDNO + SEMSTR + CRSENO, we can access the records with a partial key of student, or student and semester, but not with a partial key of course or semester. Thus, we can get a list of all courses for a given student, but not a list of all students who have taken a given course; the database file would need to be keyed differently to allow this kind of access.

Operations for Output Files

The operations we've looked at so far are appropriate for input files. A few I/O operations deal with output — that is, writing records to database files. Until now, the output of your programs has been reports. You may also designate a database file as program output. The File Specification entries in this case require the filename in positions 7-14, the type, O for output, in position 15, E in position 19 (assuming the file is externally described), K in position 31 (if the file is accessed via a key) and DISK, the device specification, in positions 40-46.

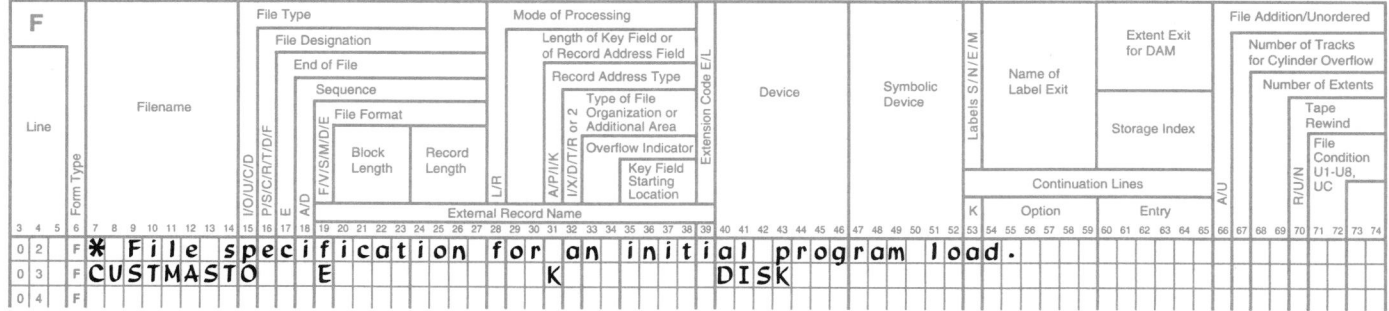

You may need to make one additional entry to the File Specifications, depending on whether your program is performing an initial file load — that is, putting records into the file for the first time — or adding records to a file that already contains records. If you are adding records to an output file that already contains records, you must signal that fact by entering an A in position 66 of the File Specification, as shown below.

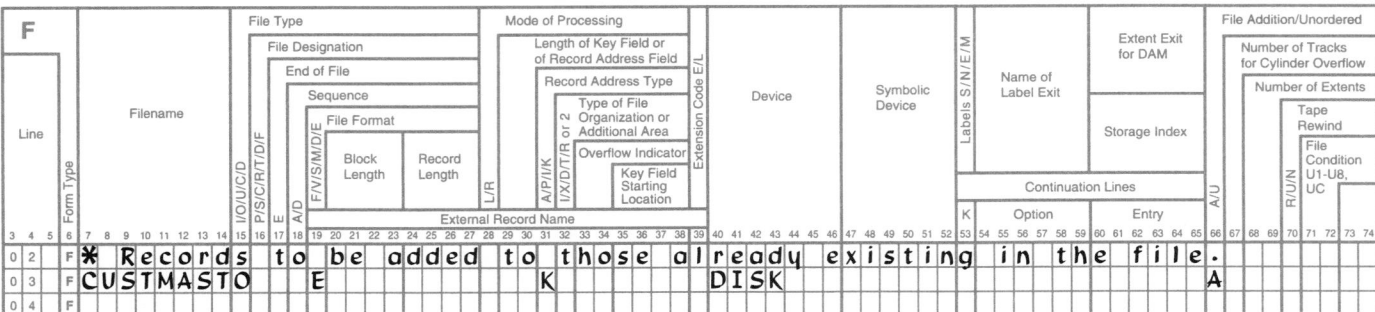

Once you have defined a database file as output, two RPG operations allow you to output records to the file: EXCPT and WRITE.

EXCPT (Calculation Time Output)

You already have used the EXCPT operation to write to printer files; EXCPT also can be used to write records to a database file. The form of the EXCPT statement that is used to write to database files is no different than the form used for printer files.

The EXCPT operation optionally can designate a named E line on the output. When the program reaches the EXCPT operation, it writes the named E line(s) (if the EXCPT includes a line name in factor 2) or all unnamed E lines (if the EXCPT operation appeared alone on the Calculation Specification) from the Output Specifications.

In the Output Specifications, you need to enter the record format name of the externally described file, rather than the file name itself, in positions 7-14. Then list either all the fields comprising the record, or simply *ALL. Omitting a field or fields from the list causes zeros or blanks, depending on the data type, to be written to the record for that field. Rather than listing all the fields, you can simply code *ALL, which has the same effect as including all the field names.

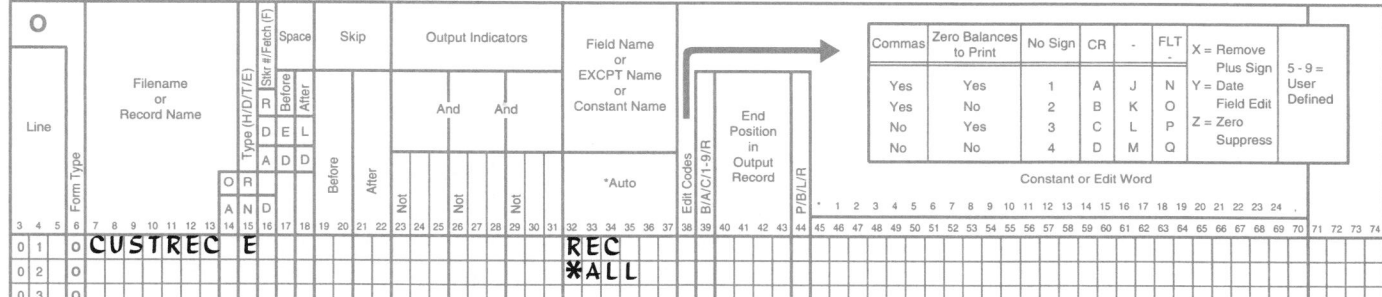

The above code examples show how you could write records to the customer file for an initial file load. If you want to add records to records already in a file, in addition to entering an A in position 66 of the File Specification, you need to include an ADD entry in positions 16-18 of the Output Specification E line, as shown below.

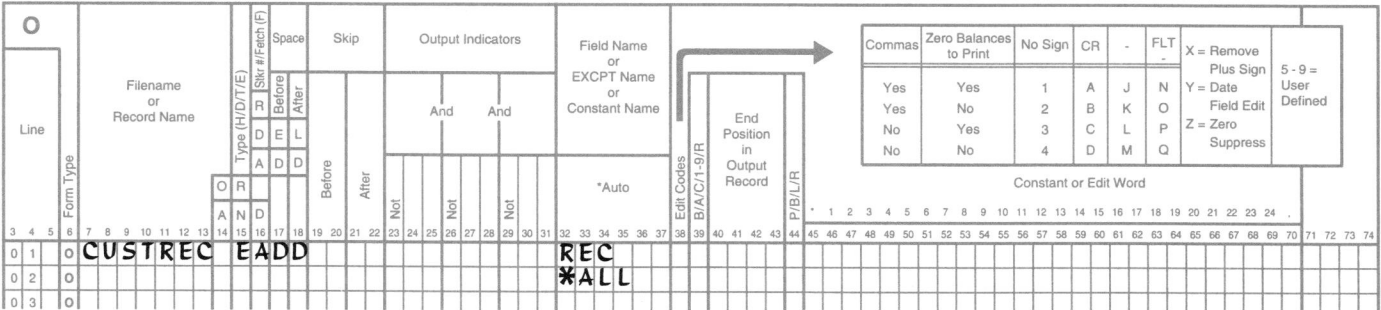

Today's RPG programmers generally output database records more directly in their calculations by using the WRITE operation. The WRITE operation must designate a record-format name, rather than a file name. If the writing is adding records to a file that already contains records, the A in position 66 of the File Specification for that file is required.

C			Indicators						Result Field			Resulting Indicators				

The specification form with columns for Line, Form Type, Control Level (L0-L9, LR,SR, AN/OR), And (Not), And (Not), Factor 1, Operation, Factor 2, Result Field (Name, Length), Decimal Positions, Operation Extender (H,N,P), Resulting Indicators Arithmetic (Plus, Minus, Zero), Compare (1>2, 1<2, 1=2), Lookup(Factor 2)is (High, Low, Equal), Comments.

0 1	C															
0 2	C						WRITECUSTREC									
0 3	C															
0 4	C															

With a WRITE operation, the current program values for all the fields comprising the record definition are written to the file. You may include an optional indicator in the LO position (56-57) for this operation to signal an error.

Update Files and I/O Operations

A common data processing task is file maintenance. File maintenance, or updating, involves adding or deleting records from database files, or changing the information in database records, to keep the information current and correct. Records that do not exist cannot be changed or deleted; if a file has unique keys, a second record with the same key should not be added to the file. Accordingly, file maintenance routines typically require first determining whether or not the record exists in the file (through a CHAIN or SETLL), and then determining what update option is valid, given the record's found status.

RPG includes an update file type, signaled by U in position 15 of the File Specifications, which allows you to read, change, and then rewrite records to the file, as well as to add and delete entire records. Any database file can be used as an update file simply by coding it as such on the File Specifications. If the maintenance procedure involves adding new records, you need to signal that fact on the File Specifications by entering an A (for Add) in position 66.

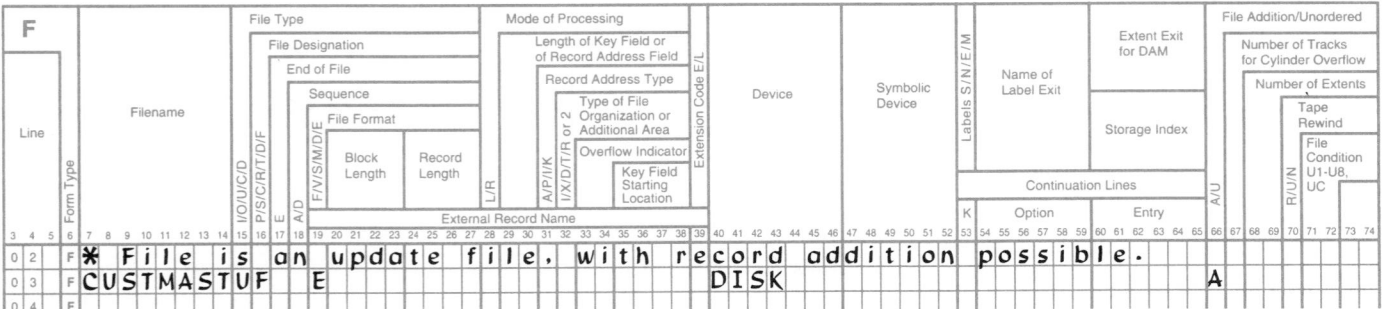

An update file supports both input and output operations. If you define a file as an update full procedural file, you can use all the input operations discussed so far — CHAIN, READ, READE, REDPE, READP, SETLL, and SETGT — to access records in the file. You also can use KLIST for externally described update files. If you defined the file for add capability (the A on the File Specifications), you can use the WRITE operation to add new records to the file. Two additional I/O operations exist that can be used only for update files: DELET and UPDAT.

DELET (Delete Record)

The DELET operation deletes a single record from the file specified in factor 2. Factor 2 can be a file name or, if the file is externally described, a record-format name. The use of factor 1 is optional. If you leave factor 1 blank, the system deletes the record most recently read. If you use factor 1 to specify which record is to be deleted, you may enter a field name, a literal, or a KLIST name. If duplicate records based on the factor 1 value exist in the file, the system deletes only the first record.

An entry in factor 1 requires the use of an indicator in positions 54-55. This indicator comes on if the record to be deleted is not found in the file. An optional indicator in the LO position (56-57) signals other error conditions.

Line	Form Type	Control Level (L0-L9, LR,SR, AN/OR)	Not	And Not	And Not	Factor 1	Operation	Factor 2	Name	Length	Decimal Positions	Operation Extender (H,N,P)	1>2 / High	1<2 / Low	1=2 / Equal	Comments
0 1	C					* This code deletes the record of customer 100 if the record										
0 2	C					* exists in the file.										
0 3	C						MOVE	'100'	CUSTNO							
0 4	C					CUSTNO	CHAIN	CUSTMAST					90			
0 5	C					*IN90	IFEQ	*OFF								
0 6	C						DELET	CUSTMAST								
0 7	C						ENDIF									
0 8	C					* The 2 lines below produce the same result.										
0 9	C						MOVE	'100'	CUSTNO							
1 0	C					CUSTNO	DELET	CUSTMAST					90			
1 1	C															

Note that if you use the DELET with factor 1 blank without first retrieving a record from the file, you will get a system error message. The DELET operation logically deletes records from a file, rather than physically removing them. Although as a result of DELET, a record is no longer accessible to programs or queries, the record actually remains on disk until the file containing the deleted record is reorganized.

UPDAT (Modify Existing Record)

The UPDAT operation modifies the record most recently read. You can use this operation only with files defined for update. This operation does not use factor 1; factor 2 must contain a record-format name, not a file name, if the file is externally described. Moreover, your program must have success- fully completed a READ, READE, READP, REDPE, or CHAIN operation retrieving that record format before it executes an UPDAT.

UPDAT causes the current program values of all the record's fields to be rewritten to the file. You cannot issue multiple UPDATs for a single read operation.

C		Indicators			Factor 1	Operation	Factor 2	Result Field			Resulting Indicators	Comments

```
0 1   C * Retrieve the customer record, add current invoice amount
0 2   C * to customer's balance due and rewrite the record to the
0 3   C * file. If customer is not in file, perform error routine.
0 4   C           CUSTNO    CHAINCUSTMAST                        90
0 5   C           *IN90     IFEQ *OFF
0 6   C                     ADD  INVAMT    BALDUE
0 7   C                     UPDATCUSTREC
0 8   C                     ELSE
0 9   C                     EXSR ERROR
1 0   C                     ENDIF
1 1   C
```

Updating through EXCPT

The UPDAT operation rewrites *all* of a database record's fields to a file. In the above example, the current value of BALDUE *and every other field in CUSTREC* is incorporated into the record by the UPDAT. If your program logic has resulted in changes in field values that you do not wish to be updated, you can use EXCPT to designate which fields are to be rewritten.

```
C   Indicators       Factor 1      Operation  Factor 2        Result Field          Resulting Indicators
01 C* Retrieve the customer record, add current invoice amount
02 C* to customer's balance due, and rewrite via EXCPT.
03 C* If customer is not in the file, perform error routine.
04 C          CUSTNO     CHAIN CUSTMAST                        90
05 C          *IN90      IFEQ  *OFF
06 C                     ADD   INVAMT      BALDUE
07 C                     EXCPT CUPDAT
08 C                     ELSE
09 C                     EXSR  ERROR
10 C                     ENDIF
11 C
```

```
O
01 O* Only the balance due field is updated; other fields retain
02 O* whatever values they originally had when the record was read.
03 OCUSTREC  E                     CUPDAT
04 O                               BALDUE
05 O
```

File and Record Locking

Any multiuser system needs to address the problems related to simultaneous use of the same database file. Otherwise, it is possible that if two users access the same record for update, make changes in the record, and then rewrite it to the file, one of the user's changes might get lost — a condition sometimes called **phantom updates**. Two approaches you can use to deal with this type of problem are **file locking** and **record locking**.

The easiest kind of locking is to limit access to a file to one user at a time — a condition known as file locking. Although OS/400 permits you to lock files at a system level by issuing CL commands, most of the time you want to allow multiple users access to the same files at the same time. RPG/400 includes built-in, automatic locking features at a record level.

If your program designates a file as an update file, RPG/400 automatically places a lock on a record when it is read within your program. Updating that record or reading another record releases the record from its locked state. While the record is locked, other application programs can access that record if they have defined the file as an input file, but not if they, too, have defined the file as an update file. This solution eliminates the problem of lost updates.

However, record locking can cause waiting and access problems for users if programmers don't structure their code to avoid locks except when absolutely necessary. The nightmare scenario you should keep in mind when designing update programs is that of the user who keys in a request to update a record, pulls up the screen of data preparatory to making changes in the record, and then realizes it's lunch time and disappears for two hours. Meanwhile, the record lock prevents all other users from accessing that record.

A common solution programmers have used to avoid this problem has been to read the record to obtain its field values and then immediately write an exception line to that record format with no fields listed. This exception output would release the record from its locked state. Then, once the program had obtained all needed update values, it would again read the same record and immediately update that record with the new values.

More recently (V2R2 of OS/400), IBM has added enhancements to RPG to deal more easily with this record-locking problem. First, by coding N in position 53 (the half-adjust position) of the Calculation Specification associated with an input operation, you can specify that the input operation to an update file be done without locking the record. You can use this feature with READ, READE, READP, REDPE, and CHAIN to avoid unnecessary locking. Second, if you've read a record with a lock and want to release the lock, you can use the operation UNLCK. UNLCK, followed by the file name in factor 2, releases all locks to that file.

C			Indicators				Operation		Factor 2	Result Field			Resulting Indicators			Comments

```
0 1  C* Random  read  with  no  lock.
0 2  C            CUSTNO      CHAINCUSTMAST                    N90
0 3  C                        ...
0 4  C* Random  read  with  lock.
0 5  C            CUSTNO      CHAINCUSTMAST                     90
0 6  C                        ...
0 7  C* Release  record  lock.
0 8  C                        UNLCKCUSTMAST
0 9  C
```

If you start releasing record locks in update procedures, however, be aware that you can easily code yourself right back into the phantom-update problem that caused systems to incorporate record-locking in the first place.

If you aren't including some provision for checking to make certain that another user has not updated a record between the time you first accessed the record and the time you are about to rewrite the record with the values from your program, leave all record locking in place.

Beyond record-locking considerations, generally accepted programming practice dictates that a program should not keep a file open any longer than it needs to access the required data from the file. RPG automatically opens your files at the beginning of processing and then closes them all at the end of processing. If your program needs access to a file for only a portion of its total running time, you should take control of the file opening and closing, rather than allowing RPG to manage those tasks for you.

RPG includes two operations to give you this capability: OPEN and CLOSE.

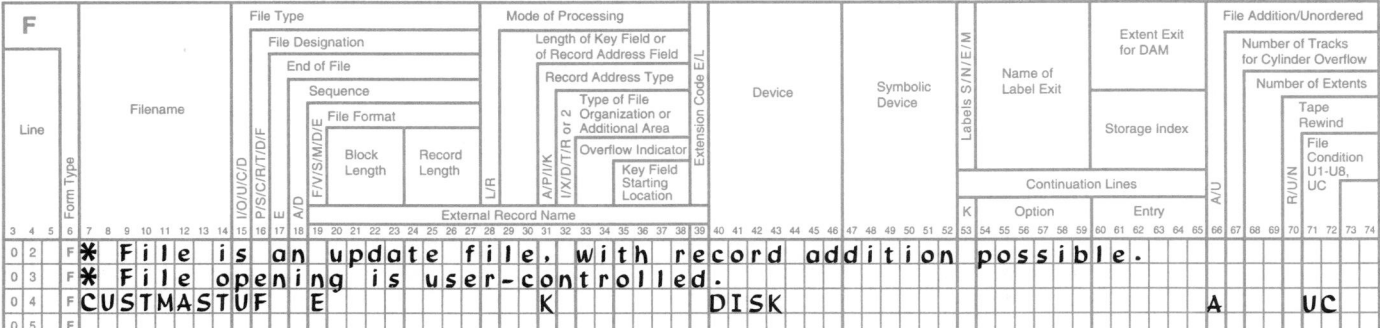

You can CLOSE a file that RPG has opened automatically. If you want to control the file opening with the OPEN operation, you must make an additional entry — UC (User Control) in positions 71-72 of the File Description for the file you wish to open.

Line	Operation	Factor 2
0 1	OPEN	CUSTMAST
0 2	...	
0 3	CLOSE	CUSTMAST
0 4		

Line	
0 2	* File is an update file, with record addition possible.
0 3	* File opening is user-controlled.
0 4	CUSTMASTUF E K DISK A UC
0 5	

Trying to open a file already open causes an error. However, you can open a given file more than once within a program, provided the file is closed prior to each successive open.

I/O Errors

Many of the I/O operations discussed above use resulting indicators to signal commonly expected results of the operation, such as reaching end-of-file, or CHAINing to a record not in the file. All the operations include the optional use of an indicator to detect errors of input or output, such as trying to read a record locked by another program, or issuing a read to a record format not next in the file. You can trap such errors as part of your operation by including an indicator in the LO resulting indicator position (56-57).

Line	Form Type	Control Level (L0-L9, LR,SR, AN/OR)	Indicators						Factor 1	Operation	Factor 2	Result Field			Resulting Indicators		Comments
			And		And							Name	Length	Decimal Positions			
0 1	C									UPDAT	CUSTREC					80	
0 2	C								*IN80	IFEQ	*ON						
0 3	C									EXSR	ERROR						
0 4	C									ENDIF							
0 5	C																

Chapter 9 will show you additional ways to detect these and other kinds of errors. Errors not handled by a program cause the program to end abnormally (abend). Abends upset users and operators and often result in frantic phone calls to the programmer, usually at 3 a.m. Good, defensive programmers always design programs to minimize the possibility of errors and then trap for unexpected errors to ensure their reputations and minimize middle-of-the-night wake-up calls.

Chapter Summary

In this chapter you learned many I/O operations appropriate to input, output, and update files. READ, READE, READP, and REDPE are input operations used to access records sequentially from a full procedural file whose type is declared as input or update. SETLL and SETGT can be used to position the file prior to a sequential read operation. CHAIN randomly retrieves a record and also positions the file for subsequent sequential reading, if desired.

The KLIST and KFLD operations allow you to position the file or retrieve a record based on a composite key. By using a partial KLIST, you can initiate access to sets of records that share a common value on the first field(s) of a composite key.

You can use WRITE or EXCPT to put records into an output file or an update file. Operations UPDAT and DELET are specific to update files. You cannot UPDAT a record without having first read it.

The AS/400 includes built-in record locking to prevent the problem of phantom updates. Techniques —including use of the UNLCK operation — exist to minimize record locking, but they should not be used if their implementation might cause lost updates to occur.

You have read about a large number of operations dealing with input and output. Although it is not difficult to remember what each operation does, it is hard to keep from confusing what indicator goes where to signal what, and whether the operation uses a file name or a record-format name. The table that follows summarizes the operations for you, to help you see more clearly the differences among the operations and to serve as a quick reference as you are writing your programs.

Summary Table of RPG/400 I/O Operations

File Types	Factor 1	Operation	Factor 2	Result	Indicators		
					HI	LO	EQ
I,U	—	**READ**	FILE/RFMT	dtastr	—	err	EOF
I,U	flck	**READE**	FILE/RFMT	dtastr	—	err	EOF
I,U	—	**READP**	FILE/RFMT	dtastr	—	err	BOF
I,U	flck	**REDPE**	FILE/RFMT	dtastr	—	err	BOF
I,U	FLCK	**SETLL**	FILE/RFMT	—	nr	err	eq
I,U	FLCK	**SETGT**	FILE/RFMT	—	nr	err	—
I,U	FLCK	**CHAIN**	FILE/RFMT	dtastr	NR	err	—
O,U	—	**WRITE**	RFMT	dtastr	—	err	—
O,U	—	**EXCPT**	ename	—	—	—	—
U	—	**UPDAT**	RFMT	dtastr	—	err	—
U	flck	**DELET**	FILE/RFMT	—	nr	err	—
I,O,U	—	**OPEN**	FILE	—	—	err	—
I,O,U	—	**CLOSE**	FILE	—	—	err	—
I,U	NAME	**KLIST**	—	—	—	—	—
I,U	—	**KFLD**	—	FIELD	—	—	—

Uppercase = required entry; lowercase = optional entry.

Indicators: eof = end-of-file; bof = beginning-of-file; nr = no record; err = error; eq = equal match found.

flck	May be a field, literal, constant, or KLIST.
FILE/RFMT	May be a file name or a record format name (for externally described files).
RFMT	Must be a record format name for externally descibed files.
FILE	Must be a file name.
dtastr	Data structure — used only with program-described files.
ename	Exception line name on output.

Terms

abend
composite key
concatenated key

file access
file locking
phantom updates

random access
record locking
sequential access

Discussion/Review Questions

1. Describe the difference between sequential and random record retrieval.

2. What does "position the file" mean?

3. What are the differences between the SETGT and SETLL operations?

4. Since READE and REDPE imply reading records with matching keys, would you ever use them in programs accessing files with UNIQUE keys? Explain your answer.

5. When is it appropriate to use a READE, as opposed to a READ operation?

6. When can you omit an A in position 66 of the File Specification of an output file? Why don't you need this A on printer files?

7. What does the term "file maintenance" mean? What kinds of files are likely to need maintenance?

8. Is there any difference possible in the results when you update a file with EXCPT rather than UPDAT?

9. Since designating a file type as update allows you maximum flexibility in which I/O operations you can use with that file, why don't programmers designate all their files as update files, just in case? That is, why bother with input and output files?

10. What is the difference between a file lock and a record lock? Which technique do you think is easier for an operating system to implement? Why? Which technique is preferable from a user standpoint? Why?

11. What is defensive programming? What defensive programming technique is described in this chapter? Name several other ways to be a defensive programmer.

Exercises

1. Assume you had a logical file of customers, CUSTL, keyed on zip code. Write the Calculation Specifications that would allow you to print an exception line CUSLIN for every customer whose zip code matched ZIPIN. If no customers have that zip code, print exception line NOCUST.

2. Your company sequentially assigns a unique customer number to each new customer. Assume customer file CUSTP is keyed on customer number,

field CUSTNO. Write the Calculation Specifications necessary for determining what number should be assigned to the next new customer.

3. You have a sales file, SALESP, keyed on a composite key of store, department, and salesman. (Duplicate keys are present, since each record represents a single sale.) Write the Calculation Specifications needed to total all the sales for a given department within a given store. Field DEPT contains the

Exercises Continued

Exercises continued

desired department, field STORE the store. The sales field that you want to accumulate is SLSAMT. Modify your code so that it totals all the sales of the store represented in STORE.

4. Write the File Specifications and Calculation Specifications needed to allow you to randomly retrieve a customer in file CUSTP based on the customer number in CUSTNO, subtract PAYMNT from BALDUE, and rewrite the record. Execute subroutine NOCUST if the customer is not found in the file.

5. You have a transaction file TRANS of records to be added, deleted, or changed in the CUSTP master file. The CODE field of the transaction record contains an A, D, or C, denoting whether the record is to be added, deleted, or changed, while the number of the customer to add, delete, or change is contained in transaction field CUSTNO. Write the File Specifications and Calculation Specifications that will allow you to appropriately process each record in the transaction file. Add is a valid option if the customer does not already exist in CUSTP; Change or Delete is valid only if the customer does exist in CUSTP. Execute subroutine ADDREC for valid adds, CHGREC for valid changes, and DELREC for valid deletions; for all invalid transactions, execute subroutine ERROR. (Don't code the details of these subroutines; stop at the point of coding the EXSR statements.)

Programming Assignments

1. GTC Telephone Company wants a program to update its Customer Master File (GTCSTP) based on data contained in the Payments Transaction File (GTPAYP). Data files are described in Appendix D. For each record in the payment file, randomly retrieve the appropriate customer, subtract the payment amount from amount owed, change the date of last payment field, and rewrite the customer record. Also prepare the audit report shown below. Notice that if a customer in the payment file is not found in the customer file, an error notation should appear on the report.

```
           1         2         3         4         5         6
 1234567890123456789012345678901234567890123456789012345678901
  XX/XX/XX      GTC PAYMENTS PROCESSED   PAGE XXØX
                     AUDIT REPORT

    CUSTOMER       DATE RECEIVED      AMOUNT

  (XXX)XXX-XXXX      XX/XX/XX       X,XXØ.XX
  (XXX)XXX-XXXX      XX/XX/XX       X,XXØ.XX ERROR
  (XXX)XXX-XXXX      XX/XX/XX       X,XXØ.XX

                     TOTAL      XXX,XXØ.XX

     XØX CUSTOMERS NOT IN MASTER FILE
```

Programming Assignments Continued

Programming Assignments continued

2. CompuSell wants a program that will generate purchase orders for those items in the inventory file that need reordering — that is, if their quantity on hand is less than or equal to their reorder point. For any inventory item that meets this criterion and that has not already been reordered (the reorder code field is still blank), include that item on a purchase order and rewrite the record to the inventory file with an R in the reorder code field to signal that it has been reordered.

   Only one purchase order should be completed per supplier — that is, all items to be purchased from the same supplier should appear on the same purchase order. The format of the purchase order is shown below. Note that the item number is the *supplier's* product number, not CompuSell's. The unit cost is the current cost figure and the quantity is the reorder quantity in the inventory file.

   You will need to use data from CompuSell's Inventory File (CSINVP) and Supplier File (CSSUPP), described in Appendix D. You will also need to create a logical file so that the inventory records can be processed in supplier number order.

```
          1         2         3         4         5         6         7         8
 12345678901234567890123456789012345678901234567890123456789012345678901234567890

        XX/XX/XX                    COMPUSELL
                                  5260 HAWORTH
                             KALAMAZOO  MI  49008-0010

    PURCHASE ORDER TO:

     SUPPLIER: XXXXXXXXXXXXXXXXXXXXXXXXXX  CONTACT: XXXXXXXXXXXXXXXXXXXXXXXXXXXXXXXXXX
               XXXXXXXXXXXXXXXXXXXXX                 (XXX)XXX-XXXX
               XXXXXXXXXXXXXXX  XX XXXXX-XXXX

     ITEM NUMBER       DESCRIPTION           UNIT COST      QTY        EXTENSION
      XXXXXXXX   XXXXXXXXXXXXXXXXXXXXXXXXXX   X,XX0.XX      X,X0X    XX,XXX,XX0.XX
      XXXXXXXX   XXXXXXXXXXXXXXXXXXXXXXXXXX   X,XX0.XX      X,X0X    XX,XXX,XX0.XX
      XXXXXXXX   XXXXXXXXXXXXXXXXXXXXXXXXXX   X,XX0.XX      X,X0X    XX,XXX,XX0.XX

                                             ORDER TOTAL    $XXX,XXX,XX0.XX


                  AUTHORIZED SIGNATURE_____
```

3. CompuSell wants you to write a program to process goods received from suppliers. As ordered goods are received from suppliers, the items are added to inventory and a record of the item received is added to the Goods Received file CSRCVP. The contents of this file are then run in batch to update the Inventory file, CSINVP. Appendix D describes these files. Note that you will need to create a logical file to access the records in CSINVP by supplier product ID.

   For each item in CSRCVP, the following changes must be made in the corresponding record of CSINVP: a) the quantity on hand must be changed to reflect the additional goods; b) the reorder code should be changed to spaces; c) if the current charge from the supplier is not identical to the current and average cost stored in the inventory file, two changes must be made. First, the Inventory file's current cost must be changed to reflect the new cost. Second, the average cost must be recalculated and updated.

Programming Assignments Continued

Programming Assignments *continued*

To calculate new average cost, multiply the old average cost by the old quantity on hand, add this to the cost of the items that have just come in, and divide by the new total quantity on hand. Thus, if you had 10 units in stock with an average cost of $3 and received 20 more units at a cost of $4, the new average cost would be $(10*3 + 20*4)/30 = \$3.67$.

In addition to updating the Inventory file, your program should produce the following report to serve as an audit trail of the updating. Note that if there is an error in an item number in CSRCVP, so that a corresponding item does not exist in CSINVP, that fact should be noted on the report printing two special lines, as shown. The second line contains an image of the problem record from CSRCVP.

```
         1         2         3         4         5         6         7         8
1234567890123456789012345678901234567890123456789012345678901234567890123456789 0

   XX/XX/XX              COMPUSELL INVENTORY UPDATE REPORT           PAGE XX0X
                           RECEIVED GOODS PROCESSED


SUPPLIER    ITEM    QTY    NEW QTY    OLD         NEW        OLD AVG.    NEW AVG.
  ID         NO    RCVD    ON HAND    COST        COST        COST        COST

XXXXXXXX   XXXXX   XX0X     XX0X    X,XX0.XX    X,XX0.XX    X,XX0.XX    X,XX0.XX
XXXXXXXX   XXXXX   XX0X     XX0X    X,XX0.XX    X,XX0.XX    X,XX0.XX    X,XX0.XX
XXXXXXXX   ITEM NOT FOUND IN INVENTORY FILE; RECHECK SUPPLIER ID
           XXXXXXXXXXXXXXXXXXXXX   RECORD NOT PROCESSED
XXXXXXXX   XXXXX   XX0X     XX0X    X,XX0.XX    X,XX0.XX    X,XX0.XX    X,XX0.XX
```

4. Wexler University wants you to write a program that will generate a transcript of completed courses for each student in the transcript request file WUTRANSP. This program will also require the use of the Student Master File (WUSTDP), the Course File (WUCRSP) and the Earned Credits File (WUCRDP). All files are described in Appendix D.

Note that the line showing graduation date and degree granted should print only if the student has, in fact, graduated, as signaled by non-blank values in those fields of the student's master record.

Courses should be listed in chronological order. Note that under semester, the school wants WIN to print for semester code 1, SUM for semester code 2, and FAL for semester code 3; the right-most XX represents the year the course was taken.

```
         1         2         3         4         5         6         7         8
1234567890123456789012345678901234567890123456789012345678901234567890123456789 0
                   WEXLER UNIVERSITY OFFICIAL TRANSCRIPT
                        DATE ISSUED: XX/XX/XX

STUDENT:   XXXXXXXXXXXXXXX XXXXXXXXXX    DATE ADMITTED: XX/XX/XX
           XXX-XX-XXXX                   MAJOR: XXX

           CREDITS EARNED: X0X           GRADE POINT AVERAGE: 0.XX
           GRADUATED:  XX/XX/XX          DEGREE GRANTED: XXX

      COURSE        TITLE               SEMESTER    CREDITS     GRADE
      XXXXX   XXXXXXXXXXXXXXXXXXXXXXXXX   XXX XX        X          XX
      XXXXX   XXXXXXXXXXXXXXXXXXXXXXXXX   XXX XX        X          XX
      XXXXX   XXXXXXXXXXXXXXXXXXXXXXXXX   XXX XX        X          XX
```

Programming Assignments Continued

Programming Assignments continued

5. Wexler University wants you to write a program that will generate class lists to distribute to all instructors. The class lists should be formatted as shown in the following printer spacing chart. Because these lists are sent to the instructors, begin each instructor's list on a new page. You will need to access data from several files to obtain the output: the Current Enrollment file (WUENRLP), the Student Master file (WUSTDP), the Current Sections File (WUSCTP), the Course File (WUCRSP), and the Instructor File (WUINSTP). These data files are described in Appendix D. Follow your instructor's directions for accessing these files of data. *Hint:* You will need to use logical files to solve this problem.

```
          1         2         3         4         5         6         7
1234567890123456789012345678901234567890123456789012345678901234567890
                   WEXLER U. CLASS LIST—19XX

INSTRUCTOR: XXXXXXXXXXXXXXX DEPT: XXX

   DEPT  COURSE   TITLE                    CREDITS    SECTION
   XXX    XXX    XXXXXXXXXXXXXXXXXXXXXXXXX     X       XXXXX

         STUDENT                 SOC. SEC.   DCODE     MAJOR
   XXXXXXXXXXXXXXX XXXXXXXXXX    XXX-XX-XXXX    X        XXX
   XXXXXXXXXXXXXXX XXXXXXXXXX    XXX-XX-XXXX    X        XXX
   XXXXXXXXXXXXXXX XXXXXXXXXX    XXX-XX-XXXX    X        XXX

             SECTION ENROLLMENT: X0X STUDENTS

   DEPT  COURSE   TITLE                    CREDITS    SECTION
   XXX    XXX    XXXXXXXXXXXXXXXXXXXXXXXXX     X       XXXXX

         STUDENT                 SOC. SEC.   DCODE     MAJOR
   XXXXXXXXXXXXXXX XXXXXXXXXX    XXX-XX-XXXX    X        XXX
   XXXXXXXXXXXXXXX XXXXXXXXXX    XXX-XX-XXXX    X        XXX
   XXXXXXXXXXXXXXX XXXXXXXXXX    XXX-XX-XXXX    X        XXX
   XXXXXXXXXXXXXXX XXXXXXXXXX    XXX-XX-XXXX    X        XXX

             SECTION ENROLLMENT: X0X STUDENTS
```

Chapter 7

Interactive Applications

Chapter Overview

In this chapter you will learn how to define display files and use them to develop interactive applications.

Batch and Interactive Programs

So far, the applications you have written were designed to run in batch. In **batch processing**, once a program begins to run, it continues to execute instructions without human intervention or control. Most batch applications in the business environment involve processing one or more transaction files sequentially; the programs end when the transaction files reach end-of-file.

Interactive applications, in contrast, are user driven. As the program runs, a user at a workstation interacts with the computer — selecting options from menus, entering data, responding to prompts, and so on. The sequence of instructions the program executes is determined in part by the user; the program continues until the user signals (s)he is ready to quit.

This dialogue between the user and the computer is mediated through what, on the AS/400, are called **display files**. Display files define the screens that the program presents as it runs. Display files allow values keyed by the user in response to the screen to be input as data to the program. Thus, display files serve as the mechanism that allows the user and program to interact.

Display Files

Display files are defined externally to the program that uses them. The procedure for creating a display file is similar to the procedure followed for creating a physical or logical file. You code display files on DDS Specification Sheets, enter the specifications using SEU to create a source member (with type DSPF), and then compile the source code to create an object.

Display files include entries at a file, record, and field level, just like database and printer file definitions. File-level entries appear at the very beginning of the definition, and apply to all the record formats within the file. Record-level entries are associated with a single record format, while field-level entries are coded for specific fields or constants within a record format. Each record format defines what is written to or read from the workstation in a single I/O operation. On an output operation, the record may fill an entire screen with prompts and/or values, or, on an input operation, the record may read in several values keyed in from the workstation.

Unless you make special provisions, only one screen displays at a time. When a different record format is written, the first screen is erased prior to the display of the second.

As an introduction to DDS coding for display files, consider the following situation: A school identifies each of its semester offerings through a section number. For each section, the school stores information about the course this section is associated with, the days and time it meets, the assigned room, the section enrollment, and the instructor. This data is stored in a file SECTIONS; its physical file definition is shown below.

		Name	Length	Data Type	Decimal Positions		Functions
A	R	SECTREC					
A		SECTNO	5				TEXT('Section Number')
A		DAYS	3				TEXT('Days class meets')
A		BEGTIM	4	0			TEXT('Time class starts')
A		ROOM	4	0			TEXT('Classroom')
A		ENROLL	3	0			TEXT('Current enrollment')
A		INSTR	15				TEXT('Section Instructor')
A		COURSE	6				TEXT('Course Identifier')
A	K	SECTNO					

The school wants a simple online inquiry program that will allow a user to enter a section number and display information about that section. The input, or entry, screen for this application is shown on the following page.

```
                                  Section Inquiry
         Type value, then Enter.

             Section number . . _____




         F3=Exit
```

The DDS of the display-file record format needed to produce the above screen is shown below.

	Form Type	And/Or/Comment (A/O/*)		Conditioning				Name Type (B/R/K/S/O)	Reserved	Name		Reference (R)	Length		Data Type (B A/P/S/B A/S/X/Y/N/I/W)	Decimal Positions	Usage (B/O/I/B/H/I/M)	Location		Functions
Sequence Number			Not (N)	Indicator	Not (N)	Indicator	Not (N)	Indicator											Line	Pos	
	A								R	SECT1											
	A																				CA03(03 'F3=Exit')
	A																		1	28	'Section Inquiry'
	A																		3	2	'Type value, then Enter.'
	A																		5	5	'Section number . .'
	A								SECTN				5A		I			5	24	
	A																		23	2	'F3=Exit'
	A																				

Notice that each record format begins with an identifier, an R in position 17, followed by a name for that format, in this case, SECT1, beginning in position 19. Below the record format line appear all the fields and literals that are to make up that format. You must indicate the location of each literal and field on this screen by specifying the screen line on which it is to appear (in positions 39-41) and its *starting* column position within that line (coded in positions 42-44).

Code the literals themselves, such as 'Section Inquiry', in positions 45-80 of the DDS line. You must enclose them in apostrophes.

You enter field names left-adjusted in positions 19-28. Each field needs an assigned usage, coded in position 38. Usage codes include I for input, O for output, or B for both input and output. SECTN, the only field part of the sample definition, is an input field, since its value is to be entered by the user and read by (input to) the program. Its usage is I.

You must further define each field by specifying its length in positions 30-34, data type in position 35, and decimal positions in positions 36-37 (if a numeric field).

Actually, column 35 for display files is more appropriately called data type/keyboard shift, because it allows many more possible values than are permitted for field definitions of physical files. These additional values affect the **keyboard-shift attribute** of different workstations to limit what characters the user can enter. Although a complete description of allowable values is beyond the scope of this text, four commonly used values are described below:

A (Alphanumeric shift): used for character fields; puts keyboard in lower shift, allows any character to be entered.

X (Alphabetic only): used for character fields; allows only A-Z, commas, periods, dashes, and spaces to be entered; lowercase letters sent as uppercase.

S (Signed numeric): used for numeric fields; allows digits 0-9; no signs; use Field- key to enter a negative value.

Y (Numeric only): can enter digits 0-9, plus or minus signs, periods, commas, and spaces.

One very important distinction between S and Y is that Y allows the use of edit codes and edit words to be associated with the field, while S does not.

Because this application treats SECTN as a character field, a decimal-position entry is not appropriate. Type is A, or character; we could have omitted the A, since A is the default type for character fields. The default type for numeric fields is S, unless you associate an edit code or word with that field; in this latter case, the system assumes a default value of Y.

The line below the record format definition, CA03(03 'F3 = Exit'), establishes a connection between function key F3 and the 03 indicator. When coding interactive applications, indicators communicate between the screen and the program that uses the screen. Control generally returns from the screen to the program when the user presses the Enter key or a function key that has been assigned a special meaning. In this screen, for instance, the user is prompted to press F3 to exit the program. But because the function key cannot be referenced directly within an RPG program, an indicator must serve as a mediator.

The DDS line CA03(03 'F3 = Exit') accomplishes three things. First, the CA03 portion establishes F3 as a valid command key in this application; only those function keys explicitly referenced within the DDS are valid, or enabled, during program execution. Second, the 03 within the parentheses associates indicator 03 with F3, so that when F3 is pressed, indicator 03 comes on. Although you can associate any indicator (01-99) with any function key, it makes good programming sense to associate a function key with its corresponding numeric indicator to avoid confusion. And finally, by referencing the function key as CA (Command Attention) rather than CF (Command Function), the code is saying to return control to the program without the input data values (if any) that the user has just entered. If the line were coded CF03(03 'F3 = Exit'), control would return to the program *with* the input data.

The information within apostrophes — 'F3 = Exit' — serves only as documentation. You could omit it (e.g., code only CA03(03)) without affecting how the screen functions. Good programming practice, however, suggests including such documentation.

We can now look at the design of the second screen the application needs. It's an information screen, or panel, to display the requested information. The specific values shown are to give you a sense of what the screen might look like when the program is running.

```
          Section Information

Section number . . . . . . 12435
Course . . . . . . . . . . BIS350
Instructor . . . . . . . . Johnson
Room . . . . . . . . . . . 1120
Meets on days  . . . . . . MWF
Starting time  . . . . . . 10:30
Enrollment . . . . . . . . 36




Press Enter to continue.

F3=Exit  F12=Cancel
```

This screen will require a second record format within the display file. The DDS for this record format is shown on the following page.

Form Type	Condition Name	Name	Reference (R)	Usage	Line	Pos	Functions
A							REF(SECTIONS)
A		R SECT2					
A							CA03(03 'F3=Exit')
A							CA12(12 'F12=Cancel')
A					1	10	'Section information'
A					3	2	'Section number . . . . . .'
A		SECTNO	R	O	3	29	
A					4	2	'Course . . . .'
A		COURSE	R	O	4	29	
A					5	2	'Instructor . . . .'
A		INSTR	R	O	5	29	
A					6	2	'Room . . . .'
A		ROOM	R	O	6	29	
A					7	2	'Meets on days . . . . .'
A		DAYS	R	O	7	29	
A					8	2	'Starting time . . . . .'
A		BEGTIM	R	O	8	29	
A					9	2	'Enrollment . . . .'
A		ENROLL	R	O	9	29	
A					21	2	'Press Enter to continue.'

Form Type	Condition Name	Name	Reference (R)	Usage	Line	Pos	Functions
A					23	2	'F3=Exit'
A					23	11	'F12=Cancel'
A							

The above code represents a "bare bones" record format to describe the screen. Note that the fields represented are given an O, for Output, usage. That's because their values are going to be sent from the program to the screen. Instead of including length and decimal-position entries, these field entries contain an R in position 29. This R (for Reference) signals that the fields are defined elsewhere, and that their definitions can be obtained from that source. The source, in this case, is the file SECTIONS, as indicated by the first line containing keyword REF, followed by the file name in parentheses. REF is a file-level keyword that should appear at the beginning of the DDS specifications, *prior* to *any* record-format definitions.

If you define a field through referencing, and if the referenced database field includes an edit code or edit word associated with it in the database file, that editing is automatically incorporated into the display file. (If the referenced field is unedited, or if the field is defined within the display file itself, you can add editing within the display file, as discussed later in this chapter.)

Notice that record format SECT2 enables F12, as well as F3. The AS/400 uses F12, Cancel, to signal that the user wants to back up to the previous screen, while F3, Exit, always means exit the entire application.

Putting the two format definitions together completes the DDS for the display file, called SECTINQR.

Page 1 of 2

```
      A                                                      REF(SECTIONS)
      A          R SECT1
      A                                                      CA03(03 'F3=Exit')
      A                                                 1 28'Section Inquiry'
      A                                                 3  2'Type value, then Enter.'
      A                                                 5  5'Section number . .'
      A            SECTN            5A  I             5 24
      A                                                23  2'F3=Exit'
      A          R SECT2
      A                                                      CA03(03 'F3=Exit')
      A                                                      CA12(12 'F12=Cancel')
      A                                                 1 10'Section Information'
      A                                                 3  2'Section number . . . . . . .'
      A            SECTNO     R                    O   3 29
      A                                                 4  2'Course . . . . . . . . . .'
      A            COURSE     R                    O   4 29
      A                                                 5  2'Instructor . . . . . . . .'
      A            INSTR      R                    O   5 29
      A                                                 6  2'Room . . . . . . . . . . .'
      A            ROOM       R                    O   6 29
```

Form Type	Name	Reference (R)	Usage	Line	Pos	Functions
A				7	2	'Meets on days . . . .'
A	DAYS	R	O	7	29	
A				8	2	'Starting time . . . . . .'
A	BEGTIM	R	O	8	29	
A				9	2	'Enrollment . . . .'
A	ENROLL	R	O	9	29	
A				21	2	'Press Enter to continue.'
A				23	2	'F3=Exit'
A				23	11	'F12=Cancel'

Before looking at some of the many additional features available for defining display files, let's develop the section inquiry program to see how display files are used in interactive programs. Recall that the user wants to enter a section number to request section information from the SECTIONS file. The program should display the retrieved information on the screen. The user may then enter another section number or signal that (s)he is finished by pressing F3.

In writing the program, you must define the display file, like any other kind of file, on the File Specifications. Display files are full procedural, externally described files. However, because the concept of "key" is not applicable to this kind of file, leave position 31 blank. What about type? You have worked with Input files, Output files, and Update files. Display files represent a new type: Combined. A **combined file** supports both input and output, but as independent operations. You cannot update a combined file. Finally, the device is WORKSTN. Below are the complete file specifications for the section inquiry program.

Line	Form Type	Filename	File Type	File Designation	File Format	Mode of Processing	Device
02	F	SECTIONS	I	F	E	K	DISK
03	F	SECTINQR	C	F	E		WORKSTN
04	F						

Because both the files are externally described, the program will have no input specifications, nor output specifications, for that matter. The only portion of the program left to code is the Calculation Specifications. Before jumping into this coding, however, it pays first to think through the logic of a solution. Interactive programs are extremely prone to "spaghetti coding," primarily because flow of control is less straight line; depending on which function key a user presses, you may need to repeat, back up, or early-exit out of different routines.

The present program will need to loop until the user presses F3 in response to either screen 1 or screen 2. If the user presses F12 at screen 2 to back up, that effectively is the same in this program as hitting the Enter key, because in both cases the user should next see screen 1 again.

A rough solution written in pseudocode is shown below.

```
WHILE user wants to continue (no Exit)
    Display first screen
    Obtain user's response to the screen
    IF user wants to continue (no Exit)
        Random read section file to get section info
        IF record found
            Display second screen
            Obtain user's response
    ENDIF
ENDIF
ENDWHILE
```

You can easily develop the RPG calculations from the pseudocode, except that you don't know how to send screens of data to the user or read user input. The allowable operations for screen I/O are WRITE, READ, and EXFMT (Execute Format). All three operations require a record-format name in factor 2.

The READ operation sends control to the currently displayed screen, waits for the end of user input (signaled by the user's pressing either the Enter key or any other enabled special keys), and returns control to the program. The WRITE operation displays a screen and returns control to the program without waiting for user input.

EXFMT combines the features of WRITE and READ; it first writes a record to the screen and then waits for user input to that screen. When the user has finished inputting, the system reads the data back from the screen and returns control to the program. Since in most screen I/O you want to display some information and then wait for a user response, EXFMT is the operation you will use most frequently in your interactive programs.

The figure on the following page shows an RPG implementation of the pseudocode solution to the section inquiry problem.

```
     C                        *IN03     DOWEQ*OFF
     C                                  EXFMTSECT1
     C                        *IN03     IFEQ *OFF
     C                        SECTN     CHAINSECTIONS                    90
     C                        *IN90     IFEQ *OFF
     C                                  EXFMTSECT2
     C                                  ENDIF
     C                                  ENDIF
     C                                  ENDDO
     C                                  MOVE *ON       *INLR
     C                                  RETRN
     C
```

In that code, indicator 03, which comes on when the user presses F3, controls the main program loop. Because the user can signal "Exit" at screen SECT1, the calculations need an IF following the return from the SECT1 screen to check for this possibility. Because the user may have keyed in a wrong section number, which would cause the CHAIN operation to fail (indicator 90 on), the program executes the information panel, SECT2, only if the chaining worked.

Additional DDS Keywords

Although the DDS definition for the example above would work, it represents a minimalist approach to screen design. It contains no "bells-and-whistles." More importantly, perhaps, as the DDS is presently coded, numeric fields would be displayed without editing, and information about a possible important program event — a section not found in the file — is not conveyed to the user. You can include these and other kinds of special effects by using keywords.

You already have been introduced to three keywords used with display files (REF, CAnn and CFnn). The AS/400 includes a long list of permissible keywords for display files to modify the screen's appearance or the screen/user interaction. This section discusses some of the major keywords. Refer to IBM's manual *Programming: Data Description Specifications Reference* (SC41-9620) for additional detail.

Keywords are always coded in positions 45-80 of the DDS specification form. Keywords apply at a file, record, or field level. Some keywords can be used with two levels, while others are appropriate to just one level. Where you code the keyword determines which level it is associated with.

File-Level Keywords

File-level keywords always must appear as the first lines in the DDS specifications, prior to any record-format information. If you have several file-level keywords, the order in which they are coded does not matter. You have already encountered one file-level keyword, REF, used to indicate a database file that contains definitions of fields used in the screen.

MSGLOC (Message Location) specifies the position of the message line for error and other messages. The keyword's format is MSGLOC(line-number). Without this keyword, the message-line position defaults to the last screen line (line 24 on a standard 24 x 80 screen).

The CAnn (Command Attention) and CFnn (Command Function) keywords, already discussed, enable the use of Function keys and associate the keys with program indicators. You can use as many function keys as are appropriate to your application by including a CAnn or CFnn keyword for each.

If you code these keywords at a file level, they apply to *all* the record formats within the file. Alternately, they can be associated with individual record formats, as in our example above. In that case, the keys are valid only during input operations for the screen or screens with which they are associated.

A commonly used file-level keyword is PRINT. This keyword enables the PRINT key during the interactive application to allow the user to print the current screen. Without this keyword, the print key is disabled. You can also use PRINT as a record-level keyword to enable the key for some screens but not others.

VLDCMDKEY is a file-level or record-level keyword used to turn on an indicator when the user presses any valid (enabled) command key. Note that command keys include any special key, such as the ROLLUP key, in addition to function keys. The format for this keyword is VLDCMDKEY(indicator ['text']). The indicator can be any numbered indicator (01-99); the text description is optional and serves only as documentation.

VLDCMDKEY is useful because it allows the program to differentiate between control returned as a result of the Enter key and control returned by any other key. You often need to set up separate logic branches based on this distinction.

Record-Level Keywords

Record-level keywords appear on the line on which the record format is named and/or on lines immediately following that line, *preceding* any field or literal definition. These kinds of keywords apply only to the screen with which they are associated. They do not carry over or influence other record formats defined within the file.

Keywords CAnn, CFnn, PRINT, and VLDCMDKEY, discussed above, can be used as record-level keywords, as well as file-level keywords. Keyword BLINK, on the other hand, is strictly a record-level keyword. BLINK causes the cursor to blink during the display of the record format with which it is associated.

OVERLAY is a record-level keyword specifying that the record format be displayed without clearing the previous display. OVERLAY works only when the record formats involved do not overlap lines on the screen.

Field-Level Keywords

A field-level keyword applies only to the specific field with which it is associated. A field can have several keywords. The first keyword appears on the same line as the field definition or on the line immediately following the definition, and each additional keyword is coded on a successive line. All keywords for a field must be coded before the next field definition line.

Two field-level keywords control the format of numeric output fields on the display: EDTCDE — Edit Code — and EDTWRD — Edit Word. Recall that only numerically defined fields may be edited, and that the field type specification in column 35 of the DDS must be Y or blank to use editing for a displayed field.

Edit codes and edit words match those used within RPG itself and have the same meaning as in RPG. EDTCDE's format is EDTCDE(edit-code [*|$]); the parentheses should contain a valid edit code, such as 1, optionally followed by a single * to provide asterisk protection or a single $ to supply a floating dollar sign. The format for EDTWRD is EDTWRD('edit-word'). To review RPG edit words and edit codes, see Chapter 2.

The following DDS sample shows the use of EDTWRD and EDTCDE.

A		Conditioning				Name		Length		Data Type / Decimal Positions / Usage		Location			Functions
	Form Type		Condition Name	Name Type	Reserved		Reference (R)					Line	Pos		
	A			R		SAMPLE									
	A					SOCSEC		9	Y 0 B			4	10		EDTWRD(' _ _ ')
	A					NAME		20	B			5	10		
	A					BILDAT		6	Y 0 B			6	10		EDTCDE(Y)
	A					AMTDUE		7	Y 2 B			7	10		EDTCDE(1 $)

Another field-level keyword, DSPATR, or Display Attribute, determines the appearance of fields on the screen. You can use DSPATR more than once for a given field, and you can include more than one attribute with the same keyword. The keyword is followed by parentheses containing the code(s) of the desired attribute(s). The following attributes can be assigned to all types of fields (Input, Output, or Both).

Attribute	Meaning
BL	Blinking field
CS	Column separator (a vertical bar separating each position within a field)
HI	High intensity
ND	Nondisplay (keyed characters don't appear on screen)
PC	Position cursor (position cursor to the first character of this field)
RI	Reverse image
UL	Underline

The sample code on the next page illustrates the use of **display attributes**. This sample is not intended to set a style standard to be followed, since a screen with so many "bells and whistles" would be distracting for the user. In general, use such features sparingly and consistently to draw attention to specific fields on the screen or to problems the user must deal with.

Sequence Number	Form Type	And/Or/Comment (A/O/*)	Not (N)	Indicator	Not (N)	Indicator	Not (N)	Indicator	Name Type (R/K/S/O)	Reserved	Name	Reference (R)	Length	Data Type (P/S/B A/S/X/Y/N/I/W)	Decimal Positions	Usage (O/I/B/H/M)	Line	Pos	Functions
	A								R		SAMPLE								
	A										SOCSEC		9Y		0	B	4	10	DSPATR(ND)
	A																		DSPATR(UL)
	A										NAME		20			B	5	10	DSPATR(BL UL)
	A										BILDAT		6Y			B	6	10	EDTCDE(Y)
	A																		DSPATR(RI)
	A																		DSPATR(PC HI BL)
	A																		

Another important set of field-level keywords concerns **data validation**. Every programmer should recognize the extreme importance of preventing invalid data from entering the system; corrupt data files can cause abnormal endings or incorrect processing. Although there is no way to completely ensure that values a user enters are correct, by validating data as tightly as possible, you can eliminate some kinds of errors.

The four major keywords used for validating user entry are VALUES, COMP, RANGE, and CHECK. Each allows you to place restrictions on what the user is allowed to enter. Violating these restrictions causes the system to display an appropriate error message on the message line and to display the field in reverse image to force the user to change the entered value.

The VALUES keyword allows you to specify the exact valid values allowed for this field. The keyword format is VALUES(value1 value2 ...). Up to 100 values can be entered. Character values must be enclosed in apostrophes.

The RANGE keyword allows you to specify a range within which the user's entry must fall to be considered valid. The format for this keyword is RANGE(low-value high-value). If you use the RANGE keyword with character fields, the low and high value must each be enclosed in apostrophes. The valid range includes the low and high value, such that the entered value must be greater than or equal to the low value and less than or equal to the high value to be considered valid.

COMP allows you to specify a relational comparison to be made with the user's entered value to determine validity. This keyword's format is COMP(relational-operator value). The relational operator can be one of the following:

Operator	Meaning
EQ	Equal to
NE	Not equal to
GT	Greater than
NG	Not greater than
LT	Less than
NL	Not less than
GE	Greater than or equal to
LE	Less than or equal to

CHECK is a field-level keyword that you can use for validity checking. Its format is CHECK(code [...]). That is, one or more validity checking codes can be associated with a single CHECK entry. Some of these validity codes are ME (Mandatory Enter), MF (Mandatory Fill), and AB (Allow blanks).

For Mandatory Entry fields, the user must enter at least one character of data (that character could be a blank); the user cannot simply bypass that field. Mandatory Fill specifies that each position in the field have a character in it. (A blank is considered a character.) AB provides the user with an override option for a field that fails a validity check. For example, if a field has a VALUES keyword associated with it and the user is not certain which value is appropriate to the record (s)he is entering, (s)he can simply enter blanks and the value will be accepted.

The CHECK keyword includes parameter values concerned with functions other than validity checking. CHECK(LC), for example, allows the user to enter lowercase letters (as well as uppercase) for character fields. Without this keyword, all user-entered alphabetic characters are returned to the program as uppercase.

This use of CHECK can appear at a field, record, or file level, depending on how broadly you want to enable lowercase data entry.

One field-level keyword of major importance is ERRMSG (Error Message). When an error message is in effect for a field, the message displays on the message line of the screen and the field with which it is associated appears on the screen in reverse image. The format for the ERRMSG keyword is ERRMSG('message text' [indicator]). If you include an indicator, that indicator is turned off as part of the input operation that follows the display of the error message. Error messages are useful for conveying information about program-processing problems to the user's screen.

Finally, two field-level keywords serve as built-in variables to display the date and/or time on the screen. TIME, entered as a keyword, along with a screen line and column position value, causes the system time to be displayed in HHMMSS format (hours, minutes, seconds). The time is displayed with default edit word '0ƀ:ƀƀ:ƀƀ' unless you specify an alternate display format. You can display the current date by using keyword DATE, along with a line and column entry. DATE appears as a six-position, unedited value unless you associate an edit code or word with it.

Conditioning Indicators

So far, field-level keywords have been discussed as though they are always in effect. However, if this were the case, many would be of little value. Why, for instance, would you want an error message to display each time a field appears on the screen? In fact, most individual field-level keywords can be conditioned by one or more indicators. The status of these indicators when the screen displays determines whether or not the keywords are in effect. Actually, not only can keywords be conditioned, but fields and literals also can be associated with indicators, to control whether or not the field or literal appears on the screen.

Moreover, you can use multiple indicators, in AND and/or in OR relationships, to condition screen events. You can include up to three indicators on a DDS line; these indicators are in an AND relationship with one another, such that all the indicators on the line would need to be on for the event they are conditioning to occur. If you need to use more than three indicators to control an event, you can signal an AND by coding A in position 7 of the DDS line.

If you want an event to occur if one of several indicators is on (i.e., you wish to express an OR relationship), code one indicator per line, with an O in position 7 of the second (and successive) lines; the keyword, field, or literal conditioned by these indicators should appear on the last line of the set.

```
A *Sample DDS showing the use of indicators.
A           R SAMPLE
A   10        FLDA          10      O  4 15
A  N10        FLDB          12      O  4 30
A             FLDC           5      O  6  5
A   20 25                              DSPATR(HI)
A   30
AO  40                                 DSPATR(UL)
A   10                              15  5'Indicator 10 is on'
A
```

In the code above, FLDA displays if indicator 10 is on, while FLDB displays only if indicator 10 is off. FLDC will always appear, but it will be displayed in high intensity only if indicators 20 and 25 are both on; it will be underlined if either indicator 30 or indicator 40 is on. The literal 'Indicator 10 is on' will display only if indicator 10 is, in fact, on.

Because indicators can be turned on or off as part of your program logic, they provide a way for program events to control screen display. For example, in our sample program, if the user-entered section number didn't exist in the SECTIONS file, it would be nice to not just return the user to the first screen, but to return with the erroneous section number in reverse video, with a message "Section not found" at the bottom of the screen, and with the cursor positioned on the field. We can easily cause that to happen by making a few changes in the first screen format. Because the program is already turning on indicator 90 when an unsuccessful chain occurs, we simply need to use indicator 90 to condition the ERRMSG keyword.

Seq	Form Type	Conditioning	Name Type	Name	Length	Ref	Data Type	Dec	Usage	Line	Pos	Functions
	A											REF(SECTIONS)
	A											PRINT
	A		R	SECT1								
	A											BLINK
	A											CA03(03 'F3=Exit')
	A									1	28	'Section Inquiry'
	A									3	2	'Type value, then Enter.'
	A									5	5	'Section number . .'
	A			SECTN	5A		B			5	24	
	A	N90										DSPATR(UL)
	A	N90										DSPATR(HI)
	A	90										ERRMSG('Section not found' 90)
	A									23	2	'F3=Exit'
	A		R	SECT2								
	A											CA03(03 'F3=Exit')
	A											CA12(12 'F12=Cancel')
	A									1	10	'Section Information'
	A									3	2	'Section number . . . .'
	A			SECTNO	R				O	3	29	
	A									4	2	'Course . . . .'

Seq	Form Type	Conditioning	Name Type	Name	Length	Ref	Data Type	Dec	Usage	Line	Pos	Functions
	A			COURSE	R				O	4	29	
	A									5	2	'Instructor . . . .'
	A			INSTR	R				O	5	29	
	A									6	2	'Room . . . .'
	A			ROOM	R				O	6	29	EDTCDE(Z)
	A									7	2	'Meets on days . . . .'
	A			DAYS	R				O	7	29	
	A									8	2	'Starting time . . . .'
	A			BEGTIM	R				O	8	29	EDTWRD(' 0: ')
	A									9	2	'Enrollment . . . .'
	A			ENROLL	R				O	9	29	EDTCDE(3)
	A									21	2	'Press Enter to continue.'
	A									23	2	'F3=Exit'
	A									23	11	'F12=Cancel'
	A											

Note that one of the changes includes changing the usage of SECTN to B(oth) so the erroneous section number will be returned to the screen. If indicator 90 is off, SECTN displays as an underlined field in bold, or high intensity. If 90 is on, the error message appears and the field automatically appears in reverse image. A few extra keywords were added to give the display file more functionality: PRINT (to enable the Print key) and BLINK (to cause the cursor to blink).

The only additions to record format SECT2 were to add editing to ROOM, DAYS, and ENROLL to achieve the format shown in the sample screen shown earlier in the chapter (page 173).

Interactive File Maintenance

A common data processing task is file maintenance — that is, adding, deleting, and changing records in a company's database files. Over the past decade an increasing amount of such updating has been implemented through interactive, rather than batch, processing.

In a typical updating program, the user specifies the key of a record and signals whether that record is to be added, changed, or deleted. Because businesses typically want key-field values to master records to be unique (e.g., they would not want the same customer number to be assigned to two customers), a user request to add a record with a key that matches the key of a record already in the file generally is handled as an error. Similarly, it is impossible to change or delete a record that does not exist in the file.

As a result, the first tasks of an updating program are to accept the user's update option request (add, delete, or change) and the key of the record to be maintained, and to check the file for the existence of a record with that key before giving the user the chance to actually enter data values.

A critical concern of interactive updates is how to detect invalid data entries to prevent corrupting the business' database files. On the AS/400, you have three methods of safeguarding against invalid data: by using validation keywords within the database definitions themselves, provided those fields are displayed for input and reference back to the database file; by including validation keywords within the display file; or by validating field values within the program, after they are read from the screen.

Some validation is handled automatically for you by the AS/400's operating system. For example, the system will not allow you to enter a nonnumeric value for a numerically defined field. Or, if you have specified type X for a character field, the system will permit alphabetic entries only. The use of validation keywords also automatically limits what the user can enter without the need for further programming on your part. For example, if you specify VALUES('A' 'C' 'D') for field CODE, attempts by the user to enter any other value will automatically cause an error message to appear on the bottom line of the screen and CODE to display in reverse video.

Always validate your data as tightly as possible, given the nature of the data. For some fields (e.g., name), the best you can do is ensure that the user enters some value, rather than skipping over the field; for other fields (e.g., sex code), you will be able to specify permissible values for the entered data. Never overlook validating data at any point where it enters the system.

To illustrate screen and program design for interactive updating, we will develop a program to update the university's SECTIONS file. To refresh your memory, the file definition is shown below.

Seq #	Form Type	A/O/C	Name Type	Name	Length	Dec Pos	Functions
	A		R	SECTREC			
	A			SECTNO	5		TEXT('Section number')
	A			DAYS	3		TEXT('Days class meets')
	A			BEGTIM	4	0	TEXT('Time class starts')
	A			ROOM	4	0	TEXT('Classroom')
	A			ENROLL	3	0	TEXT('Current enrollment')
	A			INSTR	15		TEXT('Section Instructor')
	A			COURSE	6		TEXT('Course Identifier')
	A		K	SECTNO			

The first screen of the application is shown on the following page. The user keys in a section number and an action code to specify whether (s)he wants to add, change, or delete the section.

```
                        Section File Maintenance

Type values, then Enter.

    Section number  . . _____
    Action Code   . . . _      A=Add
                               C=Change
                               D=Delete









F3=Exit
```

If the user tries to enter an invalid action code, an error message appears. If (s)he enters a section with an action code inappropriate for that section — that is, trying to add a section already in the file, or trying to change or delete a section *not* in the file — an appropriate error message appears on the screen.

If the user's entries are valid and appropriate, screen 2 displays, with blank fields if the user is in ADD mode, or with the field values from the selected record displaying if the mode is CHANGE or DELETE. A prompt appropriate to each mode displays at the bottom of the screen. Some data validation takes place as values are entered. When the user presses Enter, the program performs the appropriate action and then returns the user to the first screen. If the user presses F12 at the second screen, no maintenance is done for that record and the user returns to the first screen. Pressing F3 at the second screen causes a program exit without maintenance of the last displayed data.

```
                         Section File Maintenance          ADD

     Section number . . . . . .  XXXXX
     Course . . . . . . . . .  XXXXXX
     Instructor . . . . . . . .  XXXXXXXXXXXXXX
     Room . . . . . . . . . .  XXXX
     Meets on days  . . . . . .  XXX
     Starting time  . . . . . .  XX:XX
     Enrollment . . . . . . . .  XXX




     Press Enter to add

     F3=Exit   F12=Cancel
```

The DDS for the display file, SECTMAIN, is shown below. It contains a
DSPATR entry not yet introduced. DSPATR(PR) protects input-capable fields
(i.e., usage I or B) from input keying. Because you can condition display
attributes with indicators, this attribute can be used to permit or prevent a
user from keying a value into a field, depending on processing needs at that
point in time. The maintenance program on page 193 uses DSPATR(PR) to
prevent the user from changing field values within a record when (s)he has
selected the delete option.

```
          1         2         3         4         5         6         7         8
1234567890123456789012345678901234567890123456789012345678901234567890123456789Ø
     A                                       REF(SECTIONS)
     A                                       PRINT
     A                                       CAØ3(Ø3 'F3=Exit')
     A                                       VLDCMDKEY(1Ø)
     A          R SCREEN1
     A                                     1 28'Section File Maintenance'
     A                                     3  2'Type values, then Enter.'
     A                                     5  5'Section number . .'
     A          SECTN       5  B  5 24
     A  3Ø
     AO 31
     AO 32
     AO 91                                   DSPATR(PC)
     A  3Ø                                   ERRMSG('Record already exists' 3Ø)
     A  31                                   ERRMSG('No record for change' 31)
     A  32                                   ERRMSG('No record for delete' 32)
     A  91                                   ERRMSG('I/O error' 91)
     A                                     6  5'Action Code . . .'
     A          ACTION      1  I  6 24VALUES('A' 'C' 'D')
     A                                     6 30'A=Add'
     A                                     7 30'C=Change'
```

```
                1         2         3         4         5         6         7         8
       12345678901234567890123456789012345678901234567890123456789012345678901234567890
       A                                             8 30'D=Delete'
       A                                            24  2'F3=Exit'
       A              R SCREEN2                          CA12(12 'F12=Cancel')
       A                                             1 28'Section File Maintenance')
       A                MODE        6   0            1 60DSPATR(HI)
       A                                             3  2'Section number . . . . . .'
       A                SECTNO      R   O            3 29
       A                                             4  2'Course . . . . . . . . . .'
       A                COURSE      R   B            4 29
       A    40                                          DSPATR(PR)
       A                                             5  2'Instructor . . . . . . . .'
       A                INSTR       R   B            5 29
       A    40                                          DSPATR(PR)
       A                                             6  2'Room . . . . . . . . . .'
       A                ROOM        R   B            6 29EDTCDE(Z)
       A    40                                          DSPATR(PR)
       A                                             7  2'Meets on days  . . . . . .'
       A                DAYS        R   B            7 29VALUES('MWF' 'TTH')
       A    40                                          DSPATR(PR)
       A                                             8  2'Starting time  . . . . . .'
       A                BEGTIM      R   B            8 29EDTWRD(' 0:   ')
       A    40                                          DSPATR(PR)
       A                                             9  2'Enrollment . . . . . . . .'
       A                ENROLL      R   B            9 29EDTCDE(3)
       A    40                                          DSPATR(PR)
       A                                            21  2'Press Enter to '
       A                MODE2       6   O           21 17DSPATR(HI)
       A                                            23  2'F3=Exit'
       A                                            23 11'F12=Cancel'
```

Notice in SCREEN2 that SECTNO is Output only, to prevent the user from modifying that field. Also, SCREEN1 uses indicators to display error messages differently, depending on processing outcomes within the program. Because SECTN should display in reverse image with the cursor positioned to that field for any file error, DSPATR(PC) is conditioned by four indicators in an "OR" relation; if any one of the four indicators is on, the display attributes will be in effect. DSPATR(PR), or protected, is enabled for all SCREEN2 input-capable fields during the deletion mode to prevent the user from modifying these fields.

Before jumping into the RPG code required to implement this interactive application, let's work out the logic of what the application should do. Typically this "think-before-acting" approach to programming leads to more structured code. And remember, when coding for interactive applications, it is hard to resist falling into the GOTO habit. The pseudocode that follows illustrates the logic needed for this maintenance program. Notice that the pseudocode breaks the program into separate modules based on the function the code performs.

Program Mainline
WHILE user wants to continue
        Display screen 1
        Read screen 1
        SELECT
                WHEN user signals exit
                 Leave
                WHEN action is ADD
                 Do subroutine ADDREC
                WHEN action is CHANGE
                 Do subroutine CHGREC
                WHEN action is DELETE
                 Do subroutine DLTREC
        ENDSELECT
  ENDWHILE
  END PROGRAM

Subroutine ADDREC
  Chain to Section file
  IF record found
        Set on error indicator
  ELSE
        Zero and blank all record fields except section number
        Display screen 2
        Read screen 2
        IF not valid command key
                Write record to file
        ENDIF
  ENDIF
  END Subroutine

Subroutine CHGREC
  Chain to Section file
  IF record not found
        Set on error indicator
  ELSE
        Display screen 2
        Read screen 2
        IF not valid command key
                Update record to file
        ENDIF
  ENDIF
  END Subroutine

Subroutine DLTREC
    Chain to Section file
    IF record not found
        Set on error indicator
    ELSE
        Display screen 2
        Read screen 2
        IF not valid command key
            Delete record from file
        ENDIF
    ENDIF
    END Subroutine

Once you have the pseudocode worked out, coding the RPG is simple. In the program below, notice that indicators turned on within the program to control screen display may need to be turned off. Those indicators associated with error messages in the screen are set off automatically.

```
          1         2         3         4         5         6         7
12345678901234567890123456789012345678901234567890123456789012345678901234
     F**********************************************************************
     F* This program interactively maintains file SECTIONS.               *
     F*    Author: Judy Yaeger.   Date Written:   11-92.                   *
     F*                                                                    *
     F*  Indicators:                                                       *
     F*     03 - F03; exit                                                 *
     F*     10 - Valid command key pressed                                 *
     F*     12 - F12; cancel                                               *
     F*     30 - Invalid add; record already exists                       *
     F*     31 - Invalid change; no record for change                     *
     F*     32 - Invalid delete; no record for delete                     *
     F*     40 - Protect screen fields on delete                          *
     F*     90 - No record in file                                        *
     F*     91 - I/O failure on WRITE, UPDAT, or DELET                     *
     F**********************************************************************
     FSECTIONSUF E           K        DISK                    A
     FSECTMAINCF E                    WORKSTN
     C           *IN03     DOWEQ*OFF
     C                     MOVE *OFF     *IN40
     C           *IN91     IFEQ *OFF              If no I/O err.
     C                     MOVE *BLANKS  SECTN
     C                     ENDIF
     C                     EXFMTSCREEN1
     C                     SELEC
     C           *IN03     WHEQ *ON               If F3, then
     C                     LEAVE                  exit loop.
     C           *IN12     WHEQ *ON               If F12, then
     C                     ITER                   restart loop.
     C           ACTION    WHEQ 'A'
     C                     EXSR ADDREC            Add
     C           ACTION    WHEQ 'C'
     C                     EXSR CHGREC            Change
```

```
              1         2         3         4         5         6         7
     1234567890123456789012345678901234567890123456789012345678901234567890123 4
     C            ACTION    WHEQ 'D'
     C                      EXSR DLTREC                          Delete
     C                      ENDSL
     C                      ENDDO
     C                      MOVE *ON    *INLR
     C                      RETRN
     C***************************************************************
     C* ADDREC:  Processes an ADD action request                   *
     C***************************************************************
     CSR          ADDREC    BEGSR
     C            SECTN     CHAINSECTIONS         90
     C            *IN90     IFEQ *OFF                            If sec. exists
     C                      MOVE *ON    *IN30                    Add error
     C                      ELSE
     C                      MOVE 'ADD '  MODE
     C                      MOVE 'add '  MODE2
     C                      MOVE SECT    SECTNO
     C                      EXSR INITL                           Initialize
     C                      EXFMTSCREEN2                         Get values
     C            *IN10     IFEQ *OFF                            Not VLDCMDKEY
     C                      WRITESECTREC          91 Add record
     C                      ENDIF
     C                      ENDIF
     C                      ENDSR
     C***************************************************************
     C* CHGREC:  Processes a CHANGE request                        *
     C***************************************************************
     CSR          CHGREC    BEGSR
     C            SECTN     CHAINSECTIONS         90
     C            *IN90     IFEQ *ON                             If no section
     C                      MOVE *ON    *IN31                    CHANGE error
     C                      ELSE
     C                      MOVE 'CHANGE' MODE
     C                      MOVE 'change' MODE2
     C                      EXFMTSCREEN2                         Get values
     C            *IN10     IFEQ *OFF                            Not VLDCMDKEY
     C                      UPDATSECTREC          91 Rewrite rec.
     C                      ENDIF
     C                      ENDIF
     C                      ENDSR
     C***************************************************************
     C* DLTREC:  Processes a DELETE request                        *
     C***************************************************************
     CSR          DLTREC    BEGSR
     C            SECTN     CHAINSECTIONS         90
     C            *IN90     IFEQ *ON                             If no section
     C                      MOVE *ON    *IN32                    DELETE error
     C                      ELSE
     C                      MOVE 'DELETE' MODE
     C                      MOVE 'delete' MODE2
     C                      MOVE *ON    *IN40                    Protect
     C                      EXFMTSCREEN2                         Get confirm
     C            *IN10     IFEQ *OFF                            Not VLDCMDKEY
     C                      DELETSECTREC          91 Delete rec.
     C                      ENDIF
     C                      ENDIF
     C                      ENDSR
```

```
         1         2         3         4         5         6         7
1234567890123456789012345678901234567890123456789012345678901234567890123
        C**********************************************************
        C* INITL:  Initializes record fields to blanks and zeros  *
        C*  preparatory to an ADD                                 *
        C**********************************************************
        CSR         INITL       BEGSR
        C                       MOVE *BLANKS    COURSE
        C                       MOVE *BLANKS    INSTR
        C                       MOVE *ZEROS     ROOM
        C                       MOVE *BLANKS    DAYS
        C                       MOVE *ZEROS     BEGTIM
        C                       MOVE *ZEROS     ENROLL
        C                       ENDSR
```

Many RPG programmers feel that the fields used in the display file should not be the same as the database fields, and in some applications, depending on the program design, such separate definition in fact may be necessary to prevent losing values input by the user (or read from the database).

To implement this approach, simply define the display file fields independently, giving them new names. Then, in your RPG program add two subroutines — one that moves the screen field values to the database fields, and one that does the reverse (moves the database fields to the screen fields). Before you add or update a record, execute the subroutine that moves the screen fields to the database fields. Before you display the data entry screen for a change or delete, execute the subroutine that moves the database fields to the screen fields.

Screen Design and CUA

The screens illustrated in this chapter were based on a set of design standards called **CUA**, or **Common User Access**. IBM developed and promotes CUA as a way of standardizing user interfaces across platforms. All the AS/400 screens follow these standards.

Screens can be classified into one of four panel types: menu, list, entry, and information. Under CUA, all panels have the same general layout: a panel title on the first screen line, an optional information area, an instruction area, a panel body area (where either the menu, list, data entry fields, or informational output occur), and at the bottom of the screen, a command area, function key listing, and at the very bottom, a message line. Figure 7.1 illustrates these types of panels.

Figure 7.1
CUA Panel Layout

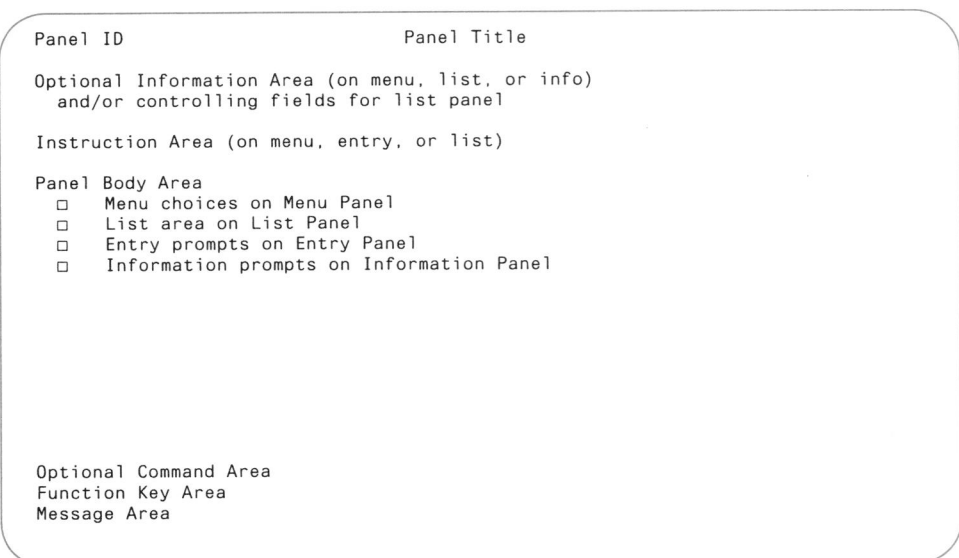

```
Panel ID                         Panel Title

Optional Information Area (on menu, list, or info)
   and/or controlling fields for list panel

Instruction Area (on menu, entry, or list)

Panel Body Area
   □   Menu choices on Menu Panel
   □   List area on List Panel
   □   Entry prompts on Entry Panel
   □   Information prompts on Information Panel




Optional Command Area
Function Key Area
Message Area
```

CUA has specific guidelines for row and column placement of screen items, vertical alignment of screen columns, capitalization and punctuation, function key use, error-condition handling, and so on. Although such standards may seem to you to stifle creativity, there are two excellent reasons for standardizing the user interface.

First, a standardized interface makes it easier for a user to learn new applications, since the interface is consistent with other applications. If F3 is always the Exit key across applications, for instance, and F12 always backs up to the previous screen, the user does not have to learn new commands counter to those used in other applications.

A second major reason for adopting CUA (or other) standards is that such standards can improve programmer productivity. If you adopt a set of design standards, you can easily develop a set of generic DDS descriptions — one for each panel type — that can then easily be tailored to your specific applications.

Chapter Summary

Interactive applications are mediated through display files defined in DDS. Each record format of a display file defines a screen. The format may include literals to display and fields for output, input, or both. Each data item is positioned on the screen based on a line and column DDS entry for each.

DDS relies on keywords to achieve specific desired effects. Some keywords are associated with the entire file, others with a specific record format, and others yet with specific fields. Keywords enable function keys, determine the appearance and format of displayed items, control what the user can enter as input values, and associate error messages with fields.

Most keywords, as well as fields and literals, can be conditioned by indicators. If the indicator is on at display time, the keyword is in effect (or the field or literal displays); if the indicator is off, the effect or data item the indicator is associated with is suppressed. The indicators are turned on within a program to control screen display. On the display side, valid command keys can be associated with indicators to convey information back to the program.

Today's businesses frequently use interactive applications to display database information or the results of processing data; more and more companies also are using interactive applications for file maintenance. In this latter case you should pay special attention to validating the user's entries, to maintain data file integrity.

IBM has developed a set of screen-design standards, called CUA (Common User Access), that can standardize AS/400 interactive applications. Such standards of screen design can make it easier for users to learn new applications and for programmers to develop new applications more efficiently.

Terms

batch processing   data validation   interactive applications
combined file   display attributes   keyboard-shift attribute
CUA (Common User Access)   display file

Discussion/Review Questions

1. Contrast batch and interactive applications.

2. What are the permissible I/O operations that can be used with record formats of display files? What are the effects of each?

3. Describe how a combined file differs from an update file.

4. What allows the system to determine whether you are using a keyword as a file-, record-, or field-level keyword?

5. What's the difference between referring to a function key as CA (Command Attention) and CF (Command Function)? How does each affect your program?

6. Explain the meaning of each of the following display-attribute codes: BL, CS, ND, HI, UL, RI, PC.

7. Why might you want to know in general whether the user pressed an enabled function or a special key (i.e., use the VLDCMDKEY keyword), when each valid key has its own indicator whose status can be checked within your program?

8. What are the relational codes used with COMP in DDS display files? Are they identical to the RPG relational codes used with IFxx?

9. What's the difference between Mandatory Enter and Mandatory Fill?

10. What happens when an Error Message (ERRMSG) is in effect for a field? Describe the screen effects.

11. How can program events influence screen display, and how can screen input influence program flow of control?

12. Describe how a record's existence affects the validity of adding, deleting, or changing the record when maintaining a file with unique keys.

13. Discuss the pros and cons of adopting IBM's CUA standards in your screen design.

14. What impact do you think Graphical User Interfaces (GUIs), as typified by the PC Windows environment, will have on future AS/400 interactive applications?

Exercises

1. Assume that your school has a student file containing name, sex, total credits accumulated, residency code, grade point average, major (or degree program), and student classification. Write the DDS for a record format that prompts the user to enter values for these fields, including as many validation keywords as are appropriate.

2. Write a DDS record format that would prompt the user to enter salesperson number, date of sale, and amount of sale. The cursor should blink, salesperson number should be underlined with column separators, date of sale should display in high intensity, and amount of sale should be in reverse image and blinking. *Exercises Continued*

Exercises continued

3. Rewrite the DDS from exercise 2 so that the salesperson number is underlined if indicator 10 *and* 12 are on, and displayed with column separators if 10 *or* 12 is on. Date of sale should display in high intensity only if indicator 10 is on. Amount of sale should be in reverse image and blinking if 10 *and* 12 are on *or* if 14 *and* 16 are on.

4. Write the pseudocode for a program to allow interactive processing of received goods. The program should allow a user to enter a product number (on SCRN1), determine whether that product number exists in the file, and either display an error message (on SCRN1) if the product number is incorrect, or display a second screen (SCRN2) that asks the user to enter the quantity of that product received. The amount entered should be added to the current quantity on hand, and the product record then updated. Include provisions for exiting and canceling.

5. Write the RPG for the pseudocode of exercise 4. Don't code the DDS. Make up whatever file and field names you need. Document whatever indicators you use.

Programming Assignments

1. CompuSell wants you to develop an interactive application that will allow the company to enter its product number for an item and display a screen of information about the supplier of that product. The screen should include all the information in the supplier file CSSUPP. You also must use inventory file CSINVP to obtain the correct supplier number for the item in question. The data files are described in Appendix D; follow your instructor's directions for obtaining the files.

   Develop the DDS and the RPG program for this application. Design your application with two screens: one inquiry screen and one informational display. Write your program to loop so that, following the display of the requested information, the program prompts the user for a new product number; continue until (s)he signals that (s)he is finished. Follow your instructor's directions for testing this program.

2. CompuSell wants you to write an interactive file maintenance program for its Customer Master File CSCSTP (see Appendix D). If the user wants to add a new customer, your program must determine the appropriate number to assign the customer (numbers are sequentially assigned) and provide the number automatically for the user; also automatically use the system date for the date of last order and assign balance due a value of zero. For a change request, allow the user to change any field except the customer number. Do not allow the user to delete a record if the customer has a balance greater than zero. Follow your instructor's directions for testing this program.

3. Wexler University wants you to write an interactive file maintenance program for its instructor file WUINSTP (see Appendix D). Design screens as appropriate for the application. Allow the users to add, delete, or change instructor records. Do not allow them to change the Social Security number or add a record with a duplicate Social Security number. Include as much data validation as you can, given the nature of the data fields being entered. Follow your instructor's directions for testing this program.

Programming Assignments Continued

Programming Assignments continued

4. CompuSell wants you to write an interactive application to enter customer orders. The application should begin by determining the appropriate starting order number, based on the last order number in Order File CSORDP. The main process loop should then begin by requesting the customer number; only orders for established customers (those in the Customer Master File CSCSTP) may be processed. If the customer exists, then the program should set up a loop to allow the user to enter ordered items until the order is complete.

   For each item, the user should enter the product number and the quantity desired. If the product is not in the Inventory File CSINVP, or if the quantity on hand is less than the quantity desired, inform the user through error messages that the item cannot be ordered; otherwise, update the quantity-on-hand field of the inventory file to reflect the new, lower quantity on hand and write a record to the Orders File (CSORDPRP) for that item.

   When the user has finished entering items for a customer, determine whether payment was included in the order, and if so, for how much. A record should be written to the CSORDP file, leaving the amount due zero. (The files CSORDP and CSORDPRP will be used by different programs to generate pick-lists and invoices.)

5. Wexler University wants you to write a program that will provide an online registration system for its students. The registration system should work as follows:

   a) The student should be prompted to enter his/her social security number. If the student is not found in the student master file, the program should not allow him/her to proceed.

   b) If the student is in the file, (s)he should be allowed to register for courses until (s)he signals that (s)he is finished.

   c) For each desired course, the student will enter the section number. If the section number is invalid, the student should be informed. If the number is valid, the course identification, title, and credits should display on the screen, along with the time and days the section meets and an indication of whether the section is full or not full (current enrollment < cap).

   d) If the section is not full, and if the student indicates that this is, in fact, the course and section into which (s)he wishes to enroll, the program should confirm the enrollment to the user, update the current enrollment figure in the Current Section record by adding 1 to it, and add a record to the Current Enrollment File for this student in this section.

   When a student has finished enrolling, the program should return to the initial screen to allow the next student to enroll. This process should continue until the user presses F3 to exit the application completely.

   Your program will use files WUSTDP, WUSCTP, WUCRSP, and WUENRLP (see Appendix D). Follow your instructor's directions for testing this program.

Chapter 8

Tables and Arrays

Chapter Overview

In this chapter you will learn how to create, store, and access tables of data. You will also learn how to define and use arrays, data structures that can simplify repetitive processing of similar data.

Tables

In common usage, a **table** is a collection of data organized into columns and rows. Similar kinds of data are stored within a column, and the data within a row of the table is related, or "belongs" together. Typically, the data in the first column of a table is organized sequentially in ascending order to facilitate finding an item. Once you find the item you want in column 1, you then read across the row to extract the data related to that item.

The three-column table below, for example, would allow you to look up a state code to extract the name and sales tax of the state associated with that state code. (Note that the full table would include 50 codes and their corresponding names and tax rates, not just the eight shown.)

State Code	State Name	Tax Rate
AK	Alaska	.0000
AL	Alabama	.0400
AR	Arkansas	.0000
AZ	Arizona	.0500
CA	California	.0725
CO	Colorado	.0300
CT	Connecticut	.0600
DE	Delaware	.0000
...	...	...

RPG allows you to define table data structures so that your program can extract data in a way analogous to how you use tables. The major difference between an RPG table and tables as we are used to thinking about them is that one RPG table represents only a single column of data. In RPG terms, our table above is actually *three* related tables.

Table Definition

Data elements within an RPG table need to have the same length, the same data type, and the same number of decimal positions (if numeric data). In the above table, state codes are all 2-byte-long character data; the state names, however, have different lengths. To use the names in an RPG table, you would have to determine the length of the longest state name (South and North Carolina both have 14 characters) and pad the names of the other states with trailing blanks to make them all 14 characters long.

Extension Specifications are used to define tables. When your program uses Extension Specifications, these specifications must follow the File Specifications, preceding the Input Specifications. Required entries on Extension Specifications vary, depending on the complexity and layout of the data you are storing in table format and where the table data values are coming from.

Consider first how RPG would handle a very simple table — a table of 50 state codes. Once you understand definitional requirements for this table, you can expand your understanding to more complex examples. The table of state codes appears below.

State Code
AK
AL
AR
AZ
CA
CO
CT
DE
...

An RPG table name must begin with TAB, followed by up to three additional characters. The name you choose is entered as the Table/Array name in positions 27-32 of the Extension Specifications. Each table definition must also include an entry in positions 36-39 stating the number of elements in the table, an entry in positions 40-42 stating the length of each element, and, if the data is numeric, an entry in position 44 stating the number of decimal positions in an element. If the table data is arranged in order, an A (for ascending) or D (descending) should be coded in position 45, although this entry is optional for most tables.

E	Line	Form Type	Record Sequence of the Chaining File / Number of the Chaining Field / From Filename	To Filename	Table or Array Name	Number of Entries Per Record	Number of Entries Per Table or Array	Length of Entry	P/B/L/R	Decimal Positions	Sequence (A/D)	Table or Array Name (Alternating Format)	Length of Entry	P/B/L/R	Decimal Positions	Sequence (A/D)	Comments
0 1	E				TABCOD		50	2			A						
0 2	E																

The Extension Specification above associates the table name TABCOD with our state codes, and states that it contains 50 elements of two-position-long character data. This table definition allocates memory so that the entire table full of data can remain in memory throughout a program's execution.

Additional entries are required to complete the above definition. These entries depend on the source of the data values to be stored in the table and the layout of this original data. You can put data values into a table in two ways: You can either hard-code the data within your program (this kind of table is often called a **compile-time table**), or you can instruct the computer to obtain the data from a separate disk file each time the program runs (a **pre-runtime**, or **pre-execution table**).

Compile-Time Tables

A compile-time table obtains its data from the program's source code; the data is bound to the table when you compile the program. The table data must be entered at the very end of the program, following the last program entries (most often the last output specification). A source line with ****b̸** (**blank) entered in positions 1-3 must precede the table values, which begin in position 1 of the next line.

How you enter the data at this point is up to you. You could put one table entry per line, two per line, three per line, and so on. In our example, since each state code is two bytes long, we could code as many as 40 entries per line. The only stipulations are that the values must be entered in the order that you want them to appear in the table, that multiple entries per line be entered contiguously, without spaces separating them, and that you are consistent in the number of entries you put on each line.

If the number of entries per line is not an even multiple of the number of total table entries, the odd number of entries goes on the last line. For example, assume that you decide to enter four state codes on one line. There would be 12 lines of four codes, with a final thirteenth line containing only two codes. The coding would look like this:

Output Specification (O form)

Column headers: Line / Form Type / Filename or Record Name / Type (H/D/T/E) / Stkr #/Fetch (F) / Space (Before/After) / Skip (Before/After) / Output Indicators (And/And, Not) / Field Name or EXCPT Name or Constant Name / *Auto / Edit Codes B/A/C/1-9/R / End Position in Output Record / P/B/L/R / Commas / Zero Balances to Print / No Sign / CR / - / FLT / X = Remove Plus Sign, Y = Date Field Edit, Z = Zero Suppress / 5-9 = User Defined / Constant or Edit Word

Commas	Zero Balances to Print	No Sign	CR	-	FLT
Yes	Yes	1	A	J	N
Yes	No	2	B	K	O
No	Yes	3	C	L	P
No	No	4	D	M	Q

Table data lines:

```
**
AKALARAZ
CACOCTDE
...
```

Each program line in your source member is a record in the source file. Accordingly, if you have entered four state codes per line, there are four table entries per record. If you had entered only one code per line, there would be one table entry per record. This distinction is important to understand, because number of entries per record is a required entry in the Extension Specification for a table. The system must know this information so it can correctly obtain the data to load into the table. This required entry goes in positions 33-35 of the Extension Specification and is the final requirement for defining a compile-time table.

Extension Specification (E form)

Line	Form Type	Record Sequence of the Chaining File	Number of the Chaining Field	From Filename	To Filename	Table or Array Name	Number of Entries Per Record	Number of Entries Per Table or Array	Length of Entry	P/B/L/R	Decimal Positions	Sequence (A/D)	Table or Array Name (Alternating Format)	Length of Entry	P/B/L/R	Decimal Positions	Sequence (A/D)	Comments
0 1	E					TABCOD	4	50	2			A						
0 2	E																	

Compile-time tables are useful for relatively small tables whose data are not likely to change over time. With large tables, it would be a waste of a programmer's time to enter the data as part of the program. Moreover, if the table data is **volatile** (i.e., frequently changing), a programmer would have to go back to the source program, change the table data at the end of the program, and recompile the program each time the data needed updating. You should avoid this practice, since each time you enter SEU to modify your source code, you run the risk of inadvertently introducing errors into the program.

Pre-Runtime Tables

An alternate way to handle data values required by a table is to store the data in a database file that is loaded into the table each time the program is run. This kind of table is called a pre-runtime or pre-execution table, because RPG automatically retrieves all the table data from the file before the program's procedural processing begins.

In this case, the Extension Specification needs an additional entry: the name of the file containing the table data, coded in positions 19-26.

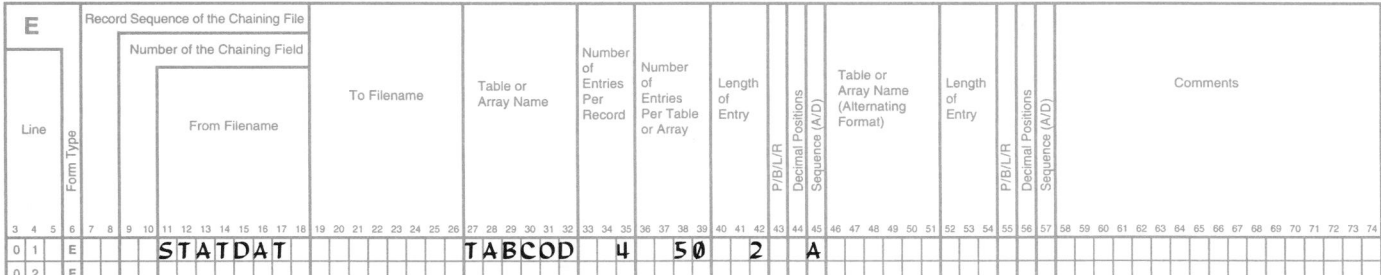

And since this means that the program is using an additional file, a definition of that file must also appear on the File Specifications.

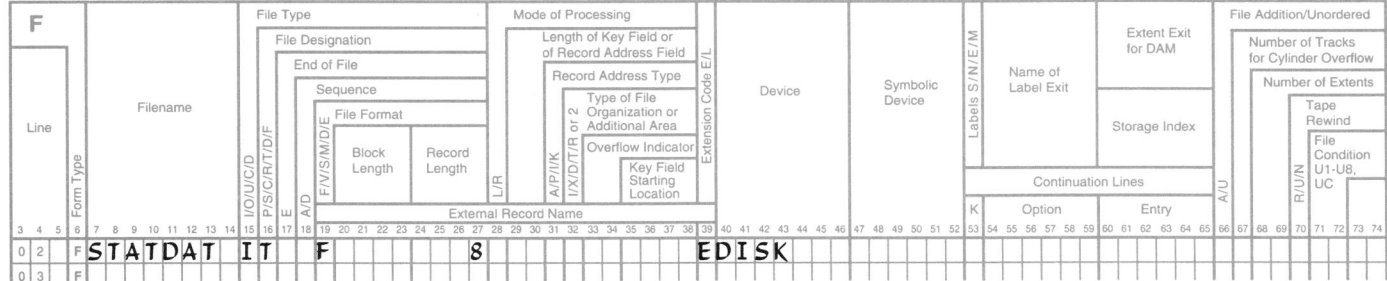

The File Specification for a table file differs somewhat from that of other files you have worked with. Although the type is Input, since the data is being read by the program, the file's designation is T for table; this entry directs the system to read all the data into a table automatically at the program's start. Because the table is defined internally within the program, rather than externally, an F for Fixed Format is coded in position 16. The appropriate record length is coded in positions 24-27. And an E in position 39 signals that this file's contents are defined on the Extension Specifications.

Table Look-Ups

Tables are used for one primary purpose: to look up data values using the LOKUP operation. Typically, you have a field, either from an input file or a result field from a calculation, that you want to find in the table; this value goes in factor 1. The name of the table goes in factor 2. The LOKUP operation requires an indicator to serve as a signal for the type of match you want to find between the table value and the factor 1 value. Most of the time you want an equal match, so you put the indicator in the EQ position (58-59).

When a LOKUP is successful, the resulting indicator comes on and an internal pointer is positioned at the matching table value. You can use the indicator's status to control subsequent processing within the program. The code below illustrates a simple **table look-up**.

```
C*Use input field CODEIN as the search argument of a look up within
C*TABCOD; indicator 50 comes on if an equal match is found.
C           CODEIN      LOKUPTABCOD                    50
C           *IN50       IFEQ *ON
C                       EXSR FOUND
C                       ELSE
C                       EXSR BADCOD
C                       ENDIF
```

A table look-up involving a single table is of limited value. Its primary purpose would be to validate the value of an input field. The more common use of tables — to look up a value in one column of a table to extract a related value from a second column — requires some additional table definition in RPG and a slight modification of the LOKUP operation.

Two Related Tables

Recall that in RPG a table corresponds to one column of information. Assume you wanted to represent the information in the following example in table format within RPG.

State Code	State Name
AK	Alaska
AL	Alabama
AR	Arkansas
AZ	Arizona
CA	California
CO	Colorado
CT	Connecticut
DE	Delaware
...	...

To represent both the state codes and the state names within RPG requires defining two tables. The form of those definitions depends on how you have entered the data supplying the table values. When you are entering pairs of related table data, it is often convenient to enter the pairs together, as shown below.

This form of table data entry is called **alternating format**. To reflect this data organization, the two tables are defined on the same line of the Extension Specifications. The second table's name, entry length (and decimal positions, if the data is numeric) are coded in the appropriate columns in positions 46-57.

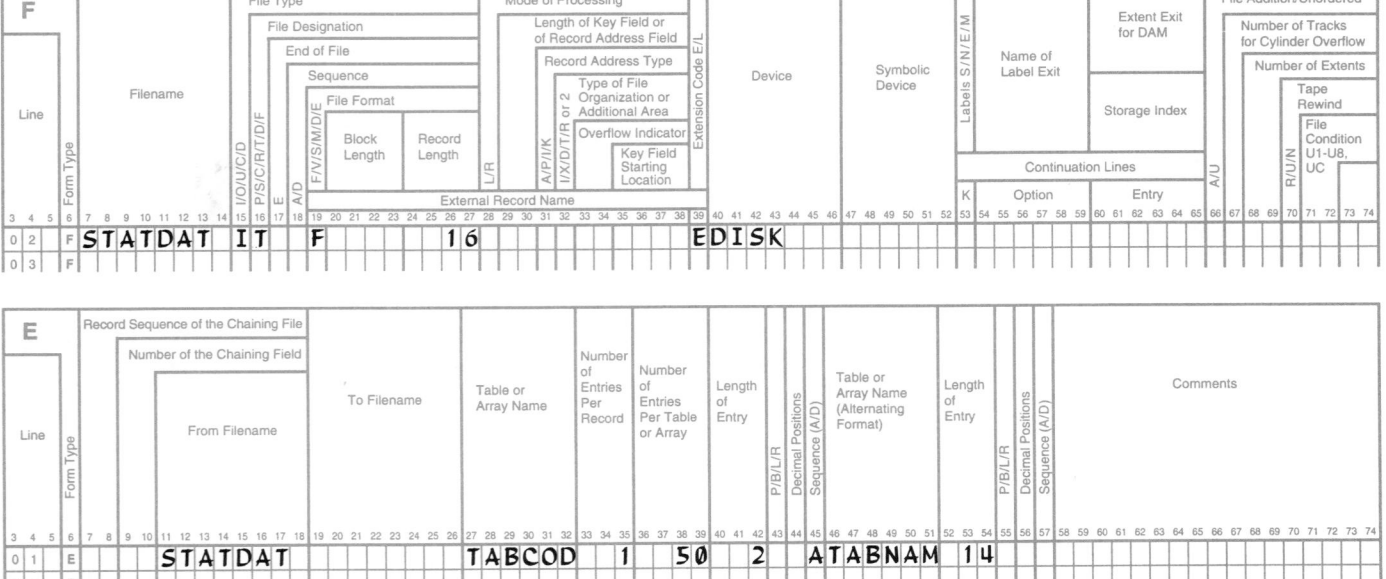

E	Record Sequence of the Chaining File		Number of the Chaining Field	From Filename	To Filename	Table or Array Name	Number of Entries Per Record	Number of Entries Per Table or Array	Length of Entry	P/B/L/R	Decimal Positions	Sequence (A/D)	Table or Array Name (Alternating Format)	Length of Entry	P/B/L/R	Decimal Positions	Sequence (A/D)	Comments
0 1 E						TABCOD	1	50	2				A TABNAM	14				
0 2 E																		

The state names are stored in TABNAM, and the length of each name is stated as 14 — the length of the longest name. Note that the number of entries per record specification in positions 33-35 is 1, because only one pair of values is coded on each line. If the data had been laid out so that several pairs of data were entered on the same line, that specification entry would need to be adjusted to accurately reflect the data layout.

Notice also that there is no separate entry to indicate the number of entries in the TABNAM table. Because TABCOD and TABNAM are tables in alternating format, the number of entries per table applies to both tables: There are 50 pairs of data.

Although the example above deals with alternating-format, compile-time tables, the same approach can be used for pre-runtime tables. Enter the data in alternating format in the table file, adjust the record-length specification on the File Specification as needed, and enter the file name in positions 11-18 of the Extension Specification line.

F	Filename	File Type	File Designation	End of File	Sequence	File Format	Block Length	Record Length	Mode of Processing	Length of Key Field or of Record Address Field	Record Address Type	Type of File Organization or Additional Area	Overflow Indicator	Key Field Starting Location	Extension Code E/L	Device	Symbolic Device	Labels S/N/E/M	Name of Label Exit	Extent Exit for DAM	Storage Index	Continuation Lines	File Addition/Unordered	Number of Tracks for Cylinder Overflow	Number of Extents	Tape Rewind	File Condition U1-U8, UC
0 2 F	STATDAT	I T				F		16								EDISK											
0 3 F																											

E	Record Sequence of the Chaining File		Number of the Chaining Field	From Filename	To Filename	Table or Array Name	Number of Entries Per Record	Number of Entries Per Table or Array	Length of Entry	P/B/L/R	Decimal Positions	Sequence (A/D)	Table or Array Name (Alternating Format)	Length of Entry	P/B/L/R	Decimal Positions	Sequence (A/D)	Comments
0 1 E				STATDAT		TABCOD	1	50	2				A TABNAM	14				
0 2 E																		

You can then use the tables to look up a state code to extract a state name. In order to extract the name related to the state code, TABNAM must appear in the result field of the LOKUP operation. A successful code look-up causes the internal pointer to be positioned in TABNAM at the name that corresponds to the matched code in TABCOD. The result is that table name TABNAM contains the desired state name, and you can print or display TABNAM or use it in any other operation for which you need the appropriate state name.

If the look-up of TABCOD is not successful, TABNAM will contain the state name from the last successful look-up. Good programming practice suggests that you should always provide for the possibility of unsuccessful look-ups within your code.

Line			Factor 1	Operation	Factor 2	Result Field Name	Length		Resulting Indicators
0 1	C	*Look up CODEIN in TABCOD to extract TABNAM.							
0 2	C		CODEIN	LOKUP	TABCOD	TABNAM			50
0 3	C	* *IN50 is on if the look up located an equal match.							
0 4	C		*IN50	IFEQ	*ON				
0 5	C			EXSR	PRTNAM				
0 6	C			ELSE					
0 7	C			EXSR	BADCOD				
0 8	C			ENDIF					

Multiple Related Tables

The Extension Specifications provide room for just two table definitions in alternating format. How can you represent the data below so you can look up a state code to extract both the state name and the sales tax rate?

State Code	State Name	Tax Rate
AK	Alaska	.0000
AL	Alabama	.0400
AR	Arkansas	.0000
AZ	Arizona	.0500
CA	California	.0725
CO	Colorado	.0300
CT	Connecticut	.0600
DE	Delaware	.0000
...	...	...

This problem has two solutions. The appropriate one depends on how your table data values are actually entered. Assume your data values are entered in alternating format, as shown below.

```
        0
**
AKAlaska        0000
ALAlabama       0400
ARArkansas      0000
AZArizona       0500
CACalifornia    0725
   ...
```

Because RPG allows you to define only two tables in alternating format, you would need to define the state names and tax rates as a single table and then split apart the two pieces after a successful look-up.

Line	Form Type	Record Sequence of the Chaining File / Number of the Chaining Field / From Filename	To Filename	Table or Array Name	Number of Entries Per Record	Number of Entries Per Table or Array	Length of Entry	P/B/L/R	Decimal Positions	Sequence (A/D)	Table or Array Name (Alternating Format)	Length of Entry	P/B/L/R	Decimal Positions	Sequence (A/D)	Comments
0 1	E			TABCOD	1	50	2				ATABTWO	18				
0 2	E															

Line	Form Type	Control Level (L0-L9, LR,SR, AN/OR)	And (Not)	And (Not)	(Not)	Factor 1	Operation	Factor 2	Result Field Name	Length	Decimal Positions	Operation Extender (H,N,P)	Resulting Indicators Plus/High	Minus/Low	Zero/Equal	Comments
0 1	C	* TABTWO contains both the state name and the tax rate.														
0 2	C					CODEIN	LOKUP	TABCOD	TABTWO						50	
0 3	C					*IN50	IFEQ	*ON								
0 4	C	* Split up the TABTWO values into right and left portions.														
0 5	C						MOVE	TABTWO	RATE	44						
0 6	C						MOVEL	TABTWO	NAME	14						
0 7	C					AMT	MULT	RATE	TAXDUE	52H						
0 8	C						ELSE									
0 9	C						EXSR	BADCOD								
1 0	C						ENDIF									
1 1	C															

A MOVE operation to a result field of the appropriate length and decimal positions allows you to split off the right-most portion of the table data — in this case the tax rate — while a MOVEL operation gives you the left-most data — state name.

An alternate way to handle multicolumn table data is to first enter all the data from one column, then all the data from the next, and so on. A separator record (**∅) needs to appear between each set of data.

```
        0                          . . .
**
AK
AL
AR
AZ
**
Alaska
Alabama
Arkansas
Arizona
**
0000
0400
0000
0500
```

With this data layout, you define each table separately on the Extension Specifications, in the same order in which the data values appear at the end of your program.

E	Record Sequence of the Chaining File			To Filename	Table or Array Name	Number of Entries Per Record	Number of Entries Per Table or Array	Length of Entry	P/B/L/R	Decimal Positions	Sequence (A/D)	Table or Array Name (Alternating Format)	Length of Entry	P/B/L/R	Decimal Positions	Sequence (A/D)	Comments
0 1					TABCOD	1	50	2			A						
0 2					TABNAM	1	50	14									
0 3					TABRAT	1	50	4		4							

The calculations would then require two separate look-ups, one to extract the appropriate state name and the other to extract the tax rate.

C		Indicators			Factor 1	Operation	Factor 2	Result Field			Resulting Indicators	Comments
		And	And					Name	Length		High Low Equal	
0 1	C				CODEIN	LOKUP	TABCOD	TABNAM			50	
0 2	C				CODEIN	LOKUP	TABCOD	TABRAT			50	
0 3	C				*IN50	IFEQ	*ON					
0 4	C				AMT	MULT	TABRAT	TAXDUE	52H			
0 5	C					. . .						
0 6	C											

Notice that if the look-up is successful, TABRAT can be directly used as a factor in a calculation. There is no need to first move it to a non-table field.

Although the sample coding above used compile-time tables, the same techniques of entering multicolumn data and performing look-ups apply to pre-runtime tables as well, where the data is stored in a table file.

There are trade-offs between these two techniques of handling multicolumn tables. When data values are entered column by column, there is a higher chance of data entry errors or of associating incorrect values than when data values are entered a row at a time, with all related data adjacent to each other.

On the other hand, if multicolumn data is handled as two alternating tables, with the second table a concatenation of several data values that need to be split apart in the calculations, the calculations are less obvious and more error-prone.

Range Tables

One final kind of table needs to be considered: a **range table**. Consider the following table of shipping charges.

Package Weight (lb)	Shipping Charge ($)
0- 1	2.50
2- 5	4.25
6- 10	7.50
11- 20	9.00
21- 40	12.00
41- 70	16.00

You would use this table to look up a package weight to determine the shipping charges for the package. Unlike the previous tables, in this table the weight column entries represent a range of values rather than discrete values. How should these values be represented, and how should the LOKUP be performed?

One solution is to represent this data as two tables, storing only the *upper* end of the range of weights in the table along with the charges, as shown below.

```
        0              . . .
**
010250
050425
100750
200900
401200
701600
```

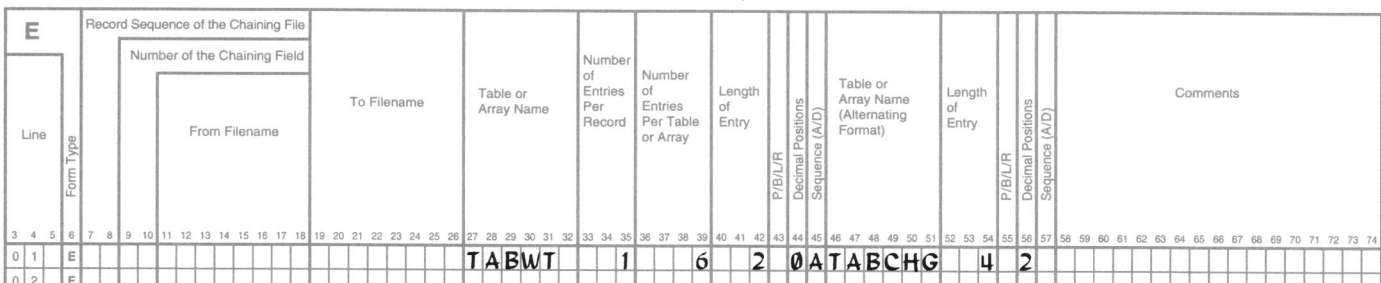

The above Extension Specification defines TABWT as a table of six elements, with one entry per record and each entry a 2-byte numeric value with no decimal positions, and TABCHG as a table in alternating format with TABWT, with each TABCHG entry a 4-byte numeric value with two decimal positions. Range tables *require* a sequence entry; the weights are in ascending sequence, so an A appears in position 45 of the Extension Specification.

You use the LOKUP operation to access range tables. Because you are no longer looking for an exact match between an input value and a table value, you enter a resulting indicator in two positions for the LOKUP operation; given the sample table's layout, the indicator is entered in the HI and EQ positions.

The look-up statement above translates to "Find the first table weight that is greater than or equal to the input weight and extract the shipping charge that corresponds to that table weight." Since the maximum table weight is 70, failure of the look-up indicates an input weight over the 70-pound limit. In such cases, the program executes subroutine NOSHIP.

Changing Table Values

Tables are generally used for extracting values. It is possible, however, to change table values — either intentionally or accidentally — during program execution. Anytime you specify a table name as the result of a mathematical or an assignment operation, the value of the entry where the table is currently positioned will be changed. Failing to understand this can sometimes lead to inadvertent program errors.

For example, consider the shipping weight problem. Assume that in the application developed, you want to add and print either the appropriate shipping charge, or, for packages weighing more than 70 pounds, to add and print 0 to indicate that the package can't be shipped. The following incorrect solution may tempt you.

C	Form Type	Control Level (L0-L9, LR,SR, AN/OR)	Indicators					Factor 1	Operation	Factor 2	Result Field				Resulting Indicators				Comments
			And		And						Name	Length	Decimal Positions	Operation Extender (H,N,P)					
			Not		Not		Not												
Line															High	Low	Equal		
0 1	C		*	This incorrect solution may change some of the values in															
0 2	C		*	TABCHG to zero.															
0 3	C							WTIN	LOKUP	TABWT	TABCHG				50		50		
0 4	C							*IN50	IFEQ	*OFF									
0 5	C								Z-ADD	0	TABCHG								
0 6	C								ENDIF										
0 7	C							PKGCHG	ADD	TABCHG	TOTCHG	72							
0 8	C																		

The result of the above code would be that each time a package weighing more than 70 pounds is processed, the TABCHG value of the most recently successful look-up would be set to 0. The next time a package of that lower weight was processed, its shipping charge would incorrectly be extracted as 0.

You can deliberately change table values, if you wish, by first executing a LOKUP to position the table correctly and then moving the new value into the table. If the table data came from a file, and you want to store the table with its revised values back in the file at the end of processing, you can accomplish this task quite simply with a few modifications of the File and Extension Specifications.

First, designate the table file as a Combined file, rather than just an Input file. Then include the file name as the To File (positions 19-28), as well as the From File, on the Extension Specifications. These two changes will cause the (changed) table values to be written back to the file upon program completion.

Arrays

An **array** is a data structure similar to a table, in that it contains multiple elements, all defined with a common name. Like a table, each element within an array must be the same data type, with the same length and number of decimal positions (if the elements are numeric). Arrays are defined on Extension Specifications; the required entries are the same as those required for tables. Like tables, you may load data into arrays at compile time, with values entered at the end of the program, or at pre-runtime, with values obtained from a table file. Array data may be obtained in alternating format, again, like tables.

Basically the only *definition* differences between **compile-time arrays** and tables and **pre-runtime arrays** and tables is that array names *cannot* begin with TAB. For reasons soon explained, programmers keep array names short, usually no more than three characters long. Examine the definitions below and you will see that other than the names, these are identical to table definitions.

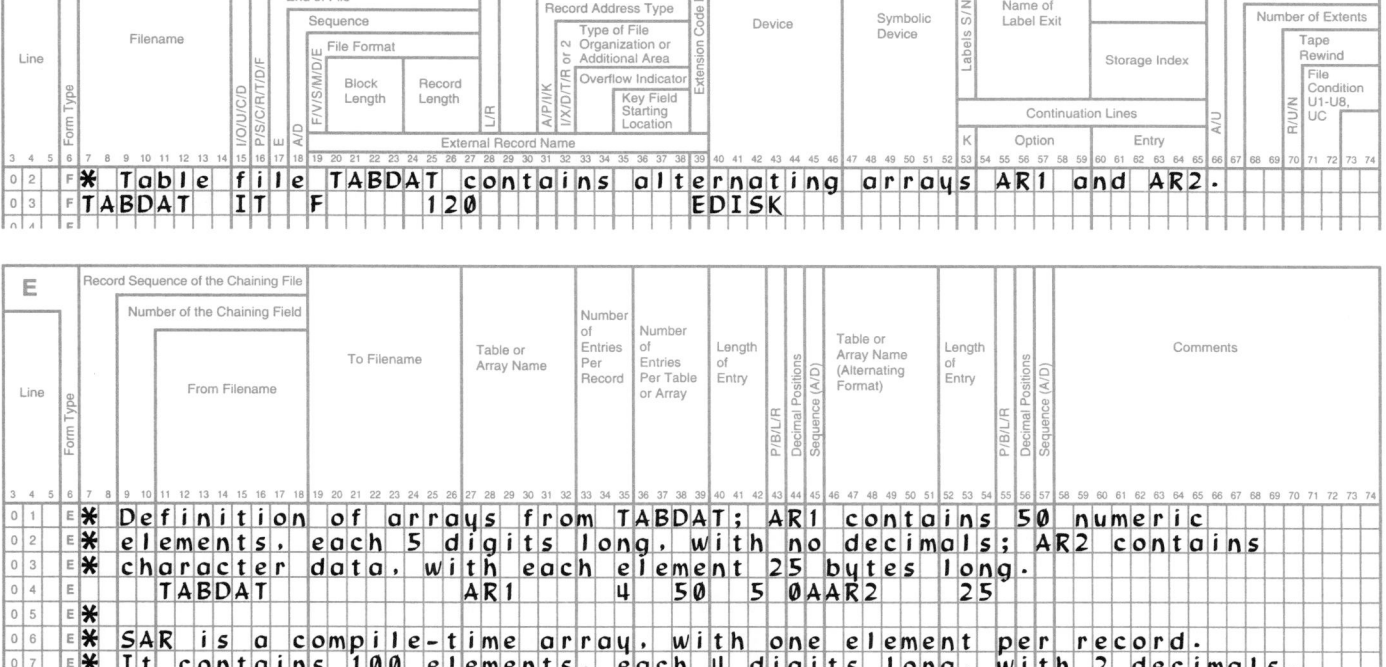

If arrays and tables are so similar, why does RPG have both data structures? Although tables and arrays bear the points of similarity identified above, the capabilities of arrays go far beyond those of tables. The first major difference is that unlike tables, arrays can be loaded with values during the course of program execution. This kind of array is called a **runtime array.**

A runtime array is distinguished on Extension Specifications by the *omission* of a "Number of entries per record" entry (positions 33-35). A "From Filename" entry also is inappropriate for a runtime array.

		Record Sequence of the Chaining File						Number of Entries Per Record	Number of Entries Per Table or Array	Length of Entry	P/B/L/R	Decimal Positions	Sequence (A/D)	Table or Array Name (Alternating Format)	Length of Entry	P/B/L/R	Decimal Positions	Sequence (A/D)	Comments
E		Number of the Chaining Field																	
Line	Form Type	From Filename			To Filename	Table or Array Name													
0 1	E	* The system recognizes the arrays below as run-time arrays.																	
0 2	E					GAR			10	7	2								
0 3	E					ARC			15	1									
0 4	E					QAR		200	3	0									
0 5	E																		

The data for a runtime array can come from fields of an input file of the program or from results of calculations. Before looking at these techniques to load an array, you must learn an additional feature about arrays: Unlike table elements, individual elements of an array can be directly referenced and manipulated, using an index, or pointer.

RPG indexing notation requires a comma between the array name and the index. Thus GAR,3 means the third element in the array GAR. ARC,10 is the 10th element in the array ARC. So they don't exceed RPG's limit of six-character data names, programmers typically restrict array names to two or three characters to allow the use of indexes with the arrays. When you reference an array without an index, the system infers that you wish to reference the entire array — that is, all its elements.

The index used to reference an element does not have to be a numeric literal. Instead, a field can serve as an index, provided it is a numeric field with 0 decimal positions. If the index is a field, the *value* of that field determines what element of the array is being referenced. Thus, if N has a value of 3, QAR,N is the 3rd element of QAR. If N's value is 10, QAR,N is the 10th element of the array. We'll demonstrate the value of this indirect referencing later in this chapter.

Runtime Arrays and Input Data

Although externally described file-record formats do not allow fields to be defined as array elements, program-described records can contain arrays. Chapter 9 will illustrate a method you can use to overcome this limitation for externally described files; meanwhile, the following example deals with a program-described input file.

Assume you have a file of sales records from all the company's sales staff. Each record contains the salesperson's identification number and the total sales for each month during the past year — 12 sales figures in all. Each sales figure is 10 digits long, with two decimal positions. Those sales figures could be defined as array elements, in the following way:

Extension Specification (E)

Line	Form Type	From Filename	To Filename	Table or Array Name	Number of Entries Per Record	Number of Entries Per Table or Array	Length of Entry	Table or Array Name (Alternating Format)	Length of Entry	Comments
0 1	E			SAL	12	10	2			
0 2	E									

You also need to build a connection between the input record and the Extension Specification array definition. This connection is made simply by giving the appropriate portion of the input record the array name.

Input Specification (I)

Line	Form Type	Filename	Sequence	Field Location From	To	Decimal Positions	Field Name
0 1	I	SALES	NS				
0 2	I			1	5		SLSNO
0 3	I	*SAL is an array defined on the Extension Specifications.					
0 4	I			6	125	2	SAL
0 5	I						

The system will correctly subdivide the values of the input record into the appropriate elements of SAL based on the Extension Specification definition. Thus, the data value in positions 6-15 of the input record will be stored in SAL,1; the value in positions 16-25 in SAL,2; etc. You could, if you want, define the location of each array element separately on the Input Specifications, as shown on the following page. Programmers generally use this technique only if the elements are not contiguous within the input record.

```
I                                                                           Field
                                    Record Identification Codes             Location
Line Filename  Seq  N  RII   Pos 1      Pos 2      Pos 3   S  From  To  DP  Field Name  CL  M  FRR  Plus Minus ZorB
01  I SALES    NS
02  I                                                   1     5      SLSNO
03  I *SAL elements are defined individually to demonstrate an
04  I *alternative technique of handling array definition.
05  I *The Extension Specification remains unchanged.
06  I                                                   6   152     SAL,1
07  I                                                  16   252     SAL,2
08  I                                                  26   352     SAL,3
09  I                                                  36   452     SAL,4
10  I                                                        . . .
11  I
```

With either method of describing the input, each time you read a record from the SALES file, the 12 sales figures from that record will be stored in array SAL. When a new input record is read, the sales figures from that record replace the previous contents of the array. Thus, the contents of SAL are continually changing as your program runs. That's the reason for calling SAL a runtime array. Runtime arrays also can obtain values as a result of calculations performed as your program runs.

Calculations with Arrays

Any of the arithmetic operations — ADD, SUB, MULT, DIV, or SQRT — or assignment operations — Z-ADD, Z-SUB, MOVE, and MOVEL — can be used with arrays or their elements. If just individual elements are referenced in the calculations, the effects are the same as if the array elements were fields.

```
C                                                        Result Field       Resulting Indicators
Line   Ind  Factor 1    Operation   Factor 2      Name    Length  DP       Comments
01  C* Multiply AR,1 by 5 and store the answer in AR,2
02  C      5           MULT        AR,1          AR,2
03  C* Zero out the 5th element of AR and add 10 to it.
04  C                  Z-ADD10                   AR,5
05  C* Add the values of two elements and store the result in a third
06  C* element.
07  C      AR,6        ADD         AR,3          AR,10
08  C
```

Entire arrays, rather than just individual elements of the arrays, also can be specified as factor 1 and/or factor 2 of calculations. In that case, the result field *must always* be an array name.

If all the factors involved in the operation are arrays, then the operation is performed successively on *corresponding elements* of the arrays until the array with the fewest number of elements has been completely processed.

Line	Form Type	Control Level	Indicators	Factor 1	Operation	Factor 2	Result Field Name	Length	Dec Pos	Op Ext	Resulting Indicators	Comments
01	C	*		Add corresponding elements of AR and PR, storing the results								
02	C	*		in corresponding elements of TR.								
03	C			AR	ADD	PR	TR					
04	C	*		Zero out each element of TR and add the corresponding element								
05	C	*		of PR to it.								
06	C				Z-ADD	PR	TR					
07	C	*		Take the square root of each element of PR and store the								
08	C	*		result in the corresponding element of TR.								
09	C				SQRT	PR	TR			H		
10	C											

When factor 1 or factor 2 is not an array, but the remaining factor (if the operation uses one) and the result are arrays, the operation works with corresponding elements of the array, along with the non-array value in each case, and continues until all the elements in the shortest array have been processed.

Line	Form Type	Control Level	Indicators	Factor 1	Operation	Factor 2	Result Field Name	Length	Dec Pos	Op Ext	Resulting Indicators	Comments
01	C	*		Divide each element of PR by 4 and store the result in the								
02	C	*		corresponding element of TR.								
03	C			PR	DIV	4	TR			H		
04	C	*		Store 'ABCDE' in each element of array STR								
05	C				MOVE	'ABCDE'	STR					
06	C											

In addition to the standard operations, three operations apply only to arrays: XFOOT, SORTA, and MOVEA.

XFOOT *(Summing the Elements of an Array)*

XFOOT, called "crossfoot," sums the elements of an array. This operation does not use factor 1. Factor 2 contains the name of the array whose elements are to be added together, and the result field contains the field where the answer is to be stored. If you half-adjust this operation, the rounding takes place just before the final answer is stored in the result field. **Crossfooting** is a term used in accounting to sum across a row of figures to develop a total for that row. The XFOOT operation is very useful in such applications, provided the figures to be added are array elements.

Line	Form Type	Control Level (L0-L9, LR,SR, AN/OR)	Indicators And Not	And Not	And Not	Factor 1	Operation	Factor 2	Result Field Name	Length	Decimal Positions	Operation Extender (H,N,P)	Resulting Indicators Arithmetic Plus	Minus	Zero	Compare 1>2	1<2	1=2	Lookup(Factor 2)is High	Low	Equal	Comments
0 1	C					* Sum the elements of array SAL and store the answer in TOTAL.																
0 2	C						XFOOT	SAL	TOTAL	92												
0 3	C																					

SORTA *(Sort an Array)*

SORTA is a simple but useful operation that rearranges the values of the elements of an array into ascending or descending sequence. The sequence used depends on the sequence entry for that array in position 45 of the Extension Specifications. If no sequence is specified (45 is blank), the operation sorts the values in ascending sequence, the default order for SORTA. D in position 45 causes the elements to be sorted in descending sequence. The Calculation Specification for this operation includes just the operation and the name of the array to be sorted, entered in factor 2.

Line	Form Type	Control Level (L0-L9, LR,SR, AN/OR)	Indicators And Not	And Not	And Not	Factor 1	Operation	Factor 2	Result Field Name	Length	Decimal Positions	Operation Extender (H,N,P)	Resulting Indicators Arithmetic Plus	Minus	Zero	Compare 1>2	1<2	1=2	Lookup(Factor 2)is High	Low	Equal	Comments
0 1	C						SORTA	SAR														
0 2	C					* SAR is 5 numeric elements, 2 long with no decimals.																
0 3	C					* Before SORTA: 10 92 33 85 12																
0 4	C					* After SORTA: 10 12 33 85 92																
0 5	C																					

MOVEA (Move Array)

The MOVEA (Move Array) operation transfers values from factor 2 to the result field of the operation. At least one of these entries — factor 2 or the result — must contain an array name. Generally MOVEA is used with character data, although it can be used with numeric values if the entries in factor 2 and the result have the same numeric length (though not necessarily the same number of decimal positions).

What makes MOVEA unusual is that the operation ignores the element boundaries of the array and moves the values, character by character, from the sending to the receiving field or array until either there is nothing left to send or there is no more room in the receiving field.

The easiest way to understand how a MOVEA operation works is to look at some examples. Assume you have two arrays: ARA, a four-element character array, with each element three characters long; and ARB, a character array of five elements, each two characters long. FIELDA is a field five characters long.

The following examples illustrate the effects of different MOVEA operations using the arrays defined above. Notice especially that the data movement takes place *from left to right* and that portions of the receiving field or array not used in the operation retain their original values.

```
Array-to-array MOVEA, different length elements, with receiving
array shorter than sending array.
                        MOVEAARA        ARB

                          ARA                         ARB
before MOVEA:   abc def ghi jkl          mn op qr st uv
after MOVEA:    abc def ghi jkl          ab cd ef gh ij
------------------

Array-to-array MOVEA, different length elements, with receiving
array longer than sending array.
                        MOVEAARB        ARA

                          ARB                         ARA
before MOVEA:   mn op qr st uv           abc def ghi jkl
after MOVEA:    mn op qr st uv           mno pqr stu vkl
------------------

MOVEA sending field to a receiving array.
                        MOVEAFIELDA     ARA

                         FIELDA                        ARA
before MOVEA:   ZYXWV                    abc def ghi jkl
after MOVEA:    ZYXWV                    ZYX WVf ghi jkl
------------------

 MOVEA sending array to a receiving field.
                        MOVEAARA        FIELDA

                          ARA                       FIELDA
before MOVEA:   abc def ghi jkl          ZYXWV
after MOVEA:    abc def ghi jkl          abcde
------------------
```

Factor 2 and/or the result field can specify an array element, rather than an entire array. In that case, the data movement *starts* at that array element; elements preceding the specified element are not involved in the MOVEA operation. Data movement continues until there is nothing left to move or until the receiving array or field has no more room. The examples below illustrate this kind of data movement.

```
MOVEA specifying sending array element, receiving array.
              MOVEAARA,3     ARB

                   ARA                        ARB
before MOVEA:  abc def ghi jkl           mn op qr st uv
after MOVEA:   abc def ghi jkl           gh ij kl st uv
------------------

MOVEA specifying sending array, receiving array element.
              MOVEAARA        ARB,4

                   ARA                        ARB
before MOVEA:  abc def ghi jkl           mn op qr st uv
after MOVEA:   abc def ghi jkl           mn op qr ab cd
------------------

MOVEA with both sending and receiving specified as array elements.
              MOVEAARA,3     ARB,2

                   ARA                        ARB
before MOVEA:  abc def ghi jkl           mn op qr st uv
after MOVEA:   abc def ghi jkl           mn gh ij kl uv
------------------
```

As you probably noticed, those positions within the result field that did not have new values moved to them by the MOVEA retained their old values. As of V2R2 of OS/400, by entering a P in position 53 (the half-adjust position) of the MOVEA, you can specify that the unused positions to the right are to be blank-padded. The sample code below illustrates this feature.

```
MOVEA with both sending and receiving specified as array elements and
padding specified for the result.
              MOVEAARA,3     ARB,2      P

                   ARA                        ARB
before MOVEA:  abc def ghi jkl           mn op qr st uv
after MOVEA:   abc def ghi jkl           mn gh ij kl ƀƀ
------------------
```

The value of the MOVEA operation lies in its ability to manipulate portions of data fields and combine bits and pieces from different data sources into a single data item.

Using Arrays

Now that you understand how to define arrays and how to use them in different calculations or special array operations, you are ready to see how arrays can simplify or expedite solutions to different kinds of programming problems. The ability to index an array with a field, rather than a literal, adds tremendous flexibility to your ability to manipulate arrays and makes arrays the preferred data structure to handle problems requiring identical processing of similar data items.

Recall, for example, the SALES file described earlier, in which each record contained a salesperson's number and 12 monthly sales totals for that salesperson. The 12 monthly sales were defined as elements of an array, as shown below. BON is an additional array required in our example to follow.

Line	Form Type	Record Sequence of the Chaining File / Number of the Chaining Field / From Filename	To Filename	Table or Array Name	Number of Entries Per Record	Number of Entries Per Table or Array	Length of Entry	P/B/L/R	Decimal Positions	Sequence (A/D)	Table or Array Name (Alternating Format)	Length of Entry	P/B/L/R	Decimal Positions	Sequence (A/D)	Comments
0 1	E			SAL	12		10		2							
0 2	E			BON	12		8		2							
0 3	E															

Line	Form Type	Filename	Sequence	Number (1/N)	Option (O)	Record Identifying Indicator or **	Record Identification Codes 1 Position / Not (N) / C/Z/D / Character	Record Identification Codes 2 Position / Not (N) / C/Z/D / Character	Record Identification Codes 3 Position / Not (N) / C/Z/D / Character / P/B/L/R / Stacker Select	Field Location From	Field Location To	Decimal Positions	Field Name	Control Level (L1-L9)	Matching Fields or Chaining Fields	Field Record Relation	Plus	Minus	Zero or Blank
0 1	I	SALES	NS																
0 2	I									1	5		SLSNO						
0 3	I									6	125	2	SAL						
0 4	I																		

Assume that the company is determining an end-of-the-year bonus. The bonus is determined on a monthly basis by the sales for that month; anytime the monthly sales exceeds $50,000, the bonus for that month is 1/2 percent of the sales; otherwise, there is no bonus for that month. The company wants to calculate total annual bonus, but also have the individual monthly bonuses print on 12 columns running across a report.

To program a solution without using arrays would require writing a set of calculations that would be replicated 12 times, each time with a different set of fields representing each of the 12 months. With the SAL array representing the 12 months' sales for a given salesperson and a BON array to store the bonus for each month, the calculations are relatively short:

Line	Form Type	Control Level (L0-L9, LR,SR, AN/OR)	Indicators							Factor 1	Operation	Factor 2	Result Field				Resulting Indicators			Comments
			And		And								Name	Length	Decimal Positions	Operation Extender (H,N,P)	Arithmetic / Compare			
0 1	C	*	Calculate 12 monthly bonuses and total bonus for a salesperson.																		
0 2	C	*	Index I is varied from 1 to 12 in DO loop to successively																		
0 3	C	*	reference elements of arrays SAL and BON.																		
0 4	C									1	DO	12	I	20						
0 5	C									SAL,I	IFGT	50000								
0 6	C									SAL,I	MULT	.005	BON,I			H				1/2% bonus
0 7	C										ELSE									
0 8	C										Z-ADD0		BON,I							bonus is 0
0 9	C										ENDIF									
1 0	C										ENDDO									
1 1	C										XFOOT	BON	TOTBON	92						total bonus
1 2	C																			

The beauty of handling data with arrays and variable indexes, as shown in the example, is that if there were 1,200 sales figures instead of 12, the calculations would be no longer; the only required changes would be to increase the number of iterations of the loop from 12 to 1,200 and to increase the lengths of fields I and TOTBON to avoid truncation.

It was stated earlier that the value of the MOVEA operation lies in its ability to manipulate portions of data fields and combine bits and pieces from different data sources into a single data item. This manipulation typically involves the use of a variable index.

Consider the following problem. A customer file contains records with a first name field FNAME and a last name field LNAME. FNAME is defined as 12 positions long and LNAME as 15 positions long. You want to use this file to generate letters to the customers, but you want the letter salutation to read:

"Dear Judy Yaeger:" — not

"Dear Judy   Yaeger   :"

How can you trim the trailing blanks following the first and the last name of each customer to get the desired effect? One method is to use an array and the MOVEA operation.

Page 1 of 2

Line	Form Type	Control Level (L0-L9, LR,SR, AN/OR)	Not	And Not	And Not	Factor 1	Operation	Factor 2	Result Field Name	Length	Decimal Positions	Operation Extender (H,N,P)	Plus	Minus	Zero	Comments
0 1	C					*Move "Dear" into array AR, defined as 35 character elements,
0 2	C					*each 1 character long.
0 3	C						MOVEA	'Dear'	AR				p			
0 4	C					*AR's contents: 'Dear '
0 5	C					*Now move FNAME into array, leaving a blank before the name.
0 6	C						MOVEA	FNAME	AR,6							
0 7	C					*AR's contents: 'Dear Judy '
0 8	C					*Now loop to inspect characters of AR, moving backwards from
0 9	C					*the last possible position for the last character of FNAME
1 0	C					*until a non-blank character is found.
1 1	C						Z-ADD	17	I	20						
1 2	C					AR,I	DOWEQ	' '	I							
1 3	C						SUB	1	I							
1 4	C						ENDDO									
1 5	C					*Given example, I is now 9.
1 6	C					*Add 2 to I so it points to where LNAME should begin.
1 7	C						ADD	2	I							
1 8	C					*Move LNAME to appropriate location in array.
1 9	C						MOVEA	LNAME	AR,I							
2 0	C					*AR's contents:'Dear Judy Yaeger '
	C					*To determine location for colon, loop to search from end of array.
	C						Z-ADD	35	I							
	C					AR,I	DOWEQ	' '								
	C						SUB	1	I							
	C						ENDDO									

Page 2 of 2

Line	Form Type	Control Level	Not	And Not	And Not	Factor 1	Operation	Factor 2	Name	Length						Comments
0 1	C					*Given example, I is now 16. Add 1 to I for colon position.
0 2	C						ADD	1	I							
0 3	C						MOVEA	':'	AR,I							
0 4	C					*AR's contents: 'Dear Judy Yaeger: '
0 5	C					

Array Look-Ups

This chapter began with a discussion of tables and LOKUP. The LOKUP operation also can be used to access arrays. Different information results from an array look-up, depending on whether or not the array is used in conjunction with an index.

If you simply want to know whether a value exists as an element in an array, without needing to know the location of the element, no index is needed.

Line	Form Type	Control Level (L0-L9, LR,SR, AN/OR)	And Not	And Not	Not	Factor 1	Operation	Factor 2	Result Field Name	Length	Decimal Positions	Operation Extender (H,N,P)	Plus	Minus	Zero	1>2	1<2	1=2	High	Low	Equal	Comments
0 1	C					VAL	LOKUP	PAR													50	
0 2	C					*IN50	IFEQ	*ON														
0 3	C						EXSR	PRESENT														
0 4	C						ELSE															
0 5	C						EXSR	ABSENT														
0 6	C						ENDIF															
0 7	C																					

If, on the other hand, you want to know not only whether a value exists in the array but also its location in the array, you need to use an index. To start the look-up at the beginning of the array, initialize the index to 1 prior to the LOKUP.

Line	Form Type	Control Level (L0-L9, LR,SR, AN/OR)	And Not	And Not	Not	Factor 1	Operation	Factor 2	Result Field Name	Length	Decimal Positions	Operation Extender (H,N,P)	Plus	Minus	Zero	1>2	1<2	1=2	High	Low	Equal	Comments
0 1	C						Z-ADD	1	I	30												
0 2	C					VAL	LOKUP	PAR,I													50	
0 3	C																					

If indicator 50 is on following the look-up, it means that the value was found in the array. Moreover, index I's value points to the location of the array element with the same value as VAL.

Indicators as Array Elements

There is one special, predefined array in RPG: array *IN. *IN is an array of 99 one-position character elements that represents the indicators 01-99. Thus, *IN,1 and *IN01 are both references to indicator 01. Note that the non-numbered indicators (e.g, *INLR or *INOF) are not represented within this array. The elements of *IN can contain only the character values '0' (*OFF) or '1' (*ON). Any operations valid for an array of character elements are valid to use with *IN. RPG programmers sometimes use this feature of indicators to turn off or on a consecutive block of indicators in a single calculation.

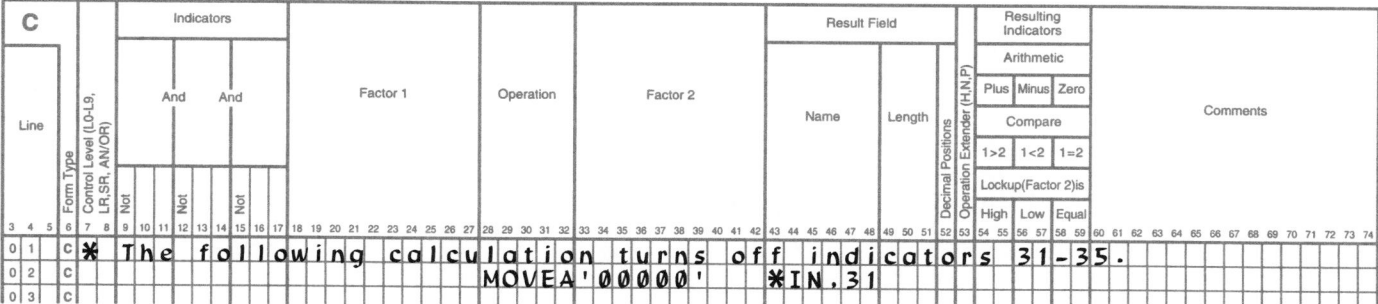

In general, it is best to avoid using this feature of RPG. It's easy to make mistakes in its use, and it results in code that is less understandable than other methods of manipulating indicator values.

Output with Arrays

When you specify a table name as part of an Output Specification, the current instance of the table (the value to which the table is positioned) prints. In contrast, when you specify an array name to print, all the elements appear, separated with two blanks, with the last element ending in the ending position specified for the array. Any editing associated with the array applies to each element. Depending on the printer spacing chart you are following, you may be able to use this shortcut; the alternative is to list each element of the array individually, with an index, and give each its own ending position.

If you need to print all the elements of an array but require more than two blanks separating the elements on the report, you can use an edit word that includes blanks (&) to increase the distance between the elements. In the following examples, array SAR stores seven numeric values (each of length six with two decimal positions), which will be printed so that the last element ends in position 76.

```
O* Given the specification below, all the elements of SAR
O* will print, separated with two spaces, and containing commas.
O* The last element will end in position 76.
O                    SAR       1      76
O                    ...
O* Alternately each element could be listed individually.
O                    SAR,1     1      16
O                    SAR,2     1      26
O                    SAR,3     1      36
O                    ...
O                    SAR,7     1      76
O                    ...
O* If you need more than two blanks between elements, you can
O* still use the entire array by using an edit word. The code
O* below results in 3 blanks separating SAR's elements.
O                    SAR             76 '&  ,  0.  '
```

Chapter Summary

Tables and arrays are both used to store sets of similar elements in RPG. Both tables and arrays can be loaded at compile time, from data hard-coded at the end of the source program, or at pre-execution time, from data contained in a table file. Arrays also can be loaded during runtime, from values contained on input records or as the result of calculations.

RPG tables are useful for performing look-ups with the LOKUP operation. You can look up a value in one table to extract information from a parallel table, provided that table is named as the result of the LOKUP operation. Using a table name in a calculation or printing operation causes the element to which the table is currently positioned to be used.

Arrays offer more flexibility than tables. You can explicitly reference an individual array element by using an index, or you can manipulate the array as a whole by using the array name without an index. You may use a numeric literal or field as an index to point to a specific array element. Three special RPG operations can be used only with arrays: XFOOT, SORTA, and MOVEA. Although you also can use LOKUP with arrays, arrays are most often used to simplify processing of identical kinds of data or to manipulate portions of data fields.

RPG's numbered indicators can be accessed as elements of a built-in array, *IN.

Terms

alternating format	Extension Specifications	runtime array
array	pre-runtime array	table
compile-time array	pre-runtime (pre-execution)	table look-up
compile-time table	table	volatile
crossfooting	range table	

Discussion/Review Questions

1. If you wanted to describe the phone book as a table in RPG, how many tables would you define?

2. If a program uses tables, what additional specification form is required and where should these specifications appear in your program?

3. What is the difference between the "number of entries per table" and "number of entries per record" entries on the Extension Specifications?

4. What factors would you use to determine whether to hard-code a table or store the table data in a disk file?

5. What are the two techniques that can be used to define tables of more than two columns? What are the advantages and disadvantages of each technique?

6. What is a "range" table? Give an example of one.

7. When would you need a "To Filename" entry in positions 19-26 of the Extension Specifications?

8. What are RPG's requirements for naming tables and arrays? What practical considerations add additional constraints to array names?

9. What do the terms *compile time*, *pre-runtime*, and *runtime* refer to when used to describe tables or arrays?

10. Give four ways that arrays can obtain data values.

11. What is the difference between using a table name and an array name in a calculation (i.e., what data is being represented)?

12. How are the effects of standard arithmetic operations dependent upon whether array elements or arrays are entered as factors in the calculations?

13. What RPG operations are used only with arrays? What does each do?

14. Compare and contrast how MOVE, MOVEL, and MOVEA work in RPG.

15. Describe appropriate uses for tables and arrays. How would you decide which (if either) to use in a given application?

Exercises

1. You are writing an application to process orders. Records include date ordered in YYMMDD format, but you want the *name* of the month ordered, rather than the number of the month, to print. a) Show how you would hard-code data for a two-column table relating month number to month name. b) Code the Extension Specifications for these compile-time tables, matching the definitions to the way in which you've laid out your data. c) Write the calculations needed to look up OMN (Order month) in one table to extract the appropriate month name.

2. Modify your work in exercise 1 by using arrays, rather than tables. Don't require your program to do more work than needed. (*Hint:* Can you think of a way to obtain the correct month name without performing a look-up?)

3. An input file contains records of sales. Each record represents one week of sales, with seven sales figures, each 10 with two decimal positions, in positions 21-90 of the input record. Code the Extension, Input, and portion of the Calculation Specifications needed to generate a weekly sales total and also to separately accumulate sales for each day of the week as input to the file is processed.

4. Write the output specification needed to produce the two lines of variable data shown below. Assume the detailed information is stored in array DAR and the totals in array TAR.

5. Assume the IRS wants you to use the following table to determine how much salary to withhold for federal taxes:

| | Tax Rate | |
If weekly salary is	Single	Married
0- $150	.18	.15
$151- $250	.25	.18
$251- $500	.28	.25
$501- $1000	.31	.28
over $1000	.33	.31

a) Hard-code this information so it can be handled with RPG tables. b) Define the Extension Specifications to reflect your hard coding. c) Write the calculations needed to assign the proper value to field RATE based on SAL (salary) and MS (Marital Status: S = single, M = married) of an employee's input record. d) Modify your code as needed if the table data were stored in a table file, rather than hard-coded.

```
          1         2         3         4         5         6         7
123456789012345678901234567890123456789012345678901234567890123456789012345

             SALES FIGURES BY REGION

      EAST          MIDWEST          SOUTH         WESTERN         MEXICO
   XXX,XX0.XX      XXX,XX0.XX      XXX,XX0.XX      XXX,XX0.XX      XXX,XX0.XX
   XXX,XX0.XX      XXX,XX0.XX      XXX,XX0.XX      XXX,XX0.XX      XXX,XX0.XX

 $X,XXX,XX$.XX    $X,XXX,XX$.XX    $X,XXX,XX$.XX   $X,XXX,XX$.XX   $X,XXX,XX$.XX
```

Programming Assignments

1. Wexler University wants a program that will produce a student grade report and assign final grades. An input file, WUEXAMP (Appendix D) contains student records with five exam grades per student. Define this input file within your program so you can handle the exams as array elements.

   The program will need to calculate an average exam grade for each student. The school also wants to know class averages for each exam and for the course as a whole. The program should also assign final grades based on the following criteria:

Average Grade	Final Grade
93 - 100	A
88 - 92	BA
83 - 87	B
75 - 82	CB
70 - 74	C
65 - 69	DC
60 - 64	D
< 60	F

   The desired report layout is shown below. Notice that the students' first and last names are to print together, with one blank between the last character of the first name and the first character of the last name.

   ```
            1         2         3         4         5         6         7         8         9
   1234567890123456789012345678901234567890123456789012345678901234567890123456789012345678Ø

       XX/XX/XX            WEXLER U. STUDENT GRADE REPORT           PAGE XXØX

                                            EXAM EXAM EXAM EXAM EXAM    AVG.  FINAL
       STUDENT ID.        NAME                1    2    3    4    5    GRADE  GRADE

       XXX-XX-XXXX  XXXXXXXXXXXXXXXXXXXXXXXXX  XØX  XØX  XØX  XØX  XØX   XØX    XX
       XXX-XX-XXXX  XXXXXXXXXXXXXXXXXXXXXXXXX  XØX  XØX  XØX  XØX  XØX   XØX    XX
       XXX-XX-XXXX  XXXXXXXXXXXXXXXXXXXXXXXXX  XØX  XØX  XØX  XØX  XØX   XØX    XX

                    CLASS AVERAGE:            XØX  XØX  XØX  XØX  XØX   XØX
   ```

2. CompuSell wants you to write an interactive program that can be used by its shipping department to calculate shipping charges based on destination and weight of package.

   Two files of table information related to shipping exist: the Zip/Zone Table File (CSZPZNP) and the Charges Table File (CSCHGP). These files are described in Appendix D.

   Your program should allow a user to enter the first three digits of the zip code of a package's destination and the pounds and ounces of the package weight, and based on the entered information, calculate the appropriate shipping charge and display the charge to the user.

   Note that any package with ounces greater than zero should get charged the rate appropriate for the next pound. That is, a package weighing 7 pounds 3 ounces should get charged at the 8-pound rate.

Programming Assignments Continued

Programming Assignments continued

3. Wexler University wants you to write a program to score student tests. Each test is a 50-question, multiple-choice test. (Possible answers for each question are A, B, C, D, and E). Student responses are scanned and stored in a database file WUTSTP. The format of these records is described in Appendix D; each record includes information about the course, the test, the student, and the student's test responses. The file is keyed on Course ID, Test, and Section number. An answer key to each test is prepared and stored in database file WUKEYP (Appendix D); this file is keyed on Course ID and Test.

There will be several sets of tests, possibly from different sections and different courses, in WUTSTP. The same key may be used to grade different sections' tests, provided the test number and course ID of the key record of WUKEYP matches those of the records to be graded.

You want to grade every record in WUTSTP; there may be keys in WUKEYP that don't match any of the current batches of tests, but there should not be any student test that does not have a corresponding key in WUKEYP.

Use arrays to do the scoring. Then use a compile-time table to assign letter grades. The table should reflect the following scale:

Score	Letter Grade
< = 29	F
30 - 34	D
35 - 39	C
40 - 44	B
45 - 50	A

Prepare a report as shown below. Start each new section and/or each new test on a new page with all headings. If a section takes more than one page, repeat all headings on successive pages. Note that an average grade for each section is required.

```
         1         2         3         4         5         6         7
1234567890123456789012345678901234567890123456789012345678901234567890123456789012345

                    WEXLER U. GRADE REPORT

 COURSE ID:  XXXXXX   TEST:  XXXX            DATE:  XX/XX/XX

 SECTION:  XXXXXX  INSTRUCTOR: XXXXXXXXXXXXXX

            STUDENT ID          TEST SCORE      LETTER GRADE
            XXX-XX-XXXX             ØX               X
            XXX-XX-XXXX             ØX               X
            XXX-XX-XXXX             ØX               X

            SECTION AVERAGE        ØX
```

4. GTC, a local telephone company, wants you to write a program to calculate costs of calls as part of a billing system. A Calls Transaction File (GTCLSP) is generated automatically as part of the company's switching system. Call data accumulates in this file during the course of the month. At the end of the month, the file is first used

Programming Assignments Continued

Programming Assignments continued

with this program and then used to print bills before being cleared for the next month's accumulation of call data. Note that the file includes a cost-of-call field, but the value for that field will be supplied by this program when it updates each record. When the record is read initially, this field contains zeros.

Cost of calls depends on two things: the area code and exchange of the number called, and the time of the call. Base daytime rates for all area codes and exchanges are contained in a rates file, GTCRATP. Each record contains the cost for the first minute and the per-minute charge for each additional minute for calls made to that area code/exchange. This file should be loaded into a table that can be used to look up the appropriate charges for each call in the calls file.

Time of call affects cost, based on the table below. This table should be incorporated into a hard-coded table so it can be used for look-ups during processing. The percents are *discounts* to the standard costs contained in the rate file.

Hours	Mon-Fri	Sat	Sun
8:00 a.m. - 4:59 p.m.	0%	60%	60%
5:00 p.m. - 10:59 p.m.	35%	60%	35%
11:00 p.m. - 7:59 a.m.	60%	60%	60%

Notice that the time of call in the calls file is based on a 24-hour clock, such that 2:15 p.m. would be stored as 1415. To apply the discount, you need to know the day of the week. The algorithm below first converts a date to a sequential century-day and then from that figure derives a value (day-of-week) from 1-7 to represent the day of week from Sunday thru Saturday, respectively. Where the algorithm says INTEGER, truncate the value to a whole number (no rounding); where it says REMAINDER, use the MVR operation.

IF month > 2
        Add 1 to month
ELSE
        Add 13 to month
        Subtract 1 from year
ENDIF

century-day = INTEGER(years * 365.25) + INTEGER(month * 30.6) + days − 63

day-of-week = REMAINDER(century-day / 7) + 1

Your program is to determine the cost of each call in GTCLSP, based on the area code and exchange of the *called* number and the time of the call; each call record should be updated with the cost calculated by your program.

Chapter 9

Advanced Data Definition

Chapter Overview

This chapter covers a miscellany of RPG features that allow you to define data in ways that facilitate data manipulation, error trapping and debugging, and program maintenance. The topics all deal with data, but they are basically independent, "stand-alone" concepts. You can incorporate any or all of these concepts within your programs to improve your programming style.

Named Constants

RPG/400 allows you to define constants on Input Specifications by specifying a value for the constant and associating a name with that value. This data element, called a **named constant**, can then be used throughout your program. You define a named constant by coding the value for the constant in positions 21-42 of the specification line, a C in position 43, and a name for the constant in positions 53-58. The name must follow the RPG rules for field names.

Enter numeric constant values with a decimal point or sign if appropriate, but never with commas. Enclose character constant values within apostrophes. Character data can be up to 256 characters long, while numeric constants have an upper limit of 30 digits (no more than nine of which may be to the right of the decimal point). If a constant value is too long to enter on one Specification line, you may continue the entry over as many lines as needed, provided the constant does not exceed the size limitation for its type.

To continue a constant, code a hyphen immediately following the last character on the line. If a continued constant is character data, each continuation line must begin with an apostrophe; the constant needs only a single ending apostrophe, on the final line containing the constant's value. The system considers any blanks within the apostrophe and the hyphen to be part of the constant, while blanks to the right of a continuation hyphen are disregarded. Examples of named constants appear on the following page.

I	Line	Form Type	Filename	O R / A N D	Sequence	Number (1/N)	Option (O)	Record Identifying Indicator or **	Record Identification Codes — 1 Position	Not (N)	C/Z/D	Character	2 Position	Not (N)	C/Z/D	Character	3 Position	Not (N)	C/Z/D	Character	Stacker Select P/B/L/R	Field Location From	To	Decimal Positions	Field Name	Control Level (L1-L9)	Matching Fields or Chaining Fields	Field Record Relation	Plus	Minus	Zero or Blank
0 1	I								.0751												C				FICA						
0 2	I	*																													
0 3	I								'DAN QUAYLE'												C				EXVP						
0 4	I	*																													
0 5	I								'ANTIDISESTABLISH-												C				LONGWD						
0 6	I								'MENTARIANISM'																						
0 7	I	*																													
0 8	I								1435159201435133145-												C				USADBT						
0 9	I								2599.39																						
1 0	I	*																													
1 1	I								'THIS LONG CONSTANT -												C				EXMPLE						
1 2	I								'HAS BLANKS -																						
1 3	I								'WHERE YOU WOULD-																						
1 4	I								' EXPECT THEM TO APP-																						
1 5	I								'EAR IN A SENTENCE.'																						
1 6	I	*The below constant can edit phone numbers.																													
1 7	I								'0( ) - '												C				PHONED						
1 8	I																														

Once you have defined a named constant, you can use it as a factor 1 or factor 2 variable in calculations appropriate to its type, or as a constant or edit word in the Output Specifications. The value of a named constant is fixed; you cannot change it during the course of program execution.

Named constants have three primary uses. The most obvious is to let you use a value within your calculations that is too long to directly enter as a literal in factor 1 or 2 on the Calculation Specifications. A second use of named constants is to define an edit word that is to be used for several different output fields. By defining the edit word once as a named constant, that editing mask can be used repeatedly on the Output Specifications simply by entering the named constant where you otherwise would have to enter the edit word itself.

Perhaps the most important advantage of named constants is that they allow you to follow standards of good programming practice by defining constants in one place, at the beginning of your program, rather than coding them as literals throughout your calculations. This practice facilitates maintenance programming. If a value, such as FICA rate, needs to be changed, it is much easier and less error-prone to locate a named constant and change the value in that one place, rather than to search through an entire program looking for each calculation in which the literal value .0751 occurs.

*LIKE DEFN (Field Definition)

Although **DEFN** is a calculation operation, rather than an Input Specification entry, this operation can help simplify and standardize your work-field definitions. More importantly, DEFN can also make program maintenance more efficient.

DEFN with the *LIKE option allows you to define a field based on the attributes of another field. The field being defined may be a character or numeric field, but it cannot be an array, array element, or table. The field providing the definition may be internally or externally defined, and may be an array or a table; if so, the attributes of one of the elements of the array or table provide the definition.

The format for this operation is simple: The word *LIKE appears in factor 1, the field *supplying* the definition appears in factor 2, and the field you are defining appears in the result position of the Calculation Specification.

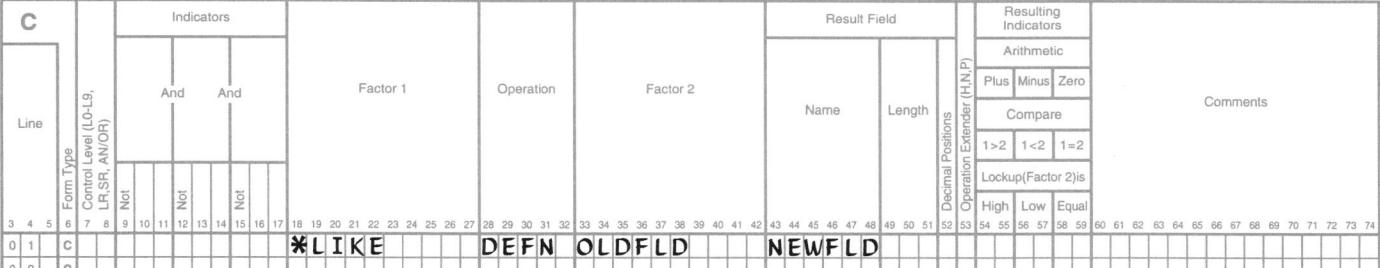

The specification above defines NEWFLD by giving it the type, length, and decimal positions (if type is numeric) of OLDFLD. A variant of this basic format allows you to lengthen or shorten the length of the field being defined by putting a plus sign (+) or minus sign (−) in position 49 to indicate the field being defined should be larger or smaller than the defining field. The increase or decrease in field length is entered (right-adjusted) in positions 50-51. You cannot change the number of decimal positions of the field being defined.

Assume you are writing a payroll program and that GROSS is an externally defined salary field. The DEFN operations define NET, FEDTAX, and STTAX relative to GROSS. Four accumulators, used for building grand totals, are each defined relative to the fields whose values they are going to accumulate. The following example illustrates these definitions.

C			Indicators			Factor 1		Operation		Factor 2		Result Field				Resulting Indicators			Comments
			And	And								Name	Length			Arithmetic			
Line	Form Type	Control Level (L0-L9, LR,SR, AN/OR)	Not	Not	Not									Decimal Positions	Operation Extender (H,N,P)	Plus	Minus	Zero	
																Compare			
																1>2	1<2	1=2	
																Lookup(Factor 2)is			
																High	Low	Equal	
0 1	C						*LIKE		DEFN	GROSS		NET							
0 2	C						*LIKE		DEFN	GROSS		FEDTAX	-	2					
0 3	C						*LIKE		DEFN	GROSS		STTAX	-	2					
0 4	C						*LIKE		DEFN	GROSS		TOTGRS	+	4					
0 5	C						*LIKE		DEFN	NET		TOTNET	+	4					
0 6	C						*LIKE		DEFN	FEDTAX		TOTFED	+	4					
0 7	C						*LIKE		DEFN	STTAX		TOTST	+	4					
0 8	C																		

The example illustrates the value of DEFN for program maintenance. Assume that the payroll program containing these definitions is put into production and that, after a few years, inflation causes salaries to become so high that the original definition for GROSS is too small. Accordingly, you modify the definition of GROSS in the database file to make it large enough to hold new salary figures.

If you had defined the work fields in this program without using DEFN, you would need to go through the program's calculations carefully to modify manually any work field whose length needs changing because of the change in GROSS. But since you used DEFN for those work fields, all you need to do is recompile the program; the work field lengths will be adjusted automatically based on the new length of GROSS.

Another common use of *LIKE DEFN is the definition of display fields in interactive applications. Rather than directly referencing database fields within a display file, many programmers use work fields in their screen definitions to handle screen input and output and then transfer the data values between the work fields and the database fields within their RPG programs. By using *LIKE DEFN to define an alternate field for each database field to be displayed, the programmer is assured that any future changes to the database field definitions will not create maintenance problems for programs containing such display fields.

DEFN is a non-executable operation, and DEFN Specifications can appear anywhere within the calculations. Good programming practice, however, dictates that all such statements appear together either at the very start of the calculations or within a subroutine that is executed once at the beginning of the program.

Data Structures

Data structures represent an additional option for addressing data within RPG/400. Data structures can give you flexibility in your handling of data by allowing you to subdivide fields into subfields, to restructure records with different field layouts, to change field data types, to define character fields longer than 256 bytes, and to add a second dimension to arrays. Thinking of a data structure as a contiguous portion of memory, which is then subdivided and referenced in different ways by the data structure's subfields, may help you conceptualize how data structures work.

Although data structures can be defined externally, this discussion focuses on program-defined data structures, since that is the kind used most often by RPG programmers.

Simple Data Structures

You define data structures on Input Specifications, following any record definitions. DS coded in positions 19-20 signals the beginning of a data structure. You also may enter a name for the data structure in positions 7-12; this name entry is optional, but would be required if you wanted to reference the data structure as a whole elsewhere in your program. Data structure names follow the same rules as field names. You can use the data structure as a whole (referencing it by name) any way that you can use a character field. Although you can enter the length of the data structure in positions 48-51 of the DS line, this entry is optional. If you omit it, the system derives the length of the structure as a whole from the lengths of its subfields.

Subfields comprising the data structure follow the data structure header line. Define each subfield entry by giving it a name (positions 53-58) and specifying its location within the data structure with "from" and "to" values (positions 44-51). The locations of subfields may overlap, and the same position within a data structure may fall within the location of several subfields.

The subfields can be unique to the data structure itself, or they can be fields or arrays also defined elsewhere in the program — as part of an input record, for example, or on the calculations or Extension Specifications. If non-unique, the definitions must match, since they are defining the same data item.

To be sure you understand data structures, consider some examples. First, assume your input file contains fields FNAME (first name — 10 bytes) and PHONE (10 digits), and that your program needs to work with just the first-name initial and the phone-number area code. A data structure could give you these capabilities.

```
I..........................................................................................
I Filename   Sq NB RI  Record Identification Codes      Field Location
I                                                        From  To  Dp Field Name
01 I OPTNAM        DS
02 I                                                        1   10    FNAME
03 I                                                        1    1    INIT
04 I                                                       11   20 0  PHONE
05 I                                                       11   13 0  AREACD
06 I                                                       14   16 0  EXCHG
07 I                                                       17   20 0  LOCAL
08 I
```

Because the data structure subfields FNAME and PHONE are identical to fields of the input record, each time a record is read those values will be stored in the data structure; subfield INIT will contain the value of the first position of the FNAME field, and AREACD will contain the value of the first three positions of PHONE. Note that you could manipulate the entire data structure by using the structure's name OPTNAM.

Another use of a data structure is to group fields from non-adjacent locations on a data record. The physical file definition below contains fields WAREHS and PARTNO, but the fields are not adjacent to one another in the record.

```
A.....................................................................................
A  Name Type  Name      Length  Dt Dp Usg  Location      Functions
A        R    PRTREC
A             PARTNO        5    0
A             DESC         20
A             QTY           7    0
A             WAREHS        3    0
A        K    PARTNO
A
```

By defining the following data structure , you can access WAREHS and PARTNO as a concatenation, or combined field, using the data structure name PRTKEY.

I	Filename		Sequence	Number (1/N)	Option (O)	Record Identifying Indicator or * *	Record Identification Codes 1 Position	Not (N)	C/Z/D	Character	2 Position	Not (N)	C/Z/D	Character	3 Position	Not (N)	C/Z/D	Character	Stacker Select	P/B/L/R	Field Location From	To	Decimal Positions	Field Name	Control Level (L1-L9)	Matching Fields or Chaining Fields	Field Record Relation	Field Indicators Plus	Minus	Zero or Blank
01	PRTKEY						DS																							
02																					1	30		WAREHS						
03																					4	80		PARTNO						
04																														

Or consider another example. An externally described file contains student answers for a 100-problem, multiple-choice exam, and a second externally described file contains a key for the exam. You want to write a program to grade the exams, using array manipulation to compare each student's answers one at a time with the correct answer for that problem.

Because externally described files do not allow fields to be defined as arrays, the student answers have been defined as one large field, STDANS, while the answers on the key have been defined as one large field, KEYANS. A data structure can be used to convert these answer fields to arrays, preparatory to processing.

E	Record Sequence of the Chaining File	Number of the Chaining Field From Filename	To Filename	Table or Array Name	Number of Entries Per Record	Number of Entries Per Table or Array	Length of Entry	P/B/L/R	Decimal Positions	Sequence (A/D)	Table or Array Name (Alternating Format)	Length of Entry	P/B/L/R	Decimal Positions	Sequence (A/D)	Comments
01				STD	100	1										
02				KEY	100	1										
03																

I	Filename		Sequence	Number (1/N)	Option (O)	Record Identifying Indicator or * *	Record Identification Codes 1 Position	Not (N)	C/Z/D	Character	2 Position	Not (N)	C/Z/D	Character	3 Position	Not (N)	C/Z/D	Character	Stacker Select	P/B/L/R	Field Location From	To	Decimal Positions	Field Name	Control Level (L1-L9)	Matching Fields or Chaining Fields	Field Record Relation	Field Indicators Plus	Minus	Zero or Blank
01							DS																							
02																					1	100		STDANS						
03																					1	100		STD						
04																					101	200		KEYANS						
05																					101	200		KEY						
06																														

Array STD provides a redefinition of field STDANS, while array KEY redefines KEYANS. Note that the system treats STD and KEY as arrays (rather than simply fields) because an Extension Specification exists for each of those data items.

Although you can also overlap field definitions or include the same positions in several fields within program-defined records, the results of these kinds of definitions are different than for data structures. When you define overlapping fields in a program-defined input record, the system establishes a separate storage location for each field, so that changing the value of one field does not affect the value of any of the other fields. With data structures, in contrast, overlapping subfields reference the same memory locations.

I							Record Identification Codes														Field Location				Field Indicators		
							1			2			3																
						Record Identifying Indicator or **	Position	Not (N)	C/Z/D	Character	Position	Not (N)	C/Z/D	Character	Position	Not (N)	C/Z/D	Character	Stacker Select	P/B/L/R	From	To	Decimal Positions	Field Name	Control Level (L1-L9)	Matching Fields or Chaining Fields	Field Record Relation	Plus	Minus	Zero or Blank
Line	Form Type	Filename	Sequence	Number (1/N)	Option (O)																								
0 1	I	* Field overlap in program-described input record.																											
0 2	I	INREC	NS																										
0 3	I																			1	10		FNAME						
0 4	I																			1	1		INIT						
0 5	I																												
0 6	I																												

Given the input record definition above, if FNAME were 'JACK' and our program moved 'M' to INIT, FNAME would still remain 'JACK'. In contrast, with a data structure, overlapping subfields reference the same area of storage, so that changing the value of one of the subfields also changes the value of any fields that overlap it. Thus, if FNAME is 'JACK', INIT is 'J'; if we then move 'M' to INIT, FNAME will become 'MACK'.

Multiple-Occurrence Data Structures

You can establish a **multiple-occurrence data structure** by entering a numeric value (1-9999) in positions 44-47 of the line on which you declare the data structure. The value you enter specifies the number of occurrences (or repetitions) of the data structure in storage. A multiple-occurrence data structure is similar to a table or array, because it enables the computer to store many values for a given field name. But because the entire data structure is repeated, you can build a much more complex data structure than you can with RPG tables or arrays.

Consider the problem of the state table data discussed in Chapter 8. When we wanted to be able to access state name and sales tax rate based on state code, we were able to access the data by defining three separate tables in RPG. As the number of kinds of data increase, however, implementing through tables becomes more and more awkward. If, for example, you wanted to be able to access the state's capital, lowest zip code, and highest zip code, in addition to state name and tax rate, based on state code, you would need to define six separate tables and perform five separate look-ups to obtain the needed information. A data structure could handle this problem more simply.

I	Line	Form Type	Filename	Sequence	Number (1/N)	Option (O)	Record Identifying Indicator or **	Record Identification Codes											Field Location			Decimal Positions	Field Name	Control Level (L1-L9)	Matching Fields or Chaining Fields	Field Record Relation	Field Indicators		
								1			2			3			Stacker Select P/B/L/R	From	To						Plus	Minus	Zero or Blank
				O R				Position	Not (N)	C/Z/D Character	Position	Not (N)	C/Z/D Character	Position	Not (N)	C/Z/D Character											
				A N D																							
0 1		I	DSTATE					DS											50								
0 2		I																1	2		CODE						
0 3		I																3	16		NAME						
0 4		I																17	20	4	SLSTAX						
0 5		I																21	35		CAPIT						
0 6		I																36	40	0	LOWZIP						
0 7		I																41	45	0	HIZIP						
0 8		I																									

The data structure above occurs 50 times; each occurrence contains CODE, NAME, SLSTAX, CAPIT, LOWZIP, and HIZIP, which are the same names as those used as fields within the STATES file. To load the data structure from the STATES file that contains the data, it is necessary to read each successive record from the file into a successive occurrence of the data structure. (This loading operation is illustrated in detail shortly.)

Multiple-occurrence data structures do not use subscripts or pointers directly to indicate which occurrence you want to work with. Instead, the OCUR operation is used to establish which occurrence of the data structure is used next within the program.

In an OCUR operation, factor 1 specifies which occurrence should be made current, while factor 2 contains the name of the data structure whose occurrence is being set. Factor 1 may contain a literal, a numeric field, or a named constant. The value of the factor 1 data item determines which occurrence, or instance, of the factor 2 data structure becomes active. Alternately, factor 1 may contain the name of a different multiple-occurrence data structure; in this case, the *current occurrence* of *that* data structure determines the occurrence of the data structure named in factor 2.

```
C        Indicators                                                    Result Field              Resulting
                                                                                                 Indicators
                                                                                                 Arithmetic
              And    And     Factor 1        Operation    Factor 2                          Plus Minus Zero
                                                                       Name    Length            Compare        Comments
 Line                                                                                       1>2  1<2  1=2
                                                                                           Lookup(Factor 2)is
         Not   Not   Not                                                                    High  Low  Equal

0 1   C  * Make  the  fifth  occurrence  of  DSTATE  active.
0 2   C              5              OCUR  DSTATE
0 3   C  * Make  the  Nth  occurrence  of  DSTATE  active.
0 4   C              N              OCUR  DSTATE
0 5   C
```

An optional indicator can be coded in positions 56-57; this indicator comes on if the specified occurrence is outside the range of the data structure.

If you want to determine which occurrence a data structure is set to, you can leave factor 1 blank and code an optional entry (which must be a numeric, integer field) in the result-field position; the result field will be given the value of the current occurrence.

```
C        Indicators                                                    Result Field              Resulting
                                                                                                 Indicators
                                                                                                 Arithmetic
              And    And     Factor 1        Operation    Factor 2                          Plus Minus Zero
                                                                       Name    Length            Compare        Comments
 Line                                                                                       1>2  1<2  1=2
                                                                                           Lookup(Factor 2)is
         Not   Not   Not                                                                    High  Low  Equal

0 1   C  * S will  indicate  which  occurrence  of  DSTATE  is  currently  active.
0 2   C                              OCUR  DSTATE       S          20
0 3   C
```

The following calculations illustrate how the state data could be obtained from a fully procedural input file to load the values into the multiple-occurrence data structure defined earlier.

```
C* Loop 50 times to load DSTATE from the STATES file.
C* Exit early if file contains fewer than 50 records.
C           1         DO   50          I         20
C           I         OCUR DSTATE
C                     READ STATES                       90
C   *IN90             IFEQ *ON
C                     EXSR ERROR
C                     LEAVE
C                     ENDIF
C                     ENDDO
C
```

Once the data structure is loaded, the information is available for "look-ups." To access the data structure information based on a match between an input state code (CODEIN) and the state codes in the data structure, you can code a loop to change the occurrence until a match is found; at that point, all the data-structure fields contain values appropriate for CODEIN. The calculations below illustrate this technique.

```
C* DSTATE is set to its first occurrence.
C                     Z-ADD1          I
C           I         OCUR DSTATE                       99
C* Loop, changing occurrence, until match is found
C* or the last occurrence has been examined.
C           CODEIN    DOWNECODE
C   *IN99             ANDEQ*OFF
C                     ADD  1          I
C           I         OCUR DSTATE                       99
C                     ENDDO
C* 99 signals the code was not found in the data structure.
C   *IN99             IFEQ *ON
C                     EXSR BADCOD
C                     ELSE
C                     EXSR FOUND
C                     ENDIF
C
```

Another use of a multiple-occurrence data structure is to provide you with the equivalent of **two-dimensional array** capabilities. Unlike most other programming languages, RPG allows arrays to be only single-dimension. Sometimes this limitation can make programming a solution to a problem more difficult than if the language included the capability to define arrays in two (or more) dimensions.

A simple analogy can help you understand the idea of a two-dimensional array. Most of you are familiar with spreadsheets. Each spreadsheet cell is addressed by a row and a column position. The row represents one dimension, the column a second. Although most spreadsheets implement this addressing with an alphabetic "pointer" for the column and a numeric "pointer" for the row (e.g., cell B4), you can see how each cell is uniquely addressed by the combination of row and column values.

Although RPG does not directly support two-dimensional arrays, you can achieve the same effect by including an array within a multiple-occurrence data structure. The array subscripts would point to a value in one dimension (the "column"), while the occurrence of the data structure would point to the second dimension (the "row").

Consider the following problem. A company has an externally described file of sales transactions for the year; each record includes AMT (amount of sale), DATE (date of sale in YYMMDD format) and LOC (numeric value, 1-50, designating the location at which the sale took place). The company wants a report that shows total monthly sales broken down by location.

One solution to this problem uses a multiple-occurrence data structure with 50 occurrences (each representing a location), and with each occurrence containing an array of 12 elements (representing each month). The portion of the program defining the data structure and showing the calculations to accumulate the sales is given below.

Line	Form Type		Table or Array Name	Number of Entries Per Record	Number of Entries Per Table or Array	Length of Entry					Comments
0 1	E	* Array to represent 12 monthly sales totals.									
0 2	E		SAR		12	10	2				
0 3	E										

I (Input Specification)

Line	Form Type	Filename	Field Location From	To	Dec	Field Name
01	I	* Multiple occurrence data structure, 50 occurrences.				
02	I	LOCAT IDS	50			
03	I		1	120		SAR
04	I	* Data structure to access month portion of input field DATE.				
05	I	DS				
06	I		1	60		DATE
07	I		1	20		YR
08	I		3	40		MN
09	I		5	60		DY
10	I					

C (Calculation Specification)

Line	Form Type	Indicators	Factor 1	Operation	Factor 2	Result Field Name	Length	Resulting Indicators	Comments
01	C		* Calcs to process SALES file to accumulate sales within						
02	C		* the appropriate month/location accumulator.						
03	C			READ	SALES			90	
04	C	*IN90		DOWEQ	*OFF				
05	C		* Set occurrence based on location.						
06	C		LOC	OCUR	LOCAT			55	55=error
07	C		* In case of invalid location or month value.						
08	C	*IN55		IFEQ	*ON				
09	C		MN	ORGT	12				
10	C		MN	ORLT	1				
11	C			EXSR	ERROR				
12	C			ELSE					
13	C			ADD	AMT	SAR,MN			
14	C			ENDIF					
15	C			READ	SALES			90	
16	C			ENDDO					
17	C								

At the end of the above routine, the year's sales have been accumulated within data structure LOCAT, with each of the 50 occurrences of LOCAT containing the 12 monthly sales totals for that location. You could then print the totals in a row/column format.

Initialization and Reinitialization of Variables

Data structures are considered character fields and, as a result, will contain blanks at the start of your program unless you explicitly initialize their subfields. In our sample code for accumulating sales, unless we had initialized all occurrences of SAR to 0, our program would end abnormally when we tried to add AMT to an SAR element.

You can initialize an entire data structure globally — so that all numeric subfields are set to zero and all character fields to spaces — by coding an I in position 18 of the data structure specification. (If you looked closely at LOCAT's definition above, you may have noticed an I that served to initialize that data structure's values.) Alternately, you can initialize only specific subfields of a data structure by coding an I in position 8 of the subfield definition line. If an I appears and you do not specify an initializing value, character subfields are initialized to blanks and numeric subfields to zero.

You can provide a different initializing value by entering a literal value or a named constant in positions 21-42 for that subfield. The value must match the type of the subfield; it cannot be longer than the subfield or have more decimal positions than the subfield (if the type is numeric). If the value is too long to fit on one line, it can be continued over several lines in the same way that values for named constants can be continued.

```
I

0 1  I * The lines below define named constants.
0 2  I                14419                          C          NUMK
0 3  I                'ACCOUNTING'                   C          CHARK
0 4  I * The entire data structure below is initialized.
0 5  I EXMPL1      IDS
0 6  I                                                1   100FLDA
0 7  I                                               11    15 FLDB
0 8  I * Subfield initialization illustrated below. Two subfields
0 9  I * initialized by named constants.
1 0  I EXMPL2       DS
1 1  I  I                                             1    42NUM1
1 2  I  I            12.34                            5    82NUM2
1 3  I  I                                             9    18 CHAR1
1 4  I  I            'ABCDEF'                        19    28 CHAR2
1 5  I  I            'This is a long -               29    59 CHAR3
1 6  I            'value for CHAR3'
1 7  I  I            NUMK                            60    640NUM3
1 8  I  I            CHARK                           65    79 CHAR4
1 9  I
```

In the sample code above, the entire data structure EXMPL1 is initialized by the I in position 18, such that any of its numeric subfields (e.g., FLDA) become 0 and any character fields (e.g., FLDB) are blank. All EXMPL2 data structure subfields are initialized individually. NUM1 is initialized to zero and

CHAR1 is initialized to blanks because no alternate values are provided for those fields. NUM2's value is initialized to 12.34, CHAR2's value is initialized to 'ABCDEF', and CHAR3's to 'This is a long value for CHAR3'. NUM3's value becomes 14419 and CHAR4's value becomes 'ACCOUNTING   ', because they have been initialized with named constants with those values.

An alternate way to handle initialization of data structure subfields, and of fields in general, is to explicitly assign them initial values within a subroutine that the program performs just once at the start of execution. RPG/400 actually provides such a subroutine, named *INZSR. If you include a subroutine with this name within your program, the subroutine is invoked automatically immediately after the program completes its other start-up tasks, such as opening the files and loading any tables or arrays. Although you can include other kinds of operations within *INZSR, good programming practice suggests that all operations within this subroutine focus on a single function — initializing variables.

C	Form Type	Control Level (L0-L9, LR,SR, AN/OR)	And		And		Factor 1	Operation	Factor 2	Result Field Name	Length	Decimal Positions	Operation Extender (H,N,P)	Resulting Indicators			Comments
0 1	C	SR						*INZSR						BEGSR			
0 2	C							Z-ADD0		RECCNT	40						
0 3	C							Z-ADD0		VALADD	30						
0 4	C							Z-ADD3.415		PI	43						
0 5	C							...									
0 6	C							ENDSR									
0 7	C																

Although RPG automatically initializes all numeric fields to 0 and all character fields to blanks at the start of a program, there are good reasons to explicitly initialize variables in an initialization subroutine. This practice makes the processing steps within your program more evident. Moreover, it relies less on the automatic features of RPG, in keeping with the movement toward complete procedural implementation of the language.

You often need to reinitialize field values during processing. For instance, in control-break programs, you need to set subtotal accumulators back to 0. Or in interactive maintenance programs, you may want to clear data fields when you add new records. RPG/400 provides two operations — CLEAR and RESET — to allow you to reinitialize variables.

CLEAR changes the values of the data item(s) it is used with to 0, blanks, or '0', depending on the field type. ('0' is appropriate for indicators.) You can CLEAR individual fields or structures (data structures, arrays, tables, record formats). A CLEAR operation requires a factor 2 entry that specifies which data item is to be cleared. If you specify an array, the system clears the entire array. If, however, you specify a multiple-occurrence data structure or a table for clearing, only the current occurrence or table element is cleared.

If the data item to be cleared is a database file-record format, you can specify *NOKEY in factor 1 to signal that all the record's fields *except* the record key are to be cleared. If you CLEAR a record format, only fields that are output in that record format are affected. This means that if you clear a display-file record format, only those fields with usage O(utput) or B(oth) would be reinitialized.

Line	Form Type	Control Level (L0-L9, LR,SR, AN/OR)	And (Not)	And (Not)	And (Not)	Factor 1	Operation	Factor 2	Result Field Name	Length	Decimal Positions	Operation Extender (H,N,P)	Resulting Indicators Plus/1>2	Minus/1<2	Zero/1=2	Comments
0 1	C					* All data structure subfields get set to blank or 0,										
0 2	C					* depending on their types.										
0 3	C						CLEAR	DATSTR								
0 4	C					* All record fields except key get set to blank or 0.										
0 5	C					*NOKEY	CLEAR	RECORD								
0 6	C					* O and B fields of screen cleared, but not I fields.										
0 7	C						CLEAR	SCREEN2								
0 8	C					* All array elements cleared.										
0 9	C						CLEAR	ARR								
1 0	C					* Only current occurrence of multiple occurrence DS is cleared.										
1 1	C						CLEAR	MLTDS								
1 2	C															

The RESET operation is similar to CLEAR, except that instead of automatically reinitializing values to blank, 0, or '0', depending on type, RESET restores the elements to whatever value they had at the end of the initialization step at the program's start. If you had initialized data structure subfields to specific values, or had turned on indicators or assigned values to fields in *INZSR, and these values had subsequently been changed during the program's execution, you can easily reassign them those same values with RESET.

The format of RESET is identical to that of CLEAR: The factor 2 value may be a data structure, record format, array, table, or variable (field, subfield, or indicator). As with CLEAR, only the current occurrence of a data structure or the current element of a table is reset. If factor 2 is a display-file record format, only those fields with usage O(output) or B(both) are reinitialized to their starting values.

C			Indicators							Result Field				Resulting Indicators				
Line	Form Type	Control Level (L0-L9, LR,SR, AN/OR)	And (Not)	And (Not)	(Not)	Factor 1	Operation	Factor 2		Name	Length	Decimal Positions	Operation Extender (H,N,P)	Arithmetic Plus/Minus/Zero; Compare 1>2/1<2/1=2; Lookup(Factor 2)is High/Low/Equal		Comments		

0 1	C		*	A l l d a t a s t r u c t u r e s u b f i e l d s g e t s e t t o t h e i r o r i g i n a l l y
0 2	C		*	i n i t i a l i z e d v a l u e s o r t o b l a n k s .
0 3	C			R E S E T D A T S T R
0 4	C		*	A l l r e c o r d f i e l d s e x c e p t k e y s e t t o i n i t i a l i z e d v a l u e s o r t o
0 5	C		*	d e f a u l t v a l u e s o f b l a n k a n d z e r o .
0 6	C			* N O K E Y R E S E T R E C O R D
0 7	C		*	U s a g e O a n d B f i e l d s o f s c r e e n r e s e t , b u t n o t I f i e l d s .
0 8	C			R E S E T S C R E E N 2
0 9	C		*	A l l a r r a y e l e m e n t s r e s e t t o i n i t i a l i z e d v a l u e .
1 0	C			R E S E T A R R
1 1	C		*	O n l y c u r r e n t o c c u r r e n c e o f m u l t i p l e o c c u r r e n c e D S i s r e s e t .
1 2	C			R E S E T M L T D S

File-Information Data Structures

A **file-information data structure** is a special data structure that can be defined for each file used by your program. A file-information data structure contains predefined subfields that can provide information to your program about the file and the outcomes of input and/or output operations to the file. The subfields vary depending on whether the data structure is associated with a physical or logical database file, a display file, or a printer file.

A file-information data structure must be linked to the file it is associated with by making some entries on that file's File Specification description. You can make these required entries either on the file description line itself or on a continuation line for that file (a line following the file line with a K in 53 to signal that it is a continuation statement). The required entries are K in position 53, letters INFDS in positions 54-59 and the name of the data structure in positions 60-65.

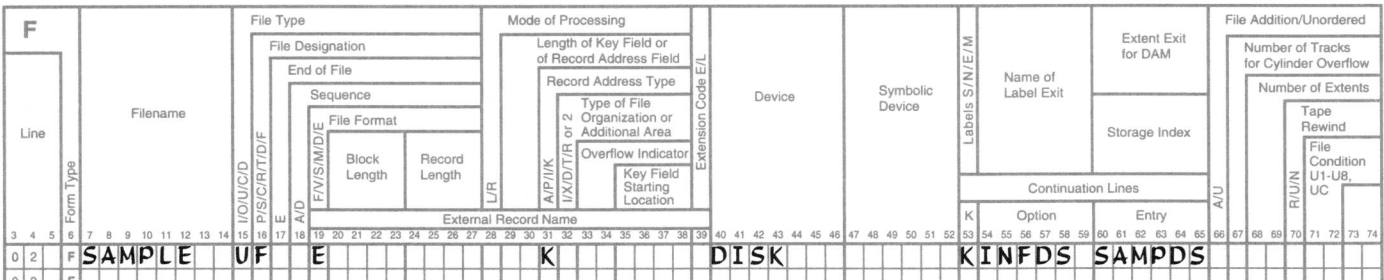

The above code defines data structure SAMPDS as the file-information data structure for file SAMPLE. Each such data structure is 528 positions long and is subdivided into predefined segments or subfields, each of which automatically will contain information about the file the data structure is associated with. To reference a particular subfield of information, you need to know its From and To position within the data structure. You can look these positions up in a reference manual.

Alternately, IBM has provided keywords, which are more easily remembered, to represent the location of those subfields most often referenced. For these subfields, you can substitute the keyword for the subfield's actual location within the data structure. You must supply a name for the subfield, regardless of whether you reference its location through actual positions or through a keyword.

Although a complete discussion of file-information data structures is beyond the scope of this text (see IBM's reference manual, *Languages: RPG/400 Reference* (SC09-1349) for each subfield and its location within the data structure), the following paragraph describes some of the subfields and what they represent to give you a sense of the potential usefulness of file-information data structures.

The subfield in positions 1-8 (or keyword *FILE) contains the name of the file. Positions 16-21 (or keyword *OPCODE) contain the name of the most recent operation processed on the file, such as READ. Positions 11-15 (or keyword *STATUS) contain a five-digit numeric field, with 0 decimal positions, that contains the status code of the most recent I/O operation.

Status codes are predefined values that signal specific I/O events. Status code 00000 reflects no error or exception. Status code 00002 indicates that a function key was used to end a display. Status code 00011 signals an end-of-file on a read. Status code 00012 signals a no-record-found condition on a chain operation. Any status code greater than 00099 is an error. Different error codes signal precisely what kind of error occurred. For example, 01211 indicates an attempt at I/O to a closed file, while status code 01021 indicates an attempt was made to write a record with a duplicate key to a file that is supposed to have unique keys.

Some of the subfields, such as the status-code subfield, are useful for testing and debugging programs. Other subfields may provide information needed by your program as part of its normal processing. For example, if you are trying to develop an interactive application that is cursor sensitive, your program will need to be able to determine the cursor's location on the screen; positions 370-371 of the file-information data structure contain (in binary representation) the row and column coordinates of the cursor upon return from a screen.

Other subfields of the file-information data structure include information about the position of the file "pointer," or current relative record number (positions 397-400); a count of the total number of records in the file (positions 156-159); or what function key was used to end a display (position 369).

The following example shows a sample file-information data structure. Notice the use of the keywords in place of location in three of the subfields. Rather than *FILE, the file name could have been accessed by coding From 1 To 8.

I	Line	Form Type	Filename	Sequence	Number (1/N)	Option (O)	Record Identifying Indicator or **	Record Identification Codes — 1 Position	Not (N)	C/Z/D	Character	2 Position	Not (N)	C/Z/D	Character	3 Position	Not (N)	C/Z/D	Character	Stacker Select	P/B/L/R	Field Location — From	To	Decimal Positions	Field Name	Control Level (L1–L9)	Matching Fields or Chaining Fields	Field Record Relation	Field Indicators — Plus	Minus	Zero or Blank
	0 1	I	SAMPDS									DS																			
	0 2	I																				*FILE			FILNAM						
	0 3	I																				*STATUS	0		FSTAT						
	0 4	I																				*OPCODE			OPCODE						
	0 5	I																			B	397	4000	RRN						
	0 6	I																			B	156	1590	RCDCNT						
	0 7	I																													

In general, anytime you write a program for which you need "behind-the-scenes" information about the files used by the program, remember file-information data structures. Chances are that the data you need can be obtained from a subfield within such a data structure.

Program-Status Data Structures

Just as you can define file-information data structures to provide you with information about data or events associated with the files used by your program, you can also define a **program-status data structure** that can provide you with information about the program itself and about exceptions/errors that occur during program execution.

Like a file-information data structure, a program-status data structure has predefined subfields that automatically are given values during the course of your program's execution. Some of these subfields are useful in testing and debugging to determine what went wrong in the program, while others provide information that might be needed to implement the logic of the program itself.

For example, a program-status data structure can supply you with the name of the program, the job name and job number, the name of the user who called the program, and the specific number of any runtime exception or error that occurs while the program is running. A status code subfield also can provide information about program problems. To give you a sense of what kinds of errors the status code can report, below is a sample of some of the possible values for the status code subfield:

Code	Meaning
00000	No error occurred
00101	Negative square root
00102	Divide by 0
00121	Array index not valid
00122	OCUR outside range
00907	Decimal data error

An S in position 18 of a data structure definition line identifies a program-status data structure. Any subfield of the data structure that you want to access must be defined within the data structure. The definition includes the location of the subfield, a decimal entry (if appropriate), and a name you assign to the subfield. IBM has provided keywords that can substitute for the location of those subfields most commonly used. A sample program-status data structure is illustrated below. For more information about program-status data structures, see IBM's reference manual, *Languages: RPG/400 Reference.*

```
I
* Sample program status data structure.
                    SDS
                                                    *STATUS OPSTAT
                                                      40  42 ERRTYP
                                                      43  46 ERRCOD
                                                     244 253 JOBNAM
                                                     264 2690JOBNUM
                                                     354 363 USER
```

Error Handling and *PSSR

Without explicit error handling within your program, regardless of whether or not you include file-information and program-status data structures, any runtime error will cause the system to suspend the program and send a message to the interactive user or the system operator (when the program is running in batch). Assume you wanted to handle errors internally within your program, rather than allowing the errors to cause such a program **abend** (abnormal ending). You could use one of several alternative methods to handle errors.

One technique is to code an error indicator in positions 56-57 of those operations that permit such an entry. If an error occurs during an operation that includes such an error indicator, the indicator comes on and the program simply continues to the next sequential instruction.

Line	Form Type	Control Level	And (Not)	And (Not)	And (Not)	Factor 1	Operation	Factor 2	Result Field Name	Length	Dec Pos	Op Ext	Resulting Indicators	Comments
0 1	C					* Error indicator 56 causes program to simply continue								
0 2	C					* if an error occurs.								
0 3	C						READ	SAMPLE					5690	
0 4	C					*IN90	DOWEQ	*OFF						
0 5	C					SAMP	CHAIN	FILEX					9556	
0 6	C						EXSR	CALCS						
0 7	C						READ	SAMPLE					5690	
0 8	C						ENDDO							
0 9	C													

Although this method prevents an abnormal end of your program, it is simply ignoring the error — a potentially dangerous practice. A better method would be to include an error routine that the program executes immediately upon encountering an error. By checking the status of your error indicator after each operation that uses it, your program could appropriately execute a special routine should any error occur.

Line	Form Type	Control Level	And (Not)	And (Not)	And (Not)	Factor 1	Operation	Factor 2	Result Field Name	Length	Dec Pos	Op Ext	Resulting Indicators	Comments
0 1	C					* Error indicator 56 checked and subroutine ERROR								
0 2	C					* executed if an error occurs.								
0 3	C						READ	SAMPLE					5690	
0 4	C					*IN56	IFEQ	*ON						
0 5	C						EXSR	ERROR						
0 6	C						ENDIF							
0 7	C					*IN90	DOWEQ	*OFF						
0 8	C					SAMP	CHAIN	FILEX					9556	
0 9	C					*IN56	IFEQ	*ON						
1 0	C						EXSR	ERROR						
1 1	C						ENDIF							
1 2	C						EXSR	CALCS						
1 3	C						READ	SAMPLE					5690	
1 4	C					*IN56	IFEQ	*ON						
1 5	C						EXSR	ERROR						
1 6	C						ENDIF							
1 7	C						ENDDO							
1 8	C													

Including all these checks, however, would greatly increase the length of your program and still would not solve the problem of errors generated by operations (such as DIV) that do not permit the use of an error indicator.

Fortunately, an alternate method of error trapping exists. RPG has built in a special subroutine name, *PSSR. If you include a subroutine named *PSSR within your program, that subroutine will automatically receive control when a *program error* occurs. To send control to this subroutine for *file* exceptions/errors, you must explicitly designate *PSSR as the error handler for the file(s). This assignment is quite straightforward; simply add a file description line designating *PSSR as the INFSR (file exception/error subroutine) for the file or files of concern. The example below illustrates this assignment.

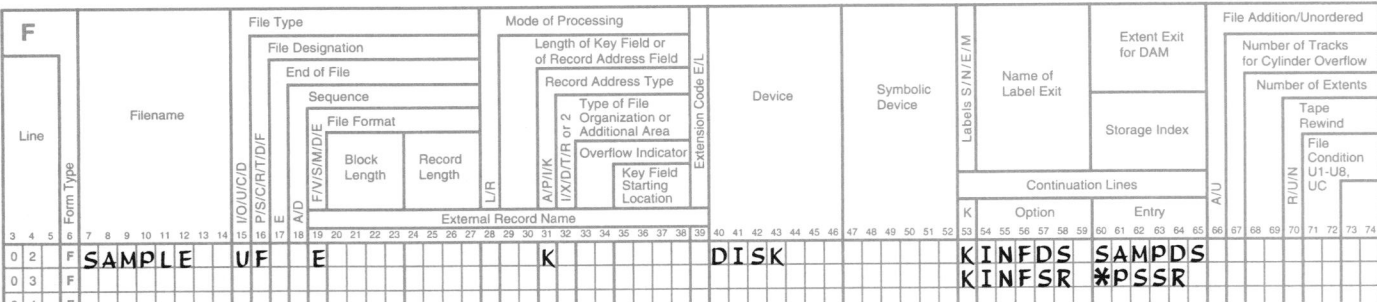

The K in position 53 of the second File Specification signals that this line is a continuation of the definition for file SAMPLE; option INFSR signals that the entry following it is to serve as the error routine automatically invoked when a file exception/error occurs. With the above addition, any kind of error encountered while your program is running will cause control to be transferred to subroutine *PSSR — without the need for including and checking error indicators.

```
     C   Indicators              Factor 1   Operation   Factor 2        Result Field        Resulting Indicators   Comments
01  C* Error routine automatically invoked on error without the
02  C* need for error indicators.
03  C                                  READ  SAMPLE                                   90
04  C           *IN90                  DOWEQ*OFF
05  C           SAMP                   CHAINFILEX                              95
06  C                                  EXSR CALCS
07  C                                  READ  SAMPLE                                   90
08  C                                  ENDDO
09  C                                  ...
10  C SR        *PSSR                  BEGSR
11  C                                  ...
12  C                                  ENDSR
13  C
```

Within *PSSR, you could check the status codes and other subfields of the file-information and program-status data structures to determine the best response to the error — perhaps ignoring the error and continuing, perhaps writing a line to an error report and continuing, or perhaps noting the error and bringing the program to a normal ending. The optimal design of *PSSR logic is beyond the scope of this text. As a programmer new to RPG, you should be aware of the need for error detection and understand the function and value of a *PSSR subroutine. As you gain more experience with the language, you will no doubt begin to incorporate such error handling within your programs.

Chapter Summary

Named constants allow you to assign fixed-character or numeric values to data names that then can be used throughout your program. Named constants are beneficial to use because they can represent data values too long to hard code as factors within your calculations and because they concentrate program maintenance to one line of code when a constant value needs to be changed.

Fields can be defined relative to other field definitions using *LIKE DEFN. A field defined in this way may have its length exactly match that of the field supplying the definition; alternately, you can specify its length in terms relative to that of the second field's length (e.g., three positions longer, or two positions shorter).

You can define data structures that represent complex definitions of a given area of memory. A data structure is composed of subfields. These subfields may represent overlapping areas of storage or subdivisions of fields. A multiple-occurrence data structure establishes repetitions of the data structure in memory to allow you to perform data manipulation more complex than what simple arrays or tables can offer. Arrays can appear as subfields of multiple-occurrence data structures; this feature provides the equivalent of two-dimensional arrays, a feature not otherwise available in RPG.

Data structures or subfields of data structures can be initialized easily as part of the data structure definition. RPG also provides subroutine *INZSR, which, if included within your program, automatically executes at the program's startup. Programmers often use *INZSR to explicitly initialize fields and other data items. The operation CLEAR can be used to initialize or reinitialize data items to zeros or blanks, depending on data type. RESET, on the other hand, reinitializes data items to whatever value they were given at the beginning of the program.

Two special data structures of predefined subfields exist in RPG to provide information about the status of files used by the program or about the processing of the program itself: file-information data structures and program-status data structures. These data structures often are accessed within RPG's *PSSR error subroutine to determine the cause of an execution error.

Terms

abend	file-information data structure	named constant
data structures	multiple-occurrence	program-status data structure
DEFN	data structure	two-dimensional array

Discussion/Review Questions

1. What is a named constant?

2. What are the advantages of using named constants in a program?

3. What is the purpose of *LIKE DEFN? Why might you use this RPG feature?

4. What kinds of capabilities can you gain by using data structures?

5. What is a multiple-occurrence data structure? Compare and contrast it to an RPG table.

6. Data structures use OCUR; what parallel for OCUR do you have when you are working with arrays? With tables?

7. What is variable initialization? What techniques are available in RPG to allow you to initialize fields and other data items?

8. Describe the difference between CLEAR and RESET operations.

9. What built-in subroutines does RPG provide for your use? When is each executed?

10. Compare and contrast a file-information data structure with a program-status data structure.

11. How many file-information data structures can you have within a program? How many program-status data structures?

12. Discuss different options for trapping errors (or not trapping errors) within a program, giving the pros and cons of each method.

Exercises

1. Code the following values as named constants: a commission rate of 2.5%; the company name "Acme Explosives Company"; the FICA cut-off income of $58,000; and an edit word for editing Social Security numbers.

2. A retail business' SALES file contains field DAYSAL, eight positions long with two decimal positions, that represents the store's sales from one day. Use *LIKE DEFN to define fields that will hold: the sales tax for a day's sales, a week's worth of sales, a week's sales tax, annual sales, and annual sales tax.

3. Data file WUTSTP contains student answers to 50-item, multiple-choice tests. The format of these records is shown below.

TEST	Test number	positions 1- 4
SECT	Section number	positions 5- 9
CRSE	Course ID	positions 10-15
STID	Social Security number	positions 16-24
ANS	Answers 1-50	positions 25-74

Exercises Continued

Exercises continued

Code a data structure that does the following: subdivides CRSE into two three-position fields (the first represents the department offering the course, the second the course number); subdivides STID — Social Security number — into three-, two-, and four-position subfields; and defines ANS as an array, with each answer a separate element of the array. (Include the Extension Specification.)

4. To determine shipping charges, CompuSell uses a table file that contains shipping charges based on weight and zone. Each record contains a weight and six charges (one each for zones 2-7).

    There are 70 records in the file, sequentially reflecting weights 1-70. The record layout of CSCHGP is:

Field	Positions	(Decimal positions)
Weight (pounds)	1 - 2	(0)
Charge zone 2	3 - 6	(2)
Charge zone 3	7 - 10	(2)
Charge zone 4	11 - 14	(2)
Charge zone 5	15 - 18	(2)
Charge zone 6	19 - 22	(2)
Charge zone 7	23 - 26	(2)

Define a multiple-occurrence data structure that will hold the contents of this file and allow you to store all the table information at once within the data structure as an alternative to storing it in tables.

5. Write the calculations that would be needed to load the data structure from exercise 4 with the contents of CSCHGP. Make up whatever data names you need, in addition to those of the data structure.

6. Write the calculations needed to locate the appropriate charge from the data structure of exercises 4 and 5 based on an input weight — field WTIN — and zone — field ZIN. (That is, do the equivalent of a table look-up, using your data structure.)

Programming Assignments

1. Acme Explosive Company tracks its product sales by month. This sales information is stored in file PRDSLSP, described in Appendix D. There is only one record per product manufactured by the company. Each record includes sales totals for that product for each month of the previous year.

    The company wants you to write a program to produce a summary report of sales, highlighting the month with the lowest sales and the month with the highest sales for each product. The name of the months, rather than the month number, is to appear on the report. At the end of the report the company wants the overall product sales for each month.

    To facilitate processing the sales figures, define the input record as a data structure containing an array. Define all work variables with *LIKE DEFN. Handle the names of the months as a compile-time array.

Programming Assignments Continued

Programming Assignments continued

```
          1         2         3         4         5         6         7
 123456789012345678901234567890123456789012345678901234567890123456789Ø

 XX/XX/XX     ACME EXPLOSIVES ANNUAL SALES SUMMARY     PAGE XXØX

 PRODUCT         BEST MONTH        WORST MONTH
 XXXXXX         XXX,XØX JANUARY    XXX,XØX SEPTEMBER
 XXXXXX         XXX,XØX MAY        XXX,XØX AUGUST
 XXXXXX         XXX,XØX JUNE       XXX,XØX DECEMBER

 TOTAL MONTHLY SALES:
 JANUARY        $XX,XXX,X$X
 FEBRUARY       $XX,XXX,X$X
 MARCH          $XX,XXX,X$X
     . . .
 DECEMBER       $XX,XXX,X$X
```

2. Honest John's Used Cars employs 20 salespeople; each salesperson has a number assigned to him/her (numbers range from 1-20). During the course of a week, each sale a salesperson makes is recorded in a transaction file, HJSLSP (see Appendix D). Each record includes information about the salesperson number, the invoice number, and the amount of the sale. Each input record in the transaction file contains a record of a single sale. The file records are not sorted in any way. There may be several input records for a given salesperson, depending on how many successful sales (s)he has had during the week.

   A salesperson file is also available, HJSLPP, keyed on salesperson number and including the salesperson's name and weekly base pay (see Appendix D).

   Honest John wants you to determine weekly pay due each salesperson. Pay is based on the weekly base pay plus a commission based on total weekly sales for each salesperson. If total sales is greater than $50,000, use a 3% commission rate; if it's between $25,000 and $50,000, use a 2% commission rate; if it's less than $25,000, use a 1% commission rate. It is possible that not every salesperson has had at least one sale this week; however, each should get paid at least his/her base pay.

   Write a program to generate the report shown below, with the following restrictions on your program: 1) Do not define a logical file over HJSLSP. Instead, use a multiple-occurrence data structure to accumulate sales for each sales person. 2) Do not hard-code commission levels or rates in your calculations; instead, handle them as named constants. 3) Use *LIKE DEFN to define any work variables needed within your program.

```
          1         2         3         4         5         6         7         8         9
 123456789012345678901234567890123456789012345678901234567890123456789012345678901234567890

      XX/XX/XX              HONEST JOHN'S USED CARS
                          WEEKLY SALESMAN PAY SCHEDULE

      SLSP.                          BASE                      TOTAL
      NO.        NAME                PAY        COMMIS.        PAY

       1    XXXXXXXXXXXXXXXXXXXXXXXX  X,XXØ.XX    X,XXØ.XX     XX,XXØ.XX
       2    XXXXXXXXXXXXXXXXXXXXXXXX  X,XXØ.XX    X,XXØ.XX     XX,XXØ.XX
       3    XXXXXXXXXXXXXXXXXXXXXXXX  X,XXØ.XX    X,XXØ.XX     XX,XXØ.XX
                              . . .

            TOTALS          $XXX,XX$.XX   $XXX,XX$.XX   $X,XXX,XXØ.XX
```

Programming Assignments Continued

Programming Assignments continued

3. Piper, a small commuter airline, runs three flights a day between two cities, seven days a week. Its plane holds 20 passengers. The airline wants an online reservation system that will do the following:

Allow the user to enter a day (1-7)[*], representing Monday-Sunday, a flight number (1-3), and the number of requested seats. If that many seats are available, allow the user to enter the name and phone number of the person making the reservation and reserve that many seats by adding a record to the reservation file. Confirm the reservation and then redisplay the original entry screen with no values showing. If that flight does not have enough vacant seats, display a message on the screen that tells how many seats are available and allow the user to change all or part of the reservation (i.e., redisplay with the old data).

A physical file, PIPRESP, exists for use by your program (Appendix D). The file contains information about reservations for the flights for the week, including information about the person who made the reservation and the number of seats (s)he reserved. This file should be updated as customers place reservations and should be used to determine availability of seats.

Hint: Load a multiple-occurrence data structure from the file at the beginning of the program before taking reservations. As you take reservations, make sure you update the data structure to keep it current, and also write a record to the reservation file.

> [*]To simplify the problem, assume that Piper does not take reservations more than a week in advance, nor does it take reservations on the day of the flight. Thus, if today is Tuesday, a reservation for day 2 would be interpreted to be for next Tuesday. Also assume that the first thing each morning a program runs that transfers all reservation records for that day's flight to another file, so you don't need to worry about mixing up today's reservations with those for a week from now.

4. Wexler University wants you to write a program to prepare tuition bills for students based on their current enrollment. You will need to use four files: WUENRLP, WUSTDP, WUCRSP, and WUSCTP. (See Appendix D). You may create whatever logical files you need to facilitate processing.

Each record in WUENRLP, which represents student current enrollment, should be processed in student order. For each section a student is enrolled in, you will need to determine the course identification and credits. Accumulate credits for the student. Then bill the student based on the total number of credits (s)he is enrolled for and the student's residency and status, using the following per-credit-hour tuition figures:

	Indistrict ($)	Out-of-District ($)	International ($)
Lower Division (<61 credits)	77.50	155.25	200.50
Upper Division (>60 credits)	87.25	195.50	225.75
Graduate	111.50	250.50	276.00

In addition to tuition fees, the school levies the following fees:

a) Enrollment fee: An enrollment fee will be charged to all students. Students enrolled in seven or more credit hours will be charged $194.00. Those enrolled in fewer than seven credit hours will be charged $72.50.

b) Student Activity fee: $8.00 is a Student Organization's assessment.

Programming Assignments Continued

Programming Assignments continued

c) MCC Fee: Michigan Collegiality Congress fee of $.50.

Define all fees and charges as named constants in your program, since as a student you know these charges are bound to change soon. Use whatever other features discussed in this chapter (such as *INZSR) that you feel will make your job easier.

Prepare a student tuition bill for each student, formatted as follows:

```
          1         2         3         4         5         6         7
 123456789012345678901234567890123456789012345678901234567890123456789Ø

   WEXLER U. TUITION BILL     BILLING DATE: XX/XX/XX

 TO: XXXXXXXXXXXXXXX XXXXXXXXXX
     XXXXXXXXXXXXXXX
     XXXXXXXXXXXXXXX XX XXXXX-XXXX

 ACCORDING TO OUR RECORDS, YOU HAVE ENROLLED IN THE
 FOLLOWING COURSES:
 COURSE     SECTION     DAYS   TIME       CREDITS
 XXXXXX     XXXXXX      XXX    XØ:XX         X
 XXXXXX     XXXXXX      XXX    XØ:XX         X
 XXXXXX     XXXXXX      XXX    XØ:XX         X
                              TOTAL CREDITS  XØ

                              AMOUNT DUE
               TUITION:          $X,XX$.XX
               ENROLLMENT FEE:    XXØ.XX
               ACTIVITY FEE:       XØ.XX
               MCC FEE:             .XX

               TOTAL DUE:        $X,XX$.XX

 FAILURE TO PAY TOTAL WITHIN 21 DAYS OF BILLING
 WILL RESULT IN YOUR BEING DROPPED FROM ALL
 CLASSES.
```

Chapter 10

Interactive Programs: Advanced Techniques

Chapter Overview

This chapter extends your ability to write interactive applications by introducing you to two new concepts: subfiles and on-line help.

Subfiles

In Chapter 7 you were introduced to interactive programs. You learned how to write inquiry and maintenance programs where the program logic required the display of information one record at a time. Some kinds of applications require the use of **list panels**, in which data from many records is displayed on a screen for review, selection, or update. RPG has a special feature called **subfiles** to handle this kind of program requirement.

A subfile is a collection of records that is handled as a unit for screen I/O. Although subfile processing can get quite complicated, basic subfile processing techniques can be learned without great difficulty. As a prelude to discussing coding requirements for subfiles, consider the following problem description.

In Chapter 7 we worked with a file of course section information and developed an interactive application to display detailed section information based on an entered section number. The record layout of that file, SECTIONS, is repeated on the following page.

Form Type	Name Type (R/K/S/O)	Name	Length	Decimal Positions	Functions
A	R	SECTREC			
A		SECTNO	5		TEXT('Section number')
A		DAYS	3		TEXT('Days class meets')
A		BEGTIM	4	0	TEXT('Time class starts')
A		ROOM	4	0	TEXT('Classroom')
A		ENROLL	3	0	TEXT('Current enrollment')
A		INSTR	15		TEXT('Section Instructor')
A		COURSE	6		TEXT('Course Identifier')
A	K	SECTNO			

Now assume that the same school wants an application in which it can enter a course name to see a list of all the sections offered for that course.

The desired screen layouts are shown below and on the next page. Notice that the second screen contains information from many section records, rather than just a single one. This fact means that you will need to use subfiles to implement the solution.

```
                              Course Inquiry

          Type value, then Enter.

              Course number . .  _____













          F3=Exit
```

```
                    XXXXXX Course Information

       Section      Instructor       Room   Days    Time    Enroll.
        XXXXX   XXXXXXXXXXXXXX        XXXX   XXX    XX:XX     XØX
        XXXXX   XXXXXXXXXXXXXX        XXXX   XXX    XX:XX     XØX
        XXXXX   XXXXXXXXXXXXXX        XXXX   XXX    XX:XX     XØX













       Press Enter to continue.

       F3=Exit  F12=Cancel
```

The first step before beginning the screen definition is to create a logical file over the SECTIONS file to access the records in order by course, and within course by section. The definition for that logical file, SECTIONL, is shown below.

Now consider the display file, SECTINQ. The first screen definition is identical to the layout from the screen in Chapter 7; only the literals need to be changed. Note, though, that CA03 has been moved to make it a file-level keyword.

| | | Conditioning | | | | | Name | | Length | | Data Type | Decimal Positions | Usage | Location | | Functions |
Sequence Number	Form Type	And/Or/Comment (A/O/*)	Condition Name	Name Type	Reserved			Reference (R)						Line	Pos	
	A															CA03(03 'F3=EXIT')
	A			R		CORINQ										
	A													1	28	'Course Inquiry'
	A													3	2	'Type value, then Enter.'
	A													5	5	'Course number . .'
	A					COURS			6A		B			5	24	
	A															DSPATR(UL)
	A	N90														DSPATR(HI)
	A	90														ERRMSG('Course not found' 90)
	A													23	2	'F3=Exit'
	A															

The second screen will require subfile definition. To use a subfile to display multiple records on a screen requires two record formats: one to define a subfile record and one to control the subfile and its display.

Subfile Record Formats

The **subfile record format** describes the fields that are to appear on the screen. Because in this example the screen and database fields are the same, the database file containing the field definitions is noted with record-level keyword REF.

A new record-level keyword is required, SFL (Subfile), which identifies this format as a subfile. The remaining information in the subfile record format describes the fields to appear, their locations on the screen, and any editing or other special keywords if desired. The line number associated with each field represents the line on which the first record of the subfile is to appear.

The figure below illustrates the subfile record format of our application.

Sequence Number	Form Type	And/Or/Comment (A/O/*)	Condition Name						Name Type (ⓑ/R/K/S/O)	Reserved	Name	Reference (R)	Length	Data Type (ⓑ A/P/S/B A/S/X/Y/N/I/W)	Decimal Positions	Usage (ⓑ/O/I/B/H/M)	Line	Pos	Functions
	A																		REF(SECTIONS)
	A							R		SUBSEC									SFL
	A									SECTNO	R				O	4	14	
	A									INSTR	R				O	4	23	
	A									ROOM	R				O	4	41	
	A									DAYS	R				O	4	49	
	A									BEGTIM	R		Y		O	4	57	EDTWRD('0 : ')
	A									ENROLL	R		Y		O	4	66	EDTCDE(3)

Subfile Control-Record Formats

The **subfile control-record format** must immediately follow the subfile record format. This record format controls the display of the subfile records through the use of special record-level keywords. In addition, programmers often include the column headings for the subfile display as part of this record format.

The subfile control-record format *requires* several record-level keywords. These required keywords and their functions are as follows:

SFLCTL (Subfile Control): This keyword identifies this as the subfile control record for the subfile named within the parentheses of the keyword.

SFLDSP (Subfile Display): If this keyword is active when an output operation is performed on the subfile control record, the subfile itself is also displayed. This keyword generally is conditioned by an indicator to control whether or not the subfile displays on a given output operation.

SFLPAG (Subfile Page): This keyword defines how many subfile records are to be displayed at one time on the screen. The number follows the keyword and is enclosed in parentheses. You generally determine this number by calculating the number of available screen lines after all other lines to be displayed along with the subfile are taken into account.

SFLSIZ (Subfile Size): this value, enclosed in parentheses immediately following the keyword, should be either equal to or greater than the SFLPAG value. If the value is greater, you may make it large enough to accommodate the maximum number of records you would normally have in the subfile. (If you underestimate, however, the subfile will automatically be extended to make room for the additional records.) A subfile cannot be greater than 9,999 records. If SFLSIZ is greater than SFLPAG, OS/400 automatically handles paging through the subfile when the user presses the roll keys, and displays a "+" on the bottom of the screen to indicate there are subfile records not yet displayed.

Subfile control record-level keywords that are optional but usually used include:

SFLDSPCTL (Subfile Display Control): This keyword enables the display of any output fields or constants described within the control-record format. This keyword generally is conditioned with the same indicator used for the SFLDSP keyword.

SFLCLR (Subfile Clear): If this keyword is active when an output operation is performed on the subfile control record, the subfile itself is cleared of records. An option indicator is required for this keyword, or the system would clear the subfile on every output operation to the control record. The indicator often is the reverse of the indicator used for SFLDSP and SFLDSPCTL, so that you clear the subfile in one output operation and display the subfile and the control-record information in a second output operation.

The figure below illustrates a subfile control-record format. Notice that when indicator 50 is on the system will clear the subfile; when 50 is off, the system will display both the subfile record format and the subfile control-record format. Also note that the control-record format includes screen column headings for the subfile.

As mentioned above, the relationship between subfile size and subfile page can be varied. There are several different approaches to defining this interrelationship and loading data into the subfile. The method used depends in part on the program's anticipated processing requirements. We will develop our sample program using four different techniques, to give you a sense of the variation and rationale for each method.

Loading the Entire Subfile

The first method involves defining the subfile size large enough to hold the maximum expected number of records and then loading all the appropriate data into the subfile prior to any record display. This method is the easiest to code but results in the slowest initial response time. Once the display begins, however, paging through the subfile is fast. This method is least appropriate when there are a large number of records to be loaded and the user is unlikely to want to see most of them.

The figure below shows the complete DDS for this application method. Notice that in addition to subfile-related keywords, the control-record format includes the record-level keyword OVERLAY so that the footer-record format, also defined below, will not be erased when the subfile is displayed.

```
          1         2         3         4         5         6         7         8
 1234567890123456789012345678901234567890123456789012345678901234567890123456789Ø
     A                                              CAØ3(Ø3 'F3=Exit')
     A                                              CA12(12 'F12=Cancel')
     A                                              REF(SECTIONS)
     A           R CORINQ
     A                                            1 28'Course Inquiry'
     A                                            3  2'Type value, then Enter.'
     A                                            5  5'Course number . .'
     A             COURS       6A  B   5 24
     A                                              DSPATR(UL)
     A N9Ø                                          DSPATR(HI)
     A  9Ø                                          ERRMSG('Course not found' 9Ø)
     A                                           23  2'F3=Exit   F12=Cancel'
     A           R SUBSEC                            SFL
     A             SECTNO      R     0 4 14
     A             INSTR       R     0 4 23
     A             ROOM        R     0 4 41
     A             DAYS        R     0 4 49
     A             BEGTIM      R  Y  0 4 57EDTWRD('Ø :   ')
     A             ENROLL      R  Y  0 4 66EDTCDE(3)
     A           R CTLSEC                            SFLCTL(SUBSEC)
     A                                              SFLPAG(15)
     A                                              SFLSIZ(8Ø)
     A  5Ø                                          SFLCLR
     A N5Ø                                          SFLDSPCTL
     A N5Ø                                          SFLDSP
     A                                              OVERLAY
     A             COURS       6A  O   1 28
     A                                            1 35'Course Information'
     A                                            3 12'Section'
     A                                            3 24'Instructor'
     A                                            3 41'Room'
     A                                            3 49'Days'
```

```
              1         2         3         4         5         6         7         8
     12345678901234567890123456789012345678901234567890123456789012345678901234567890
     A                                                       3 57'Time'
     A                                                       3 64'Enroll.'
     A              R FOOTER
     A                                                      21  2'Press Enter to continue.'
     A                                                      23  2'F3=Exit   F12=Cancel'
```

With the display-file definition complete, we can turn to the requirements for the program that will use it.

In all subfile applications, you need to make some additions to the File Specifications, because RPG requires that you associate a subfile with its display file. This association occurs on a continuation line — a separate specification line with a K in position 53. That continuation line needs to include the keyword SFILE in positions 54-59 (Option) and the record-format name of the subfile in positions 60-67 (Entry). Additionally, a field that will serve as the subfile records' relative record number is required in positions 47-52 (Symbolic Name).

In the example above, subfile SUBSEC is the subfile record-format name, and RRN serves as the field that will store relative record numbers of the subfile.

Next, you need to design the calculations. In our application, once the user has entered the desired course, the program needs to use that value to access the appropriate records in SECTIONL and write them to the subfile; loading the subfile continues until there are no more appropriate records (i.e., no more sections for that course). Then the subfile can be displayed by executing the subfile control-record format. Because SLFPAG is less than SLFSIZ, the system will handle any user request to roll up or roll down. Upon return the program should either end or request another course, depending on whether the user pressed F3 or Enter.

The pseudocode on the following page illustrates the logic needed for this application.

```
WHILE user wants to continue
        Display inquiry screen
        IF user doesn't want to exit
                Access start of appropriate sections
                IF section not found
                        Turn on error indicator
                ELSE
                        Clear subfile
                        Load subfile
                        Display subfile
                ENDIF
        ENDIF
ENDWHILE
```

The pseudocode for loading the subfile using this method of handling subfiles is as follows:

```
Read a matching section record
WHILE there are more appropriate section records
        Increment relative record number
        Write a record to the subfile
        Read a matching section record
ENDWHILE
```

The following figure illustrates the RPG implementation of the design depicted above in pseudocode.

Line	Form Type	Control Level	Indicators (And/And Not)	Factor 1	Operation	Factor 2	Result Field Name	Length	Dec Pos	Op Ext	Resulting Indicators	Comments
01	C			CRSKEY	KLIST							
02	C				KFLD		COURS	6				
03	C			*IN03	DOWEQ	*OFF						
04	C				EXFMT	CORINQ						Inquiry screen
05	C			*IN03	IFEQ	*OFF						Not exit
06	C			CRSKEY	SETLL	SECTIONL					10	Match found
07	C			*IN10	IFEQ	*OFF						
08	C				MOVE	*ON	*IN90					For errmsg
09	C				ELSE							SETLL worked
10	C				EXSR	CLRSFL						Clear subfile
11	C				EXSR	LODSFL						Load subfile
12	C				WRITE	FOOTER						Display footer
13	C				EXFMT	CTLSEC						Display subfile
14	C				ENDIF							
15	C				ENDIF							
16	C				ENDDO							
17	C				MOVE	*ON	*INLR					
18	C				RETRN							
19	C			****Subroutine to clear the subfile and reset RRN to 0 ****								
20	C	SR		CLRSFL	BEGSR							
	C				MOVE	*ON	*IN50					
	C				WRITE	CTLSEC						
	C				MOVE	*OFF	*IN50					
	C				Z-ADD	0	RRN	40				
	C				ENDSR							

Line	Form Type	Control Level	Indicators (And/And Not)	Factor 1	Operation	Factor 2	Result Field Name	Length	Dec Pos	Op Ext	Resulting Indicators	Comments
01	C			****Subroutine to load subfile until no more records.								
02	C	SR		LODSFL	BEGSR							
03	C			CRSKEY	READE	SECTIONL					95	READE failed
04	C			*IN95	DOWEQ	*OFF						
05	C				ADD	1	RRN					
06	C				WRITE	SUBSEC						
07	C			CRSKEY	READE	SECTIONL					95	
08	C				ENDDO							
09	C				ENDSR							
10	C											

Note in the above calculations that the subfile is loaded by writing records to the subfile record format based on the relative record number field, which is incremented prior to each successive write operation. The program displays the subfile by executing the subfile *control*-record format. A WRITE to the control format clears the subfile (as long as the indicator for SFLCLR is on); the program also uses WRITE — rather than EXFMT — to display the FOOTER format because a user response to that display is not required. The KLIST allows you to access the file by a partial key.

In the subfile application above, subfile size was greater than subfile page, and the size was large enough to handle the maximum number of records the subfile normally would be expected to hold. The program stored all relevant database records in the subfile prior to any display. With this approach, OS/400 automatically enables the roll keys and signals through a + in the lower screen corner that more subfile records are available for viewing. From a programmer's viewpoint, this technique is the simplest to code. Unfortunately, this method can result in poor response time when the application is used.

The cause of the slow system response is that this technique requires the system to access all the records that meet the selection criterion and store them in the subfile prior to displaying the first page of the subfile. If the subfile size is small, the performance will be satisfactory, but as the subfile size increases, response time will degrade noticeably. In that case, especially if the user typically does not roll much throughout the subfile, it may make sense to build the subfile a page at a time, as the user requests additional pages.

Loading the Subfile a Page at a Time

The other methods of subfile building load the subfile a page at a time. There are three variants on this technique.

Variation #1 — Subfile Size One Greater than Page
This method of subfile handling relies on the fact that the system will automatically expand a subfile, regardless of its stated size, as your program adds more records to it. Because this additionally allocated room is not contiguous on disk, performance degrades as the number of pages in the subfile increases, but the technique works well when the number of records usually required within the subfile is small.

This method entails loading the subfile one page at a time, based on the user's request for additional pages. Rolling within the subfile records already loaded is handled automatically by the operating system. When the user attempts to roll up past the last page in the subfile, however, control returns to the program, which must load an additional page (if more appropriate records exist).

To use this method, you must add three additional keywords to the subfile control-record format. First, the ROLLUP keyword must be associated with an indicator to allow the system to send control back to the program when a roll-up request exceeds the current limits of the subfile. You must also add the SFLEND (Subfile End) keyword, conditioned by an indicator.

This keyword, its associated indicator, and the Rollup key work in conjunction with one another to determine what happens when the user tries to roll past the current limits of the subfile. If the SFLEND indicator is off, the system displays a + sign and returns control to your program to load the next page; if the SFLEND indicator is on, the plus sign is not displayed, and control is not returned to your program for additional loading. Thus, your program should turn on the SFLEND indicator when no additional records remain to be put into the subfile. The system will then prohibit user attempts to roll past the last page of records in the subfile.

The third keyword needed is SFLRCDNBR (subfile record number), coded within the subfile control-record format opposite a hidden field. The value of the hidden field determines which page of the subfile is displayed when the subfile control format is written. Without this keyword and its associated field, when your program writes the control record after loading a new page into the subfile, it will display the first page of the subfile by default. Using parameter value CURSOR with SFLRCDNBR causes the cursor to be positioned on that record upon display.

Note that you signify a field is hidden by entering an H in position 38 (Usage) of the DDS specifications. Hidden fields do not include a screen-location specification, because although they are part of the screen, they are not displayed. Your program can write a value to the field and read the field's value, but the user cannot see or change the value of a hidden field.

The changes this method requires in the subfile control-record format are shown on the following page. Note that the DDS does not repeat the portion of the control-record format defining the column headings, since those lines remain unchanged from our first example.

A	Form Type	And/Or/Comment	Condition Name Indicators	Name Type	Reserved	Name	Reference (R)	Length	Data Type	Decimal Positions	Usage	Location Line	Location Pos	Functions
	A			R		SUBSEC								REF(SECTIONS)
	A													SFL
	A					SECTNO	R				O	4	14	
	A					INSTR	R				O	4	23	
	A					ROOM	R				O	4	41	
	A					DAYS	R				O	4	49	
	A					BEGTIM	R			Y	O	4	57	EDTWRD('0 : ')
	A					ENROLL	R			Y	O	4	66	EDTCDE(3)
	A			R		CTLSEC								SFLCTL(SUBSEC)
	A													SFLPAG(15)
	A													SFLSIZ(16)
	A		50											SFLCLR
	A		N50											SFLDSPCTL
	A		N50											SFLDSP
	A													OVERLAY
	A													ROLLUP(21 'ROLLUP')
	A		95											SFLEND
	A					SFLRCD		4S	0		H			SFLRCDNBR(CURSOR)
	A								. . .					

The major logic changes in the program center on loading the subfile a page at a time. Each time control returns to the program from the screen, if the return was triggered by the roll key, the program must load the next page of the subfile and return control back to the screen.

When there are no more records left to load, the program should turn on the SFLEND indicator to disable rolling past the last subfile page. To determine whether additional pages can be built, the program needs to read one additional record after loading an entire subfile page before displaying the new page. The following figure illustrates this technique. Note that the CLRSFL subroutine is not included, because it is identical to that of our first example.

Line	Form Type	Control Level	Indicators (And / And)	Factor 1	Operation	Factor 2	Result Field Name	Length	Decimal Positions	Operation Extender	Resulting Indicators	Comments
01	C			CRSKEY	KLIST							
02	C				KFLD		COURS					
03	C			*IN03	DOWEQ	*OFF						
04	C				EXFMT	CORINQ						Inquiry screen
05	C			*IN03	IFEQ	*OFF						Not exit
06	C			CRSKEY	CHAIN	SECTIONL					10	10=not found
07	C			*IN10	IFEQ	*ON						CHAIN failed
08	C				MOVE	*ON	*IN90					For errmsg
09	C				ELSE							CHAIN worked
10	C				EXSR	CLRSFL						Clear subfile
11	C				EXSR	LODSFL						Load page
12	C				WRITE	FOOTER						Display footer
13	C				EXFMT	CTLSEC						Display subfile
14	C			*IN21	DOWEQ	*ON						Loop while ROLL
15	C				EXSR	LODSFL						Load page
16	C				EXFMT	CTLSEC						Display subfile
17	C				ENDDO							
18	C				ENDIF							
19	C				ENDIF							
20	C				ENDDO							
	C				MOVE	*ON	*INLR					
	C				RETRN							
	C			**** Load one page of subfile or until no more records to load ****								
	C	SR			LODSFL	BEGSR						
	C			* First record of page already read by CHAIN or prev. READE								

Line	Form Type	Control Level	Indicators (And / And)	Factor 1	Operation	Factor 2	Result Field Name	Length	Decimal Positions	Operation Extender	Resulting Indicators	Comments
01	C			RRN	ADD	1	SFLRCD	40				Set SFLRCD
02	C				DO	15						Loop 15 times
03	C				ADD	1	RRN					
04	C				WRITE	SUBSEC						
05	C			CRSKEY	READE	SECTIONL					95	READE failed
06	C			*IN95	IFEQ	*ON						Early exit
07	C				LEAVE							if no more
08	C				ENDIF							records.
09	C				ENDDO							
10	C				ENDSR							
11	C											

Notice that in the above code, in contrast to the code of the first method, the subroutine LODSLF reads and writes only 15 records to the subfile — that is, one page. If no more appropriate sections remain before the page is full, the looping ends. In the mainline, a loop of load-and-display continues until the user presses some key other than the rollup key (*IN21).

Variation #2 — Size Much Bigger Than Page
This method of building subfiles a page at a time, setting size much bigger than page, is really just a variant of loading the entire subfile at once. However, like variation #1, this method builds the subfile just a page at a time, instead of putting all the appropriate records in the subfile prior to any display.

This method is appropriate when a large number of records need to be stored in a subfile, because the large specified size allocates adjacent disk space for faster access during subfile processing. Although each user request for an additional page still requires loading that page of the subfile, the system does not have to allocate additional disk space before each page load (unless the subfile begins to exceed the declared size). You should probably not use this method if the expected subfile size exceeds 100 records.

To use this technique, you need only to make slight modifications to the display file; the program logic for this implementation remains identical to that of variation #1. In the display file, you merely need to change the subfile size and move the ROLLUP keyword from the subfile control-record format to the subfile record format. These changes are illustrated on the following page; note that the figure does not repeat the footer record nor that portion of the subfile control record that describes the screen file headings because these entries remain unchanged.

```
A  Conditioning        Name         Length        Location         Functions
                                                  Line  Pos
   A                    R SUBSEC                                    REF(SECTIONS)
   A                                                                SFL
   A                                                                ROLLUP(21  'ROLLUP')
   A                    SECTNO    R         O   4  14
   A                    INSTR     R         O   4  23
   A                    ROOM      R         O   4  41
   A                    DAYS      R         O   4  49
   A                    BEGTIM    R     Y   O   4  57 EDTWRD('0  :     ')
   A                    ENROLL    R     Y   O   4  66 EDTCDE(3)
   A                    R CTLSEC                                    SFLCTL(SUBSEC)
   A                                                                SFLPAG(15)
   A                                                                SFLSIZ(80)
   A  50                                                            SFLCLR
   A  N50                                                           SFLDSPCTL
   A  N50                                                           SFLDSP
   A                                                                OVERLAY
   A  95                                                            SFLEND
   A                    SFLRCD          4S  0H                      SFLRCDNBR(CURSOR)
   A                    ...
```

Variation #3 — Subfile Size Equals Page

Setting subfile size equal to page is most appropriate when the user is likely to want to roll through a large number of records, for example, to do generic searches. Response time is medium and consistent, regardless of the number of records viewed.

With this method, the subfile stores only one page of records. Rolling forward requires replacing the existing page with the next page through loading; because rolling backward requires replacing the existing page with records already read, the program logic required by this technique is more complicated than that of the other methods. Moreover, the method of backward rolling used will depend on whether you are accessing records by unique keys, non-unique keys, partial keys, or relative record numbers. As an alternative to enabling ROLLDOWN, often programmers require users to restart the subfile at the beginning to review records already displayed. This is the method illustrated here.

The DDS for this implementation is similar to that used when subfile size is one greater than subfile page, except that subfile size equals subfile page and keyword SFLRCDNBR is not used. (Because the subfile is only one page long, positioning the subfile upon redisplay is not a problem with this technique.) Note that the control-record format includes keywords ROLLUP and SFLEND, and function key 04 is enabled to signal restarting the course display. (Also note that the illustration omits the screen column headings from the subfile control-record format and the footer-record format, which remain identical to those of the previous methods.)

Sequence Number	Form Type	And/Or/Comment (A/O/*)	Not (N)	Indicator	Not (N)	Indicator	Not (N)	Indicator	Name Type (b/R/K/S/O)	Reserved	Name	Reference (R)	Length	Data Type (b A/P/S/B A/S/X/Y/N/I/W)	Decimal Positions	Usage (b/O/I/B/H/M)	Line	Pos	Functions
	A								R		SUBSEC								REF(SECTIONS)
	A																		SFL
	A										SECTNO	R				O	4	14	
	A										INSTR	R				O	4	23	
	A										ROOM	R				O	4	41	
	A										DAYS	R				O	4	49	
	A										BEGTIM	R		Y		O	4	57	EDTWRD('0 : ')
	A										ENROLL	R		Y		O	4	66	EDTCDE(3)
	A								R		CTLSEC								SFLCTL(SUBSEC)
	A																		SFLPAG(15)
	A																		SFLSIZ(15)
	A		50																SFLCLR
	A		N50																SFLDSPCTL
	A		N50																SFLDSP
	A																		OVERLAY
	A																		ROLLUP(21 'ROLLUP')
	A		95																SFLEND
	A																		CA04(04 'F4=Restart Course')
	A																		VLDCMDKEY(05)
	A																		

This method does require some major changes to the RPG program, however. First, before each loading of the subfile, the subfile must be cleared, since the new records should completely replace the previously displayed records. Second, the program must check the roll-key indicator and indicator 04 upon return from the screen to determine whether to build the next page of the subfile or to restart at the beginning of the subfile.

Line	Form Type	Control Level (L0-L9, LR,SR, AN/OR)	Indicators And Not	And Not	Not	Factor 1	Operation	Factor 2	Result Field Name	Length	Decimal Positions	Operation Extender (H,N,P)	Resulting Indicators Plus	Minus	Zero	Comments
0 1	C					CRSKEY	KLIST									
0 2	C						KFLD		COURS							
0 3	C					*IN03	DOWEQ	*OFF								
0 4	C						EXFMT	CORINQ								Inquiry screen
0 5	C					*IN03	IFEQ	*OFF								Not exit
0 6	C					CRSKEY	CHAIN	SECTIONL							10	10=not found
0 7	C					*IN10	IFEQ	*ON								CHAIN failed
0 8	C						MOVE	*ON	*IN90							For errmsg
0 9	C						ELSE									CHAIN worked
1 0	C	* Loop until user exits or hits Enter.														
1 1	C					*IN03	DOUEQ	*ON								Until exit
1 2	C					*IN05	OREQ	*OFF								or no valid cmd
1 3	C					*IN04	IFEQ	*ON								Restart at
1 4	C					CRSKEY	CHAIN	SECTIONL							10	beginning
1 5	C						ENDIF									
1 6	C						EXSR	CLRSFL								Clear subfile
1 7	C						EXSR	LODSFL								Load subfile
1 8	C						WRITE	FOOTER								Display footer
1 9	C						EXFMT	CTLSEC								Display subfile
2 0	C						ENDDO									
	C						ENDIF									
	C						ENDIF									
	C						ENDDO									
	C						MOVE	*ON	*INLR							
	C						RETRN									

Line	Form Type	Control Level	And/Not	And/Not	Factor 1	Operation	Factor 2	Result Name	Length	Dec	Resulting Indicators	Comments
01	C				* Subroutine to clear the subfile and reset RRN to 0.							
02	C				*							
03	C	SR			CLRSFL	BEGSR						
04	C					MOVE	*ON	*IN50				
05	C					WRITE	CTLSEC					
06	C					MOVE	*OFF	*IN50				
07	C					Z-ADD	0	RRN	20			
08	C					ENDSR						
09	C				*							
10	C				* Subroutine to load one page of subfile or until no more records							
11	C				* remain to be loaded. First record of page already read by							
12	C				* CHAIN or previous READE.							
13	C				*							
14	C	SR			LODSFL	BRGSR						
15	C					DO	15					Loop 15 times
16	C					ADD	1	RRN				
17	C					WRITE	SUBSEC					
18	C				CRSKEY	READE	SECTIONL				95	READE failed
19	C		*IN95			IFEQ	*ON					Early exit
20	C					LEAVE						if no more
	C					ENDIF						records.
	C					ENDDO						
	C					ENDSR						

Subfiles and Change

Assume you wanted to list sections of a course not just to inspect the data, but to make changes in the data; perhaps you need to assign different instructors to sections, or to reschedule some sections to different rooms. An RPG operation — READC (Read Next Changed Record) — used only with subfiles, allows you to develop such an application.

The READC operation requires a subfile name in factor 2 and an indicator in positions 58-59 to signal end-of-subfile. Generally used within a loop, the READC operation will read only those records from a subfile that have been modified during a prior EXFMT operation; when no changed subfile records remain to be read, the indicator associated with the operation comes on.

Because of the READC operation, a user can make as many changes as are necessary to various records in the subfile in a single display; all these changes can then be processed when control returns to the program.

You can use READC regardless of the technique used to load and display the subfile. For simplicity's sake, we'll modify the first version of the program, in which all the relevant records are loaded into the subfile at one time, to demonstrate how to use this operation.

We need to make a few changes in the display file. First, the subfile fields need to be different from the database fields. Without this change, rereading a database record preparatory to updating it would obliterate any changes to subfile field values. Also, the usage of most of the subfile fields needs to be B, to allow the user to modify their values; section number remains output only, to prevent changes to the key. Finally, some of the screen captions and prompts require changes to better suit the new application.

```
          1         2         3         4         5         6         7         8
1234567890123456789012345678901234567890123456789012345678901234567890123456789 0
A                                          CA03(03 'F3=Exit')
A                                          CA12(12 'F12=Cancel')
A            R CORINQ
A                                        1 20'Course Section Update'
A                                        3  2'Type value, then Enter.'
A                                        5  5'Course number . .'
A              COURS           6   B   5 24
A                                          DSPATR(UL)
A N90                                       DSPATR(HI)
A  90                                       ERRMSG('No such course' 90)
A                                       23  2'F3=Exit'
A            R SUBSEC                        REF(SECTIONS)
A                                           SFL
A              SECTNO      R        O   4 14
A              SINSTR         15  B     4 23
A              SROOM          4  0B     4 41
A              SDAYS              B     4 49
A              SBEGTI         4Y 0B     4 57EDTWRD('0 :  ')
A              SENROL         3Y 0B     4 66EDTCDE(3)
A            R CTLSEC                        SFLCTL(SUBSEC)
A                                           SFLPAG(15)
A                                           SFLSIZ(80)
A  50                                        SFLCLR
A N50                                        SFLDSPCTL
A N50                                        SFLDSP
A                                           OVERLAY
A              COURS                    1 28
A                                        1 35'Course Information'
A                                        3 12'Section'
A                                        3 24'Instructor'
A                                        3 41'Room'
A                                        3 49'Days'
A                                        3 57'Time'
A                                        3 64'Enroll.'
A            R FOOTER
A                                       21  2'Change values as desired;-
A                                             ' press Enter to continue.'
A                                       23  2'F3=Exit  F12=Cancel'
```

The program requires a few changes to enable the updating to take place. First, remember that the database file will be an update type, so that records can be read and then rewritten to the file with any changes.

The program logic also will remain basically the same. The major difference occurs when control returns to the program following the subfile display. At that point, provided the user did not press F3 or F12, the program needs to loop, using READC to read any modified subfile record and use that data to update the data file. The loop should continue until there are no more changed records.

Because specific database records need to be accessed by their complete key, the program needs a second KLIST, with both course and section as KFLDs. Finally, because the subfile and database fields are different, the program needs to move values back and forth between corresponding fields at appropriate times.

```
          1         2         3         4         5         6         7         8
 1234567890123456789012345678901234567890123456789012345678901234567890123456789Ø
     FSECTIONLUF  E          K          DISK
     FSECTINQ CF  E                     WORKSTN
     F                                       RRN    KSFILE SUBSEC
     C           CRSKEY    KLIST
     C                     KFLD          COURS
     C           FULKEY    KLIST
     C                     KFLD          COURS
     C                     KFLD          SECTNO
     C           *INØ3     DOWEQ*OFF
     C                     EXFMTCORINQ                        Inquiry screen
     C           *INØ3     IFEQ *OFF                          Not exit
     C           CRSKEY    SETLLSECTIONL                 10 10=found
     C           *IN10     IFEQ *OFF                          SETLL failed
     C                     MOVE *ON      *IN90                For errmsg
     C                     ELSE                               SETLL worked
     C                     EXSR CLRSFL                        Clear subfile
     C                     EXSR LODSFL                        Load subfile
     C                     WRITEFOOTER                        Display footer
     C                     EXFMTCTLSEC                        Display subfile
     C           *INØ3     IFEQ *OFF
     C           *IN12     ANDEQ*OFF
     C                     EXSR UPDATE
     C                     ENDIF
     C                     ENDIF
     C                     ENDIF
     C                     ENDDO
     C                     MOVE *ON      *INLR
     C                     RETRN
     C****Subroutine to clear the subfile and reset RRN to Ø ******
     CSR         CLRSLF    BEGSR
     C                     MOVE *ON      *IN50
     C                     WRITECTLSEC
     C                     MOVE *OFF     *IN50
     C                     Z-ADDØ        RRN      40
     C                     ENDSR
     C***Subroutine to load subfile until no more records or subfile full
     CSR         LODSLF    BEGSR
     C           CRSKEY    READESECTIONL                 95 READE failed
     C           *IN95     DOWEQ*OFF
     C                     ADD  1        RRN
     C                     EXSR MOVDB                         trans. to s.f.
     C                     WRITESUBSEC
     C           CRSKEY    READESECTIONL                 95 READE failed
     C                     ENDDO
     C                     ENDSR
     C***Subroutine to read changed records in subfile and update
     C* database records.
     CSR         UPDATE    BEGSR
     C                     READCSUBSEC                   99
     C           *IN99     DOWEQ*OFF
```

```
         1         2         3         4         5         6         7         8
1234567890123456789012345678901234567890123456789012345678901234567890123456789Ø
         C          FULKEY     CHAINSECTIONL             1Ø
         C          *IN1Ø      IFEQ *OFF
         C                     EXSR MOVSF
         C                     UPDATSECREC               5Ø
         C                     ENDIF
         C                     READCSUBSEC                    99
         C                     ENDDO
         C                     ENDSR
         C*****************************************************************
         C* Subroutine to transfer values from database fields to        *
         C* subfile fields.                                              *
         C*****************************************************************
         CSR        MOVDB      BEGSR
         C                     MOVE DAYS       SDAYS
         C                     Z-ADDBEGTIM     SBEGTI
         C                     Z-ADDROOM       SROOM
         C                     Z-ADDENROLL     SENROL
         C                     MOVE INSTR      SINSTR
         C                     ENDSR
         C*****************************************************************
         C* Subroutine to transfer values from subfile fields to         *
         C* database fields.                                             *
         C*****************************************************************
         CSR        MOVSF      BEGSR
         C                     MOVE SDAYS      DAYS
         C                     Z-ADDSBEGTI     BEGTIM
         C                     Z-ADDSROOM      ROOM
         C                     Z-ADDSENROL     ENROLL
         C                     MOVE SINSTR     INSTR
         C                     ENDSR
```

Uses of Subfiles

You can use subfiles in a variety of ways. They can simply display data, when the user only needs to review information. You can use them for display with selection, so the user can select one of the entries for more detailed information about the selected record; the user can then update the selected record, if (s)he wishes to.

Subfiles can be used for data entry of new records to database files, with or without validity checking. A given workstation file can have multiple subfiles associated with it. Two subfiles can be displayed simultaneously on the screen. You can transfer data between the program and the subfile by using CHAIN, UPDAT, and WRITE operations, as well as READC; such processing is always based on relative record numbers of the subfile records. Finally, you can display system messages through special message subfiles.

It should be obvious from the above discussion that subfile processing can become complex, and that mastery of programming with subfiles, like any kind of programming, comes with practice and experience.

On-Line Help

Well-designed interactive applications often allow the user to obtain additional information about what (s)he is supposed to do. This kind of information, called *help*, normally does not appear on the standard display because of space limitations, but can be evoked by pressing the Help key.

The AS/400 allows you to build such help into your applications as part of your display file DDS. The actual help text may reside in an Office-Vision/400 document, in records within a separate display file, through panel groups defined within UIM (User Interface Manager), or as records within the display file used in the interactive application. We will look at only this last technique; for information on the other techniques, consult IBM's AS/400 manual *Programming: Data Description Specifications Reference* (SC41-9620).

First, you need to include the keyword HELP, at either the file or record level, to enable the Help key. With the Help key enabled, pressing it will display help information associated either with the entire display or with a specific area of the display, depending on how you have implemented this feature. The simplest kind of help to code is help associated with the entire screen. For this kind of implementation, all you need in addition to the keyword HELP is file-level keyword HLPRCD, coupled with the name of the record format containing the help text.

Form Type	Name Type	Name	Line	Pos	Functions
A					HELP
A					HLPRCD(RCD02)
A	R	RCD01			
A		. . .			
A	R	RCD02			
A			4	5	'This is the record format'
A			5	5	'containing the help text'
A			6	5	'that will display when the'
A			7	5	'user presses the Help key.'
A					

You often want to be able to associate specific help text with specific portions of the screen, rather than having global help. You can provide such cursor-sensitive help by including a new kind of format within your DDS — the **help-specification format** — which will associate a specific portion of the screen with a specific record of help text. Signal this kind of specification by entering an H in position 17 and the keyword HLPARA in positions 45-80. Help specifications are associated with standard record formats; the H line must appear after any record-level keywords but before any fields of the associated record.

The HLPARA (Help area) associated with the help specification defines a rectangular area on the screen; if the cursor is within this area when the user presses the Help key, the text of the record associated with this help specification is displayed. Define the rectangular area by specifying within parentheses four numeric values representing the line and column position of the upper-left corner of the rectangular area and the line and column position of the lower-right corner of the area.

A	Form Type	Conditioning						Name Type (b/R/K/S/O)	Reserved	Name		Reference (R)	Length	Data Type (b A/P/S/B A/S/X/Y/N/I/W)	Decimal Positions	Usage (b/O/I/B/H/M)	Location		Functions
		And/Or/Comment (A/O/*)	Condition Name														Line	Pos	
			Indicator	Not (N)	Indicator	Not (N)	Indicator	Not (N)											
	A																		CA03(03 'F3=Exit')
	A																		HELP
	A																		HLPRCD(GENHLP)
	A							R	INQREC										
	A							H											HLPARA(2 10 4 40)
	A																		HLPRCD(REC1)
	A							H											HLPARA(5 15 20 70)
	A																		HLPRCD(REC2)
	A								. . .										
	A							R	REC1										
	A																1	5	'Help text 1'
	A							R	REC2										
	A																1	5	'Help text 2'
	A							R	GENHLP										
	A																1	5	'General help'
	A																		

In addition to the HLPARA, the help specification includes keyword HLPRCD to designate which record should be displayed when the user requests help from within the designated screen area.

In the generic example above, two different help areas are associated with record format INQREC. Each help area, in turn, evokes a different help record. If the user presses the Help key while viewing INQREC and his/her cursor is in the rectangular area defined by screen line 2, column 10 and line 4, column 40, the contents of REC1 display; if the cursor is within the area defined by line 5, column 15 and line 20, column 70, REC2 displays. If the cursor is outside both these areas, record GENHLP displays.

To further demonstrate on-line help, the display file from the course-inquiry application is partially duplicated on the following page with the addition of specific help (if the user's cursor is on the screen line asking for course input) and general help instructions (if the cursor is anywhere else on the screen).

```
                1         2         3         4         5         6         7         8
       12345678901234567890123456789012345678901234567890123456789012345678901234567890
       A                                              CA03(03 'F3=Exit')
       A                                              HELP
       A                                              HLPRCD(GENHLP)
       A         R CORINQ
       A         H                                    HLPARA(5 5 5 24)
       A                                              HLPRCD(CORHLP)
       A                                         1 20'Course Section Update'
       A                                         3  2'Type value, then Enter.'
       A                                         5  5'Course number . .'
       A           COURS          6   B     5 24
       A                                              DSPATR(UL)
       A N90                                          DSPATR(HI)
       A  90                                          ERRMSG('No such course' 90)
       A         R GENHLP
       A                                         4  5'To get Help, position the'
       A                                         4 30' cursor within the item f'
       A                                         4 55'or which you want more   '
       A                                         5  5'information and press Hel'
       A                                         5 30'p.'
       A         R CORHLP
       A                                         5  5'Enter the 6 character ID '
       A                                         5 30'of the course whose secti'
       A                                         5 55'ons you want to see.     '
       A                                         6  5'(For example, BIS264)'
       A
```

You can have as many help specifications, each describing a different screen area, as you need. The area can be as big or small as you wish to make it. If the user presses the Help key outside all defined help areas, the file-level help record is displayed, if you have included one; otherwise, the system informs the user that no help is available. You cannot use help specifications within subfile record formats but may include them as part of subfile control-record formats.

Chapter Summary

Subfiles allow users to work with more than one database record at a time in an interactive application. Records stored in a subfile are displayed in a single output operation to the workstation file; changes made to subfile records are returned to the program in a single input operation.

To define subfiles within DDS requires two kinds of record formats: one that defines the fields within the subfile and describes the field locations within a screen line; and a second format, called a subfile control-record format, that actually manages the displaying of the subfile information.

Several required keywords are used with subfiles: Record-level keyword SFL identifies a record format as a subfile record, while record-level keyword SFLCTL identifies a format as a subfile control-record format. Additional required keywords determine how many records appear on the screen at the same time, how much total storage the system allocates to the subfile, and when the subfile and its control record are displayed.

Several different techniques exist for loading and displaying subfiles. These methods differ in the relationship they establish between subfile page and subfile size and in when they write records to the subfile relative to when the subfile display begins. Regardless of the technique you use, all applications involving subfiles require additional entries on the File Specifications for the workstation files using the subfiles. All input to and output from a subfile is done through relative record numbers. The READC operation allows your application program to process just those subfile records that the user has changed.

The AS/400 allows you to associate on-line help with an entire screen or with specific areas of the screen that the user can access through the Help key.

Terms

help-specification format
list panels

subfiles
subfile record format

subfile control-record format

Discussion/Review Questions

1. What is a subfile?

2. What are the functions of a subfile record format and a subfile control-record format in a display file?

3. What are the meanings of the following display file keywords, and which record format is each used with? SFL, SFLCTL, SFLPAG, SFLSIZ, SFLDSP, SFLCLR, SFLDSPCTL.

4. In subfile processing, how are column headings for the subfile and screen footings (i.e., information to display below the subfile) generally handled?

5. What is a File Specification continuation line? What information is required on a continuation line when you develop an application using subfiles?

6. What's a hidden field?

7. When do you need to use the keyword SFLRCDNBR?

8. Discuss the relative merits of different approaches to subfile definition and loading.

9. Discuss roll-key control and action with the different approaches to subfile definition and loading.

10. How does the READC operation differ from the other read operations of RPG?

11. In using subfiles for updating, why do you need to use fields for the subfile that are different from the fields of the database file you are updating?

12. How do you establish cursor-sensitive help?

Exercises

1. Design the screens and write the DDS for an interactive application that allows the user to enter a zip code and lists the names of all the company's customers residing within that zip code. Create whatever fields you may need and make subfile size much greater than page.

2. Write the RPG for Exercise 1. Make up whatever file and field names you need, but be consistent with definitions used in Exercise 1. Use the technique of loading the entire subfile prior to display.

3. Revise the DDS from Exercise 1 to make subfile size and page equal. Modify the RPG code from Exercise 2 to suit this change.

4. Write the pseudocode for an interactive application that will display a list of all a company's product numbers and their descriptions and allow the user to place an X in front of those products for which (s)he wants more information. The program should then display a screen of detailed production information (quantity on hand, cost, selling price, reorder point, reorder quantity) for each product selected by the user.

5. Write the generic pseudocode needed to use subfiles for data entry (i.e., for adding large numbers of records to a file).

Programming Assignments

1. Write an interactive application for Wexler University that will allow the user to enter a department number to display all the instructors working within that department. Use a logical file built over WUINSTP (see Appendix D).

2. Write an interactive application for CompuSell that will allow a user to locate a customer based on a generic name search. That is, the user can enter one or more starting letters of the last name and the program will display the customers by last name, starting with the first customer whose name meets the generic specification and ending when a customer's name no longer matches that specification.

   The subfile of customers displayed should include just the last name, first name, and identification of the customers, plus a selection field. If the user chooses (selects) one of the records, the program then should display all the detailed information about that customer (all the data fields of the customer master file). You will need to use CSCSTP and a logical file keyed on last name built over CSCSTP (see Appendix D). Include a generic help screen in your application.

3. Write an application for Wexler University that will allow a user to interactively add or change (but not delete) a course and/or its description in files WUCRSP and WUCRSDSP (see Appendix D). Do not allow the user to change the course identification, or add a duplicate identification. All other fields of either file may be changed. Do not display the line numbers of the description on the screen.

4. GTC Telephone Company wants you to develop an interactive application to process payments from customers. The program should allow the user to enter a screen full of payments at one time by entering for each payer his phone number and amount paid. This information should be used for two purposes: 1) to update the Customer Master File (GTCSTP) amount owed and data of last payment fields; and 2) to write a record to the Payments Archive File (GTPAYP). Use the system date for date fields. See Appendix D for file layouts.

Chapter 11

Byte- and Bit-Level Operations

Chapter Overview

This chapter introduces you to several RPG operations that allow you to inspect or manipulate individual positions or bytes within a field. You will also learn about operations that allow you to work with individual bits, including what you need to know to understand when such operations are needed.

Field Character Inspection

Often a field is defined as "the smallest unit of data that can be manipulated within a program." It would be more accurate to say that a field is the unit most often manipulated by a program. In fact, RPG offers a way to access data at subfield levels, through data structures. Additionally, RPG includes operations that allow you to inspect or manipulate individual bytes, or even bits of bytes, within data fields. Although these operations are not needed as often as other operations discussed so far, they do provide options for processing data at a level that otherwise would be beyond our capabilities.

Several RPG operations allow you to inspect, or test, the individual positions, or bytes, within a character field.

TESTN (Test Numeric)

The TESTN operation can be used to determine whether a character field contains all numeric characters, leading blanks followed by all numeric characters, or all blanks. The operation is useful for validating fields before you use them in mathematical operations or attempt to edit the fields to prevent an abnormal program ending that would occur if the data were non-numeric. Because you can use the TESTN operation only with character fields, you would need to move the field's value to a numeric field following validation or redefine the field as a numeric variable within a data structure, before you use it for arithmetic or editing.

The TESTN operation does not use factors 1 and 2; the field to be tested occurs as the result field. You must use at least one resulting indicator with this operation. Where you position that indicator depends on what you are trying to test for. You can, if you wish, use indicators in all three resulting indicator positions.

An indicator specified in positions 54-55 comes on if all the characters within the field are numeric. An indicator in positions 56-57 comes on if the result field contains numeric characters and one or more leading blanks. An indicator in positions 58-59 comes on if the result field contains all blanks.

Because of the way RPG handles signed numbers, the right-most character of the field may contain the EBCDIC representation of A-R and still be considered numeric, since these are the same representations as signed (+ or –) digits 0-9.

Study the examples below to understand the use of indicators with this operation.

Line	Form Type	Control Level (L0-L9, LR,SR, AN/OR)	Indicators And Not	And Not	Not	Factor 1	Operation	Factor 2	Result Field Name	Length	Decimal Positions	Operation Extender (H,N,P)	Resulting Indicators Arithmetic Plus	Minus	Zero	Comments
0 1	C						TESTN		FLDA				10			
0 2	C															

FLDA	*IN10	Explanation
'123'	ON	Every character is numeric.
'1A3'	OFF	A is not numeric.
'12C'	ON	C interpreted as positively signed 3.

Line	Form Type	Control Level (L0-L9, LR,SR, AN/OR)	Indicators And Not	And Not	Not	Factor 1	Operation	Factor 2	Result Field Name	Length	Decimal Positions	Operation Extender (H,N,P)	Resulting Indicators Arithmetic Plus	Minus	Zero	Comments
0 1	C						TESTN		FLDA				102030			
0 2	C															

FLDA	*IN10	*IN20	*IN30	Explanation
'1 2 3'	ON	OFF	OFF	All characters are digits.
' 23'	OFF	ON	OFF	Leading blank is present.
' 3'	OFF	ON	OFF	Both blanks are leading.
'1 3'	OFF	OFF	OFF	Blank is not leading.
' '	OFF	OFF	ON	All characters are blanks.
'A2C'	OFF	OFF	OFF	A is not a digit.

SCAN (Scan Character String)

The SCAN operation allows you to look for a character or string of characters within a character field. The direction of the SCAN is left to right. SCAN requires entries in both factors 1 and 2; a result field is optional, as are indicators in positions 56-57 and 58-59.

Factor 1 contains the string you are looking for, sometimes called the **compare string**. This may be represented by a character field, array element, named constant, data structure name, literal, or table name. Moreover, you can specify that only a portion of that data item be used as the string to search for by following the data item with a colon (:), followed by an integer length, expressed either as a literal, field, named constant, array element, or table name. The length determines how much of the factor 1 entry the operation scans for.

For example, factor 1 could be CODE, in which case the entire value of the CODE field would be the compare string, or it could be CODE:3, in which case the first three characters of the CODE field would be the compare string. If factor 1 were CODE:X, the value of X would determine how many characters of CODE comprised the compare string.

Factor 2 contains the string to be scanned, sometimes called the **base string**. The base string may be a character field, array element, named constant, data-structure name, literal, or table name. The base string may be followed by a ":", followed in turn by an integer literal, field, named constant, or array element that represents the *starting location* for the SCAN within the string. For example, if factor 2 contains NAME, the entire NAME field will be scanned, whereas if it contains NAME:4, the scan will begin at the fourth character in the NAME field.

The optional result field may contain a numeric integer field, array element, array name, or table name. If a result field is present and it is anything other than an array name, the SCAN operation will stop as soon as it locates an occurrence of the compare string within the base string, and a number representing the starting position of the compare string within the base string will be stored in the result field. If the compare string is not found within the base string, the result field is set to 0.

If the result field is an array name, the SCAN continues to the end of the base field, and the starting locations of each occurrence of the compare string within the base string are stored in successive elements of the array. If the array contains more elements than the number of compare string occurrences within the base string, the unneeded array elements are set to 0.

You can use an indicator in positions 58-59; this indicator comes on if the SCAN succeeds in finding the compare string within the base string. An optional indicator in positions 56-57 comes on if an error occurs in the SCAN operation.

The SCAN is case-sensitive; that is, "A" is not the same as "a". If the compare string includes blanks, whether leading, trailing, or embedded, the blanks are considered part of the SCAN pattern to look for.

To get a feeling for how SCAN works, consider the following examples.

C		Indicators			Factor 1	Operation	Factor 2	Result Field			Resulting Indicators				Comments
		And	And					Name	Length		Arithmetic				
Line	Form Type	Control Level (L0-L9, LR,SR, AN/OR)	Not	Not	Not						Decimal Positions	Operation Extender (H,N,P)	Plus	Minus	Zero	
													Compare			
													1>2	1<2	1=2	
													Lookup(Factor 2)is			
													High	Low	Equal	
0 1	C					FLDA	SCAN	FLDB	FLDC	20					50	
0 2	C															

Field Values   **Results**

FLDA	FLDB	FLDC	*IN50	Explanation
'my'	'Do it my way'	7	ON	Match of 'my' and 'my'
'my'	'Amy knows best.'	2	ON	Match of 'my' and 'my'
'my'	'It may harm you.'	0	OFF	'my' is not 'may' or 'm y'
'my'	'My way is best.'	0	OFF	'my' is not 'My'

C		Indicators			Factor 1	Operation	Factor 2	Result Field			Resulting Indicators				Comments
0 1	C *	The examples below are based on the case where													
0 2	C *	FLDA is 'abcde' and FLDB is 'mabcdeabczab'. The comment													
0 3	C *	below each calculation explains the result and why.													
0 4	C *														
0 5	C				FLDA:3	SCAN	FLDB	FLDC							50	
0 6	C *	Compare value is 'abc', so FLDC is 2 and 50 is on.													
0 7	C *														
0 8	C				FLDA:3	SCAN	FLDB:8	FLDC							50	
0 9	C *	FLDC is 0 and 50 is off, because scan starts at 8th byte of FLDB													
1 0	C *														
1 1	C				FLDA:2	SCAN	FLDB	ARR							50	
1 2	C *	ARR is a 5-element array. Results of scan are ARR,1 is 2;													
1 3	C *	ARR,2 is 7; ARR,3 is 11; ARR,4 and ARR,5 are 0. 50 is on.													
1 4	C														

The SCAN operation is useful for inspecting text data. It could also be used, for example, to scan addresses to locate all businesses or customers residing on the same street.

CHECK (Check)

The format of the CHECK operation is similar to that of SCAN. Factor 1 contains a character compare field, and factor 2 contains a source or base string, while the result field contains a numeric field or array name.

There are significant differences between CHECK and SCAN, however. SCAN looks for the *presence* of the *entire* compare string within the base string and notes the location of its occurrence in the result field. CHECK notes *discrepancies* between the *individual characters* of the compare field and the base string and signals the *absence* of a base character from the set of compare characters by storing its location in the result field.

SCAN is used for locating substrings within a base string, while CHECK is useful for verification of characters within the base string.

The factor 1 value of CHECK, represented in a character field, literal, named constant, data structure, array element, or table name, contains a list of valid characters. Factor 2 contains the character field, literal, named constant, data structure, array element, or table name whose characters you want checked against those of the data item in factor 1. The result field contains a numeric field, array element, data structure name, table name, or array name.

The CHECK operation proceeds from left to right as it checks the characters of the base string against those in the compare string. If the result field is anything other than an array name, CHECK stores in it the position of the first character of the base string not found in the compare string. If all the base string characters are present in the compare string, the result field is set to 0. If the result field is an array name, the CHECK operation does not stop at the first mismatch, but continues to store the positions of unmatched base-string characters in successive elements of the named array. Unneeded array elements are set to 0.

As with the SCAN operation, you can use the colon notation with the base string to specify the position within the base string where the CHECK operation is to begin; the value represented by the field or literal following the colon determines the starting location for the CHECK.

If you don't need to know the position of invalid characters but simply want to know whether the base string contains one or more invalid characters, you can omit a result-field entry and code an indicator in positions 58-59 of the specification. This indicator will come on if CHECK finds one or more unmatched characters in the base string.

```
C                 Indicators          Factor 1        Operation      Factor 2          Result Field       Resulting Indicators

01 C* Assume field CODE contains 'X'.
02 C            'ABCDE'    CHECK CODE                             50
03 C* 50 comes on, because X does not appear within factor 1.
04 C*
05 C* Assume DIGITS contains '0123456789' and AMT contains '$125.50'.
06 C            DIGITS     CHECK AMT             RSLT    10
07 C* RSLT's value is 1, because the $ of AMT is not in DIGITS.
08 C*
09 C* Assume DIGITS contains '0123456789', AMT contains '$125.50', and
10 C* ARR is a four-element array.
11 C            DIGITS     CHECK AMT             ARR
12 C* ARR,1 contains 1 (position of $); ARR,2 contains 5 (Position of
13 C* the decimal point); ARR,3 and ARR,4 are 0.
14 C*
15 C            DIGITS     CHECK AMT:2           ARR
16 C* ARR,1 is 5 (position of the decimal point); remaining elements
17 C* are 0. The $ is not noted because the CHECK begins with position
18 C* 2 of AMT.
19 C
```

CHEKR (Check Reverse)
CHEKR works exactly like CHECK, except that it checks the base string from right to left, rather than from left to right. This operation can be used to locate the right-most invalid character in a string or to determine the length of a string of non-blank characters within a field.

C	Line	Form Type	Control Level (L0-L9, LR,SR, AN/OR)	Indicators (Not/And/Not/And/Not)	Factor 1	Operation	Factor 2	Result Field — Name	Length	Decimal Positions	Operation Extender (H,N,P)	Resulting Indicators	Comments
	01	C*			Assume field CODE contains 'X'.								
	02	C			'ABCDE'	CHECKCODE						50	
	03	C*			50 comes on, because X does not appear in factor 1.								
	04	C*											
	05	C*			Assume DIGITS contains '0123456789' and AMT contains '$125.50'.								
	06	C			DIGITS	CHEKRAMT		RSLT	10				
	07	C*			RSLT's value is 5, because the decimal point is not in DIGITS.								
	08	C*											
	09	C*			Assume DIGITS contains '0123456789', AMT contains '$125.50', and								
	10	C*			ARR is a four-element array.								
	11	C			DIGITS	CHEKRAMT		ARR					
	12	C*			ARR,1 is 5 (position of the decimal point); ARR,2 is 1 (position								
	13	C*			of $); ARR,3 and ARR,4 are 0.								
	14	C*											
	15	C*			Assume NAME contains 'Jones '.								
	16	C			' '	CHEKRNAME		LEN	20				
	17	C*			LEN is 5, the position of the right-most non-blank character								
	18	C*			of NAME.								
	19	C											

Field Character Manipulation

The operations we've discussed so far in this chapter allow you to look at, or inspect, individual characters or substrings of character fields. Several operations allow you to actually manipulate or change characters or strings of characters within a field.

SUBST (Substring)

The SUBST operation copies a portion of a character string into a different field. Factor 1, required for this operation, represents the length of the string to be copied. It must be an integer field, array element, table name, or literal. Factor 2, also required, contains the base character string *to be copied*; it may be represented by a field, array element, named constant, data-structure name, table name, or literal. The copying begins with the left-most character of the base string, unless the data item representing the base string is followed by a colon, followed by a start location. The result field serves as the receiving field for the SUBST operation. It must be a character field, array element, data structure, or table name. An optional indicator in positions 56-57 comes on if an error occurs during the SUBST operation.

If the specified starting location is greater than the actual length of the base character string, the SUBST operation does not take place. If the length specified in factor 1 causes the substring to extend beyond the end of factor 2, the error indicator comes on. If the substring is shorter than the result field, the unused positions of the result field will retain their previous contents unless you code a P (Pad) in position 53 of the specification. In that case, the unused portion is padded with trailing blanks.

Some examples illustrating the SUBSTR operation are explained below.

Line	Form Type	Control Level (L0-L9, LR,SR, AN/OR)	And Not	And Not	And Not	Factor 1	Operation	Factor 2	Result Field Name	Length	Decimal Positions	Operation Extender (H,N,P)	Plus	Minus	Zero	1>2	1<2	1=2	High	Low	Equal	Comments
0 1	C					* The examples below are based on a FLDA value of 'abcdefgh'																
0 2	C					* and a value of '12345' in RESULT prior to the SUBST operation.																
0 3	C					*																
0 4	C					3	SUBST	FLDA	RESULT	5											90	
0 5	C					* RESULT contains 'abc45', because just the first 3 characters of																
0 6	C					* FLDA are copied. Indicator 90 is off.																
0 7	C					*																
0 8	C					3	SUBST	FLDA	RESULT	5		P									90	
0 9	C					* RESULT is 'abc ' because of the padding specification.																
1 0	C					*																
1 1	C					4	SUBST	FLDA:3	RESULT	5		P									90	
1 2	C					* RESULT is 'cdef ' because 4 characters are copied, starting																
1 3	C					* with the third position of FLDA. 90 stays off.																
1 4	C					*																
1 5	C					3	SUBST	FLDA:9	RESULT	5		P									90	
1 6	C					* The operation is not executed, because the starting position																
1 7	C					* exceeds the length of FLDA.																
1 8	C					*																
1 9	C					6	SUBST	FLDA:5	RESULT	5		P									90	
2 0	C					* Indicator 90 comes on, because the length, in conjunction with																
	C					* the starting position, goes beyond the length of FLDA																

CAT (Concatenate Two Character Strings)

The CAT operation is useful for concatenating (i.e., combining) the values of two strings to form a third string. The two character-data items to be combined are specified in factor 1 and factor 2; either factor can be a field, array element, named constant, data structure name, table name, or literal. The result-field entry specifies where the results of the concatenation are to be placed. It can be a field, array element, data structure name, or table name.

You have the option of specifying the number of blanks you want to appear between the non-blank characters of the concatenated fields by appending a colon (:) to the factor 2 item, followed by an integer literal, field, named constant, array element, or table name specifying the desired number of blanks. If you do not specify the number of desired blanks, all the trailing blanks (if they exist) within factor 1 are included in the concatenation.

If the concatenation is too large to fit in the result field, truncation occurs from the right of the string. No indicators are used with the CAT operation. As was the case for SUBST, CAT leaves residual characters in the unused left-most positions of the result field unless you enter a P in position 53 to pad those unused positions with blanks.

You can get a sense of how CAT works by examining the examples below.

```
C
     Line
 3 4 5 6 7 8 9...                                                              74
0 1  C* The examples below are based on FNAME (10 positions) with a value
0 2  C* of 'John        ', LNAME (12 positions) with a value of
0 3  C* 'Johnson      ', and WNAME (25 positions) with a value of
0 4  C* 'abcdefghijklmnopqrstuvwxy'.
0 5  C*
0 6  C        FNAME      CAT  LNAME        WNAME    25
0 7  C* WNAME contains 'John      Johnson       wxy', since nothing about
0 8  C* blanks or padding was specified.
0 9  C*
1 0  C        FNAME      CAT  LNAME:1      WNAME    25
1 1  C* WNAME contains 'John Johnson       rstuvwxy', because 1 blank was
1 2  C  requested.
1 3  C*
1 4  C        FNAME      CAT  LNAME:1      WNAME    25 P
1 5  C* WNAME contains 'John Johnson             ', because 1 blank was
1 6  C* requested, along with padding.
1 7  C*
1 8  C        FNAME      CAT  LNAME:0      WNAME    25 P
1 9  C* WNAME contains 'JohnJohnson              ', because 0 blanks were
2 0  C* requested.
     C*
     C        FNAME      CAT  LNAME:1      SNAME    10 P
     C* SNAME contains 'John Johns', because it can only store 10
     C* characters.
     C
```

XLATE

XLATE is an operation that allows you to translate, or convert, characters within a string to other characters. Factor 2 contains the source string to be converted, and the result field specifies where the results of the translation should be placed; this field can be the same as the source field. This effectively means that the conversion can take place right within the string field itself, without using an additional target field. As with SUBSTR, you can use a colon and a value to designate the position where the translation is to begin. If you do not specify a starting location, the conversion starts at the first position of the factor 2 string.

How do you specify which characters should be translated, and what they should be changed to? A factor 1 entry supplies this information by including first a From string, then a colon, and then a To string. The From and To strings serve as translation tables. The two strings must have the same number of characters, with the characters ordered so that each character in the From string has a corresponding character in the To string that represents the desired substitute for the From character.

During the XLATE operation, any character in the source string found in the From string is converted to the corresponding character in the To string and stored in the result field. If a source string character does not appear in the From string, the character is transferred unchanged to the result field.

The factor 2 source string and the result field can be character fields, array elements, or table names. The factor 1 From and To strings may be named constants, fields, literals, array elements, or table names. An optional P in position 53 of the operation ensures that residual characters are not left in the result field, should its length be larger than that of the source string.

If this sounds confusing, looking at the examples below should help clarify how the operation works. The examples convert uppercase letters to lowercase letters and vice versa; this kind of translation is the most frequent application of XLATE. The From and To strings of alphabetic characters are defined through named constants UC and LC.

Line						1 Position				2 Position				3 Position				From	To		Field Name							
0 1	I	* Two named constants to serve as translation "tables".																											
0 2	I					'ABCDEFGHIJKLMNOP-												C			UC							
0 3	I					'QRSTUVWXYZ'																						
0 4	I					'abcdefghijklmnop-												C			LC							
0 5	I					'qrstuvwxyz'																						
0 6	I																											

```
C    Indicators              Factor 1      Operation    Factor 2      Result Field        Resulting Indicators
     And  And                                                         Name   Length

01  C*  LNAME  (15 positions) contains 'BRYNE-SMITH            '; NAME (20
02  C*  positions) contains 'XXXXXXXXXXXXXXXXXXXX'.
03  C*
04  C           UC:LC      XLATELNAME       NAME      20
05  C*  NAME now is 'bryne-smith       XXXXX'; all upper-case letters
06  C*  of LNAME are changed to lower-case; the hyphen is not changed;
07  C*  the X's remaining are residual characters because padding was
08  C*  not specified.
09  C*
10  C           UC:LC      XLATELNAME:2     NAME             P
11  C*  Name now is 'Bryne-smith            '; the starting position of 2
12  C*  leaves the B unchanged; padding removes trailing characters.
13  C*
14  C           UC:LC      XLATELNAME:2     LNAME
15  C*  LNAME now contains 'Bryne-smith', because the source field was
16  C*  also designated the result.
17  C*
18  C*  Consider FLDA, which contains 'abc123ABC'.
19  C           LC:UC      XLATEFLDA        FLDA
20  C*  FLDA is now 'ABC123ABC', because LC is the From String, UC the
    C*  To String in factor 1. Had they been reversed (i.e., UC:LC),
    C*  FLDA would be 'abc123abc'.
    C
```

Using Arrays for String Manipulation

Before the introduction of string operations in RPG, programmers used arrays to inspect and manipulate characters within string fields. This approach, discussed in Chapter 8, was widely adopted and is still in use today, especially by programmers who are not yet comfortable with the operations discussed above.

This technique, you will recall, involves first moving the field whose characters are to be manipulated into an array of one-character-long elements. By looping through the elements, you can check each of the original field characters, while the array index serves as a positional locator of the character within the field. In this way, you can count, modify, or re-arrange individual field characters or substrings, depending on the processing required by the problem.

To compare this approach with RPG/400's string operations, let's work through a series of examples requiring string manipulation. For simplicity's sake, assume that all the array examples are using an array AR, defined as shown on the following page.

Extension Specification (E)

Line	Form Type	From Filename	To Filename	Table or Array Name	Number of Entries Per Record	Number of Entries Per Table or Array	Length of Entry	Table or Array Name (Alternating Format)	Length of Entry	Comments
0 1	E			AR		25	1			
0 2	E									

First, consider a common requirement of programming involving addresses: concatenating CITY (15 positions), a comma, STATE (2 positions) and ZIP (5 positions) into a common field CTYZIP for printing labels. The trailing blanks of CITY need to be eliminated to prevent an unsightly gap between the city and the comma. A solution using array manipulation is shown below. The routine checks the city field from right to left for the first non-blank character, rather than moving from left to right, so that it can handle city names which include a blank, like Des Moines.

Calculation Specification (C)

```
Line  Form  Factor 1   Operation  Factor 2   Result Field  Length  Dec
 01   C                MOVEACITY              AR                   P
 02   C* Initialize I to the length of the city field.
 03   C                Z-ADD15                I             20
 04   C* Move to the left through AR, stopping when a non-blank character
 05   C* is found or when the first element of the array is reached.
 06   C     AR,I       DOWEQ*BLANK
 07   C     I          ANDGT1
 08   C                SUB  1                 I
 09   C                ENDDO
 10   C* I now points to the right-most non-blank character (or to first
 11   C* element of AR, if CITY was blank).
 12   C* Increment I and move a comma to that array element.
 13   C                ADD  1                 I
 14   C                MOVEA','               AR,I
 15   C* Add 2 to I to skip to where STATE goes and move STATE.
 16   C                ADD  2                 I
 17   C                MOVEASTATE             AR,I
 18   C* Add 3 to I to position zip code correctly.
 19   C                ADD  3                 I
 20   C                MOVEAZIP               AR,I
      C* Move array to field where the concatenated value is desired.
      C                MOVEAAR                CTYZIP        25
      C
```

You can accomplish the same effect much more simply using RPG's CAT operation.

C		Indicators			Factor 1	Operation	Factor 2	Result Field		Operation Extender (H,N,P)	Resulting Indicators	Comments
		And	And					Name	Length		Arithmetic / Plus Minus Zero / Compare / 1>2 1<2 1=2 / Lookup(Factor 2)is / High Low Equal	
Line	Form Type	Control Level (L0-L9, LR,SR, AN/OR)	Not	Not	Not						Decimal Positions		
0 1	C	✱ Preparing an address line using CAT.										
0 2	C				CITY	CAT	',':0	WRK1	16			
0 3	C				STATE	CAT	ZIP:1	WRK2	8			
0 4	C				WRK1	CAT	WRK2:1	CTYZIP	25			
0 5	C											

Or consider the problem of left-justifying a value within a character field to remove any leading blanks. You might, for example, want a routine to guarantee that all addresses are left-adjusted (e.g., '124 N. 25th Street   '), regardless of whether or not they were entered with leading blanks (e.g., '   124 N. 25th Street '). Before RPG's string operations were possible, programmers would use arrays to left-justify values within a field, as shown below.

C		Indicators			Factor 1	Operation	Factor 2	Result Field		Operation Extender (H,N,P)	Resulting Indicators	Comments
		And	And					Name	Length		Arithmetic / Plus Minus Zero / Compare / 1>2 1<2 1=2 / Lookup(Factor 2)is / High Low Equal	
Line	Form Type	Control Level (L0-L9, LR,SR, AN/OR)	Not	Not	Not						Decimal Positions		
0 1	C					MOVEA	STADD	AR		P		
0 2	C					Z-ADD	1	I	20			
0 3	C	✱ Loop to move from left to right until first non-blank is found.										
0 4	C				AR,I	DOWEQ	' '					
0 5	C				I	ANDLT	25					
0 6	C					ADD	1	I				
0 7	C					ENDDO						
0 8	C	✱ I now points to left-most non-blank character or to 25th element.										
0 9	C	✱ Use I as starting point to move array's contents back to STADD.										
1 0	C					MOVEA	RR,I	STADD		P		
1 1	C											

Again, you can use string operations rather than array manipulation to accomplish left-justification.

Line	Form Type	Control Level (L0-L9, LR,SR, AN/OR)	Indicators			Factor 1	Operation	Factor 2	Result Field		Operation Extender (H,N,P)	Resulting Indicators			Comments
			And (Not)	And (Not)	(Not)				Name	Length / Decimal Positions		Arithmetic / Compare / Lookup			
01	C	*				Left justification using string operations.									
02	C	*				Locate the first non-blank character and store its position in I.									
03	C					' '	CHECKST	RADD	I	20					
04	C	*				Subtract I from STADD length plus 1 to get the length of address.									
05	C					26	SUB	I	LEN	20					
06	C	*				Use substring to move the address starting with first non-blank.									
07	C					LEN	SUBST	STADD:I	STADD		P				
08	C														

You can develop work-arounds for all the string operations using arrays and MOVEA. However, RPG/400's string operations provide a more direct way to inspect and manipulate individual characters or substrings within character data items than methods available in earlier versions of the language.

Working with Bits

Three RPG operations allow you to manipulate or test the status of individual bits within a character. These operations are useful when you need to work with EBCDIC values that cannot be directly entered from the keyboard. These generally are values below hexadecimal 40 (X'40'). Many of these hex values represent display attributes for screen output or control characters for printers. The standard way to assign one of these hexadecimal values to a field is by setting on and off the appropriate bits in the field.

Bits are numbered 0-7, with bits 0, 1, 2, and 3 called "high-order" or **zone bits** and 4, 5, 6, and 7 "low-order" or **decimal bits**. To set bits off, use the BITOF (Set Bits Off) operation. The field whose bits are to be affected must be a one-position character field or a one-position character array element.

A factor 2 entry specifies which bits are to be turned off. This entry can be a direct reference to the bits in question; in this case, the number of the bit(s) to be set off must be enclosed in apostrophes. The bits to be set off can also be specified by using a named constant in factor 2. Or factor 2 can contain the name of a one-position character field, table element, or array element. In this case, the bits that are *on* in that field are set *off* in the result field. Bits off in the factor 2 field are not affected.

The BITON (Set Bits On) operation works identically to the BITOF operation except that the factor 2 entry determines which bits of the result field are set *on*.

Line	Form Type	Control Level	Indicators	Factor 1	Operation	Factor 2	Result Field Name	Length	Resulting Indicators	Comments
0 1	C	*		Assume the following bit settings:			FLDA=11111111			
0 2	C	*					FLDB=00000000			
0 3	C	*					FLDC=11110000			
0 4	C	*								
0 5	C				BITON	'0123'	FLDB			
0 6	C	*		After operation FLDB=11110000						
0 7	C	*								
0 8	C				BITOF	'047'	FLDA			
0 9	C	*		After operation FLDA=01110110						
1 0	C	*								
1 1	C				BITOF	'01234567'	FLDA			
1 2	C	*		FLDA now 00000000						
1 3	C	*								
1 4	C				BITON	FDLC	FLDA			
1 5	C	*		FLDA now 11110000; same bits are on as in FDLC.						
1 6	C									
1 7	C									

You can use the TESTB (Test Bit) operation to turn on indicators based on a comparison between a factor 2 entry and the result field. The result field must be a one-character field, while factor 2 can specify directly the bits to be tested, or it can contain the name of a one-position character field, table name, or array element. In this case, the bits on in the factor 2 entry are compared with the corresponding bits in the result field; bits that are off in factor 2 are not considered.

Resulting indicators reflect the results of the comparison, and you must assign at least one indicator to be used with this operation. An indicator in positions 54-55 comes on if *all* bits specified or on in factor 2 are *off* in the result field. That is, the HI indicator signals that all specified bits are off. An indicator in positions 56-57 (LO) comes on if *some* of the bits specified on in factor 2 are *on* in the result field, while others are off. Finally, an indicator in positions 58-59 (EQ) comes on if *all* the bits specified on in factor 2 are *on* in the result field.

```
     C                                                  Result Field    Resulting Indicators
Line C* Assume the following bit patterns: FLDA=11110000
     C*                                                 FLDB=11000000
     C           TESTB'23'         FLDA       203040
     C* Indicator 40 comes on, because all factor 2 bits on in FLDA.
     C*
     C           TESTB'567'        FLDA       203040
     C* Indicator 20 comes on, because all factor 2 bits are off in FLDA.
     C*
     C           TESTB'04'         FLDA       203040
     C* Indicator 30 comes on, because some factor 2 bits are on in FLDA.
     C*
     C           TESTBFLDB         FLDA       203040
     C* Indicator 40 comes on, because all the on bits of FLDB are
     C* on in FLDA.
     C
```

For those of you uncomfortable with manipulating data at the bit level, take heart. In Version 2, Release 2 of OS/400, IBM has enhanced RPG to allow the direct assignment of hexadecimal values to fields.

Hexadecimal is a system of representing values based on powers of 16, in contrast to **binary** representation, based on powers of 2, and **decimal** representation, based on powers of 10. Digits 0-9 are used to represent 0-9 in hexadecimal; hex also uses characters A-F to represent values 10-15, respectively. Hex B (usually represented as X'0B') is the equivalent of decimal 11, for example.

Hexadecimal representation often is used with computers because of the convenient relationship between hexadecimal and binary representation: You can represent four bits as a single hexadecimal digit. Thus, the bits of a byte can always be translated into exactly two hex digits. 1111 1110, for example, is X'FE'.

Because you can represent the bits of any character — displayable or non-displayable — with two hexadecimal characters, this new RPG enhancement that allows direct manipulation of hex values eliminates the need to turn off or on individual bits to achieve a specific bit pattern of values.

Instead, you can express the desired value in hexadecimal by entering an X, followed by the hex value within apostrophes. You can manipulate hex values within your calculations, or you can assign them as values to named constants and then work with the named constants within your calculations. With this convenient addition to RPG, the use of bit operations should fade dramatically over the next few years.

The example below contrasts using bit operations and hexadecimal literals to assign the value X'38' (binary 0011 1000) to a field. Note that two hex digits fill one RPG position (or byte).

C		Indicators				Factor 1	Operation	Factor 2	Result Field				Resulting Indicators				Comments
		And	And						Name	Length		Arithmetic					
Line	Form Type	Control Level (L0-L9, LR,SR, AN/OR)	Not	Not	Not						Decimal Positions	Operation Extender (H,N,P)	Plus	Minus	Zero		
													Compare				
													1>2	1<2	1=2		
													Lookup(Factor 2)is				
													High	Low	Equal		
0 1	C						BITOF	'01234567'	FLDA	1							
0 2	C						BITON	'234'	FLDA								
0 3	C	* FLDA is now 00111000, or X'38'.															
0 4	C	*															
0 5	C						MOVE	X'38'	FLDA								
0 6	C	* Moving the hex value has the same effect as the bit operations.															
0 7	C																

Chapter Summary

RPG includes several operations used to check or manipulate characters within fields. You can use these operations only with character fields. TESTN determines whether the characters within a field are all numeric, blanks, or leading blanks followed by numeric characters. The most common use of this operation is to validate fields to make sure they contain numeric data.

SCAN, CHECK, and CHEKR are operations that allow you to inspect fields. SCAN looks for the presence of a specified character or string of characters, while CHECK and CHEKR detect the presence of non-specified characters. All three operations allow you to store the position of the located character or string within the field for subsequent use.

SUBST, CAT, and XLATE allow you to change characters within a field. SUBST copies a portion of a field into a second field, CAT combines two fields' values into a third field, and XLATE transforms characters based on a translation table you provide.

RPG also allows you to turn off or on individual bits within a one-character field using BITON and BITOF. The TESTB operation allows you to determine the status of bits within a one-character field. These bit operations are likely to fall into disuse now that RPG allows you to manipulate hexadecimal values directly.

Terms

base string	decimal	zone bits
binary	decimal bits	
compare string	hexadecimal	

Discussion/Review Questions

1. Do you need to use TESTN to assure that input fields entered interactively are numeric? Why or why not?

2. What does "case-sensitive" mean?

3. Discuss the differences between SCAN, CHECK, and CHEKR.

4. Explain the differences between SUBST, XLATE, and CAT.

5. Which operation(s) would you use if you wanted to determine whether or not data fields included lowercase letters?

6. Which operation(s) would you use if you wanted to guarantee that a data field contained only uppercase letters?

7. What is the usefulness of the bit-level operations?

8. Discuss the relationship between hexadecimal values and binary values.

9. Many companies that send out mass mailings are plagued with duplicates on their mailing lists. Why is this often the case? Describe specifically how some of the operations discussed in this chapter help eliminate the duplication. Do you think you could eliminate all duplication? Why or why not?

Exercises

1. Use TESTN to determine whether PAYIN (8-byte character) is numeric or blank. If all characters are numeric, move the value to a numeric field; if all characters are blank, execute subroutine MISSSR; otherwise, execute subroutine ERRSR.

2. Write the code needed to determine whether PTDESC (part description) contains the word "washer."

3. Assume you have two fields, ZIP and ZIP4, and that you want a third field, ZIP10, to include the zip code in the form '12345-6789' if ZIP4 is not blank or zero, but '12345   ' if the ZIP4 value is not present. Write the code to accomplish this processing.

4. Write the code needed to change a date stored in DATE in YYMMDD format to NDATE in the new format of name of month, day, 4-digit year (examples: June 1, 1993 and January 31, 1992).

5. Write the code needed to make sure that bits 1, 4, and 7 of field FLD are on and the other bits are off.

Programming Assignments

1. Wexler University needs a program to print mailing labels for its instructors (file WUINSTP, Appendix D). Depending on the instructor's preferred mode of address, the label should be addressed to "DR.," "MR.," "MRS.," or "MS.," followed by the name. As shown in the example below, all trailing blanks should be trimmed from first name and city. Note that the form of the zip code depends on whether or not the plus-4 digits are present. The university uses 3-across labels, each of which is 30 characters wide and five print lines long. The printer spacing chart shows the desired format for the labels.

```
          1         2         3         4         5         6         7         8         9
1234567890123456789012345678901234567890123456789012345678901234567890123456789012345678901234567890

DR. HAL HOLLOWAY              MRS. DONNA SMITH              DR. JO ANNE CERTAIN
3345 N. WESTERN AVE.          213 E. WILSON BLVD.          19000 S. WOODLAND DR.
KALAMAZOO, MI  49005-1010     PAW PAW, MI  49045           MATTAWAN, MI  49069

MR. ARNOLD VON RIEGLE
1221 E. BROAD ST.
PORTAGE, MI  49008-0010
```

2. Wexler University is very embarrassed. It seems that the user who entered the course descriptions didn't know how to spell "receive," and as a result, the word is misspelled "RECIEVE" in several places within the description file WUCRSDSP. (See Appendix D.) Write a program that will check through the records of WUCRSDSP and change any misspelled instances of "RECEIVE." Note that your code should correct "RECIEVING," "RECIEVES," and "RECIEVED," as well as "RECIEVE."

3. The president of Wexler University has just seen the labels from Program 1 (above) and he says they're not elegant enough. He doesn't want all the lettering to appear in uppercase. You point out that this is going to take a lot more programming effort, but he is adamant. Read the specifications for Program Assignment 1, but incorporate lowercase lettering within your labels, as shown below, to produce mailing labels for the instructors in WUINSTP.

```
          1         2         3         4         5         6         7         8         9
1234567890123456789012345678901234567890123456789012345678901234567890123456789012345678901234567890

Dr. Hal Holloway              Mrs. Donna Smith              Dr. Jo Anne Certain
3345 N. Western Ave.          213 E. Wilson Blvd.          19000 S. Woodland Dr.
Kalamazoo, MI  49005-1010     Paw Paw, MI  49045           Mattawan, MI  49069

Mr. Arnold Von Riegle
1221 E. Broad St.
Portage, MI  49008-0010
```

4. Wexler University is even more embarrassed. They just realized that the person who didn't know how to spell "receive" also consistently misspelled "QUANTITY" as "QUANITY" throughout the course descriptions. This error also appears as "QUANITATIVE" and "QUANITIES." Write a program that will check through the records of WUCRSDSP (Appendix D) and change any of these misspellings.

Programming Assignments Continued

Programming Assignments continued

Note that because you are adding a letter, in some instances this might make your description line too long for the 50-position field and you will need to word-wrap to the next description line. This wrapping may have to continue until you encounter a line with enough trailing blanks to include the wrapped word. Conceivably, you might even have to enter an additional description line for that course to handle the wrapping. Assume that hyphenation was not used in the original descriptions.

Chapter 12

Interprogram Communications

Chapter Overview

This chapter discusses how RPG programs can communicate with one another by passing data values as parameter arguments. It also introduces you to two other RPG capabilities: executing Command Language commands from within an RPG program, and sharing data among programs through data areas.

Modular Programming

As concern about program development and maintenance efficiencies has grown, programmers have become increasingly interested in developing small, stand-alone units of code (rather than writing monolithic programs thousands of lines long). There are many advantages to this approach, which is often called **modular programming**.

First, if you develop code in small, independent units, you often can reuse these units, since it is common for several applications to share identical processing requirements for some portions of their logic. Furthermore, small programs are easier to test than large programs are. Moreover, changes made to code are less likely to cause unexpected — and unwanted — side effects if the changes are made within a small, stand-alone module, rather than in a routine that is embedded within a gigantic program. And finally, because such modules can be separately developed and tested, a modular approach to programming makes it easier to divide an application development project among a team of programmers, each with responsibilities for developing different modules.

Calling Programs

RPG allows you to break an application system into small, self-contained modules of code by including the CALL operation. The CALL (Call a Program) operation passes control to the program named in factor 2. Factor 2 may contain a literal specifying the program to be executed (the "called program"). Alternately, factor 2 may contain a field, array element, or named constant that specifies the name of the program to be executed. When the program name is determined through a variable value, the program to be called is not fixed, or constant, but may change from one call to the next.

C			Indicators							Result Field			Resulting Indicators			
			And	And	Factor 1	Operation	Factor 2		Name	Length		Arithmetic			Comments
Line	Form Type	Control Level (L0-L9, LR,SR, AN/OR)	Not	Not	Not						Decimal Positions	Operation Extender (H,N,P)	Plus Minus Zero Compare 1>2 1<2 1=2 Lookup(Factor 2)is High Low Equal		
0 1	C		✱ A CALL to a program specified as a literal.												
0 2	C					CALL	'GL001R'								
0 3	C		✱ A CALL to a program using a variable.												
0 4	C					CALL	PRGNAM								
0 5	C														

Assume PRGNAM is an 8-position character field, with value 'GL001R'. In that case, the two CALL statements in the above examples will have identical effects: the execution of program GL001R. However, with the second method the value of PRGNAM could change during execution so that a repetition of that same CALL statement could invoke a different program.

Calling a program by supplying its name as a field value rather than as a literal causes more system overhead than coding its name as a literal. Accordingly, you should use a literal unless the program to be called actually may change within a run or between runs of the calling program.

You can include an optional indicator in the LO positions (56-57) to signal an error occurred when the program attempted the call.

When program execution reaches a CALL statement, control passes to the called program, which in turn begins to execute. The called program continues to execute until it reaches a RETRN statement; at this point, control returns to the calling program, at the statement immediately following the CALL. The figure below illustrates this flow of control among calling and called programs.

Figure 12.1
Flow of Control with CALLS

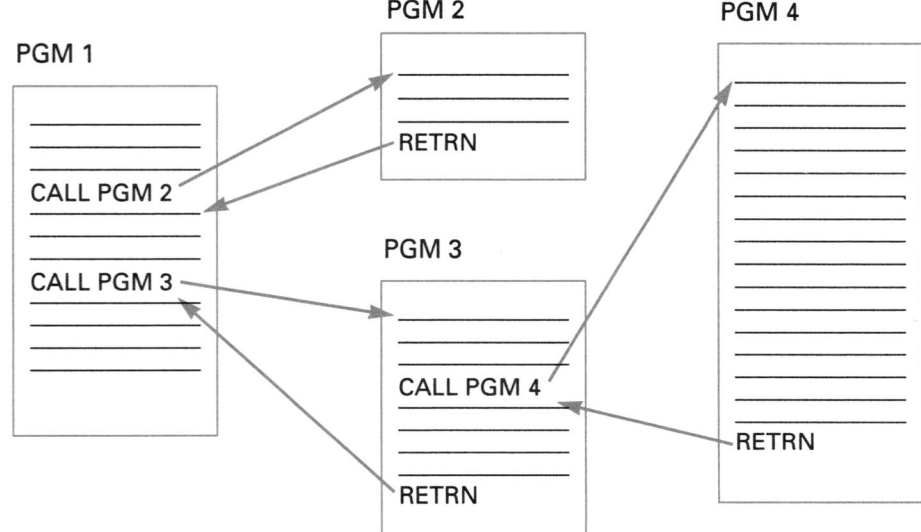

As you can see, the flow of control of a CALL is like that of an EXSR, except that CALL evokes an external module, rather than a subroutine internal to the program. A called program may in turn call other programs, but it should not recursively call its calling program.

The CALL to an external routine offers one additional significant advantage over an EXSR operation: The routine called does not have to be an object created from RPG source. You can write a program in any high-level language (HLL) supported by the AS/400, or in OS/400's CL, compile it, and then call it from an RPG program.

Similarly, you can call an RPG program from a CL program or a program written in a different HLL supported by the AS/400. The RPG program's RETRN statement returns control to whatever program called it.

This flexibility allows you to break a problem down into logical units, write each unit in the language best suited for developing the algorithm required by that unit, and then call the units to perform their processing as needed. Although this multilanguage approach to program development is not widely used in the AS/400 world today, its use may grow as cooperative processing and the use of Graphical User Interfaces (GUIs) demand more sophisticated capabilities than those RPG has to offer.

As mentioned above, the system returns control to the calling program from a called program when it encounters a RETRN statement in the called program. If the LR indicator is also on when the RETRN is executed, the system's resources tied up by the called program are released; a subsequent call to that program causes the program to start up again as though for the first time. On the other hand, if LR is not on within the called program upon return, that called program remains activated. As a result, a subsequent call to that program will find all the fields and indicators of the called program to have the values they had at the time of the previous RETRN. Moreover, any files used by the called program also will still be open as a result of the previous call.

```
     C                                                                    Resulting Indicators
                Indicators                                  Result Field
     C                                                                    Arithmetic
           And   And    Factor 1    Operation   Factor 2    Name  Length  Plus Minus Zero
     Line                                                                 Compare
                                                                          1>2  1<2  1=2
                                                                          Lookup(Factor 2)is
                                                                          High  Low  Equal

01   C* Partial calcs showing called program where RETRN is executed
02   C* without LR on; the called program will remain active with files
03   C* open and variables and indicators retaining their current values
04   C* at the time of the RETRN.
05   C      ...
06   C      RETRN
07   C******************
08   C* Partial calcs in which LR is set on prior to RETRN; called program
09   C* is deactivated, so that it will start from "scratch" the next
10   C* time it is called.
11   C      ...
12   C      MOVE *ON              *INLR
13   C      RETRN
14   C
```

Whether or not you should turn on LR before returning from a called program, then, depends on whether you want the called program to start afresh each time the calling program evokes it or whether you want the called program to pick up from where it had left off on the previous call. Failure to correctly handle this indicator can cause undesired effects in the called program.

If LR is on, the program automatically returns to the calling program at the ending point of the fixed-logic cycle (Chapter 13 describes this cycle), even though no RETRN has been encountered. In other words, LR provides an implicit return. However, when using a procedural approach to RPG programming, you should always explicitly include a RETRN operation to indicate exactly when you want the called program to terminate.

You also can deactivate a called program from the calling program by using the FREE operation. FREE (Deactivate a Program) removes the program from the list of activated programs and ensures that the called program will begin anew each time it is called. The format of the FREE operation requires a factor 2 entry containing the name of the program to deactivate, coded directly as a literal, or as the value of a field, named constant, or array element.

C		Indicators						Result Field				Resulting Indicators			
Line	Form Type	Control Level (L0-L9, LR,SR, AN/OR)	And	And	Factor 1	Operation	Factor 2	Name	Length	Decimal Positions	Operation Extender (H,N,P)	Arithmetic / Compare / Lookup			Comments
0 1	C						CALL	'WYCSTPR'							
0 2	C						FREE	'WYCSTPR'							
0 3	C						CALL	PRGNAM							
0 4	C						FREE	PRGNAM							
0 5	C														

As with CALL, you can include an optional indicator in positions 56-57 of a FREE operation. This indicator will come on if the attempt to FREE the program fails.

Passing Data Between Programs

A CALL operation would be of limited value if it did not permit the called and calling programs to share data. Within a single RPG program, all variables are globally defined; that is, the value of any variable can be accessed from anywhere within the program. This global feature of variables does not extend across program boundaries, however. That means if you want a called program to process some data and send the results of the processing back to the calling program, you need to make special provisions to allow this sharing to take place.

RPG uses the PARM (Identify Parameters) operation to indicate which field's values are to be shared between programs. A list of **PARMs** in the calling program must have a list of corresponding PARMs in the called program.

Each PARM requires an entry in the result field of the Calculation Specification. This entry may be a field, data structure, or array that is to serve as the parameter. It cannot be an indicator, a literal, a label, a constant, or a table name. If the field is a multiple-occurrence data structure, all occurrences of the data structure are passed as a single field.

Although the data names of the calling and called programs' PARMs do not need to be the same, corresponding PARMs in the two programs should have the same type and length, since in fact these corresponding parameters are referencing the same storage location within the computer.

PARMs can appear only immediately after a CALL operation or following a PLIST operation; PLIST (Identify a Parameter List) is a declarative operation that identifies a list of parameters to be shared between programs. PLIST requires an identifying entry in factor 1; that entry may be a PLIST name, if the PLIST is within a calling program, or the reserved word *ENTRY, if the PLIST is within a called program and signals the arguments the called program is to receive from the calling program upon its invocation.

Before we discuss PARMs in more detail, let's clarify the relationship between calling and called programs, PLISTs, and PARMs by looking at some examples. In the illustration below, the calling program calls PROG2, passing it PARMs FLDA, FLDB, and FLDC. Since the PARMs appear immediately following a CALL operation, they do not require a PLIST operation preceding them.

```
C*  This is a calling program. Notice how the PARMs follow the
C*  CALL without a PLIST operation.
C              CALL    'PROG2'
C              PARM              FLDA
C              PARM              FLDB
C              PARM              FLDC
```

An alternate way to code the same logic is to include the PARMs within a PLIST and name the PLIST to be used as part of the CALL operation, as shown below. Both examples accomplish the same effect — passing the addresses of FLDA, FLDB, and FLDC to the called program PROG2.

```
C*  This is a calling program. The PARMs appear in a PLIST, which
C*  is referenced in the call operation.
C              CALL    'PROG2'   PLSTA
C              ...
C    PLSTA     PLIST
C              PARM              FLDA
C              PARM              FLDB
C              PARM              FLDC
```

To access those storage locations passed by the calling program, the called program also must include PARMs. These PARMs occur within a PLIST labeled *ENTRY, as shown on the following page. A called program can contain only one *ENTRY PLIST.

C			Indicators									Result Field				Resulting Indicators			
			And	And	Factor 1		Operation		Factor 2			Name	Length			Arithmetic			
Line	Form Type	Control Level (L0-L9, LR,SR, AN/OR)	Not	Not	Not									Decimal Positions	Operation Extender (H,N,P)	Plus	Minus	Zero	Comments
																Compare			
																1>2	1<2	1=2	
																Lookup(Factor 2)is			
																High	Low	Equal	

0 1	C	* This is the called program PROG2. It includes an *ENTRY PLIST.
0 2	C	. . .
0 3	C	*ENTRY	PLIST
0 4	C	PARM	FLD1
0 5	C	PARM	FLD2
0 6	C	PARM	FLD3
0 7	C	

Note that although the variable names in the corresponding PARMs of the calling and called program may be different, they should agree in data type and length, since they reference the same storage location. The variables declared as PARMs must be defined within their respective programs, either within the PARM statements themselves or in other specifications within the programs.

Because RPG passes parameter arguments by passing the address of the storage location represented by the field, rather than by passing the field's value, changes in the parameter fields within the called program result in the same changes in the parameter fields of the calling program. For example, assume in the above illustration that FLDA had a value of 150 before the CALL to PROG2, and that as part of its processing, PROG2 changed the value of FLD1 to 0. Upon return to the calling program, FLDA now would have a value of 0, since that field and FLD1 of the called program reference the same storage location.

If this possible change in parameter field values could cause undesired effects, the option exists to use factor 2 with the PARM operation to eliminate this kind of side effect. Simply enter the field whose value you want passed to the called program as factor 2 and enter a different field as the result field. When the CALL takes place, the system copies the value of the factor 2 field into the result field and passes the address of the result field to the called program. Upon return from the called program the result field's value may be changed, but the factor 2 field value remains undisturbed.

C			Indicators			Factor 1	Operation	Factor 2	Result Field			Resulting Indicators				Comments

The RPG coding form shows the following entries:

Line	Form Type												
0 1	C	✱	To pass FLDA's value to PROG1 without the possibility of FLDA's										
0 2	C	✱	value being changed by PROG1, code the PARM as shown below.										
0 3	C					CALL	'PROG1'						
0 4	C					PARM	FLDA	FLDX	30				
0 5	C												

You will find a wide variation in the extent to which different companies make use of RPG's CALL feature. Some companies incorporate calls within menu programs that present application choices to users; the menu programs will then call the selected programs to perform the desired processing. Typically, this kind of program does not require passing data between the calling program and the programs it calls.

Another common use of called programs is to perform date conversion. Many accounting programs, for example, need to determine the number of elapsed days between two dates. To perform this arithmetic, the dates typically are converted to a **Julian** or **Julianized format** in which dates are represented as sequential numbers so that one value can be subtracted from the other.

This date conversion often is done within a called program. The calling program includes two parameters — one containing the date in its **Gregorian format**, and one to store the date in its Julianized representation. The called program does the conversion of the value represented in the first parameter, stores the results in the second parameter, and returns control to the calling program.

Another example of a program that might be called by many programs is one that converts a numeric value representing dollars and cents (e.g., 123.43) to its representation in words (e.g., One Hundred Twenty-three Dollars and 43 cents). The logic required for such a conversion is not trivial, and companies do not want to continually reinvent that particular wheel.

Calling QCMDEXC

Occasionally within an RPG program, you would like to be able to communicate directly with the operating system to issue a CL command. You might, for example, want to override one database file with another or send a message reporting on the program's progress to the user. IBM has supplied a program, QCMDEXC, which allows you to run a single CL command from within a HLL program.

Any program can call QCMDEXC. QCMDEXC expects to receive arguments for two parameters: The first parameter should contain the command the system is to execute, and the second should contain the command length.

Putting the desired command in a form that can be passed to QCMDEXC as a parameter argument is not a straightforward process. The result field of a PARM cannot contain a named constant, and most system commands are too long to assign to a field via MOVE or MOVEL. As a consequence, programmers typically use a compile-time array to build the command and then specify the array as the result field of the first parameter. The length of the array is then passed as the second parameter's argument.

In the sample program shown below, one display file is substituted for another by defining the command as array OVR and passing the command to QCMDEXC. Notice the use of factor 2 in the second PARM statement to assign a value of 80 to PARM LEN.

```
            1         2         3         4         5         6         7
   1234567890123456789012345678901234567890123456789012345678901234567890

       FSCREEN1 CF  E                       WORKSTN
       F                          ...
       E                          OVR    80  80  1
       C                          ...
       C                          CALL 'QCMDEXC'
       C                          PARM              OVR
       C                          PARM 80           LEN    155
       C                          ...
    **
    OVRDSPF SCREEN1 SCREEN2
```

Data Areas

PARMs allow data to be shared between calling and called programs. **Data areas** are AS/400 objects used to communicate data between programs within a job or between jobs; one program does not have to call another to access the same data if the data resides in a data area. Data areas can be used to store information of limited size, independent of database files or programs.

The system automatically creates a **local data area (LDA)** for each job in the system. Each LDA is 1,024 positions long, with type character; initially, blanks fill the LDA. When you submit a job with the SBMJOB command, the value of your LDA is copied into the LDA of the submitted job, so that the submitted job can access any data values stored in the LDA by your initial job. When a job ends, its LDA ceases to exist.

You also can create more permanent data areas with the CL command CRTDTAARA (Create Data Area). A data area created in this way remains an object on the system and can be accessed by any program regardless of its job.

Programmers use data areas for storing small quantities of data that are frequently used by several programs or by the same program each time it is run. For example, they might prefer storing within a data area the next order number or customer number to be assigned, to avoid having to retrieve that information from a database file of orders or customers. Programmers sometimes use a data area to store constant values used by several programs, such as tax rates or discounts, or to transfer the processing results of one program to another.

Data-Area Data Structures

As an RPG programmer, you should understand how you can access data areas from within an RPG program. One way to make a data area accessible to an RPG program is to define a data structure for the data area. A U in position 18 of a data structure identifies it as a **data-area data structure**.

If you do not name the data structure, the data structure contains information from the LDA. If you want the data structure to contain data from a different data area, you must provide a program name for the data structure that matches the name of the data area in the system. The figure below illustrates two data-area data structures.

Line	Form Type	Filename	Sequence	Number (1/N)	Option (O)	Record Identifying Indicator or **	Position 1	Not (N)	C/Z/D	Character	Position 2	Not (N)	C/Z/D	Character	Position 3	Not (N)	C/Z/D	Character	Stacker Select P/B/L/R	From	To	Decimal Positions	Field Name	Control Level (L1-L9)	Matching Fields or Chaining Fields	Field Record Relation	Plus	Minus	Zero or Blank
0 1	I	* The data structure below represents the LDA.																											
0 2	I		UDS																										
0 3	I																			1	80		INVNO						
0 4	I										. . .																		
0 5	I	* The data structure below represents data area RECPTS.																											
0 6	I	RECPTS	UDS																										
0 7	I																			1	102		STOR1						
0 8	I																			11	202		STOR2						
0 9	I																			21	302		STOR3						
1 0	I																												

A data area defined as above is read into the program at program initialization and is locked to prevent other programs from accessing it. When the program ends, the system writes back the contents of the data structure to the data area and removes the lock.

Using *NAMVAR DEFN

You do not have to define a data-area data structure to access data areas within your program. Contents of a data area are also accessible through the *NAMVAR DEFN operation. This operation requires *NAMVAR in factor 1 and a field to receive the data area's contents in the result field.

The result field can be a field, a data-structure subfield, or a data structure *not* defined as a data-area data structure (i.e., no U in position 18). You must define this result field, either as part of the DEFN operation or elsewhere within your program, and the definition should match that of the data area itself.

Factor 2 normally contains the external name of the data area whose contents you want to access. If you leave factor 2 blank, the result field represents both the external data-area name and the name you use to represent the data area within your program. If you want to use this operation with the LDA, code *LDA in factor 2.

```
Line  C  Factor 1        Operation  Factor 2    Result Field       Length  Comments
                                                Name
01 C *  Data area INVOICE associated with field INVNO.
02 C              *NAMVAR  DEFN  INVOICE              INVNO    50
03 C *  Data area name CHKNO to be used also as the field name.
04 C              *NAMVAR  DEFN                       CHKNO    60
05 C *  Local Data Area associated with LOCAL.
06 C              *NAMVAR  DEFN  *LDA                 LOCAL
07 C
```

There is one important difference between accessing data areas with *NAMVAR DEFN and accessing them through a data-area data structure: The contents of the data area are not automatically retrieved into the variables at the start of the program with *NAMVAR DEFN, the way they are with data-area data structures, nor are the field contents automatically written back out to the data areas at program termination. Instead, you must explicitly retrieve and write the contents of the data areas in your calculations. Specific operations exist to allow this explicit I/O of data areas.

Before we look at those operations, you need to understand one more use of *NAMVAR DEFN. Recall that the contents of a data-area data structure are automatically, or implicitly, read from the data area at the start of your program and automatically (implicitly) written back out to the data area at the close of your program. If, in addition, you *explicitly* want to access the contents of such a data area during the course of your program's execution, you must use the *NAMVAR DEFN feature to associate the data-area data structure with an additional field.

```
Line  C  Factor 1        Operation  Factor 2    Result Field       Length  Comments
                                                Name
01 C *  This DEFN assigns an alternate name to the RECPTS data area
02 C *  data structure.
03 C              *NAMVAR  DEFN  RECPTS               SALES    30
04 C
```

Any explicit I/O from or to the data area then takes place through this field (SALES, in our example), rather than through the data-area data structure identifier (e.g., RECPTS).

With that background complete, we can now look at the RPG operations used for explicit I/O with data areas.

IN (Retrieve a Data Area)

IN "reads" the contents of the data area into your program. Factor 2 must contain the result field of a *NAMVAR DEFN statement. By including the optional entry *LOCK as a factor 1 entry, you can lock the data area from update by another program. If you leave factor 1 blank and the data area has been retrieved previously, the locked status associated with the previous retrieval remains in effect. That is, if the data area was locked before this IN operation, it remains locked; if it was not locked, it remains unlocked. *LOCK cannot be used with the LDA.

Line	Form Type	Control Level (L0-L9, LR,SR, AN/OR)	And Not	And Not	Not	Factor 1	Operation	Factor 2	Result Field Name	Length	Decimal Positions	Operation Extender (H,N,P)	Resulting Indicators Arithmetic Plus / Compare 1>2 / Lookup High	Minus / 1<2 / Low	Zero / 1=2 / Equal	Comments
0 1	C	*				Retrieves contents of the LDA into LOCAL.										
0 2	C						IN	LOCAL								
0 3	C	*				Retrieves data area RECPTS into SALES with lock now in effect.										
0 4	C					*LOCK	IN	SALES								
0 5	C	*				Retrieves data area CHKNO into CHKNO with lock now in effect.										
0 6	C					*LOCK	IN	CHKNO								
0 7	C															

OUT (Write Out a Data Area)

OUT updates the data area specified in factor 2. Factor 2 must contain the result field of a *NAMVAR DEFN statement. Moreover, the operation cannot be used unless the data area already has been retrieved — either through the execution of an IN operation, or through the implicit retrieval that results for data-area data structures.

If you include the optional entry *LOCK in factor 1, a lock remains in effect for the data area following the OUT operation; if you leave factor 1 blank, the data area is unlocked after it is updated. As with the IN operation, you cannot include a *LOCK entry for the LDA.

```
Line  Form Type
01  C *LDA is updated but the lock remains.
02  C         OUT  LOCAL
03  C *Data area RECPTS is updated but lock remains in effect.
04  C *LOCK    OUT  SALES
05  C *Data area CHKNO is updated and lock removed.
06  C         OUT  CHKNO
07  C
```

UNLCK (Unlock a Data Area)
UNLCK unlocks the data area specified in factor 2. This factor 2 entry must be the result field of a *NAMVAR DEFN statement. Executing an UNLCK operation on a data area already unlocked does not cause a system error. You cannot use the UNLCK operation with the LDA.

```
Line  Form Type
01  C *Data area RECPTS is unlocked.
02  C         UNLCK SALES
03  C
```

For all three data area operations — IN, OUT, and UNLCK — if you enter *NAMVAR as the factor 2 entry, *all* the data areas appearing as result fields in *NAMVAR DEFN operations participate in the operation. All three operations also allow you to include an optional error indicator in positions 56-67 to signal that an error occurred during the operation.

Chapter Summary

One way to implement a modular approach to programming is to break required processing into separate programs, each focused on accomplishing a single function. These programs then can be used by other programs through the CALL operation. The AS/400 allows calling and called programs to be written in any mix of languages available on the system, including CL.

In RPG, all variables are global within a program, but local to the program. To share data between a calling and called program, PARMs are used in both programs to define the shared data. These PARMS appear either immediately following a CALL operation or as part of a named PLIST in the calling program and within an *ENTRY PLIST in the called program. The corresponding PARM variables in the calling and called programs share a common storage location. As a result, changes to a parameter's value in one of the programs affects that corresponding parameter's value in the other program.

You can call a special program supplied by IBM, QCMDEXC, to execute a CL command. You must pass the command as a parameter to QCMDEXC, along with a parameter specifying the command's length.

The AS/400 also provides data areas for sharing values between programs. The programs do not have to call one another to access the same data area. A Local Data Area (LDA) is automatically available for each job; additionally, you can define permanent data areas that any program can subsequently access. You can access the contents of a data area within an RPG program by defining a special data structure — a data-area data structure — or by referencing the data area in a *NAMVAR DEFN statement.

Data contained in data-area data structures is automatically retrieved at the start of a program and written back to the data area at the end of the program. To retrieve data from data areas referenced only through *NAMVAR DEFN, you must explicitly use the IN operation. OUT writes data values back to a data area, while UNLCK can release a lock on a data area to allow its access for update by other programs.

Terms

data area   Julian format   PARMs
data-area data structures   local data area (LDA)
Gregorian format   modular programming

Discussion/Review Questions

1. What does "modular programming" mean?

2. What are the advantages of a modular approach to application development?

3. What effect does LR have on a called program? What's the chief difference between turning on LR and the FREE operation?

4. What is the function of a PARM operation?

5. When do PARMs need to occur as part of a PLIST?

6. When is *ENTRY used as a PLIST name?

7. When would you call QCMDEXC?

8. What is an LDA?

9. Why might you use a data area rather than a database file to store values?

10. What is an advantage of accessing data areas through a data-area data structure?

11. What are the two uses of the DEFN operation that you have learned in this text?

Exercises

1. Write the RPG code to call either PROGA, PROGB, or PROGC, depending on whether OPTION is 1, 2, or 3. No parameters are needed with any of the calls.

2. Write that portion of a calling program that passes a date in YYMMDD format to a called program to convert the date to a date in month-name, day, 4-digit-year format (e.g., January 1, 1993).

3. Write the entire RPG program that would be called in Exercise 2 to convert the date to the desired format.

4. Assume a data area named CHKVALS contains a 6-position number representing the last check number used, a 6-position date reflecting the most recent date on which the check-writing program was run, 10 positions containing the name of the last user running the check-writing program, and

four positions reflecting the number of checks written during the last program run. Code a data-area data structure to enable access to this data area.

5. At a certain point in an RPG program you need to delete a database file. The name of the file to be deleted is contained in field FILNAM, a 10-position character field. The CL command to delete a file is:

```
DLTF FILE(*CURLIB/XXXXXXXXXX)
```

where *XXXXXXXXXX* represents where a file name should appear.

Write the RPG code to incorporate the file from FILNAM in the proper location within the command and then call QCMDEXC to carry out the command. Show the extension specifications and the compile-time array, as well as any needed calculations.

Programming Assignments

1. Develop an interactive menu application that presents the user with a choice for executing one of four programs you have written this semester. (Your instructor may tell you which applications to include; preferably, the programs will be part of the same application system and include at least one interactive application.) Your program should call the appropriate program based on the user's choice. Upon return from the called program, the user should again see the menu for another selection. This should continue until the user signals Exit at the menu. Design your menu to be user friendly and to include informational messages signaling the results of processing for non-interactive applications, so that the user knows the selected program has executed.

2. As part of its billing procedure, GTC needs to convert military time to standard time in several programs. The company decides to do this conversion through a called program. Write such a called program that will receive as a parameter argument the time in HHMM format, where the hours are based on a 24-hour clock (i.e., military time), convert that value to time expressed on a 12-hour clock, with a.m. or p.m. noted, and pass that converted value back to the calling program. For example, if the called program was passed 1530, it should convert that value to 3:30 p.m.

    To test your program, use GTC's Calls Transaction File (GTCLSP) as the input file to a calling program that passes the time-of-call value from each record to the called program and generates the following report to reflect the converted time returned by the called program:

```
          1         2         3         4
1234567890123456789012345678901234567890112345
XX/XX/XX                PAGE XX0X
     GTC TIME CONVERSION TEST REPORT

   MILITARY TIME   CONVERTED TIME

      XXXX          0X:XX A.M.
      XXXX          0X:XX P.M.
      XXXX          0X:XX A.M.
```

3. GTC needs to convert time from military to standard time and determine the day of the week from a given date, both as part of its billing procedure. The programmers decide to implement each of these conversions as called programs. Write two called programs to accomplish these tasks. More details of the time conversion are described in Assignment 2 above. For the called program that determines day of week, use the algorithm below:

Algorithm for determining day of week from date stored in YYMMDD format:

```
IF month > 2
    Add 1 to month
ELSE
    Add 13 to month
    Subtract 1 from year
ENDIF
```

Programming Assignments Continued

Programming Assignments continued

century-day = INTEGER(years * 365.25) + INTEGER(month * 30.6) + days – 63

day-of-week = REMAINDER(century-day ⁄ 7) + 1

IF day-of-week = 1
    name-of-day = "Sunday"
ELSE
IF day-of-week = 2
    name-of-day = "Monday"
ELSE
IF day-of-week = 3
    name-of-day = "Tuesday"
    ... etc. ...
ENDIF

Where the algorithm says INTEGER, truncate the value without rounding. Where it says REMAINDER, use the MVR operation.

Test your two called programs by generating the report shown below, using the date-of-call and time-of-call fields of GTC's Call Transaction File (GTCLSP) for your test data. For the report column "DAY", print the appropriate name of the day (e.g., SUNDAY).

```
            1         2         3         4         5
1234567890123456789012345678901234567890123456789012345
XX/XX/XX                                    PAGE XXØX
   GTC DATE AND TIME CONVERSION TEST REPORT

 DATE        DAY      MILITARY TIME   CONVERTED TIME

 XX/XX/XX   XXXXXXXXX    XXXX         ØX:XX A.M.
 XX/XX/XX   XXXXXXXXX    XXXX         ØX:XX P.M.
 XX/XX/XX   XXXXXXXXX    XXXX         ØX:XX A.M.
```

4. CompuSell wants you to write a label-printing program for its customers in file CSCSTP (Appendix D); the company wants your program to print 2-across labels. Each of the labels reading across should represent the same customer. The printer will be loaded with continuous-label stock when this program is run. Each label is five print lines long. The desired format for the labels is shown below. Note that the information within parentheses is included to let you know what should appear on the label, but that information should not appear within your output.

Programming Assignments Continued

Programming Assignments continued

```
            1         2         3         4         5         6         7         8         9        10
1234567890123456789012345678901234567890123456789012345678901234567890123456789012345678901234567890
1
2    XXXXXXXXXX XXXXXXXXXXXXXXX           XXXXXXXXXX XXXXXXXXXXXXXXX        (first, last name)
3    XXXXXXXXXXXXXXXXXXXXX                XXXXXXXXXXXXXXXXXXXXX             (street address)
4    XXXXXXXXXXXXXXX  XX XXXXX-XXXX        XXXXXXXXXXXXXXX  XX XXXXX-XXXX    (city, state, zip)
5
6
7    XXXXXXXXXX XXXXXXXXXXXXXXX           XXXXXXXXXX XXXXXXXXXXXXXXX
8    XXXXXXXXXXXXXXXXXXXXX                XXXXXXXXXXXXXXXXXXXXX
9    XXXXXXXXXXXXXXX  XX XXXXX-XXXX        XXXXXXXXXXXXXXX  XX XXXXX-XXXX
10
```

This is a repeat of program assignment 2.3, except that now management has decided the labels will look nicer if the names, addresses, and city print in lowercase (except for the first letter of each word). Rather than writing a conversion routine repeatedly for each of the fields, you decide to write the routine once as a called program so that it will be available for use in other programs as well.

Write a called program that converts a string of uppercase letters to a string in which the first character in the field and any other character immediately following a blank remains uppercase, but all other letters are converted to lowercase. Include as parameters two character fields each 25 positions long. The program should process the value passed in the first parameter and store the converted string in the second PARM field prior to returning.

Once you have written the called program, in your label program successively call that program to convert first name, last name, street address, and city to the desired format for each customer before printing the label.

Chapter 13

Looking Backward: RPG II

Chapter Overview

This chapter will provide you with a basic understanding of RPG II and RPG's fixed-logic cycle. It will show you how programmers express complex logic without structured operations by relying on indicators and GOTOs. It also demonstrates control-break processing with level indicators.

RPG II: An Initial Look

You may validly wonder, "Why bother with RPG II?", since RPG/400 has become the standard implementation in most of today's RPG installations. The primary reason why you should be familiar with RPG II is that you often will be asked to maintain programs that have been based in part or entirely on older features of the language. Some of the programs may be old, written before RPG III or RPG/400 existed; others may be more recent, but written by programmers who have not entirely embraced RPG/400 standards. If you don't understand how the RPG II features work, you will have little chance of success modifying programs that rely on them.

Recognize that the inclusion of RPG II in this book is not an endorsement to use these methods. However, all the features discussed in this chapter can be implemented in RPG/400. The newer versions of RPG enhanced, rather than replaced, those features present in earlier versions of the language. In general, using the techniques offered by RPG/400 will result in programs easier to understand and modify than the ones presented here.

To demonstrate the differences between RPG/400 and RPG II, let's revisit the first program we wrote in Chapter 2 to see how it would be implemented in RPG II. The program is reproduced on the next page.

```
             1         2         3         4         5         6         7
    12345678901234567890123456789012345678901234567890123456789012345678901234567890
        F********************************************************************
        F*  This program produces a weekly sales report.  The       *
        F*  report data come directly from input file SALES.         *
        F*     Author:  J. Yaeger    Date written: 10/10/92.         *
        F*                                                           *
        F*      Indicator 90:  End-of-file SALES                     *
        F********************************************************************
        FSALES    IF  F      63           DISK
        FQPRINT   O   F     132           PRINTER
        I*****************Input Specifications*****************
        ISALES    NS
        I                                         1    40SLSMNO
        I                                         5    34 NAME
        I                                        35    50 ITEM
        I                                        51   560SDATE
        I                                        57   632PRICE
        C*****************Calculations*************************
        C                   EXCPTHEADS
        C                   READ SALES                        90
        C*
        C         *IN90     DOWEQ*OFF
        C                   EXCPTDETAIL
        C                   READ SALES                        90
        C                   ENDDO
        C*
        C                   MOVE *ON       *INLR
        C                   RETRN
        O***************Output Specifications*****************
        OQPRINT   E  202          HEADS
        O                                         8 'PAGE'
        O                            PAGE        13
        O                                        50 'WEEKLY SALES REPORT'
        O                                        64 'DATE'
        O                            UDATE Y     73
        O         E   1            HEADS
        O                                         5 'SLSM.'
        O                                        48 'DATE OF'
        O                                        77 'SALE'
        O         E   2            HEADS
        O                                         3 'NO.'
        O                                        21 'NAME'
        O                                        46 'SALE'
        O                                        61 'ITEM SOLD'
        O                                        77 'PRICE'
        O         E   1            DETAIL
        O                            SLSMNO       4
        O                            NAME        37
        O                            SDATE Y     48
        O                            ITEM        67
        O                            PRICE 1     79
```

The program represents a simple read/write program. The calculations of the program focus on setting up a loop to read records and write report lines. To express this logic in RPG II will require a few modifications to our program.

First, RPG II programs rely on RPG's **fixed-logic cycle.** All versions of RPG (including RPG/400) have a built-in read-process-write cycle that can be used to automate part of the processing requirements. This read-process-write cycle repeats until all the desired records have been processed. To plug into the automated reading portion of the fixed-logic cycle, the main input file needs to be assigned P (for Primary) as designation, rather than F (Full procedural). RPG automatically handles the reading of records from a primary file, so you do not (in fact, cannot) explicitly issue an input instruction to that file.

The File Specifications for our revised program appear below. Notice that the specification for the output file includes an overflow indicator that will help determine when it is time to advance to a new page of the report.

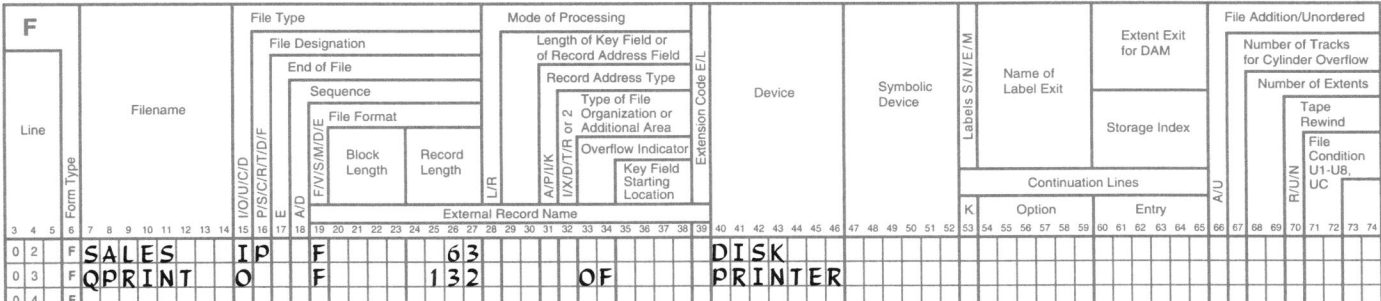

We also need to make a minor addition to the Input Specifications of our program: adding a Record Identifying Indicator in positions 19-20 of the record identification line of the input file description. The indicator that we designate as the record identifying indicator will come on (i.e., have a value of '1' or *ON) each time RPG successfully reads a record from the file; the indicator is automatically turned off (i.e., assumes a value of '0', or *OFF) just prior to the next automatic attempt to read the next record. If the system retrieves another record, the indicator comes back on. On the other hand, if the system detects end-of-file, the record identifying indicator remains off and indicator LR automatically comes on instead.

You can use any one of RPG's numbered indicators (01-99) to serve as a record identifying indicator. In our sample program, indicator 01 will serve this purpose. Note that you enter all indicators as two-digit numbers, even if the first digit is a zero.

I	Filename	Sequence	Number (1/N)	Option (O)	Record Identifying Indicator	**	Record Identification Codes — Position 1 · Not(N) · C/Z/D · Character	Position 2 · Not(N) · C/Z/D · Character	Position 3 · Not(N) · C/Z/D · Character · Stacker Select P/B/L/R	Field Location — From	To	Decimal Positions	Field Name	Control Level (L1-L9)	Matching Fields or Chaining Fields	Field Record Relation	Field Indicators — Plus	Minus	Zero or Blank
01 I	SALES	NS			01														
02 I										1	4	0	SLSMNO						
03 I										5	34		NAME						
04 I										35	50		ITEM						
05 I										51	56	0	SDATE						
06 I										57	63	2	PRICE						
07 I																			

To automate the output portion of the cycle, so that writing is done automatically without explicit output operations, you need to change the record format type on the Output Specifications from E to the type appropriate for a given line: H for heading line, D for detail, or T for total. Also remove the line names, because names are permitted only for exception lines.

In addition to changing the line types and removing the line names, you now also will need to use indicators to specify whether a given line should print during the output portion of the fixed-logic cycle. Associating an indicator with an output line means that the indicator must be on for the line to print during the output phase of the current pass of the fixed-logic cycle. Enter indicators in positions 23-31 of the Output Specifications. Multiple indicators on a line are in an AND relationship, such that they all must be on for the line to print. To express an OR relationship between indicators, code one indicator on a line, drop down a line and enter OR in positions 14-15, and enter the second indicator on this second line.

In the sample program, you want headings each time the overflow indicator comes on. There is also a special indicator, 1P (First Page), which is on for a very brief time at the beginning of the program. This indicator normally is used to produce headings on the first page (because the overflow indicator does not come on until the first page is full). You condition heading lines, then, with 1P or OF. Note that when you work with the fixed-logic cycle, OF turns off automatically after use, so that you do not need to explicitly turn it off within your calculations.

Because you want a detail line to print each time an input record is processed, use indicator 01, the record-identifying indicator, to condition the detail line.

Page 1 of 2

```
O    Filename    Type  Space  Skip   Output        Field Name    End    Edit   Constant or Edit Word
     or          Stkr# Before After  Indicators    or EXCPT      Pos.   Codes
Line Record Name       Before        And And       Name or       in
                       After                        Constant     Output
                                     Not Not Not    *Auto         Record

01 O QPRINT   H   202         1P
02 O          OR              OF
03 O                                               8    'PAGE'
04 O                                 PAGE          13
05 O                                               50   'WEEKLY SALES REPORT'
06 O                                               64   'DATE'
07 O                                 UDATE  Y      73
08 O          H   1           1P
09 O          OR              OF
10 O                                               5    'SLSM'
11 O                                               48   'DATE OF'
12 O                                               77   'SALE'
13 O          H   2           1P
14 O          OR              OF
15 O                                               3    'NO.'
16 O                                               21   'NAME'
17 O                                               46   'SALE'
18 O                                               61   'ITEM SOLD'
19 O                                               77   'PRICE'
20 O          D   1           01
   O                                 SLSMNO        4
   O                                 NAME          37
   O                                 SDATE  Y      48
```

Page 2 of 2

```
O    Filename    Type  Space  Skip   Output        Field Name    End
     or                              Indicators    or EXCPT      Pos.
Line Record Name                     And And       Name or       in
                                     Not Not Not   Constant      Output
                                     *Auto                       Record

01 O                                 ITEM          67
02 O                                 PRICE  1      79
03 O
```

What changes are required in the Calculation Specifications? Since this is a simple read/write program, there would be no calculations! In the RPG/400 version of the program, the calculations pertained to setting up a processing loop, reading, and writing. All those steps are built into the fixed-logic cycle, so that none of these steps need to be explicit in your program. And when you use the fixed-logic cycle with a primary input file, indicator LR comes on automatically at end-of-file; this signal serves to end the program automatically.

If the program had required arithmetic operations or decision or repetitive processing for a given input record, these operations would appear on Calculation Specifications. In general, for a simple detailed report, the only Calculation Specifications needed are those that describe the processing required for each input record. Remember that the record retrieval, writing, and main process looping occurs automatically with the fixed-logic cycle.

The entire RPG II version of the sample program is shown below.

```
          1         2         3         4         5         6         7
 123456789012345678901234567890123456789012345678901234567890123456789012345678901234567890
       F*****************************************************************
       F*  This program produces a weekly sales report using     *
       F*  RPG II techniques and the fixed-logic cycle.          *
       F*     Author:  J. Yaeger    Date written: 10/10/92.      *
       F*****************************************************************
       FSALES   IP  F    63            DISK
       FQPRINT  O   F    132      OF   PRINTER
       I*****************Input Specifications******************
       ISALES   NS  01
       I                                      1    40SLSMNO
       I                                      5   34 NAME
       I                                     35   50 ITEM
       I                                     51   560SDATE
       I                                     57   632PRICE
       O****************Output Specifications******************
       OQPRINT  H  202      1P
       O          OR        OF
       O                                  8 'PAGE'
       O                          PAGE   13
       O                                 50 'WEEKLY SALES REPORT'
       O                                 64 'DATE'
       O                          UDATE Y 73
       O          H   1      1P
       O          OR         OF
       O                                  5 'SLSM.'
       O                                 48 'DATE OF'
       O                                 77 'SALE'
       O          H   2      1P
       O          OR         OF
       O                                  3 'NO.'
       O                                 21 'NAME'
       O                                 46 'SALE'
       O                                 61 'ITEM SOLD'
       O                                 77 'PRICE'
       O          D   1      01
       O                          SLSMNO  4
       O                          NAME   37
       O                          SDATE Y 48
       O                          ITEM   67
       O                          PRICE 1 79
```

RPG's Fixed-Logic Cycle

As mentioned above, the fixed-logic cycle provides a built-in logical structure of read-process-write over the descriptions that you enter through your program specifications. The steps of the logic cycle can be depicted as shown on the next page:

Pseudocode of RPG's Fixed-Logic Cycle
Turn on 1P indicator
WHILE LR is off
        Print detail output (H and D lines)
        Turn off 1P, record identifying, and level indicators
        Read record from primary file
        IF end of file
                Turn on LR and all level indicators
        ELSE
                Turn on record identifying indicator
                IF change in control field
                        Turn on level indicator(s)
                ENDIF
        ENDIF
        Perform total calculations
        Perform total output (T lines)
        IF LR is not on
                IF overflow indicator is on
                        Print lines conditioned by overflow
                ENDIF
                Move data into input fields
                Perform detail calculations
        ENDIF
ENDWHILE

If you examine the above cycle carefully, you see that characterizing the fixed-logic cycle as read-calculate-write is a simplification. For one thing, at various points in the cycle different indicators automatically come on or are turned off. For another, the calculations and writing each are actually broken down into two segments — total time and detail time, with total-time calculations and output preceding detail calculations and output. A more accurate characterization, then, would be read-calculate-write-calculate-write.

Total-time calculations are characterized by special indicators, called level indicators, coded in positions 7-8 of the calculation specifications; calculations without an indicator in positions 7-8 are treated as detail calculations. On the Calculation Specifications, all detail calculations should be coded first, followed by total-time calculations, with subroutines appearing last within the calculations.

On the output, total-time output is represented by those lines designated as T lines, while H and D lines are considered detail output.

The Fixed-Logic Cycle and Control Breaks

The primary reason for breaking the fixed-logic cycle into two segments — total-time and detail-time — is to facilitate the automatic preparation of control-break reports. You'll recall from Chapter 4 that control-break reports require detecting a change in a control-field value, and when such a change is detected, executing special break processing: printing a subtotal line, rolling over accumulators, zeroing out accumulators, and resetting the hold field.

The figure below reprints the control-break program developed procedurally in Chapter 4.

```
          1         2         3         4         5         6         7
1234567890123456789012345678901234567890123456789012345678901234567890
      F***************************************************************
      F* This program produces a Sales Report listing subtotals for *
      F* each salesperson.                                           *
      F* Author:  Yaeger      Date Written:  Dec. 1992               *
      F***************************************************************
      FSALESFILIF  F    19              DISK
      FQPRINT  O   F   132      OF      PRINTER
      ISALESFILNS   Ø1
      I                                      1    4 SLSMAN
      I                                      5    7 DEPT
      I                                      8  132SALES
      I                                     14  19ØSALDAT
      C***************************************************************
      C*  Calculations required to produce the Sales Report.
      C*  Main-line logic.
      C***************************************************************
      C                   EXSR INIT
      C*
      C         *IN9Ø     DOWEQ*OFF
      C         SLSHLD    IFNE SLSMAN                    Check for
      C                   EXSR SLSBRK                    control break
      C                   ENDIF
      C                   EXSR DETL
      C                   READ SALESFIL              90
      C                   ENDDO
      C*
      C                   EXSR TERM
      C                   MOVE *ON      *INLR
      C                   RETRN
      C***************************************************************
      C* Subroutine to read first record, set up hold, and print
      C* first page headings.
      C***************************************************************
      CSR       INIT      BEGSR
      C                   READ SALESFIL              90
      C                   MOVE SLSMAN   SLSHLD  4
      C                   EXCPTHEADS
      C                   ENDSR
      C***************************************************************
      C* Subroutine done when salesman changes; print subtotal,
      C* rollover accumulator, zero out accumulator, and reset hold.
      C***************************************************************
      CSR       SLSBRK    BEGSR
      C                   EXCPTBRKLIN
      C                   ADD  SALTOT   GNDTOT 82
      C                   Z-ADDØ        SALTOT
      C                   MOVE SLSMAN   SLSHLD
      C                   ENDSR
      C***************************************************************
      C* Subroutine executed for each input record.
      C***************************************************************
      C         DETL      BEGSR
      C         *INOF     IFEQ *ON                     Page overflow
```

```
         1         2         3         4         5         6         7
1234567890123456789012345678901234567890123456789012345678901234567890
         C                         EXCPTHEADS
         C                         MOVE *OFF      *INOF
         C                         ENDIF
         C                         EXCPTDETAIL
         C                         ADD  SALES     SALTOT 62      Saleman Tot.
         C                         ENDSR
         C***********************************************************
         C* Subroutine done at end of file; execute SLSBRK one last
         C* time and print grand total line.
         C***********************************************************
         CSR           TERM        BEGSR
         C                         EXSR SLSBRK
         C                         EXCPTTOTAL
         C                         ENDSR
         O***********************************************************
         OQPRINT  E  2Ø2           HEADS
         O                         UDATE Y  17
         O                                  33 'SALES REPORT'
         O                                  40 'PAGE'
         O                         PAGE     44
         O        E  2             HEADS
         O
         O                                  19 'SLSM.'
         O                                  37 'AMT.'
         O        E  1             DETAIL
         O                         SLSMAN   18
         O                         SALES 1  39
         O        E 12             BRKLIN
         O                                  24 'TOTAL'
         O                         SALTOT1  39
         O                                  40 '*'
         O        E                TOTAL
         O                                  26 'GRAND TOTAL'
         O                         GNDTOT1  39
         O                                  41 '**'
```

Let's rework this program using RPG II. First, you need to know that RPG has special level indicators, L1-L9, that can be associated with control fields and that come on automatically when a change in the value of these fields is detected. Level indicators eliminate the need for explicit hold fields, because RPG automatically detects changes in control fields' values and turns on the appropriate level indicator(s) when it detects a change.

You can use those level indicators to condition any calculations that would need to be done as part of break processing and also to condition the appropriate subtotal line to print when a change in the control field occurs.

Again, you will recall that when you procedurally code a control-break problem, when a break occurs you need to complete the processing for the prior group before continuing with the detail processing of the record that triggered the break. It is for this reason that the fixed-logic cycle performs total calculations and output before detail calculations and output. It is also why, once end-of-file is detected, the cycle runs through total-time before ending. These final steps allow the wrap-up for the very last group in the report and the printing of grand totals, if the report requires them.

Because all total calculations are performed before total output, you cannot zero out a level's accumulator as part of total-time calculations; otherwise, the subtotals would always print as 0. RPG provides an alternate method of zeroing out these fields on the Output Specifications. By coding a B in position 39, for Blank after printing, the field is automatically set to zeros (if its type is numeric) or blanks (if its type is character) immediately after its value is printed.

The figure below illustrates the sales report program written using the fixed-logic cycle and indicators. Notice that the sales amount is rolled over into the grand-total accumulator as a total-time calculation conditioned by L1. As a result, the program executes that calculation each time SLSMAN changes. Also note that the grand-total line is conditioned by LR, so that it prints just once, just before the program ends.

```
          1         2         3         4         5         6         7
  1234567890123456789012345678901234567890123456789012345678901234567890
        F************************************************************
        F* This program produces a Sales Report listing subtotals for *
        F* each salesperson.                                          *
        F*  Author: Yaeger        Date Written:  Dec. 1992            *
        F************************************************************
        FSALESFILIP F      19              DISK
        FQPRINT  O  F     132      OF      PRINTER
        ISALESFILNS  01
        I                                     1    4 SLSMANL1
        I                                     5    7 DEPT
        I                                     8  132SALES
        I                                    14  190SALDAT
        C************************************************************
        C*  Calculations required to produce the Sales Report.
        C************************************************************
        C                    ADD  SALES     SALTOT  62        Salesman Tot.
        CL1                  ADD  SALTOT    GNDTOT  72
        O************************************************************
        OQPRINT  H  202    1P
        O        OR         OF
        O                           UDATE Y   17
        O                                     33 'SALES REPORT'
        O                                     40 'PAGE'
        O                           PAGE      44
        O        H   2      1P
        O        OR         OF
        O                                     19 'SLSM.'
        O                                     37 'AMT.'
        O        D   1      01
        O                           SLSMAN    17
        O                           SALES 1   39
        O        T  12      L1
        O                                     24 'TOTAL'
        O                           SALTOT1B  39
        O                                     40 '*'
        O        T          LR
        O                                     26 'GRAND TOTAL'
        O                           GNDTOT1   39
        O                                     41 '**'
```

If the sales file were sorted by department, and within department by salesman, we could easily convert this program to a two-level control-break problem by associating L2 with department and adding a department accumulator and a department total line (printed when L2 is on). Calculation modifications would be minimal: Instead of rolling SALTOT into GNDTOT, we'd roll it into DPTTOT when L1 was on; when L2 came on, we'd roll DPTTOT into GNDTOT.

Note that a file does not have to be program-described to use level indicators. If SALESFIL were externally described, we could still use level indicators; all we would need to do is include just those input specifications needed to make the association between the control field and L1.

Although RPG II did not make use of externally described files, as a maintenance programmer, you may encounter this mix of RPG II and RPG/400 techniques.

The figures below show all the File and Input Specifications needed for our program if SALESFIL were externally described. Notice that on the Input Specifications you use the record format name, not the file name, and the positions 15-16 are left blank. Also notice that From and To positions are omitted from the SLSMAN field definition, since that field is externally described.

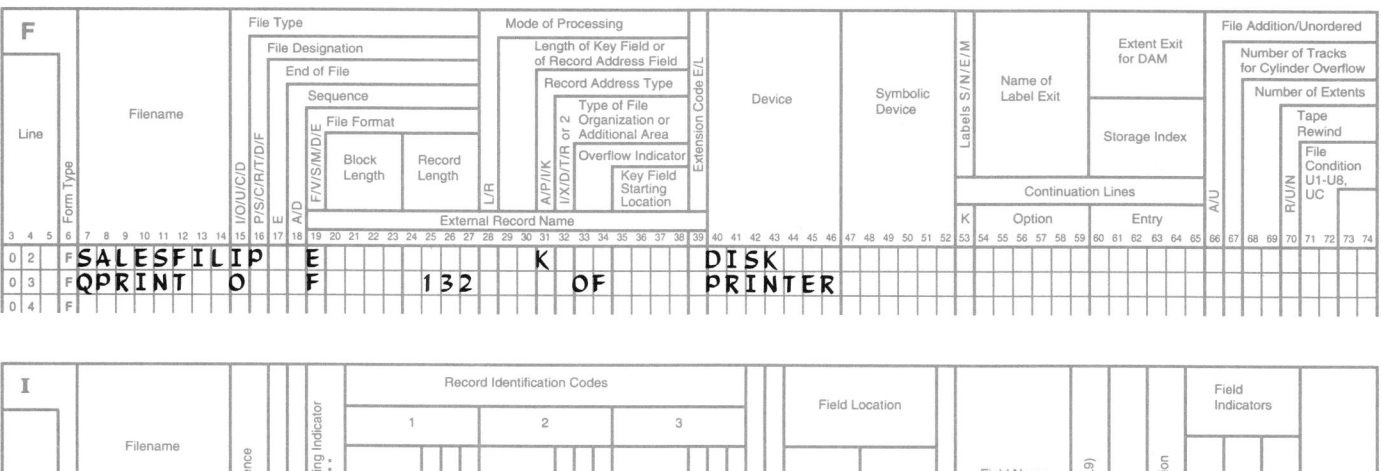

At this point, you may be wondering why RPG II techniques are no longer used much. After all, they seem to allow you to write code that is a lot shorter, and the code doesn't seem so difficult to understand. However, RPG II had many drawbacks. One of its major problems was a complete lack of any structured operators for decisions and iteration. The techniques required to implement such logical structures led to code that could be confusing.

Decisions in RPG II

Without IFxx, CASxx, SELEC, or CABxx operators, RPG II still needed some way to perform a relational test between two values and then perform alternate courses of action based on the outcome of that test. To provide that function, this earlier version of the language relied on the COMP (Compare) operation and indicators.

COMP compares the values of factor 1 and factor 2 and turns on an indicator in the HI (positions 54-55), LO (positions 56-57), or EQ (positions 58-59) columns, depending on whether factor 1 is greater than, less than, or equal to factor 2. You can enter an indicator in just one or several of those locations, and use one, two, or three different indicators, depending on the kind of comparison you are trying to make.

You then could use those indicators in positions 9-17 of calculations following the COMP to condition whether or not the operation was to be performed. Any calculation conditioned by an indicator is executed only if its associated indicator(s) is (are) on at that time.

Consider the RPG/400 IF logic below:

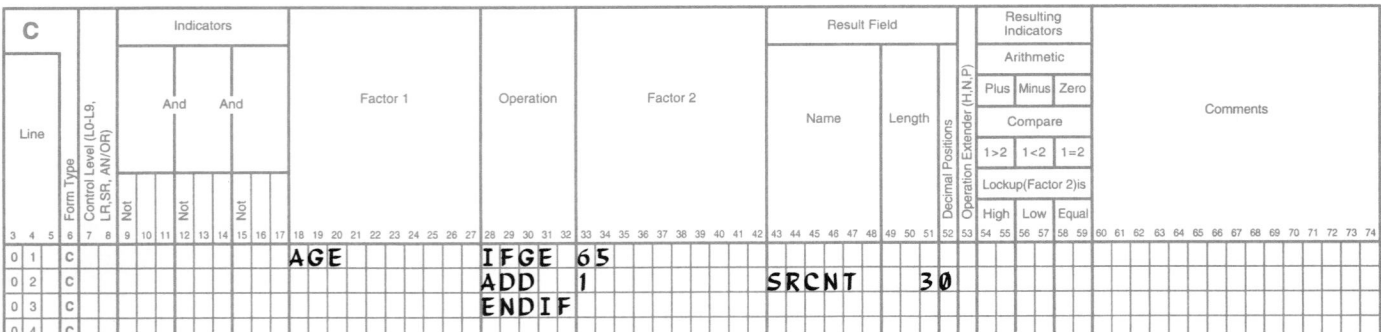

To express that same logic in RPG II would require the following lines. Indicator 65 turns on if AGE is greater than or equal to 65; indicator 65 conditions the addition operation.

Line	Form Type	Control Level (L0-L9, LR,SR, AN/OR)	Indicators And (Not)	And (Not)	And (Not)	Factor 1	Operation	Factor 2	Result Field Name	Length	Decimal Positions	Operation Extender (H,N,P)	Resulting Indicators Arithmetic / Compare — Plus / 1>2 / High	Minus / 1<2 / Low	Zero / 1=2 / Equal	Comments
0 1	C					AGE	COMP	65					65		65	
0 2	C		65				ADD	1	SRCNT	30						
0 3	C															

That doesn't look too bad, does it? But let's make the decision logic a little more complex:

Line	Form Type	Control Level (L0-L9, LR,SR, AN/OR)	Indicators And (Not)	And (Not)	And (Not)	Factor 1	Operation	Factor 2	Result Field Name	Length	Decimal Positions	Operation Extender (H,N,P)	Resulting Indicators Arithmetic / Compare — Plus / 1>2 / High	Minus / 1<2 / Low	Zero / 1=2 / Equal	Comments
0 1	C					AGE	IFGE	65								
0 2	C					SEX	IFEQ	'F'								
0 3	C						Z-ADD	84	LIFE	30						
0 4	C						ELSE									
0 5	C						Z-ADD	79	LIFE							
0 6	C						ENDIF									
0 7	C						ELSE									
0 8	C					SEX	IFEQ	'F'								
0 9	C						Z-ADD	81	LIFE							
1 0	C						ELSE									
1 1	C						Z-ADD	78	LIFE							
1 2	C						ENDIF									
1 3	C						ENDIF									
1 4	C															

The following sample expresses that decision logic using COMPs and indicators.

C	Control Level	Indicators (And / And / Not)	Factor 1	Operation	Factor 2	Result Field Name	Length	Dec. Pos.	Resulting Indicators (1>2 Plus / 1<2 Minus / 1=2 Zero)
01 C			AGE	COMP	65				65 65
02 C			SEX	COMP	'F'				70
03 C		65 70		Z-ADD	84	LIFE	30		
04 C		65N70		Z-ADD	79	LIFE			
05 C		N65 70		Z-ADD	81	LIFE			
06 C		N65N70		Z-ADD	78	LIFE			
07 C									

In the example above, multiple indicators on a line of calculations signal an "AND" condition; that is, all the indicators on a line must be on for the calculation to be performed. "OR" relations could be signaled by using the following method:

C	Control Level	Indicators	Factor 1	Operation	Factor 2	Result Field Name	Length
01 C		05					
02 C	OR	10	A	ADD	B	C	52
03 C							

The above line means, "Add A and B, giving C, if either indicator 05 or indicator 10 is on." AND relationships can be similarly represented by coding AN in positions 7-8, rather than OR. This can be useful if you have more than three indicators conditioning a calculation.

As the decision logic's complexity increases, the number of indicators needed in RPG II increases, and with that, the difficulty of understanding the code. For example, can you figure out what the following code is trying to do?

Line	Form Type	Control Level	Ind And	Ind And	Factor 1	Operation	Factor 2	Result Name	Length	Dec	Resulting Indicators
0 1	C					Z-ADD	.15	RATE	22		
0 2	C				SAL	COMP	25000				60 20 30
0 3	C		60		SAL	COMP	40000				60 30 60
0 4	C		20		SAL	COMP	15000				20 20
0 5	C		20			Z-ADD	.18	RATE			
0 6	C		30			Z-ADD	.25	RATE			
0 7	C		60			Z-ADD	.31	RATE			
0 8	C										

Conditioning indicators on calculations apply only to the code line on which they occur. If each of three calculations, for example, is to be executed only if indicator 10 is on, indicator 10 must appear with each calculation. Programmers sometimes tried to avoid this repetitive use of indicators on calculations by using the GOTO operation to branch around, or bypass, a group of calculations.

Line	Form Type	Control Level	Ind And	Ind And	Factor 1	Operation	Factor 2	Result Name	Length	Dec	Resulting Indicators
0 1	C				SAL	COMP	15000				10
0 2	C		10			Z-ADD	.15	RATE	22		
0 3	C		10			GOTO	EXT				
0 4	C				SAL	COMP	25000				20
0 5	C		20			Z-ADD	.18	RATE			
0 6	C		20			GOTO	EXT				
0 7	C				SAL	COMP	40000				60 30 60
0 8	C		30			Z-ADD	.25	RATE			
0 9	C		60			Z-ADD	.31	RATE			
1 0	C				EXT	TAG					
1 1	C										

The two preceding figures both express the same logic. You can see that using the structured operations, as shown in the next figure, results in code that is much easier to understand.

Line	Form Type	Factor 1	Operation	Factor 2	Result Field Name	Length	Resulting Indicators
01	C		SELEC				
02	C	SAL	WHLT	15000			
03	C		Z-ADD	.15	RATE	22	
04	C	SAL	WHLT	25000			
05	C		Z-ADD	.18	RATE		
06	C	SAL	WHLT	40000			
07	C		Z-ADD	.25	RATE		
08	C		OTHER				
09	C		Z-ADD	.31	RATE		
10	C		ENDSL				
11	C						

Resulting Indicators and Arithmetic

Another common use of indicators in RPG II was to include them as resulting indicators in conjunction with arithmetic operations. You can associate resulting indicators with any arithmetic or assignment operation; they are commonly used with ADD, SUB, MULT, and DIV.

Resulting indicators will go on or off automatically when the operation with which they are associated is executed, depending on the value of the result of that operation. If the result is a positive value, an indicator in positions 54-55 will come on; if the result is negative, an indicator in positions 56-57 will come on; and if the result is zero, an indicator in positions 58-59 will come on. Any resulting indicator in a position that does not reflect the sign of the result goes off (or stays off). The figure below demonstrates the use of resulting indicators.

Line	Form Type	Factor 1	Operation	Factor 2	Result Field Name	Plus	Minus	Zero
01	C	* Indicator 10 comes on if C is 0.						
02	C	A	MULT	B	C			10
03	C	* Indicator 10 comes on if C is less than 0; otherwise 20 comes on.						
04	C	A	DIV	B	C		20	10	20
05	C	* Indicator 10 comes on if C is greater than 0, 20 if C is less						
06	C	* than 0, and 30 if C equals 0.						
07	C	A	SUB	B	C	10	20	30
08	C							

As you can see from the examples above, one or more of these indicator positions can be used with a given calculation, with the same indicator repeated (e.g., if you want it to signal the result is greater than or equal to zero), or with a unique indicator in each position.

The main use of resulting indicators was to eliminate the need for a COMP operation in RPG II, in which the result field would be compared to zero, or to eliminate the need for an IF operation in RPG/400.

Line	Form Type	Control Level (L0-L9, LR,SR, AN/OR)	Indicators And / Not	And / Not	And / Not	Factor 1	Operation	Factor 2	Result Field Name	Length	Decimal Positions	Operation Extender (H,N,P)	Resulting Indicators Plus/1>2 High	Minus/1<2 Low	Zero/1=2 Equal	Comments
0 1	C *					Three equivalent ways of specifying that if taxable income										
0 2	C *					is less than Ø, set taxable income to Ø.										
0 3	C *					The method below uses a resulting indicator.										
0 4	C					GROSS	SUB	DEPDEN	TAXABL	72				20		
0 5	C		20				Z-ADD0		TAXABL							
0 6	C *															
0 7	C *					This method uses COMP rather than a resulting indicator.										
0 8	C					GROSS	SUB	DEPDEN	TAXABL	72						
0 9	C					TAXABL	COMP	0						20		
1 0	C		20				Z-ADD0		TAXABL							
1 1	C *															
1 2	C *					This method uses IF in place of a resulting indicator or comp.										
1 3	C					GROSS	SUB	DEPDEN	TAXABL	72						
1 4	C					TAXABL	IFLT	0								
1 5	C						Z-ADD0		TAXABL							
1 6	C						ENDIF									
1 7	C															
1 8	C															

Iteration and RPG II

Without DO, DOWxx, and DOUxx, even with its built-in processing cycle RPG II still needed a way to create loops to perform repetitive processing for a single input record. In RPG II, programmers implemented loop logic with COMP and indicators; the indicators conditioned a GOTO that sent control back to prior calculations to repeat processing steps.

The following illustrates an RPG II technique of adding all the numbers from 1 to 100.

```
C                      Factor 1      Operation  Factor 2        Result Field   Resulting Indicators
01  C * Initialize NUM and SUM to 0.
02  C                                 Z-ADD0                     NUM      30
03  C                                 Z-ADD0                     SUM      40
04  C * Loop while NUM is less than 100.
05  C                      LOOP        TAG
06  C * Increment NUM by 1.
07  C                                 ADD   1                    NUM
08  C * Add NUM to accumulator SUM.
09  C                                 ADD   NUM                  SUM
10  C                      NUM         COMP  100                              50
11  C           50                    GOTO  LOOP
12  C
```

Another pair of operations often used in RPG II was SETON and SETOF. Because RPG II did not allow indicators to be referenced directly as fields, the only way to change the value of an indicator directly was to SETON or SETOF the desired indicator(s).

With these operations, factors 1 and 2 and the result are always blank, but up to three indicators can be specified in positions 54-59 of the specification.

```
C
01  C * Turns on indicators 10, 20, and 30.
02  C                                 SETON                                 102030
03  C * Turns off indicators 10 and 20.
04  C                                 SETOF                                 1020
05  C
```

Most of the features discussed in this chapter — features that at one time in RPG's history were the only means to accomplish a given programming solution — have alternate, more modern counterparts to accomplish the same end in RPG/400. In RPG/400, COMP, conditioning indicators, and GOTOs should be avoided.

Whether or not to completely abandon the fixed-logic cycle in RPG/400 is an interesting problem. RPG's fixed-logic cycle still underlies every RPG program written, but more and more, today's programmers are ignoring its automatic features. The figure below contrasts program flow using the fixed-logic cycle with the procedural approach favored today. Rather than "riding" the basic process loop built into RPG, contemporary RPG programmers structure their own loops that execute repeatedly during the first (and only) pass through RPG's cycle.

Figure 13.1
Contrast of RPG II and modern RPG process logic vis-à-vis the underlying Fixed-Logic Cycle

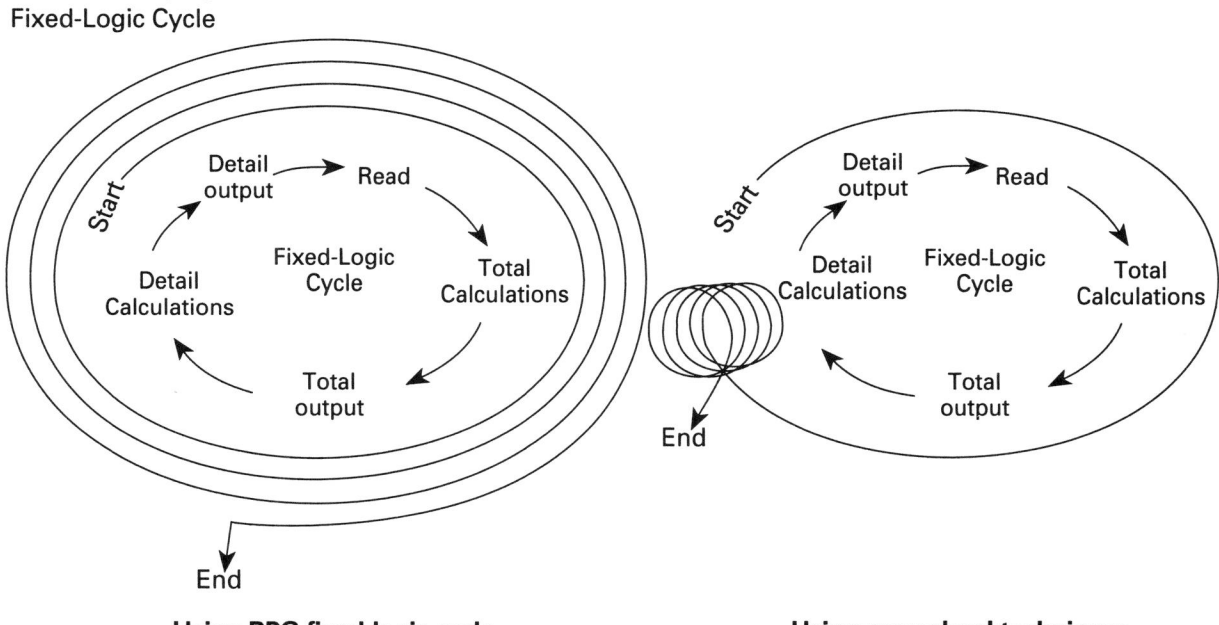

**Using RPG fixed-logic cycle
and RPG II techniques**

**Using procedural techniques
of modern RPG**

The fixed-logic cycle truly is worthless for interactive applications, since the cycle presupposes that you have a primary data file that you want to sequentially process from beginning to end-of-file. On the other hand, when all you require is a straightforward report of a data file's contents — with or without subtotals, using RPG's fixed-logic cycle may result in somewhat shorter programs, perhaps more quickly developed than if you coded fully procedural programs. Whether these shorter programs are as easy to maintain as procedural programs is open to debate.

Ultimately more important than whether or not you incorporate the fixed-logic cycle into your report programs, regardless of the method you use, is that you think before you code and that your work reflects a structured, modular approach to program design.

Chapter Summary

RPG has evolved since its introduction in the early 1960s. Language features that were once necessary but are now obsolete include using the COMP operation to turn on indicators and then using those indicators to condition calculations. In the past, programmers also used resulting indicators with arithmetic operations to test the value of the result field. These indicators then conditioned subsequent calculations and/or output. The GOTO operation — once used for both decisions and iteration — has become superfluous with the introduction of structured operations in RPG.

Use of the fixed-logic cycle upon which RPG is based has also diminished through time. The logic cycle automatically retrieved and processed records sequentially from a file designated as primary. The cycle automatically wrote output described on the Output Specifications. The cycle actually consists of two separate calculate-and-write segments — one, called "total time," appropriate for control-break processing and grand totals, and one, "detail time," for the calculations and output associated with each input record.

Although today's programmers no longer rely on these older techniques, all RPG programmers should be able to maintain older programs that use these techniques.

Terms

fixed-logic cycle

Discussion/Review Questions

1. Describe RPG's fixed-logic cycle.

2. What is a primary input file?

3. How does RPG differentiate between detail output and total output?

4. How does RPG differentiate between detail calculations and total calculations?

5. Why did RPG II include a COMP operation?

6. Give several contemporary alternatives to conditioning calculation lines with indicators.

7. What's a resulting indicator?

8. Describe the general steps of the fixed-logic cycle.

9. Why is the fixed-logic cycle inappropriate for most interactive applications?

Exercises

For each of the exercises below, rewrite the RPG code to include just those features available in RPG II.

1.

Line	Form Type		Factor 1	Operation	Factor 2	Result Field Name	Length		Comments
0 1	C	*	This code uses nested IFs to assign a value to
0 2	C	*	RATE based on level of sales.
0 3	C		SALES	IFLE	5000
0 4	C			Z-ADD	.005	RATE	44
0 5	C			ELSE
0 6	C		SALES	IFLE	10000
0 7	C			Z-ADD	.0075	RATE
0 8	C			ELSE
0 9	C		SALES	IFLE	20000
1 0	C			Z-ADD	.01	RATE
1 1	C			ELSE
1 2	C			Z-ADD	.015	RATE
1 3	C			ENDIF
1 4	C			ENDIF
1 5	C			ENDIF

Exercises Continued

Exercises continued

2.

Line	Form Type	Control Level (L0-L9, LR,SR, AN/OR)	And (Not)	And (Not)	(Not)	Factor 1	Operation	Factor 2	Result Field Name	Length	Decimal Positions	Operation Extender (H,N,P)	Resulting Indicators Plus	Minus	Zero / 1>2	1<2 / Low	1=2 / Equal	Comments
01	C					* This code uses CASxx to send control to different												
02	C					* subroutines based on the level of gross sales.												
03	C					GROSS	CASGT	40000	SRHI									
04	C					GROSS	CASGE	30000	SRMED									
05	C					GROSS	CASGT	15000	SRLO									
06	C						CAS		SRVLO									
07	C						ENDCS											
08	C																	

3.

Line	Form Type	Control Level	And	And		Factor 1	Operation	Factor 2	Result Field Name	Length	Dec	Ext	Resulting Indicators					Comments
01	C					* If no overtime hours, total pay is hours * rate.												
02	C					HRS	IFLE	40										
03	C					HRS	MULT	RATE	TOTPAY	62H								
04	C						ELSE											
05	C					* Figure regular pay and overtime pay, then add for total pay.												
06	C					40	MULT	RATE	REGPAY	62H								
07	C					HRS	SUB	40	OTHRS	20								
08	C					RATE	MULT	1.5	OTRATE	42H								
09	C					OTHRS	MULT	OTRATE	OTPAY	62H								
10	C					REGPAY	ADD	OTPAY	TOTPAY									
11	C						ENDIF											
12	C																	

Exercises Continued

Exercises continued

4.

Line	Form Type	Control Level (L0-L9, LR,SR, AN/OR)	And (Not)	And (Not)	(Not)	Factor 1	Operation	Factor 2	Result Field Name	Length	Decimal Positions	Operation Extender (H,N,P)	Plus	Minus	Zero	1>2	1<2	1=2	High	Low	Equal	Comments
01	C					* Reorder, depending on region, code, and number of																
02	C					* spare parts.																
03	C					REGION	IFEQ	'W'														
04	C					REGION	OREQ	'S'														
05	C					CODE	IFEQ	12														
06	C					REORD	SUB	QTYOH	SPARE	60												
07	C					SPARE	IFLE	0														
08	C						EXSR	ORDSR														
09	C						ENDIF															
10	C						ENDIF															
11	C						ENDIF															
12	C																					

5. (For this exercise omit those calculations that could be handled automatically as part of the fixed-logic cycle if the input file were a primary file.)

Line	Form Type	Control Level (L0-L9, LR,SR, AN/OR)	And (Not)	And (Not)	(Not)	Factor 1	Operation	Factor 2	Result Field Name	Length	Decimal Positions	Operation Extender (H,N,P)	Plus	Minus	Zero	1>2	1<2	1=2	High	Low	Equal	Comments
01	C					* This routine processes all records in CUSTFILE and																
02	C					* prints a detail line for those customers whose																
03	C					* AMTDUE is not equal to zero.																
04	C					*IN90	DOWEQ	*OFF														
05	C						READ	CUSTFILE												90		
06	C						SELEC															
07	C					*IN90	WHEQ	*ON														
08	C						LEAVE															
09	C					AMTDUE	WHEQ	0														
10	C						ITER															
11	C						OTHER															
12	C						EXCPT	DETAIL														
13	C						ENDSL															
14	C						ENDDO															
15	C																					

Programming Assignments

1. Wexler University wants a department directory. Write a program using the fixed-logic cycle to develop this directory, shown below.

```
          1         2         3         4         5         6         7         8
12345678901234567890123456789012345678901234567890123456789012345678901234567890123456789012345

                              WEXLER UNIVERSITY
                            DIRECTORY OF DEPARTMENTS
                                    19XX

       DEPT.    NAME                 CHAIR                      OFFICE       PHONE

       XXX   XXXXXXXXXXXXXXXXXXXX  XXXXXXXXXXXXXXXXXXXXXXXXXX  XXXXXXXXXX  (XXX)XXX-XXXX
       XXX   XXXXXXXXXXXXXXXXXXXX  XXXXXXXXXXXXXXXXXXXXXXXXXX  XXXXXXXXXX  (XXX)XXX-XXXX
```

2. CompuSell wants a report that shows the current value of its inventory based on the product costs. For each record in the Inventory Master File (CSINVP), multiply quantity on hand by average cost to get the inventory value for that product. Use the report layout shown below. Implement this program using the fixed-logic cycle.

```
          1         2         3         4         5         6         7         8         9         10
12345678901234567890123456789012345678901234567890123456789012345678901234567890123456789012345678901234567890

       XX/XX/XX                    COMPUSELL               PAGE XX0X
                                INVENTORY REPORT

       PROD.       DESCRIPTION         QUANTITY  AVERAGE        TOTAL
       NUMBER                          ON HAND    COST          VALUE

       XXXXXX  XXXXXXXXXXXXXXXXXXXXXXXXX  XX0X   X,XX0.XX   X,XXX,XX0.XX
       XXXXXX  XXXXXXXXXXXXXXXXXXXXXXXXX  XX0X   X,XX0.XX   X,XXX,XX0.XX

                                        GRAND TOTAL   $XXX,XXX,XX$.XX
```

3. At the end of the semester Wexler University distributes mark-sensitive grade reports to its instructors based on the records in the Current Enrollment File; these reports are scanned to add the final grade to each record in file WUENRLP. Wexler University wants you to write a program that updates students' grade-point-average and credits-earned fields of the Student Master File (WUSTDP) based on the credits and grades earned by each student represented in the Current Enrollment File.

The school uses the following grade values to determine grade points:

A: 4.0	CB: 2.5	D: 1.0
BA: 3.5	C: 2.0	F: 0
B: 3.0	DC: 1.5	

Build a logical file over WUENRLP keyed on student number and use RPG II's fixed-logic cycle and control-break features to update the Student Master File.

4. GTC wants you to write a program that prepares customers' phone bills and updates two fields in the Customer Master File: current billing amount and balance owed. For current billing amount, replace previous contents with the amount due calculated for this month's charges; for the balance owed, add this month's charges to the previous amount.

Programming Assignments Continued

Programming Assignments continued

Billing charges:

There is a set monthly charge for local service of $15.00 per month, regardless of calls made. Additionally, there is an intrastate access charge of $4.39 per month, regardless of calls. A 3 percent federal excise tax applies to the total *cost of calls only,* but not to service charges. A 4 percent state sales tax applies to the cost of calls and the services charges.

You will need to use files GTCSTP (Customer Master) and GTCLSP (Calls Transaction) for this application; you can create whatever logical files you find helpful. Note that because of the monthly service charges, you will need to bill every customer, even if (s)he has made no calls this month.

If you have written program 12.2, call that program to convert the time from military time to standard time for printing; if you have not written that program, change the printer spacing chart to reflect military time (HHMM as stored in GTCLSP).

Implement this program using either RPG/400 or RPG II, based on your instructor's directions.

Your bills should be formatted as shown below:

```
            1         2         3         4         5         6         7
   12345678901234567890123456789012345678901234567890123456789012345678901234567890

   GTC INC    PO BOX 123  LAWRENCE  MI  49067

       BILL FOR:  X. XXXXXXXXXXXXXX
                  XXXXXXXXXXXXXXXXXXXX
                  XXXXXXXXXXXXXX XX XXXXX
                  (XXX)XXX-XXXX

   GTC CURRENT CHARGES
        LOCAL SERVICE                                  15.00
        INTRASTATE ACCESS                               4.39

   DATE        CALLS MADE     #MIN    TIME         COST
   MMMDD       XXX-XXX-XXXX   XXØ     HHMMA.M.     XXØ.XX
   MMMDD       XXX-XXX-XXXX   XXØ     HHMMP.M.     XXØ.XX
   MMMDD       XXX-XXX-XXXX   XXØ     HHMMP.M.     XXØ.XX

                                             CALLS TOTAL  X,XXØ.XX

           3% FEDERAL EXCISE TAX ON X,XXØ.XX             XXØ.XX
           4% STATE TAX ON X,XXØ.XX                      XXØ.XX
                                                   --------------------
   CHARGES FOR THIS BILLING PERIOD                     X,XXØ.XX
   BALANCE PAST DUE                                    X,XXØ.XX
   AMOUNT DUE                                          X,XXØ.XX
```

Chapter 14

Looking Forward: RPG IV

Chapter Overview

This chapter introduces you to changes in RPG/400 and to new features not previously available in the language. Through samples of program code the chapter will give you a sense of the "look and feel" of this new version of RPG. Finally, the chapter includes a discussion of how RPG IV should affect your programming style.

Introduction to RPG IV

In Chapter 1 you learned that in conjunction with V3R1 of OS/400, IBM introduced a version of RPG called RPG IV. If you have judiciously been reading each chapter, including the notes in Appendix E on RPG IV modifications, by now you have an idea of specific ways in which RPG IV differs from RPG/400. This chapter unites the concepts presented in Appendix E and elaborates on them to allow you to consolidate and expand your understanding of RPG IV.

First, you should realize that part of IBM's motivation for introducing a new version of RPG was to address criticisms of RPG's syntax. Many programmers accustomed to the **free-form** structure of languages like Pascal and C chafed over the restrictive, somewhat cryptic features of RPG caused by its fixed-position format and the limited space for entries within their allotted positions. Other strong — and justified — complaints focused on the patchwork approach to data definition that had taken place over the decades, as IBM added enhancements to the language.

Accordingly, a large percentage of the changes in RPG IV represent attempts to "clean up" the language. These features really contribute no additional functionality to RPG; they simply restructure the language to make it more internally consistent and closer in format to other modern programming languages. Consequently, as a result of your work during this course, you should already understand the concepts themselves and know how to express them in RPG/400; all you need to do now is learn how RPG IV handles those same concepts.

The most obvious change is that specification lines are now 100 characters long, rather than 80, with positions 81-100 on all specification types reserved for comments. Along with this change, more room has been allocated for some entries; the relative positions of some entries have been modified;

and some entries have been changed from fixed-position specifications to a more free-form format through the use of **keywords** (a concept new to RPG, although standard in DDS and CL).

Variable names can now be up to 10 characters long. To further increase the readability of RPG code, **mixed-case entry** (the use of lower-case letters as well as uppercase letters) is now permissible, although the language is not **case sensitive** (i.e., the compiler does not differentiate between NetPay and NETPAY, for example). You can now validly use the underscore character (_) within variable names (e.g., Cust_Name).

In addition to lengthened variable names, other general RPG limits have been extended as well. The maximum number of decimal positions in a numeric variable has been increased to 30. Named constants can now be up to 1,024 bytes long, while the length of character variables, the number of elements in an array, the number of occurrences in a multiple-occurrence data structure, and the length of one such occurrence all now have 32,767 as an upper limit. You can now use as many files as you wish within a single application (previously there had been a limit of 50 files), and no upper limit exists (for all practical purposes) for the number of subroutines your program can include.

The RPG compiler now interprets three different kinds of lines as comments to be ignored: lines with a specification type in position 6 and an asterisk (*) in position 7 (regardless of what else appears within the line), lines that contain a specification type in position 6 and are blank from positions 7-80, and lines that are completely blank between positions 6 and 80. The first two types of lines must appear in that portion of your program appropriate to the specification type they indicate, while the last kind can appear anywhere within your program.

Given the syntactical changes introduced in RPG IV, older RPG source code can no longer be correctly interpreted by the ILE RPG/400 compiler. Rather than requiring programmers to make the necessary code changes by hand, IBM has provided a utility to help RPG shops migrate source code to RPG IV as effortlessly as possible. As a result, in V3R1, the AS/400 operating system includes CL command CVTRPGSRC (Convert RPG Source) that converts pre-RPG IV source code to RPG IV syntax. This conversion program automatically increases specification length to 100 characters, re-arranges fixed-position entries to appropriate locations, changes obsolete positional entries to suitable keywords, and in general corrects any obsolete syntax to the form applicable to RPG IV.

Traditionally, many companies using AS/400s have stored their RPG source code as members in source file QRPGSRC. One recommended practice now is to store members converted via CVTRPGSRC, as well as any new RPG IV source code that you write, in a source file named QRPGLESRC (RPG IV participates in ILE, IBM's Integrated Language Environment). This method of member organization will easily help you keep track of those source members that still need to be converted to RPG IV.

Before we look at changes specific to the different specification types, we need to address one additional topic that affects RPG generally: **data types.** As discussed earlier in this text, RPG historically was a language that did not differentiate much between categories of data. It recognized just two types of data, numeric and character, with three classes of numeric data — zoned (or signed), packed, and binary. Most modern programming languages offer a variety of data types, with different operations appropriate to the different types. IBM has made an attempt to address this issue by including additional data types in RPG IV and by formalizing their classification and permissible operations.

The data types and their subclasses that are available with the first release of RPG IV are as follows:

- Numeric
    Zoned
    Packed
    Binary
- Character
    Fixed length
- DBCS
- Date
- Time
- Timestamp
- Basing Pointer
- Procedure Pointer

You are already familiar with the numeric and character data types from your work with RPG/400. **DBCS** (Double Byte Character Set) data is a graphic data type in which two bytes are required to represent any one character of the character set. This data type allows easy manipulation and display of graphic characters. It is especially suited for languages whose character sets are more complicated than that of English, such as Japanese. The declared type of DBCS data, on specifications where it is relevant, is G.

Three data types pertaining to time now exist: **date, time,** and **timestamp.** Date (type D) is a 10-byte data item with a default display form of yyyy-mm-dd. Time (type T), with an 8-byte length, has the default form hh.mm.ss. Timestamp (type Z), with a 26-byte length, has the default form yyyy-mm-dd-hh.mm.ss.mmmmmm.

When declaring data of these types, you do not need to specify length, since each has a built-in default. In conjunction with these data types to facilitate calculations involving time, IBM has added three operations to RPG: ADDDUR, SUBDUR, and EXTRACT. These operations will be discussed in the section on Calculation Specifications.

Finally, IBM has introduced two types of pointers: **basing pointers** and **procedure pointers**. Both kinds of pointers are used to access dynamically allocated storage of either variable data (basing pointers) or program modules (procedure pointers). Procedure pointers are useful for calling program modules, especially across different languages. Basing pointers allow based variables to reference different storage locations during program execution. Pointers are of type *, with a predefined length of 16 bytes. More information about both kinds of pointers follows in the discussion of Definition Specifications and Calculation Specifications.

With these general changes noted, let's take a look at specific changes that affect each RPG specification type.

Modifications to File Specifications

To provide a context within which you can understand the changes to File Specifications introduced with RPG IV, assume we want to write an interactive program that allows a user to display, modify, or add customer records to a customer master file. The program should also allow the display of a subfile showing all the orders any existing customer has placed with the company. Further, assume that for control purposes the application will print a report listing which customer records have been added or modified during the program run. Finally, assume that we need to control the opening of the customer file, to access a file-information data structure concerning the customer file, and to evoke the *PSSR subroutine in case of errors associated with I/O errors for both the order and the customer file.

The figure below illustrates the File Specifications for the four files required by our hypothetical application as they would be coded in the 80-column format of RPG/400. Notice that the code sample includes two header lines; one indicates column position, and one contains "prompts" similar to those given in SEU. The required **continuation lines** (K in position 53) signal additional information about the order, the customer, and the display files. Two of these continuation "lines" actually appear on the main file description lines, while two appear on separate specifications, either because of lack of room (for CUSTFILE) or because RPG/400 required that a separate line be used (the subfile description for CUSTDSP). If you do not recall the meaning of the entries below, you might refer to Chapters 6, 9, and 10 to refresh your memory.

```
          1         2         3         4         5         6         7         8
 12345678901234567890123456789012345678901234567890123456789012345678901234567890
     FFilenameIPEAF....RlenLK1AIOvKlocEDevice+......KOptionEntry+A....UI........
     F* File Specifications coded in RPG/400
     FORDERFILIF  E        K        DISK        KINFSR *PSSR
     FCUSTFILEUF  E        K        DISK        KINFDS CUSTDSA    UC
     F                                          KINFSR *PSSR
     FQPRINT   O  F   132    OF     PRINTER
     FCUSTDSP CF  E                 WORKSTN
     F                                    RRN   KSFILE CUSSFL
```

Now let's see how specifications for those same files would look in RPG IV. Let's further assume that we have taken advantage of the ability to use longer file names when we created the database and the display files.

```
          1         2         3         4         5         6         7         8         9         10
 1234567890123456789012345678901234567890123456789012345678901234567890123456789012345678901234567890
     FFilename++IPEASFRlen+LKlen+AIDevice+.Functions+++++++++++++++++++++++++++++Comments++++++++++++
     F* File Specifications coded in ILE RPG
     FOrderFile IF   E           K DISK      INFSR(*PSSR)
     FCustFile  UF A E           K DISK      INFDS(CustDS) INFSR(*PSSR) USROPN
     FQprint    O    F 132         PRINTER   OFLIND(*INOF)
     FCustDsp   CF   E             WORKSTN   SFILE(CustSfl:Rrn)
```

In comparing the two sets of File Specifications, you can see that file name, type, designation, format, record length, record address type, file addition, and device entries remain the same, except their positions on the lines have changed. (The most extreme change among these entries is that A, which denotes addition of records to the file, has shifted from position 66 to position 20, as shown for CustFile.)

RPG IV now expresses the rest of the entries as keywords in positions 44-80. The order in which you list the keywords is arbitrary, and you can put as many on one line as will fit. If insufficient room exists on one line, additional continuation lines can follow. Continuation lines have an F in position 6, blanks in positions 7-43, one or more keywords in positions 44-80, and (optional) comments in positions 81-100. Some keywords have parameters enclosed within parentheses; others do not. If a keyword has more than one parameter, a colon is used as a separator.

Looking at our example, you can see that the name of the information data structure for file errors is the parameter for keyword INFDS; the name of the subroutine to handle file errors is the parameter for keyword INFSR. Keyword SFILE has two parameters: the first signals the name of the subfile, while the second names the variable to be used to access that subfile by relative record number.

Keyword OFLIND replaces the fixed-position entry for overflow indicator, with the indicator to be used to signal page overflow as the parameter of this keyword. Keyword USROPN, which does not require a parameter, indicates that the opening of this file is under user control.

There are additional keywords used with File Specifications that go beyond the scope of this text. One keyword, however, brings to RPG a new feature that you should know about. When keyword PREFIX(prefix name) is associated with an externally described file, the prefix given as the parameter value is automatically attached to the beginning of all field names defined in that file for use in this program. This feature lets you use the same name for a given data item in every file within which that data item is stored (e.g., CustNbr); at the same time, you can differentiate within your program which file the value is coming from (e.g., CCustNbr and OCustNbr, where C is the prefix designated for the file CustFile and O is the prefix for the OrderFile). Note that the external field name plus the prefix together cannot exceed 10 characters.

Modifications to Extension Specifications

This section is very short, because Extension Specifications have been eliminated in RPG IV. The definition functions they provided have been assumed by a new specification type: **Definition Specifications**.

Introducing Definition Specifications

Definition Specifications reflect IBM's intent to consolidate data definition in a single place within your program (between File Specifications and Input Specifications) and to make the definitions of various kinds of data items more consistent. In RPG/400, tables and arrays were defined in one way on Extension Specifications; data structures and named constants were defined another way on Input Specifications; and *LIKE DEFN, which defined one variable in terms of another, used still a different approach on the Calculation Specifications!

With RPG IV, Definition Specifications provide the means for defining tables, arrays, data structures, and named constants. As was the case for File Specifications, converting the definitions of these data items to the format required on Definition Specifications requires little, if any, new understanding. Instead, for the most part it is a simple matter of learning the format of the new specification.

Let's first look at several table and array definitions, as we are accustomed to seeing them on Extension Specifications.

```
         1         2         3         4         5         6         7         8
12345678901234567890123456789012345678901234567890123456789012345678901234567890
E....FromfileTofile++ArrnamN/rN/tbLenPDSArrnamLenPDSComments++++++........
E* Tables and arrays defined in RPG/400
E                     SAR       100 9 2              Runtime array
E                     PAR     5 40 10  A             Compile-time array
E     ARRYFIL         XAR     1 400  5 0D            Pre-Runtime array
E     TABLEFILTABLEFILTABX    10 500 20              Pre-Runtime Table
E                     TABZON   1 20  1 0ATABRAT  5 2 Comp-time, alter. fmt.
```

As you will recall, based on the above definitions, SAR is a runtime array of 100 elements, each of which is 9 bytes long with 2 decimal positions. Array PAR is a compile-time array with its data hardcoded at the end of the program, 5 entries per record. There are 40 elements in the array, each of which is 10 bytes long, and the data is arranged in ascending sequence. The data for array XAR is coming from file ARRYFIL, where each of XAR's 400 elements (5 bytes long with 0 decimal positions) is entered one per record in descending sequence. The data for TABX is coming from TABLEFIL file and will be written back to that same file at the end of the processing; the table has 10 entries per record and 500 20-byte character elements in all. TABZON and TABRAT are two tables in alternating format; their data is entered one set per line at the end of the program, in ascending order based on TABZON values.

How would we represent these same definitions on RPG IV's Definition Specifications? The parallel definitions are shown in the figure below. Because RPG IV allows data names on Definition Specifications to "float" within positions 7-21 to enhance program readability, the data names in the figure begin in position 8 to make them stand out more clearly.

```
          1         2         3         4         5         6         7         8         9         10
 1234567890123456789012345678901234567890123456789012345678901234567890123456789012345678901234567890
     DName++++++++++ETDsFrom+++To/L+++IDc.Functions++++++++++++++++++++++++++++++Comments++++++++++++
 D* Tables and arrays in RPG IV
 D Sar           S             9 2 DIM(100)
 D Par           S            10   DIM(40) PERRCD(5) ASCEND
 D Xar           S             5 0 DIM(400) FROMFILE(ArryFil) PERRCD(1)
 D                                 DESCEND
 D TabX          S            20   DIM(500) FROMFILE(TableFil)
 D                                 TOFILE(TableFil) PERRCD(10)
 D TabZon        S             1 0 DIM(20) ASCEND PERRCD(1)
 D TabRat        S             5 2 DIM(20) ALT(TabZon)
```

Several differences between the two sets of definitions are worth noting. RPG IV defines each table and array on a separate specification line, even if that table or array is in alternating format with another table/array. Each entry requires an S in position 24 to indicate that it is a **stand-alone field** (i.e., not part of a data structure). And finally, in contrast to RPG/400, the only other positional entries in RPG IV indicate the length and the number of decimal positions of a single element of the array or table. All the other definition entries have been changed to free-format keywords that are coded in positions 44-80 of the specification line.

The relevant keywords are DIM, which denotes the dimension or number of elements in the table/array; ASCEND and DESCEND, which specify if the data values are in ascending or descending order; PERRCD, which indicates the number of elements entered per record (for compile-time and pre-runtime tables/arrays); FROMFILE, which designates pre-runtime tables/arrays; and TOFILE, which indicates whether or not the data is to be written back to the table file when the program has finished running. Finally, keyword ALT is used to show that the table/array data is stored in alternating format with another, primary table/array; you indicate the name of the primary table/array as the parameter value of ALT. Because a table/array in alternating format "inherits" the PERRCD, FROMFILE, and TOFILE values from the table/array it is associated with, you cannot use these keywords in association with ALT.

Also notice that if there is not enough room on a given line for all the keywords required for a given definition, you simply use a second, continuation Definition Specification line for the remaining keywords, as shown for array Xar and table TabX.

Definitions of named constants and data structures have likewise been ported from Input Specifications to Definition Specifications in RPG IV. Let's first take a look at how named constants are handled in the two versions of

RPG. The first figure below shows named constants in RPG/400 style, while the second illustrates those same named constants defined in RPG IV.

```
          1         2         3         4         5         6         7         8
 12345678901234567890123456789012345678901234567890123456789012345678901234567890
 I..............Namedconstant++++++++C.........Fldnme....................
 I* Named constants in RPG/400
 I             .Ø6                   C        SLSTAX
 I             'SUPERCALIFRAGILIST-  C        LNGWRD
 I             'ICEXPIALIDOCIOUS'
 I             'ZEN AND THE ART OF - C        TITLE
 I             'MOTORCYCLE MAINTENA-
 I             'NCE'
 I             1824622563312345-     C        BIGNUM
 I             1.431
```

```
          1         2         3         4         5         6         7         8         9        1Ø
 12345678901234567890123456789012345678901234567890123456789012345678901234567890123456789012345678901234567890
 DName++++++++++ETDsFrom+++To/L+++IDc.Functions+++++++++++++++++++++++++++++Comments+++++++++++
 D* Named constants in RPG IV
 D SlsTax          C                   CONST(.Ø6)
 D LngWrd          C                   'SUPERCALIFRAGILISTICEXPIALIDOCIOUS'
 D Title           C                   CONST('ZEN AND THE ART OF MOTORCYCLE-
 D                                        MAINTENANCE')
 D BigNum          C                   18246225633123451.431
```

Other than a re-arrangement of the order of information between the older and newer named constant definitions, the only difference in named constant implementation in RPG IV is that you can optionally include the keyword CONST, with the constant value as the keyword's parameter, rather than entering only the constant's value. (The above figure illustrates named constants defined with and without this optional keyword.)

Next let's consider the definition of data structures. The following figure illustrates several data structures defined on Input Specifications using RPG/400.

```
          1         2         3         4         5         6         7         8
 12345678901234567890123456789012345678901234567890123456789012345678901234567890
 I..............Ext-field+............PFromTo++DField+....................
 I* Data structures defined in RPG/400
 I* Data structures to access subfields of NAME and SOCSEC
 I             DS
 I                                       1  15 NAME
 I                                       1   1 INITL
 I                                      16  24ØSOCSEC
 I                                      16  18ØSS1
 I                                      19  2ØØSS2
 I                                      21  24ØSS3
 I* Data structure to combine two fields into a single CRSSEC
 ICRSSEC       DS
 I                                       1   3ØCRSNO
 I                                       4   8ØSECT
 I* Multiple-occurrence data structure consisting of array SAR;
 I* SAR defined on extension specs
 ILOCAT        DS                       5Ø
 I                                       1 12Ø SAR
```

As with named constants, the basic approach to data structure definition in RPG IV has not changed much from RPG/400, other than moving
the entries to Definition Specifications, re-arranging some of the entries,
and substituting keywords for what originally were positional entries. The
figure below shows the same data structures from the figure above as they
would be defined in RPG IV.

```
          1         2         3         4         5         6         7         8         9        10
 1234567890123456789012345678901234567890123456789012345678901234567890123456789012345678901234567890
    DName++++++++++ETDsFrom+++To/L+++IDc.Functions+++++++++++++++++++++++++++++Comments++++++++++++
    D* Data structures defined in RPG IV
    D* Data structure to access subfields of Name and SocSec
    D                 DS
    D Name                    1     15
    D   Initl                 1      1
    D SocSec                 16     24 0
    D   SS1                  16     18 0
    D   SS2                  19     20 0
    D   SS3                  21     24 0
    D* Data structure to combine two fields into a single CrsSec
    D CrsSec           DS
    D   CrsNo                  1      3 0
    D   Sect                   4      8 0
    D* Multiple-occurrence data structure consisting of array SAR
    D Locat            DS               OCCURS(50)
    D   SAR                    1    120 0 DIM(12)
```

Notice from the above example that entries within the Name area of
the Definition Specifications can float within the allocated positions (7-21).
This feature lets you indent subfields to visually reflect the hierarchical
structure of the data. Keyword OCCURS now signals a multiple-occurrence
data structure, with the number of occurrences as the parameter value. Also
note that arrays can appear within a data structure and that you define them
through the keyword DIM. Thus, SAR is an array of 12 integers (10 positions, 0 decimal positions), and Locat is a multiple-occurrence data structure containing 50 occurrences of the SAR array.

A feature new to RPG IV data structures is that their subfields can now
be defined in terms of length or number of bytes (just as fields are defined
in DDS), rather than their definition requiring From and To positions. A
blank From entry signals that you are using length notation, which you
enter in the To/L area (positions 33-39). The following figure shows how
our previously defined data structures would look using this option.

```
          1         2         3         4         5         6         7         8         9        10
123456789012345678901234567890123456789012345678901234567890123456789012345678901234567890
DName++++++++++ETDsFrom+++To/L+++IDc.Functions+++++++++++++++++++++++++++++Comments+++++++++++
D* Data structures defined with length notation in RPG IV
D                   DS
D Name                            15
D   Initl                          1     OVERLAY(Name)
D SocSec                           9 0
D   SS1                            3 0   OVERLAY(SocSec:1)
D   SS2                            2 0   OVERLAY(SocSec:4)
D   SS3                            4 0   OVERLAY(SocSec:6)
D CrsSec              DS
D   CrsNo                          3 0
D   Sect                           5 0
D Locat               DS                 OCCURS(50)
D   SAR                           10 0   DIM(12)
```

With this notation, to indicate that Initl is a subfield of Name and that SS1, SS2, and SS3 are subfields of SocSec, you need to use keyword OVERLAY, with the name of the field to be overlayed in parentheses. An optional positional parameter specifies where the overlay is to begin within the field; if that second parameter is omitted, the default assumption is that the overlay should start with the first byte of the overlayed field.

Also observe that when you use length notation for arrays (e.g., array SAR), you indicate the length of one *element* of the array, rather than the length of the array as a whole.

Program-status and data-area data structures require the same entries on Definition Specifications as they previously did on Input Specifications. They are declared by coding an S or a U, respectively, in position 23 (Type of data structure) of the Definition Specifications.

You have already been introduced to the concept of stand-alone fields in the discussion of RPG IV's handling of tables and arrays. Stand-alone fields — that is, fields that are not contained within a data structure — are new to RPG IV. Their use is not limited to tables and arrays; you can define any field as a stand-alone field on Definition Specifications by including an S (for Stand-alone) in position 24 of its definition. The inclusion of stand-alone fields allows you to separate the definition of work fields from their use in calculations. Prior to RPG IV, you had to define such fields as part of Result field entries on Calculation Specifications.

```
          1         2         3         4         5         6         7         8         9        10
123456789012345678901234567890123456789012345678901234567890123456789012345678901234567890
DName++++++++++ETDsFrom+++To/L+++IDc.Functions+++++++++++++++++++++++++++++Comments+++++++++++
D* Stand-alone fields defined in RPG IV
D Counter         S              5 0
D SaleAmt         S              7 2
D SalesTax        S             -1     LIKE(SalesAmt)
D Charge          S                    LIKE(SalesAmt)
D TotSales        S             +4     LIKE(SalesAmt)
D TotSlsTax       S             +4     LIKE(SalesTax)
D TotChrge        S             +4     LIKE(Charge)
```

The length of stand-alone fields must be specified in terms of an absolute length, rather than based on From and To positions. You can also, however, specify a field's length relative to that of another field by using keyword LIKE, with the name of the referenced field as the parameter. In this case, a blank length entry means the two fields are to have the same length, while a digit entry in the To/L+++ position, preceded by a + or a − sign, signals how much larger or smaller the field is to be relative to the referenced field.

Finally, you can use keyword INZ to initialize any item defined on Definition Specifications (except named constants). If the keyword is used without an optional parameter, the data item it is associated with is initialized to default values appropriate for the data type of the item (e.g., blanks for character fields, zero for numeric). If you associate INZ with a data structure as a whole, all subfields of the data structure are appropriately initialized based on their type. For subfields, arrays, and stand-alone fields, you can optionally include a constant as a parameter of INZ to initialize the data item to a value other than its default.

```
          1         2         3         4         5         6         7         8         9        10
 1234567890123456789012345678901234567890123456789012345678901234567890123456789012345678901234567890
     DName++++++++++ETDsFrom+++To/L+++IDc.Functions++++++++++++++++++++++++++++Comments++++++++++++
     D* Examples using initialization and overlay keywords in RPG IV
     D Counter        S              5  0 INZ(50)                               Initial. to 50
     D SaleAmt        S              7  2 INZ                                   Initial. to 0
     D SalesTax       S             -1    LIKE(SalesAmt) INZ                    Initial. to 0
     D Sar            S              9  2 DIM(100) INZ(20.05)                   All elements = 20.5
     D                DS                  INZ                                   Initial subflds.
     D Name                         15
     D SocSec                        9  0
     D   SS1                         3  0 OVERLAY(SocSec:1)
     D   SS2                         2  0 OVERLAY(SocSec:3)
     D   SS3                         4  0 OVERLAY(SocSec:5)
```

Although RPG IV still allows you to define character or numeric fields within Calculation Specifications (by using that field as a result field of an operation and specifying the field's length and decimal positions or by using *LIKE DEFINE), I would recommend that you confine all data definition required within your programs to Definition Specifications. This practice will result in programs that you can more easily maintain and modify.

In the first section of this chapter, we introduced the concept of pointer data types. You must define pointers on Definition Specifications. You can define them explicitly, as stand-alone data items, as subfields of a data structure, or as elements in an array of pointers; however, you can also implicitly define a based pointer by naming it as the pointer upon which an entity is based. Some examples of pointer definitions are shown in the following figure.

```
          1         2         3         4         5         6         7         8         9         10
 123456789012345678901234567890123456789012345678901234567890123456789012345678901234567890123456789
 DName++++++++++ETDsFrom+++To/L+++IDc.Functions++++++++++++++++++++++++++++Comments++++++++++++
 D* Definition of pointers in RPG IV
 D Ptr1           S               *                              Based pointer
 D DataStruct     DS                                             Data structure of
 D   Ptr2                         *                              2 based pointers
 D   Ptr3                         *
 D Ptr4           S               *    PROCPTR                   Procedure pointer
 D Field2                       25A    BASED(Ptr5)               Ptr5 implicitly def.
 D ArrayPtr       S               *    DIM(10)                   Array of pointers
```

Note that because all pointers are 16 bytes long, you do not need to include a length entry as part of a pointer's definition; the * in position 40 denoting the pointer data type suffices. You use the keyword PROCPTR to differentiate procedure pointers from basing pointers.

The contents of the address to which a basing pointer "points" can only be accessed through a data item that is based on that pointer; you need to declare such basing on the Definition Specifications as part of the data item's definition. The figure below illustrates definitions of based variables through the use of keyword BASED.

```
          1         2         3         4         5         6         7         8         9         10
 123456789012345678901234567890123456789012345678901234567890123456789012345678901234567890123456789
 DName++++++++++ETDsFrom+++To/L+++IDc.Functions++++++++++++++++++++++++++++Comments++++++++++++
 D* Definition of based variables in RPG IV
 D FieldX         S             8 2    BASED(Ptr1)
 D DataStruct     DS                   BASED(Ptr2)
 D   FieldY                     15
 D   FieldZ                      9 4
 D Array1         S             10      DIM(20) BASED(Ptr3)
 D Array2         S             20      DIM(15) BASED(Ptr4)
```

Modifications to Input Specifications

Other than an adjustment of the positions of entries that the new 100-position specification lines mandate, no differences exist in Input Specifications between RPG/400 and RPG IV.

The two figures below show a typical program-described input record and field definitions, respectively, as they would appear in RPG IV.

```
          1         2         3         4         5         6         7         8         9         10
 123456789012345678901234567890123456789012345678901234567890123456789012345678901234567890123456789
 IFilename++SqNORiPos1+NCCPos2+NCCPos3+NCC...............................Comments++++++++++++
 I* Record-level input description of a program-described file in RPG IV
 ISalesTransNS
```

```
          1         2         3         4         5         6         7         8         9         10
 123456789012345678901234567890123456789012345678901234567890123456789012345678901234567890123456789
 I......................Fmt+SPFrom+To+++DcField++++++++L1M1FrP1MnZr......Comments++++++++++++
 I* Field-level input descriptions of a program-described file in RPG IV
 I
 I                             1     4 0SlsmNo
 I                             5    10 0Date
 I                            11    20 2SalesAmt
```

Modifications to Calculation Specifications

Calculation Specifications have been redesigned in RPG IV to allow sufficient room for longer variable names and operation codes. To facilitate this adjustment, room for only one conditioning indicator per line now exists. With the expanded room for operation codes, IBM has changed the following operation codes to conform to their correct English spelling (much to the delight of language purists, who grimaced every time they had to key in OCUR!):

RPG/400	RPG IV
BITOF	BITOFF
CHEKR	CHECKR
DEFN	DEFINE
DELET	DELETE
EXCPT	EXCEPT
LOKUP	LOOKUP
OCUR	OCCUR
REDPE	READPE
RETRN	RETURN
UNLCK	UNLOCK
SELEC	SELECT
SETOF	SETOFF
UPDAT	UPDATE
WHxx	WHENxx

Using the older version of these operation codes within RPG IV will result in syntax errors.

Two notational differences appear on the Calculation Specifications between the two versions of the language. First, operation extenders H (Half-adjust), P (Pad), and N (No lock) now should appear enclosed in parentheses immediately following the relevant operation. Instead of being coded in a fixed position on the specification line, these extenders can float to the right of the operation code (as far as position 35). Second, instead of referencing individual elements of an array using a comma separator, you now reference array elements with an index contained within parentheses that follow the array name. (You would also use this notation on Output Specifications.)

The figure that follows shows some calculations involving these operations or features as you would code them in RPG/400.

```
         1         2         3         4         5         6         7         8
1234567890123456789012345678901234567890123456789012345678901234567890123456789Ø
         CLØNØ1NØ2NØ3Factor1+++OpcdeFactor2+++ResultLenDEHiLoEqComments++++++......
         C* Calculations coded in RPG/400
         C           CUSTNO    REDPECUSTMAST                     9Ø
         C                     MOVEASAR,1      TAR,3        P
         C                     SELEC
         C           AGE       WHLT BOTLMT
         C                     MULT 1.1        CHARGE       H
         C                     UPDATCUSTREC
         C           AGE       WHGT TOPLMT
         C                     DELETCUSTREC
         C                     ENDSL
         C                     RETRN
```

The following figure reflects the same calculations as they would be coded
in RPG IV.

```
       1         2         3         4         5         6         7         8         9        10
1234567890123456789012345678901234567890123456789012345678901234567890123456789012345678901234567890
         CLØNØ1Factor1++++++Opcode(E)+Factor2++++++Result++++++++Len++D+HiLoEq....Comments++++++++++++
         C     CustNo       READPE    CustMast                          9Ø
         C                  MOVEA (P) SAR(1)      Tar(3)
         C                  SELECT
         C     Age          WHENLT    BotLmt
         C                  MULT(H)   1.1         Charge
         C                  UPDATE    CustRec
         C     Age          WHENGT    TopLmt
         C                  DELETE    CustRec
         C                  ENDSL
         C                  RETURN
```

Of more significance in signaling a change in direction of the language, RPG IV introduces a second form of the Calculation Specifications,
called the **extended factor 2 format**, and four new operations that are used
with this format: EVAL, DOW, DOU, IF, and WHEN. This change represents
RPG's movement toward a more free-form language. These features let you
code, within a single specification, complex calculations and/or logical
expressions that would take two or more separate calculations in the older
versions of RPG.

The operations supported within expressions include the following:

Operation	Effect	Data Type
+	Addition	Numeric
−	Subtraction	Numeric
*	Multiplication	Numeric
/	Division	Numeric
**	Exponentiation	Numeric
+	Concatenation	Character

You can also use any of the following comparison operations within the
extended factor 2 calculation:

Operation	Code Equivalent
=	EQ
>	GT
<	LT
>=	GE
<=	LE
<>	NE

Logical operations AND and OR and unary operation NOT are also supported. When you combine these operations within an expression, the expression is evaluated based on rules of precedence that determine the order in which the operations are executed. You can use parentheses to give operations higher precedence than they would normally have. The order of precedence (or execution) is parentheses, NOT, exponentiation, multiplication and division, addition and subtraction, relational comparisons, AND, and OR.

With that background, let's look first at the EVAL operation. EVAL (Evaluate) is another assignment operation. It signals that the extended factor 2 portion of the Calculation Specification will include a target field, followed by an equal sign, followed by an expression whose value is to be evaluated and assigned to the target field. The figure below gives some examples of EVAL.

```
          1         2         3         4         5         6         7         8         9        10
 1234567890123456789012345678901234567890123456789012345678901234567890123456789012345678901234567890
     CLØNØ1Factor1++++++Opcode(E)+Extended-factor2++++++++++++++++++++++++++++++Comments++++++++++++
 C* Assign Count the value Ø
 C                   EVAL      Count = Ø
 C* Calculate the volume of a cube.
 C                   EVAL (H)  Volume = Length * Height * Width
 C* Calculate Economic Order Quantity
 C                   EVAL (H)  EOQ = ((2*D*O)/C)**(1/2)
 C* Convert Fahrenheit to Centigrade
 C                   EVAL(H)   C = 5 * (F - 32) / 9
 C* The example below demonstrates the use of a continuation line.
 C                   EVAL  (H) OvrtimePay = 1.5 * HourlyRate *
 C                                          (HrsWorked - 4Ø)
```

Note that to round the results of an expression, the extended operator (H) must follow the EVAL operation, as shown above. Also note that the number of blanks between fields and operators is not fixed and that if an expression is too long to fit on a single Calculation Specification line, you can continue it on an additional line (or lines), as shown in the above calculation of overtime pay.

New operations DOW, DOU, IF, and WHEN work identically to their RPG/400 counterparts DOWxx, DOUxx, IFxx, and WHxx. They have been added to RPG's lexicon to be used with the extended factor 2 format of the Calculation Specification. They allow you to build complex expressions to form the logical comparisons that determine flow of control in these looping or branching structures. You can use any of the operations discussed for

EVAL to create an expression that can be evaluated as true or false. The system evaluates the expression to determine its next course of action.

The figure below illustrates some of these operations and provides samples of possible expressions.

```
          1         2         3         4         5         6         7         8         9        10
1234567890123456789012345678901234567890123456789012345678901234567890123456789012345678901234567890
    CLØNØ1Factor1++++++Opcode(E)+Extended-factor2+++++++++++++++++++++++++++++++++Comments++++++++++++
    C* Extended factor2 logical comparisons
    C               IF        Count > 100
    C               ...                                                         Do whatever
    C               ELSE
    C               ...                                                         Do something else
    C               ENDIF
    C               DOW       ((A + B) > 2ØØ) AND (Y = 5)
    C               ...
    C               ENDDO
    C               DOU       *IN9Ø = *ON OR Amount <=25
    C               ...
    C               ENDDO
```

RPG IV introduced three new operations to perform time, date, and timestamp calculations. These operations are ADDDUR (Add Duration), SUBDUR (Subtract Duration), and EXTRCT (Extract). All three of these operations use duration codes *YEARS (or *Y), *MONTHS (*M), *DAYS (*D), *HOURS (*H), *MINUTES (*MN), *SECONDS (*S), and *MSECONDS (*MS) to indicate which portion of time data you want to manipulate.

The ADDDUR operation lets you add a duration coded in factor 2 to the time specified in factor 1 and store the answer in the date, time, or timestamp field specified as the result field. Factor 1 can contain any data item representing one of the three time data types; if factor 1 is blank, the duration is simply added to the result field.

Factor 2 must contain both an integer field (or constant) expressing the number to add and one of the six duration codes listed above to indicate the kind of duration the number represents; you separate these two portions of factor 2 with a colon. If the numeric portion of factor 2 represents a negative value, the duration is subtracted, rather than added.

The figure below illustrates the use of ADDDUR. Assume that fields BillDate, StartDate, and EndDate were defined as type D (date) and fields StartTime and EndTime as type T (time).

```
          1         2         3         4         5         6         7         8         9        10
1234567890123456789012345678901234567890123456789012345678901234567890123456789012345678901234567890
    CLØNØ1Factor1++++++Opcode(E)+Factor2++++++Result++++++++Len++D+HiLoEq....Comments++++++++++++
    C* Add 3Ø days to BillDate to determine DueDate
    C       BillDate    ADDDUR    3Ø:*DAYS     DueDate
    C* Add field Min, containing minutes, to StartTime to determine EndTime
    C       StartTime   ADDDUR    Min:*MN      EndTime
    C* Add 5 years to DueDate
    C                   ADDDUR    5:*YEARS     DueDate
    C* Subtract 5 months from EndDate to get StartDate
    C       EndDate     ADDDUR    -5:*MONTHS   StartDate
```

Operation SUBDUR has two uses. One use is to subtract a factor 2 duration from a time data item in factor 1 and store the answer in the result; this use is analogous to ADDDUR, except the duration is subtracted, rather than added. However, SUBDUR can also be used to calculate the duration between two time units. With this format, both factor 1 and factor 2 must contain data items of compatible time types, while the result field must contain an integer receiving field and a duration code to denote the unit of time involved in the operation. Again, a colon separates these two subfactors. Both uses of SUBDUR are shown in the figure below.

```
          1         2         3         4         5         6         7         8         9        10
1234567890123456789012345678901234567890123456789012345678901234567890123456789012345678901234567890
    CLØNØ1Factor1++++++Opcode(E)+Factor2++++++Result+++++++Len++D+HiLoEq....Comments+++++++++++
    C* Subtract 30 days from DueDate to determine BillDate
    C      DueDate          SUBDUR    3Ø:*DAYS       BillDate
    C* Subtract 5 years from DueDate
    C                       SUBDUR    5:*YEARS       DueDate
    C* Subtract birthday from today to get age in years
    C      TodayDate        SUBDUR    BirthDate      Age:*YEARS
    C* Determine number of days left to study
    C      ExamDate         SUBDUR    TodayDate      CramTime:*D
```

Finally, EXTRCT (the third new operation for manipulating time) extracts a portion of a Date, Time, or Timestamp data item and stores it in the result field, which can be any numeric or character receiving field. The factor 2 time data item must be coupled with a duration code to signal which portion of the time unit is to be extracted. Factor 1 is always blank for EXTRCT operations.

```
          1         2         3         4         5         6         7         8         9        10
1234567890123456789012345678901234567890123456789012345678901234567890123456789012345678901234567890
    CLØNØ1Factor1++++++Opcode(E)+Factor2++++++Result+++++++Len++D+HiLoEq....Comments+++++++++++
    C* Determine birthyear.
    C                       EXTRCT    BirthDate:*Y   BirthYear
    C*Extract month of loan.
    C                       EXTRCT    LoanDate:*M    LoanMonth
```

RPG IV also extends operations MOVE, MOVEL, and MOVEA to allow their use in moving values between dates and/or numeric or character fields. The rules for these kinds of movements depend on the kinds of data types involved in the move and are somewhat complicated. For example, when moving data from a character field to one of the time data types, the sending field must contain the separator characters appropriate to the receiving field, whereas if the sending field is numeric, the separator characters should not be present in the sent value. In both cases, factor 1 of the operation must include a format code (e.g., *MDY *YMD, *JUL) indicating the layout of the data to be sent. Consult the RPG IV manual for additional detail.

Another feature introduced in RPG IV is a set of **built-in functions.** Each function returns a value based on what the function does and the value used as the argument of the function. Built-in functions can also appear within the arguments of built-in functions. You can use these functions within expressions on the extended factor 2 format of the Calculation Specifications; you can also use them within the Functions area — positions 44-80 — of Definition Specifications to provide parameter values for the definitions.

All function names begin with a percent sign (%). Functions require one or more parameters, enclosed within a set of parentheses, to indicate what data the function should operate on. At present, eight built-in functions are recognized within V3R1 of RPG IV.

Four of the functions directly address string handling. %TRIM removes leading and trailing blanks from its argument; %TRIMR removes trailing (or rightmost) blanks; and %TRIML removes leading (or leftmost) blanks. Function %SUBST works the same way as operation SUBST to extract a substring from a string. %SUBST requires two parameters: the base string and the starting position of the substring operation. An optional additional parameter specifies the length of the substring to be extracted from the base string. Colons are used to separate the string, the starting position, and the length portions of the argument. The figure below shows some uses of these functions.

```
          1         2         3         4         5         6         7         8         9        10
 1234567890123456789012345678901234567890123456789012345678901234567890123456789012345678901234567890
    CLØN01Factor1+++++++Opcode(E)+Extended-factor2+++++++++++++++++++++++++++Comments++++++++++++
    C* Concatenate trimmed name for letter salutation
    C                   EVAL      Salutation = 'Dear ' + %TRIM(FirstName) + ' '
    C                                     + %TRIM(LastName) + ','
    C* Ensure that address is left-adjusted
    C                   EVAL      Address = %TRIML(Address)
    C* Extract area code from phone number
    C                   EVAL      AreaCode = %SUBST(Phone:1:3)
```

Two built-in functions let you more easily modify your programs by eliminating the need to hardcode literals within your calculations. Function %ELEM returns the number of elements of an array or a multiple-occurrence data structure, while %SIZE returns the length in bytes of a variable or literal. Both of these functions can appear anywhere that a numeric constant is permitted.

Assume that array Sales contains sales figures and array Tax is to contain sales taxes for those sales. The number of elements in the arrays is defined on the Definition Specifications, but you want to use a DO operation to calculate all the taxes without directly referencing the total number of elements in the array. The figure below shows how you can use %ELEM to accomplish this processing.

```
          1         2         3         4         5         6         7         8         9        10
 1234567890123456789012345678901234567890123456789012345678901234567890123456789012345678901234567890
    CLØN01Factor1+++++++Opcode(E)+Extended-factor2+++++++++++++++++++++++++++Comments++++++++++++
    C                   DO        %ELEM(Sales)  Cnt
    C                   EVAL (H)  Tax(Cnt) = Sales(Cnt) * Taxrate
    C                   ENDDO
```

Similarly, if you needed to know the length of a variable (LastName, for example), you could use %SIZE, as shown below.

```
          1         2         3         4         5         6         7         8         9        10
1234567890123456789012345678901234567890123456789012345678901234567890123456789012345678901234567890
    CLØN01Factor1++++++Opcode(E)+Extended-factor2++++++++++++++++++++++++++++Comments++++++++++++
    C                 EVAL      Length = %SIZE(LastName)
```

The remaining two functions, %PADDR and %ADDR, return addresses, or storage locations, and are used to assign values to pointers. %ADDR is used with basing pointers, while %PADDR is appropriate for procedure pointers. The figure below illustrates how %ADDR can be used to assign values to pointers and how the based variables are subsequently affected.

```
          1         2         3         4         5         6         7         8         9        10
1234567890123456789012345678901234567890123456789012345678901234567890123456789012345678901234567890
    CLØN01Factor1++++++Opcode(E)+Extended-factor2++++++++++++++++++++++++++++Comments++++++++++++
    C* Assume Ptr1 is a basing pointer, and Field1 is based on that pointer.
    C                 EVAL      Ptr1 = %ADDR(Field2)
    C                 IF        Field1 = Field2
    C* The above IF is true, because Field1's pointer contains Field2's address.
    C                 ...
```

The concept of pointers can be very confusing to beginning (and even more advanced!) programmers, and a complete discussion of them is beyond the scope of this text. A full understanding (in fact, even a slight knowledge) of pointers is not necessary to master RPG IV. (When you're ready to tackle pointers, their use is well-documented in IBM's *ILE RPG/400 Reference*, SC09-1526). For now, just know that pointers store the addresses of variables and procedures and can be used to indirectly reference or modify a variable's value or to dynamically reference a procedure.

One final new calculation operation — CALLB — has major implications for program design and reflects an important change in IBM's approach to executable programs. RPG IV now allows calling programs and the programs they call to be bound (or connected) *before* execution, rather than requiring them to be bound at runtime. To enable this feature, IBM has added a mandatory "binding step" between the compiling and running steps of a program. Before RPG IV, compiling directly created an executable object of type *PGM. Now, compiling creates a **program module** object (type *MODULE), which must be operated on with the CRTPGM (Create Program) command to create an executable object (type *PGM).

Most significantly, the CRTPGM command allows separately compiled modules that need to call each other at runtime to be linked together before execution to form a single *PGM object; this process is called **static binding**. In **dynamic binding**, a separate *PGM object would be created for each module, and the programs would be connected *during* execution.

Static binding improves runtime call performance tremendously over dynamic binding, because *resolving a call* (i.e., locating the called program and checking its authorities) can be completed *before* runtime. The availability of static binding should encourage a modular approach to program development among those who (until now) eschewed the use of dynamic program calls because of performance considerations.

To call a statically bound ILE procedure from an RPG IV program, use the CALLB operation, rather than CALL. Factor 2 must contain a literal (or constant) specifying the name of the called procedure or a procedure pointer; it cannot be a field that will contain the name of the called program at runtime. The bound procedure(s) called with CALLB can be written in any ILE language available on the AS/400.

```
          1         2         3         4         5         6         7         8         9        10
 1234567890123456789012345678901234567890123456789012345678901234567890123456789012345678901234567890
     CLØNØ1Factor1++++++Opcode(E)+Factor2++++++Result++++++++Len++D+HiLoEq....Comments+++++++++++
     C                   CALLB     'MYPROGRAM'
     C                   PARM      ARG1
     C                   PARM      ARG2
```

Parameters are passed from programs called with CALLB by using the PARM operation, just as they are with the CALL operation.

Data defined within a procedure is local to that procedure; it is not automatically available to other procedures bound with it. To pass data between procedures, you can use PARMs and PLIST with CALLB, just as you can with CALL. Additionally, you can define variables whose values are available across procedures by including the data item within the Definition Specifications of each procedure that needs to reference it. Include keyword EXPORT with the definition in the procedure you want responsible for storage allocation for that data item and keyword IMPORT with the definition in the remaining procedures that need to reference that data item. Data items so defined should *not* also appear as PARMs within the modules.

Modifications to Output Specifications

RPG IV's Output Specifications, like its Input Specifications, bring few new features to RPG. Aside from the changed positions of entries, caused by the expanded field lengths and 100-position specification line, the most significant change likely to affect your code is that an Output Specification continuation line now exists. As a result, you can continue a given constant or edit word from one line to the next, rather than having to break it into separate pieces, each with its own ending position. You must use a continuation character — a plus sign (+) or a minus sign (–) — to signal the continuation; "+" indicates that the constant/edit word continues with the first non-blank character within the continuation area on the following line, whereas "–" indicates that the constant/edit word continues with the first position in the next specification's continuation area. In addition, both space and skip entries, whether before or after, now have a maximum limit of 255.

```
          1         2         3         4         5         6         7         8         9         10
123456789012345678901234567890123456789012345678901234567890123456789012345678901234567890
O..............NØ1NØ2NØ3Field+++++++++YB.End++PConstand/editword/DTformat++Comments+++++++++++
O*The example below shows the use of a continuation line for long output constants.
O                                        100 'THE NATIONAL ASSURANCE +
O                                            AND TRUST COMPANY'
```

Putting It All Together

Now that you have read about the individual changes to RPG introduced with RPG IV, you may find it useful to examine an entire program written in this version of the language. Such an examination should consolidate your understanding of the enhancements introduced by IBM and prepare you for using RPG IV in your own coding. The sample RPG IV program below is based on the following scenario.

Assume CompuSell, the mail order computer reseller, allows some large customers to pay after shipping. The company needs a program to generate invoices for those customers. Assume that shipped-order information is stored in files CSORDP (header information) and CSORDPRP (order details), while customer information is stored in CSCSTP and inventory information is stored in CSINVP. (You will find detailed record layouts of these files in Appendix D.)

The company offers discounts to these customers based on the size of the order. No discount is applied to orders less than $1,000; if the order total is at least $1,000 but less than $5,000, the company gives a 0.5 percent discount; if the total is at least $5,000 but less than $10,000, the company gives a 1 percent discount; and orders totaling $10,000 or more receive a 3 percent discount.

CompuSell charges a flat rate of $10 per 100 pounds (or fraction there-of) for shipping. Finally, payment is due within 30 days of the invoice date, and the company offers a 2 percent cash discount from the net due for customers who remit payment within 10 days of the invoice date.

If (because of some error) an order exists whose customer is not in the customer master file or no items are found to be associated with an order, the error should be noted on an error report, and the invoice should not be prepared. However, if an item within an order cannot be found in the inventory file, the problem should be noted on the error report and the item should be excluded from the invoice, but the rest of the invoice should be completed. The layouts of the desired invoices and error report are shown in the following figures.

Printer Spacing Chart for Invoices:

```
        1         2         3         4         5         6         7         8
1234567890123456789012345678901234567890123456789012345678901234567890123456789Ø

        ORDER NO. XXXXX            COMPUSELL              DATE XX/XX/XX
        CUST. NO. XXXXXX           INVOICE                PAGE XXØX

    BILL TO:
    XXXXXXXXXXXXXXXXXXXXXXXXXXXXXX
    XXXXXXXXXXXXXXXXXX
    XXXXXXXXXXXXXXXXXXXXXXXXXXXXXX

    PROD                          UNIT
    NO        DESCRIPTION         PRICE     QTY         EXTENSION
    XXXXXX  XXXXXXXXXXXXXXXXXXXXXX  X,XXØ.XX  X,XØX    XX,XXX,XXØ.XX
    XXXXXX  XXXXXXXXXXXXXXXXXXXXXX  X,XXØ.XX  X,XØX    XX,XXX,XXØ.XX
    XXXXXX  XXXXXXXXXXXXXXXXXXXXXX  X,XXØ.XX  X,XØX    XX,XXX,XXØ.XX
    XXXXXX  XXXXXXXXXXXXXXXXXXXXXX  X,XXØ.XX  X,XØX    XX,XXX,XXØ.XX

                                         TOTAL       XXX,XXX,XXØ.XX
                              LESS XØ.X% DISCOUNT      X,XXX,XXX.XØ
                                                     ---------------
                                       NET DUE      $XXX,XXX,XX$.XX
                                  PLUS SHIPPING          XXX,XXØ.XX
                                                     ---------------
                                    TOTAL DUE    $X,XXX,XXX,XX$.XX
        PAYMENT DUE BY XX/XX/XX
        $XX,XXX,XX$.XX CASH DISCOUNT IF PAID BY XX/XX/XX
```

Printer Spacing Chart for Error Report:

```
        1         2         3         4         5         6         7         8
1234567890123456789012345678901234567890123456789012345678901234567890123456789Ø
            COMPUSELL INVOICING ERROR LOG    XX/XX/XX

ORDER     CUST      PRODUCT          PROBLEM

XXXXX     XXXXX                      CUSTOMER MISSING FROM FILE CSCSTP
XXXXX     XXXXX     XXXXX            ITEM MISSING FROM FILE CSINVP
XXXXX     XXXXX                      ORDER HAS NO ITEMS IN FILE CSORDP
```

The pseudocode below represents a solution to the above problem.

Pseudocode for Invoice Program

Program Mainline
Do Date Calculations
Read Orders file
WHILE not end-of-file for Orders file
        Do Process Order
        Read Orders file
ENDWHILE
End Program

Process Order
Randomly read Customer file based on Cust. No. in order record
IF customer not found
>   Write appropriate error message on error report

ELSE
>   Chain on Order No. to first matching record in Ord/Prod file
>   IF match not found
>>   Write appropriate error message on error report
>
>   ELSE
>>   Initialize invoice accumulators
>>   Format customer name and address for printing invoice
>>>   Write invoice headings
>>   WHILE more matching Ord/Prod records
>>>   Do Process Order Item
>>>   Read next matching record from Ord/Prod file
>>   ENDWHILE
>>   Do Process Invoice Footers
>   ENDIF

ENDIF

Process Order Item
Randomly access Product file based on Product No. of item
IF product not found in Product file
>   Write appropriate error message on error report

ELSE
>   Calculate extension
>   Accumulate invoice item total cost, total pounds, total ounces
>   IF overflow on
>>   Write invoice headings
>   ENDIF

Write invoice item (detail) line

Process Invoice Footers
Calculate discount
Calculate net
Determine number of packages for shipping
Calculate shipping charge
Calculate total due
Calculate cash discount
Write invoice footers

Date Calculations
Calculate due date
Calculate discount date

The program implementing the above pseudocode is shown below. To shorten the program code, assume that external definitions for the required printer files exist, so that we do not need to include output specifications in the program.

```
          1         2         3         4         5         6         7         8         9         10
1234567890123456789012345678901234567890123456789012345678901234567890123456789012345678901234567890
     F******************************************************************************
     F*  This program generates invoices for CompuSell's charge customers based *
     F*  on orders contained in order file CsOrdP.  It also generates an error  *
     F*  report for problems encountered during invoice preparation.            *
     F*          Author:  J. Yaeger     Date Written:  Nov., 1994               *
     F******************************************************************************
     FCsOrdP    IF   E           K DISK
     FCsOrdPrP  IF   E           K DISK
     FCsCstP    IF   E           K DISK
     FCsInvP    IF   E           K DISK
     FQprint    O    E             PRINTER OFLIND(*IN10)
     FErrRpt    O    E             PRINTER OFLIND(*IN20)
     D******************************************************************************
     D*  All fields and constants are defined below; no definition occurs       *
     D*  within the Calculation Specifications.                                  *
     D******************************************************************************
     D                 DS
     D ShipWt              1      4 0
     D  Lbs                       2 0 OVERLAY(ShipWt)
     D  Ozs                       2 0 OVERLAY(ShipWt:3)
     D Extension      S         +4   LIKE(SellPr)
     D GrssTotal      S         +1   LIKE(Extension)
     D QtyDscnt       S         -2   LIKE(GrssTotal)
     D NetDue         S              LIKE(GrssTotal)
     D ShipChrg       S          8 2
     D TotalDue       S         +1   LIKE(GrssTotal)
     D CashDscnt      S         -2   LIKE(TotalDue)
     D DiscntPctW     S          3 3
     D DueDate        S          D
     D DiscntDate     S          D
     D InvDate        S          D
     D CityStZip      S         30
     D CustName       S         30
     D TotalLbs       S          8 0
     D TotalOzs       S          8 0
     D MessageOut     S         35
     D DiscPrint      S          3 1
     D PkgsFrac       S         15 10
     D PkgsWhole      S          5 0
     D ErrCnt         S          7 0 INZ(0)
     D StrZip         S          9
     D******** Named Constants ***********
     D DiscLvl#1      C              1000
     D DiscPct#1      C              0
     D DiscLvl#2      C              5000
     D DiscPct#2      C              .005
     D DiscLvl#3      C              10000
     D DiscPct#3      C              .01
     D DiscPct#4      C              .03
     D CshDscPct      C              .02
     D ShipUCst       C              10
     D ShipUWt        C              100
     D MessCust       C              'CUSTOMER MISSING FROM FILE CSCSTP'
     D MessProd       C              'ITEM MISSING FROM FILE CSINVP'
     D MessOrd        C              'ORDER HAS NO ITEMS IN FILE CSORDPRP'
```

```
            1         2         3         4         5         6         7         8         9        10
   12345678901234567890123456789012345678901234567890123456789012345678901234567890123456789012345678901234567890

       C*****************************************************************************
       C     Order         KLIST
       C                   KFLD                      Ord#
       C*******  Mainline of program  ********
       C                   EXSR      CalcDates
       C                   READ      CsOrdP                                    90
       C                   DOW       *IN90 = *OFF
       C                   EXSR      PrcssOrder
       C                   READ      CsOrdP                                    90
       C                   ENDDO
       C                   EVAL      *INLR = *ON
       C                   RETURN
       C
       C*** Subroutine to process each order ****
       C     PrcssOrder    BEGSR
       C     CustNo        CHAIN     CsCstP                                    95
       C                   IF        *IN95 = *ON
       C                   EVAL      MessageOut = MessCust
       C                   EXSR      ErrDetail
       C                   ELSE
       C     Order         CHAIN     CsOrdPrP                                  96
       C                   IF        *IN96 = *ON
       C                   EVAL      MessageOut = MessOrd
       C                   EXSR      ErrDetail
       C                   ELSE
       C*        **** Initialize variables ****
       C                   EVAL      TotalLbs = 0
       C                   EVAL      TotalOzs = 0
       C                   EVAL      GrssTotal = 0
       C                   EVAL      Page = 1
       C*        **** Format name and address for printing ****
       C                   MOVE      CZIP          StrZip
       C                   EVAL      CustName  = %TRIMR(CFName)    + ' '  +
       C                                         %TRIMR(CLName)
       C                   EVAL      CityStZip = %TRIMR(CCity)    + ', ' +
       C                                         CState            + ' '  +
       C                                         %SUBST(StrZip:1:5) + '-'  +
       C                                         %SUBST(StrZip:6:4)
       C                   WRITE     InvHeads
       C                   DOW       *IN96 = *OFF
       C                   EXSR      PrcssItem
       C     Order         READE     CsOrdPrP                                  96
       C                   ENDDO
       C                   EXSR      InvFooters
       C                   ENDIF
       C                   ENDIF
       C                   ENDSR
       C
       C*** Subroutine to process one invoice item ***
       C     PrcssItem     BEGSR
       C     ProdNo        CHAIN     CsInvP                                    97
       C                   IF        *IN97 = *ON
       C                   EVAL      MessageOut = MessProd
       C                   EXSR      ErrDetail
       C                   ELSE
       C                   EVAL      Extension = QtyOrd * SellPr
       C                   EVAL      GrssTotal = GrssTotal + Extension
       C                   EVAL      TotalLbs = TotalLbs + Lbs
       C                   EVAL      TotalOzs = TotalOzs + Ozs
       C                   ENDIF
       C
```

```
          1         2         3         4         5         6         7         8         9        10
 1234567890123456789012345678901234567890123456789012345678901234567890123456789012345678901234567890
        C                   IF        *IN10 = *ON
        C                   WRITE     InvHeaders
        C                   EVAL      *IN10 = *OFF
        C                   ENDIF
        C                   WRITE     InvDetail
        C                   ENDSR
        C
        C*** Subroutine to process invoice footer lines ***
        C     InvFooters    BEGSR
        C*         **** Determine discount percent based on gross total ****
        C                   SELECT
        C                   WHEN      GrssTotal < DiscLvl#1
        C                   EVAL      DiscntPctW = DiscPct#1
        C                   WHEN      GrssTotal < DiscLvl#2
        C                   EVAL      DiscntPctW = DiscPct#2
        C                   WHEN      GrssTotal < DiscLvl#3
        C                   EVAL      DiscntPctW = DiscPct#3
        C                   OTHER
        C                   EVAL      DiscntPctW = DiscPct#4
        C                   ENDSL
        C
        C                   EVAL (H)  QtyDscnt = DiscntPctW * GrssTotal
        C                   EVAL      DiscPrint = DiscntPctW * 100
        C                   EVAL      NetDue = GrssTotal - QtyDscnt
        C*     *** Determine number of packages required, including any fractional portion ***
        C                   EVAL      PkgsFrac = (TotalLbs + TotalOzs/16)
        C                                 / ShipUWt
        C                   EVAL      PkgsWhole = PkgsFrac
        C                   IF        PkgsFrac > PkgsWhole
        C                   EVAL      PkgsWhole = PkgsWhole + 1
        C                   ENDIF
        C
        C                   EVAL      ShipChrg = ShipUCst * PkgsWhole
        C                   EVAL      TotalDue = NetDue + ShipChrg
        C                   EVAL (H)  CashDscnt = CshDscPct * NetDue
        C
        C                   WRITE     InvTotals
        C                   ENDSR
        C
        C*** Subroutine to print error report details ***
        C     ErrDetail     BEGSR
        C                   IF        ErrCnt = 0 OR *IN20 = *ON
        C                   WRITE     ErrHeads
        C                   EVAL      *IN20 = *OFF
        C                   ENDIF
        C                   WRITE     ErrDet
        C                   EVAL      ErrCnt = ErrCnt + 1
        C                   ENDSR
        C
        C*** Subroutine to perform date calculations ***
        C     CalcDates     BEGSR
        C     *MDY          MOVE      UDATE       InvDate
        C     InvDate       ADDDUR    30:*DAYS    DueDate
        C     InvDate       ADDDUR    10:*DAYS    DiscntDate
        C                   ENDSR
```

As you compare the pseudocode with the RPG implementation, notice that the code uses date data types and date calculations to determine the due date and the discount date. It also uses functions %TRIMR and %SUBST, along with + as a string concatenation operation, to format the customer name, city, state, and zip code for printing.

Moreover, as you examine the program, recognize that it suggests some programming standards that RPG IV makes possible. First, all variable names are entered in mixed case, with the first letter of each abbreviated word capitalized to facilitate understanding. All RPG reserved words are entered in uppercase letters. Whenever possible, the calculations use EVAL followed by a free-form expression, rather than using the individual RPG operations for arithmetic or assignment. No field definition occurs within the Calculation Specifications; data definition takes place exclusively on the Definition Specifications. Similarly, no numeric literals representing values that might be later changed appear directly in the calculations; instead, each is defined as a named constant for ease of future program maintenance. Standards such as these are important to adopt to produce programs that are easy to understand and easy to modify.

At this point, if this chapter represents your first real introduction to RPG IV, you are probably feeling overwhelmed by the large number of features discussed in the chapter. Although it may seem as though you must absorb a vast amount of new information, you will find that you will adapt very rapidly to those minor changes that are based on enlargements or re-arrangements of specifications. For those changes that represent features entirely new to RPG (e.g., built-in functions, pointers, time data types), as long as you are aware that they are now available, you can begin to feel comfortable with them as the need to use them in your programs arises.

Chapter Summary

RPG IV enhancements to RPG/400 include longer variable names, mixed-case entry, and 100-position specification lines. The new compiler interprets completely blank lines, lines with just a specification type in position 6, and lines with a specification type in position 6 and an asterisk in position 7 as comment lines. Extension Specifications have been eliminated, and data definition has been consolidated on the new specification type, Definition Specifications, which can be used to define tables and arrays, named constants, data structures, and stand-alone fields. CL command CVTRPGSRC converts pre-RPG IV source code to RPG IV syntax to minimize conversion efforts.

File Specifications, Definition Specifications, Calculation Specifications, and Output Specifications now offer continuation lines so code that will not fit on a single line can easily be carried over to additional lines. The use of keywords has replaced many positional entries on the specification forms. Moreover, the longer specification lines allow calculation operations to be up to six positions long; concomitant with the expansion, operations such as EXCPT, RETRN, and OCUR are no longer abbreviated and instead appear as EXCEPT, RETURN, and OCCUR.

A new assignment operation, EVAL, uses free-form expressions to determine the value to be assigned to the target field. New variants of decision operations (IF, WHEN) and looping operations (DOU, DOW) similarly allow conditions to be expressed as free-form expressions.

RPG IV introduces new data types, including DBCS (Double Byte Character Set or Graphic), basing pointers, procedure pointers, date, time, and timestamp. Three new operations, ADDDUR, SUBDUR, and EXTRACT facilitate manipulation of the three date data types; operations MOVE, MOVEL, and MOVEA have extensions that allow you to use them to assign numeric or character values to date, time, and timestamp data items (and vice versa).

RPG now includes eight built-in functions. %TRIM, %TRIML, %TRIMR, and %SUBST are functions used primarily for string manipulation, while functions %ADDR and %PADDR return addresses for basing pointers and procedure pointers, respectively. You can use function %ELEM to determine the number of elements in an array or in a multiple-occurrence data structure, while %SIZE returns the number of bytes in a field or constant.

Compiling now creates a program module (type *MODULE), rather than an executable program (type *PGM). A module needs to go through a binding step to turn it into an executable object. As part of this binding step, two or more modules that call one another can be bound together into a single *PGM; this process is called static binding, and its use results in better runtime performance than dynamic binding. Program modules to be statically bound require the use of the new CALLB operation (rather than the CALL operation) to invoke one another.

Many of RPG IV's new features let you develop a programming style that emphasizes ease of understanding and program maintainability that was not possible in earlier versions of the language.

Terms

basing pointer	Double Byte Character Set	procedure pointer
built-in function	(DBCS) data type	program module
case sensitive	dynamic binding	stand-alone field
continuation line	extended factor 2 format	static binding
data type	free-form	time data type
date data type	keywords	timestamp data type
Definition Specifications	mixed-case entry	

Discussion/Review Questions

1. What factors served as impetus to the development of RPG IV? Does the new version of the language completely quiet criticisms of RPG as a language? Why or why not?

2. What features of RPG IV represent innovations to RPG, in contrast to a reworking of concepts present in earlier versions of the language?

3. Could/should you use EVAL to determine the difference between two dates? Explain your answer.

4. Discuss the pros and cons of using the new operations IF, WHEN, DOW, and DOU.

5. Why do you suppose IBM introduced free-form entry on the Calculation Specifications through the EVAL operation, while retaining much of the fixed-position notation of RPG as a whole?

6. Do you think that the use of indicators is diminished or increased as a result of RPG IV? Support your answer.

7. What's the difference between CALL and CALLB?

8. What is the value of allowing the definition of stand-alone fields on Definition Specifications?

Exercises

To increase your understanding of the differences between RPG/400 and RPG IV, rework the following exercises from earlier chapters, this time making use of appropriate features offered by RPG IV.

Chapter	Exercises
3	1, 2, 3, 4
4	3
9	1, 2, 3, 4
13	3, 4

Programming Assignments

1. Wexler University wants a report showing faculty members' earnings and length of employment in years. The data is contained in physical file WUINSTP (see Appendix D). The printer spacing chart of the desired report is shown below. Note that you are to list the faculty members in order of increasing salary within their respective departments. Also note that the names on the report represent a trimmed concatenation of last name, comma, and first name (e.g., Doe, John). The number of years employed should represent the number of whole years completed when you consider date of hire and the current system date.

```
         1         2         3         4         5         6         7         8
1234567890123456789012345678901234567890123456789012345678901234567890123456789012345678901234567890

   XX/XX/XX                        WEXLER UNIVERSITY                   PAGE XX0X
                               FACULTY EARNINGS REPORT

                                                               NO. YEARS
       DEPT.        NAME                    RANK  SEX   SALARY   EMPLOYED

       XXX    XXXXXXXXXXXXXXXXXXXXXXXXXX     X     X   XXX,XX0.XX    0X
              XXXXXXXXXXXXXXXXXXXXXXXXXX     X     X   XXX,XX0.XX    0X

       XXX    XXXXXXXXXXXXXXXXXXXXXXXXXX     X     X   XXX,XX0.XX    0X
              XXXXXXXXXXXXXXXXXXXXXXXXXX     X     X   XXX,XX0.XX    0X
              XXXXXXXXXXXXXXXXXXXXXXXXXX     X     X   XXX,XX0.XX    0X
```

2. GTC needs a listing of all customers who owe a balance and have not sent in a payment within the past 30 days. They would like this listing to be in descending order by amount owed, so they can concentrate on collecting from those customers who owe them the most money first. The data upon which you are to base the report is stored in GTC's customer master file GTCSTP (see Appendix D). The desired listing format appears below; the customer name should be a trimmed concatenation of first name followed by last name (with a blank separator).

```
         1         2         3         4         5         6         7         8
1234567890123456789012345678901234567890123456789012345678901234567890123456789012345678901234567890
   XX/XX/XX            GTC OVERDUE PAYMENTS LISTING        PAGE XX0X

       CUSTOMER               PHONE          AMOUNT       DAYS SINCE
         NAME                 NUMBER          OWED       LAST PAYMENT

   XXXXXXXXXXXXXXXXXXXXXXXXXX  (XXX) XXX-XXXX   X,XX0.XX       X0X
   XXXXXXXXXXXXXXXXXXXXXXXXXX  (XXX) XXX-XXXX   X,XX0.XX       X0X
   XXXXXXXXXXXXXXXXXXXXXXXXXX  (XXX) XXX-XXXX   X,XX0.XX       X0X
   XXXXXXXXXXXXXXXXXXXXXXXXXX  (XXX) XXX-XXXX   X,XX0.XX       X0X
```

3. CompuSell wants an aged accounts receivable report of customer balances, based on the date of the last order placed and the balance due. The report should only list those customers with a positive balance due. The amount still owed by each customer should appear in the appropriate column of the report based on when (s)he last placed an order. Data for the report resides in file CSCSTP (see Appendix D). The printer spacing chart below indicates the desired report layout. Notice that management wants column totals to print.

Programming Assignments Continued

Programming Assignments continued

```
          1         2         3         4         5         6         7         8
 12345678901234567890123456789012345678901234567890123456789012345678901234567890
     XX/XX/XX                       COMPUSELL                    PAGE XX0X
                    AGED ACCOUNTS RECEIVABLE REPORT

                    --------------------AMOUNTS OWED--------------------
       CUST. NO.    0-30 DAYS     31-60 DAYS     61-90 DAYS     OVER 90 DAYS

        XXXXX       X,XXX.X0      X,XXX.X0       X,XXX.X0       X,XXX.X0
        XXXXX       X,XXX.X0      X,XXX.X0       X,XXX.X0       X,XXX.X0
        XXXXX       X,XXX.X0      X,XXX.X0       X,XXX.X0       X,XXX.X0
        XXXXX       X,XXX.X0      X,XXX.X0       X,XXX.X0       X,XXX.X0

        TOTALS      XXX,XX0.XX    XXX,XX0.XX     XXX,XX0.XX     XXX,XX0.XX
```

4. Wexler University needs a program to clean up its student master file, WUSTDP (see Appendix D). It wants to move records of all students who graduated more than five years ago to file WUSTDG and remove them from WUSTDP. The school also wants to archive records of inactive students (those who have not yet graduated but who have not taken a course within the past five years — based on data in file WUCRDP, the earned credits file) into file WUSTDI and remove them from WUSTDP. Note that the archive files do not exist; you will have to create them before you run your program. Both files should have the same record layout as WUSTDP.

In addition to writing the records to the appropriate archive file and removing them from WUSTDP, Wexler also wants the program to generate two report listings to serve as an audit trail. One report should list those students removed to WUSTDG, while the other should list those students moved to the inactive file WUSTDI. These reports should simply echo the record data and not be broken down into individual fields of data. The report layouts are shown below. In each layout, X...X represents a 126-byte record image.

Report 1:

```
XX/XX/XX    WEXLER UNIVERSITY GRADUATE ARCHIVE REPORT    PAGE XX0X

RECORDS REMOVED FROM FILE WUSTDP AND STORED IN FILE WUSTDG:

X........................................................................X
X........................................................................X
```

Report 2:

```
XX/XX/XX    WEXLER UNIVERSITY INACTIVE STUDENT ARCHIVE REPORT    PAGE XX0X

RECORDS REMOVED FROM FILE WUSTDP AND STORED IN FILE WUSTDI:

X........................................................................X
X........................................................................X
```

Appendix A

Developing Programs on the AS/400

As described in Chapter 1, once you have written a program, you must enter it on the system, compile it, and then run the program. This Appendix is designed to introduce you to those features of the AS/400 that you need to know to complete the above tasks.

The AS/400 has a set of commands, called Control Language (CL), that allows you to direct its activities. It also has a series of menus that allow you to work on the AS/400 without knowing CL. This Appendix introduces you to two alternate menus — the Programmer Menu and Programming Development Manager — that you can use to complete your assignments.

Before you look at these menus, you need a basic understanding of AS/400 terminology. The AS/400 uses libraries to organize stored information, called objects. A library is analogous to a PC directory (and is itself an object). The AS/400 stores many kinds of objects — data files, job descriptions, commands, output queues, programs, and so on. The type associated with an object determines what kinds of actions can be performed on the object. All object types begin with an asterisk (*).

You will be working with two primary kinds of objects: *PGM and *FILE. An object with type *PGM is a program of machine-executable code. When you call an object with this type, you are telling the computer to carry out the instructions contained in the object.

Objects with type *FILE are files; files are further differentiated by attributes, which categorize the nature of the file: The attribute PF-SRC indicates the file is a source physical file that contains source code. Attribute PF-DTA indicates that the object is a physical database file; attribute LF indicates that the object is a logical database file.

The contents of all files, regardless of attribute, can be organized into members. A member is like a subdivision of a file. A file must exist before members can be added to it. Each program that you enter will be stored as a member within a source physical file; when you compile that member (or program), you will create a *PGM object with the same name as the member.

It is not unusual for installations to store their source code in libraries separate from their object (executable) code, although in the typical school environment each student has a single library for storing all his/her own work. Your instructor will supply you with the name of the source file and the library name within which you will be working.

The Programmer Menu

The **Programmer Menu** is easy to use, although it is not as versatile as the **Programming Development Manager**. How you reach this menu will depend on how your user profile is set up; if you see the AS/400 Main Menu upon sign-on, select Option 5, Programming, and then at the resulting Programming panel select Option 1, Programmer Menu. You should see the following display:

```
                        Programmer Menu
                                                System:    S1034373
        Select one of the following:
            1. Start AS/400 Data File Utility
            2. Work with AS/400 Query
            3. Create an object from a source file    object name, type, pgm for CMD
            4. Call a program                         program name
            5. Run a command                          command
            6. Submit a job                           (job name), , ,(command)
            7. Go to a menu                           menu name
            8. Edit a source file member              (srcmbr), (type)
            9. Design display format using SDA        (srcmbr), ,(mode)
           90. Sign off                               (*nolist, *list)

        Selection . . . . .  ___          Parm . . . .  _____
        Type  . . . . . . .  _____      Parm 2 . . .  _____
        Command . . . . . .  _____

        Source file . . . .  _____   Source library . . . . . . .   *LIBL
        Object library . .   _____   Job description  . . . . . .   *USRPRF


        F3=Exit        F4=Prompt              F6=Display messages    F10=Command entry
        F12=Cancel     F14=Work with submitted jobs                  F18=Work with output
```

The **Programmer Menu** presents a list of options. You need to use just three of these options to enter, compile, and run your program.

TO ENTER/EDIT A PROGRAM: Select Option 8 (Edit a Source File Member) from the menu. Key the name you wish to call your program (the member name) on the line to the right of the first Parm prompt. Before pressing the Enter key, make sure that the following entries on the bottom of the screen are complete: Source Library; Source File; Object Library; and Type; and use the arrow, tab, or field-exit keys to position your cursor to the proper location for entry.

TO COMPILE A PROGRAM: Select Option 3 (Create an Object From a Source File) from the menu. The Member Name, Type, Source File and Library, and Object Library entries must be present before you press the Enter key.

Most systems are set up to compile in batch, so that your workstation is free for other tasks while the system is compiling your program. However, your program will not be ready to run until the compiling has completed. Wait for a message-waiting sign at the bottom of your screen and make sure the compiling has successfully completed before running the program. The compiler generates a compile listing of your program (and errors, if any were found) that will be in your output queue when the compiling has completed.

If you have previously compiled the program successfully, so that an object already exists for that program, the system will prompt you to delete the object and then recompile by pressing F11.

TO RUN A PROGRAM: Select Option 4 (Call a program) from the menu. Because this option is interactive, your workstation will be locked up until the program completes.

In addition to the menu options, you will use some of the function keys noted at the bottom of the screen.

TO VIEW OR PRINT OUTPUT: Pressing F18 will display your output queue. The output queue contains reports generated by the system or by your programs. These reports are called spooled files, because they are stored temporarily on disk rather than automatically being sent to the printer. You can display these reports, delete them, or release them to the printer by entering the appropriate number to the left of the spooled file. For more detailed information on printing, refer to the printing instructions within the next section.

TO DISPLAY MESSAGES: F6 shows you a list of any messages the system has sent you.

Programming Development Manager (PDM)

PDM is a little more complex to use than the Programmer Menu, but it provides you with much more flexibility for accessing and manipulating libraries, objects, and members. This discussion focuses only on those features of PDM you need to complete your assignments.

To access PDM from the Main Menu of the AS/400, first select Option 5, Programming and at the resulting Programming panel, select Option 2, Programming Development Manager (PDM). You will see the PDM menu on the following page:

```
                    AS/400 Programming Development Manager (PDM)

  Select one of the following:

        1. Work with libraries
        2. Work with objects
        3. Work with members

        9. Work with user-defined options




  Selection or command
  ===>_____
  _____
  F3=Exit       F4=Prompt      F9=Retrieve         F10=Command entry
  F12=Cancel    F18=Change defaults
```

TO ENTER/EDIT A PROGRAM: Select Option 3, Work with Members, from the PDM menu. You will see the resulting display:

```
                      Specify Members to Work With

  Type choices, press Enter

     File  . . . . . . . . .   CMD*_____    Name, F4 for list

       Library . . . . . . .   ATEST_____  *LIBL, *CURLIB, name

     Member:
       Name  . . . . . . . .   *ALL_____    *ALL, name, *generic*
       Type  . . . . . . . .   *ALL_____    *ALL, type, *generic*, *BLANK








  F3=Exit     F4=Prompt     F5=Refresh     F12=Cancel
```

You may either enter the desired source file or position your cursor on the file prompt and press F4 to get a list of the possible files. Once you have entered or selected the desired file, the system will display all the members of that file.

```
                        Work with Members Using PDM
 File  . . . . .     QCLSRC____
   Library . . . .   WORKLIB___             Position to  . . . . .  _____

 Type options, press Enter.
   2=Edit           3=Copy        4=Delete        5=Display       6=Print
   7=Rename         8=Display description         9=Save          13=Change text ...

 Opt  Member       Type          Text
  __   AP0010C      CLP_____   Audit report on daily entries_____
  __   ATTNPGM      CLP_____   ATTN pgm for group jobs_____
  __   CAMON        CLP_____   message monitor_____
  __   CHGPRTFC     CLP_____   Find/then change print files on System_____
  __   CL0010C      CLP_____   Chg security on selected files_____
  __   CLCMPSRC     CLP_____   check source last change dates in version libs____
  __   COMPC        CLP_____   Compare_2_files_up_to_1024_in_length_____
  __   CONFIG       CLP_____   _____
                                                                   More...

 Parameters or command
 ===> _____
 F3=Exit           F4=Prompt              F5=Refresh          F6=Create
 F9=Retrieve       F10=Command entry      F23=More options    F24=More keys
```

From this screen you can select a source member to edit, print, or compile by keying in a 2, 6, or 14 adjacent to the member you want to work with. (Note that Option 14 does not appear on the initial screen; pressing F23, more options, reveals this and other additional options for working with members. However, an option does not have to appear on the screen to use it — provided it is a valid option.)

TO EDIT/ENTER A MEMBER: To Edit an existing member, enter a 2 to the left of the member name to bring that member into SEU and continue work on it. If you are creating a new member, pressing F6 (Create) will take you to the Start SEU screen. You will need to enter the source file name, the member name, and the type.

TO COMPILE A MEMBER: Enter 14 to the left of the name of the member you want to compile. If the compiled object already exists, a Confirm Compile of Member screen (see following page) appears; to compile your new version, you must respond Yes to "Delete existing object".

```
                        Confirm Compile of Member

The following object already exists for the compile operation:

    Object which exists  . . . . . . . . :    ADDL
        Library  . . . . . . . . . . . . :      SRCLIB
    Object type  . . . . . . . . . . . . :    *PGM

    Member to compile  . . . . . . . . . :    ADDL
    File . . . . . . . . . . . . . . . . :    CMDSRC
        Library  . . . . . . . . . . . . :      ATEST

Type choice, press Enter.
Press F12=Cancel to return and not perform the compile operation.

    Delete existing object . . . . . . . .    Y    Y=Yes, N=No




F12=Cancel
```

Your program will not be ready to run until the system returns a message to you that the compile completed successfully. If the message says that the compile ended abnormally, you must correct program errors and then recompile the program.

TO RUN A PROGRAM: Select Work with Objects from the PDM screen. The resulting screen will display a list of objects in your library. Enter 16 in the left column adjacent to the program object you want to run. The following figure shows the Work with Objects Using PDM screen. Note that although 16 does not appear as an initial option, pressing F23 would reveal it (and other options, as well).

```
                          Work with Objects Using PDM

    Library . . . . .   QUSRSYS___       Position to . . . . . . . .   _____
                                         Position to type . . . . .    _____

    Type options, press Enter.
      2=Change      3=Copy         4=Delete      5=Display      7=Rename
      8=Display description         9=Save       10=Restore     11=Move ...

    Opt  Object       Type      Attribute    Text
    __   QAALERT      *FILE     PF-DTA       Data base file for alerts processing
    __   QAALHLSN     *FILE     LF           Logical file for alerts processing
    __   QAALRCLC     *FILE     LF           Logical file for alerts processing
    __   QAALRSCN     *FILE     LF           Logical file for alerts processing
    __   QAALRSCT     *FILE     LF           Logical file for alerts processing
    __   QAALSOC      *FILE     PF-DTA       Data base file for SOC processing
    __   QAEABKMT     *FILE     PF-DTA       System Delivered Education Bookmark F
    __   QAEACRSI     *FILE     PF-DTA       System Delivered Education Course Ind
                                                                            More...

    Parameters or command
    ===> _____
    F3=Exit          F4=Prompt            F5=Refresh            F6=Create
    F9=Retrieve      F10=Command entry    F23=More options      F24=More keys
```

Alternately, you can enter CALL progname on any command line.

TO VIEW OR PRINT OUTPUT: Type sp in any option column on any of PDM's screens to obtain a list of your spooled files. (You can also key in WRKSPLF on any command line.) You will see the screen shown below, which includes a list of all spooled output.

```
                          Work with Printer Output
                                                        System:    S1034373
    User . . . . . .   YAEGER        Name, *ALL, F4 for list

    Type options below, then press Enter.  To work with printers, press F22.
      2=Change   3=Hold   4=Delete   5=Display           6=Release   7=Message
      9=Work with printing status    10=Start printing   11=Restart printing

           Printer/
    Opt    Output         Status
           Not Assigned
           REMUSRS        Held (use Opt 6)
           GENUSRS2       Held (use Opt 6)
           GENUSERS3      Held (use Opt 6)
           GENUSRS3       Held (use Opt 6)
           GENUSRS3       Held (use Opt 6)
           QSYSPRT        Held (use Opt 6)
           QSYSPRT        Held (use Opt 6)



    F1=Help    F3=Exit        F5=Refresh    F6=Completed printed output
    F11=Dates/pages/forms      F12=Cancel    F22=Work with printers    F24=More keys
```

You can see the dates, times, and pages of the output by pressing F11. The screen below shows the result of this action.

```
                        Work with Printer Output
                                                  System:   S1034373
User . . . . . .   YAEGER        Name, *ALL, F4 for list

Type options below, then press Enter.  To work with printers, press F22.
   2=Change   3=Hold   4=Delete   5=Display          6=Release   7=Message
   9=Work with printing status      10=Start printing   11=Restart printing

      Printer/
Opt   Output      Date      Time      Pages   Copies   Form Type
      Not Assigned
      REMUSRS     01/08/93  11:22:10    3       1      *STD
      GENUSRS2    01/08/93  11:35:22    4       1      *STD
      GENUSERS3   03/18/93  13:45:30    3       1      *STD
      GENUSRS3    03/24/93  13:52:10    3       1      *STD
      GENUSRS3    03/24/93  13:56:37    3       1      *STD
      QSYSPRT     04/08/93  14:00:14    1       1      *STD
      QSYSPRT     04/08/93  14:01:10    1       1      *STD


                                                          More...
F1=Help   F3=Exit   F5=Refresh    F6=Completed printer output
F14=Select other printer output   F22=Work with printers   F24=More keys
Printer output REMUSRS moved to printer PRT01.
```

To look at a spooled file, enter 5 adjacent to the file. To delete a spooled file, enter 4, and then press Enter at the resulting screen to confirm the deletion request. If you want to print a file, depending on how your system is set up, you may first have to assign the file to a printer by entering 10 adjacent to the file name. At the resulting screen (see below), enter PRT01 — or the name your instructor provides you.

```
                    Assign Output to a Printer

    Printer output . . :   REMUSRS

This printer output is not assigned to a printer.
To print the output, type the printer name below and then press Enter.

    Printer  . . . . . .  _____   Name, F4 for list
```

You will return to the Work with Printer Output screen, and the message *Attempting to start should appear next to the spooled file you chose to print. Pressing F5 (refresh) will show you the progress the system is making in printing the file.

TO DISPLAY MESSAGES: Type DSPMSG on the command line and press Enter. Or type dm in any option column of your current screen.

Appendix B

Source Entry Utility (SEU)

SEU Overview

RPG programs generally are entered into the computer interactively through an AS/400 editor called Source Entry Utility (SEU). An editor is like a limited word processor, in that it allows you to easily enter, modify, and delete text. Because the editor has been designed specifically to facilitate entry of program source code, it includes some special features, such as line prompting and syntax checking, that would not be available in a standard word processor.

Source programs are stored as members of a source file. The file generally used to store RPG programs is QRPGSRC; the member type is RPG. The name that you supply your program is the name that identifies that member. You can enter SEU by selecting Option 8 from the Programmer Menu, from PDM's Work with Members screen, or by directly entering the command STRSEU (Start SEU) on a command line. You can use SEU to create a new member or to edit, browse, or print an existing member.

When you enter SEU to create a new member, you see a screen like that on the following page. The SEU command line is at the top of the screen; the middle of the screen is used for code entry; and the bottom of the screen reminds you of enabled function keys and their uses and delivers system messages to you.

```
Columns . . . :   1  71              Edit                       BIS264/SOURCE
SEU==>                                                                 DEMO
FMT F    .....FFilenameIPEAF....RlenLK1AIOvKlocEDevice+......KExit++Entry+A....U
         *************** Beginning of data ***************************************
. . . . . . .
. . . . . . .
. . . . . . .
. . . . . . .
. . . . . . .
. . . . . . .
. . . . . . .
. . . . . . .
. . . . . . .
. . . . . . .
. . . . . . .
. . . . . . .
. . . . . . .
. . . . . . .
. . . . . . .
. . . . . . .
         ***************** End of data *******************************************
   F3=Exit   F4=Prompt   F5=Refresh   F9=Retrieve    F10=Cursor
   F16=Repeat find       F17=Repeat change           F24=More keys
 Member DEMO added to file BIS264/SOURCE.
```

Press Enter to remove the blank lines between the beginning and end of data lines. You are ready to begin entering your program. As you enter your program, SEU tries to detect syntax errors in your code. When you enter a line containing such an error, the error will appear in reverse video and the system provides a brief explanation of the error on the message line of the screen. When you have successfully corrected the error, the entry will display normally.

SEU, like other parts of the AS/400, has lavish on-line help available. The help is cursor-position sensitive. When you find yourself in trouble, or don't know what response is appropriate, try using the Help key.

Using Prompts

SEU can provide you with prompts to facilitate your code entry. To obtain a line prompted appropriately for File Specifications, key IPF (Insert with Prompts for File Specifications) to the left on the Beginning Data line and press Enter. A prompted line appropriate for File specifications appears at the bottom of the screen. Enter your first File Specification, using the Field Exit key to move from entry to entry. When you have keyed in the first line, press Enter. SEU assigns the line a sequence number and moves it to the main portion of the screen; it also provides another prompted line for your next File Specification.

```
⎛  Columns . . . :    1  71              Edit                    BIS264/SOURCE
   SEU==>                                                                DEMO
   FMT F  .....FFilenameIPEAF....RlenLK1AIOvKlocEDevice+......KExit++Entry+A....U
          *************** Beginning of data ************************************
   0001.00      FDEMO   IF  F    100           DISK
   .......
   Prompt type . . .    F       Sequence number . . .  .......

                 File          File         End of                    File
   Filename      Type      Designation       File      Sequence      Format

   Record      Mode of       Length of       Record
   Length      Processing    Key Field    Address Type

     File              Overflow     Key Field     Extn
   Organization        Indicator    Start Loc     Code     Device
                                                            DISK
                                              File          File
   Continuation    Exit    Entry    Addition      Condition


   F3=Exit   F4=Prompt   F5=Refresh        F11=Previous record
   F12=Cancel               F23=Select prompt  F24=More keys
⎝
```

Each RPG specification form has one or more appropriate prompt formats available in SEU. (A summary of the prompt formats appears below.) To change the prompt format, press F23 and select the new format you want. Once selected, a prompt form will continue until you press F23 for a new prompt, F12 to cancel the prompt and return to the Edit display, or press Enter without entering anything. This latter method also returns your cursor to the Edit display.

RPG Prompt Formats

H:	Control (H)
F:	File
FC:	File Continuation/Subfile
FK:	File, Continuation
FX:	File, External Description
U:	Auto Report
E:	Extension
L:	Line Counter
I:	Input, Record ID
IX:	Input, Record ID-External
J:	Input, Field Description
JX:	Input, External Field
DS:	Data Structure
SS:	Data Structure Subfield
SV:	Data Structure Subfield
C:	Calculation
O:	Output, File ID & Control

RPG Prompt Formats

OD:	Output, Disk
P:	Output, field/constant
N:	Named Constant
*:	Comment lines

Working Within the Edit Display

Sometimes it is more efficient to enter or edit code without the help of the prompts. The list of features below summarizes what you can do in edit display mode and how to do it.

Position cursor: Use arrow keys to move within a screen; use Roll keys to page up or down between screens.

Move to a specific line of code: Key the sequence number of the line you want to move to over the sequence number of a line currently on the screen and press Enter. The source will be repositioned to display the source code containing the desired line.

Insert within a line: The Insert key toggles insertion on.

Delete within a line: Use the Delete key to delete individual characters.

All the bold letter commands described below must be keyed over the sequence number of the line(s) involved in the operation.

Insert a line: Key an **I** on a line and press Enter. A blank line will appear below the line you are on.

Delete a line: Key a **D** on the line you want to delete and press Enter.

Delete a block of lines: Key **DD** on the first line of the block, move the cursor to the last line of the block, again key **DD**, and press Enter.

Move a line: Key **M** on the line to be moved, reposition the cursor to the desired location, key either **A** or **B**, and press Enter. The line will be moved either A(fter) or B(efore) the target line, depending on what you keyed.

Move a block of lines: Key **MM** on the first line of the block to be moved, position the cursor to the last line of the block and key **MM**; then position the cursor to the target line, key **A** or **B**, and press Enter. The block will be moved either A(fter) or B(efore) the target line, depending on what you keyed.

Copy a line: Key **C** on the line to be copied, reposition the cursor to the desired location, key either **A** or **B**, and press Enter. The line will be copied either A(fter) or B(efore) the target line, depending on what you keyed.

Copy a block of lines: Key **CC** on the first line of the block to be copied, position the cursor to the last line of the block and key **CC**; then position the cursor to the target line, key **A** or **B**, and press Enter. The block will be copied either A(fter) or B(efore) the target line, depending on what you keyed.

Repeat a line: Key an **RP** and press Enter to repeat the line once immediately below the line on which you entered the R.

Repeat a line _x_ times: Key **RPx**, where _x_ is any number, and press Enter to repeat the line _x_ number of times immediately below the line on which you entered the command.

Prompt an entered line: Key **Pf** on the line, where _f_ is the prompt format you want, and press Enter.

Insert prompted lines: Key **IPf**, where _f_ is the prompt format you want, and press Enter. This will return you to prompted mode.

Function Keys in SEU

Several function keys are active within SEU. Those you will use most often are summarized below.

F3: Used to go to the SEU exit screen (described below).

F4: Places the line the cursor is on when the key is pressed into an appropriate prompt format.

F10: Toggles the cursor between the SEU command line and the edit display.

F12: Cancels the current action; generally used to return to display editing from a prompted format.

F13: Takes you to a screen that allows you to change the SEU defaults for the current session. Among other things, allows you to enable or disable lowercase alphabetic entry.

F15: Splits the screen in two to allow you to browse a second member or a compile output while working in your source code, or to copy code from one member into another.

F23: Displays all possible prompt formats and allows you to select the one you want to activate.

SEU's Command Line

To position the cursor on the command line, press F10. Once there, you can enter an SEU command. Some of the possible commands are:

SAVE: To save the member without exiting SEU.

CANCEL: To leave SEU without saving and return to the previous menu.

TOP or **T**: To move to the top of your source member.

BOTTOM or **B**: To move to the bottom of your source member.

FIND or **F**: To search for a string of characters in the source member. The string does not need to be enclosed in apostrophes unless it contains blanks, special values, apostrophes, or quotation marks.

CHANGE or **C**: To change a string of characters to some other string.

Working with a Split Screen

Pressing F15 takes you to a screen that allows you to divide your screen into two halves, with your current member on the top and another member or spool file on the bottom.

```
                          Browse/Copy Options

      Type choices, press Enter.

         Selection . . . . . . . . . .    2          1=Member
                                                     2=Spool file
                                                     3=Output queue
         Copy all records  . . . . . .    N          Y=Yes, N=No
         Browse/copy member  . . . . .    SALESRPT    Name, F4 for list
           File  . . . . . . . . . .      QRPGSRC     Name, F4 for list
             Library . . . . . . . . .      YAEGER    Name, *CURLIB, *LIBL

         Browse/copy spool file  . . . .  SALESRPT    Name, F4 for list
           Job . . . . . . . . . . . .    SALESRPT    Name
             User  . . . . . . . . . .      YAEGER    Name, F4 for list
             Job number  . . . . . . .      *LAST     Number, *LAST
           Spool number  . . . . . . .      *LAST     Number, *LAST, *ONLY

         Display output queue  . . . . .  QPRINT      Name, *ALL
           Library . . . . . . . . . .      *LIBL     Name, *CURLIB, *LIBL


      F3=Exit        F4=Prompt       F5=Refresh       F12=Cancel
      F13=Change session defaults    F14=Find/Change options
```

At the above screen, if you choose Option 1, member, you then should enter the name of the member you want to appear in the lower half of the screen. This option is very useful for copying portions of code from one member to another, or for checking on field names in a database file while entering a program that uses that file. To copy lines from one member to the other in split-screen mode, use the same technique as when you are working within a single member; the arrow keys will take your cursor across the mid-screen boundary. The roll keys affect the member in either the top or the bottom half of the screen, depending on where your cursor is positioned.

If you choose Option 2, spool file, from the Browse Options Display, the default values are such that the most recent compile listing of this member is brought into the lower half of the display. This feature is very useful for correcting compile errors, because it allows you to scroll through the

```
Columns . . . :   1  71              Edit                      YAEGER/QRPGSRC
SEU==>                                                             SALESRPT
*************** Beginning of data ********************************************
0001.00      F***********************************************************************
0002.00      F* This program produces a weekly sales report.  The report
0003.00      F* data come directly from input file SALES.
0004.00      F*     Author: J. Yeager     Date Written: 10/10/92
0005.00      F*
0006.00      F* Indicator 90: End-of-file SALES


Columns . . . :   1  71            Browse          Spool file . . :   SALESRPT
SEU==>
*************** Beginning of data ***************************✦************
0000.01  5738RG1 V2R1MØ  910329            IBM SAA RPG/400
0000.02  Compiler . . . . . . . . . . . :  IBM SAA RPG/400
0000.03  Command options:
0000.04    Program  . . . . . . . . . . :  YAEGER/SALESRPT
0000.05    Source file  . . . . . . . . :  *LIBL/QRPGSRC
0000.06    Source member  . . . . . . . :  *PGM



 F3=Exit   F5=Refresh    F9=Retrieve  F10=Cursor    F12=Cancel
 F16=Repeat find         F17=Repeat change          F24=More keys
```

compile listing and make corrections in your source member based on the errors noted in the listing without the need for a hard-copy version of the compile listing.

Exiting SEU

When you press F3 to exit SEU, an exit screen (shown on the following page) appears that allows you to accept preset default values or change them, as you wish. By changing defaults you can save the member with a name different from that with which you began the editing session, or you can cancel editing changes by specifying N to "Change/create member". You also can get a printout of your member without having to compile it by changing the Print Member option to Y. Note that the "Return to editing" default is N if you exited with no syntax errors in your source but Y if errors remained. You can exit with errors remaining if you change the default to N.

```
                                        Exit

   Type choices, press Enter.

      Change/create member  . . . . . . .    N          Y=Yes, N=No
         Member  . . . . . . . . . . . .     SALESRPT   Name, F4 for list
         File  . . . . . . . . . . . . .     QRPGSRC    Name, F4 for list
            Library . . . . . . . . . . .       YAEGER  Name
         Text  . . . . . . . . . . . . .

      Resequence member . . . . . . . .      Y          Y=Yes, N=No
         Start . . . . . . . . . . . .       0001.00    0000.01-9999.99
         Increment . . . . . . . . . .       01.00      00.01-99.99

   Print member  . . . . . . . . . .        N          Y=Yes, N=No

   Return to editing . . . . . . . .        N          Y=Yes, N=No

   Go to member list . . . . . . . .        N          Y=Yes, N=No



   F3=Exit    F4=Prompt    F5=Refresh    F12=Cancel
```

Appendix C

Program Testing and Debugging

A major portion of a programmer's time is spent ensuring that the program (s)he has written is, in fact, accurately producing the desired results. This procedure involves carefully checking the program's correctness and fixing any errors the checking uncovers — a process often referred to as "debugging."

Syntax Errors

Program errors fall into one of two broad categories: syntax errors and logic errors. Syntax errors are errors in your usage of the programming language. Because the system points out these kinds of errors for you, they are simple to detect and easy to correct, once you have mastered the rules of the language in which you are programming.

On the AS/400, SEU detects some kinds of syntax errors as you enter program statements. For example, failing to make a required entry within a specification line, forgetting to right-adjust a numeric entry within its allocated columns, or including an invalid value in a column (e.g., an F instead of an I, O, U, or C for file type on the File Specifications) will cause SEU to display the erroneous entry in reverse video, display an error message on the bottom of the screen, and lock the keyboard. You will need to press the reset key before the system allows you to proceed. Moreover, until you correct the error, it will remain in reverse video as a reminder of a problem.

Once you have completely entered your program and have eliminated all syntax errors detected by SEU, your next step is to compile the program. Compiling is a process that translates the statements in your source member into an object of machine-code instructions the AS/400 can then execute. In attempting to complete this translation process, the RPG/400 compiler often detects additional syntax errors unnoticed by SEU.

If your program contains compile errors, the system sends you a message that your job ended abnormally. You can find the cause(s) of the difficulties by printing or displaying the compile listing, a report of the compilation generated by the compiler. A compile listing includes a listing of your program. The compiler numbers the program statements sequentially in increments of 100 and also indicates the date on which the statement was entered (or modified).

Within the program listing, the compiler also indicates how it is interpreting any nesting of structured operators by inserting B at the beginning of the structure, E at the end of the structure, and an X for any ELSE it encounters within the structure. It also prints a digit with each of these codes representing the level of nesting the structure establishes. By cross-checking these digits, you can make sure that the computer has matched the beginnings and ends of the structures as you had intended.

The compiler also provides a cross-reference listing to help you diagnose problems. A cross-reference listing is a list of all fields and indicators used in your program showing every program statement within which each of the fields or indicators occurs. The statement defining the field is annotated with D (for define), while any statement within which the field or indicator's value is changed is annotated with M (for modify). This listing can be useful for quickly locating field and/or indicator usage within your program listing.

If your program contains syntax errors, the compiler notes errors by inserting an asterisk and a numeric error code either under the line in error or within the cross-reference listing. At the end of the compile listing, a message summary lists these error codes and provides a message detailing the cause of the problem. Problems vary in severity. A message with a severity of 00 is an informational message noting a condition that will not prevent the program from compiling; errors with severity of 10 or above need to be corrected before the program will compile normally.

Once you have obtained a "clean compile," that is, once the system has successfully translated your program into machine language, you can begin to check for logic errors your program may contain.

Logic Errors

Logic errors are caused by faulty program design. You detect these kinds of errors by having the computer execute your program and then carefully checking the results of the execution. There are two broad classes of logic errors, sometimes called runtime errors and output errors.

Runtime Errors

Runtime errors are errors that prevent your program from reaching a normal end. Runtime errors are easy to detect: Either the program abruptly stops in the middle (an abend, or abnormal ending), or the program runs and runs and runs, until finally you or the operator intercedes to terminate the job. (This latter kind of a problem signals an infinite loop.) Although detecting the presence of a runtime error is not a problem, sometimes discovering the cause of the error can be difficult. Moreover, the kinds of logic problems that cause abends are different from those that cause infinite loops.

Diagnosing Abends

When your program ends abnormally, the system sends you an error message to inform you of the cause of the problem and where the problem occurred within your program. Sometimes these error messages are not completely clear; by putting your cursor on the message and pressing the

Help key you can obtain additional information about the problem. Typical causes of such runtime problems are trying to divide by zero, attempting to carry out a numeric operation on a field that contains non-numeric data, trying to reference an array element beyond the defined limits, or size, of the array, attempting to read past end-of-file, or trying to update a record before you have read a record.

Once you have located the problem statement and determined the nature of the problem, you often have to trace through your program logic to determine how your program allowed that problem to occur. For example, if program statement A DIV B C is causing an abnormal ending because of an attempt to divide by zero, you need to determine why field B has a value of zero at the time the system is attempting the division operation. Is B an input field? If so, have you forgotten to read a record prior to the division? Or, if B is a work field, have you neglected to assign it a non-zero value prior to the division? Or have you inadvertently Z-ADDed 0 to B at the wrong time in your program?

If you cannot locate the cause of the problem, you may find it useful to run the program in debug mode, discussed later in this appendix.

Diagnosing Infinite Loops

If you have had to cancel your job to prevent it from running forever, you know that you have an infinite loop within your program. An infinite loop is a faulty logic structure that causes the computer to repeat the same set of instructions over and over again, and that does not allow the computer to break out of the loop. The code below shows two obvious infinite loops.

```
         1         2         3         4         5         6         7
123456789012345678901234567890123456789012345678901234567890
         C* Obvious examples of infinite loops.
         C           LOOP      TAG
         C                     ADD  1         CNT
         C                     GOTO LOOP
         C                     ...
         C                     MOVE *OFF       *IN90
         C           *IN90     DOWEQ*OFF
         C                     ADD  1         CNT
         C                     ENDDO
```

In the examples above, the cause of the infinite looping is simple; the GOTO unconditionally (that is, always) transfers control up to the tag, while in the case of the DOWEQ, there is no statement within the loop that can change the value of *IN90 to *ON — the condition needed to end the loop.

Generally, the cause of an infinite loop within a real program is less obvious. The first thing to realize in trying to diagnose the cause of your problem is that you can narrow your focus to the iterative operations in your program: DOWxx, DOUxx, DO, and perhaps GOTO and CABxx (if you have used them to create loops). The second thing to realize is that somehow the condition that specifies when the looping should stop is not occurring. Forgetting to include a READ operation, for example, within a DOWxx loop that continues until end-of-file is reached will result in an infinite loop. Or forgetting to increment a counter in a count-controlled loop based on an operation other than DO will likewise prevent the loop from ever ending.

Finally, a common cause of infinite loops more easily over-looked is defining a counter too small. Study the example below to see if you can detect the cause of the infinite loop that would result if that program were run.

```
          1         2         3         4         5         6         7
 1234567890123456789012345678901234567890123456789012345678901234567890

        C                      Z-ADD0         CNT     20
        C           CNT        DOUEQ100
        C                      ...
        C                      ADD  1         CNT
        C                      ENDDO
```

The example results in an infinite loop because CNT can never attain a value of 100; because it is defined as 2 positions, with 0 decimals, the largest value CNT can store is 99. Adding 1 to 99 causes the resulting value, 100, to be truncated to 00.

Output Errors

The most insidious kinds of logic errors are those that do not cause abnormal program endings or infinite loops but simply result in incorrect output. Some of these kinds of errors are very obvious: neglecting to print heading lines on reports, for instance, or omitting an output entry that causes an entire column of information to be missing from a report. Other kinds of output errors are less easily detected and require careful checking by hand to discover. You are unlikely to notice errors in complex calculations, for example, if you simply scan the output visually.

Detecting Output Errors

Carefully checking output generated by the computer against the results of your hand calculations is called desk checking. How much hand checking is required depends on the complexity of the logic the program expresses. Generally, you should check out enough sets of data to test each logic branch within your program at least once. That is, if you have written a payroll program that processes workers with overtime hours differently from those workers without overtime, you should hand check at least one worker with overtime hours and one without. The more conditional logic within your program, the more desk checking is required to ensure that your program is processing each case correctly.

Don't forget to check the accuracy of subtotals and grand totals. If you have a large number of columns with totals, generally you do not have to hand calculate the total for all columns; if you are doing all your accumulation in the same place within your program, and the calculations are all set up in the same way, if one column's total is correct, the rest should be correct also — provided that you are using the correct fields in the calculations and referencing the correct accumulators in your Output Specifications.

The final step in output checking is to rigorously compare the computer-generated output with design documents, such as printer spacing charts, to ensure that your output exactly matches the requested format. Are the column headings appropriately centered over the columns? Are the literals spelled correctly (e.g., "Quantity," not "Quanity")? Does the report's vertical alignment exactly match that of the printer spacing chart? Did you edit the output correctly? The programmer's job is to give the designer exactly what (s)he requested. Although concern with these kinds of formatting details may seem "picky," careful attention to detail is one facet of the kind of preciseness required to be a top-rate programmer.

Correcting Output Errors

Once you have discovered an output error, your next job is to discover the cause of the error so you can correct it. A good programmer never makes changes within a program without having a specific reason to make a change. That is, you should try to locate the precise cause of the problem and then fix it, rather than base your changes on hunches or trial and error.

To discover the error, focus your attention initially on those calculations specifically involved in generating the incorrect output. If, after carefully checking these program statements, you still have not found a statement that is not correct, broaden your search to those portions of the program that may be influencing the output more remotely.

Although it is impossible to list every possible cause of erroneous output, you should be alert to a number of common errors when you are trying to debug your program.

Field problems: Variables are defined too small, causing truncation. This problem is most likely to occur with fields used as accumulators or fields that are the result of complex calculations. Another common field-related problem is failure to appropriately initialize or reinitialize fields. Forgetting to reset an indicator, counter, or flag-variable during repetitive processing is a common cause of erroneous output.

Loops: Off-by-one errors, resulting in a count-controlled loop repeating one too few or one too many times, occur frequently in programs. This kind of error stems from incorrectly establishing the conditional test to end the looping process. It often is related to incorrectly initializing the counter field used to control the looping.

For example, both pseudocode examples below, designed to add all the numbers between 1 and 100, are erroneous. The first example would sum the numbers 1 through 101, while the second would add the values 1 through 99.

```
Initialize I to 0
Initialize SUM to 0
WHILE I is less than 101
    Add 1 to I
    Add I to SUM
END WHILE

Initialize I to 1
Initialize SUM to 0
WHILE I < 100
    Add I to SUM
    Add 1 to I
END WHILE
```

Another common loop problem is failing to enter the loop. When you use a looping operator that tests the condition prior to executing the steps within the loop, your program may fail to enter the loop. For example, assume you want to read a file sequentially until you locate a desired code value within a record, process that record, and then resume reading until you find the next record with that same code value. The following pseudocode will correctly find the first record containing the desired code, but then will continue to process the same first record infinitely.

```
WHILE not end-of-file
    WHILE code <> desired value and not end-of-file
        Read a record
    END WHILE
    Process the record
END WHILE
```

The cause of the problem is that once the first appropriate record is located, the code field contains the desired value. As a result, the test of the inner loop will always be false and the inner loop will not be executed, thereby preventing additional records from being read.

IF Logic. Programmers often incorrectly specify the relational comparison used within an IF that is testing for a range of values. For example, if specifications state that pay rate should be less than $45.00, the following pseudocode would be incorrect:

```
IF rate > 45
    Perform error routine
END IF
```

Sometimes output errors are caused by incorrectly nesting IFs. Know how the system matches IFs, ELSEs, and ENDIFs, and check the notation of the compiler listing to make sure the system is interpreting your nested IFs the way you intended.

Another common IF problem is incorrectly using AND, OR, or NOT in compound IFs. NOTs in particular are error-prone. For example, if you want to validate a code field that should have a value of S, H, or R, the pseudocode below would falsely signal valid values as errors:

> IF code NOT = 'S' OR code NOT = 'H' OR code NOT = 'R'
>   Perform error routine
> END IF

Calculations: Steps in complex calculations are not executed in the correct order. Also, programmers sometimes overlook the possibility that a calculation may result in a negative value. This can be a difficult problem to locate, because RPG prints or displays all values as absolute (unsigned) values unless field editing includes provision for a negative sign; however, during calculations, negative values are handled as negative values.

For example, in figuring income tax withholding, a dependent allowance often is subtracted from gross earnings before applying the withholding tax percentage. If the relationship between gross earnings and number of dependents is such that this subtraction results in a negative value, failure to consider this possibility will cause the tax to be added (subtracting a negative number) to gross earnings; on the payroll register report, the same negative tax liability will appear to be a positive value, unless the tax field is edited with a code specifying that negative signs should print.

Debug

Sometimes despite your best efforts, you may not be able to locate the source of an output error by visually examining your program. Rather than resorting to making random changes in the program to see how they affect your output, you should use the AS/400's debugging facility. A "debugger" allows you to trace a program as it is executing, stepping through the program a statement at a time or stopping it at "breakpoints" that you designate so you can examine the values of fields at that point in execution. This procedure often can help you locate program errors that otherwise might elude you.

To run a program in debug mode, you must first enter the CL (Control Language) command STRDBG PGM(program-name), where program-name is the name of the program you are trying to debug. Your program then remains in debug mode until you issue the command ENDDBG. Once in debug mode, you can approach debugging in two ways. First, you can specify "breakpoints," statements within your program where you want execution to halt so you can examine the value of various variables at that point in execution. Or you can follow the flow of control in your program by issuing trace commands.

Breakpoints

Within debug mode, you specify breakpoints with the CL command ADDBKP (Add Breakpoint). The basic format of this command is ADDBKP STMT(statement-identifier), where statement-identifier represents a minimum of one and a maximum of 10 statement identifiers included as parameter values. These statement identifiers can be the statement numbers as they appear on the compile listing or labels (TAG statements) within the program.

ADDBKP STMT(2500 3000 4250) would cause the program to stop successively at statements 2500, 3000, and 4250, in each case just prior to that statement's execution. Upon stopping, the system shows you the breakpoint display, indicating which breakpoint has been reached and, optionally, the current value of specified program values.

By including an optional parameter with your ADDBKP command, PGMVAR, you can specify up to 10 program variables whose values you want to examine at the breakpoints. ADDBKP STMT(2000) PGMVAR(CNT TOTPAY) would stop your program just before executing statement 2000 and display the current values of variables CNT and TOTPAY. Pressing the Enter key causes your program to resume execution.

At the breakpoint display, you also can enter additional commands to control the debugging session by pressing F10. You can, for example, add additional breakpoints by issuing another ADDBKP statement, or you can remove breakpoints with the command RMVBKP STMT(statement-identifier). You can specify specific statements to remove, or use *ALL as the STMT parameter value to remove all breakpoints.

You also can issue a DSPPGMVAR (Display Program Variable) to view the contents of variables not specified in an ADDBKP command. The format of this CL command is

```
DSPPGMVAR PGMVAR(var1 var2 ...)
```

where var1 and var2 represent a list of the names of up to 10 program variables you want to examine.

Another useful feature of debug is that you can actually change the value of a variable or variables to determine how your program executes when processing that value. To use this feature, you would generally wait until your program had reached the desired breakpoint and then issue the command:

```
CHGPGMVAR  PGMVAR(variable name) VALUE(desired value)
```

where variable name represents the name of the field whose value you want to change and desired value is the value you want that field to assume. You can use this command with character or numeric fields; enclose character values with apostrophes.

Trace Commands

The second approach to using debug is to trace the flow of statement execution. The command ADDTRC (Add Trace) tells the system to trace the flow of the program for the range of statements you specify. The format for this command is

```
ADDTRC STMT(start-statement-identifier                          +
            stop-statement-identifier) PGMVAR(var1 var2...)
```

where the parameter values for STMT indicate the beginning and ending points of the desired trace and PGMVAR includes up to 10 variables whose values are to be tracked during the trace.

Once you have added a trace, as you run your program the system stores the traced statement numbers and the variable values in a special trace file. To view the results of the trace, issue a DSPTRCDTA (Display Trace Data) command. This command displays the statements traced by the most recent trace operation and displays the variables' values within that range of statements. Other associated trace commands are CLRTRCDTA (Clear Trace Data), to clear trace data from a previous trace command, and DSPTRC (Display Trace), to show what traces you have currently defined for the program. Command RMVTRC (Remove Trace) removes all or part of the traces you have specified with ADDTRC.

A special kind of tracing is called "stepping," in which you want all or a portion of your program to execute one line at a time and then stop so that you can examine the logic flow and program variables after each operation. To specify this single-stepping through your program, issue the STRDBG command with additional parameter MAXTRC(1) to specify that only a single trace statement is to be executed before returning control to your terminal. Thus, to single-step through statements 1000-2000 of program SALESRPT and allow you to check out the values of fields A and B, you would enter the following commands:

```
STRDBG PGM(SALESRPT) MAXTRC(1)
ADDTRC STMT(1000 2000) PGMVAR(A B)
CALL SALESRPT
...
DSPTRCDTA
```

Once you are finished with a debugging session, remember to issue the command ENDDBG to end the session; this command automatically removes all traces and breakpoints.

For additional information about working in debug mode, see IBM's reference manual *Programming: Control Language Programmer's Guide* (SC41-8077).

As a beginning programmer you sometimes will feel frustrated at your initial inability to locate the cause of program errors. With practice, you will find that you begin to recognize what kinds of logic errors cause various kinds of output errors and as a result, you will be able to correct your programs with increasing ease. And remember, even seasoned programmers make logic mistakes. The sign of an excellent programmer is detecting such problems when they occur, rather than overlooking output errors due to careless or incomplete testing.

Appendix D

Data Files

This Appendix contains definitions of the data files used in the programming assignments throughout the book. Most of the assignments focus on three companies to give you a sense of what it is like to develop an application system for a company. An application system is a series of programs that use the same set of data files to record and maintain data important to some facet of the company's business, process that data, permit on-line queries of the data, and produce needed reports. Depending on what programs your instructor assigns you, you will be working with several of the data files described below.

An overview of each company precedes the descriptions of the company's files so you will have a context within which to understand each company's data and program needs. The key fields of each file, if any, are preceded by an asterisk (*).

Case 1: CompuSell

CompuSell is a small mail-order company specializing in computers and computer supplies. The company needs an integrated system of programs to handle its orders and inventory, as well as to generate needed reports for management. An analyst already has done the preliminary design work and determined the files needed as part of the system. The files, and their record layouts, are described below.

CSCSFINP: *Customer Finance File*
This file contains information about customers who are financing purchases.

Record layout of CSCSFINP:

Field	Description	Positions	(Decimal Positions)
* CUSTNO	Customer number	1- 6	(0)
PURAMTE	Purchase amount	7- 12	(2)
DWNPAY	Down payment	13- 18	(2)
PDATE	Purchase date	19- 24	(0) YYMMDD

CSCSTP: *Customer Master File*

This file stores basic information about its customers. A unique customer number is assigned each new customer and serves as that customer's identifier. In addition to storing name, address, and phone information, this file tracks date of last order (for marketing purposes) and balance owed (for billing purposes). (Although most customers are cash customers, occasionally a customer will under- or over-pay on an order).

Record layout of CSCSTP:

Field	Description	Positions	(Decimal Positions)
* CUSTNO	Customer number	1- 6	(0)
CFNAME	First name	7- 16	
CLNAME	Last name	17- 31	
CSTRET	Street address	32- 51	
CCITY	City	52- 66	
CSTATE	State	67- 68	
CZIP	Zip+4	69- 77	(0)
CPHONE	Phone	78- 87	(0)
ORDDAT	Last order date	88- 93	(0) MMDDYY
BALDUE	Balance due	94- 99	(2 implied)

CSINVP: *Inventory Master File*

This file is used to maintain inventory records. When a company adds a new product to its line, the information is recorded in this file. Each item carried has a unique product number. As items are sold, they are subtracted from inventory; as stock comes in from suppliers, the stock is added to inventory. When quantity on hand drops to reorder quantity, the item is reordered from the appropriate supplier. The reorder code field is used to prevent the same item from accidentally being reordered more than once. Supplier code is a supplier identification number assigned by CompuSell; supplier product ID is the supplier's identifier for that product. Current cost reflects the most recent cost paid for the item, while average cost is the average cost of the items in inventory. Selling price is what CompuSell currently charges for the item.

Record layout of CSINVP:

Field	Description	Positions	(Decimal Positions)
* PRODNO	Product number	1- 6	(0)
DESCRP	Description	7- 31	
SELLPR	Selling price	32- 37	(2 implied)
SHIPWT	Shipping weight	38- 41	First 2 positions are pounds; last 2 are ounces

Continued

Record layout of CSINVP *continued*:

Field	Description	Positions	(Decimal Positions)
QTYOH	Quantity on hand	42- 45	(0 implied)
RORPNT	Reorder point	46- 49	(0 implied)
RORQTY	Reorder quantity	50- 53	(0 implied)
RORCOD	Reorder code	54	Blank or R
SUPCOD	Supplier code	55- 57	(0)
SUPPID	Supplier product ID	58- 65	
CURCST	Current cost	66- 71	(2 implied)
AVGCST	Average cost	72- 77	(2 implied)

CSORDP: *Orders File*

This file contains "header" information about each order placed with Compu-Sell. The detailed information about items ordered is stored in CSORPRP.

Record layout of CSPRDP:

Field	Description	Positions	(Decimal Positions)
* ORD#	Order number	1- 5	(0)
ODATE	Date ordered	6- 11	(0)
CUSTNO	Customer number	12- 17	(0)
PAYMNT	Payment included	18- 24	(2)
ORDTOT	Total cost of order	25- 31	(2)

CSORDPRP: *Order/Products File*

This file, in conjunction with file CUSTORD, contains information about customer orders.

Record layout of CSORDPRP:

Field	Description	Positions	(Decimal Positions)
* ORD#	Order number	1- 5	(0)
* PRODNO	Product number	6- 11	(0)
QTYORD	Quantity ordered	12- 15	(0)

CSRCVP: *Goods Received File*

The company uses a file of received goods. Each time goods are received from a supplier, the information is stored in this file until it can be processed in batch to update the inventory file.

Record layout of CSRCVP:

Field	Description	Positions	(Decimal Positions)
* SUPCOD	Supplier code	1- 3	(0)
* SUPPID	Supplier product ID	4- 11	
QTYRCV	Quantity received	12- 15	(0)
COST	Item cost	16- 21	(2)

CSSUPP: *Supplier File*

This file stores information about the suppliers of CompuSell's products.

Record layout of CSSUPP:

Field	Description	Positions	(Decimal Positions)
* SUPCOD	Supplier code	1- 3	
SNAME	Supplier name	4- 28	
CONTAC	Contact person	29- 58	
SSTRET	Street address	59- 78	
SCITY	City	79- 93	
SSTAT	State	94- 95	
SZIP	Zip	96-104	(0)
SPHONE	Phone	105-114	(0)

In addition to the above files, CompuSell will need two "table" files to help it determine what to charge its customers for shipping.

CSZPZNP: *Zip/Zone Table File*

This file will be used to determine the correct shipping zone based on the first three digits of a customer's zip code. Zones range from 2 to 7, depending on zip code. This is a range table file, such that each zip code record represents the highest of a range of zip codes.

Record layout of CSZPZNP:

Field	Description	Positions	(Decimal Positions)
TZIP	3 Zip digits	1- 3	(0)
TZONE	Related shipping zone	4	(0)

CSCHGP: *Charges Table File*

This second "table" file contains shipping charges based on weight and zone. Each record contains a weight and six charges (one each for zones 2-7).

Record layout of CSCHGP:

Field	Description	Positions	(Decimal Positions)
TWGT	Weight in pounds	1- 2	(0)
TCHG2	Charge zone 2	3- 6	(2)
TCHG3	Charge zone 3	7- 10	(2)
TCHG4	Charge zone 4	11- 14	(2)
TCHG5	Charge zone 5	15- 18	(2)
TCHG6	Charge zone 6	19- 22	(2)
TCHG7	Charge zone 7	23- 26	(2)

Case 2: Wexler University

Wexler University is a small midwestern university that wants a system for student records and registration. The system will store information about departments, instructors, courses, sections, students, and enrollment. The files required as part of the system are described below.

WUCRDP: *Earned Credits File*

This file contains a record for each course each student has completed.

Record layout of WUCRDP:

Field	Description	Positions	(Decimal Positions)
* STUNO	Social Security number	1- 9	(0)
DEPT	Course department	10- 12	
CRSNO	Course number	13- 15	(0)
GRADE	Grade	16- 17	
SEMES	Semester taken	18- 20	First two positions YY; third position is semester code, where 1 = Winter; 2 = Summer; 3 = Fall

WUCRSDSP: *Course Description File*

Each course has a description of varying length; the description may include an overview of the course, prerequisites, etc. A description for a given course is represented by one or more records in this file; the records for a given course are sequentially assigned a line number.

Record layout of WUCRSDSP:

Field	Description	Positions	(Decimal Positions)
* DEPT	Course department	1- 3	
* CRSNO	Course number	4- 6	(0)
* LINE	Description line number	7- 8	(0)
CRSDSC	Description	9- 58	

WUCRSP: *Course File*

Each course the university offers is represented by a record in this file. Each course is uniquely identified by a 6-position identification of course department and course number (e.g., CIS264).

Record layout of WUCRSP:

Field	Description	Positions	(Decimal Positions)
* DEPT	Course department	1- 3	
* CRSNO	Course number	4- 6	
CRSTTL	Course title	7- 31	
CREDIT	Credits	32	(0)

WUDPTP: *Department File*

This file contains information about each department of Wexler University.

Record layout of WUDPTP:

Field	Description	Positions	(Decimal Positions)
DEPT	Department code	1- 3	
DNAME	Department name	4- 23	
CHAIR	Name of chair	24- 48	
DOFFIC	Department office	49- 58	
DPHONE	Department phone	59- 68	(0)

WUENRLP: *Current Enrollment File*

A record is entered in this file for each student for each section (s)he is enrolled in. At the end of the semester, scanned grades are added to this file before preparing semester grade reports.

Record layout of WUENRLP:

Field	Description	Positions	(Decimal Positions)
SECT	Section number	1- 5	(0)
STUNO	Social Security number	6- 14	(0)
GRADE	Grade received	15- 16	

WUEXAMP: *Student Exam File*

Record layout of WUEXAMP:

Field	Description	Positions	(Decimal Positions)
STUNO	Social Security number	1- 9	(0)
SFNAME	First name	10- 19	
SLNAME	Last name	20- 34	
EXAM1	Exam 1 grade	35- 37	(0)
EXAM2	Exam 2 grade	38- 40	(0)

Field	Description	Positions	(Decimal Positions)
EXAM3	Exam 3 grade	41- 43	(0)
EXAM4	Exam 4 grade	44- 46	(0)
EXAM5	Exam 5 grade	47- 49	(0)

WUHRLYP: *Hourly Employees File*

Field	Description	Positions	(Decimal Positions)
EMPNO	Social Security number	1- 9	(0)
LNAME	Last name	10- 24	
FNAME	First name	25- 34	
REGHRS	Regular hours	35- 37	(1)
OTHRS	Overtime hours	38- 40	(1)
RATE	Regular pay rate	41- 44	(2)

WUINSTP: *Instructor File*

Each instructor at Wexler University has a record in this file.

Record layout of WUINSTP:

Field	Description	Positions	(Decimal Positions)
IFNAME	First name	1- 10	
ILNAME	Last name	11- 25	
* INSTNO	Social Security number	26- 34	(0)
DEPT	Department	35- 37	
SALARY	Salary	38- 45	(2)
RANK	Academic rank	46	1 = Instructor; 2 = Assistant professor; 3 = Associate professor; 4 = Full professor
SEX	Sex	47	M = male; F = female;
HIRDAT	Date of hire	48- 53	(0) YYMMDD
MARSTS	Marital status	54	M = Married; S = Single; H = Head of house
DEPEND	Number of dependents	55- 56	(0)
TENURE	Tenured faculty	57	Y = yes; N = no
TITLE	Preferred title	58	1 = Dr.; 2 = Mr.; 3 = Mrs.; 4 = Ms.
STREET	Street address	59- 78	
CITY	City	79- 93	
STATE	State	94- 95	
ZIP	Zip	96-104	(0)

WUKEYP: *File of Keys to Tests in WUTSTP*
This file contains the keys (answers) to the tests contained in WUTSTP. There is one answer key (record) for each test. The file is keyed on Course-ID and Test number; these values match those in the Student Test File.

Record layout of WUKEYP:

Field	Description	Positions	(Decimal Positions)
*TESTNO	Test number	1- 4	(0)
*CRSID	Course ID	5- 10	
ILNAME	Instructor's last name	11- 25	
KEY	Correct answers 1-50	26- 75	

WULOANP: *Faculty Credit Union Loan File*
This file contains records for loan applications to the credit union.

Input record format for WULOANP:

Field	Description	Positions	(Decimal Positions)
*LOANNO	Loan number	1- 5	(0)
CNAME	Customer name	6- 20	
LAMT	Loan amount	21- 27	(2)
ANNRAT	Annual interest rate	28- 31	(4)
YEARS	Years for loan	32- 33	(0)

WUSCTP: *Current Sections File*
Every section of each course currently being offered is represented by a record in this file. Each section has been assigned a unique number.

Record layout of WUSCTP:

Field	Description	Positions	(Decimal Positions)
*SECT	Section number	1- 5	(0)
DEPT	Course department	6- 8	
CRSNO	Course number	9- 11	
SECTIM	Meeting time	12- 15	(0) HHMM
SECDAY	Meeting days	16- 18	
ROOM	Meeting room	19- 22	
CAP	Maximum enrollment	23- 25	(0)
CURENL	Current enrollment	26- 28	(0)
ILNAME	Instructor's last name	29- 43	

WUSTDP: *Student Master File*

This file contains information about all Wexler University's students who are actively enrolled and those who have graduated within the past five years.

Record layout of WUSTDP:

Field	Description	Positions	(Decimal Positions)
* STUNO	Social Security number	1- 9	(0)
SLNAME	Student last name	10- 24	
SFNAME	Student first name	25- 34	
SMNAME	Student middle name	35- 44	
STREET	Street address	45- 64	
CITY	City	65- 79	
STATE	State	80- 81	
ZIP	Zip	82- 90	(0)
PHONE	Telephone	91-100	(0)
CRDTOT	Credits earned	101-103	(0)
DCODE	District code	104	I = Indistrict; O = Out-of-district; F = International
ADMDAT	Date admitted	105-110	YYMMDD
CLASS	Classification	111	U = Undergraduate; G = Graduate
GRDDAT	Date graduated	112-117	Blanks or YYMMDD
SDEPT	Department of major	118-120	
GPA	Grade point average	121-123	(2)
DEGREE	Degree granted	124-126	

WUTRANSP: *Transcript Request File*

Record layout of WUTRANSP:

Field	Description	Positions	(Decimal Positions)
* STUNO	Social Security number	1- 9	(0)

WUTSTP: *Student Test File*

This file contains student answers to 50-question, multiple-choice tests. The file is keyed on Course ID, Test, and Section number.

Record layout of WUTSTP:

Field	Description	Positions	(Decimal Positions)
* TESTNO	Test number	1- 4	(0)
* SECTN	Section number	5- 9	(0)
* CRSID	Course ID	10- 15	
STUID	Student ID	16- 24	(0)
ANS	Answers 1-50	25- 74	Values A, B, C, D, E

Case 3: GTC, Inc.

GTC is a small regional telephone company that needs an application system to maintain customer accounts, bill for calls, process payments, generate management reports, and so on. Four main files will be needed as part of the system. The files, and their record layouts, are described below.

GTCLSP: *Calls Transaction File*

This file is generated automatically by the telephone switching system. Records accumulate in the file during the month; once a month the file is processed to determine monthly billing. The file is then cleared at the beginning of each new billing period.

Record layout of GTCLSP:

Field	Description	Positions	(Decimal Positions)
CPHONE	Caller's number	1- 10	(0)
CALLED	Called number	11- 20	(0)
CALDAT	Date of call	21- 26	(0) YYMMDD
CALLEN	Length of call (in minutes)	27- 29	(0)
CALTIM	Time of call	30- 33	(0) HHMM based on 24-hour clock
CALCST	Call cost	34- 38	(2)

GTCSTP: *Customer Master File*

This file contains a record for each of GTC's customers.

Record layout of GTCSTP:

Field	Description	Positions	(Decimal Positions)
* CPHONE	Customer phone number	1- 10	(0)
CLNAME	Last name	11- 25	
CFNAME	First name	26- 35	
CSTRET	Street address	36- 55	
CCITY	City	56- 70	
CSTAT	State	71- 72	
CZIP	Zip	73- 77	(0)
CURBIL	Current billing amount	78- 83	(2)
AMTOWE	Amount owed	84- 89	(2)
PAYDAT	Date last payment	90- 95	(0) YYMMDD

GTPAYP: *Payments Transaction File*
This file is generated through OCR and manual entry techniques. Records are used once to update the customer account figures and generate a payment report and then archived.

Record layout of GTPAYP:

Field	Description	Positions	(Decimal Positions)
* CPHONE	Payer's phone number	1- 10	(0)
AMTPD	Amount paid	11- 16	(2)
DATRCV	Date payment received	17- 22	(0) YYMMDD

GTRATP: *Rates Table File*
This is a sequential file used as a table to determine cost of calls to a given area code and exchange.

Record layout of GTRATP:

Field	Description	Positions	(Decimal Positions)
TAREA	Area code called	1- 3	(0)
TEXCH	Exchange called	4- 6	(0)
TCITY	City called	7- 16	
TSTATE	State called	17- 18	
CST1ST	Cost for first minute	19- 20	(2)
CSTADL	Cost for each additional minute	21- 22	(2)

Miscellaneous Files

The files described below are not part of any of the above application systems. They represent "stand-alone" applications included as programming exercises to demonstrate certain programming concepts.

ACP001: *Acme Work File, used in Chapter 4, problem 4*
Input record format for ACP001:

Field	Description	Positions	(Decimal Positions)
* SOCSEC	Social Security number	1- 9	(0)
NAME	Name	10- 25	
WKDATE	Date worked	26- 31	(0) MMDDYY
HOURS	Hours worked	32- 33	(0)
QTY	Quantity produced	34- 36	(0)

BIDS: *Bids File, used in Chapter 3, problem 4*

Record layout for BIDS:

Field	Description	Positions	(Decimal Positions)
JOBNO	Job number	1- 4	(0)
PCODE	Paint code	5- 9	(0)
PCOST	Per gallon cost	10- 13	(2)
COVRG	Coverage per gallon	14- 16	(0)
LENFT	Room length, feet	17- 18	(0)
LENIN	Room length, inches	19- 20	(0)
WIDFT	Room width, feet	21- 22	(0)
WIDIN	Room width, inches	23- 24	(0)
HTFT	Room height, feet	25- 26	(0)
HTIN	Room height, inches	27- 28	(0)
PCT	Percent windows, doors	29- 30	(2)

HJSLPP: *Salesperson File, used in Chapter 9, problem 2*

Record layout for HJSLPP:

Field	Description	Positions	(Decimal Positions)
* SLSMNO	Salesperson number	1- 2	(0)
SNAME	Name	3- 27	
BASPAY	Weekly base pay	28- 33	(2)

HJSLSP: *Sales File, also used in Chapter 9, problem 2*

Record layout for HJSLSP:

Field	Description	Positions	(Decimal Positions)
SLSMNO	Salesperson number	1- 2	(0)
INVNO	Invoice number	3- 7	(0)
AMT	Sale amount	8- 14	(2)

MWC001P: *Meter Reading File, used in Chapter 4, problem 3*

Record layout for MWC001P:

Field	Description	Positions	(Decimal Positions)
CNAME	Customer name	1- 20	
CUSTNO	Customer number	21- 25	(0)
OLDMTR	Old meter reading	26- 29	(0)
NEWMTR	New meter reading	30- 33	(0)
RCODE	Residency code	34	1 = City resident; 2 = Non-city resident

PIPRESP: *Airline Reservation File, used in Chapter 9, problem 3*

Record layout for PIPRESP:

Field	Description	Positions	(Decimal Positions)
*DY	Day of week	1	(0)
*FLIGHT	Flight number	2	(0)
RESERV	Seats reserved	3- 4	(0)
FNAME	First name of reserver	5- 14	
LNAME	Last name of reserver	15- 29	
PHONE	Phone number of reserver	30- 39	(0)

PRDSLSP: *Sales Volume File, used in Chapter 9, problem 1*

This file contains a record for each of the company's products, showing the sales volume for each month.

Record layout for PRDSLSP:

Field	Description	Positions	(Decimal Positions)
PRODNO	Product number	1- 6	(0)
SLS	12 monthly sales[1]	7- 78	(0)

[1] Represent 12 monthly total sales figures for that product, arranged sequentially from January to December; each sales figure is a 6-digit integer.

Appendix E

RPG IV and RPG/400

This appendix highlights how RPG IV affects the material presented in this text. The changes are discussed within the context of individual chapters of the book, so that you can easily reference the appropriate section of this appendix as you study various chapters from the body of the text. Throughout the appendix, "Mandatory Changes" indicate features described in the chapters that need to be modified to work with OS/400 V3R1's SEU and/or the ILE RPG/400 compiler, while "Optional Changes" note features that are available but do not directly affect RPG/400 syntax.

Chapter 1 Modifications
Mandatory Changes

As a result of the Integrated Language Environment introduced along with RPG IV, compiling a program no longer results in an executable program; instead, it creates what is called a "module." The module, in turn, must be bound (with other modules if appropriate) to produce an executable program. However, V3R1 includes a command, CRTBNDRPG, which allows you to combine the compiling and binding into a single step if your RPG IV source code represents an entire program.

Chapter 2 Modifications
Mandatory Changes

The 80-column specification lines of RPG have been expanded to 100 columns to allow longer entries and to include room for comments. (All specification forms now reserve positions 81-100 for internal documentation.) In addition, the locations of some entries have been shifted, while in a few cases, the entries have been eliminated completely from the specification. Let's consider the new layout of each specification used in this chapter.

The new File Specification line with sample entries appears on the next page. Notice that although all entries introduced in this chapter are retained, their positions have been changed. Filename now occurs in positions 7-16; File Type, position 17; File Designation, position 18; File Format, position 22; Record Length, positions 23-27; and Device, positions 36-42.

```
          1         2         3         4         5         6         7         8         9        10
 1234567890123456789012345678901234567890123456789012345678901234567890123456789012345678901234567890
     FFilename++IPEASFRlen+LKlen+AIDevice+.Functions+++++++++++++++++++++++++++Comments+++++++++++
     FSALES    IF   F  63        DISK
     FQPRINT   O    F 132        PRINTER
```

The new 100-position specifications for Input similarly result in the repositioning of entries. The Input Specification line for record descriptions now locates Filename in positions 7-16, while the Sequence entry falls in positions 17-18, as illustrated below.

```
          1         2         3         4         5         6         7         8         9        10
 1234567890123456789012345678901234567890123456789012345678901234567890123456789012345678901234567890
     IFilename++SqNORiPos1+NCCPos2+NCCPos3+NCC................................Comments+++++++++++
     ISALES    NS
```

The new locations for field description entries on Input Specifications are: From, positions 37-41; To, positions 42-46; Decimal positions, positions 47-48; and Field name, positions 49-62.

```
          1         2         3         4         5         6         7         8         9        10
 1234567890123456789012345678901234567890123456789012345678901234567890123456789012345678901234567890
     I.......................Fmt+SPFrom+To+++DcField++++++++L1M1FrP1MnZr......Comments+++++++++++
     I                                    1    4 0SLSMNO
     I                                    5   34 NAME
```

The figure below shows how the calculation entries discussed in this chapter would be coded using the new 100-position Calculation Specification line.

```
          1         2         3         4         5         6         7         8         9        10
 1234567890123456789012345678901234567890123456789012345678901234567890123456789012345678901234567890
     CL0N01Factor1++++++Opcode(E)+Factor2++++++Result+++++++Len++D+HiLoEq....Comments+++++++++++
     C                 EXCEPT    HEADS
     C                 READ      SALES                                   90
     C     *IN90       DOWEQ     *OFF
     C                 EXCEPT    DETAIL
     C                 READ      SALES                                   90
     C                 ENDDO
     C                 RETURN
```

Because the new Calculation Specifications allow six-character-long operations, IBM has lengthened the operation EXCPT to EXCEPT and RETRN to RETURN, as coded above. Note that the calculation entries are now located in the following positions: Factor 1, positions 12-25; Factor 2, positions 36-49; Result field, positions 50-63; Operation (and extender), positions 26-35; and the Resulting indicators, positions 71-76.

The new 100-position Output Specification forms follow. Notice in the first form that Filename now falls in positions 7-16; Type of Line in position 17; the Exception name in positions 30-39; Space before, positions 40-42; Space after, positions 43-45; Skip before, positions 46-48; and Skip after, positions

49-51. In the second form, the Field name occurs in positions 30-43; Edit code, position 44; End position, positions 47-51; and Constant or Edit word, positions 53-80.

```
         1         2         3         4         5         6         7         8         9        10
1234567890123456789012345678901234567890123456789012345678901234567890123456789012345678901234567890
 OFilename++DF..NØ1NØ2NØ3Excnam++++B++A++Sb+Sa+.............................Comments++++++++++++
 OQPRINT    E        HEADS        2 2

         1         2         3         4         5         6         7         8         9        10
1234567890123456789012345678901234567890123456789012345678901234567890123456789012345678901234567890
 O..............NØ1NØ2NØ3Field++++++++YB.End++PConstant/editword/DTformat++Comments++++++++++++
 O                                    8 'PAGE'
 O                  PAGE         Y   13
```

Optional Changes

For all specification entries, RPG IV now supports mixed-case entry, rather than restricting entries to uppercase letters. File names and field names may be up to 10 characters long. The underscore (_) is also now an allowable character within an RPG variable name, as long as the name does not begin with an underscore. The decimal position entry has been expanded to two columns, and RPG will now support numeric variables with up to 30 decimal positions.

A continuation form of the Output Specification now exists, so that you can easily continue a constant or edit word from one line to the next. You signal such a continuation by terminating the entry on the first line with a hyphen (–) or a plus (+). A hyphen signals that the constant resumes with the first position of the continuation area (positions 53-80) on the next line, while a plus signals that the continuation resumes with the first non-blank character encountered in the continuation area of the next line.

```
         1         2         3         4         5         6         7         8         9        10
1234567890123456789012345678901234567890123456789012345678901234567890123456789012345678901234567890
 O..............NØ1NØ2NØ3Field++++++++YB.End++PConstant/editword/DTformat++Comments++++++++++++
 O*The two examples below would produce the same output because of the use of the + and -.
 O* Example 1: + as continuation character
 O                                           90 'ACME EXPLOSIVES SALES +
 O                                              REPORT'
 O* Example 2: - as continuation character
 O                                           90 'ACME EXPLOSIVES SALES -
 O                                              REPORT'
```

To facilitate using blank lines within your code to make the code more readable, RPG now supports two additional kinds of comment lines. First, if positions 6-80 are all blank, the line is treated as a comment and can appear anywhere within your code. Alternately, position 6 may contain a valid specification type, while positions 7-80 are blank. In this second case, the specification type must be appropriate for its location within the program.

Also note that all the specification forms now include a comment area in positions 81-100, so that you can easily document any line of code. Finally, on the Output Specifications, the permissible upper limit of the Space before and/or Space after entries have been extended to 255; in RPG/400 the maximum value you could enter was 3. The new range for Skip before and Skip After is also now 1-255.

Chapter 3 Modifications

Mandatory Changes

As a concomitant of the changed format of the Calculation Specification line, the placement and method of expressing rounding and padding have changed. These operation extenders now must follow the operation code and be written within parentheses. They may float, however, anywhere to the right of the operation, providing they fall within the prescribed positions for the operation (positions 26-35), as illustrated below.

```
          1         2         3         4         5         6         7         8         9        10
 1234567890123456789012345678901234567890123456789012345678901234567890123456789012345678901234567890
    CLØNØ1Factor1++++++Opcode(E)+Factor2++++++Result++++++++Len++D+HiLoEq....Comments++++++++++++
    C     RATE        MULT(H)    LOAN         INTRST        6 2
    C     TOTAMT      DIV  (H)   NUM          AVGAMT        5 2
    C                 MOVE (P)  '12'          EXMPLE
    C                 MOVEL(P)'ABCD'          EXMPLE2
```

Optional Changes

Because of the expanded factor 1 and factor 2, the maximum length of numeric and character literals is now 14.

A new operation, EVAL (Evaluate), provides a relatively free-form technique for expressing complicated calculations in a single step. The operation uses the extended factor 2 format of the Calculation Specification. In this format, EVAL appears as the operation code (with rounding or padding, if appropriate), while the expanded factor 2 area contains a target (result) field, followed by the assignment operator (=), followed by an expression. (Note that the target field needs to be defined elsewhere — preferably on a D-spec; it cannot be defined as part of the EVAL operation.)

The expression can contain the arithmetic operators +, –, *,/, and ** (exponentiation), as well as relational symbols, logical operators, and built-in functions. (See Chapters 11 and 14 for additional details about functions.) You can use parentheses to change the order in which the computer executes the operations within the expression. In general, the evaluation of the expression follows the precedence rules of mathematics; parentheses have the highest precedence, followed by exponentiation, multiplication and division, and addition and subtraction, in that order.

Within the extended factor 2 area (positions 36-80), RPG IV allows free-form entry, so that you can include as many (or as few) blanks between fields, literals, and operations as you would like. If necessary, the expression may be continued to one or more extended factor 2 continuation lines; these kinds of lines must be blank between positions 7 and 35, with the expression continued in positions 36-80. The figure below illustrates the EVAL operation and the use of a continuation line.

```
          1         2         3         4         5         6         7         8         9        10
 12345678901234567890123456789012345678901234567890123456789012345678901234567890123456789012345678901234567890
     CL0N01Factor1++++++Opcode(E)+Extended-factor2+++++++++++++++++++++++++Comments+++++++++++
 C                   EVAL(H)   GRPFT = COST * .6 * QTY
 C* The example below demonstrates the use of a continuation line.
 C                   EVAL  (H) OVRTIM_PAY = 1.5 * HRLY_RATE *
 C                                          (HRS_WORKED - 40)
```

Chapter 4 Modifications

Mandatory Changes

The RPG/400 SELEC and WHxx operations have been changed to SELECT and WHENxx, respectively.

Optional Changes

The operation codes DOUxx, DOWxx, IFxx, and WHENxx have new, optional analogous operation codes — DOU, DOW, IF, and WHEN — which can be used to more clearly depict the condition(s) being tested as part of the operation. These alternate forms use the extended factor 2 form of the Calculation Specifications to depict the condition(s) being tested as a logical expression. The figure below illustrates the use of these operations.

```
          1         2         3         4         5         6         7         8         9        10
 12345678901234567890123456789012345678901234567890123456789012345678901234567890123456789012345678901234567890
     CL0N01Factor1++++++Opcode(E)+Extended-factor2+++++++++++++++++++++++++Comments+++++++++++
 C                   IF        AGE >= 65 AND STATUS = 'R'
 C                   ...
 C                   ELSE
 C                   ...
 C                   ENDIF
 C
 C                   DOW       *IN90 = *OFF AND *IN99 = *OFF
 C                   ...
 C                   ENDDO
 C
 C                   DOU       NUM = 100
 C                   ...
 C                   ENDDO
```

Finally, there is no longer any limit on how many subroutines a given program may contain.

Chapter 5 Modifications

Mandatory Changes

With the new 100-position File Specification line, the definitions for externally described database files and printer files now appear as follows:

```
          1         2         3         4         5         6         7         8         9        10
 12345678901234567890123456789012345678901234567890123456789012345678901234567890123456789012345678901234567890
     FFilename++IPEASFRlen+LKlen+AIDevice+.Functions++++++++++++++++++++++++++Comments+++++++++++
     FSALESFIL  IF   E           K DISK
     FSALESRPT  O                  PRINTER OFLIND(*INOF)
```

Notice that instead of entering an overflow indicator in a fixed position within the code line, you now signal the use of an overflow indicator through keyword OFLIND (with your selected indicator noted within parentheses), entered anywhere within the Functions area of the line.

Optional Changes
RPG IV now supports file names up to 10 characters long, and the characters may include underscores, so the rules of file naming of DDS and RPG now coincide.

Chapter 6 Modifications

Mandatory Changes
On the File Specifications, the place to indicate that you want to allow the addition of records to an output or update file has shifted to position 20. Moreover, to indicate that you want user control over opening a file, you no longer code UC in positions 71-72. Instead, you now denote this feature through keyword USROPN, coded in the Functions area of the specification line. The figure below shows what the File Specification from earlier in the chapter would look like in RPG IV.

```
        1         2         3         4         5         6         7         8         9        10
123456789012345678901234567890123456789012345678901234567890123456789012345678901234567890
     FFilename++IPEASFRlen+LKlen+AIDevice+.Functions+++++++++++++++++++++++++Comments+++++++++++
     F* File is an update file, with record addition possible.  File opening is user-controlled.
     FCUSTMAST  UF A E          K DISK     USROPN
```

On the Calculation Specifications, recall that with the new 6-position operations, EXCPT has become EXCEPT. Similarly, UPDAT is now UPDATE, DELET is now DELETE, REDPE is READPE, and UNLCK is UNLOCK. The old, 5-letter versions of these operations will not work. Also, you now code operation extender N (the signal that no record locking should occur when the record is read) within parentheses, following the input operation, as shown in the figure below.

```
        1         2         3         4         5         6         7         8         9        10
123456789012345678901234567890123456789012345678901234567890123456789012345678901234567890
     CL0N01Factor1++++++Opcode(E)+Factor2++++++Result++++++++Len++D+HiLoEq....Comments+++++++++++
     C     CUSTNO        CHAIN (N) CUSTMAST                     90
```

Chapter 7 Modifications
No RPG IV language changes affect the material presented in this chapter.

Chapter 8 Modifications

Mandatory Changes
A major change in RPG IV has been to consolidate several different kinds of data definition onto a single, new Definition Specification. As part of this consolidation, Extension Specifications have been eliminated, and all table and array definitions that in the past appeared on E-specs now have functionally

equivalent entries on Definition Specifications instead. Definition Specifications, if used within a program, should appear following the File Specifications and before any Input Specifications. The layout of a D-spec is shown below.

```
          1         2         3         4         5         6         7         8         9         10
 1234567890123456789012345678901234567890123456789012345678901234567890123456789012345678901234567890
    DName++++++++++ETDsFrom+++To/L+++IDc.Functions++++++++++++++++++++++++++++Comments+++++++++++++
```

To define any non-alternating format table or array, enter the name of the table or array anywhere in positions 7-21; enter an S (for stand-alone field) in position 24; enter the length of one element of the table or array right adjusted within positions 33-39; and for numeric data, enter the number of decimal positions in positions 41-42. Then, in positions 44-80, you need to enter one or more keywords, depending on the kind of table or array you are defining. These keywords are entered free-form, in any order. You may use a continuation Definition Specification if it's needed to hold all the required keywords.

The first keyword, required as part of the definition of every table and array, is DIM (dimension), followed by the number of elements of the table/array noted within parentheses. If you want to declare that the table/array is in ascending or descending order, include keyword ASCEND or DESCEND.

```
          1         2         3         4         5         6         7         8         9         10
 1234567890123456789012345678901234567890123456789012345678901234567890123456789012345678901234567890
    DName++++++++++ETDsFrom+++To/L+++IDc.Functions++++++++++++++++++++++++++++Comments+++++++++++++
    D* Definitions of three run-time arrays: two of the arrays are to be ordered.
    D GAR             S              7 2 DIM(10)
    D ARC             S              1   DIM(15)   DESCEND
    D QAR             S              3 0 DIM(200)  ASCEND
```

If the table/array data is hardcoded at the end of your program (a compile-time table/array), you need an additional keyword, CTDATA (for compile-time data). If the table/array data is loaded from a file (a pre-runtime table/array), you need to include keyword FROMFILE, with the name of the file containing the data in parentheses following the keyword. For both these kinds of tables/arrays, you specify the data layout by using the PERRCD keyword, with the number of entries per record enclosed in parentheses. If you omit this keyword for compile-time or pre-runtime tables, the default assumption is one entry per record.

If the data from these kinds of tables/arrays is to be written to a file at the end of the program's execution, use keyword TOFILE with the receiving file's name in parentheses.

```
          1         2         3         4         5         6         7         8         9        10
 1234567890123456789012345678901234567890123456789012345678901234567890123456789012345678901234567890
     DName++++++++++ETDsFrom+++To/L+++IDc.Functions++++++++++++++++++++++++++++Comments++++++++++++
     D* Compile-time table of 50 elements; elements entered 1 per record in ascending sequence.
     D TABCOD          S              2    DIM(50) ASCEND CTDATA
     D* Pre-runtime table of 200 elements, entered 5 per record.  Data read from and written back
     D* to TAXFILE.
     D TABTAX          S              3  3 DIM(200) FROMFILE(TAXFILE)
     D                                     TOFILE(TAXFILE) PERRCD(5)
```

If you are defining a table or array that is in alternating format with another (primary) table or array, you must include the keyword ALT and specify the name of the primary table/array. The DIM keyword is a required entry for both the alternating table/array and the primary table/array. However, you cannot include the PERRCD, FROMFILE, and TOFILE keywords in the alternate table/array's definition; the alternating table "inherits" these keywords from the primary table/array.

```
          1         2         3         4         5         6         7         8         9        10
 1234567890123456789012345678901234567890123456789012345678901234567890123456789012345678901234567890
     DName++++++++++ETDsFrom+++To/L+++IDc.Functions++++++++++++++++++++++++++++Comments++++++++++++
     D* Two compile-time tables in alternating format; each table has 50 elements, entered 1 per
     D* record.  TABCOD is in ascending sequence.
     D TABCOD          S              2    DIM(50) CTDATA ASCEND PERRCD(1)
     D TABNAM          S             14    DIM(50) ALT(TABCOD)
```

Within the Calculation and Output Specifications, you now reference individual array elements using parentheses, rather than the comma notation. And on the Calculation Specifications, the LOKUP operation is now LOOKUP.

```
          1         2         3         4         5         6         7         8         9        10
 1234567890123456789012345678901234567890123456789012345678901234567890123456789012345678901234567890
     CL0N01Factor1++++++Opcode(E)+Factor2++++++Result+++++++Len++D+HiLoEq....Comments++++++++++++
     C* Calculations involving individual array elements.
     C     AR(6)         ADD       AR(3)         AR(10)
     C                   MOVEA     ARA(3)        ARB
     C* A table lookup.
     C     CODEIN        LOOKUP    TABCOD        TABNAM                   50
```

You can no longer define a run-time array within the Input Specifications. Instead, the Input Specifications would handle the array as a simple field; this field, in turn, would be redefined as an array through a data structure defined on the Definition Specifications. (See Chapter 9 to learn about data structures.)

With all of the MOVE operations, including MOVEA, you now code the Pad option (P) as an operation extender following the operation, as shown below.

```
          1         2         3         4         5         6         7         8         9        10
 1234567890123456789012345678901234567890123456789012345678901234567890123456789012345678901234567890
     CL0N01Factor1++++++Opcode(E)+Factor2++++++Result+++++++Len++D+HiLoEq....Comments++++++++++++
     C                   MOVEA (P) ARAB          ARAA
```

Optional Changes

The delimiter line that separates your program source code from the hard-coded data of a compile-time table/array can now more specifically identify the data by using a **keyword record. To use this format, code asterisks in positions 1 and 2 of a line following your last line of code; in positions 3-8 enter CTDATA. Leave position 9 blank. Starting in position 10, enter the name of the table/array whose data follows. Although this method is optional, within a program **keyword records cannot be mixed with the older ** delimiter.

Also note that with the new 100-character specification lines, you can now enter up to 100 characters of compile-time data per line.

Chapter 9 Modifications

Mandatory Changes

You now have to code all the advanced data definition features discussed in this chapter on the new Definition Specifications. Let's look at how each specific type of definition would be handled.

You define a named constant by entering its name anywhere in positions 7-21 and placing a C (for constant) in position 24. Enter the value of the constant in positions 44-80, optionally using the keyword CONST. A named constant can now be up to 1,024 bytes long; a numeric constant can have up to 30 decimal positions. To enter a named constant that is too long to fit on a single line, continue the value onto the Functions area of one (or more) continuation lines.

```
          1         2         3         4         5         6         7         8         9        10
 1234567890123456789012345678901234567890123456789012345678901234567890123456789012345678901234567890
     DName++++++++++ETDsFrom+++To/L+++IDc.Functions+++++++++++++++++++++++++++++Comments++++++++++++
     D* Examples of valid named constants.
     D FICA             C                   CONST(.Ø751)
     D PI               C                   3.142
     D EXVP             C                   CONST('DAN QUAYLE')
     D LONGWORD         C                   'ANTIDISESTABLISHMENTARIANISM'
     D EXMPLE           C                   CONST('THIS LONG CONSTANT HAS -
     D                                      BLANKS WHERE YOU WOULD EXPECT THEM-
     D                                      TO APPEAR IN A SENTENCE.')
```

The basic approach to data structure definition has not changed much, except that some of the entries are repositioned to match the Definition Specifications' layout, and keywords are substituted for what originally were positional entries. Data structures are signalled by entering DS in positions 24-25; providing a name for the data structure remains optional. (An S in position 23 declares a data structure to be a program-status data structure.) Subfields of the data structure are coded on successive lines, with the subfield names coded in positions 7-21. The names may float within these positions to allow the hierarchical layout of the data structure to be easily visible. You can now define the length of subfields either using From and To entries as in RPG/400 (entered in positions 26-32 and 33-39, respectively), or you can simply enter the length of the subfield in positions 33-39.

```
          1         2         3         4         5         6         7         8         9        10
 1234567890123456789012345678901234567890123456789012345678901234567890123456789012345678901234567890
     DName++++++++++ETDsFrom+++To/L+++IDc.Functions++++++++++++++++++++++++++++++Comments++++++++++++
     D* One method of specifying length of subfields of a data structure.
     D PRTKEY          DS
     D   WAREHS                     1      3 0
     D   PARTNO                     4      8 0
     D* An alternate method of defining the same structure.
     D PRTKEY          DS
     D   WAREHS                            3 0
     D   PARTNO                            5 0
```

The maximum size of a single-occurrence data structure is 32,767 bytes. You can now directly define run-time arrays as part of a data structure, using the DIM keyword.

```
          1         2         3         4         5         6         7         8         9        10
 1234567890123456789012345678901234567890123456789012345678901234567890123456789012345678901234567890
     DName++++++++++ETDsFrom+++To/L+++IDc.Functions++++++++++++++++++++++++++++++Comments++++++++++++
     D* The data structure below redefines fields STDANS and KEYANS as arrays of 100 elements each.
     D                 DS
     D STDANS                       1    100
     D STD                          1    100     DIM(100)
     D KEYANS                     101    200
     D KEY                        101    200     DIM(100)
```

Specify a multiple-occurrence data structure by using the keyword OCCURS, with the number of occurrences coded within parentheses (the maximum allowable occurrences is now 32,767).

```
          1         2         3         4         5         6         7         8         9        10
 1234567890123456789012345678901234567890123456789012345678901234567890123456789012345678901234567890
     DName++++++++++ETDsFrom+++To/L+++IDc.Functions++++++++++++++++++++++++++++++Comments++++++++++++
     D STATE           DS                          OCCURS(50)
     D   CODE                              2
     D   NAME                             15
     D   SLSTAX                            4 4
     D   CAPIT                            15
     D   LOWZIP                            5 0
     D   HIZIP                            5 0
```

You can use keyword INZ on the data structure definition line to initialize all the structure's subfields. The initialization values used are zero for numeric subfields and blanks for character fields. You can also associate keyword INZ with individual subfields. In this case you can use the keyword with a constant to specify any desired initial value appropriate to the subfield's data type.

You signal file-information data structures on the file specs, as before, but now you make use of the free-form function area of the revised File Specifications. Use the keyword INFDS, along with the name of the appropriate data structure in parentheses, to associate the data structure with a file. To declare a subroutine as the desired error routine for file errors, use keyword INFSR, with the name of the error subroutine in parentheses. (*PSSR can be the designated error handler, if you want.)

```
          1         2         3         4         5         6         7         8         9         10
  1234567890123456789012345678901234567890123456789012345678901234567890123456789012345678901234567890
      FFilename++IPEASFRlen+LKlen+AIDevice+.Functions++++++++++++++++++++++++++++Comments++++++++++++
      F* File spec. declaring data structure SAMPDS as the file-information data structure, and
      F* the *PSSR subroutine as the error handler in case of errors occurring for this file.
      FSAMPLE    UF  E          K DISK    INFDS(SAMPDS) INFSR(*PSSR)
```

The format of both the CLEAR and the RESET operations has been changed somewhat. You now specify the name of the variable to be cleared or reset in the result position, rather than in factor 2. You can also now define the variable in conjunction with CLEAR or RESET by including a length and a decimal position entry (if appropriate) along with the result. If you CLEAR or RESET a table or multiple-occurrence data structure, only the current table element or occurrence is cleared/reset, unless you include *ALL as a factor 2 entry.

```
          1         2         3         4         5         6         7         8         9         10
  1234567890123456789012345678901234567890123456789012345678901234567890123456789012345678901234567890
      CL0N01Factor1++++++Opcode(E)+Factor2++++++Result++++++++Len++D+HiLoEq....Comments++++++++++++
      C* Count, defined as part of the CLEAR operation, is cleared to 0.
      C                   CLEAR                   COUNT            4 0
      C* Only the current occurrence of data structure STATE is cleared.
      C                   CLEAR                   STATE
      C* Every occurrence of data structure STATE is cleared.
      C                   CLEAR     *ALL          STATE
```

Optional Changes

Field definitions can now occur within the Definition Specifications. You can define these fields, called *stand-alone fields* because they are not part of a data structure, independently or relative to the definition of another field (as in *LIKE DEFN). In either case, in addition to the name of the field, an S (for stand-alone) must appear in position 24, and you must complete the field's definition by specifying its length and type.

You cannot use From and To entries to define the length of a stand-alone field. Instead, there are two ways to signal its length. First, you can enter the actual length of the field in positions 33-39. Alternately, you can use the LIKE keyword to define the field relative to another field. In this case, the name of the referenced field must appear as the parameter of the keyword LIKE. If you want to base one field's definition upon that of another but increase or decrease its size, you can indicate the relative increase or decrease by coding an entry in positions 33-39 with a + or – followed by the increase or decrease in desired bytes.

For stand-alone fields not using LIKE, you must make a decimal position entry in positions 41-42 if the field is numeric. You can also specify a data type in position 40 for this kind of field. (If you leave the data type column blank, the default types are packed decimal for numeric fields and character for non-numeric fields.)

```
         1         2         3         4         5         6         7         8         9        10
1234567890123456789012345678901234567890123456789012345678901234567890123456789012345678901234567890
    DName++++++++++ETDsFrom+++To/L+++IDc.Functions++++++++++++++++++++++++++++++Comments+++++++++++
    D* Examples of definitions of stand-alone fields.
    D NAME_WK         S             25
    D COUNT           S              6 0
    D NEWFLD          S                     LIKE(OLDFLD)
    D FEDTAX          S             -2     LIKE(GROSS)
    D TOTGRS          S             +4     LIKE(GROSS)
```

You can still define fields on Calculation Specifications using *LIKE DEFN, except that the operation code has been changed to DEFINE.

Chapter 10 Modifications

Mandatory Changes

With the change in File Specifications layout, you now associate a subfile and a relative record number field with a workstation file by using keyword SFILE in the Functions area. The subfile record format name, a colon, and the field to be used for the relative record numbers appear within parentheses following the keyword, as shown below.

```
         1         2         3         4         5         6         7         8         9        10
1234567890123456789012345678901234567890123456789012345678901234567890123456789012345678901234567890
    FFilename++IPEASFRlen+LKlen+AIDevice+.Functions++++++++++++++++++++++++++++++Comments+++++++++++
    FSECTIONL  IF  E           K DISK
    FSECTINQ   C   E             WORKSTN SFILE(SUBSEC:RRN)
```

Chapter 11 Modifications

Mandatory Changes

Operations CHEKR and BITOF each have been expanded to six characters: CHECKR and BITOFF.

Optional Changes

RPG IV now includes built-in functions %SIZE, %TRIM, %TRIMR, %TRIML, and %SUBST. These functions return specific values based on evaluation of their arguments (parameters within parentheses following the function). If more than one argument is used for a given function, a colon is used to separate the arguments. Although you may use these functions to define data within Definition Specifications, you are more likely to use them within calculations to manipulate strings. On Calculation Specifications, functions can only appear within an extended factor 2 entry. In that case, the argument of the function can be a variable, a constant, or a free-form expression that can itself include built-in functions.

%SIZE returns the number of bytes occupied by its argument. If the argument has only a single parameter and that parameter is the name of an array, a table, or a multiple-occurrence data structure, the value returned is the size of a single element or occurrence. If a second parameter, *ALL, follows the first, the returned value is the size of the entire table, array, or data structure. Following are some examples of %SIZE.

```
            1         2         3         4         5         6         7         8         9        10
   1234567890123456789012345678901234567890123456789012345678901234567890123456789012345678901234567890
      CLØN01Factor1++++++Opcode(E)+Factor2++++++Result+++++++Len++D+HiLoEq....Comments+++++++++++++
      C                 EVAL      SIZ = %SIZE(FIELDA)                         Length of FIELDA
      C                 EVAL      SIZ = %SIZE(TABLEX)                         Length of 1 element
      C                 EVAL      SIZ = %SIZE(TABLEX:*ALL)                    Bytes of whole table
```

The three trim functions work similarly to remove trailing and/or leading blanks from their arguments. %TRIML removes leading, or left-most blanks; %TRIMR removes trailing, or right-most blanks; and %TRIM removes both trailing and leading blanks. The value returned by these functions is the trimmed result. You can use these functions with character variables, constants, or expressions. You can see how these trim functions work from the examples below.

Function	Returned Value
%TRIML(' 1234 N. 25th St. ')	'1234 N. 25th St. '
%TRIMR(' 1234 N. 25th St. ')	' 1234 N. 25th St.'
%TRIM(' 1234 N. 25th St. ')	'1234 N. 25th St.'

Finally, function %SUBST (substring) works like the SUBST operation, but its expression is more direct than SUBST. Within parentheses following the function, you include as a first parameter the string from which you want to extract some portion. The required second parameter follows a colon separator and represents the starting position of the substring. This starting position can be represented by a numeric variable, a constant, or an expression that evaluates to an integer greater than zero. A third parameter (optional, following a colon separator) indicates the length of the substring to extract. If you omit the third parameter, the substring includes all the bytes from the starting position to the final byte of the string.

```
            1         2         3         4         5         6         7         8         9        10
   1234567890123456789012345678901234567890123456789012345678901234567890123456789012345678901234567890
      CLØN01Factor1++++++Opcode(E)+Factor2++++++Result+++++++Len++D+HiLoEq....Comments+++++++++++++
      C                 EVAL      AREACODE = %SUBST(PHONE:1:3)                First 3 digits
      C                 EVAL      EXCHANGE = %SUBST(PHONE:4:3)                4th-6th digits
      C                 EVAL      LOCAL = %SUBST(PHONE:7)                     7th-end of field
```

Like the other functions already discussed, %SUBST can be used to return a value needed within a calculation, as shown in the above examples. Unlike the other functions, %SUBST can also be used as the *target* of an assignment operation using EVAL to change the value of the designated substring. For this usage, the designated string must be a variable that can be assigned a value; a constant, for example, would be inappropriate. The following figure illustrates this use of %SUBST.

```
        1         2         3         4         5         6         7         8         9        10
123456789012345678901234567890123456789012345678901234567890123456789012345678901234567890
  CLØNØ1Factor1++++++Opcode(E)+Factor2++++++Result++++++++Len++D+HiLoEq....Comments++++++++++++
  C                 EVAL      %SUBST(PHONE:1:3) = '616'
```

Chapter 12 Modifications

Mandatory Changes

As mentioned in Chapter 9, operation code DEFN has been changed to DEFINE. Operation UNLCK has been changed to UNLOCK. In addition, RPG IV no longer recognizes the FREE operation.

Optional Changes

RPG IV now allows calling programs and the programs they call to be *statically bound* (or connected) before execution, rather than dynamically bound at runtime. Static binding significantly improves runtime call performance over that of dynamic binding.

At a source-code level, to indicate static binding, use the operation CALLB, rather than CALL. Factor 2 must contain a literal or constant specifying the name of the called procedure; it cannot be a field that will contain the name of the called program at runtime.

```
        1         2         3         4         5         6         7         8         9        10
123456789012345678901234567890123456789012345678901234567890123456789012345678901234567890
  CLØNØ1Factor1++++++Opcode(E)+Factor2++++++Result++++++++Len++D+HiLoEq....Comments++++++++++++
  C                 CALLB     'MYPROGRAM'
```

To actually "connect" these program modules or procedures (each of which has been separately compiled into an object of type *MODULE through the CRTRPGMOD command) you would issue the CRTPGM (or bind) command and specify the modules to be linked.

Data defined within a procedure is local to that procedure; it is not automatically available to other procedures bound with it. To pass data between procedures, you can use PARMs and PLIST with CALLB, just as with CALL. Additionally, you can use variables whose values are available across procedures by defining the data item on Definition Specifications of each relevant procedure; include keyword EXPORT within the definition of the procedure that you want responsible for storage allocation and include keyword IMPORT within the variable's definition in the remaining procedures that need to reference it. Data items so defined should *not* be included as PARMs.

Chapter 13 Modifications

Mandatory Changes

RPG IV continues to allow you to condition calculations with indicators. However, to make more room within Calculation Specifications for other kinds of entries (and to acknowledge the trend away from this use of indicators), the redesigned specification has room for only a single conditioning indicator per specification line. To signal that a calculation should be executed if two (or more) indicators are on, you will need to use two (or more) lines of code (with one indicator per line) and place AN in positions 7-8 of all but the first line of the calculation.

```
          1         2         3         4         5         6         7         8         9        10
1234567890123456789012345678901234567890123456789012345678901234567890123456789012345678901234567890
CL0N01Factor1+++++++Opcode(E)+Factor2+++++++Result+++++++Len++D+HiLoEq....Comments++++++++++++
C* Assign LIFE the value of 84 only if indicators 65 and 70 are both on.
C   65
CAN 70              Z-ADD     84        LIFE
```

The SETOF operation has been changed to SETOFF.

Glossary

abend — the condition in which a program prematurely terminates, or ends abnormally, after issuing an error message indicating the problem that prevented the program from reaching its normal ending point. (Chapters 6; 9)

algorithm — a step-by-step procedure for solving a problem. (Chapter 1)

alphanumeric data — data treated as characters, rather than numbers, regardless of the actual make-up of the data; may be alphabetic, special characters, or digits. (Chapter 1)

alternating format — the form of data entry in tables or arrays in which pairs of related data are entered together. (Chapter 8)

array — a data structure similar to a table in that it contains multiple elements defined with a common name; unlike tables, individual elements of arrays may be referenced by using an index. Also unlike tables, arrays can be loaded with values during the course of program execution — called runtime arrays. (Chapter 8)

arrival sequence — the sequence in which database records are accessed in the order in which they were placed in the database file (first-in, first-out), rather than based on the value of a key field. (Chapter 5)

assignment operations — those operations that allow you to simply assign a value to a variable. RPG has four assignment operations: Z-ADD (Zero and Add), Z-SUB (Zero and Subtract), MOVE (Move), and MOVEL (Move Left). (Chapter 3)

"backwards" sequential access — accessing records in a database file in descending key order through the READP or REDPE operations. (Chapter 6)

base string — the factor 2 value of string operations (e.g., SCAN, CHECK, XLATE), which serves as the focus or target of the string operation. (Chapter 11)

basing pointer — a data type that allows you to access variables whose storage is dynamically allocated based on the value of the associated pointer. (Chapter 14)

batch processing — computer processing in which the computer processes a "batch" of data (typically representing business transactions) without user intervention, in contrast to applications that are interactively controlled by the user during execution. (Chapters 1; 7)

binary — a system of representing values based on powers of 2. For example, decimal value 8 is 1000 in binary. (Chapter 11)

binary data type — numeric data stored directly in base 2 representation, rather than through EBCDIC encoding. (Chapter 5)

bits (binary digits) — either 0 or 1. A group of eight adjacent binary digits represents one EBCDIC character and equals one byte. See also decimal bits; zone bits (Chapters 1; 11)

built-in function — a construct that is predefined by a programming language to return a specific value for use in an expression; the nature of the returned value depends on which built-in function is used. (Chapter 14)

Calculation Specifications — lines in RPG programs that detail the procedural processing steps, including calculations, to be performed by your program. Each Calculation Specification line of code must include a C in position 6. (Chapter 2)

CALL operation — Call a Program operation in RPG invokes the execution of another program. CALL allows an application system to be broken into small, self-contained modules of code. (Chapter 12)

CASE logic — a logic construct that allows multiple alternate branches of processing to be specified, in contrast to an IF structure, which allows only a single alternate branch. (Chapter 4)

case sensitive — a characteristic of programming languages that means the compiler differentiates between an uppercase letter and its lowercase version; the two are not treated as equivalent. (Chapter 14)

character data type — a declaration that a field will contain alphanumeric data. (Chapter 5)

character field — a field defined to represent alphanumeric characters. (Chapter 2)

character literals — non-numeric elements used in factor 1 and/or factor 2 of the Calculation Specifications when working with character-oriented operations. Any character you can represent via the keyboard, including a blank, can comprise a character literal. To indicate that a value is a character literal and not a field name, simply enclose it with apostrophes. (Chapter 3)

check-protection — a technique most commonly used in printing checks in which insignificant leading zeros in a number are replaced by asterisks rather than simply suppressed to prevent tampering with the check's face value. (Chapter 2)

combined file — a file that supports both input and output, but as independent operations. Display files are combined files. (Chapter 7)

comment lines — *See* internal documentation. (Chapters 1; 2; 3)

compare string — the factor 1 value of a string operation (e.g., SCAN, CHECK, CHEKR) that contains the value to be checked for in the base string contained in factor 2. (Chapter 11)

compile — to translate the source code of a program into machine language, or object code. (Chapter 1)

compile-time array — an array whose values are hard-coded at the end of the source program and whose values are bound to the array when the program is compiled. (Chapter 8)

compile-time table — a table whose values are entered at the end of the source program and are bound to the table when the program is compiled. (Chapter 8)

compiler — a special computer program that translates a program written in a high-level programming language (HLL) into machine language that the computer can understand. (Chapter 1)

composite key — a key for a file or record format composed of more than one field. (Chapters 5; 6)

concatenated key — same as composite key. (Chapter 6)

concatenation — an operation that joins two character strings in the order specified, forming a single string. (Chapters 5; 11)

constants — in an RPG program, those characters that do not change, representing the actual values that will be processed or printed out on a report; also called literals. (Chapter 2)

continuation line — a line that allows you to continue a line of code; continuation lines can be used with File, Definition, Calculation, and Output Specifications for completing keyword and free-form entries that are too long to fit on a single line. (Chapter 14)

control-break problem — a special type of batch processing problem for files whose records are grouped by values of a control field and that require special processing based on a change in the control field's value; generally the special processing involves printing subtotals for each group of records. (Chapter 4)

crossfooting — a term used in accounting to sum across a row of figures to develop a total for that row. (Chapter 8)

CUA — Common User Access; a set of IBM design standards that were developed to promote standardizing user interfaces across platforms. (Chapter 7)

data area — an AS/400 object used to communicate data between programs within a job or between jobs. One program does not have to call another to access the same data if the data resides in a data area. (Chapter 12)

data-area data structures — data structures defined specifically for data areas. See also data area; data structure (Chapter 12)

Data Description Specifications (DDS) — the name given to the RPG specification form on which database and display file definitions are developed. (Chapter 5)

data dictionary — a central repository for storing definitions of data independent of programs and widely used in a database approach to data management; on the AS/400, a data dictionary can be developed through a special kind of physical file, called a field-reference file. (Chapters 1; 5)

Data File Utility (DFU) — an AS/400 program that facilitates entering data values into database files without the need for writing a HLL data-entry program. (Chapter 5)

data structure — a contiguous portion of memory, which is then subdivided and referenced in different ways by the data structure's subfields. (Chapter 9)

data type — a declared characteristic of data items; a field's data type determines what kinds of values it can store and what operations can be performed on it. (Chapter 14)

data validation — attempting to determine that data is correct prior to accepting it as input. In RPG, the four major keywords used for validating user-entered data are VALUES, COMP, RANGE, and CHECK. (Chapter 7)

date data type — a data type used to store dates; fields of this type (type D) are 10 bytes long with the default format yyyy-mm-dd. (Chapter 14)

debugging — correcting any error found in a computer program. (Chapter 1; Appendix C)

decimal bits — the right-most 4 bits of a byte, numbered 4, 5, 6, and 7; also called low-order or digit bits. *See also* bits. (Chapter 11)

decimal — a system of representing values based on powers of 10. (Chapter 11)

decision operations — the options for sending control to alternate statements within a program. *See also* selection. (Chapter 4)

Definition Specifications — lines used in RPG IV programs for defining fields, constants, arrays, tables, and data structures used within a program; Definition Specifications require a D in position 6. (Chapter 14)

detail line — an output line based on data contained in a single record of an input file; the line prints detailed information about the data record being processed. (Chapter 2)

digit bits — the right-most four bits of a byte; also called low-order or decimal bits. (Chapter 5)

display attributes — special characteristics that can be assigned to fields to affect their appearance on the screen; includes such features as underlining, high intensity, and blinking. (Chapter 7)

display file — files that define the screens that the program presents as it runs. Display files allow values keyed by the user in response to the screen to be input as data to the program; therefore, display files serve as the mechanism that allows the user and the program to interact. (Chapter 7)

Double Byte Character Set (DBCS) data type — a graphic data type in which two bytes (rather than a single byte) are required to represent any one character of the character set being represented. (Chapter 14)

dynamic binding — the process of interconnecting programs (that call one another) at execution time, rather than when the programs are created; the CALL operation is used with this kind of binding. (Chapter 14)

EBCDIC — Extended Binary Coded Decimal Interchange Code; the data-representation format used by IBM. EBCDIC assigns a unique 8-bit binary pattern to each representable character or digit. The left-most four bits are called zone or high-order bits; the right-most four bits are called digit or low-order bits. In this format, A is less than B, B less than C, and so on. Lowercase letters are "smaller" than uppercase letters, letters are smaller than digits, and blank is smaller than any other displayable character. (Chapters 4; 5)

edit code — a letter or number that specifies how numeric values are to be formatted to make them more readable upon output; different edit codes evoke different formatting. (Chapter 2)

edit words — an alternative to edit codes for signaling the desired format for numeric output; an edit word supplies a template into which a numeric value is inserted and may include instructions for zero-suppression and insertion of special characters. Edit codes and edit words are never used together for the same field. (Chapter 2)

editor — a computer program designed to allow you to enter, rearrange, change, and delete source program statements (or other text) interactively. SEU, the AS/400's editor, also performs basic syntax checking as you enter program statements. (Chapter 1)

end-of-file — in sequential record access, when an attempt to read another record fails because no records remain unprocessed. (Chapter 2)

exponentiation — the operation in which a value is raised to a power. (Chapter 3)

extended factor 2 format — a form of the Calculation Specifications in which there is no result entry; instead, positions 36-80 are used for a free-form expression. (Chapter 14)

Extension Specifications — specifications used in RPG/400 to define tables and arrays; RPG IV eliminated these specifications, transferring the definition function to the Definition Specifications. (Chapter 8)

external documentation — material added to, but not a direct part of, a program that is useful for understanding, using, or modifying the program, such as system and program flowcharts, user manuals, or operator instructions. (Chapter 1)

externally described file — a file whose records are defined at a field level to the system when the file is created and whose external definition is used by a program referencing that file. (Chapter 5)

field — generally represents the smallest unit of data to be manipulated within a program, such as a customer account number, last name, first name, street address, city, state, zip code, phone number, and so on. *See also* Program Variable. (Chapter 1)

field definition — the specification of variables to be used within a program by assigning the variable a name, length, and data type. (Chapter 2)

field-definition lines — also called field-description lines; lines in an RPG program that describe the content of a given input record for program-described files. (Chapter 2)

field-level keywords — keywords that are associated only with a specific field within a file in DDS Specifications. (Chapter 5)

field-reference file — another name for a centralized data dictionary of the fields in a physical file. *See* data dictionary. (Chapter 5)

figurative constants — implied literals that can be used without a specified length. Figurative constants assume the length and decimal positions of the fields they are associated with. RPG's figurative constants are *BLANK (or *BLANKS), *ZERO (or *ZEROS), *HIVAL, *LOVAL, *OFF, *ON, and *ALL'X..'. (Chapter 3)

file — a named set of records stored or processed as a unit. In RPG, files are either physical files or logical files. *See* physical file; logical file. (Chapter 1)

file access — the means by which a file can be read, written to, or updated; methods include sequential and random access. *See* sequential access; random access (Chapter 6)

File Description Specifications — program lines that describe the files your program uses and how the files will be used within the program. File Description Specifications generally begin RPG programs, and all file specifications include an F in position 6. Each file used by a program requires its own file specification line. (Chapter 2)

file designation — refers to the way the program will access, or retrieve, the data in an input, combined, or update file. (Chapter 2)

file-information data structure — a special data structure that can be defined for each file used by a program. File-information data structures contain predefined subfields that provide information about the file following I/O operations. (Chapter 9)

file-level keywords — in DDS Specifications, keywords that apply to the file as a whole. (Chapter 5)

file locking — limiting access to a file to one user at a time. (Chapter 6)

File Specifications — a shortened synonym for File Description Specifications. (Chapter 2)

fixed dollar sign — in numeric data, where the dollar sign is positioned in a set column of the output, regardless of the number of significant digits in the number following the sign. (Chapter 1)

fixed-form — *See* fixed-position. (Chapter 2)

fixed format — in File Specifications, an indication that a file's records will be described within the program and that each record of the file has the same, fixed length. (Chapter 2)

fixed-logic cycle — RPG's built-in read-process-write cycle that repeats until all the desired records have been processed. (Chapter 13)

fixed-position — also called *fixed-form*, means that the location of an entry within a program line is critical to its interpretation by the RPG compiler. (Chapter 2)

floating dollar sign — in numeric data, where the dollar sign prints next to the left-most significant digit of the number; the position of the dollar sign varies, or floats, depending on the value of the number with which it is associated. (Chapter 1)

Fourth-generation languages (4GLs) — languages designed to make programming easier by allowing the programmer to specify the desired results to be accomplished instead of the detailed processing required to achieve the desired results; often also referred to as non-procedural languages. (Chapter 1)

free-form — a term used to characterize program syntax; free-form implies that the meaning of the code is not dependent on the location of the code within a line (i.e., the meaning is not positionally dependent). (Chapter 14)

full procedural — the term used for a file whose records are explicitly read within the program, as opposed to using the built-in retrieval of RPG's fixed-logic cycle. Such files are identified by an F in position 16 of the entry for file designation on the File Specifications. (Chapter 2)

graphical user interface (GUI) — a visual computer interface that uses icons to represent actual objects; the user accesses and manipulates these icons via a pointing device. The PC Windows environment typifies a GUI. (Chapter 7)

Gregorian format — date format in which a date is expressed in terms of the year, month, and day of the month on which the date falls, based on the calendar system established in 1582 by Pope Gregory XIII. (Chapter 12)

half-adjusting — the term often used to mean "rounding" a numeric answer on the computer. The computer adds half the value of the right-most desired decimal position to the digit immediately to the right of that decimal position before storing the answer in the result field. Because the value added is half the value of the least-significant digit position of the result, the term half-adjust evolved. (Chapter 3)

help-specification format — a format within the Data Description Specifications (DDS) that will associate a specific portion of the screen with a specific record of help text. (Chapter 10)

hexadecimal — a system of representing values based on powers of 16. Digits 0-9 are used to represent 0-9 in hexadecimal; characters A-F are used to represent values 10-15, respectively. Hex B (usually represented as X'0B') is the equivalent of decimal 11, for example. (Chapter 11)

hierarchical decomposition — *See* top-down design. (Chapter 4)

high-level languages (HLLs) — programming languages designed to make it easier for programmers to express instructions to computers; contrasted to low-level languages such as machine language or assembler. Programs written in an HLL need to be translated into machine language, a process called compiling, before the computer can actually execute the program. (Chapter 1)

high-order bits — *See* zone bits; EBCDIC. (Chapter 5)

high-order truncation — the loss of digits from the left end of a result field. (Chapter 3)

indicator — an internal switch, or variable, with only two states or values — off or on (or '0' or '1'), used by a program to signal whether a particular event has occurred within the program and to control, or condition, subsequent processing within the program. (Chapters 1; 2)

input file — a file that contains data to be read by the program. (Chapter 2)

Input Specifications — those specifications that follow File Specifications in an RPG/400 program and Definition Specifications in an RPG IV program. Input Specifications describe the records within the program-described input files and define the fields within the records; they are identified by an I in position 6. (Chapter 2)

integer data — data representing whole numbers. (Chapter 2)

integer numeric field — a numeric field defined with 0 decimal positions, such that it can only store whole numbers. (Chapter 2)

interactive applications — those applications in which a user interacts with the computer directly through a terminal or workstation to control the actions of a computer program as it is running. (Chapters 1; 7)

internal documentation — comments included within the source code of a program to aid in understanding, using, or modifying the program. In RPG, coding an asterisk (*) in position 7 designates that line to be a comment. (Chapters 1; 2; 3)

iteration — a control structure within a program that permits instructions within the program to be repeated until a condition is met or is no longer met; also called "repetition" or "looping". (Chapter 4)

join-logical file — a logical file that combines fields from different physical files into a single record. (Chapter 5)

Julian format — date format in which dates are represented as sequential numbers, so that one value can be subtracted from the other. (Chapter 12)

key field — a field in a record whose contents are used to build access paths to records such that the records appear to be in sequence based on that field's values. (Chapter 5)

key sequence — an access method in which database records are retrieved based on the key field defined for the records. (Chapter 5)

key specifications — DDS specifications that declare which field (or fields) is to serve as the key to the file. (Chapter 5)

keyboard-shift attribute — an entry associated with fields within display files that determines what kinds of data a user can input into that field or be displayed. (Chapter 7)

keywords — reserved words that have special meanings within RPG and DDS; keywords are used on File Specifications to signal attributes of the file and on Definition Specifications to specify characteristics of the data item being defined. Some keywords require the inclusion of parameter values to indicate which of several allowable options you are selecting. In DDS, keywords may be associated with a whole file, with record formats within a file, or with fields within a record format to enable special functions, designate display attributes, and so on. *See also* file-level keywords, record-level keywords, and field-level keywords. (Chapters 5; 7; 14)

leading-decision loop — a program loop in which the test to determine whether the instructions within the loop are to be performed is made before the instructions within the loop are executed for the first time. (Chapter 4)

level checking — a feature of the AS/400 that prevents running a program if changes have been made to the definition of a physical or logical file used by that program unless the program is first recompiled. This feature prevents executing a program using an obsolete or inaccurate definition of a database file. (Chapter 5)

list panels — term referring to the screen display of data from many records for review, selection, and update. (Chapter 10)

literals — *See* constants. (Chapter 2)

local data area (LDA) — a data area created for each job in the system. Each LDA is 1,024 positions long, with type character. *See also* data area. (Chapter 12)

logic errors — program errors caused by faulty program design that cause the program to end abnormally, loop infinitely, or process data incorrectly to produce incorrect output. (Chapter 1; Appendix C)

logical files — files that describe how data appears to be stored in the database. Logical files do not actually contain data records, but rather access paths, or pointers, to records in physical files. Logical files must have one or more fields designated as a key, by which the access paths are identified. (Chapter 5)

low-order bits — the four right-most bits of a byte, also known as decimal or digit bits. *See* high-order bits; EBCDIC. (Chapter 5)

low-order truncation — the loss of digits from the right end of a result field. (Chapter 3)

master files — sets of data or files, of long-term or permanent, importance; such files contain vital information for an organization's ongoing operations. (Chapter 1)

mixed-case entry — a characteristic of programming languages that allows you to enter alphabetic characters as either uppercase or lowercase. (Chapter 14)

modular programming — approach to programming in which small, stand-alone units of code are developed (as opposed to monolithic programs thousands of lines long). (Chapter 12)

multiple-occurrence data structure — similar to a table or an array, a multiple-occurrence data structure enables multiple repetitions of the data structure in storage. (Chapter 9)

named constant — in RPG, a constant value that has been provided with a name; this value can then be used throughout the program by referring to it by name, rather than entering the value itself. (Chapter 9)

numeric data — pertaining to non-alphabetic information — i.e., numbers; arithmetic calculations can be performed on numeric data. (Chapter 1)

numeric field — fields that contain numeric values; numeric fields may be used in calculations and edited for output. (Chapters 2; 3)

numeric literals — a number *per se* whose value remains fixed throughout a program. A numeric literal can be up to 10 positions long and may include the digits 0 through 9, and a decimal point and/or a sign. (Chapter 3)

object code — a program's code translated into executable machine language. (Chapter 1)

output editing — refers to formatting numeric output values by suppressing leading zeros and adding special characters, such as decimal points, commas, and dollar signs to make the values easier to comprehend for people looking at the output. (Chapters 1; 2)

output file — the destination for writing operations of a computer program. (Chapter 2)

Output Specifications — specifications used to define the desired format of output files when described within a program; they are identified by an O in position 6. (Chapter 2)

overflow indicators — special built-in indicators in RPG that signal end-of-page. RPG/400's overflow indicators include OA, OB, OC, OD, OE, OF, OG, and OV. (Chapter 4)

packed-decimal data type — the numeric representation of data in EBCDIC format in which only the digit, or low-order, bits of a number are stored, with the sign of the number represented by an additional four bits. The sign bits always occupy the right-most four-bit positions of a packed-decimal value. (Chapter 5)

PARMs — RPG's method of designating fields to be shared between a calling and called program. (Chapter 12)

phantom updates — the condition that occurs if two users access the same record for update at the same time and as a result of this concurrent access, one of the user's changes are lost; modern multiuser operating systems are designed to prevent phantom updates. (Chapter 6)

physical files — database files that actually store data records. (Chapter 5)

PLIST operation — an RPG declarative operation that identifies a list of parameters to be shared between programs. PLIST requires an identifying entry in factor 1. (Chapter 12)

pre-runtime array — an array whose values are obtained from a disk file at the start of a program's execution. (Chapter 8)

pre-runtime/pre-execution table — a table whose values are obtained from a disk file at the start of a program's execution. (Chapter 8)

priming read — an initial read operation prior to the main process loop of a program, designed to provide the instructions within the loop with their first set of data to process. (Chapter 2)

printer spacing chart (PSC) — a detailed representation of the desired report layout when desired output includes a report. The PSC shows all constants the report should include (e.g., report headings, column headings) and where on the report the constants should appear. Variable information is generally indicated by Xs, where each X represents one character of data. (Chapter 1)

problem definition — the first step in the Program Development Cycle, the process of identifying the problem in terms of the programming specifications. (Chapter 1)

procedural languages — programming languages that require explicit, step-by-step statements or instructions to the computer of the procedure required to produce a specific result or product (e.g., a sales report). (Chapter 1)

procedure pointer — a data type that is used to point to a program (or a procedure) whose storage is dynamically allocated. (Chapter 14)

program design — the second — and crucial — step in the Program Development Cycle, this phase encompasses working out the solution (algorithm) to the problem using sound programming logic prior to expressing the solution in a given programming language. (Chapter 1)

Program Development Cycle — the sequence of activities required to develop a program, including defining the problem, designing the solution, writing the program, entering the program, testing and debugging the program, documenting the program, and maintaining the program. (Chapter 1)

program maintenance — making modifications to a program once it is actually being used, or "in production." (Chapter 1)

program module — an object of type *MODULE that is the result of a compile operation in RPG IV; a program module must be bound (either alone or with other modules) to produce an executable program. (Chapter 14)

program-status data structure — a data structure that can provide information about the program itself and about exceptions/errors that occur during program execution. (Chapter 9)

program variable — a program-defined construct that represents a location in the computer's memory; referencing a variable within a program causes the computer to access the memory location that corresponds to that variable and appropriately manipulate the data value stored at that location. In RPG, the term *field* is usually used instead of *variable*. Such fields, or variables, may represent alphanumeric (character) or numeric data. (Chapter 1)

pseudocode — a tool of program design that uses stylized English to detail the underlying logic needed for a program. (Chapters 1; 2)

random access — the term applied to file access by just "reaching into" a file and extracting only the specific record you want (as opposed to retrieving database records sequentially). (Chapter 6)

range table — a table in which the entries represent a range of values rather than discreet values. (Chapter 8).

record — a set of one or more related data items grouped for processing. (Chapter 1)

record-format descriptions — a term used to describe those entries on Input and Output Specifications that describe one record type of a program-described input or output file. (Chapter 2)

record layouts — descriptions of the record formats of input files to be used by a program, including the beginning and ending positions of data fields within records, the order and length of the fields, and the number of decimal positions for numeric data. (Chapter 1)

record-level keywords — in DDS, those keywords that apply to a specific record format within a file. (Chapter 5)

record locking — a mechanism for preventing two users from accessing the same database record for update at the same time. RPG automatically puts a lock on a record of an Update file when the record is read. Updating that record or reading another record releases the record from the locked state. While the record is locked, other application programs can access the record if they have defined the file as an input file, but not if they have defined it as an update file. (Chapter 6)

recursion — a programming technique in which subroutines execute or invoke themselves, either directly or indirectly through an intermediate subroutine; this technique is not permitted in RPG. (Chapter 4)

redundancy — the duplication of data across files. (Chapter 5)

relational codes — in RPG programming, one of six two-letter codes used in making a relational comparison between two values. The six codes are GT (Greater Than), LT (Less Than), EQ (Equal To), NE (Not Equal To), LE (Less Than or Equal To) and GE (Greater Than or Equal To). (Chapter 4)

relational comparison — testing a condition to determine the appropriate course of action within a program by making a comparison between two values via one of six criteria: Greater Than (GT), Less Than (LT), Equal To (ET), Not Equal To (NE), Less Than or Equal To (LE), and Greater Than or Equal To (GE). (Chapter 4)

Report Program Generator (RPG) — a high-level programming language introduced by IBM in the early 1960s. As originally designed, RPG included a fixed-logic cycle that eliminated the need for programmers to detail each processing step required for the computer to execute the program. Another unique characteristic of RPG was its use of a special class of built-in, pre-defined variables called indicators. (Chapter 1)

runtime array — an array that obtains or changes its values during the course of program execution, as a result of either input or calculations. (Chapter 8)

selection — the logic structure that lets you establish alternate paths of instructions within a program; which alternate the program executes depends on the results of a test or condition within the program. (Chapter 4)

sequence — the logic structure that lets you instruct the computer to execute operations serially. (Chapter 4)

sequential access — a method of retrieving or reading records serially, either in key order (if the file is keyed and so noted in position 31 on the File Specifications) or in arrival or FIFO (First-In-First-Out) order (for non-keyed files). (Chapter 6)

simple logical file — a logical file whose records are based on a single physical file. *See* logical file. (Chapter 5)

source code — the statements/instructions of a program expressed in a high-level language. (Chapters 1; 7)

Source Entry Utility (SEU) — the AS/400 editor you use to enter your RPG program. *Also see* Appendix B. (Chapters 2; 7)

source member — on the AS/400, a subset of a file that contains a set of source statements/instructions representing a single program. (Chapters 1; 7)

spaghetti code — a program whose flow of control is difficult to follow; usually caused by undisciplined, haphazard transfer of control from one part of the program to another. (Chapters 1; 4; 7)

stand-alone field — a field whose definition is independent of any data structure definition. (Chapter 14)

static binding — a method of interconnecting separate program modules (that call one another) at a binding step prior to execution; the CALLB operation is used with this kind of binding. (Chapter 14)

structured design — a program development methodology that advocates a systematic approach to program design and emphasizes limiting flow-of-control structures within a program to three basic logic structures: sequence, selection (also called decision), and iteration (also called repetition or looping). (Chapters 1; 4)

subfile control-record format — the record format immediately following the subfile record format that controls the display of the subfile records through the use of special record-level keywords. Column headings for the subfile display also are often included as part of this record format. (Chapter 10)

subfile record format — describes the subfile fields that are to appear on the screen. (Chapter 10)

subfiles — a collection of record data from a database file that is handled as a unit for screen I/O. (Chapter 10)

subroutine — a set of operations coded elsewhere within the calculations of a program and invoked as a unit by referencing the subroutine's name with an EXSR (Execute Subroutine) operation. (Chapter 4)

subschemas — in database terminology, users' views of data. (Chapter 5)

syntax errors — errors in programming caused by misuse of the rules of the programming language that prevent the creation of an object program for the computer to execute. *See* Appendix C. (Chapter 1)

table — conceptually, a collection of data organized into columns and rows. Similar kinds of data are stored within a column, and the data within a row of a table is "related," or belongs together. In RPG, one column of such a conceptual table. (Chapter 8)

table look-up — an operation to locate a specified value within a table. In RPG, the common use of tables is to look up a value in one table to extract a related value from a second table. (Chapter 8)

time data type — a data type used to store time data; fields of this type (type T) are 8 bytes long with the default format hh.mm.ss. (Chapter 14)

timestamp data type — a data type used to store date and time to the nearest microsecond; fields of this type (type Z) are 26 bytes long with the default form yyyy-mm-dd-hh.mm.ss.mmmmmm. (Chapter 14)

top-down design — the term used for program development that starts with a broad "outline" of the solution followed by successively breaking the big pieces into smaller and smaller units. Also sometimes called hierarchical decomposition. (Chapter 4)

trailing-decision loop — a program loop in which a test based on a comparison is made after the instructions within the loop have been executed; the outcome of the test determines whether or not the instructions within the loop are again executed. (Chapter 4)

transaction files — relatively temporary data files, usually generated during the course of a day's business, that often need to be processed only a single time. (Chapter 1)

truncation — the loss of digits from the right or the left ends of a result field. (Chapter 3)

two-dimensional array — an array that requires two indexes (or subscripts) to determine the identity of a given element of the array; one index points to the row and the second to the column location of the element. (Chapter 9)

volatile — in terms of programming, refers to data that is frequently changing. (Chapter 8)

Warnier-Orr diagram — a tool of program design that uses a notation relying on brackets to indicate program level and logic structures, such as iteration and decision. (Chapter 1)

zero suppression — the elimination of leading, non-significant zeros when printing or displaying numeric data. For example, 000123 would print as " 123" if zero suppression were in effect. (Chapter 1)

zone bits — the left-most four bits in IBM's EBCDIC coding scheme, bits 0, 1, 2, and 3. *See also* bits; decimal bits; high-order bits; EBCDIC. (Chapters 5; 11)

zoned-decimal data type — the numeric representation of data in EBCDIC format in which a full byte is required to store each digit of a numeric value, except that the zone of the right-most digit is used to store the sign of the data (1111 represents a + sign and 1101 represents a − sign). (Chapter 5)

Index

* (asterisk)
  as check-protection, 37
  EDTCDE/EDTWRD keywords and, 180
  as object type designation, 389
  in printer spacing chart, 8
  as syntax error designation, 408
+ (plus sign), continuation character, 376, 433
: (colon), concatenated fields and, 300
, (commas)
  edit words and, 38
  indexing notation, 216
' (apostrophes)
  character literals and, 59
  display file documentation, 173
− (minus sign)
  continuation character, 376, 433
  floating negative sign and, 8
/ (slash)
  dates and, 8, 36
  "divided by" sign, 48
_ (underscore), 433

A

Abends, 142, 254
  diagnosing, 408-409
  See also Errors
Access. *See* File access
Accumulating, 45, 50
  See also Addition
Accumulators
  RPG II and, 340-341
  setting, 249
%ADDR function, 375
ADD (Add) operation, 44-46
  code example, 45-46
  rounding for, 53
ADDBKP (Add Breakpoint) command, 414

ADDDUR (Add Duration) operation, 359, 372, 384
  code example, 372
  defined, 372
Addition, 44-46
  result field size for, 50-51
ADDTRC (Add Trace) command, 414-415
Algorithms, 9
*ALL, 64, 152
Alphanumeric data, 5
ALT keyword, 363
AND operation, 371
AND relationship, 334, 344
Apostrophes (')
  character literals and, 59
  display file documentation, 173
Application System/400, 3
Applications
  batch, 169
  interactive, 2, 169-200, 349
Arithmetic operations, 44-49, 65
  ADD, 44-46
  arrays and, 218-219
  coding, 44
  DIV, 48
  MVR, 48-49, 52
  SQRT, 49
  SUB, 46
  using, 54-57
  See also Calculations
Array look-ups, 225-226
  indexes and, 225-226
Arrays, 214-228
  arithmetic operations and, 218-219
  calculations with, 218-222
  compile-time, 215
  corresponding elements of, 219
  defined, 214-215
  Definition Specification and, 362-363

elements for, 216-217, 223
  indicators as, 226-227
  printing, 227
example using, 223-225
*IN, 226-227, 228
for left-justifying field values, 305
length notation for, 366
loading data into, 215
names of, 215
operations, 219-222
output with, 227-228
pre-runtime, 215
required entries for, 215
RPG IV definition, 362-363, 437
runtime, 215-218
for string manipulation, 303-306
two-dimensional, 246
using, 222-225
See also Indexes; Tables
Arrival sequence, 108
AS/400, 389-397
  Programmer Menu, 389, 390-391
  Programming Development Manager (PDM), 389, 391-397
ASCEND keyword, 363, 437
Assignment operations, 57-63, 65
  defined, 57
  MOVE, 59-61
  MOVEL, 62-63
  Z-ADD, 57-58
  Z-SUB, 58
Asterisk (*)
  as check-protection, 37
  EDTCDE/EDTWRD keywords and, 180
  as object type designation, 389
  in printer spacing chart, 8
  as syntax error designation, 408

B

Base string, 295
BASED keyword, 368
Basing pointers, 359-360
Batch processing, 2, 80, 169
Binary digits, 1
Binary format, 111, 134, 308
  storage and, 113
  use of, 113
Binding. *See* Dynamic binding;
  Static binding
BITOF (Set Bits Off) operation, 306,
  309
BITON (Set Bits On) operation, 306,
  309
Bits, 1
  decimal, 112, 306
  manipulating, 293
  numbering of, 306
  setting off, 306
  setting on, 306
  testing, 307
  working with, 306-309
  zone, 112, 306
*BLANK (*BLANKS), 63
Blanks, 74, 433
BLINK keyword, 179, 187
Breakpoints, 414
Built-in functions, 373-375, 442-444
  %ADDR, 375
  defined, 373
  %ELEM, 374
  name format, 374
  %PADDR, 375
  %SIZE, 374-375, 442
  %SUBST, 374, 383, 442, 443
  %TRIM, 374, 442, 443
  %TRIML, 374, 442, 443
  %TRIMR, 374, 383, 442, 443
  using, 373-374
Bytes, manipulating, 293

C

CABxx (Compare and Branch)
  operation, 89-90

  code example, 90
  multiple, 89
  transfer of control, 89
Calculation Specifications, 17, 28-32, 38
  for externally described files, 124
  illustrated, 30
  indicators and, 30
  operations, 30, 31-32
  RPG II, 335-336
  RPG IV, 369-376, 432
  use of, 28
  See also Specifications
Calculations
  with arrays, 218-222
  commenting on, 54
  complex, 54
  errors in, 413
  indicators and, 30-31
  total-time, 337, 340
  See also Arithmetic operations
CALL (Call a Program) operation,
  313-317, 325-326
  code example, 314
  defined, 313
  to external routine, 315
  factor 2, 313
  flow of control, 314-315
  repetition of, 314
  See also RETRN (Return to Caller)
    operation
CALLB operation, 375-376, 384, 444
  code example, 376
  defined, 375
  PARM operation with, 376
  PLIST operation with, 376
CAnn keyword, 173, 178, 179
CASE logic, 77, 79
Case sensitivity, RPG IV, 358
CASxx operation, 80, 92
  ENDCS, 80
  subroutines, 80
CAT (Concatenate Two Character
  Strings) operation, 300-301, 305, 309
  code examples, 301
  defined, 300

  residual characters, 301
CFnn keyword, 173, 178, 179
CHAIN (Random Retrieval from a
  File) operation, 147-148, 286
  code example, 148
  defined, 147
  successful, 148, 151
  unsuccessful, 148
Character data, 111
Character fields, 22, 309
  comparing, 297
  inspection of, 293-299
  manipulation, 299-303
  numeric, 293
  scanning, 295
  See also Fields
Character literals, 59-63
  length of, 59
  MOVE, 59-61
  MOVEL, 61-62
  using, 59
  See also Literals
Characters
  discrepancies between, 297
  right-most invalid, 298
  translating, 301-302
CHECK (Check) operation, 297-298,
  309
  code example, 298
  format, 297
  uses, 297
CHECK keyword, 183
  code example, 183
  defined, 183
  parameter values, 183
Check-protection, 37
CHEKR (Check Reverse) operation,
  298-299, 309
  code example, 299
  defined, 298
CL commands
  ADDBKP (Add Breakpoint), 414
  ADDTRC (Add Trace), 414-415
  CLRTRCDTA (Clear Trace Data),
    415

CRTDTAARA (Create Data Area), 321

CRTLF (Create Logical File), 122

CRTPF (Create Physical File), 122

CRTPGM (Create Program), 375

CVTRPGSRC (Convert RPG Source), 358, 383

DSPMSG (Display Message), 397

DSPPGMVAR (Display Program Variable), 414

DSPTRC (Display Trace), 415

DSPTRCDTA (Display Trace Data), 415

ENDDBG (End Debugger), 413

RMVBRK (Remove Breakpoint), 414

RMVTRC (Remove Trace), 415

STRDBG (Start Debugger), 413

STRSEU (Start SEU), 399

CLEAR operation, 249-250, 258
  code example, 250
  defined, 249
  factor 2 entry, 249-250
  NOKEY option, 250
  for record formats, 250
  RPG IV, 441

CLOSE operation, 159
  code example, 159
  defined, 159
  See also OPEN operation

CLRTRCDTA (Clear Trace Data) command, 415

Code. See Object code; Source code

Colon (:), concatenated fields and, 300

Combined files, 176

Commas (,)
  edit words and, 38
  indexing notation, 216

Comment lines, 33, 39
  DDS, 109
  on calculations, 54

Common User Access (CUA), 195-196, 197
  reasons for adopting, 196
  row and column placement, 196

See also Screens

Communications, interprogram, 313-330

COMP (Compare) operation, 342-345, 350
  code examples, 343, 344, 345
  defined, 342
  indicators, 342-345

COMP keyword, 117-118
  code example, 183
  defined, 182
  relational operators, 183

Compare string, 295

Comparisons
  character, 74
  between field values, 118
  relational, 73-74

Compile errors, 407

Compilers, 11, 13
  defined, 1
  syntax errors and, 407-408

Compile-time arrays, 215
  See also Arrays

Compile-time tables, 203-204
  coding example, 204
  defined, 203
  entering data for, 203-204
  uses for, 204
  See also Tables

Compiling, 11
  defined, 11
  members, 393-394
  RPG IV, 431

Composite keys, 108
  defining, 149-150
  defining parts of, 149-150
  KFLD and, 150
  referencing, 148-151

Concatenated keys, 148

Concatenation, 108
  character string, 300-301

Conditioning indicators, 184-187, 197
  multiple, 184
  on calculations, 345
  turning off/on, 185

See also Indicators

CONST keyword, 364

Constants, 27
  continuing, 235
  figurative, 63-65, 74
  named, 235-236, 257

Continuation lines, 360

Control language. See CL commands

Control structures, 71
  illustrated, 72
  iteration, 71, 80-86
  selection, 71, 74-77
  sequence, 71, 72
  types of, 71

Control-break logic, 94-100
  pseudocode, 95-96
  routines, 96

Control-break problem, 95, 338-339
  multiple-level, 98
  RPG II, 339-341

Counter-controlled loops, 84

Counters, 84-85
  starting value of, 85
  upper limit of, 84

Counting, 45, 50

Crossfooting, 220

CRTDTAARA (Create Data Area) command, 321

CRTLF (Create Logical File) command, 122

CRTPF (Create Physical File) command, 122

CRTPGM (Create Program) command, 375

CTDATA keyword, 437, 439

CVTRPGSRC (Convert RPG Source) command, 358, 383

D

Data
  alphanumeric, 111
  date, 359
  DBCS, 359, 384
  dictionary, 124
  displaying, 286

integer, 22
numeric, 111, 134
passing, between programs, 317-320
for runtime arrays, 216
storage, 111-114
table
    alternate format entry, 207
    changing values for, 213-214
    entering values for, 210-211
    multicolumn, 210-212
    splitting, 210
    volatile, 204
time, 359
timestamp, 359
types of, 111-114, 359
validation, 182, 187
Data areas, 321-322, 326
    accessing contents of, 322
    defined, 321
    explicit I/O with, 324
    local (LDA), 321, 326
    uses of, 321
    See also Data-area data structures
Data Description Specification. See DDS
Data File Utility (DFU), 123
Data files, 5-6
Data hierarchy, 5-6, 12-13
    illustrated, 6
Data structures, 238-254, 257-258
    data-area, 322-325
    defined, 238-239
    defining, 239-240, 257-258
    Definition Specification and, 365
    examples, 239-242
    file-information, 251-253, 258
    function of, 238-239
    grouping fields and, 240
    initializing, 247-249
    multiple-occurrence, 242-247
    occurrence of, 243-244
        changing, 245
        current, 243
        indicator for, 244
    program-defined, 239
    program-status, 253-254, 258

reinitializing, 249-251
RPG IV definition of, 364-367,
    439-440
simple, 239-242
subfields, 239, 247-254
Data-area data structures, 322
    *NAMVAR DEFN vs., 322-325
    reading contents of, 323
    RPG IV Definition Specification, 366
Database design, 126, 134
Database files, 124-126
    accessing via partial key list, 151
    creating, 122-123
    as update file, 154
Date
    conversion, 320
    data type, 359
    formats, 62
    Gregorian format, 320
    Julian format, 320
DATE keyword, 129, 184
    code example, 184
DBCS (Double Byte Character Set)
    data, 359, 384
DDS, 109-110, 196
    comment lines, 109
    components, 109
    defined, 109
    display file coding, 170-178
    of display file record, 171
    entering, statements, 122
    field beginning position, 129
    field length, 113
    keywords. See Keywords
    line positioning, 130
Debugging, 10, 13, 413-415
    breakpoints, 414
    trace commands, 414-415
    See also Testing
Decimal bits, 112, 306
Decimals
    position of, 22
    representation, 308
Decision operations. See Selection
    operations

Definition Specifications, 362-368, 383,
    436-437
    data structure definitions, 364-367,
        439-440
    data-area data structure entries, 366
    defined, 362
    Name area, 365
    named constant definitions,
        363-364, 439
    pointers and, 367-368
    program-status entries, 366
    table and array definitions, 362-363
    See also RPG IV
DEFN operation, 237-238, 257
    with *LIKE option, 237-238, 442
        code example, 238
        defined, 237
        use of, 238
    with *NAMVAR option, 322-325,
        326
        code example, 323
        defined, 322
        result field, 322
        use of, 323
    for program maintenance, 238
    RPG IV, 444
    Specifications, 238
DELET (Delete Record) operation,
    155-156
    code example, 155
    defined, 155
DESCEND keyword, 363, 437
Detail line, 24, 334
Digit bits, 112
DIM keyword, 363, 365, 437, 440
Display attributes, 181
Display files, 169-178, 196
    attributes, 172
    DDS coding for, 170-178
    defined, 169
    defining, 176
    documentation, 173
    entries, 169
    information screen, 173-174
    pseudocode for, 177

record formats for, 171, 173-174

records for, 171

screen displays and, 170

See also Interactive applications

DIV (Divide) operation, 48

code example, 48

rounding for, 53

Division, 48

remainder field, 52

result field size for, 51-52

See also Rounding

DO (Do) operation, 83-86

ENDO, 84, 85

format, 84-85

Documentation, 13

display file, 173

external, 10

internal, 10, 32-33

overview, 33

Dollar signs, 7-8

EDTWRD/EDTCDE keywords and, 180

fixed, 7, 37

floating, 8, 36-37, 57

printing, 36-37

DOU operation, 371

DOUxx (Do Until) operation, 82-83

DOWxx vs., 82

example, 83

flowchart, 83

DOW operation, 371

DOWxx (Do While) operation, 32, 80-82

ANDxx and, 81

DOUxx vs., 82

flowchart, 83

loops, 81, 410

ORxx and, 81

relational codes, 81

DSPATR keyword, 181-182, 191

attributes, 181

code example, 182

defined, 181

DSPMSG (Display Messages) command, 397

DSPPGMVAR (Display Program Variable) command, 414

DSPTRC (Display Trace) command, 415

DSPTRCDTA (Display Trace Data) command, 415

Duration codes, 372

Dynamic binding, 375, 384

E

EBCDIC, 73-74, 112, 134

codes, 112

values, working with, 306

Edit codes, 35-37

defined, 28

list of, 35

Output Specification and, 28, 35

sample use of, 36

X, 36

Y, 36

Z, 36

See also EDTCDE keyword

Edit words, 37-38

coding, 37-38

defined, 37

as named constants, 236

See also EDTWRD keyword

Editing

numeric values, 39

output, 35

Editor, 10, 13

See also Source Entry Utility (SEU)

EDTCDE keyword, 129-130

code example, 181

format, 180

See also Edit codes

EDTWRD keyword, 129

code example, 181

format, 180

See also Edit words

%ELEM function, 374

END statements, 92-94

operation-specific, 93-94

ENDDBG (End Debugger) command, 413

ENDDO (End Do Group) operation, 32

End-of-file condition, 29

Entering programs, 10-11

Entries

field description, 22-23, 26-28

fixed-position, 17

record identification, 21, 24-26

SKIP, 25-26

SPACE, 25-26

ERRMSG keyword, 184

conditioning, 185

Error indicators, 254-256

status of, 255

Errors

compile, 407

with error indicator, 254

file exception, 256

I/O, 160

logic, 11, 408

minimizing, 160

output, 410-413

program, 10-11, 256

*PSSR and, 254-257

runtime, 408

syntax, 10-11, 407-408

See also Abends

EVAL operation, 371, 384, 434

Exception lines, 25

EXCPT (Calculation Time Output) operation, 31, 131, 146, 432

code example, 153

for database files, 152-154

updating through, 156-157

EXFMT (Execute Format) operation, 177-178

code example, 178

defined, 177

Exponentiation, 47

EXPORT keyword, 376, 444

EXSR (Execute Subroutine) operation, 92

Extended Binary Coded Decimal Interchange Code. *See* EBCDIC

Extended factor 2 format, 270-271
 comparison operations, 371
Extension Specifications, 202-203
 defined, 202
 EQ position, 206, 213
 From File position, 214
 HI position, 213
 illustrated, 203
 number of entries per record, 204
 required entries on, 202
 RPG IV, 362
 runtime arrays and, 215
 table definitions in alternating
  format, 209
 Table/Array name position, 202
 To File position, 214
 See also Arrays; Specifications; Tables
External documentation, 10
Externally described files, 107-139
 file description, 107-108
 printer files, 127-131, 134
 RPG programming with, 123-124
 See also Files
EXTRCT (Extract) operation, 359, 372,
373, 384
 code example, 373
 defined, 373

F

Field characters, 293-303, 309
 inspection of, 293-299
 manipulation of, 299-303
 See also Fields
Field description entries
 Input Specification, 22-23
 Output Specification, 26-28
Field-level keywords, 109, 180-184
Field-reference files, 124-126
 defined, 124, 134
 uniformity of, 126
Fields, 5
 character, 22
 control, 100, 339
 defined, 5
 defining, 5

fixed-length, 12
 grouping, 240
 hidden, 276
 initializing, 249
 key, 108
 left-justifying values, 305-306
 location of, 22
 name of, 22, 26-27
 numeric, 22, 43-44
 overlapping definitions of, 242
 PAGE, 27
 parameter, 319
 result, 50-52
 screen, 195
 splitting, 62
 stand-alone, 363, 366-367, 441
 subfile, 284
 UDATE, 27
 See also Subfields
FIFO (First-In-First-Out) order, 141
Figurative constants, 63-64, 65
 *ALL, 64, 152
 *BLANK (*BLANKS), 63
 defined, 63
 *HIVAL, 63
 list of, 63
 *LOVAL, 63
 *OFF, 64, 74
 *ON, 64, 74
 *ZERO, 64
 See also Constants
*FILE objects, 252, 389
File access, 141-148
 random, 147-148
 sequential, 141-147
File Description Specifications, 17,
18-20, 38
 defined, 18
 DEVICE, 20
 for externally described files, 123
 FILE DESIGNATION, 19
 FILE FORMAT, 19-20
 FILE TYPE, 19
 FILENAME, 19
 illustrated, 20

RECORD LENGTH, 20
 RPG II, 333
 RPG IV, 360-362, 431
 for table files, 205
File locking, 157-158
 defined, 157
 See also Record locking
File maintenance, 154-156
 interactive, 187-195
  critical concern of, 187
  example, 188-195
  pseudocode, 192
  source code, 193-195
File-information data structure,
251-253, 258
 code example, 251
 defined, 251
 example, 252-253
 subfields, 251-252
 See also Data structures
File-level keywords, 109, 179
Files
 closing, 159
 combined, 176
 data, 5-6
 database, 124-126
  accessing via partial key list, 151
  creating, 122-123
 defined, 5
 display, 169-178, 196
  attributes, 172
  DDS coding for, 170-178
  defined, 169
  defining, 176
  documentation, 173
  entries, 169
  information screen, 173-174
  pseudocode for, 177
  record formats for, 171, 173-174
  records for, 171
  screen displays and, 170
 exception errors, 256
 externally described, 107-139
  printer files, 127-131, 134
  RPG programming with, 123-124

field-reference, 124-126, 134
input, 6, 19, 20-21
  operations for, 141-148
logical, 108-109, 134
  advantages of, 114
  coding, 114
  defined, 108
  defining, 114-122, 267
  field specifications, 116
  join, 120-122
  keyed sequential access, 115
  with multiple-record formats,
    119-120
  record selection/omission,
    116-119
  simple, 114-116
master, 5
name of, 21, 25, 436
opening, 159
output, 19, 24-26
physical, 108-109, 134
  changing definition of, 123
  defined, 108
  defining, 110-111
record types and, 6
spooled, 395-396
table, 205, 214
transaction, 5
update, 154-157
  See also File maintenance
Fixed dollar sign, 7
  specifying, 37
Fixed-logic cycle, 332-333, 336-342, 350
  control breaks and, 337-342
  defined, 336
  interactive applications and, 349
  procedural techniques vs., 349
  pseudocode, 337
  RPG/400 and, 348-349
  segments, 337
  steps, 336-337
  See also RPG II
Fixed-position entries, 17
Floating dollar sign, 8, 36, 57
  specifying, 37

Floating negative sign, 8
Fourth Generation Languages (4GLs), 1
FREE (Deactivate a Program)
  operation, 316-317, 444
  code example, 317
  defined, 317
  formatting, 316-317
  indicator, 317
  See also CALL (Call a Program)
    operation
FROMFILE keyword, 363, 437
Full procedural files, 19
Function keys
  indicators associated with, 173
  SEU, 403

G

GOTO operation, 72, 87-88, 350
  calculation indicators and, 345
  code example, 88
  IF logic and, 88
  TAG operation and, 87
  transfer of control and, 89
"GOTO-less programming," 72
Gregorian format, 320

H

Half-adjusting. *See* Rounding
Help, 290
  area, 287-288
  defined, 286-287
  entire screen, 287
  general, 288
  global, 287
  on-line, 286-289
  specific, 288
  specifications, 289
  text, 287
Help key, 287, 288, 290
  help areas and, 289
HELP keyword, 287
Help-specification format, 287
Hexadecimal representation, 308
  example use of, 309
  uses, 308

Hidden fields, 276
Hierarchical decomposition, 90-91
  defined, 90
High-level languages (HLLs), 1, 315
*HIVAL, 63
HLPARA (Help Area) keyword,
  287-288
HLPRCD keyword, 287, 288
Hyphen (-). *See* Minus sign (–)

I

I/O errors, 160
I/O operations, 154-157, 161
  RPG/400, 162
IF operation, 371
IFxx (If) operation, 74-79
  ANDxx variant, 75-76
  ELSE and, 75
  ENDIF, 76
  general form, 74
  logic errors, 412-413
  nested, 76-77
  ORxx variant, 75-76
  page overflow and, 78-80
  relational codes, 74
ILE RPG/400 Reference, 375
IMPORT keyword, 376, 444
*IN array, 226-227, 228
IN (Retrieve a Data Area) operation,
  324, 326
  code example, 324
  defined, 324
Indexes, 216
  array look-ups and, 225-226
  as positional locator, 303
  variable, 224
  See also Arrays
Indexing notation, 216
Indicators, 30-31
  as array elements, 226-227
  coding, 30-31
  COMP, 342-344
  conditioning, 184-187, 197, 345
  defined, 2
  EQ, 342

error, 254-256
FREE operation, 317
with function keys, 173
GOTO operation and, 345
HI, 342
level, 337, 339
LO, 342
LR, 315-316, 335
numbered, 226, 228
overflow, 78
record identifying, 333
in relational comparisons, 74
resulting, 293, 346-347
roll-key, 281
SFLEND, 276, 277
TESTB operation, 307
TESTN operation, 294
using, 31
INFDS keyword, 361, 440
Infinite loops, 408
    code examples, 409
    defined, 409
    diagnosing, 409-410
    See also Loops
INFSR keyword, 361, 440
Initialization
    numeric field, 149
    subfields, 148-149
    variable, 247-249
Input files, 6, 19, 20-21
    operations for, 141-148, 151
Input Specifications, 20-23, 38
    DECIMAL POSITIONS, 22
    defined, 20
    for externally described files, 124
    field description entries, 22-23
    FIELD LOCATION, 22
    FIELD NAME, 22
    FILE NAME, 21
    illustrated, 23
    line types, 21
    record identification entries, 21
    RPG II, 333
    RPG IV, 368, 432
    SEQUENCE, 21

See also Specifications
Insertion characters, 38
Integer data, 22
Integrated Language Environment
    (ILE), 3, 358, 431
Interactive applications, 2, 169-200
    defined, 169
    file maintenance, 181-185
    fixed-logic cycle and, 349
    See also Display files
Interactive file maintenance, 187-195
    critical concern of, 187
    example, 188-195
    pseudocode for, 192-193
    source code for, 193-195
Internal documentation, 10, 32-33
    comment lines, 33
*INZSR subroutine, 249, 258
INZ keyword, 367, 440
ITER operation, 86-87
    code example, 87
    function of, 86
Iteration, 71
    function of, 80
    RPG II and, 347-349
Iteration operations, 80-86
    Do, 83-86
    DOUxx, 82-83
    DOWxx, 81-82
    required formats for, 101

J

JFILE keyword, 122
JFLD keyword, 122
JOIN keyword, 122
Join-logical files, 120-122
    defined, 120
Julian format, 320

K

Key field, 108
Key sequence, 108
Keyboard-shift attribute, 172
Keys
    composite, 148-151

concatenated, 148
duplicate, 148
Help, 287, 288, 290
lists, partial, 150-151
non-unique, 280
partial, 280
PRINT, 179
ROLLUP, 179
unique, 280
Keywords, 109, 178-184, 196-197
    ALT, 363
    ASCEND, 363, 437
    BASED, 368
    BLINK, 179, 187
    CAnn, 178, 179
    CFnn, 178, 179
    CHECK, 183
    coding, 178
    COMP, 117-118, 182
    conditioning, 184
    CONST, 364
    CTDATA, 437, 439
    DATE, 129, 184
    DESCEND, 363, 437
    DIM, 363, 365, 437, 440
    DSPATR, 181-182, 191
    EDTCDE, 129-130, 180-181
    EDTWRD, 129-130, 180-181
    ERRMSG, 184, 185
    EXPORT, 376, 444
    field-level, 109, 180-184
    *FILE, 252
    file-level, 109, 179
    FROMFILE, 363, 437
    HELP, 287
    HLPARA, 287-288
    HLPRCD, 287, 288
    IMPORT, 376, 444
    INFDS, 361, 440
    INFSR, 361, 440
    INZ, 367, 440
    JFILE, 122
    JFLD, 122
    JOIN, 122
    LIKE, 367, 441

MSGLOC, 179
OCCURS, 365, 440
OFLIND, 361, 436
*OPCODE, 252
OVERLAY, 180, 271, 366
PAGNBR, 129, 130
PERRCD, 363, 437
PFILE, 114
PREFIX, 361
PRINT, 179, 187
PROCPTR, 368
RANGE, 117, 182
record-level, 109, 179-180
REF, 174
ROLLUP, 275-276, 279, 280
RPG IV and, 358, 383
SFILE, 361, 442
SFL, 268, 289
SFLCLR, 270
SFLCTL, 269, 289
SFLDSP, 269
SFLDSPCTL, 270
SFLEND, 276, 280
SFLPAG, 269, 272
SFLRCDNBR, 276
SFLSIZ, 269-270, 272
SKIPA, 130
SKIPB, 130
SPACEA, 130
SPACEB, 130
*STATUS, 252
subfile-related, 269-270
TEXT, 111
TIME, 184
TOFILE, 363, 437
UNIQUE, 110
USROPN, 361, 436
validation, 187
VALUES, 116, 182
VLDCMDKEY, 179
KFLD (Define Parts of a Key)
operation, 149-151
    code example, 149, 150
    composite key field, 150
    defined, 149

KLIST (Define a Composite Key)
operation, 149-151, 275
    code example, 149, 150
    declaring, 150
    defined, 149

L

Languages: RPG/400 Reference, 252, 254
Leading-decision loops, 82
LEAVE operation, 86-87
    code example, 87
    function of, 86
Left-justification, 305-306
Level checking, 124
Level indicators, 337
    control fields and, 339
LIKE keyword, 367, 441
List panels, 265
Literals, 27
    character, 59-63
    numeric, 43-44
Loading subfiles, 271-283
    entire, 271-275
        pseudocode, 273
        source code, 274
        system response and, 275
    page at a time, 275-283
        size much bigger than page, 279-280
        subfile size equals page, 280-283
        subfile size one greater than page, 275-279
Local data areas (LDAs), 321, 326
Locking
    file, 157-158
    record, 158-159
Logic
    decision, 100
    errors, 10, 11, 408
    looping, 100
Logical files, 108-109, 134
    advantages of, 114
    coding, 114
    defined, 108

defining, 114-122, 267
    based on two physical files, 120
    field specifications, 116
    join, 120-122
    keyed sequential access, 115
    with multiple-record formats, 119-120
    record selection/omission, 116-119
    simple, 114-116
    subschemas, 108
    See also Physical files
LOKUP operation, 206, 209, 213, 225-226, 228, 438
Look-ups, 228
    array, 225-226
    table, 206-209
Loops
    counter-controlled, 84
    DOWxx, 410
    early exits and, 86-87
    errors, 411-412
    infinite, 408, 409-410
    leading-decision, 82
    specific execution times of, 83-84
    trailing-decision, 82
*LOVAL, 63

M

Maintenance
    file, 154-156, 187-195
    program, 10
Master files, 5
Members, 11
    compiling, 393-394
    editing, 393
    entering, 393
Messages, displaying, 397
Minus sign (−)
    continuation character, 376, 433
    floating negative sign and, 8
Mixed-case entry, 358, 433
Modular programming, 313
MOVE (Move) operation, 32, 59-61, 210
    code example, 60-61

for converting data type, 61
    decimal positions and, 61
    extension, 60
MOVEA (Move Array) operation,
    221-222, 224, 228
    defined, 221
    examples, 221, 222
    importance of, 222
MOVEL (Move Left) operation, 62-63,
    210
    decimal positions and, 62
MSGLOC keyword, 179
MULT (Multiply) operation, 47
    code example, 47
    rounding for, 53
Multiple-occurrence data structures,
    242-247
    establishing, 242
    example, 243-245
    pointers and, 243
    subscripts and, 243
    two-dimensional array capabilities
        and, 246
    See also Data structures
Multiple-record formats, 119-120
Multiplication, 47
    result field size for, 51
MVR (Move Remainder) operation,
    48-49
    code example, 49
    result fields and, 52

N

Named constants, 235-236, 257
    advantages of, 236
    continuing, 235
    defined, 235
    defining, 235-236
        edit word as, 236
    RPG IV definitions of, 363-364, 439
    uses of, 236
    See also Constants
Nested IFs, 76-77
    code example, 77
    pseudocode, 76

See also IFxx (If) operation
Non-unique keys, 280
NOT operation, 371
Numbers, signed, 294
Numeric data, 5
    editing, 39
Numeric fields, 22, 43-44
    defining, 44
    initialization of, 249
    length of, 44
    See also Fields
Numeric literals, 43-44
    defined, 43
    left-justified, 43
    signs, 43
    See also Literals
Numeric truncation. See Truncation

O

Object code, 11
Objects
    *FILE, 389
    *MODULE, 444
    *PGM, 389
OCCURS keyword, 365, 440
OCUR operation, 243
*OFF, 64, 74
OFLIND keyword, 361, 436
Omit Specification, 116
*ON, 64, 74
On-line help, 286-289
*OPCODE keyword, 252
OPEN operation, 159
    code example, 159
    defined, 159
    See also CLOSE operation
Operations, 65
    ADD, 44-46
    ADDDUR, 359, 372, 384
    AND, 371
    BITOF, 306, 309
    BITON, 306, 309
    CABxx, 89-90
    CALL, 313-317, 325-326
    CALLB, 375-376, 384, 444

CASxx, 80, 92
CAT, 300-301, 305, 309
CHAIN, 147-148, 286
CHECK, 297-298
CHEKR, 298-299, 309
CLEAR, 249-250, 258, 441
CLOSE, 159
COMP, 342-345, 350
DEFN, 237-238, 444
DELET, 155
DIV, 48
DO, 83-86
DOU, 371
DOUxx, 82-83
DOW, 371
DOWxx, 32, 81-82, 410
ENDDO, 32
EVAL, 371, 384, 434
EXCPT, 31, 131, 146, 152-154,
    156-157, 432
EXFMT, 177-178
EXSR, 92
EXTRCT, 359, 372, 373, 384
FREE, 316-317, 444
GOTO, 87-88, 350
IF, 371
IFxx, 74-79
IN, 324, 326
ITER, 86-87
KFLD, 149-151
KLIST, 149-151, 275
LEAVE, 86-87
LOKUP, 206, 209, 213, 225-226,
    228, 438
MOVE, 32, 59-61, 210
MOVEA, 221-222, 224, 228
MOVEL, 62-63, 210
MULT, 47
MVR, 48-49, 52
NOT, 371
OCUR, 243
OPEN, 159
OR, 371
OUT, 324-325, 326
PARM, 317-319, 325-326

PLIST, 317-318, 326
READ, 29, 31, 141-142, 177, 410
READC, 283-284, 286, 290
READE, 145-146
READP, 146-147
REDPE, 146-147
RESET, 250-251, 258, 441
RETRN, 32, 314-316, 432
RPG IV code changes, 369
SCAN, 295-296, 309
SELEC, 79, 435
SETGT, 144-145
SETLL, 142-144
SETOF, 348, 445
SETON, 348
SORTA, 220, 228
SQRT, 49
SUB, 46
SUBDUR, 359, 372, 373, 384
SUBST, 299-300, 309
TAG, 87-88
TESTB, 307, 309
TESTN, 293-294, 309
UNLCK, 158, 325, 326, 444
UPDAT, 156, 286
WHEN, 371
WHxx, 435
within expressions, 370
WRITE, 131, 177, 275, 286
XFOOT, 220, 228
XLATE, 209, 301-303
Z-ADD, 57-58
Z-SUB, 58
OR operation, 371
OR relationship, 334, 344
OTHER reserved word, 79
OUT (Write Out a Data Area)
operation, 324-325, 326
code example, 325
defined, 324
*LOCK option, 324
Output editing, 7, 35
Output errors, 410-413
calculation errors, 413
correcting, 411-413

detecting, 410-411
field problem errors, 411
IF logic errors, 412-413
loop errors, 411-412
types of, 411-413
Output files, 19, 24-26
operations for, 151-154, 161
Output Specifications, 23-28, 38-39
CONSTANTS, 27
defined, 23
EDIT CODES, 28
END POSITION IN OUTPUT
RECORD, 27-28
EXCPT NAME, 25
for externally described files, 124
field description entries, 26-28
FIELD NAME, 26-27
FILE NAME, 25
illustrated, 24
record identification entries, 24-26
RPG II, 334
RPG IV, 376-377, 432-433
SPACE AND SKIP ENTRIES, 25-26
table name in, 227
TYPE, 25
See also Specifications
Overflow indicators, 78
OVERLAY keyword, 180, 271, 366

P
Packed decimal, 111, 134
illustrated, 113
%PADDR function, 375
PAGNBR keyword, 129, 130
Panels
list, 265
screen, 195
Parameters
fields, 319
passing arguments, 319
PARM (Identify Parameters)
operation, 317-319, 325-326
with CALLB, 376
code examples, 318-319
data names of, 317

defined, 317
placement of, 317
result field, 321
within PLIST operation, 318
Partial key lists, 150-151
Partial keys, 280
PDM. See Programming Development
Manager (PDM)
PERRCD keyword, 363, 437
PFILE keyword, 114
*PGM objects, 389
Phantom updates, 157
See also File locking; Record locking
Physical files, 108-109, 134
changing definition of, 123
defined, 108
defining, 110
See also Logical files
PLIST (Identify a Parameter List)
operation, 317-318, 326
with CALLB, 376
code examples, 318-319
defined, 317
Plus sign (+), continuation character,
376, 433
Pointers, 252
basing, 359-360
Definition Specifications and,
367-368
multiple-occurrence data structures
and, 243
procedure, 359-360
PREFIX keyword, 361
Pre-runtime arrays, 215
Pre-runtime tables, 205
coding example, 205
defined, 205
entering data for, 208
Priming read, 30
PRINT keyword, 179, 187
Printer files, externally described,
127-131
Printer spacing charts (PSCs), 7-9
arrays and, 227
defined, 7

illustrated, 9
negative values and, 8
RPG IV, 378
sample problem, 55
Xs in, 7-8
Printing
  array elements, 227
  dollar signs, 36-37
  from PDM, 395-397
  type of, 25
  See also Printer spacing charts
    (PSCs); Spooled files
Procedural languages, 1
Procedure pointers, 359-360
PROCPTR keyword, 368
Program Development Cycle, 9-10, 13
  elements, 9
Program errors, 10-11
  logic errors, 11
  *PSSR subroutine and, 256
  syntax errors, 10-11
  See also Errors
Program module, 375, 384
Program variables, 4-5
  defined, 4
Programmer Menu, 389, 390-391
  accessing, 390
  F6=Display messages, 391
  F18=Work with output, 391
  illustrated, 390
  Option 3 (Create an Object From a
    Source File), 390-391
  Option 4 (Call a Program), 391
  Option 8 (Edit a Source File
    Member), 390, 399
*Programming: Control Language
Programmer's Guide*, 415
*Programming: Data Description
Specifications Reference*, 119, 178, 287
Programming, 1
  illustrated flowchart, 12
  modular, 313
  specifications, 6-9
Programming Development Manager
  (PDM), 389, 391-397

accessing, 391
Assign Output to a Printer screen,
  396
Confirm Compile of Member
  screen, 394
F4=Prompt, 392
F6=Create, 393
F23=More options, 393
illustrated, 392
Option 2 (Work with Objects), 394
Option 3 (Work with Members),
  392-393
Work with Members Using PDM
  screen, 393
Work with Objects Using PDM
  screen, 395
Work with Printer Output screens,
  395, 396
Programs
  abend, 142, 254
  abnormal end of, 160
  calling, 313-317
    flexibility, 315
    menu, 320
  compiling, 11
  completed sample, 33-34
  debugging, 413-415
  designing, 9-10
  documenting, 10
  entering, 10
  maintaining, 10
  passing data between, 317-320
  running, 394-395
  specifications for, 18
  testing, 10, 407-415
  writing, 10
Program-status data structure,
  253-254, 258
  code example, 254
  defined, 253
  defining, 253-254
  sample, 254
  See also Data Structures
Prompts, 400-402
  formats, 401-402

Pseudocode
  for control-break logic, 95-96
  defined, 28
  for display files, 177
  for fixed-logic cycle, 337
  for interactive file maintenance,
    192
  for loading entire subfile, 273
  for RPG IV sample program,
    378-379
  for two-level control-break problem,
    98-99
*PSSR subroutine, 256-257, 258
  checking status codes and subfields
    with, 257
  code example, 256
  using, 257

Q

QCMDEXC, 320, 326
  calling, 320-321
QPRINT, 19-20, 23, 130
QRPGLESRC source file, 358
QRPGSRC source file, 358, 399

R

Random access, 147-148
  CHAIN operation, 147-148
  defined, 147
RANGE keyword, 117
  code example, 183
  defined, 182
Range tables, 212-213
  code examples, 213
  defined, 212
  look-up statement for, 213
  sequence entry, 213
  See also Tables
READ (Read a Record) operation, 29,
  31, 141-142, 410
  display files, 177
  externally described files and, 142
READC (Read Next Changed Record)
  operation, 283-284, 286, 290
  defined, 283

using, 283
READE (Read Equal Key) operation, 145-146
  code example, 146
  defined, 145
Reading, sequentially, 141-147
READP (Read Prior Record)
  operation, 146-147
  code example, 147
  defined, 145
  using, 146-147
Record formats, 6
  clearing, 250
  display file, 171, 173-174
  name of, 153
Record identification entries
  Input Specification, 21
  Output Specification, 24-26
Record layouts, 6-7
  illustrated, 7
Record locking, 158-159
  code example, 158
  defined, 158
  releasing, 158
  See also File locking
Record-level keywords, 109, 179-180
Records, 5
  accessing, 155
  data entry of, 286
  defining fields of, 111
  deleting, 155
  detailed information on, 286
  display file, 171
  with duplicate keys, 148
  footer, 279
  identification indicators, 333
  selection/omission of, 116-119
  separator, 211
  sequence of, 21
  subfile, 272
  types of, 6
  updating, 156-157
  See also Record formats; Record
    locking
Recursion, 92

REDPE (Read Prior Equal) operation, 146-147
  defined, 146
  using, 146-147
Redundancy, 107
REF keyword, 174
Referencing, 216
Relational codes, 73, 100
Relational comparisons, 73-74
  defined, 73
  indicators in, 74
Relational operators, 118
Report Layout Utility (RLU), 127,134
Report Program Generator. *See* RPG;
  RPG/400; RPG II; RPG III; RPG IV
Reserved words, 383
RESET operation, 250-251, 258
  code example, 251
  defined, 250
  format of, 250
  RPG IV, 441
Result fields
  MVR operation and, 52
  SCAN operation and, 295
  size for addition, 50-51
  size for division, 51-52
  size for multiplication, 51
  size for subtraction, 51
  TESTN operation and, 293
  truncation and, 50
Resulting indicators, 293, 346-347
  RPG II arithmetic operations and, 346-347
  use of, 346-347
RETRN (Return to Caller) operation, 32, 314-316, 432
  code example, 316
  See also CALL (Call a Program)
    operation
RLU User's Guide and Reference, 127
RMVBKP (Remove Breakpoint)
  command, 414
RMVTRC (Remove Trace) command, 415
Roll-key indicator, 281

ROLLUP keyword, 275-276, 279, 280
  moving from control-record format
    to record format, 279
Rounding, 52-53
  defined, 52
  examples, 53
  when to use, 53
  See also Division
RPG
  defined, 12
  fixed-logic cycle, 332-333, 336-342, 350
  history of, 1-4
  program comparison, 4
  read-process-write cycle, 332-333
RPG II, 4, 331-355
  accumulators and, 340-341
  Calculation Specifications, 335-336
  control-break problem, 339-341
  decisions in, 342-346
  File Specifications, 333
  Input Specifications, 333
  iteration and, 347-349
  Output Specifications, 334
  resulting indicators and, 346-347
  RPG/400 vs., 331-336
  sample program, 336
  techniques, 342
RPG III, 331
RPG IV, 3, 357-387
  array definition in, 437
  built-in functions, 373-375
  Calculation Specifications, 369-376, 432
  compiling programs and, 431
  continuation lines, 360
  data structures and, 364-367, 439-440
  data type, 359
  Definition Specifications, 362-368
  extended factor 2 format, 370-371
  Extension Specifications, 362
  file names, 436
  File Specifications, 360-362, 431
  free-form entry, 434
  Input Specifications, 368, 432

keywords and, 358, 383
mixed-case entry, 358, 433
operation code changes, 369
operation extenders, 369
Output Specifications, 376-377,
    432-433
reasons for introducing, 37
sample program, 377-383
    printer spacing charts, 378
    pseudocode, 378-379
    source code, 380-382
specification lines, 357-358, 431
stand-alone fields, 363, 366-367
subfields in, 365-366, 439-440
table definition in, 437
variable names, 358
RPG/400
    fixed-logic cycle and, 348-349
    I/O operations summary table, 162
    introduction of, 3
    RPG II vs., 331-336
    RPG IV vs., 357-387, 431-445
Runtime arrays, 215-218
    calculation values and, 218
    data for, 216
    defined, 215
    Extension Specification and, 215
    input data and, 216-218
    See also Arrays
Runtime errors, 408

S

SCAN (Scan Character String)
    operation, 295-296, 309
    base string, 295
    case sensitivity, 295
    code example, 296
    compare string, 295
    defined, 295
    result field, 295
    uses of, 296
Scope terminators, 92-94
Screen fields, 195
Screens
    definition of, 267

design of, 195-196
layouts of, 266
panel types, 195
See also Common User Access
    (CUA)
SELEC (Select) operation, 79, 435
    OTHER and, 79
    RPG IV, 435
Select Specification, 116
Selection operations, 74-80
    CASxx, 80
    defined, 71
    IFxx, 74-79
    required formats for, 101
    SELEC, 79
Separator records, 211
Sequence, 71
    arrival, 108
Sequential access, 141-147
    defined, 141
    READ operation, 141-142
    READE operation, 145-146
    READP operation, 146-147
    SETGT operation, 144-145
    SETLL operation, 142-144
Sequential flow of control, 72-73
    defined, 71
    illustrated, 73
SETGT (Set Greater Than) operation,
    144-145
    code example, 145-146
    defined, 144
    file position and, 145
    with *HIVAL, 145
SETLL (Set Lower Limit) operation,
    142-144
    code example, 143-144
    defined, 142
    file positioning and, 143
    uses, 143-144
SETOF operation, 348, 445
SETON operation, 348
SEU. See Source Entry Utility (SEU)
SFILE keyword, 361, 442
SFL (Subfile) keyword, 268, 289

SFLCLR (Subfile Clear) keyword, 270
SFLCTL (Subfile Control) keyword,
    269, 289
SFLDSP (Subfile Display) keyword, 269
SFLDSPCTL (Subfile Display Control)
    keyword, 270
SFLEND (Subfile End) keyword, 276,
    280
    indicator, 276, 277
SFLPAG (Subfile Page) keyword, 269,
    272
SFLRCDNBR (Subfile Record
    Number) keyword, 276
    CURSOR parameter with, 276
SFLSIZ (Subfile Size) keyword,
    269-270, 272
Signed numbers, 294
%SIZE function, 374-375, 442
SKIPA keyword, 130
SKIPB keyword, 130
Slashes (/)
    dates and, 8, 36
    "divided by" sign, 48
SORTA (Sort an Array) operation, 220,
    228
Source code, 11, 13
    for interactive file maintenance,
        193-195
    for loading entire subfile, 274
    for RPG IV sample program,
        380-382
Source Entry Utility (SEU), 17, 399-406
    Browse Options display, 404
    command line, 399, 403-404
    defined, 399
    edit display mode, 402-403
    entering, 399
    exiting, 405-406
    function keys, 403
    illustrated, 400, 401
    on-line help, 400
    prompt formats, 401-402
    prompts, 400-402
    split screens and, 404-405
Source members, 11, 393-394

SPACEA keyword, 130

SPACEB keyword, 130

Specifications, 17-31
  Calculation, 17, 28-32, 38, 335-336, 369-376
  Data Description, 109-110
  defined, 17
  Definition, 362-368, 383, 436-437
  example, 18
  Extension, 202-203, 362
  File Description, 17, 18-20, 38, 333, 360-362
  fixed-form, 38
  help, 289
  Input, 20-23, 38, 333, 368
  Omit, 116
  Output, 23-28, 38-39, 334, 376-377
  Select, 116

Spooled files
  list of, 395-396
  viewing, 396
  See also Printing

SQRT (Square Root) operation, 49

*STATUS keyword, 252

Stand-alone fields, 363, 366-367
  defined, 441
  Definition Specification and, 366
  length of, 367
  LIKE keyword and, 441
  See also Fields

Static binding, 375-376, 384
  call performance and, 375
  defined, 375
  using, 376

Status codes, 252
  defined, 252
  file-information data structure subfield, 252
  program-status data structure subfield, 254
  *PSSR subroutine and, 257
  subfield, 253

STRDBG (Start Debugger) command, 413

Strings

base, 295
compare, 295
concatenating values of, 300
copying, 299
manipulating, 299-306
  arrays for, 303-306
translating characters in, 301-302

STRSEU (Start SEU) command, 399

Structured design, 2-3, 71-72, 100
  defined, 71
  See also Top-down design

%SUBST function, 374, 383, 442, 443

SUB (Subtract) operation, 46-47
  code example, 46-47
  rounding for, 53

SUBDUR (Subtract Duration) operation, 359, 372, 373, 384
  code example, 373
  defined, 373

Subfields, 62
  data structure, 239
  definition line, 248
  file-information data structure, 251-252
  initializing, 247-249
  numeric, 248
  overlapping, 242
  program-status data structure, 253-254
  *PSSR subroutine and, 257
  referencing, 252
  RPG IV and, 365-366, 439-440
  status code, 252
  See also Fields

Subfile control-record format, 269-271, 289
  coding example, 270
  executing, 272
  identifying, 269
  keywords, 269-270
  loading page at a time, 276-277
  screen column headings, 270, 280-281

Subfile footer-record format, 271, 281
  displaying, 275

Subfile record formats, 268-269
  defined, 268
  output operation, 269
  See also Subfile control-record format; Subfile footer-record format

Subfiles, 265-286, 289-290
  change and, 283-286
  clearing, 270, 281
  for data entry of new records, 286
  defined, 265
  defining, 289
    records, 268
  displaying, 268-270, 290
    control of, 270
    multiple records, 268
    simultaneously, 286
  fields, 284
  loading, 271-283, 290
    entire, 271-275
    page at a time, 275-283
  page of, 269, 271
  record display, 269
  records, 272
  ROLLDOWN and, 280
  size of, 269-270, 271
    equals page, 280-283
    loading entire subfile and, 271-275
    much bigger than page, 279-280
    one greater than page, 275-279
    system response and, 275
  updating, 284-286
  uses of, 286

Subroutines, 80
  break, 98
  coding, 91
  defined, 91
  defining, 91-92
  ENDSR and, 91
  *INZSR, 249, 258
  number limit of, 91
  *PSSR, 256-257, 258
  subroutines executing, 92

Subschemas, 108

Subscripts
  multiple-occurrence data structures and, 243
  two-dimensional arrays and, 246
SUBST (Substring) operation, 299-300, 309
  code examples, 300
  defined, 299
Subtraction, 46-47
  result field size for, 51
Syntax errors, 10-11, 407-408
System/38 mini-computer, 3

T

Table data
  alternate format entry, 207
  changing values for, 213-214
  entering values for, 210-211
  multicolumn, 210-212
  splitting, 210
  volatile, 204
Table look-ups, 206
  for range table, 213
Tables
  compile-time, 203-204
  defined, 201
  defining, 202-203
  Definition Specifications and, 362-363
  Extension Specifications and, 202
  files for, 205, 214
  function of, 206
  multicolumn, 210-212
  multiple related, 209-212
  pre-runtime, 205
  range, 212-213
  RPG IV definition, 362-363, 437
  two related, 206-209
  types of, 203
  See also Arrays; Table data
TAG operation, 87-88
TESTB (Test Bit) operation, 307, 309
  code examples, 308
  defined, 307
Testing, 407-415

program, 10-11
  between two values, 342
  See also Debugging
TESTN (Test Numeric) operation, 293-294, 309
  defined, 293
  indicators, 294
  result field and, 293
TEXT keyword, 111
Time data type, 359
TIME keyword, 184
  code example, 184
Timestamp data type, 359
TOFILE keyword, 363, 437
Top-down design, 90-92, 100
  advantages of, 91
  defined, 90
  example, 94-100
  subroutines and, 91-92
  See also Structured design
Total-time calculations, 337
Tracing, 414-415
Trailing-decision loops, 82
%TRIM function, 374, 442, 443
%TRIML function, 374, 442, 443
%TRIMR function, 374, 383, 442, 443
Truncation, 49-50
  defined, 49
  during execution, 50
  high-order, 49
  low-order, 50
  result fields and, 50
Two-dimensional arrays, 246
  defined, 246
  defining, 246-247
  subscripts, 246
  See also Arrays

U

UIM (User Interface Manager), 287
Underscore (RPG IV), 433
Unique keys, 280
UNIQUE keyword, 110
UNLCK (Unlock a Data Area) operation, 158, 325, 326

code example, 325
defined, 325
RPG IV, 444
Unstructured operations, 87-90
  CABxx, 89-90
  GOTO, 87-88
  TAG, 87-88
UPDAT (Modify Existing Record) operation, 156-157, 286
  code example, 156
  defined, 156
Update files, 154-157
  I/O operations and, 154-155
Updates, interactive, 187-195
  critical concern of, 187
  example, 188-195
  subfiles and, 284-286
USROPN keyword, 361, 436

V

Validation keywords, 187
Validity checking, 286
VALUES keyword, 116
  code example, 183
  defined, 182
Variables, 5, 12
  initialization of, 247-249
  names of, 383
  reinitialization of, 249-251
VLDCMDKEY keyword, 179

W

WHEN operation, 371
WHILE, 29-30
WHxx operation, 435
WRITE operation, 131, 153-154, 275, 286
  code example, 153-154
  display files, 177

X

X edit code, 36
XFOOT (Summing the Elements of an Array) operation, 220, 228

XLATE operation, 301-303, 309
    code examples, 302-303
    defined, 301
    uses of, 302

Y

Y edit code, 36

Z

Z edit code, 36
Z-ADD (Zero and Add) operation,
  57-58
    code example, 58
*ZERO, 64
Zero suppression, 7, 36
    edit codes and, 36
Zone bits, 112, 306
Zoned decimal, 111, 134
    illustrated, 113
Z-SUB (Zero and Subtract) operation,
  58

0	3	**H**
1	4	Line
	5	
H	6	Form Type
	7	Size to Compile
	8	
	9	
	10	Object Output
	11	Listing Options
	12	Size to Execute
	13	
	14	
	15	Debug
	16	Reserved
	17	
	18	Currency Symbol
	19	Date Format
	20	Date Edit
	21	Decimal Notation
	22	Reserved
	23	Number of Print Positions
	24	
	25	
	26	Alternate Collating Sequence
	27	Reserved
	28	
	29	
	30	
	31	
	32	
	33	
	34	
	35	
	36	
	37	Inquiry
	38	Reserved
	39	
	40	Sign Handling
	41	1P Forms Position
	42	Indicator Setting
	43	File Translation
	44	Punch MFCU Zeros
	45	Nonprint Characters
	46	Reserved
	47	Table Load Halt
	48	Shared I/O
	49	Field Print
	50	Formatted Dump
	51	RPG to RPG II Conversion
	52	Number of Formats
	53	
	54	S/3 Conversion
	55	Subprogram
	56	CICS/DL/1
	57	Transparent Literal
	58	
	59	
	60	
	61	
	62	
	63	
	64	
	65	
	66	
	67	
	68	
	69	
	70	
	71	
	72	
	73	
	74	

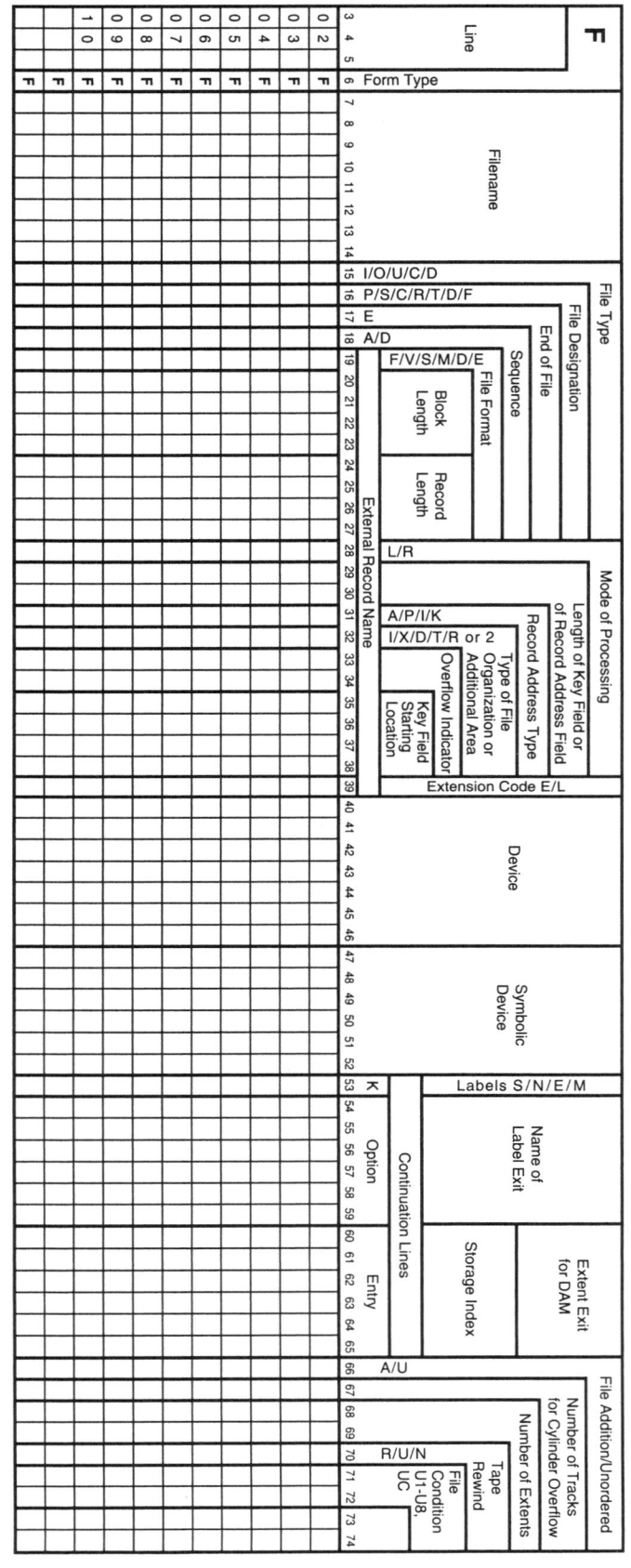

I — Input Specifications form

Column(s)	Field
3 4 5	Line
6	Form Type
7 8 9 10 11 12 13	Filename
14	Sequence — AND / OR
15	
16	
17	Number (1/N)
18	Option (O)
19 20	Record Identifying Indicator or * *
21 22 23 24	Position (Record Identification Codes 1)
25	Not (N)
26	C/Z/D
27	Character
28 29 30 31	Position (Record Identification Codes 2)
32	Not (N)
33	C/Z/D
34	Character
35 36 37 38	Position (Record Identification Codes 3)
39	Not (N)
40	C/Z/D
41	Character
42	Stacker Select
43	P/B/L/R
44 45 46 47	Field Location — From
48 49 50 51	Field Location — To
52	Decimal Positions
53 54 55 56 57 58	Field Name
59 60	Control Level (L1-L9)
61 62	Matching Fields or Chaining Fields
63 64	Field Record Relation
65 66	Field Indicators — Plus
67 68	Field Indicators — Minus
69 70	Field Indicators — Zero or Blank
71 72 73 74	

Line numbers down the left side: 01, 02, 03, 04, 05, 06, 07, 08, 09, 10, 11, 12, 13, 14, 15, 16, 17, 18, 19, 20

Form Type column: I (for each line)

C

Line			Form Type	Control Level (L0-L9, LR,SR, AN/OR)	Indicators					Factor 1	Operation	Factor 2	Result Field					Resulting Indicators			Comments

Line: 3 4 5

Form Type: 6

Control Level (L0-L9, LR,SR, AN/OR): 7 8

Indicators: 9 Not, 10 11 And, 12 Not, 13 14 And, 15 Not, 16 17

Factor 1: 18 19 20 21 22 23 24 25 26 27

Operation: 28 29 30 31 32

Factor 2: 33 34 35 36 37 38 39 40 41 42

Result Field — Name: 43 44 45 46 47 48

Result Field — Length: 49 50 51

Decimal Positions: 52

Operation Extender (H,N,P): 53

Resulting Indicators:
Arithmetic — Plus / Minus / Zero
Compare — 1>2 / 1<2 / 1=2
Lookup(Factor 2)is — High / Low / Equal
54 55 56 57 58 59

Comments: 60 61 62 63 64 65 66 67 68 69 70 71 72 73 74

Line numbers (left column): 01/02 03/04 05/06 07/08 09/10 11/12 13/14 15/16 17/18 19/20

Form Type column (row of C's): C C C C C C C C C C C C C C C C C C C C C

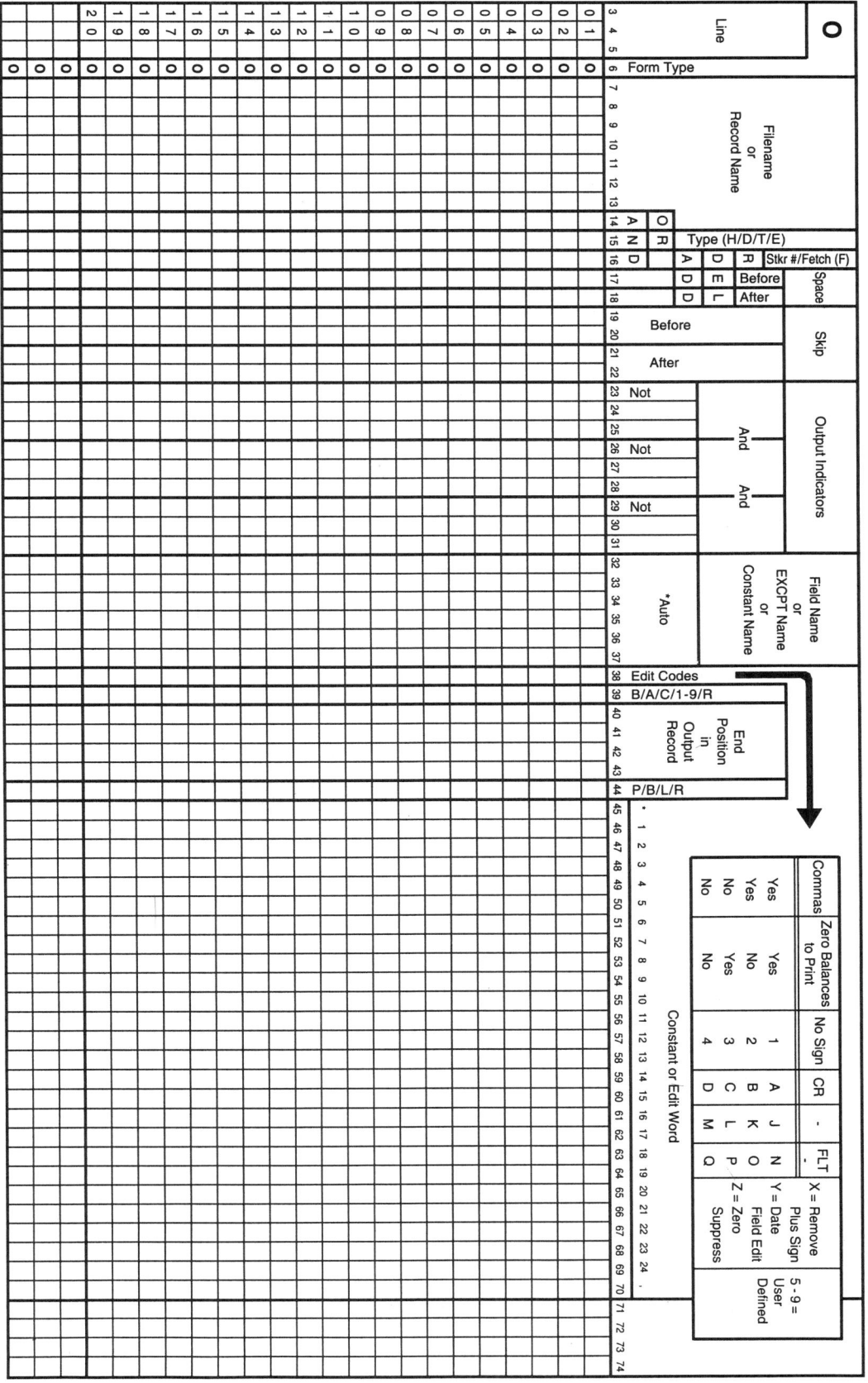

E									
Line	3 4 5								
Form Type	6	E	E	E	E	E	E	E	E	E
Record Sequence of the Chaining File	7 8								
Number of the Chaining Field	9 10								
From Filename	11 12 13 14 15 16 17 18								
To Filename	19 20 21 22 23 24 25 26								
Table or Array Name	27 28 29 30 31 32								
Number of Entries Per Record	33 34 35								
Number of Entries Per Table or Array	36 37 38 39								
Length of Entry	40 41 42								
P/B/L/R	43								
Decimal Positions	44								
Sequence (A/D)	45								
Table or Array Name (Alternating Format)	46 47 48 49 50 51								
Length of Entry	52 53 54								
P/B/L/R	55								
Decimal Positions	56								
Sequence (A/D)	57								
Comments	58 59 60 61 62 63 64 65 66 67 68 69 70 71 72 73 74								

Line numbers: 01 02 03 04 05 06 07 08

A

Column	Label
1–5	Sequence Number
6	Form Type
7	And/Or/Comment (A/O/*)
8	Not (N)
9–10	Indicator
11	Not (N)
12–13	Indicator
14	Not (N)
15–16	Indicator
17	Name Type (b̸/R/K/S/O)
18	Reserved
19–28	Name
29	Reference (R)
30–34	Length
35	Data Type (b̸ A/P/S/B A/S/X/Y/N/I/W)
36–37	Decimal Positions
38	Usage (b̸/O/I/B/H/M)
39–41	Line
42–44	Pos
45–80	Functions

Conditioning

Condition Name

Location

Form Type row: A A A A A A A A A A A A A A A A A A A A

Also Published by *NEWS/400*

Visit our web site at **www.dukepress.com** for a more detailed listing of all Duke Press books

THE A TO Z OF EDI

By Nahid M. Jilovec

Electronic Data Interchange (EDI) can help reduce administrative costs, accelerate information processing, ensure data accuracy, and streamline business procedures. Here's a comprehensive guide to EDI to help in planning, startup, and implementation. The author reveals all the benefits, challenges, standards, and implementation secrets gained through extensive experience. She shows how to evaluate your business procedures, select special hardware and software, establish communications requirements and standards, address audit issues, and employ the legal support necessary for EDI activities. 263 pages.

APPLICATION DEVELOPER'S HANDBOOK FOR THE AS/400

Edited by Mike Otey, a **NEWS/400** *technical editor*

Explains how to effectively use the AS/400 to build reliable, flexible, and efficient business applications. Contains RPG/400 and CL coding examples and tips, and provides both step-by-step instructions and handy reference material. Includes diskette. 768 pages, 48 chapters.

AS/400 DISK SAVING TIPS & TECHNIQUES

By James R. Plunkett

Want specific help for cleaning up and maintaining your disk? Here are more than 50 tips, plus design techniques for minimizing your disk usage. Each tip is completely explained with the "symptom," the problem, and the technique or code you need to correct it. 72 pages.

AS/400 SUBFILES IN RPG

On the AS/400, subfiles are powerful and easy to use, and with this book you can start working with subfiles in just a few hours — no need to wade through page after page of technical jargon. You'll start with the concept behind subfiles, then discover how easy they are to program. The book contains all of the DDS subfile keywords announced in V2R3 of OS/400. Five complete RPG subfile programs are included, and the book comes complete with a 3.5" PC diskette containing all those programs plus DDS. The book is an updated version of the popular *Programming Subfiles in RPG/400*. 200 pages, 4 chapters.

C FOR RPG PROGRAMMERS

By Jennifer Hamilton, a **NEWS/400** *author*

Written from the perspective of an RPG programmer, this book includes side-by-side coding examples written in both C and RPG to aid comprehension and understanding, clear identification of unique C constructs, and a comparison of RPG op-codes to equivalent C concepts. Includes many tips and examples covering the use of C/400. 292 pages, 23 chapters.

CL BY EXAMPLE

By Virgil Green

CL by Example gives programmers and operators more than 850 pages of practical information you can use in your day-to-day job. It's full of application examples, tips, and techniques, along with a sprinkling of humor. The examples will speed you through the learning curve to help you become a more proficient, more productive CL programmer. 864 pages, 12 chapters.

CLIENT ACCESS TOKEN-RING CONNECTIVITY

By Chris Patterson

Attaching PCs to AS/400s via a Token-Ring can become a complicated subject — when things go wrong, an understanding of PCs, the Token-Ring, and OS/400 is often required. *Client Access Token-Ring Connectivity* details all that is required in these areas to successfully maintain and trouble-shoot a Token-Ring network. The first half of the book introduces the Token-Ring and describes the Client Access communications architecture, the Token-Ring connection from both the PC side and the AS/400 side, and the Client Access applications. The second half provides a useful guide to Token-Ring management, strategies for Token-Ring error identification and recovery, and tactics for resolving Client Access error messages. 125 pages, 10 chapters.

COMMON-SENSE C
Advice and warnings for C and C++ programmers
By Paul Conte, a **NEWS/400** *technical editor*

C programming language has its risks; this book shows how C programmers get themselves into trouble, includes tips to help you avoid C's pitfalls, and suggests how to manage C and C++ application development. 100 pages, 9 chapters.

CONTROL LANGUAGE PROGRAMMING FOR THE AS/400
By Bryan Meyers and Dan Riehl, **NEWS/400** *technical editors*

This comprehensive CL programming textbook offers students up-to-the-minute knowledge of the skills they will need in today's MIS environment. Progresses methodically from CL basics to more complex processes and concepts, guiding readers toward a professional grasp of CL programming techniques and style. 512 pages, 25 chapters.

DDS BY EXAMPLE
By R S Tipton

DDS by Example provides detailed coverage on the creation of physical files, field reference files, logical files, display files, and printer files. It includes more than 300 real-life examples, including examples of physical files, simple logical files, multi-format logical files, dynamic selection options, coding subfiles, handling overrides, creating online help, creating reports, and coding windows. 360 pages, 4 chapters.

DDS PROGRAMMING FOR DISPLAY & PRINTER FILES
By James Coolbaugh

Offers a thorough, straightforward explanation of how to use Data Description Specifications (DDS) to program display files and printer files. Covers basic to complex tasks using DDS functions. The author uses DDS programming examples for CL and RPG extensively throughout the book, and you can put these examples to use immediately. Focuses on topics such as general screen presentations, the A specification, defining data on the screen, record-format and field definitions, defining data fields, using indicators, data and text attributes, cursor and keyboard control, editing data, validity checking, response keywords, and function keys. A complimentary diskette includes all the source code presented in the book. 446 pages, 13 chapters.

DATABASE DESIGN AND PROGRAMMING FOR DB2/400
By Paul Conte

This textbook is the comprehensive guide for creating flexible and efficient application databases in DB2/400. The author shows you everything you need to know about physical and logical file DDS, SQL/400, and RPG IV and COBOL/400 database programming. Clear explanations illustrated by a wealth of examples, including complete RPG IV and COBOL/400 programs, demonstrate efficient database programming and error handling with both DDS and SQL/400. Each programming chapter includes a specific list of "Coding Suggestions" that will help you write faster and more maintainable code. In addition, the author provides an extensive section on practical database design for DB2/400. This is the most complete guide to DB2/400 design and programming available anywhere. Approx. 600 pages, 18 chapters.

DESKTOP GUIDE TO THE S/36
By Mel Beckman, Gary Kratzer, and Roger Pence, **NEWS/400** *technical editors*

This definitive S/36 survival manual includes practical techniques to supercharge your S/36, including ready-to-use information for maximum system performance tuning, effective application development, and smart Disk Data Management. Includes a review of two popular Unix-based S/36 work-alike migration alternatives. Diskette contains ready-to-run utilities to help you save machine time and implement power programming techniques such as External Program Calls. 387 pages, 21 chapters.

THE ESSENTIAL GUIDE TO CLIENT ACCESS FOR DOS EXTENDED
By John Enck, Robert E. Anderson, and Michael Otey

The Essential Guide to Client Access for DOS Extended contains key insights and need-to-know technical information about Client Access for DOS Extended, IBM's strategic AS/400 product for DOS and Windows client/server connectivity. This book provides background information about the history and architecture of Client Access for DOS Extended; fundamental information about how to install and configure Client Access; and advanced information about integrating Client Access with other types of networks, managing how Client Access for DOS Extended operates under Windows, and developing client/server applications with Client Access. Written by industry experts based on their personal and professional experiences with Client Access, this book can help you avoid time-consuming pitfalls that litter the path of AS/400 client/server computing. 430 pages, 12 chapters.

ILE: A FIRST LOOK

By George Farr and Shailan Topiwala

This book begins by showing the differences between ILE and its predecessors, then goes on to explain the essentials of an ILE program — using concepts such as modules, binding, service programs, and binding directories. You'll discover how ILE program activation works and how ILE works with its predecessor environments. The book covers the new APIs and new debugging facilities and explains the benefits of ILE's new exception-handling model. You also get answers to the most commonly asked questions about ILE. 183 pages, 9 chapters.

IMPLEMENTING AS/400 SECURITY, SECOND EDITION
A practical guide to implementing, evaluating, and auditing your AS/400 security strategy

By Wayne Madden, a **NEWS/400** *technical editor*

Concise and practical, this second edition brings together in one place the fundamental AS/400 security tools and experience-based recommendations that you need and also includes specifics on the latest security enhancements available in OS/400 Version 3 Release 1. Completely updated from the first edition, this is the only source for the latest information about how to protect your system against attack from its increasing exposure to hackers. 389 pages, 16 chapters.

INSIDE THE AS/400
An in-depth look at the AS/400's design, architecture, and history

By Frank G. Soltis

The inside story every AS/400 developer has been waiting for, told by Dr. Frank G. Soltis, IBM's AS/400 chief architect. Never before has IBM provided an in-depth look at the AS/400's design, architecture, and history. This authoritative book does just that — and also looks at some of the people behind the scenes who created this revolutionary system for you. Whether you are an executive looking for a high-level overview or a "bit-twiddling techie" who wants all the details, *Inside the AS/400* demystifies this system, shedding light on how it came to be, how it can do the things it does, and what its future may hold — especially in light of its new PowerPC RISC processors. 475 pages, 12 chapters.

INTRODUCTION TO AS/400 SYSTEM OPERATIONS

by Patrice Gapen and Heidi Rothenbuehler

Here's the textbook that covers what you need to know to become a successful AS/400 system operator. System operators typically help users resolve problems, manage printed reports, and perform regularly scheduled procedures. *Introduction to AS/400 System Operations* introduces a broad range of topics, including system architecture; DB2/400 and Query; user interface and Operational Assistant; managing jobs and printed reports; backup and restore; system configuration and networks; performance; security; and Client Access (PC Support).

The information presented here covers typical daily, weekly, and monthly AS/400 operations using V3R1M0 of the OS/400 operating system. You can benefit from this book even if you have only a very basic knowledge of the AS/400. If you know how to sign on to the AS/400, and how to use the function keys, you're ready for the material in this book. 234 pages, 10 chapters.

AN INTRODUCTION TO COMMUNICATIONS FOR THE AS/400, SECOND EDITION

By John Enck and Ruggero Adinolfi

This second edition has been revised to address the sweeping communications changes introduced with V3R1 of OS/400. As a result, this book now covers the broad range of AS/400 communications technology topics, ranging from Ethernet to X.25, and from APPN to AnyNet. The book presents an introduction to data communications and then covers communications fundamentals, types of networks, OSI, SNA, APPN, networking roles, the AS/400 as host and server, TCP/IP, and the AS/400-DEC connection. 210 pages, 13 chapters.

JIM SLOAN'S CL TIPS & TECHNIQUES

By Jim Sloan, developer of QUSRTOOL's TAA Tools

Written for those who understand CL, this book draws from Jim Sloan's knowledge and experience as a developer for the S/38 and the AS/400, and his creation of QUSRTOOL's TAA tools, to give you tips that can help you write better CL programs and become more productive. Includes more than 200 field-tested techniques, plus exercises to help you understand and apply many of the techniques presented. 564 pages, 30 chapters.

MASTERING THE AS/400
A practical, hands-on guide

By Jerry Fottral

This introductory textbook to AS/400 concepts and facilities has a utilitarian approach that stresses student participation. A natural prerequisite to programming and database management courses, it emphasizes mastery of system/user interface, member-object-library relationship, utilization of CL commands, and basic database and program development utilities. Also includes labs focusing on essential topics such as printer spooling; library lists; creating and maintaining physical files; using logical files; using CL and DDS; working in the PDM environment; and using SEU, DFU, Query, and SDA. 484 pages, 12 chapters.

OBJECT-ORIENTED PROGRAMMING FOR AS/400 PROGRAMMERS

By Jennifer Hamilton, a **NEWS/400** *author*

Explains basic OOP concepts such as classes and inheritance in simple, easy-to-understand terminology. The OS/400 object-oriented architecture serves as the basis for the discussion throughout, and concepts presented are reinforced through an introduction to the C++ object-oriented programming language, using examples based on the OS/400 object model. 114 pages, 14 chapters.

PERFORMANCE PROGRAMMING — MAKING RPG SIZZLE

By Mike Dawson, CDP

Mike Dawson spent more than two years preparing this book — evaluating programming options, comparing techniques, and establishing benchmarks on thousands of programs. "Using the techniques in this book," he says, "I have made program after program run 30%, 40%, even 50% faster." To help you do the same, Mike gives you code and benchmark results for initializing and clearing arrays, performing string manipulation, using validation arrays with look-up techniques, using arrays in arithmetic routines, and a lot more. 257 pages, 8 chapters.

POWER TOOLS FOR THE AS/400, VOLUMES I AND II

Edited by Frederick L. Dick and Dan Riehl

NEWS 3X/400's Power Tools for the AS/400 is a two-volume reference series for people who work with the AS/400. Volume I (originally titled *AS/400 Power Tools*) is a collection of the best tools, tips, and techniques published in *NEWS/34-38* (pre-August 1988) and *NEWS 3X/400* (August 1988 through October 1991) that are applicable to the AS/400. *Volume II* extends this original collection by including material that appeared through 1994. Each book includes a diskette that provides load-and-go code for easy-to-use solutions to many everyday problems. *Volume I*: 709 pages, 24 chapters; *Volume II*: 702 pages, 14 chapters.

PROGRAMMING IN RPG IV

By Judy Yaeger, Ph.D., a **NEWS/400** *technical editor*

This textbook provides a strong foundation in the essentials of business programming, featuring the newest version of the RPG language: RPG IV. Focuses on real-world problems and down-to-earth solutions using the latest techniques and features of RPG. Provides everything you need to know to write a well-designed RPG IV program. Each chapter includes informative, easy-to-read explanations and examples as well as a section of thought-provoking questions, exercises, and programming assignments. Four appendices and a handy, comprehensive glossary support the topics presented throughout the book. An instructor's kit is available. 450 pages, 13 chapters.

PROGRAMMING SUBFILES IN COBOL/400

By Jerry Goldson

Learn how to program subfiles in COBOL/400 in a matter of hours! This powerful and flexible programming technique no longer needs to elude you. You can begin programming with subfiles the same day you get the book. You don't have to wade through page after page, chapter after chapter of rules and parameters and keywords. Instead, you get solid, helpful information and working examples that you can apply to your application programs right away. 204 pages, 5 chapters.

THE QUINTESSENTIAL GUIDE TO PC SUPPORT

By John Enck, Robert E. Anderson, Michael Otey, and Michael Ryan

This comprehensive book about IBM's AS/400 PC Support connectivity product defines the architecture of PC Support and its role in mid-range networks, describes PC Support's installation and configuration procedures, and shows you how you can configure and use PC Support to solve real-life problems. 345 pages, 11 chapters.

RPG ERROR HANDLING TECHNIQUE
Bulletproofing Your Applications

By Russell Popeil

RPG Error Handling Technique teaches you the skills you need to use the powerful tools provided by OS/400 and RPG to handle almost any error from within your programs. The book explains the INFSR, INFDS, PSSR, and SDS in programming terms, with examples that show you how all these tools work together and which tools are most appropriate for which kind of error or exception situation. It continues by presenting a robust suite of error/exception handling techniques within RPG programs. Each technique is explained in an application setting, using both RPG III and RPG IV code. 164 pages, 5 chapters.

RPG IV BY EXAMPLE

By George Farr and Shailan Topiwala

RPG IV by Example addresses the needs and concerns of RPG programmers at any level of experience. The focus is on RPG IV in a practical context that lets AS/400 professionals quickly grasp what's new without dwelling on the old. Beginning with an overview of RPG IV specifications, the authors prepare the way for examining all the features of the new version of the language. The chapters that follow explore RPG IV further with practical, easy-to-use applications. 500 pages, 15 chapters.

RPG IV JUMP START
Moving ahead with the new RPG

By Bryan Meyers, a **NEWS/400** *technical editor*

Introducing the "new" RPG, in which the columnar syntax has been challenged (all the specifications have changed, some vestigial specifications from an earlier era have been eliminated, and new specifications and data types have been added), this book shows you RPG IV from the perspective of a programmer who already knows the old RPG. Points out the differences between the two and demonstrates how to take advantage of the new syntax and function. 193 pages, 12 chapters.

RPG/400 INTERACTIVE TEMPLATE TECHNIQUE

By Carson Soule, CDP, CCP, CSP

Here's an updated version of Carson Soule's *Interactive RPG/400 Programming*. The book shows you time-saving, program-sharpening concepts behind the template approach, and includes all the code you need to build one perfect program after another. These templates include code for cursor-sensitive prompting in DDS, for handling messages in resident RPG programs, for using the CLEAR opcode to eliminate hard-coded field initialization, and much more. There's even a new select template with a pop-up window. 258 pages, 10 chapters.

S/36 POWER TOOLS

Edited by Chuck Lundgren, a **NEWS/400** *technical editor*

Winner of an STC Award of Achievement in 1992, this book contains five years' worth of articles, tips, and programs published in *NEWS 3X/400* from 1986 to October 1990, including more than 290 programs and procedures. Extensively cross-referenced for fast and easy problem solving, and complete with diskette containing all the programming code. 737 pages, 20 chapters.

STARTER KIT FOR THE AS/400, SECOND EDITION
An indispensable guide for novice to intermediate AS/400 programmers and system operators

By Wayne Madden, a **NEWS/400** *technical editor*
with contributions by Bryan Meyers, Andrew Smith, and Peter Rowley

This second edition contains updates of the material in the first edition and incorporates new material to enhance it's value as a resource to help you learn important basic concepts and nuances of the AS/400 system. New material focuses on installing a new release, working with PTFs, AS/400 message handling, working with and securing printed output, using operational assistant to manage disk space, job scheduling, save and restore basics, and more basic CL programming concepts. Optional diskette available. 429 pages, 33 chapters.

SUBFILE TECHNIQUE FOR RPG/400 PROGRAMMERS

By Jonathan Yergin, CDP, and Wayne Madden

Here's the code you need for a complete library of shell subfile programs: RPG/400 code, DDS, CL, and sample data files. There's even an example for programming windows. You even get some "whiz bang" techniques that add punch to your applications. This book explains the code in simple, straightforward style and tells you when each technique should be used for best results. 326 pages, 11 chapters, 3.5" PC diskette included.

TECHNICAL REFERENCE SERIES

Edited by Bryan Meyers, a **NEWS/400** *technical editor*

Written by experts — such as John Enck, Bryan Meyers, Julian Monypenny, Roger Pence, Dan Riehl — these unique desktop guides put the latest AS/400 applications and techniques at your fingertips. These "just-do-it" books (featuring wire-o binding to open flat at every page) are priced so you can keep your personal set handy. Optional online Windows help diskette available for each book.

Desktop Guide to CL Programming

By Bryan Meyers, a **NEWS/400** *technical editor*

This first book of the **NEWS/400** *Technical Reference Series* is packed with easy-to-find notes, short explanations, practical tips, answers to most of your everyday questions about CL, and CL code segments you can use in your own CL programming. Complete "short reference" lists every command and explains the most-often-used ones, along with names of the files they use and the MONMSG messages to use with them. 205 pages, 36 chapters.

Desktop Guide to AS/400 Programmers' Tools

By Dan Riehl, a **NEWS/400** *technical editor*

This second book of the **NEWS/400** *Technical Reference Series* gives you the "how-to" behind all the tools included in *Application Development ToolSet/400* (ADTS/400), IBM's Licensed Program Product for Version 3 of OS/400; includes Source Entry Utility (SEU), Programming Development Manager (PDM), Screen Design Aid (SDA), Report Layout Utility (RLU), File Compare/Merge Utility (FCMU) — *new in V3R1*, and Interactive Source Debugger — *new in V3R1*. Highlights topics and functions specific to Version 3 of OS/400. 266 pages, 30 chapters.

Desktop Guide to DDS

By James Coolbaugh

This third book of the **NEWS/400** *Technical Reference Series* provides a complete reference to all DDS keywords for physical, logical, display, printer, and ICF files. Each keyword is briefly explained, with syntax rules and examples showing how to code the keyword. All basic and pertinent information is provided for quick and easy access. While this guide explains every parameter for a keyword, it doesn't explain every possible exception that might exist. Rather, the guide includes the basics about what each keyword is designed to accomplish. The *Desktop Guide to DDS* is designed to give quick, "at your fingertips" information about every keyword — with this in hand, you won't need to refer to IBM's bulky *DDS Reference* manual. 132 pages, 5 major sections.

Desktop Guide to RPG/400

By Roger Pence and Julian Monypenny, **NEWS/400** *technical editors*

This fourth book in the *Technical Reference Series* provides a variety of RPG templates, subroutines, and copy modules, sprinkled with evangelical advice, that will help you write robust and effective RPG/400 programs. Highlights of the information provided include string-handling routines, numeric editing routines, date routines, error-handling modules, tips for using OS/400 APIs with RPG/400, and interactive programming techniques. For all types of RPG projects, this book's tested and ready-to-run building blocks will easily snap into your RPG. The programming solutions provided here would otherwise take you days or even weeks to write and test. 211 pages, 28 chapters.

Desktop Guide to Creating CL Commands

By Lynn Nelson

In this most recent book in the *Technical Reference Series*, author Lynn Nelson shows you how to create your own CL commands with the same functionality and power as the IBM commands you use every day, including automatic parameter editing, all the function keys, F4 prompt for values, expanding lists of values, and conditional prompting. After you have read this book, you can write macros for the operations you do over and over every day or write application commands that prompt users for essential information. Whether you're in operations or programming, don't miss this opportunity to enhance your career-building skills. 164 pages, 14 chapters.

UNDERSTANDING BAR CODES

By James R. Plunkett

One of the most important waves of technology sweeping American industry is the use of bar coding to capture and track data. The wave is powered by two needs: the need to gather information in a more accurate and timely manner and the need to track that information once it is gathered. Bar coding meets these needs and provides creative and cost-effective solutions for many applications. With so many leading-edge technologies, it can be difficult for IS professionals to keep up with the concepts and applications they need to make solid decisions. This book gives you an overview of bar code technology including a discussion of the bar codes themselves, the hardware that supports bar coding, how and when to justify and then implement a bar code application, plus examples of many different applications and how bar coding can be used to solve problems. 70 pages.

USING QUERY/400

By Patrice Gapen and Catherine Stoughton

This textbook, designed for any AS/400 user from student to professional with or without prior programming knowledge, presents Query as an easy and fast tool for creating reports and files from AS/400 databases. Topics are ordered from simple to complex and emphasize hands-on AS/400 use; they include defining database files to Query, selecting and sequencing fields, generating new numeric and character fields, sorting within Query, joining database files, defining custom headings, creating new database files, and more. Instructor's kit available. 92 pages, 10 chapters.

USING VISUAL BASIC WITH CLIENT ACCESS APIs

By Ron Jones

This book is for programmers who want to develop client/server solutions on the AS/400 and the personal computer. Whether you are a VB novice or a VB expert, you will gain by reading this book because it provides a thorough overview of the principles and requirements for programming in Windows using VB. Companion diskettes contain source code for all the programming projects referenced in the book, as well as for numerous other utilities and programs. All the projects are compatible with Windows 95 and VB 4.0. 680 pages, 13 chapters.

FOR A COMPLETE CATALOG OR TO PLACE AN ORDER, CONTACT

NEWS/400
Duke Communications International
221 E. 29th Street • Loveland, CO 80538-2727
(800) 621-1544 • (970) 663-4700 • Fax: (970) 669-3016